THE CAMBRIDGE HISTORY OF EIGHTEENTH-CENTURY PHILOSOPHY

More than thirty eminent scholars from nine different countries have contributed to *The Cambridge History of Eighteenth-Century Philosophy* – the most comprehensive and up-to-date history of the subject available in English.

In contrast with most histories of philosophy and in keeping with preceding Cambridge volumes in the series, the subject is treated systematically by topic, not by individual thinker, school, or movement, thus enabling a much more historically nuanced picture of the period to be painted. As in previous titles in the series, the volume has extensive biographical and bibliographical research materials.

During the eighteenth century, the dominant concept in philosophy was human nature, and so it is around this concept that the present work is centered. This allows the contributors to offer both detailed explorations of the epistemological, metaphysical, and ethical themes that continue to stand at the forefront of philosophy and to voice a critical attitude toward the historiography behind this emphasis in philosophical thought. At the same time, due attention is paid to historical context, with particular emphasis on the connections among philosophy, science, and theology.

This judiciously balanced, systematic, and comprehensive account of the whole of Western philosophy during the period will be an invaluable resource for philosophers, intellectual historians, theologians, political theorists, historians of science, and literary scholars.

Knud Haakonssen is Professor of Intellectual History at the University of Sussex.

The Cambridge History of Eighteenth-Century Philosophy

Volume I

EDITED BY

KNUD HAAKONSSEN

University of Sussex

CAMBRIDGE UNIVERSITY PRESS
Cambridge, New York, Melbourne, Madrid, Cape Town, Singapore, São Paulo

Cambridge University Press
40 West 20th Street, New York, NY 10011-4211, USA

www.cambridge.org
Information on this title: www.cambridge.org/9780521418546

First published 2006

Printed in the United States of America

A catalog record for this publication is available from the British Library.

Library of Congress Cataloging in Publication Data
The Cambridge history of eighteenth-century philosophy / edited by Knud Haakonssen.
p. cm.
Includes bibliographical references and index.
ISBN 0-521-41854-2 (alk. paper)
1. Philosophy – History – 18th century. I. Haakonssen, Knud, 1947–
B802.C24 2005
190′.9′033–dc22   2004054878

Volume I ISBN-13 978-0-521-86742-9
Volume I ISBN-10 0-521-86742-8

Available only as a set: ISBN-13 978-0-521-41854-6 hardback
Available only as a set: ISBN-10 0-521-41854-2 hardback

CONTENTS

VOLUME I

Preface		ix
Methods of reference and abbreviations		xi
List of contributors		xv

I: The Concept of Eighteenth-Century Philosophy

1 The History of Eighteenth-Century Philosophy: History or Philosophy? 3
KNUD HAAKONSSEN

2 Concepts of Philosophy 26
WERNER SCHNEIDERS

3 Schools and Movements 45
CARL HENRIK KOCH

4 The Institutionalisation of Philosophy in Continental Europe 69
T. J. HOCHSTRASSER

5 The Curriculum in Britain, Ireland, and the Colonies 97
M. A. STEWART

6 Informal Networks 121
ANN THOMSON

II: The Science of Human Nature

7 Philosophical Methods 137
REINHARD BRANDT

 8 Human Nature   160
    AARON GARRETT

 9 Perception and Ideas, Judgement   234
    KENNETH P. WINKLER

10 Self-Consciousness and Personal Identity   286
    UDO THIEL

11 Reason   319
    MICHEL MALHERBE

12 Substances and Modes, Space and Time   343
    HEINER F. KLEMME

13 Causality   368
    HEINER F. KLEMME

14 Knowledge and Belief   389
    MANFRED KUEHN

15 Scepticism   426
    RICHARD H. POPKIN

16 Philosophy of Language   451
    HANS AARSLEFF

17 Rhetoric   496
    PETER FRANCE

18 Aesthetics   516
    RUDOLF A. MAKKREEL

19 The Active Powers   557
    JEROME B. SCHNEEWIND

20 Education   608
    GERAINT PARRY

VOLUME II

III: Philosophy and Theology

21 Natural and Revealed Religion   641
    B. A. GERRISH

22 Revealed Religion: The Continental European Debate   666
    MARIA ROSA ANTOGNAZZA

23 Revealed Religion: The British Debate   683
    M. A. STEWART

24 Arguments for the Existence of God: The British Debate   710
    M. A. STEWART

25 Arguments for the Existence of God: The Continental
    European Debate   731
    MARIA ROSA ANTOGNAZZA

26 The Problem of Theodicy   749
    LUCA FONNESU

27 Religion and Society   779
    SIMONE ZURBUCHEN

IV: Natural Philosophy

28 Artifice and the Natural World: Mathematics, Logic, Technology   815
    JAMES FRANKLIN

29 The Study of Nature   854
    JOHN GASCOIGNE

30 Natural Philosophy   873
    PIERRE KERSZBERG

31 Natural History   903
    PHILLIP R. SLOAN

V: Moral Philosophy

32 The Foundations of Morality 939
DAVID FATE NORTON AND MANFRED KUEHN

33 Norm and Normativity 987
STEPHEN DARWALL

34 Politics 1026
WOLFGANG KERSTING

35 Social Sciences 1069
ROBERT BROWN

36 Philosophical Reflection on History 1107
DARIO PERINETTI

Biobibliographical Appendix 1141
KNUD HAAKONSSEN AND CONTRIBUTORS

Bibliography 1237

Index nominum 1343

Index rerum 1363

PREFACE

Like its predecessors, *The Cambridge History of Eighteenth-Century Philosophy* has a considerable history of its own and certainly more than its editor, contributors, and publisher would have wanted. However, with the help of my wife, Åsa Söderman, and the understanding and extraordinary patience of Cambridge University Press's editor, the late Terence Moore, the volume is now ready to seek its place alongside its distinguished predecessors in the series. I hope it is worthy of the company.

I have found the advice and support extended by many colleagues and friends indispensable. The plan for the volume was discussed with an advisory board consisting of Henry Allison, Michael Ayers, Michel Malherbe, David Fate Norton, Jerome B. Schneewind, Werner Schneiders, and M. A. Stewart, and I am grateful for all the advice I received from them. I am particularly indebted to the many suggestions by Professor Stewart at a formative stage of the planning. As far as the contents are concerned, I extend my warm thanks to the contributors for their fine chapters, their cooperation in revising them, and their great patience and kindness when faced with delay upon delay. A special acknowledgment is due to Aaron Garrett, who took over the longest chapter in the book at a time when my private circumstances prevented me from writing it as planned. In the early phase of the project, I benefited from the research assistance of Elizabeth Short, while Åsa Söderman assisted me with the completion of the work, especially the compilation of the massive bibliography and the indices.

It is a pleasure to acknowledge the institutions that have supported me during work on the *History*. The Research School of Social Sciences within the Institute for Advanced Studies at the Australian National University provided me with a part-time assistant. The Provost of Boston University granted me funding for casual research assistance. The Swedish Collegium for Advanced Studies in the Social Sciences awarded me a visiting fellowship.

KNUD HAAKONSSEN
Boston, April 2004

ix

METHODS OF REFERENCE AND ABBREVIATIONS

The full title (as generally understood) is given on the first reference to a work in each chapter; subsequent references are to readable shorter versions of the title. This does not apply to the works for which standardized abbreviations have been adopted; see the list below. All works referred to in the chapters are listed in the bibliography. Where contributors have indicated facsimile editions of works, bibliographical details of the facsimile reprint are given in the bibliography; the notes to the text give only the original place and year of publication.

Abbreviations

Encyclopédie refers to *Encyclopédie ou Dictionnaire raisonné des sciences des arts et des métiers*, eds. D. Diderot and J. d'Alembert, 35 vols. (Paris and Amsterdam, 1751–80).

GEORGE BERKELEY

Works refers to *The Works of George Berkeley*, eds. A. A. Luce and T. E. Jessop, 9 vols. (Edinburgh, 1948–57).

JOHANN GOTTLIEB FICHTE

Gesamtausgabe refers to *Gesamtausgabe der Bayerischen Akademie der Wissenschaften*, eds. R. Lauth and H. Jacob (Stuttgart-Bad Cannstatt, 1962–). (I Werke – II Nachgelassene Schriften – III Briefe – IV Kollegnachschriften; vol. numbers in Arabic numerals.)
Werke refers to *Sämtliche Werke*, ed. I. H. Fichte, 8 vols. (Berlin, 1845–56).

DAVID HUME

The Clarendon Edition refers to *The Clarendon Edition of the Works of David Hume*, eds. T. L. Beauchamp, D. F. Norton, and M. A. Stewart (Oxford, 1998–).
References to Hume's *A Treatise of Human Nature* cite Book.Part.Section.Paragraph (1.1.1.1) according to the *Clarendon Edition*, eds. D. F. Norton and M. J. Norton, followed by the page number(s) of the edition by L. A. Selby-Bigge and P. H. Nidditch (SBN 1).
References to Hume's *Enquiries* cite Part.Section.Paragraph (1.1.1) followed by the corresponding page number(s) of the edition by Selby-Bigge and Nidditch (SBN 1).
Works refers to *The Philosophical Works*, eds. T. H. Green and T. H. Grose, 4 vols. (London, 1882; Facsim. Aalen 1954).

IMMANUEL KANT

Ak refers to the Akademieausgabe of *Kants gesammelte Schriften*, ed. the Königlichen Preussischen (later Deutschen) Akademie der Wissenschaften (Berlin, 1900–); all translations are, unless otherwise stated, from the *Cambridge Edition of the Works of Immanuel Kant (Works)*, eds. P. Guyer and A. W. Wood (Cambridge, 1992–). All references are to the Ak, the pages of which are in the margins of the Cambridge translation. Regarding citations from *Kritik der reinen Vernunft (Critique of Pure Reason)*, A and B refer respectively to the 1781 and 1787 editions.

GOTTFRIED WILHELM LEIBNIZ	*Akademieausgabe* refers to *Sämtliche Schriften und Briefe*, ed. der Deutschen Akademie der Wissenschaften zu Berlin (Berlin, 1923–). VI.6: 345 = Reihe.vol: page. *Phil. Schriften* refers to *Die philosophischen Schriften*, ed. C. I. Gerhardt, 7 vols. (Berlin, 1875–90).
JOHN LOCKE	*An Essay Concerning Human Understanding*, ed. P. H. Nidditch (Oxford, 1975); in *The Clarendon Edition of the Works of John Locke* (*Works*). References are to Book. Chapter.Paragraph (III.x.2). Other *Collected Works* are referred to by publication year.
JEAN-JACQUES ROUSSEAU	*Oeuvres* refers to *Oeuvres complètes*, eds. B. Gagnebin and M. Raymond, 5 vols. (Paris, 1959–95).
ADAM SMITH	*Works* refers to *Glasgow Edition of the Works and Correspondence*, 7 vols. (Oxford, 1976–2001).
CHRISTIAN WOLFF	*Werke* refers to *Gesammelte Werke*, ed. J. École (Hildesheim, 1962–); 3 *Abteilungen*: Abt. I, Deutsche Werke; Abt. II, Lateinische Werke; Abt. III, Materialien und Dokumente.

CONTRIBUTORS

HANS AARSLEFF
Department of English
Princeton University

MARIA ROSA ANTOGNAZZA
Department of Theology and
    Religious Studies
King's College London

REINHARD BRANDT
Institut für Philosophie
Philipps-Universität-Marburg

ROBERT BROWN
Research School of Social Sciences
Australian National University

STEPHEN DARWALL
Department of Philosophy
University of Michigan

LUCA FONNESU
Dipartimento di Filosofia
Università di Pavia

PETER FRANCE
Department of French
University of Edinburgh

JAMES FRANKLIN
School of Mathematics
University of New South Wales

AARON GARRETT
Department of Philosophy
Boston University

JOHN GASCOIGNE
Department of History
University of New South Wales

B. A. GERRISH
The Divinity School
University of Chicago

KNUD HAAKONSSEN
Department of History
University of Sussex

T. J. HOCHSTRASSER
Department of International History
London School of Economics and
    Political Science

WOLFGANG KERSTING
Philosophisches Seminar
Universität Kiel

PIERRE KERSZBERG
Département de Philosophie
Université de Toulouse

HEINER F. KLEMME
Institut für Philosophie
Otto-von-Güricke-Universität
    Magdeburg

CARL HENRIK KOCH
Institut for Filosofi, Pædagogik og
  Retorik
Københavns Universitet

MANFRED KUEHN
Department of Philosophy
Boston University

RUDOLF A. MAKKREEL
Department of Philosophy
Emory University

MICHEL MALHERBE
Département de Philosophie
Université de Nantes

DAVID FATE NORTON
Department of Philosophy
McGill University

GERAINT PARRY
Department of Government
University of Manchester

DARIO PERINETTI
Département de Philosophie
Université du Québec à Montréal

RICHARD H. POPKIN
Department of Philosophy
Washington University, St. Louis

JEROME B. SCHNEEWIND
Department of Philosophy
The Johns Hopkins University

WERNER SCHNEIDERS
Philosophisches Seminar
Westfälische Wilhelms-Universität
  Münster

PHILLIP R. SLOAN
General Program of Liberal Studies
University of Notre Dame

M. A. STEWART
Department of Philosophy
University of Aberdeen

UDO THIEL
Department of Philosophy
Faculty of Arts
Australian National University

ANN THOMSON
Département d'études des pays
  anglophones
Université Paris 8

KENNETH P. WINKLER
Department of Philosophy
Wellesley College

SIMONE ZURBUCHEN
Département de Philosophie
Université de Fribourg

Some of the contributors are emeriti from the institutions indicated. Sadly Richard Popkin died shortly before the publication of this volume.

I

THE CONCEPT OF EIGHTEENTH-CENTURY PHILOSOPHY

THE HISTORY OF EIGHTEENTH-CENTURY PHILOSOPHY: HISTORY OR PHILOSOPHY?

KNUD HAAKONSSEN

The history of eighteenth-century philosophy is a subject with its own history. However, the idea of what constitutes eighteenth-century philosophy has been remarkably stable over the two centuries that have elapsed since the period in question, and this stability has obscured the simple fact of its historicity and made it peculiarly difficult to question the historical adequacy of that idea. What is more, even now, when detailed scholarship has undertaken such questioning in earnest, tradition is so strong that works of synthesis and overview – not to mention teaching – have to pay it considerable respect in order to find an identifiable audience.

During the last two centuries, two factors above all have lent the philosophy of the eighteenth century an identity, other than its place in time, and these two factors have often reinforced each other. One is the idea that the philosophy in question is the core of a wider cultural and social movement, namely 'the Enlightenment'. The other is that the eighteenth century has to be seen as part of – in fact, as the high point of – a development of early-modern philosophy from Francis Bacon and René Descartes to Thomas Reid and Immanuel Kant.

I. THE ENLIGHTENMENT AND PHILOSOPHY

The attempt to identify the philosophy of the eighteenth century by means of the Enlightenment is as inadequate as it is popular. Apart from the danger of tautology – namely that the philosophy of the eighteenth century is the philosophy of the Enlightenment because the Enlightenment is the eighteenth century – the concept of Enlightenment is either too wide or too narrow to capture the philosophical riches of the century. It is too wide when it reflects the scholarship of the last half century, which has made the Enlightenment into an ever more

I would like to thank the following for helpful discussions of the topics of this chapter: Hans Aarsleff, Leo Catano, Aaron Garrett, Alfredo Ferrarin, Charles Griswold, Ian Hunter, Jonathan Rée, James Schmidt, Åsa Söderman, and M. A. Stewart.

complex phenomenon that, it has been suggested, cannot be talked about in the singular since it makes sense to talk not only of any number of national Enlightenments but also of provincial, professional, popular, confessional, and several other Enlightenments.[1] Furthermore, modern scholarship has widened the idea of Enlightenment far beyond what can be recognised as in any sense a philosophical culture. While this in itself has proved to be an enormous enrichment of historical scholarship and cultural debate, it clearly makes the concept of Enlightenment useless as a tool for identifying a coherent philosophy. On the contrary, such work has a tendency to reinforce a pluralistic understanding of eighteenth-century philosophy, a topic we will return to.

If contemporary scholarship has rendered the concept of Enlightenment too wide to characterise a philosophy, traditional polemics has given us an idea too narrow and primitive to serve the purpose. The idea of Enlightenment as a style of thinking and as a cultural process that were typical of, but not exclusive to, the eighteenth century was common in European debate at the turn of that century under such labels as *Aufklärung, eclaircissement*, and illumination, but the idea of the Enlightenment as a particular period was slower to take hold, apparently first in Georg Wilhelm Friedrich Hegel's lectures in Berlin in the 1820s on the history of philosophy and on the philosophy of history, and it was not until 1910 that the idea of the period secured – and was secured by – its present English label.[2] The French period-concept of *le siècle des lumières* was largely parochial, referring to a relatively small group of Paris intellectuals who were active during a forty-year period from the late 1740s until the Revolution of 1789, but this was just the most extreme case of the general problem with the traditional narrow understanding of the Enlightenment.

For more than two centuries, it has been those critical of one or another aspect of eighteenth-century thought who have taken the lead in shaping the concept of the Enlightenment. We may mention three particularly important episodes here. First, the immediate reaction to the French Revolution across Europe included rejection of the French *philosophes* who had been invoked by the revolutionaries, and this rejection had its parallel in the three remarkable series of philosophical lectures that signalled a new era in Britain, France, and Germany, those by Samuel Taylor Coleridge (1818), Victor Cousin (1815), and Hegel (1805, or, at least, in the 1820s), to which we will return. This criticism had a shaping influence on the idea of the Enlightenment's political and religious tenor and French focus, and was so forceful that even thinkers whom we might consider cognate spirits with much of the Enlightenment, such as John Stuart Mill, accepted it. The fact that the *philosophes* on the whole had cautioned against revolution – and that those of them who lived long enough had rejected the great Revolution[3] – made no difference, and it still makes little difference.

Secondly, German scholarship from the 1870s onwards invented the idea that German culture from the 1770s to the 1830s had made a decisive break with earlier European culture, especially that of the 'West', meaning France and Britain and their derivatives in Germany itself. This fault line came to be seen as the division between Enlightenment on one hand and Romanticism, historicism, and idealism on the other. Friedrich Meinecke's *Die Entstehung des Historismus* (1936) was a late expression and summary of this scholarship; in it, Meinecke saw the German supersession of the Enlightenment as a second Reformation, which he, significantly, called *Die deutsche Bewegung* (the German Movement).[4] It is a line of thinking that has had a curiously extended life in the English-speaking world thanks to the influence of Sir Isaiah Berlin, who, however, shifted the historical parallels and saw the German Movement as a 'Counter-Enlightenment'.[5] But, whatever the labels, it was a thin Enlightenment that was left once the German Movement had deprived it of thinkers such as Gotthold Ephraim Lessing and Johann Gottfried von Herder.[6]

Both of the episodes mentioned here portray an Enlightenment that is quite limited. It was either purely French or heavily derived from French ideas, and it was a relatively brief period in European history, well short of the full eighteenth century. A third episode in the saga of how the common idea of the Enlightenment has been shaped by its enemies, namely late twentieth-century post-modernism, has tended in the opposite direction. Here the Enlightenment is often stretched to mean something like 'leading features of seventeenth- and eighteenth-century intellectual culture in Europe'. As has been pointed out, in this approach

utility trumps chronology: certain thinkers prove irresistible to critics of the Enlightenment project because they offer more forceful formulations of what are assumed to be central components of the project than can typically be found among thinkers whose works fall more squarely within the historical Enlightenment. Bacon is irreplaceable as an advocate for the scientific domination of nature, Hobbes is priceless as a representative of that individualist, rights- and contract-centered theory that critics assume lies at the heart of Enlightenment political thought, and Descartes serves as the epitome of that foundationalist and subject-centered conception of reason that philosophers have spent most of this century dismantling.[7]

At the same time, it is common in the post-modernist image of the Enlightenment to take Kant as the exemplary representative. The extreme vagueness concerning the who, where, and when of the Enlightenment is, it has been shown, easily matched by the characterisation of its intellectual content.[8] However, post-modernism shares with its critical predecessors the idea that the Enlightenment in one way or another was characterised by a very narrow outlook on human life.[9] In this regard, the most common charges are rationalism (meaning intellectualism) at the expense of passion and imagination; the idea of a universal human nature, to the detriment of individuality; individualism, disregarding social and spiritual holism; scientistic generalising, in ignorance of historical understanding of the particular; and universalism and internationalism without respect for the local and the national. Without entering into the complications arising from the *differences* between the various deriders of the Enlightenment,[10] it should be obvious that it is pointless to shackle the philosophy of the century to a concept that to such a degree has been shaped and reshaped by the culture wars of later periods.

A much more serious issue is the second factor mentioned at the beginning of this chapter, namely, the attempt to identify the philosophy of the eighteenth century as the gradual culmination of a distinctively early-modern philosophy. This general idea has commonly been relied upon by such critics of the Enlightenment as those cited earlier, but it has been shared by most people who would not see themselves in this light. It has, in fact, been the backbone of most general histories of philosophy in the post-Renaissance and post-Reformation period, and it is certain that it, in one way or another, has an influence on both authors and readers of the present volume. It is the paradigm within which we work, or, at least, from which we set out, even when we want to be critical of it, and, as will be evident from several aspects of this work, much scholarship has been devoted to such criticism. As is so often the case with general paradigms of old vintage, this one is vague and endlessly flexible, and any brief delineation of it is correspondingly difficult. However, it is possible to indicate the historicity of the standard concept of eighteenth-century philosophy and thus to alert the reader not to take the subject of this work for granted.

II. THE CONCEPT OF EARLY-MODERN PHILOSOPHY

The most basic of the ideas that have dominated the writing[11] of the history of philosophy during the last two centuries is that the theory of knowledge is at the core of all sound philosophy, the true *prima philosophia*. Furthermore, the significance of early-modern philosophy is commonly considered in this historiography to be that the roughly three centuries from the late Renaissance to 1800 were the period when philosophers increasingly came to understand this true nature of philosophy. The problem of knowledge which philosophy was supposed to deal with was that posed by scepticism conceived as a denial of the possibility of justified beliefs or scientific explanations. The philosophical history of the period has therefore commonly been told as the story of an ever-deepening struggle with scepticism that culminated in a total rejection of the premises upon which the contest had taken place, or, rather, in two such rejections, that by Immanuel Kant and that by Thomas Reid.

For these two thinkers, the central question of philosophy was not how we could acquire true knowledge. Rather, given that we do have knowledge (especially science), how is this possible, or what are its presuppositions? This standpoint inspired subsequent generations to a view of the trajectory of early-modern philosophy according to which traditional ontology was largely an encumbrance on epistemology, and the development from the seventeenth to the eighteenth century consisted in shedding this burden. It was the Hegelian transition from substance to subject, from the so-called 'great systems' within which Descartes, Spinoza, Malebranche, and Leibniz had fought scepticism, to the theories of perception, ideas, and judgement with which Locke, Leibniz (again), Wolff, Berkeley, Condillac, Hume, and many others tried to found the new sciences. In other words, it was a development that confirmed and underlined one of the most elementary assumptions of the historians who traced it, namely, that knowledge is to be understood in terms of the individual person's mind, an assumption that remained remarkably unshaken despite Hegel.

Integral to the view indicated here is that the epistemological approach divided post-Renaissance philosophy into two major schools or directions, namely, rationalism and empiricism. The former has commonly been seen as characteristic of the European continent, though one of the defining features of eighteenth-century philosophy, on this view, was that France gradually switched from Cartesian rationalism to Lockean empiricism, embodied by Condillac. Germany, however, was supposed to maintain a continuous development of rational system-building through Leibniz, Wolff, and their followers and opponents. In contrast, the English-speaking world was seen to pursue the empiricist view in ever-finer detail from Bacon and Hobbes through Locke, Berkeley, and Hume.

This way of understanding the core of early-modern philosophy is what I call the epistemological paradigm. It sees philosophy as essentially concerned with the justification of beliefs and judgements; it understands such justification in terms of events, whether perceptive or inferential, in the mind – or, as if in the mind – of the individual person; and it tends to apply this idea of epistemological justification as the criterion for what is properly included within the discipline of philosophy.

This basic model is familiar to everyone who has looked into the general histories of early-modern philosophy, both current and past, and to any teacher of the subject. Needless to say, there are a great many variations on this interpretative theme, often with acknowledgement of important exceptions and additions, such as the presence of an empiricist strain in German Enlightenment thought, but the general features have been remarkably pervasive. Furthermore, the paradigm has reigned for a long time. The emphasis on the struggle against scepticism was already a prominent feature of the philosophical historiography of the Kantians at the close of the eighteenth century, and it has inspired some of the most appreciated contemporary scholarship in the form given to the thesis by Richard Popkin. Similarly, the pre-eminence given to epistemology is comparable in the Kantian Wilhelm Gottfried Tennemann's twelve-volume *Geschichte der Philosophie* (1798–1819) and Father Frederick Copleston's nine-volume *A History of Philosophy* (1946–74). It is also noticeable that while morals, politics, law, and art have gained status as objects of past philosophical inquiry in some recent general histories of philosophy, they are more often treated in the same stepmotherly manner as they were in the great nineteenth-century works, such as those by Friedrich Ueberweg and Kuno Fisher. Often they have been treated as separate disciplines with their own histories, obviously so in the case of the many histories of political thought, but also in major histories of ethics from, for instance, Christian Garve's *Uebersicht der vornehmsten Principien der Sittenlehre, von dem Zeitalter des Aristoteles an bis auf die unsre Zeiten* (1798), through Sir James Mackintosh's *Dissertation on the Progress of Ethical Philosophy, Chiefly during the Seventeenth and Eighteenth Centuries* (1830) and Friedrich Jodl's *Geschichte der Ethik in der neueren Philosophie* (1882–9), to J. B. Schneewind's *The Invention of Autonomy: A History of Modern Moral Philosophy* (1998).

III. THE HISTORY OF THE EPISTEMOLOGICAL PARADIGM

The epistemological paradigm for the history of early-modern philosophy has held sway so universally, at least until recently, that it may be surprising to suggest that it itself has a history; in fact, that it can be traced back to a particular episode or couple of episodes at the close of the eighteenth century. The paradigm became so widely accepted because it was propagated by two remarkably successful philosophical movements in which a useful past was an integral part, namely, as mentioned, the Scottish Common Sense philosophy formulated by Thomas Reid and Dugald Stewart and the critical philosophy of Immanuel Kant. As far as the latter is concerned, the way had been cleared in one fundamental respect by Jacob Brucker's and the Wolffians' downgrading of practical philosophy relative to theoretical philosophy, as Tim Hochstrasser has shown.[12] However, it was the Kantians who had the decisive influence on the writing of the histories.[13]

The pattern of philosophical history laid down by Reid, Kant, and their followers became prescriptive far beyond their own heyday. One reason for this continuing impact seems to have been that the history of philosophy became the subject of more or less basic university courses on the European continent during the early and middle parts of the nineteenth century. It was during this period that it became widely accepted that the best introduction to the discipline of philosophy was through its history, and the textbooks for these courses were written under the influence of the views indicated here. Thus was created a teaching and textbook tradition that, as Ulrich Johannes Schneider has shown in great detail, swept through German- and French-dominated Europe.[14] It also crossed the Channel, for although the English and Scottish universities were much slower to adopt systematic tuition in the history of philosophy, there was clearly an interest in the subject sufficient to sustain public lecture series, such as the early ones by Coleridge and Hazlitt, as well as general texts, both domestic products such as Dugald Stewart's *Dissertation Exhibiting the Progress of Metaphysical, Ethical and Political Philosophy since the Revival of Letters in Europe* (1815–21), George Henry Lewes's *A Biographical History of Philosophy* (1845), Frederick Denison Maurice's several histories, and a large number of more specialised or limited histories, and imported works, such as William Enfield's version of Brucker, and translations of Tennemann, Hegel, Erdmann, Ueberweg, Windelband, Lefevre, Alfred Weber, Cousin, Høffding, and many more. However, it is clear that the acceptance of the subject was much slower in England than on the Continent. The English long considered the history of philosophy a recent German invention, in a sense quite rightly. It may be a sign of the time it took for the epistemological paradigm to conquer Britain that Enfield's (that is, Brucker's) distinctly pre-Kantian history (Brucker first published in 1742–4) remained acceptable so late in Britain: the fifth and last edition appeared in 1839.[15]

The epistemological paradigm has had a remarkable ability to transcend most major shifts in philosophy for nearly a couple of centuries. To take just one obvious example, often there was virtually no difference in views between the neo-Kantians and the logical positivists when it came to the general shape of the history of early-modern philosophy. Indeed, when a philosopher switched from the Kantian to the positivist camp, his idea of historical development might well remain unchanged (even though his *appraisals* changed). Similarly, the paradigm has been able to straddle the major confessional divides. There is not a whole lot of difference between, say, Karl Vorländer, Father Copleston, Bertrand Russell, and Anders Wedberg when it comes to deciding what is the mainstream of philosophy from Descartes to Kant.[16]

The philosophical differences between the two founders of the modern concept of the history of philosophy, Reid and Kant, were, of course, profound, but there was a striking similarity in their reactions to the immediate philosophical past. They both considered that David Hume had brought the modern philosophical tradition to a sceptical crisis because he reduced knowledge to perceptually derived ideas whose representational warrant was impossible to establish. And they both rejected this notion of knowledge as ideas in favour of a concept of knowledge as judgements that are warranted by features of undeniability on the part of any individual who wants to claim any beliefs at all. At the same time, although there is a gulf between Reid's establishment of the first principles of common sense and Kant's transcendental deduction of the pure forms of sensible intuition and of the categories, they both retained a fundamental feature of what they took to be Hume's approach, namely, that knowledge is a matter of the activity of the individual mind. Both sides of this, the individualism and the mentalism, were to remain dominant assumptions in subsequent philosophy and, not least, in interpretations of the history of early-modern philosophy.

Kant's and Reid's views of how modern philosophy had reached what they considered the impasse of Hume's scepticism were not the same but they were compatible. Neither thinker wrote a history of philosophy, yet both developed their views in often intense dialogue with their predecessors. However, their discussions were generally conducted as if with contemporaries. Both of them were distinct 'presentists' for whom the philosophy of the past had to be overcome by making it a moment in their own thought. In Kant's case, this meant that we should deal with the history of philosophy not as 'historical and empirical' but as 'rational, i.e., possible a priori' – a 'philosophical archaeology' of 'the nature of human reason'. (Loses Blatt F 3, in Ak 20: 341). When Kant does approach the history of philosophy as 'historical and empirical' in his *Lectures on Logic*, his surveys are not dramatically different from those of his contemporaries, and his own promise of progress, namely the critical establishment of metaphysics as 'the real, true philosophy', itself seems to be within empirical history.[17] However, when we turn to the treatment of the same history in the *Kritik der reinen Vernunft*, we find the critical overcoming of dogmatism and scepticism and the stalemate, 'indifferentism', to which they have fought each other, to be inherent in reason itself. 'The critical path alone is still open.'[18] Of course, it was this well-known idea of an unavoidable dialectical opposition between Leibniz's and Wolff's rationalism and dogmatism on one hand and Locke's empiricism tending to Hume's scepticism on the other that became the prototype of the canonical philosophical histories we have mentioned.

The foundational history in this vein was the already mentioned twelve-volume work by Wilhelm Gottlieb Tennemann.[19] Springing from Tennemann's own lectures in Marburg, the work was of central importance to the three significant lecture series on the history of philosophy – mentioned earlier – that signalled the changing status of the subject at the opening of the nineteenth century, namely Hegel's in Berlin in the 1820s (and perhaps already in Jena in 1805), Cousin's in Paris in 1815, and Coleridge's in London in 1818.[20] Of these, Hegel's were undoubtedly the most significant; they were an important step in Hegel's philosophical development and they helped establish the central role of the history of philosophy in the philosophical curriculum.[21] However, although they were certainly more catholic in their conception of philosophy than many of the Kantian histories, one cannot say that Hegel substantially changed the contours of early-modern philosophy and its priorities, which had been laid down by the Kantian revolution. Something similar may be said about Schelling's lectures 'On the History of Modern Philosophy', probably from 1833–4 (but with much earlier predecessors, now lost). Despite their title, the lectures are devoted to the development of German idealism and its ancestry in Descartes, Spinoza, Leibniz, and Wolff, but they do devote a couple of pages to Bacon and Hume, mainly so as to invoke the formula that 'From the beginning of modern philosophy . . . , rationalism and empiricism move parallel to each other, and they have remained parallel until now.'[22]

True to his ardent empiricism, Reid made the history of philosophy a moment in his own philosophy by thinking of it as, in Kant's words, 'historical and empirical', and, more particularly, as something that could be discarded in the discussion of mental philosophy once this had rid itself of silly metaphysical squabbles as natural philosophy had done. But until that day, Reid was sure that he had to 'build with one hand, and hold a weapon with the other.'[23] Reid's warfare was predominantly against the emergence of scepticism in modern thought.[24] From René Descartes via Nicholas Malebranche, John Locke, and George Berkeley to Reid's own time, philosophical views of how the human mind acquires knowledge of the world that enables people to conduct the business of life had become, as Reid saw it, more and more at variance with common understanding.

Reid thought that philosophers had been misled by the triumph of natural sciences into drawing an analogy between matter and mind and thus to using the methods of these sciences to explain both the cognitive and the active faculties of the mind. The very language that was being used in talking of mental phenomena was 'physicalistic', as we might say. The mental world was thus said to be composed of elements called ideas, and the composition was explained in spatial and mechanistic terms. Although few philosophers were materialists in the strict sense, most tended to understand the connection among ideas, passions, the will, and behaviour in causal or quasi-causal terms. When driven to its final, absurd conclusions, which Reid found in the work of David Hume, modern philosophy had created a phantom world of so-called ideas that sprang from objects of observation; the self was a conglomeration of perceived ideas; and the will as the source of action was nothing but the balance of passionate impulses at any given moment.

This was Reid's understanding of modern philosophy, which he considered not only false but dangerous.[25] It is well-known that Dugald Stewart elaborated considerably on this scheme in his influential Introduction to the *Encyclopaedia Britannica*, the above-mentioned *Dissertation* which Victor Cousin was instrumental in having published in French.[26] It is less well-known that a Reidian view of the history of philosophy was being propagated to the French-reading public already in the 1790s by the professor of philosophy at the Academy of Geneva, Pierre Prevost.[27]

The impact of Common Sense philosophy in France became significant, however, mainly through the efforts of Pierre-Paul Royer-Collard and, as far as the writing of the history of philosophy is concerned, through his pupil Victor Cousin.[28] Royer-Collard had used the idea of common sense as a means of going beyond any of the established schools of philosophy to an underlying general rationality, and Cousin in effect developed this idea into a philosophical eclecticism with explicit reference to the long German tradition of eclecticism (especially in Brucker). In such a scheme, all philosophising was directly dependent upon the history of the various philosophical standpoints, and Cousin's preaching of the eclectic gospel gave a tremendous boost to the history of philosophy as a subject of teaching and scholarship in France. Soon he came under the influence of German idealism, especially that of Hegel and Schelling, and created his own less than perspicuous ego-philosophy as an amalgam of the Germans, the Scots, and, first and last, Descartes. His idea of the shape of the philosophical past remained more or less stable, namely that there were four fundamental forms of philosophy: 'sensualism' (that is, what was commonly taken to be Condillac's sensationalism), 'idealism', common-sense, and mysticism.[29] From these the eclectic philosopher could distil the appropriately knowing subject.

Although widely different, Kant's critical philosophy, Reid's Common Sense, and Cousin's eclecticism had similar views of the role that the history of philosophy should play. All three saw it as their mission to overcome and go beyond the problems that had made up the history of philosophy. But while the past was history, it served well to make their own philosophies intelligible, to show the point in their argument. Consequently, there was a *philosophical* justification – indeed, a philosophical need – for the 'pedagogical' use of the history of philosophy. In shaping this history, the philosophical priorities of Kant and Reid were the fundamental factor. Each in his own way, they created the epistemological paradigm for the history of early-modern philosophy that has dominated the subject ever since they wrote. Our notion of the history of post-Renaissance philosophy is, in other words, itself the outcome of a particular episode in that history.

IV. LIMITS OF THE EPISTEMOLOGICAL PARADIGM

The epistemological paradigm for early-modern philosophy has been an immensely powerful vehicle for scholarship and for the self-understanding of the discipline of philosophy. Nevertheless, the paradigm is arguably at considerable variance with the philosophical self-understanding common in that period, and this, combined with the fact that the paradigm, as indicated earlier, is an historical accident, suggests that it is part of the philosophical historian's task to question it. Without pretending to have any magic formula for finding out *wie es eigentlich gewesen*, one is led by a great deal of modern scholarship to query not only the detail but also the general lines of the paradigmatic view of seventeenth- and eighteenth-century philosophy.

We may begin with a simple observation about the geographic comprehensiveness of modern (nineteenth- and twentieth-century) versus early-modern history of philosophy, namely, that the former is overwhelmingly Eurocentric. It may not be surprising that the philosophy of the North American colonies and the early American Republic generally has been treated as an extension of British thought, when noticed at all in general histories and university courses. But it is remarkable how suddenly all interest in non-European thought dropped out of the general histories of philosophy. Commonly, the pre-Enlightenment histories as well as the major eighteenth-century works, such as Brucker's *Historia critica philosophiae* (1742–4), as a matter of course were 'universal' in their ambitions and included chapters not only on ancient 'barbarian' thought but also on Near and Far Eastern thought of the Christian era. However, once the idea of the distinctiveness of 'modern' philosophy took over, the non-European world disappeared from sight.[30] The epistemological paradigm may here have had support from retrograde steps in the philosophy of mind and the philosophy of language in both the idealist and the emerging positivist world. It is thus remarkable that, for example, both Kant and James Mill were of the opinion that 'barbarians' could not have a philosophy because they thought concretely in images, not abstractly in concepts, a feat reserved for the Greeks and their European heirs.[31] Closely associated with such views was the linguistic racism that gained strength in the nineteenth century.[32]

A more complicated issue is the effect of gender bias on the writing of the history of philosophy during the last two centuries. Here feminist scholarship has gone to the roots of the epistemological paradigm. Through scrutiny of the standard idea of body-mind dualism and the associated masculinity of mind and reason, feminist scholars have questioned the tradition's emphasis on the solitary rational mind as the focus of knowledge.[33] This has happened especially through attention to early-modern theories of the passions.[34] Such work has connected

easily with the increasing attention to philosophical anthropology, which will
be noted later. However, feminist scholarship has largely shadowed the canon by
adding figures to be analysed, and insofar as it has questioned the over-all shape
of early-modern philosophy, this has not yet had a major impact on general
histories and courses.[35]

Another general limitation in the common histories of philosophy is, as mentioned earlier, the treatment to which ethics, politics, and aesthetics have been
subject, at least until quite recently. Ethics and aesthetics (when discussed at all)
have mostly been dealt with to the extent that they could be seen to raise modern meta-ethical and meta-aesthetic issues of relevance to the general theory
of knowledge. This is clearly the consequence of the combined Kantian and
Reidian legacy. Both thinkers in effect subsumed ethics and aesthetics under
epistemology by making the former two disciplines centrally concerned with
the justification of moral and aesthetic judgements (which is not to deny that
such justification and philosophy as a whole ultimately had a moral purpose).
However, as we will see, it is a considerable simplification of early-modern
ethical and aesthetic concerns to reduce them to questions of justification. In
addition, it has until recently been forgotten that moral philosophy very often
had a pedagogic priority as a 'foundation course' in university studies. Partly
because of this status, it had its own historiography that shows a completely different idea of the shape of philosophy from the one assumed by later historians of
ethics.[36] This finding is amply confirmed by Christian Garve's above-mentioned
general history of ethics from the close of the eighteenth century.[37]

Political theory, in contrast, has either been treated as a subject separate from
the main line of philosophical argument or simply excluded from general histories of philosophy, a tendency reinforced by the development of political science
as an independent discipline with a need for its own canon and a useful past. The
idea that a concern with the possibility of social living and its political implications could be *the* fundamental problem in philosophy, and that metaphysics
and epistemology were to be seen as esoteric learning without claim to primacy and universality, has therefore been more or less incomprehensible. Those
thinkers who pursued such a line of argument, notably Samuel Pufendorf and
Christian Thomasius, have not only not been taken seriously as philosophers
but have commonly been written out of the history of philosophy altogether,
a process that had already begun with the Wolffian takeover of the German
universities and has continued ever since. In the 1760s, Formey's brief history
of philosophy could still spare Grotius and Pufendorf, though not Thomasius, a
couple of pages, but only as reformers of natural law. A century later, Friedrich
Ueberweg made do with less than a page each for Pufendorf and Thomasius –
and identified them under the characteristic section heading 'Zeitgenossen von

Leibniz' (contemporaries of Leibniz).[38] In our own time, the following declaration is probably representative of common opinion: 'Had Kant not lived, German philosophy between the death of Leibniz in 1716 and the end of the eighteenth century would have little interest for us, and would remain largely unknown'.[39] Only in recent years has this extraordinary distortion of the whole shape of German philosophical development in the eighteenth century begun to be rectified.[40]

The narrowing effect of many histories of philosophy may be indicated by contrasting some structural features of early-modern philosophy with those imposed on it subsequently. Of the four traditional disciplines into which philosophy continued to be divided, namely, logic, metaphysics, and natural and moral philosophy, none was a natural place for the epistemological endeavours that subsequently came to be seen as the hallmark of the period's thought. Right through the eighteenth century, many epistemological questions turn up in the context of metaphysics, while the rest are to be found in logic. However, this was a logic that had largely become a mental classification scheme. Of the two other disciplines, natural philosophy was wholly classificatory and explanatory, and moral philosophy was much more so than its modern heirs. The issues that are considered 'philosophical' in our histories of philosophy, such as the epistemic adequacy of ideas or the normative warrant of obligation, have been picked out of these contexts. It is not at all clear in what sense we can be said to understand such pickings divorced from their explanatory framework, but it is clear that we have excluded a major part of what our forebears thought of as philosophy. It is equally clear that they did not have room for subdisciplines of either epistemology or meta-ethics. Indeed, 'epistemology' as the label for the theory of knowledge was not invented until 1854 by James Frederick Ferrier. Sadly, his idea of agnoiology, or the theory of ignorance, has never caught on.[41]

Natural philosophy has its own historiography in the form of what is now called the history of science. However, it is still rare to see general histories of philosophy making more than highly selective use of this discipline. The historical gains have made the subject awkward for the epistemological high road from Descartes to Kant. An equivalent history of moral philosophy, understood as the 'science of morals', has been much slower to develop, but the intense study of Enlightenment anthropology in recent times has provided means to remedy the situation. It will be very difficult, however, to integrate much of this material into the standard history of ethics, for eighteenth-century moral science in general had a much wider scope than the issues that are the core of contemporary ethics, especially the ground of normativity and obligation. Much of moral philosophy was as descriptive, classificatory, and explanatory in intent as natural philosophy, and the basic justificatory mode of argument was often the same in both branches, namely, teleological and, generally, providential. The major novelty of eighteenth-century moral thought prior to Kant's critical turn, namely, the idea that a law-governed ethics could be rejected by showing that morals were a matter of sentiment, was in itself an important element in the re-invigoration of the teleology of natural religion. When Hume pointed out to Hutcheson the fragility of this foundation, he was making it clear that such moral justification could not be part of the science of morals and that this science had to be part of a 'true' scepticism. Much of early-modern ethics was simply not concerned with the justification of moral beliefs and judgements in the way that Kant, Reid, and subsequent philosophers were. And insofar as the earlier thinkers were dealing with the moral faculties of the human mind, they were doing so as part of a wider science of morals – indeed, a general anthropology. The Copernican revolution which Hume saw as necessary in the moral sciences was fundamentally different from the more famous one proclaimed by Kant. Hume wanted the mind explained by means of general principles similar to those applied elsewhere in nature. Kant wanted an epistemic certification that objects conform to knowledge.[42]

All this is not to say that early-modern philosophers were not concerned with questions of how to lead the good life, but these questions have tended to lie outside the interests of contemporary histories of ethics, at least until very recently. We may approach the question of how early-modern thinkers pursued normative concerns, as we would call them, by means other than the justification of belief through a consideration of early-modern ideas of the practice of being a philosopher. The ancient idea that the value of a philosophy had to show itself in the life of its proponent retained great significance. While there is an established literature that approaches ancient philosophy in this light, it is only recently that something similar has been attempted with some aspects of early-modern thought. It has been argued, for instance, that even the more recondite parts of Descartes's philosophy, such as his geometry, are to be properly understood as a spiritual exercise in the service of self-cultivation.[43] At the other end of our period, the three sections of Kant's *Groundwork of The Metaphysics of Morals*, it has been suggested, are to be seen as 'stages in the spiritual grooming of a par-ticular intellectual deportment – one that will regard true morality in terms of the commands of a pure rational being acceded to through the purifying dis-cipline of metaphysics.'[44] More broadly, the continued function of metaphysics as a spiritual exercise that has both personal and social aims has been analysed in detail.[45]

Closely associated with such ideas was the notion that the philosopher's proper role was to undergo such exercises so as to live an exemplary life. The depth of this understanding of the nature of philosophy can be illustrated in many ways.

It is clearly shown through the reaction which Pierre Bayle was able to provoke with his presentation of Spinoza's life as exemplary, a feat studiously repeated by Adam Smith nearly a century later in his 'obituary' for David Hume, who himself was deeply concerned with properly presenting the sort of life his philosophy entailed.[46] Shaftesbury was ever in pursuit of the appropriately stoic stance, as he saw it, and Berkeley obviously considered it a particularly sore point to assail that stance as a sham.[47] It is telling also to notice the parallel between the philosopher's and the preacher's concern with the importance of conspicuously filling their roles. Francis Hutcheson was never unmindful of the dignity of his office, and the biography of him by his clerical colleague William Leechman reinforced the point.[48] The significance of the phenomenon is further underlined by the universal success of Fontenelle's invention of the *éloge*.[49] Considered in a wider perspective, the proper conduct of the philosophical life was just a special – and especially important – case of the general method of approaching normative, practical, 'applied' ethics by delineating the ideal fulfilment of the offices of life.[50]

These ideas of the intimate connection between life and philosophy and the associated conception of the historical passage of philosophy clearly lie outside the purview of the epistemological paradigm for early-modern philosophy. In the common perspective, the exemplary philosophical life and its historiographical significance is, at best, a quaint detail. Similarly, the practical ethics formulated through the notion of fulfilling one's offices is not going to be a concern for those who are in pursuit of early forms of deontology and consequentialism.

In view of this role of the life of the philosopher, three other structural features of early-modern philosophy fall into place. First, the pervasive use of the ad hominem argument is significant. Wave after wave of undesirables – epicureans, deists, sceptics – was supposedly stemmed by the argument that they could not 'live' their philosophy. Secondly, if philosophy is viewed as inherently connected with the conduct of life, it is not so strange that the ancient arrangement of the history of philosophy into 'sects', or schools, should have remained influential through the seventeenth and eighteenth centuries. The pivot of a sect was the founding figure whose example in self-cultivation was what made the school cohere. Not only was this approach maintained in the writing of the history of ancient philosophy, but it was also a persistent concern during the period under consideration to see early-modern philosophy in light of the traditional sect system. This is conspicuously the case in the histories of philosophy, such as Brucker's. It was clear to these historians, as it was to most people, that it was difficult to extend the ancient system unaltered to modern times, yet it remained the obvious classificatory system. This dilemma led them to a new development, and this is the third point I want to mention in this connection. I am thinking of the role of eclecticism.

Although this was a complex phenomenon, it is probably safe to say that the eclecticism which came to the fore in the late seventeenth and early eighteenth centuries, especially in Germany but with interesting features in common with English deism, was basically concerned with the possibility that a modern philosophy could be above the sects without itself being a sect if it could define the philosophical life as a non-dogmatic (non-sectarian) utilisation of all the sects.[51] This has significance for two changes in the perception of the overall structure of philosophy. First, the eclectic ideal of going beyond sectarianism in philosophy lent the history of philosophy temporal direction; instead of the traditional largely a-temporal comparison of schools, the promise of progress and the threat of decline became prominent features of debate and quickly merged with more general ideas of humanity's progressivism. This was, however, a highly ambivalent attitude, for the eclectic idea of learning through methodical comparison soon led to a renewed form of the a-temporal ideal, namely, that of not only learning systematically (in the sense of methodically) from the sects but of overcoming them by the creation of a *systematic* philosophy, a philosophy that need not pay attention to the argumentative situation in which it finds itself among the various schools of thought.

The most obvious place to observe this paradoxical development is in the work of Brucker, who contrived to see Leibniz and Wolff as eclectics, mainly because he saw the whole of post-Renaissance philosophy as attempts at eclecticism and then celebrated the two great neo-scholastics as the apogee of that development.[52] In other words, although he saw modern philosophy as liberation from an authoritarian sectarianism, he also saw it as undergoing doctrinal progress in a straight line from Descartes through Leibniz to Wolff, a line relative to which other forms of philosophy were incidental. As has been pointed out, Brucker, despite his eclectic starting point, thus paved the way for Kant's simplification of the history of modern philosophy to an epistemological clash between rationalism and empiricism by serving up a ready-made model of the former.[53] We may add that Formey's above-mentioned brief history of philosophy, which drove Brucker's argument to an extreme, seems to have been Kant's most direct source.

This idea of systematic philosophy, achieved by the inversion of eclecticism, was unusually potent both immediately and in the longer term. Philosophy proper was philosophy that had overcome sectarianism and come of age by being the systematic, timeless, context-free search for truth. Thinking that did not fulfil these requirements simply was not real philosophy. This more than anything else bolstered epistemology's status as the core of genuine philosophy, and the systematic drive became particularly strong in the German tradition, with its metaphysical underpinning of epistemological endeavour.

Once this is entrenched in the historiographical canon from the nineteenth century onwards, non-systematic forms of philosophising become marginalised or excluded. The Renaissance is at best covered as a somewhat chaotic period of transition; seventeenth- and eighteenth-century eclecticism itself disappears completely from historical view; the messy French *philosophes* are taken less than seriously; the 'civic philosophers' in the Pufendorfian tradition are, as mentioned, dismissed; and so forth. In fact, from this point of view, most of moral and political thought was unphilosophical because it was unsystematic. In addition, the passion for systematicity that grew out of the eighteenth century itself and conquered most historical scholarship for the subsequent couple of centuries meant that the Cartesian-Newtonian ideal of natural philosophy until recently completely overshadowed the other form of theorising about the natural world which in fact was so important in the eighteenth century and whose greatest representative was Linnaeus, as Phillip Sloan explains:

The importance of Linnæan science as an *alternative* eighteenth-century scientific pro-gramme to Cartesian-Newtonian natural philosophy has rarely been appreciated. In terms of the familiar categories of eighteenth-century natural philosophy – experimental method, quantitative idealization, belief in an underlying mathematical structure of re-ality, primary-secondary qualities distinction, mechanistic and reductive explanations – Linnæan science presented almost a point by point contrast. Pervaded by a direct episte-mological realism, in which the object of true science was 'to know things in themselves', Linnæan science was qualitative, non-experimental and descriptive. It denied a radical subject-object dichotomy; it admitted no 'problem of knowledge' that troubled over epistemological scepticism and problems of sensation. It was theocentric, teleological, and more in touch with classical sources (Roman Stoicism, Scholastic logic) and Re-naissance nature-philosophy than with the science of Descartes or Newton. The natural world, as it was experienced by the interested layman in all its colours, shapes, even in its anthropomorphic analogies, took precedence over material and mathematical analysis.[54]

Philosophical thought that was intertwined with human, civil history has had an equally hard time keeping a presence in the histories of philosophy and for no less interesting philosophical reasons. Here we touch upon what is perhaps the most deep-rooted element in the epistemological paradigm I referred to above as its individualism and mentalism, the assumption that knowledge has to be accounted for in terms of the activity (or passivity) of the individual person's mind. This assumption has made it difficult to give satisfactory accounts of some debates that were absolutely central in early-modern philosophy. First, there was the never-ending concern with history, sacred and profane, that demanded a theory of testimony, or of knowledge as something shared interpersonally.

This is the key to understanding the philosophical debates of such things as the status of miracles, the authority of Scripture, and the possibility of civic history.[55] In view of the difficulties of fitting these matters into the framework of traditional histories of philosophy, it is not so strange that even a figure of Vico's stature either is ignored or is treated without much connection to the rest of philosophical culture during the period. In connection with testimony and non-mentalistic ideas of knowledge, it would also be worth attending to what we may call the literary cultivation of memory in the form of the commonplace book and the like, a combination of some relevance to Locke's idea of personal identity.[56]

Secondly, the late seventeenth and eighteenth centuries saw a revolution in the theory of language whose wider importance goes unacknowledged in the common history of philosophy. Samuel Pufendorf had already formulated the basic idea that reasoning is linguistic in nature, that language originates in social interaction, and that mental ratiocination as a consequence is derived from social life.[57] Furthermore, even as he formulated the classic theory of language as, at its core, labels of ideas, John Locke admitted that some key elements in language could only be accounted for in functional, not referential, terms. However, it was Étienne Condillac who worked out a sophisticated theory of language as performative behaviour. In doing so, Condillac made it possible to make connections between language in the narrower sense and other forms of communicative behaviour which had been studied intensely for both their cognitive and practical significance, such as rhetoric, theatre, dance, music, and art. Moreover, it was this approach to linguistic behaviour that helped philosophers in their attempts to understand folk culture and the 'primitive' mind.[58]

In other words, it is necessary to set aside the epistemological paradigm in order to understand the philosophical discussions of 'social' forms of knowledge ranging from revealed religion and scriptural criticism through secular history to language, the arts, and anthropology.

V. IN THE ABSENCE OF A PARADIGM

These reflections are not meant to imply that there is no such thing as a 'true' concept of philosophy. The point is rather that if we want the history of philosophy to have a chance of being more than a collection of successful and unsuccessful illustrations of our own philosophical preconceptions, then we cannot let these preconceptions dictate what counts as philosophy irrespective of time and place. This does not mean that we can avoid the responsibility of seeing the past from our own present, nor that we cannot, or should not, ask a-historical or anachronistic questions of past works – for instance, whether an author understood what he was saying – if we think that this may ferret out content that otherwise would remain hidden.[59] But that is very different from shaping the past, such as early-modern philosophy, in the image of the present.

In the case of the present work, the blind spots of the epistemological paradigm indicated earlier are obviously not meant as an alternative paradigm or an agenda, except in a very general sense. The core of the volume is philosophical anthropology (see Part II on Human Nature), and extensive space is devoted to a concept of philosophy that is wider than that current today. Thus philosophical ideas relating to religion, nature, and moral and social relations are each allotted a Part. However, within each of these Parts, there are discussions of a wide variety of philosophical and historiographical styles, including several secured by the solid moorings of the epistemological paradigm. In addition, in Part I, which looks at philosophical arguments 'from the outside', there are two overviews clearly and happily at variance with the ideas put forward in the present chapter. This is not a work at peace with itself, nor was it meant to be. The very pluralism of approaches to eighteenth-century philosophy illustrates very well the historical and contingent nature of the subject.

In writing the history of philosophy in general and that of the early-modern period in particular, we have a choice. We can begin with a more or less fixed notion of what philosophy is (persuaded, for example, by Kant or Reid) and proceed to find historical instantiations of and approximations to it. Or we can let the concept of philosophy itself be part of the object for historical investigation. In the former case, it is not clear in what sense the enterprise is history; in the latter case, it is an open question whether it has a more than locally identifiable object.

However, the latter choice, the way of history, does have its own philosophical rationale, namely a form of what Hume called 'true scepticism.' The point of such history is to query the predominant concept of philosophical history and to make the historical coherence of the concept of philosophy itself into an object of historical investigation. It is not to deny the possibility of such coherence but to make it a fruitful question of empirical history. This mode of 'philosophierende Geschichte der Philosophie' (philosophising history of philosophy) is certainly critique, but it is historical critique.

NOTES

1 See J. G. A. Pocock, 'Enthusiasm: The Antiself of Enlightenment', in *Enthusiasm and Enlightenment in Europe, 1650–1850*, eds. L. E. Klein and A. J. La Vopa (San Marino, CA, 1998), 7–28.

2 See James Schmidt, 'Inventing the Enlightenment: Anti-Jacobins, British Hegelians, and the *Oxford English Dictionary*', *Journal of the History of Ideas*, 64 (2003): 421–43.

3 See Alan Charles Kors, *D'Holbach's Coterie: An Enlightenment in Paris* (Princeton, NJ, 1976), ch. 9.

4 Friedrich Meinecke, *Die Entstehung des Historismus*, 4th edn. (Munich, 1965), 2 and 285.

5 Isaiah Berlin, 'The Counter-Enlightenment', in his *Against the Current: Essays in the History of Ideas* (London, 1980), 1–24; J. G. A. Pocock, 'Enlightenment and Counter-Enlightenment, Revolution and Counter-Revolution: A Eurosceptical Enquiry', *History of Political Thought*, 20 (1999): 125–39. For an analysis of French reaction, see Darrin M. McMahon, *Enemies of the Enlightenment: The French Counter-Enlightenment and the Making of Modernity* (Oxford, 2001).

6 Compare Jonathan Knudsen, 'The Historicist Enlightenment', in *What's Left of Enlightenment?: A Postmodern Question*, eds. K. M. Baker and P. H. Reill (Stanford, CA, 2001), 39–49.

7 James Schmidt, 'What Enlightenment Project?', *Political Theory*, 28(6) (2000): 734–57 at 739.

8 In addition to the previous reference, see James Schmidt, 'Introduction: What Is Enlightenment? A Question, Its Context, and Some Consequences', in *What is Enlightenment? Eighteenth-Century Answers and Twentieth-Century Questions*, ed. J. Schmidt (Berkeley, CA, 1996), 1–44; *The Enlightenment and Modernity*, eds. N. Geras and R. Wokler (Basingstoke, Hampshire, London, New York, NY, 2000).

9 Compare Daniel Gordon, 'Introduction: Postmodernism and the French Enlightenment', and his 'On the Supposed Obsolescence of the French Enlightenment', both in *Postmodernism and the Enlightenment: New Perspectives in Eighteenth-Century French Intellectual History*, ed. D. Gordon (New York, NY and London, 2001), 1–6 and 201–21.

10 Most notably, whereas the earlier rounds of Enlightenment critique accused it of subjectivism and relativism, the post-modernist critique has generally been aimed at the opposites of these.

11 The most important historiographical works include *Storie delle storie generali della filosofia*, ed. G. Santinello, 5 vols. (Brescia and Padua, 1979–2004); English translation in progress: *Models of the History of Philosophy*, vol. 1, eds. C. W. T. Blackwell and P. Weller (Dordrecht, 1993); Lucien Braun, *Histoire de l'histoire de la philosophie* (Paris, 1973); *Philosophy and Its Past*, eds. J. Rée, M. Ayers, and A. Westoby (Brighton, 1978); U. J. Schneider, *Die Vergangenheit des Geistes: Eine Archäologie der Philosophiegeschichte* (Frankfurt am Main, 1990); same, *Philosophie und Universität: Historisierung der Vernunft im 19. Jahrhundert* (Hamburg, 1998); Johannes Freyer, *Geschichte der Geschichte der Philosophie im achtzehnten Jahrhundert* (Leipzig, 1912).

12 T. J. Hochstrasser, *Natural Law Theories in the Early Enlightenment* (Cambridge, 2000), 170–5.

13 Although Karl Ameriks may well be right that the interpretation of Kant's own philosophy was distorted by Karl Leonhard Reinhold, Johann Gottlieb Fichte, and Georg Wilhelm Friedrich Hegel, I do not think that this was the case with the Kantian view of philosophical history; see Ameriks, *Kant and the Fate of Autonomy* (Cambridge, 2000).

14 Schneider, *Philosophie und Universität*.

15 See my Introduction in William Enfield, *The History of Philosophy from the Earliest Periods: Drawn up from Brucker's 'Historia critica philosophiæ'* [1837], 2 vols. (Bristol, 2001).

16 Karl Vorländer, *Geschichte der Philosophie*, 2 vols. (Leipzig, 1903); Frederick Copleston, *A History of Philosophy*, 9 vols. (London, 1946–74); Bertrand Russell, *A History of Western Philosophy* (New York, NY, 1945); Anders Wedberg, *A History of Philosophy*, 3 vols. (Oxford, 1982–4).

17 Immanuel Kant, 'Logik Jäsche', Ak 9: 32; translated in Kant, *Works/Lectures on Logic*, trans. J. M. Young (1992). Kant gives three general overviews of the history of philosophy in the lectures as published: 'Logik Blomberg', Ak 24: 31–7; 'Wiener Logik', Ak 24: 800–4; and 'Logik Jäsche', Ak 9: 27–33; all are in *Lectures*. In the first and earliest of these, from around

1770, Kant divides modern philosophy into dogmatic and critical, the latter represented by Locke. While Kant clearly drew on Jean Henri Samuel Formey's *Kurzgefassete Historie der Philosophie* (Berlin, 1763; first in French, Amsterdam, 1760), it is to Kant's merit that he brings Locke up to parity with Leibniz. Formey devotes only a few lines to Locke as a 'logician' in a work which is heavily dependent upon Brucker, including the latter's perverse view that Wolff is the epitome of eclecticism.

18 Kant, *Kritik der reinen Vernunft*, A855/B883, translated as *Works/Critique of Pure Reason*, trans. P. Guyer and A. W. Wood (1998). See also and especially Preface A.

19 Wilhelm Gottlieb Tennemann, *Geschichte der Philosophie*, 12 vols. (Leipzig, 1798–1819).

20 See Schneider, *Philosophie und Universität*, 213–14. For Coleridge, see *Lectures, 1818–19: On the History of Philosophy*, ed. J. R. de J. Jackson (*The Collected Works of Samuel Taylor Coleridge*, vol. 8, London and Princeton, NJ, 2000); lectures 11–13 are on early-modern philosophy.

21 Hegel's manuscripts were compiled by Karl Ludwig Michelet and published as *Vorlesungen über die Geschichte der Philosophie* (1833–6), now vols. 18–20 of *Werke*, eds. E. Moldenhauer and K. L. Michelet, 20 vols. (Frankfurt am Main, 1969–72). Translation in *Lectures on the History of Philosophy*, trans. E. S. Haldane and F. H. Simson, 3 vols. (London 1892–6). Re-established texts, based on the 1825–6 course, in *Vorlesungen über die Geschichte der Philosophie*, vols. 6–9 of *Vorlesungen*, eds. P. Garniron and W. Jaeschke (Hamburg, 1983–6), here 9: 71–148. See also Alfredo Ferrarin, *Hegel and Aristotle* (Cambridge, 2001), 31–3.

22 Friedrich Wilhelm Joseph Schelling, *Zur Geschichte der neueren Philosophie: Münchener Vorlesungen* (Berlin, 1986), 54; quoted from Schelling, *On the History of Modern Philosophy*, trans. A. Bowie (Cambridge, 1994), 61.

23 Thomas Reid to James Gregory, 8 June 1783, in *The Correspondence of Thomas Reid*, ed. P. B. Wood (Edinburgh, 2002), 163.

24 Reid does not seem to have availed himself of any of the standard histories of philosophy. In *Essays on the Intellectual Powers of Man*, eds. D. R. Brookes and K. Haakonssen (Edinburgh, 2002), 28, he refers to Brucker's first major work, *Historia philosophica doctrinae de ideis* (Augsburg, 1723), but I know of no references to the *Historia critica philosophiæ* nor to Thomas Stanley's *History of Philosophy*, 4 vols. (London, 1655–62).

25 Reid's engagement with the history of modern philosophy was so extensive that he toyed with James Gregory's suggestion that he should turn this material into a separate work. See the letter referred to in note 23 and my Introduction in Reid, *Essays on the Intellectual Powers of Man*.

26 Dugald Stewart, *Histoire Abrégée des sciences metaphysiques, morales et politiques depuis la renaissance des lettres*, trans. J. A. Buchon (Paris, 1820).

27 See Daniel Schulthess, 'L'école écossaise et la philosophie d'expression française: Le rôle de Pierre Prevost (Geneva 1751–1839)', *Annales Benjamin Constant*, 18–19 (1996): 97–105; 'L'impact de la philosophie écossaise sur la dialectique enseignée à Genève: Un cours latin inédit (1793–1794) de Pierre Prevost', in *Nomen Latinum: Mélanges de langue, de literature et de civilisation latines offerts au professeur André Schneider*, ed. D. Knoepfler (Geneva, 1997), 383–90. Common Sense philosophy also had an extraordinary influence in the United States for several decades of the nineteenth century. For a general overview, see Benjamin W. Redekop, 'Reid's Influence in Britain, Germany, France, and America', in *The Cambridge Companion to Reid*, eds. T. Cuneo and R. van Woudenberg (Cambridge, 2004), 326–39.

28 Pierre-Paul Royer-Collard, *Les fragments philosophiques de Royer-Collard*, ed. A. Schimberg (Paris, 1913), first appended to Thomas Reid, *Œuvres complètes*, 6 vols. trans. T. Jouffroy (Paris, 1828–36). See Schneider, *Philosophie und Universität*, 180–212; Donald R. Kelley, *The Descent of Ideas: The History of Intellectual History* (Aldershot, 2002), ch. 1.

29 Later he incorporated this into a world-historical scheme of cultural cycles.

30 Those, such as Hegel and Cousin, who made philosophy part of grand cycles of civilisation, would often find room for an 'oriental' epoch some time in the grey past, and as the Middle Ages became established as an object for philosophical scholarship, the Arab contribution began to be noticed.

31 Kant, 'Wiener Logik', Ak 24: 800, and 'Jäsche Logik', Ak 9: 27; James Mill, *History of British India*, 6 vols. in 4 (New York, NY, 1968), 1: 232, 2: 240, 242; etc.; and see Mill, *Selected Economic Writings*, ed. D. Winch (Edinburgh, London, 1966), ch. 5.

32 See Hans Aarsleff, Introduction, in Wilhelm von Humboldt, *On Language: The Diversity of Human Language Structure and Its Influence on the Mental Development of Mankind*, trans. P. Heath (Cambridge, 1988), x and lxiii; same, Review Essay, in *Anthropological Linguistics*, 43 (2001): 491–507; Ruth Römer, *Sprachwissenschaft und Rassenideologie in Deutschland*, 2nd edn. (Munich, 1989).

33 See especially Genevieve Lloyd, *The Man of Reason: 'Male' and 'Female' in Western Philosophy* (Minneapolis, MN, 1993).

34 See Susan James, *Passion and Action: The Emotions in Seventeenth-Century Philosophy* (Oxford, 1997), and Annette Baier's interpretation of Hume; for instance, 'Hume, the Women's Moral Theorist?', in *Moral Prejudices: Essays on Ethics* (Cambridge, MA, 1994), 51–75.

35 See the body of work reviewed in Nancy Tuana, 'The Forgetting of Gender and the New Histories of Philosophy', and Eileen O'Neill's Comments on Tuana, in *Teaching New Histories of Philosophy*, ed. J. B. Schneewind (Princeton, NJ, 2005).

36 See Hochstrasser, *Natural Law Theories*.

37 Christian Garve's *Uebersicht der vornehmsten Principien der Sittenlehre, von dem Zeitalter des Aristoteles an bis auf die unsre Zeiten* (Breslau, 1798).

38 Friedrich Ueberweg, *Grundriss der Geschichte der Philosophie* (1863), 5 vols., 12th edn. (Berlin, 1923–8), 3: 344–6.

39 Lewis White Beck, 'From Leibniz to Kant', in *The Age of German Idealism*, eds. R. C. Solomon and K. M. Higgins, vol. 6 of *Routledge History of Philosophy* (London, 1993), 5.

40 See Hochstrasser, *Natural Law Theories*; Ian Hunter, *Rival Enlightenments: Civil and Metaphysical Philosophy in Early Modern Germany* (Cambridge, 2001); and my 'German Natural Law', in *The Cambridge History of Eighteenth-Century Political Thought*, eds. Mark Goldie and Robert Wokler (Cambridge, forthcoming). For the status of early-modern natural law in a wider perspective, see my 'Protestant Natural Law Theory: A General Interpretation', in *New Essays on the History of Autonomy*, eds. Natalie Brender and Larry Krasnoff (Cambridge, 2004): 92–109.

41 James Frederick Ferrier, *Institutes of Metaphysics: The Theory of Knowing and Being* (Edinburgh, 1854), in his *Philosophical Works*, 3 vols. eds. A. Grand and E. L. Lushington (Edinburgh, 1875), vol. 2.

42 David Hume, *A Treatise of Human Nature*, II.1.3; Kant, *Kritik der reinen Vernunft*, B xvi. I am indebted to Aaron Garrett for reminding me of this contrast.

43 Matthew L. Jones, 'Descartes's Geometry as Spiritual Exercise', *Critical Inquiry* 28 (Autumn 2001): 40–71.

44 Ian Hunter, 'The Morals of Metaphysics: Kant's *Groundwork* as Intellectual *Paideia*', *Critical Inquiry*, 28 (Summer 2002): 908–29. See also G. Felicitas Munzel, *Kant's Conception of Moral Character: The 'Critical' Link of Morality, Anthropology, and Reflective Judgement* (Chicago, IL, 1999); and Kant's emphasis on character building is a basic theme in Manfred Kuehn, *Kant: A Biography* (Cambridge, 2001).

45 Ian Hunter, *Rival Enlightenments*.

46 Pierre Bayle, *The Dictionary Historical and Critical*, trans. Pierre Des Maizeux, 5 vols. (London, 1734–8), article 'Spinoza', 5: 199–224; Adam Smith to William Strahan,

9 November 1776, in *The Correspondence of Adam Smith*, eds. E. C. Mossner and I. S. Ross, in *Works* (1977), 217–21.

47 George Berkeley, *Alciphron, or the Minute Philosopher*, Third Dialogue, in *Works*, 3: 112–40.

48 William Leechman, 'The Preface, giving some Account of the Life, Writings, and Character of the Author', in Francis Hutcheson, *A System of Moral Philosophy*, 2 vols. (London, 1755), for example at xxx–xxxii and xxxviii–xxxix.

49 See Charles B. Paul, *Science and Immortality: The Eloges of the Paris Academy of Sciences, 1699–1791* (Berkeley, CA, Los Angeles, CA, and London, 1980).

50 It is telling that when Reid was performing his role as teacher, this traditional form of practical ethics was his organizing method; see the lectures reconstructed in Thomas Reid, *Practical Ethics: Being Lectures and Papers on Natural Religion, Self-Government, Natural Jurisprudence, and the Law of Nations*, ed. K. Haakonssen (Princeton, NJ, 1990). For the significance of this form of practical ethics in the development of professional ethics, see Lisbeth Haakonssen, *Medicine and Morals in the Enlightenment: John Gregory, Thomas Percival, and Benjamin Rush* (Amsterdam and Atlanta, GA, 1997). For historical background, see, for example, Paul Marshall, *A Kind of Life Imposed on Man: Vocation and Social Order from Tyndale to Locke* (Toronto, 1996).

51 See Michael Albrecht, *Eklektik: Eine Begriffsgeschichte mit Hinweisen auf die Philosophie- und Wissenschaftsgeschichte* (Stuttgart-Bad Cannstatt, 1994); Horst Dreitzel, 'Zur Entwicklung und Eigenart der "Eklektischen Philosophie"', *Zeitschrift für Historische Forschung*, 18 (1991): 281–343; Hochstrasser, *Natural Law Theories*, passim; Kelley, *The Descent of Ideas*, especially ch. 5.

52 Concerning Brucker in general, see *Jacob Brucker (1696–1770): Philosoph und Historiker der europäischen Aufklärung*, eds. W. Schmidt-Biggemann and T. Stammen (Berlin, 1998); see also Constance Blackwell, 'Diogenes Laërtius's 'Life of Pyrrho' and the Interpretation of Ancient Scepticism in the History of Philosophy – Stanley through Brucker to Tennemann', in *Scepticism and Irreligion in the Seventeenth and Eighteenth Centuries*, eds. R. H. Popkin and A. Vanderjagt (Leiden, 1993), 324–57.

53 See Hochstrasser, *Natural Law Theories*, ch. 5; see also Richard Tuck, 'The "Modern" Theory of Natural Law', in *The Languages of Political Theory in Early-Modern Europe*, ed. A. Pagden (Cambridge, 1987), 99–119 at 99–102.

54 See Phillip R. Sloan, Chapter 31, this volume.

55 See C. A. J. Coady, *Testimony: A Philosophical Study* (Oxford, 1992). For the theological aspects, see M. A. Stewart, 'Revealed Religion: The British Debate', in Chapter 23, this volume. For testimony and history, see Dario Perinetti, 'Philosophical Reflection on History', Chapter 36, this volume.

56 See Richard Yeo's suggestion that Enlightenment efforts to organise knowledge, such as Ephraim Chambers's *Cyclopaedia*, were closely connected to the commonplace book, in 'A Solution to the Multitude of Books: Ephraim Chambers's *Cyclopaedia*' (1728) as 'the Best Book in the Universe', *Journal of the History of Ideas*, 64(1) (2003): 61–72.

57 See Hochstrasser, *Natural Law Theories*, 83–95.

58 Hans Aarsleff, *From Locke to Saussure: Essays on the Study of Language and Intellectual History* (Minneapolis, MN, 1982), 146–224; same, Introduction in Étienne Bonnot de Condillac, *Essay on the Origin of Human Knowledge*, trans. and ed. H. Aarsleff (Cambridge, 2001), xi–xxxviii; and 'Philosophy of Language', Chapter 16, this volume.

59 In praise of anachronism, see Jonathan Rée, 'The Vanity of Historicism', *New Literary History*, 22 (1991): 961–83. For testing authors' self-comprehension, see my *Natural Law and Moral Philosophy: From Grotius to the Scottish Enlightenment* (Cambridge, 1996), 8–14, and my 'Reason and Will in the Humanities', in *Is There a Human Nature?*, ed. L. S. Rouner (Notre Dame, IN, 1997): 63–77.

2

CONCEPTS OF PHILOSOPHY

WERNER SCHNEIDERS

I. INTRODUCTION

Modern philosophy began as a protest against the traditional philosophy of the schools. The Italians turned to classical antiquity, whereas the English, the French, and the Germans turned to the emerging natural sciences. Bacon, Descartes, Leibniz, Locke, and many others were, of course, students of philosophy, but they all distanced themselves from scholastic philosophy and its theological dominance. They did not teach 'school-philosophy' but remained laymen in both senses of the term, non-theologians and non-professionals. Their interest in natural science was an expression of disgust with traditional textual scholarship; they turned from terminological wrangles to the direct study of the world. Obscure and inaccurate discourse was to be replaced by exact and, where possible, quantifiable knowledge. Modern philosophers no longer searched for truth in the past or in ancient texts but expected to find it in the future, through new research into facts, causes, and principles. In this way, they hoped to establish a new and secure foundation for philosophy, closely associated with science as the model, which even was to be exceeded wherever possible. This concern with certain knowledge was virtually never theoretical; it was generally practical, motivated, for example, by hopes of medical and technological advances. Frequently its aim was a general reform of society, a new politics. At the same time, the awkward problem of religion (the reform of which universally had led to conflict) was set aside by emphasising the distinction between reason and revelation. Subsequently it was gradually reintroduced into the discussion, with the declared intention of reconciling philosophy and religion.

Eighteenth-century philosophy was clearly based on these seventeenth-century foundations. But even before the turn of the century, new theoretical and practical interests emerged, for example, epistemological and sociological ones. These inevitably implied criticism, particularly of theological or ecclesiastical tradition. Philosophy replaced theology as the foundational discipline and changed its focus of interest from metaphysics to the problems of knowledge and from natural religion – as recently distinguished from revealed religion – to ethics. The trinity of virtue, happiness, and usefulness became the central theme of reference; the appeal to reason as universally valid science turned into the self-assertion of individual reason which could call upon experience against all dogmatic rationality. The critique of unreason in the shape of superstition and prejudice, enthusiasm and fanaticism, and to some extent of tradition and authority, corresponds to the drive towards autonomy of thought and responsibility, which was particularly manifest in the German Enlightenment. A new belief in progress, the consciousness of living in a new age, became the prevailing mood. Thus began the Enlightenment, in the narrower sense of the word, as an intellectual and social movement characterised by a series of common problems and solutions and by a relatively coherent complex of normative concepts and metaphors. This process of enlightenment, in spite of all counter-movements, defines the eighteenth century, which, at least in Germany, established itself early as the Age of Enlightenment with its own strong period awareness.

The Enlightenment saw itself as the age of critique and philosophy and fostered a certain type of philosophy and philosophical self-understanding, even though this was not immediately reflected in the definitions of philosophy. Although the formal concept of philosophy remained fairly unchanged, the concept was, as always, historically influenced and acquired a new colouring during the Enlightenment. As the approximation of 'philosophy', 'critique', and 'enlightenment' shows, philosophy was understood as applied or practical knowledge, and the definitions of 'philosophy' tended to be purposive or instrumental. However, during the Enlightenment, it was also the tacit implications and the actual applications that, above all, characterised philosophy. In describing it, we must moreover presuppose a very broad concept of philosophy, corresponding to the self-perception of the age. Thus philosophy still, as a matter of course, included physics as 'natural' or even 'experimental' philosophy and, indeed, as practical speculation in the widest possible sense.

Because of its critique of different forms of belief, the Enlightenment strongly emphasised the universality of human reason and dreamt of a kinship of humankind and cosmopolitan citizenship. Even so, it was during the eighteenth century that the national traits of philosophy were reinforced. The thematic and linguistic unity of philosophy deriving from scholasticism continued well into the seventeenth century but gradually disintegrated. Of course, the Enlightenment was still relatively coherent in its defensive reaction against the past, but the very different political, religious, cultural, and social situations in its three heartlands led to quite distinct developments. Furthermore, the Enlightenment urge for improvement fostered a need for popular appeal and thus for use of the national languages; the result was a sort of national philosophy.

II. GREAT BRITAIN

Although English society was as dominated by religion and as rent by religious wars as the rest of early-modern Europe, it also saw remarkably early attempts to develop something akin to modern science, and these attempts were supported by a long tradition of nominalist and empiricist philosophy. It is notable that these developments took place outside the homes of school philosophy, that is, outside the great universities of Cambridge and Oxford. In England, the gentleman scholar and philosopher appeared early and predominantly among the social elite; later he was found chiefly among the gentry and the bourgeoisie. With the Glorious Revolution of 1688, which marked the end of the wars of religion and absolutist ambitions, the intellectual and political situation was consolidated under a constitutional monarchy with extensive intellectual liberties. Thus in Great Britain – as it became in 1707 – the Enlightenment began with a political victory.

English philosophy in the seventeenth century provided all the main foundations for that of the eighteenth; it is characterised by three features which are not found on the Continent and can only partly be explained by the religious and political situation or the empiricist and nominalist tradition. First, since the time of Francis Bacon, philosophy had been strongly oriented towards the sciences, making philosophy practically a higher form of science, while Isaac Newton and Robert Boyle in turn regarded physics and chemistry as philosophy (*philosophia naturalis et experimentalis*). Secondly, as a counterpoint to this there was an early development (especially with Edward Herbert, Lord Cherbury) of the idea of religion as natural, based on reason, common to humanity, and inherently tolerant; and these latitudinarian and deistic ideas eventually led to a free and critical exploration of religion in general. This development has to be seen against the background of the religious constellation of High Anglicanism, strong Non-conformism, and weak Roman Catholicism and the religious wars arising from this. Thirdly, as a result of the explosive political situation and the civil and religious wars, there was a rapidly developing interest in political philosophy on a grand scale and with wide perspectives. With Thomas Hobbes, this produced a theory of the modern state that was ambivalently absolutist and liberal. These factors characterise seventeenth-century philosophy; it is partly concerned with developing a new scientific philosophy based on a new method, partly with the emphatic separation of philosophy and religion. At the same time, however, the new philosophy was to have practical and especially political effects. Naturally, the importance of these factors varied from person to person and generation to generation. But they all remained significant into the eighteenth century; the scientific status of philosophy became less of a focus, while the issue of religion remained an absorbing concern in the philosophy of the early English Enlightenment.

English Enlightenment philosophy, in the narrower sense, seems at first to be characterised by two old interests and one new. First, the strong interest in religious questions acquired a distinctly critical cast and, at the expense of religion as such, took the relationship between reason and religion as its theme. Secondly, there continued to be a strong political interest in the basis for the modern state's self-understanding and in the civil liberties of its citizens. However, this gradually gave way first to ethical and then to practical (economic) discussions. Alongside these two concerns, a completely new epistemological discussion developed. This was undoubtedly grounded in the old 'nominalist' tradition and in the results of modern science, but it quickly changed direction by emphasising the phenomenal nature of the world; in fact, it drifted away from the natural sciences and the concomitant conception of knowledge (in spite of all the encomia of Newton). The rejection of scholastic philosophy, and with it all metaphysics, continued to play a significant part in all this. Early English Enlightenment philosophy prided itself on its emancipation from the universities. Joseph Addison and Richard Steele, in *The Spectator*, no. 10 (12 March 1711), boasted that they 'have brought Philosophy out of Closets and Libraries, Schools and Colleges, to dwell in Clubs and Assemblies, at Tea-Tables and in Coffee-Houses'. English philosophy in the eighteenth century initially aimed at reconciling philosophy and common sense.

John Locke may be taken as the founder of English Enlightenment philosophy in the narrower sense. In his principal work, *An Essay Concerning Human Understanding*, which appeared in 1690, almost at the same time as Newton's *Philosophia naturalis* (1687), Locke intended to explore the limits and possibilities of human reason. As is well-known, he turned against Cartesian rationalism, in the sense of apriorism, and substituted an empiricism which leaves only mathematics and ethics inviolate. Furthermore, he criticised all previous philosophies as obscure and useless: 'Schoolmen and Metaphysicians' were for him 'the great Mint-Masters' (*Essay*, III.x.2).[1] Locke identified philosophy with knowledge or science. True knowledge was based upon experience of the sort found in 'experimental philosophy'; but although this was enough for common needs, it offered no knowledge of the principles of reality – that is, science in the metaphysical sense – an ideal that Locke seems to have retained as a matter of course. While he saw his own philosophy as scientific, he seems to have understood science in a more traditional sense. At least he concludes his work with a time-honoured division of the subjects of our understanding – that is, of knowledge and thus of the sciences in the widest sense, that is to say, of philosophy. Natural philosophy, 'in a little more enlarged Sense of the Word' (IV.xxi.2), is now in first place. It deals with all things as such, including God, angels, and spirits, as well as bodies and matter, and is in fact theoretical philosophy in the sense of physics and metaphysics. In second place is practical philosophy and its most important branch, ethics; its other branches are no longer mentioned. Third is logic, now known as semiotics because it is essentially 'the Doctrine of Signs' (IV.xxi.4). This is Locke's chief interest here, and his own work may be interpreted as a 'logic' or 'semiotics' that has been developed into a theory of knowledge. But however Locke might evaluate philosophy in general and his own in particular, whether as based on experience or on principle, he obviously had enough philosophical self-awareness to employ philosophy, reason, and the 'light in the Understanding' (IV.xix.13–14) emphatically against enthusiasm and indirectly against revealed religion.

The critique of religion, which frequently led to the assertion that philosophy was the true religion, implied various theses with a general demand for the free pursuit of philosophy or free thinking in general. Freedom was necessary for independent thought and the enlightenment of others. The best example of this position is Anthony Collins's *A Discourse of Free-Thinking* (1713). Collins was not a systematic philosopher who offered reflections on the concept of philosophy; he was concerned with concrete criticism of the Bible and religion and with the defence of natural belief. For him, philosophy was above all free thought, understood as criticism: 'By Free-Thinking then I mean, the Use of the Understanding, in endeavouring to find out the Meaning of any Proposition whatsoever, in considering the nature of the Evidence for or against it, and in judging of it according to the seeming Force or Weakness of the Evidence' (sect. I).[2]

Locke's philosophy was, for many of his contemporaries in Britain, a signal to pursue new lines of thought in epistemology and the philosophy of religion as well as in ethics and politics. Whereas the philosophy of religion turned into radical criticism of religion (see, in addition to Collins, John Toland and Matthew Tindal) from which Locke had to distance himself, ethics, which had been rather neglected by Locke, was pursued along an independent path by Anthony Ashley Cooper, 3rd Earl Shaftesbury. This involved to some extent different ideas of philosophy. Shaftesbury basically inclined to a mystical-aesthetic Platonism and consequently, unlike Locke, had a positive appreciation of enthusiasm. His fervor for the good and the beautiful did not, however, prevent him from wanting to submit everything to the test by ridicule. His philosophy is in general an optimistic psychology, a 'plain home-spun Philosophy, of looking into our-selves' (*Works*, I.43).[3] As an independent gentleman-philosopher, Shaftesbury shared the aversion of his contemporaries and peers for scholasticism, which had ruined the social standing and therefore the political importance of philosophy.[4]

Dogmatic rationalists were a particular target, but even Locke was too speculative for Shaftesbury, who detested all systematic philosophy – 'The most ingenious way of becoming foolish is by *a system*' – and strove for a more worldly and livable philosophy 'by confronting this super-speculative Philosophy with a more practical sort, which relates chiefly to our Acquaintance, Friendship and good Correspondence with *our-selves*.'[5] He understood philosophy as the most sublime striving for a happiness which for him was naturally linked with virtue, so that, once again, philosophy was *vitae dux, virtutis indagatrix* (the guide to life, the explorer of excellence),[6] and philosophising everyone's business.[7] Since Shaftesbury based virtue on a moral sense which must be educated, he saw the philosopher as essentially a gentleman in the best sense of the word. 'To *philosophize*, in a just Signification, is but To carry *Good-Breeding* a step higher'.[8] As regards content, the philosopher must first of all study humanity, and especially the individual, its way of life, and its relationship to nature and society. In this way, philosophy makes us 'comprehensible to our-selves',[9] and teaches us to live in harmony with the whole world: '[T]he Sum of Philosophy is, To learn what is *just* in Society and *beautiful* in Nature, and the Order of the World'.[10]

At the same time as Shaftesbury began, or at least inspired, a series of moral-philosophical discussions, a significant new approach was taking place in epistemology. Even more than with Shaftesbury, George Berkeley's philosophy is unthinkable without Locke, but his religiously motivated intentions led in a diametrically opposite direction. His epistemologically based immaterialism was intended to defend God against all false philosophy and especially against the modern critic of religion, the 'minute philosopher' with a talent for ridicule and mockery.[11] In the middle of an Enlightenment critical of religion, philosophy could thus become the advocate of faith. Like Locke, Berkeley sees modern science as a purely superficial form of knowledge, but a dangerous one, because potentially atheistic. Thus, despite the Enlightenment's hostility to metaphysics, Berkeley is led to rehabilitate *philosophia prima*, though he naturally distinguishes between sound and unsound metaphysics: True philosophy will act like 'a medicine for the soul of man'.[12]

The epistemology begun by Locke and pursued for other ends by Berkeley was radicalised by David Hume and turned into a moderate scepticism according to which religion itself was only a form of philosophy.[13] For Hume, philosophy was understanding of phenomena and their derivation from human nature, in other words, critique in the form of anthropology. And his procedure was 'cold and unentertaining'. At the beginning of his *Enquiry Concerning Human Understanding* (1748), without any mention of natural philosophy, Hume divides 'moral philosophy, or the science of human nature' into two types.[14] One type considers man as born for action and seeks above all to improve his morals;

the other considers him as an essentially rational creature and tries to shape his intellect. Both types are of merit in contributing to conversation, instruction, and improvement. The first is a philosophy for common life, pleasant, easy, and plausible. The second is more exact and abstract; as an ascent to principles it is difficult, if not incomprehensible to common sense. Its themes are obviously identical with Hume's interests: 'to find those principles, which regulate our understanding, excite our sentiments, and make us approve or blame any particular object, action, or behaviour' (*First Enquiry*, 1.2, SBN 6). Its subtleties are far removed from daily life and therefore easily mislead, whereas the philosopher of common sense remains rooted in everyday living. The latter has therefore always been more highly regarded than 'the mere philosopher' (1.5, SBN 8) with his principles and concepts, who is disliked because he seems to give the world neither utility nor pleasure. Hume wavered between a wish to found true philosophy and his appreciation of the social wish for something useful and entertaining; he therefore tendered a balance of the two. A well-rounded personality moves between extremes, equally at home with books, in society, and in business. 'Be a philosopher; but, amidst all your philosophy, be still a man' (1.6, SBN 9). In fact, however, Hume's argument ends up as a defence of 'what is commonly called *metaphysics*' (1.7, SBN 9), although he inveighed against metaphysics and wanted to see all metaphysical books burnt. The spirit of philosophy – that is, the spirit of accuracy – will finally penetrate all of society, however introverted and averse from business the philosopher may be.[15] Hume is convinced, too, that philosophical principles will finally also determine politics. In this way, his defence of exact philosophy – not least in contending against popular superstition – becomes a programme of enlightenment: 'Accurate and just reasoning is the only catholic remedy, fitted for all persons and all dispositions' (1.12, SBN 12). Hume manifestly oscillates between a desire for immediate happiness through improvement of the world on the one hand and a striving for exact philosophy on the other.[16] He would like to reconcile common sense with philosophy as the highest form of the former and believes that a careful sceptical philosophy is the best defence against error. Such a philosophy is also a defence against superstition and a guide to living.[17]

Hume was one of the few Scottish philosophers who, in the fashion of English contemporaries, remained outside the university. But even he tried – and failed – to get a university chair, and the so-called Scottish School, which in debate with him developed a new Common Sense philosophy, was mainly an academic philosophy with certain conservative characteristics, as shown by Thomas Reid, its chief representative. Reid divided reality into body and mind, 'the Material world' and 'the Intellectual world'. Correspondingly, he divided philosophy into 'natural philosophy, as that word is now used', and the philosophy of mind, or pneumatology. Natural philosophy was older and better developed, but it was in the field of the philosophy of the (human) mind that the most important advances were to be expected.[18]

The aversion of British philosophy to all metaphysics early on produced a turn towards humanity: 'The proper study of mankind is', in Pope's words, 'Man'.[19] Epistemology and ethics were thus developed in psychological terms. At the same time, the philosophy of human nature matched the ideal of the worldly philosopher who neither sat in his study hatching new principles nor indulged in the amusements of society. The philosopher should stand in the midst of life but preserve a critical distance to all untested opinions. Thus he would be neither a bigot nor a radical but, in the final analysis, in agreement with common sense. Philosophy is the reflection of sound common sense.

III. FRANCE

The special character of French Enlightenment philosophy is largely the result of the intellectual and social situation of the French philosophers. The repeal of the edict of Nantes in 1685 and the driving out of the Huguenots had apparently welded the country, with its centralist and absolutist government, into a monolithic block. State and church were very closely linked and opposition banished or silenced. The early Enlightenment therefore was a protest by exiles from within and without France; those who were Protestant had to emigrate, and those who were Catholic could act only with extreme care. Not until the death of Louis XIV and the regency of Philip, Duke of Orléans, was there a brief period of intellectual and political liberalisation. A certain reaction followed under Louis XV, but the onset of the Enlightenment and the beginnings of social and intellectual criticism could no longer be suppressed, especially since they were promoted by Madame de Pompadour, the king's mistress. The era usually known as the *Siècle de Lumières* had thus begun already before mid-century, and after 1750 its protagonists, the *philosophes*, were centered around the great project of the *Encyclopédie*. They determined the picture of the French Enlightenment as essentially a Parisian phenomenon up until the French Revolution and, in fact, until the present day. But even at the peak of the French Enlightenment, not just before and after, there were thinkers whose intentions went beyond those of the *philosophes*.

In eighteenth-century France, there were almost no major original philosophers in the stricter sense and, consequently, no original definitions of philosophy. Furthermore, there seems to have been a greater interest in the philosophers than in their philosophy, no doubt due to the distinctive court and salon culture. At all events, even before mid-century, interest was concentrated on the *philosophe*, who was not a philosopher in the traditional sense but a man of society, no solitary sage but a committed man of letters who, while theoretically active, was principally concerned with working in society for society. In this way, philosophy became an enlightened programme for improving the world, although this can mostly be inferred indirectly from the self-portrayal of the *philosophe*. Apart from that, the classical definitions of philosophy, such as 'study of wisdom' or 'investigation of causes', persisted also in France.

French Enlightenment philosophy sets out from Cartesianism and its criticism but was already before the turn of the century distinguished by a rapid decline of interest in metaphysics and theology. In theology, the great battles between Catholics and Protestants and, within Catholicism, between Jesuits and Jansenists, had been fought; in philosophy, Cartesianism dissolved, and it had, in any case, only been accepted with reservations. The drive towards a system had still led Nicolas Malebranche and Baruch Spinoza to great schemes, but it was plainly weakening and the Enlightenment established itself as an anti-Cartesian, anti-metaphysical, anti-dogmatic rationalism. That, in turn, changed the ideal of philosophy and science. René Descartes himself had, of course, already striven for a popular notion of knowledge in his *Discours de la méthode*, but at the same time he had propagated an ideal of philosophy as a methodically constructed, strict science derived, if possible, from a single clear principle. In theory, philosophy became a universal science, representing an unshakeable system. But this ideal had lost support even before 1700. Protestant and Catholic philosophers, such as Bayle and Fontenelle, completed the break with Cartesian rationalism and prepared the way for the critical rationalism, to some extent even empiricism and sensationalism, of the Enlightenment.

Pierre Bayle took up the criticism of superstition and prejudice and attempted an historical critique of contemporary knowledge in writings that also defended toleration and a strict distinction between religion and morals.[20] He thus initiated a popular as well as scholarly Enlightenment critique of both religion and reason. Although he recognised the evidence of certain rational principles, his scrutiny of theses and facts brought him closer to scepticism so that philosophy became de facto critique understood as a sceptical method.

Bernard le Bovier de Fontenelle had turned to journalism and popular writing in early youth, and it was principally these early efforts – for example, his critique of superstition – that were significant for future intellectual development in France.[21] In the preface to his defence of the possibility of a multitude of worlds, addressed to the whole world (*à tout le monde*), also women, he proclaims an ideal of philosophy that is midway between profound scholarship and easy entertainment.[22] Philosophy should not stick to obvious phenomena but should open up the unknown by means of hypotheses. True philosophers do not believe in the visible but seek the invisible (*Entretiens sur la pluralité des mondes*, 3, 10–11). In the *Dialogues des morts*, Anacreon appears as the true sage, the Epicurean, teaching the scholastic philosopher, Aristotle, that philosophy is concerned with humanity, not with the rest of the world; the object of the philosopher is himself as a person.[23]

The *Siècle des lumières* in the narrower sense begins with François-Marie Arouet de Voltaire. As a young man, he got into trouble with the authorities because of his impudent and free-thinking criticism. He took refuge in England for some years, which decisively influenced him, as he showed in *Lettres philosophiques ou Lettres sur les Anglais* (1734) and in *Eléments de la philosophie de Newton* (1738). This popularised English empiricism and Newtonianism in France and prepared the way for the Anglomania of the French Enlightenment, which primarily identified philosophy with the way of thinking of the empirical sciences. Voltaire's *Dictionnaire philosophique portatif* (1764), on the other hand, is a partly satirical attack on the enemies of enlightenment, in which philosophy is understood mainly as moral wisdom and its chief opponents and persecutors as enthusiasts and fanatics.[24]

Even before Voltaire, a highly critical discussion of the *philosophe* as a new type of philosopher had begun in France. A small anonymous collection, *Nouvelles libertés de penser*, from 1743 contained the treatise *Le Philosophe*, now generally attributed to the grammarian C. C. Du Marsais. In this the philosopher is presented in plainly materialistic and mechanistic terms as a human thinking machine that reflects (on) its own motion. The philosopher is, as it were, a periodically self-winding clock. Reflection, or reason, determines his actions and raises him above ordinary people, yet his main goal is to live in and serve society; he is *honnête homme*. His chief service as friend of humankind is to combat prejudice and superstition, backed by a knowledge of reality.

Le Philosophe went through numerous editions and revisions and was of great significance for the self-perception of French Enlightenment philosophers, although it was criticised by them as well as by their opponents.[25] Diderot and Voltaire prized it and undertook new editions, though with important revisions. Voltaire, whose estate on his death included a text with corrections in his own hand, posthumously published, abbreviated and toned down the edition of 1773 and in the process the 'human machine' became an 'organised being'. Diderot included the treatise in abbreviated and sharpened form in the *Encyclopédie*, as the article 'Philosophe', but he dropped the sentence about the *philosophe* as thinking machine altogether.[26] However, both Voltaire and Diderot have in other contexts expressed quite different views on philosophers and philosophy.

Also, d'Alembert's *Discours préliminaire de l'Encyclopédie* (1751) presented a different concept of philosophy. Primarily a mathematician, Jean le Rond d'Alembert emphasised the technical and practical aspects in this attempt at a survey and genetic derivation of all arts and sciences. Following Bacon, he made use of the old division of mental powers into memory, imagination, and reason as the organ of philosophy and science; the two were not yet clearly distinguished. Without further definition, philosophy was then as usual divided according to its three subjects: God (and the spirits created by him), humankind, and nature. In addition, the separate disciplines are prefaced by an *ontologie ou science de l'être, ou métaphysique générale* (ontology or science of being, or general metaphysics), presumably under the influence of the German philosopher Christian Wolff. The three main divisions of philosophy in turn are designated partly as 'science' and partly (just as by Wolff) as *métaphysique particulière*. These are theology or *science de Dieu*, which here includes revealed theology; the *science de l'homme*, whose first part is *pneumatologie ou métaphysique particulière* and which includes epistemology and ethics; and the *science de la nature*, which is the science of bodies.[27] In other words, despite the common celebration of its revolutionary character, this view of philosophy is on the whole surprisingly traditional. True, d'Alembert does not doubt the advances in philosophy and science, but his praise of the new *esprit philosophique* and *esprit de discussion*, of analysis and enlightenment, does not lead to any particular criticisms of church or state. Though he cautiously disapproves of philosophers' fondness for systems (*esprit de système*), he nevertheless expects philosophy to instruct as well as entertain and is obviously concerned to rise above the *philosophie commune* of the salons.[28] In his later *Essai sur les éléments de philosophie ou sur les principes des connaissances humaines* (1759), d'Alembert is even more systematic in his promotion of the idea of metaphysics as the science of principles.

About the middle of the century, the French Enlightenment took on a new shape; it increased in both intensity and reach, becoming at once more radical and more widespread. In 1751, the first volume of the *Encyclopédie* appeared, and for many years it was the focus of the French Enlightenment, not least because it constantly had to battle for its own survival. Significant writers such as Voltaire and Rousseau kept their distance; so did Étienne Bonnot de Condillac, who did see philosophy as metaphysics in the sense of a knowledge of principles. Even d'Alembert abandoned the enterprise after some years, though partly for tactical reasons. Furthermore, just then the whole concept of the Enlightenment, and with it the idea of a philosophy that could change the world for the better, was being questioned by an outsider, the Swiss-born Jean-Jacques Rousseau. In 1750, he answered in the negative the prize question of the Academy in Dijon, whether the renewal of science and the arts had contributed to the improvement of morals, and for that he won the prize. For Rousseau, the *philosophe* was not an ideal but the illusion of a degenerate culture that had lost all solidarity. Philosophers, for him, were a rabble of charlatans (*une troupe de charlatans*).[29]

Rousseau's fundamental questioning of the Enlightenment and its supporting ordinary philosophy, and indeed of cultural and scientific progress in general, could not prevail in France. The salon scene belonged to the *philosophes*, to the few important and many unimportant writers whose critique of faith and society grew appreciably more radical. Materialism, too, first propagated by the physician Julien Offray de La Mettrie (*L'homme machine*, 1747) and then by the tax farmer Claude-Adrien Helvétius (*De l'esprit*, 1758), found a tireless systematiser in the German-born Baron d'Holbach (*Système de la nature, ou des Loix du monde physique et du monde moral* 1770). These materialists identified philosophy with scientific knowledge, which they saw as a condition for virtue and happiness.

The year 1789 brought change also to the philosophic scene in France. Most of the well-known philosophers were already dead by then and only a few, such as the Marquis de Condorcet, tried to maintain the ideals of the Enlightenment amid the confusion of the French Revolution. Condorcet's *Esquisse d'un tableau historique des progrès de l'esprit humain* (1793) is a panegyric on the progress of philosophy, the sciences, and the arts, in which the last epoch of history is the age from Descartes, who is thereby rehabilitated and glorified, through the French Revolution, which is praised as the beginning of true social freedom. Its advances are the work of the new 'analytical' philosophy and the new class of *philosophes*, the Enlighteners. This new philosophy, which is more or less lumped together with the other sciences by Condorcet, would continue its progress and organise the perfection of the human race.

The peculiar characteristics of French eighteenth-century philosophy and its concept of philosophy must largely be explained by the political and religious conditions in France as a literary reaction against an unacceptable situation. Most French philosophical writers were not thinking of eternal and ultimate matters: they were demanding change in the present world. Of course, there were always attempts at pure philosophy, even metaphysics, but most theory was only of interest as it affected practice. The *philosophes* were generally excluded from all real power relations in society, but they constituted themselves as an intellectual force that might shape society. Thus they generally favoured enlightened absolutism as an opportunity for an advisory role in politics, but they were nearly always disappointed. In fact, they remained a part of the aristocratic and upper-class culture while undermining its foundations. The truly significant and original political philosophy (Montesquieu, Rousseau) developed on the fringes of literary society.

IV. GERMANY

The philosophical situation in eighteenth-century Germany was markedly different from that in England or France. The German Enlightenment began at the end of the seventeenth century, in political and social, cultural, and intellectual conditions brought about by the catastrophe of the Thirty Years War and the continuation of territorialism and sectarianism dictated by the Peace of Westphalia (1648). Nominally, of course, the Holy Roman Empire continued under the Hapsburgs, but in fact what is known today as Germany was broken up into about 350 more or less independent political units of the most varied kinds. At the same time, the country was divided into three distinct denominations – Catholic, Lutheran, and Calvinist – sharply separate in some areas, coexisting in others. The danger of religious wars was dispelled, but there was no likelihood of further political or religious reform. Germany had no capital and no active social groups of any size. Only with the rise of Prussia, which began at the close of the seventeenth century, and the mid-eighteenth-century clash between it and the preceding big power, Austria, did the political and intellectual situation in Germany change fundamentally. Prussia became the protagonist of the new state system and absolutism, eventually enlightened absolutism.

An important feature of the German territorial system was the necessity of separate administrations in each state and territory. Given the confessional divisions, it was necessary to have separate, denominationally linked universities in which to educate the required lawyers, physicians, and pastors. So Germany early became and long remained a land of universities; at times there were about 50 universities (*Hohe Schulen, Illustre Gymnasien*). These universities, sometimes contrary to the intentions of their founding, became places of intellectual resort and debate, a third force in relation to court and church. Here the German intelligentsia gathered and those who did not enter the service of the state or the church generally sought a university professorship. In spite of their provincialism, it was in the universities that the new spirit of enlightenment developed.

Without an eye for wider social implications – for state and church – the German Enlightenment first of all proceeded as a moral argument; ethics took the lead, so to speak, over religion and politics. Gradually, philosophy replaced theology as the leading academic discipline, the lectern challenged the pulpit, and philosophy emphatically saw itself as 'worldly wisdom' and secular learning.

The philosophy of university professors is different from that of freelance authors; they write for their colleagues and students, inclining to scholarly, thorough, and systematic texts. Consequently, much of German philosophy in the eighteenth century remained a school and scholastic philosophy, in both a good and a bad sense, and the German Enlightenment was, for good and for bad, an academic Enlightenment. However, enlightened academic philosophy, because of its urge to influence society, was supplemented by a popular philosophy for the world. Although much of this remained a popularisation of school philosophy, it did make a few professors of philosophy virtual instructors to the German nation.

The great exceptional personality in Germany is Leibniz, who saw himself as the mediator between scholastic and 'modern' seventeenth-century metaphysics, and who, in spite of many enlightened characteristics, is a transitional figure to the eighteenth century. As an independent writer in court service who did not need to concern himself with academic philosophy, he had no external reason for systematic reflection on the concept of philosophy. From his sporadic comments it is clear that he understood philosophy as the science of rational principles, or *scientia*, in traditional contrast with empirical knowledge, or *historia*. While Leibniz understood science as the new physics, he saw philosophy as the higher science of transphenomenal being, a science whose ultimate aim was to glorify God.

German Enlightenment philosophy begins, at least symbolically, with Christian Thomasius's announcement of lectures in German in 1687. Thomasius understood philosophy as a practical science. At first, in his *Introductio ad philosophiam aulicam* (1688), he defined it traditionally, as an auxiliary science in the quest for knowledge of all things and their causes – 'for the good of humanity', as he added.[30] He increasingly stressed this practical purpose of learning in general and philosophy (*Weltweisheit*, or worldly wisdom) in particular. The definition of philosophy was thus primarily finalistic. It was to promote worldly happiness through knowledge of the true and the good. And such a philosophy was so easy that it could be understood by people of all levels of society and by both men and women, even though a special profession was necessary for its proper development. In the end, Thomasius even believed that all that mattered was an existential recognition of the true good; purely theoretical truth might actually have harmful effects, as exemplified by the potential for atheism in the sciences. However, compared with the Christian theology of revelation, philosophy is a 'philosophic faith'.

Thomasius was originally a lawyer and had his main influence in jurisprudence, but he was also a great inspiration in philosophy because of his break with the scholastic tradition. His followers, on the other hand, were on the whole more cautious and academic than he. Thomasian philosophy was generally not oriented towards science, particularly since it commonly saw the natural sciences as nothing but probable and empirical knowledge. Philosophy on this view was above all concerned with living – that is, with knowledge that is practical, necessary, and useful but also critical. Its subjective purpose, not its objective character, was the focus of interest. Broadly speaking, there were two branches of Thomasianism. The first, in Jena, derives from the theologian Johann Franz Budde, and its best-known member is the lexicographer Johann Georg Walch. The second, in Leipzig, derives from the physician Andreas Rüdiger and is best-known through the anti-Wolffian Christian August Crusius. Budde understood philosophy as living knowledge aimed at attaining beatitude; against Thomasius's popular philosophy he stressed the need to distinguish between academic and worldly philosophy – a distinction that still was important for Immanuel Kant. To Rüdiger, philosophy was a *cognitio judiciosa*, aimed at knowledge of hidden truths, but of qualities as opposed to the quantities measured by the natural sciences. Walch, too, described philosophy as *judicieuse*, critical knowledge but he maintained that its purpose was not only the well-being of the human race but also the glory of God. Crusius, in contrast, understood philosophy as the rational knowledge of man-independent, quasi-eternal objects, and against Wolff he stressed that philosophy was knowledge of the existing rather than the possible.

The most significant philosopher of the German Enlightenment, who dominated its second and, in part, its third generation, was Christian Wolff. Originally he taught mathematics in Halle; gradually he switched to philosophy though without, as is often suggested, becoming a disciple of Leibniz. His intention was to establish the whole of philosophy as a systematic and universal foundational science and to develop it step by step according to a so-called mathematical method. With this aim of conclusive knowledge, he published basic texts for all disciplines in ascending order. Initially, under the influence of Thomasius, he did so in German; subsequently he set out his philosophy in Latin and in more detail (because of his internal compulsion towards a comprehensive system). In the end, his work remained unfinished and necessarily fragmented.

For Wolff, philosophy above all had to be thorough. From the old Aristotelian distinction between knowledge of facts and knowledge of causes, he developed the idea of three levels of knowledge. The first level is purely historic (the establishment of experience and facts). At the second level, knowledge is mathematical (the exact determination of quantity). At the third level, it is philosophic (the fundamental science of causes and principles). Such philosophy is indebted to the mathematical method in that it is based upon exact knowledge, exact concepts, and exact conclusions. Although a specific form of knowledge, mathematics thus provides a method that is valid also for philosophy. The latter, however, is a knowledge of reasons and, consequently, of the condition of the possibility of all things – or knowledge of all things possible or of all possibilities. Philosophy is *scientia possibilium*, and God is the final reason for the possible. In this context, 'possible' means first of all that which is without contradiction, then that which is actually possible because it has a sufficient reason, and finally even the possibility of being, or that which makes possible the reality of being (*essentia qua potentia*). As the knowledge of all possible things, of whether and how they are or are not, philosophy becomes absolute knowing, and Wolff describes God as *philosophus absolute summus*.[31] Human philosophy is only part of the divine, of the omniscience of God.

Wolff was seen even in his lifetime as the prototype of the German philosophy professor, still praised by Kant for his 'thoroughness', but in his day he exerted an influence far beyond the bounds of philosophy. His pupils included A. G. Baumgarten, who established systematic aesthetics as a theory of the perfection of sense impressions, and M. Knutzen, who influenced Kant. Many of Wolff's followers, such as Georg Friedrich Meier and the poet and literary critic Johann Christoph Gottsched, soon began to reduce his doctrines to a more comprehensible form, ignoring their often laborious deductions. They all adhered more or less to Wolff's definition of philosophy as the science of the possible but tended also to reemphasise its character as a science of causation. The division into three branches of knowledge, though at first generally accepted, was increasingly questioned; doubt was cast on the so-called mathematical method so that the division in fact was reduced to the old Aristotelian distinction between knowledge of facts and of causes. This is the historical root of the Kantian distinction between philosophy and mathematics.

By mid-century, interest in a comprehensive and final system of philosophy as absolute science decreased markedly. The scientific character of philosophy, which Wolff had stressed, lost credibility, and the hope of achieving a final system of knowledge lost its fascination. Once more, the need emerged for a livable, immediately useful philosophy, a philosophy for all, not just for those of highest learning or deepest scholarship. In short, a new (exoteric) popular philosophy arose alongside the (esoteric) academic philosophy and usurped its position. This new development included such philosophical authors as Moses Mendelssohn and Christian Garve. It was, however, largely a popularisation of academic philosophy, combining in a new eclecticism elements of Thomasian and Wolffian teachings, with the latter providing most of the foundation and formal structure. This philosophy was almost exclusively written in German as a 'sound philosophy' aimed at good common sense. Although 'popular', it was a philosophy that retained a strongly finalistic character aimed as it was at achieving beatitude through virtuous behaviour. Samuel Reimarus, for example, understood philosophy as a science of all theoretical and practical truths important for human happiness.[32] Instead of the Wolffian ideal of omniscience, we find the ideal of a living knowledge, which only takes into consideration the necessary and the useful.

Although Kant occasionally adopted the elegant style, he was fundamentally opposed to the reduction of philosophy to the popular mode, and various attacks on his difficult style caused him to reflect explicitly on this. Without denying popular and popularising philosophy its right to exist, he differentiated, for example, between the difficulty of the research and the plausibility of the result. He also acknowledged that the *Kritik der reinen Vernunft* would never become popular, though its insights might. In addition, Kant followed in the footsteps of German Enlightenment philosophy since Thomasius by distinguishing also between academic philosophy and worldly philosophy. For Kant, the latter was not just popular philosophy for everyone but also philosophy in the cosmopolitan sense – existential philosophising, as it were, which also had a learned and academic expression in the university. For in the last resort philosophy for Kant was a theory, even a system, of rational principles. At least that was the aim, for no such complete philosophy yet existed and hence it was impossible to teach philosophy. Certainly Kant himself, through his critique of reason, called into question any systematic knowledge of reality, of the thing in itself. In fact, and even explicitly, his philosophical practice was criticism, and he made this the chief concern of philosophy; thus philosophical critique, in several senses, became the centre of Enlightenment in Kant's time. Although as far as his own philosophy was concerned Kant saw the 'business of critique' as a preliminary stage to real science, in the end he inclined to see critique itself, at least its content or outcome, as the desired science.

Kant still saw himself largely as part of the Enlightenment and with him its philosophy comes to an end. While German idealism took its point of departure from his philosophy, it was in fact opposed to his critique which had made the question 'What is it to be human?' into the central problem of philosophy. As a speculative transcendental philosophy and philosophical theology, idealism provided a complete contrast with the academic wisdom of the Enlightenment. Self-conscious of divine blessing, inspiration, and, occasionally, also condemnation, the philosopher – genius and professor at once – sought to understand the world in and through God, an Absolute that was bound to relativise Enlightenment's philosophy as superficial trivia.[33]

NOTES

1 John Locke, *An Essay Concerning Human Understanding*, ed. P. H. Nidditch, in the *Clarendon Edition* (*Works*) (Oxford, 1975).
2 Anthony Collins, *A Discourse of Free-Thinking* (London, 1713), 5.
3 Anthony Ashley Cooper, 3rd Earl of Shaftesbury, *Complete Works, Selected Letters and Posthumous Writings* (*Works*), in English with parallel German translation, trans. and eds. G. Hemmerich and W. Benda, vols. 1–2 (Stuttgart-Bad Cannstatt, 1981), 1.1: 360.
4 Shaftesbury, 'The Moralists', in *Works*, 2.1: 20–34.

5 Shaftesbury, 'Soliloquy: Or, Advice to an Author', in *Works* 1.1: 210–12.

6 Shaftesbury, 'Soliloquy', 220.

7 Shaftesbury, 'The Moralists', 376.

8 Shaftesbury, 'Miscellaneous Reflections', in *Works*, 1.2: 196.

9 Shaftesbury, 'Soliloquy', 202.

10 Shaftesbury, 'Miscellaneous Reflections', 196.

11 George Berkeley, *Alciphron, or the Minute Philosopher*, in *Works*, 3: 87–8.

12 Berkeley, *The Analyst*, in *Works*, 4: 94–5; *Siris*, §§285, 293 in *Works*, 5: 133, 136; *Alciphron*, §16, 3: 139.

13 David Hume, *An Enquiry Concerning Human Understanding* (*First Enquiry*), 11.27, SBN 146.

14 Hume, *First Enquiry* 1.1–2, SBN 5–6. See Hume, *A Treatise of Human Nature*, Intro. 1–8, SBN xiii–xvii.

15 Hume, *First Enquiry*, 1.9, SBN 10: 'And though a philosopher may live remote from business, the genius of philosophy, if carefully cultivated by several, must gradually diffuse itself throughout the whole society, and bestow a similar correctness on every art and calling'.

16 In his letter of 17 September 1739 to Francis Hutcheson, Hume distinguished two ways of investigating the mind: 'One may consider it either as an Anatomist or as a Painter....I imagine it impossible to conjoin these two views.' However, just as the anatomist can help the painter, so may the metaphysician help the moralist. Hume, who here obviously identifies with the metaphysician, still wants, as a friend to virtue, to stress good taste in writing and to try 'if it be possible to make the Moralist and Metaphysician agree a little better'. In *The Letters of David Hume*, ed. J. Y. T. Greig, 2 vols. (Oxford, 1932), 1: 32–3.

17 *First Enquiry*, 1.6–12, SBN 8–13; 5.1.1–9, SBN 40–7; 11.8–10, 28–9, SBN 134–5, 147; *Treatise*, 1.4.7.11–13, SBN 270–2.

18 Thomas Reid, *Essays on the Intellectual Powers of Man* (Edinburgh, 1785), eds. D. R. Brookes and K. Haakonssen (Edinburgh, 2002), Preface, 11–13.

19 Alexander Pope, *An Essay on Man*, Epistle II.i, v. 1–2, in Alexander Pope, *Poetical Works*, ed. H. Davis (Oxford, 1966), 250.

20 [Pierre Bayle], *Lettre sur le comète* (Rotterdam, 1682); *Dictionnaire historique et critique*, 2 vols. (Rotterdam, 1697); see his critical journal, *Nouvelles de la République des Lettres* (Amsterdam, 1684–7).

21 See Bernard le Bovier de Fontenelle, *Histoire des oracles* (1686), in *Oeuvres complètes*, ed. G-B. Depping, 3 vols. (Geneva, 1968), 2: 85–167; and *De l'origine des fables* (1723), in 2: 388–98.

22 Fontenelle, *Entretiens sur la pluralité des mondes* (1686), ed. R. Shackleton (Oxford, 1955), in *Oeuvres complètes*, 2: 1–83.

23 Fontenelle, *Dialogues des morts* (1683), ed. G-B. Depping, in *Oeuvres*, 2: 178 ff.

24 François-Marie Arouet de Voltaire, *Dictionnaire philosophique* (1752), eds. J. Benda and R. Naves (Paris, 1954), 342.

25 *Le Philosophe: Texts and Interpretation*, ed. H. Dieckmann (St. Louis, 1948), 30–2.

26 See *Le Philosophe*, 30–1.

27 Jean le Rond d'Alembert, *Discours préliminaire de l'Encyclopédie* (1751) in *Oeuvres de d'Alembert*, 5 vols. (Paris, 1821–2), 1: 46 ff., 49f.

28 d'Alembert, *Discours*, 77f.

29 Jean-Jacques Rousseau, 'Si rétablissement des Sciences et des Arts a contribué à épurer les moeurs', *Discours sur les sciences et les arts*, in *Oeuvres*, 3: Pt. II, 27.

30 Christian Thomasius, *Introductio ad philosophiam aulicam* (Leipzig, 1688), ch. 2, §31, p. 59.

31 Christian Wolff, *Theologia naturalis, methodo scientifica pertractata*, Pt. I (1736), in *Werke*, II.7.1: §268 (p. 244); see also *Philosophia rationalis sive logica*, Pt. I: *Discursus praeliminaris de philosophia in genere* (1728), in *Werke*, II.1.1: 1.

32 Hermann Samuel Reimarus, *Die Vernunftlehre*, 2 vols. (Hamburg, 1766), 1: 13.

33 Apart from the English, French, and German philosophers considered here, Giovanni Battista
   Vico of Italy made the greatest contribution to the development of philosophy in the eighteenth century. Though he evolved no explicit new concept of philosophy, he clarified philosophy as a historical and anthropological phenomenon by virtue of his anti-Cartesianism,
   his historical and anthropological approach, and in spite of his view of philosophy as a matter
   of principles.

3

SCHOOLS AND MOVEMENTS

CARL HENRIK KOCH

The periodisation of the history of philosophy into centuries is no easy matter. A new departure in philosophy is often determined by recourse to something earlier, and not until it is viewed from a distance does any general pattern arise. Thus, an account of the philosophical thought in a previous era will nearly always be influenced by philosophical views characteristic of the century in which they are examined. Philosophers who in former days were praised to the skies are nowadays forgotten, whereas others who made only little impact on their own times are today regarded as being of major importance.

In this chapter, simple, broad lines will be drawn within eighteenth-century philosophy as seen from the close of the twentieth century. Therefore, it will not take into account how eighteenth-century thinkers rated themselves or one another; these thinkers will be regarded not from their own but from a contemporary point of view.

I. THE EIGHTEENTH-CENTURY EUROPEAN ENLIGHTENMENT

The period from 1700 to 1800 is usually termed the Age of Enlightenment. In the great encyclopedias – from Johann Heinrich Zedler's *Grosses vollständiges Universal-Lexikon* (1732–50) to Denis Diderot and Jean le Rond d'Alembert's famous *Encyclopédie* (1751–65) and the somewhat more modest first edition of the *Encyclopædia Britannica* (1771) – the knowledge of that age was communicated to the new intellectual elite, the upper-middle classes. Enlightenment, upbringing, education, and the transmission of knowledge were the key words. In his *Considerations sur les mœurs de ce siècle* (1749), the French writer Charles Pinot Duclos characterised the century as one of violent ferment, and to a dominant strand of the Enlightenment it was possible to direct and nurture this ferment by way of education.[1] In his main work, *De l'homme* (1772), Duclos's countryman, Claude-Adrien Helvétius, formulated the slogan that education is capable of everything.[2] Most of the philosophical works of the earlier German Enlightenment (*Aufklärung*) – the systematic works of Christian Wolff and his pupils – were written with an eye to education. At the time, there was another side to the Enlightenment, represented by Diderot's attack on Helvétius's work, according to which genius is unpredictable and the individuality of each person limits what education can achieve. This points forward to Romanticism.

In his *Essais sur les éléments de philosophie* (1759), Jean le Rond d'Alembert termed his own century the century of philosophers and philosophy, and the philosophers were particularly concerned with humanity.[3] In *An Essay on Man* (1732–4), Alexander Pope had written 'Know then thyself, presume not God to scan;/ The proper study of mankind is Man', and the words 'man' or 'human' entered into the titles of many of the great philosophical works of that time.[4] In this respect, the Enlightenment was a direct continuation of the previous century. Inspired by Michel Montaigne, Pierre Charron wrote in his *De la sagesse* (1601) that the object of true science and of true study is man.[5] René Descartes, Thomas Hobbes, Baruch Spinoza, and John Locke enquired into and analysed human knowledge, emotions, and actions. But whereas Descartes, Hobbes, and Spinoza framed an a priori science of man, in the eighteenth century the science of human nature became instead an empirical psychology and anthropology inspired by Locke's charting of the human mind. As Voltaire wrote in *Lettres philosophiques* (1734), many people had written novels about the soul, but now a sage (Locke) had arrived who had modestly written its history.[6]

The eighteenth century has often also been called the century of reason. The reason so termed was not the constructive reason of the seventeenth century, as manifested in the philosophical systems of Descartes, Hobbes, and Spinoza, but a critical analytical reason whose task – to quote Locke's own words about himself in the 'Epistle to the Reader' from *An Essay Concerning Human Understanding* (1690) – was to act as 'an Under-Labourer in clearing Ground a little, and removing some of the Rubbish, that lies in the way to Knowledge'.[7] It was this critical reason that was portrayed allegorically during the French Revolution as a naked goddess. Truth appeared without the veil of prejudice that had hitherto concealed it.

The knowledge the eighteenth-century philosophers were trying to acquire was not an a priori knowledge derived by means of reason from reason it-self. Whereas mathematics and geometry constituted the seventeenth-century epistemological ideal realised in Descartes's rational mechanics – described by Voltaire as a well-written novel – the eighteenth-century ideal was, if anything, an empirically based science. In his politico-philosophical works, Hobbes, for example, established a rational basis for the type of state conceivable by reason as best suited to maintaining the social order, whereas, in his *De l'esprit des lois* (1748), Charles de Secondat de Montesquieu was to a far greater extent the empiricist who attempted to explain and justify his political science on the basis of experience.

In the seventeenth century, reason and science were regarded as factors possessing a stabilising and preserving effect on the life of the community, if indeed they were considered to have any effect on social and political life at all. In his essay 'Of Atheism', Francis Bacon had already maintained that 'a little philosophy inclineth man's mind to atheism, but depth in philosophy bringeth men's minds about to religion', and in *New Atlantis* (1629) he had described how a flourishing development in the natural sciences is fully compatible with a static society.[8] In his *History of the Royal Society* (1667), Thomas Sprat wrote in agreement with Bacon: 'A little knowledge is subject to make men headstrong, insolent and untractable; but a great deal has quite contrary effect, inclining them to be submissive to their Betters, and obedient to the Sovereign Power.'[9] In the eighteenth century, however, science was regarded as a dynamic social and political factor, which could contribute towards changing the social order, thereby paving the way for the glorious future of humankind. Knowledge does not, as Bacon considered, merely give humanity power over nature; it also gives political power. With this conception (which was not, however, allowed to remain uncontested by, for example, Jean-Jacques Rousseau and Edmund Burke), the Age of Enlightenment points towards nineteenth-century utopian socialism and Marxism.

In the seventeenth century, a philosophical-anthropological notion of man as primarily a rational being had provided the basis for the unification of the sciences of nature and man, of morality and religion within a single system. As rational beings, humankind combines thought and action, emotion and belief; and whereas emotion and belief were reduced, in this synthesis, to confused ideas, or in other words to imperfect knowledge, reason – sometimes disguised as wisdom – became the principle for human action. Art, which did not become the bugbear of reason until the nineteenth century, could be reduced – as in the classicist aesthetics that Nicolas Boileau expounded in his *L'art poétique* (1674) – to a rule-bound and thereby rationally determined activity. Blaise Pascal was one of the few thinkers to raise objections to the current cultivation of reason. In a famous sentence in *Les pensées* (1670), he writes that 'The heart [that is to say, the passions] has its reasons which reason itself does not know.'[10]

The philosophical-anthropological definition of humanity as rational was also reflected in the seventeenth-century discussion about the difference between men and animals. While Descartes regarded animals as mere machines, and thus as part of mechanical nature, he regarded man as a rational being that is neither part of nature nor produced by it. Gottfried Wilhelm Leibniz and, later, Wolff described the ability of animals to act instinctively and purposefully as an '*analogon rationis*'. The discussion continued until well into the eighteenth century and inspired the German philosopher Hermann Samuel Reimarus to evolve an empirically based animal psychology.[11]

The seventeenth century was in many ways the century of science – of Galileo Galilei, Johannes Kepler, and Isaac Newton. Descartes and Spinoza and the Port-Royal methodology of logic all established rules for expanding human knowledge. Human imperfection consisted in lack of knowledge (according to Bacon, a consequence of the Fall, which the new science was to rectify), and the rules of methodology would enable us to remedy this lack in the same way as aesthetic rules would enable us to produce art.

The eighteenth century may likewise be characterised in terms of its science. The Enlightenment was precipitated by the extension of human knowledge in all fields. But whereas seventeenth-century thought sought to provide man with the tools for procuring knowledge – that is, with a Baconian art of invention – eighteenth-century philosophers, especially from about mid-century in France, were interested in two other aspects of the Baconian conception of reform: in removing the obstacles that hindered the growth of science – both subjective prejudices and the socially created, religious obstacles – and in solving the practical problem with regard to communicating the knowledge acquired. Whereas the notion of a universal art of invention dominated seventeenth-century methodology from Bacon to Ehrenfried Walter Tschirnhausen, the eighteenth century was characterised by reflections on the transmission of knowledge, especially in a pedagogical sense. Bacon's brilliant idea of combining the method of invention with that of the transmission of knowledge was largely forgotten. Underlying the spirit of the Enlightenment was the idea of the increase in knowledge being made available to man and society in order to liberate the individual. This led in two directions. To the radical Enlightenment, as personified by the French *philosophes* such as Paul-Henri Thiry, baron d'Holbach, Claude-Adrien Helvétius, and Julien Offray de La Mettrie, philosophy became a fight against handed-down prejudices and political conditions that prevented the communication and dissemination of human knowledge. In France, it was especially the political organisation of religious and social institutions that became the target. But the ideal of progress through the spread of knowledge could also be turned into the proper objective for existing institutions and regimes, and such a conservative Enlightenment found expression across Europe in establishments ranging from royally sponsored academies to parish schools.

The first third of the eighteenth century may largely be characterised as a critical continuation of seventeenth-century rationalism, which was gradually being supplanted on the Continent by an empiricism and materialism inspired by Locke, although Locke himself was strongly influenced by various forms of

Cartesianism, as much modern scholarship has shown. There are distinct rationalist features to be found in British deism, in German Wolffianism, and in Voltaire's works in France. But the synthesis of thought, emotion, and belief under the hegemony of reason was slowly beginning to crack. In Pierre Bayle's *Dictionnaire historique et critique* (1697), the problem of the existence of evil in a world created by God was raised as a stumbling block to thought, and the rational world order was replaced by a reality resulting from the clash of two opposing principles. When correlated with the actual circumstances, the optimism that characterised Leibniz's thinking, for example, became naivety in the hands of Voltaire. The same reason that could form the basis of rational and moral action in such different thinkers as Hobbes and Ralph Cudworth was perverted by Bernard de Mandeville into pure selfishness. And La Mettrie singled out sexuality as possibly the most important factor in human existence. In his *Traité de la vie heureuse par Sénèque avec un Discours du traducteur sur le même sujet* (1748),[12] La Mettrie maintained, in perfect accordance with contemporary French reflections on happiness, that human happiness does not consist in a virtuous life under the control of reason and the will but in pleasure and lust. This conception was expressed in its most extreme form in the pornographic novels of the Marquis de Sade. The attempt of British Newtonians to combine science and religious faith with eighteenth-century physico-theology was shaken by David Hume's attack on natural theology in *Dialogues concerning Natural Religion* (1779).

Emotions, which in rationalist psychology were largely regarded merely as exercising restraint on man's rationality, became for British moral sense philosophers such as Francis Hutcheson an autonomous part of the human constitution, and for him, as for Lord Shaftesbury in England and the German aestheticians, they became furthermore a sense of beauty. This helped to bestow upon art an autonomy it had never previously had. Art no longer needed either to represent reality in order to teach us about the good and the useful or to serve as decoration but acquired a reality of its own. As opposed to the German aesthetician Johann Christoph Gottsched, who placed the purpose of art outside the work of art itself, Johann Elias Schlegel, for example, asserted that a work of art should be evaluated according to internal criteria.[13]

Thus the task of eighteenth-century philosophy was to create a new synthesis based on a new philosophical anthropology. Hume regarded human beings as products of nature which have implanted in them the ability to survive. This ability is one of feeling and not reason, the latter being capable only of constructing mathematics, which does not represent reality. Correspondingly, Rousseau sketched an anthropology in which the Cartesian *cogito* is rejected and emotions are given priority over thought. Being is the same as feeling, Rousseau wrote in his main pedagogical work, *Émile* (1762), and human sensitivity is developed

prior to the intellect.[14] We feel before we are able to think. Both Hume and
Rousseau criticised that part of the philosophy of the Enlightenment that was
rooted in rationalism. The individual who is to be liberated and raised to maturity and independence by way of enlightenment is not solely characterised
by reason but is the whole person, who thinks, feels, desires, and detests. The
Holsteiner Johann Nicolas Tetens[15] divided consciousness accordingly into the
faculties of feeling, will, and imagination. Immanuel Kant later based his critical
philosophy on Tetens's classical threefold division.

The criticism of reason in the late Enlightenment was clearly reflected in the
current interest in aesthetics; the eighteenth century in this respect resembled
the twentieth. Belief in reason was shaken in the eighteenth century in the same
way as belief in science has been shaken in the twentieth. In both cases, this has
resulted in an increased interest in aesthetics.

In the second half of the eighteenth century, the philosophical-
anthropological conception of humanity, which had previously manifested itself
in discussions as to whether animals were rational or not, figured in a discussion
of language and its origins. In his *Discours de la méthode* (1637), Descartes implied that one of the differences between humans and animals consisted in man's
making use of words (that is, his possession of a language). Hobbes, and especially Locke, had attempted to provide rational reconstructions of how sounds
are associated with ideas by way of convention, while the French Port-Royal
grammarians had attempted to formulate a universal grammar. This interest
in language was associated with the wish to acquire an unambiguous form
of communication and led, among other things, to attempts to create artificial languages. In the eighteenth century, interest was concentrated partly on a
discussion as to how far animals possess a language and partly on attempts to
discover the origin of language. Many of the eighteenth-century philosophers,
such as Étienne Bonnot de Condillac, Rousseau, and Pierre-Louis Maupertius
in France, Tetens and Johann Gottfried Herder in Germany, and Giambattista
Vico in Italy, rejected the idea of language as a rational construction.[16] According
to the thinker who above all determined the development of language theory,
Condillac, the source of language was a combination of emotions, expressed in
gestures, and reflection. Language thus founded developed in social interaction
and could not be seen as the result of rational construction.

Thus the important revolution in eighteenth-century philosophy was the
break with the philosophy of the early Enlightenment, which was rooted in
seventeenth-century rationalism. Hume and Rousseau attempted, each in his
own way, to replace the rationalist conception of man with a new philosophical
anthropology and thus with a new synthesis of thought, feeling, and action.
Whereas Hume's attempt was at the expense of revelation and reason, Rousseau's

was at the expense of science and art. As a cultural critic, Rousseau was obliged to say that art and science had perverted man. Others thought differently. Edward Gibbon, for example, wrote in his *Essai sur l'étude de littérature* (1762) that the history of nations is the account of the misfortunes of mankind, whereas the history of science is the account of their grandeur and happiness.[17]

Hume's naturalism and the ensuing critique of religion and the founding of knowledge and morality in emotional life, as well as Rousseau's definition of man as primarily a feeling individual and the ensuing criticism of modern culture, are two different aspects of eighteenth-century philosophy. Rousseau maintains in his political philosophy that the purpose of society is to realise the essence of man – his freedom. Man does not, according to Rousseau, have a specific nature. He is perfectible and not bound to nature, and he is able to develop in whatever direction he chooses. Thus man is by nature free. According to Hume, man is subject to the laws that apply to conscious biological beings. Hume, too, regards man as free, but in a sense different from that of Rousseau: man acts freely when acting in accordance with his nature (that is, in the absence of any external coercion). Whereas for Hume man is a piece of nature, for Rousseau he is absolutely free.

Kant's critical philosophy, which is the eighteenth century's most important and ever-topical contribution to the history of philosophical thought, builds on a conception of humanity that is a synthesis of Hume's and Rousseau's philosophical anthropologies: man is both nature and a free being. In it the movements of the age converge. Kant's theory of knowledge is a synthesis of rationalism and empiricism on a Leibnizian basis; his moral philosophy combines Wolffian a priori ethics with the English moral sense school, and his aesthetics combines Lessing's formal aesthetics with the English and German aesthetics inspired by Shaftesbury. Finally, Kant's natural teleology is an attempt to reconcile Newtonian causality with biological explanations based on the concept of final cause – in other words, to reconcile mechanism with physico-theology. Underlying these syntheses is the Kantian anthropology: man is both nature and reason. As nature, he is subject to the dimension of time and to the law of causality; as reason, he is timeless and free.

Although many common elements can be found in the eighteenth-century philosophy of Britain, France, and Germany, there are also characteristic features, reflecting the different influences in these countries. In Britain, for example, in Hume, Adam Smith, and Jeremy Bentham, philosophy and enlightenment were regarded as instruments for the benefit and happiness of mankind within the framework of a liberal society viewed as a perfection of the established one. The British Enlightenment had only a modest revolutionary potential. Both Hume's and Burke's political ideas were clearly conservative. In France, however,

Lockean empiricism, which like all empiricism was anti-authoritarian, became a revolutionary and essentially materialistic philosophy in the hands of philosophers such as Holbach and Helvétius. In Germany, the spirit of enlightenment was converted by Wolff and his disciples into a didactic tool for educating ministers and civil servants and thus for stabilising established society.

Despite national and political differences, there was a close connection between the three countries. In France, the Enlightenment developed under the influence of Locke and Newton. German Enlightenment philosophy was certainly, in its first stage, influenced by Leibnizian rationalism, and this stagnated in Wolff as a neo-scholastic philosophy. Wolff in his turn was refuted by Kant under the influence of Hume, and other critics of the Leibnizo-Wolffian philosophy were also influenced by the Scot. While France was at the centre of the philosophical debate in the seventeenth century, and Germany likewise in the nineteenth century, the inspiration behind eighteenth-century European philosophy came from Britain. In Spain and Italy, the dominant role of the Roman Catholic Church and the latter's grip on educational establishments prevented the breakthrough of enlightenment tendencies. Neither the Protestant North nor the New World (with the partial exception of Jonathan Edwards) could boast of original philosophical thought during the eighteenth century.

II. EIGHTEENTH-CENTURY BRITISH PHILOSOPHY

Eighteenth-century British philosophy may be divided into two periods, where 1740, the year in which Hume finished publishing *A Treatise of Human Nature* (1739–40), is the watershed. Although, as Hume himself wrote in his essay 'My Own Life' (1777), the *Treatise* 'fell dead-born from the press without reaching such distinction as even to excite a murmur among the zealots',[18] it marked the start of a philosophical oeuvre that made its originator known all over Europe and had an important influence on the further development of European philosophy.

The development in British philosophy from Locke to Hume is often described as a national matter. Locke had upheld a Cartesian dualism combined with an empirical variant of Descartes's theory of ideas, according to which knowledge is the perception of mental phenomena or of their interrelations. The resulting scepticism as to the possibility of obtaining certain knowledge about the external world had caused George Berkeley to refute the existence of a material substance, which he considered to be a philosophical fiction thought up by hair-splitting philosophers. Thus, for Berkeley the mind was the only thing of substance. Hume rejected the very idea of substance and developed a consistent phenomenalism.

Although this description is correct, the story is more complicated. Locke was a stumbling block for Berkeley in the sense that Lockean scepticism seemed to be a threat to religion. But Malebranche had realised that it was possible to circumvent the psycho-physical problem altogether by assuming that changes in material objects do not directly cause mental phenomena; they simply constitute 'occasions' for God to create such phenomena.[19] Berkeley realised that the material substance thereby became superfluous. Moreover, Bayle's treatment of the classical distinction between primary and secondary qualities enabled Berkeley to refute the idea that sense quantities were objective while sense qualities were subjective: both are simply conceptions of the mind.[20] Berkeley developed his immaterialism on this basis in *A Treatise concerning the Principles of Human Knowledge* (1710).

The influence of Malebranche on British philosophy during the eighteenth century was immense. All of Malebranche's most important works had been translated into English by the end of the seventeenth century, and Locke had already tried to refute his metaphysics.[21] Both the Cambridge Platonist John Norris, and Arthur Collier, who in his *Clavis universalis* (1713) had argued independently of Berkeley in favour of immaterialism, were supporters of Malebranche. The fact that both Berkeley and Hume criticised Malebranche, although he was in many ways their philosophical teacher, also vouched for his influence. Later, the Scottish Common Sense philosopher Thomas Reid expressed his admiration for the Frenchman.[22]

Berkeley turned not only against Lockean scepticism but also, in his *Alchiphron, or the Minute Philosopher* (1732), against the deists who were inspired by Locke's philosophy of religion. In this Locke had tried to demonstrate that the Christian faith did not embrace anything that conflicted with human reason.[23] In *Christianity not Mysterious* (1696), John Toland went a step further and maintained that nothing contrary to reason, and nothing above reason, can be part of the Christian doctrine. Later, in *Christianity as Old as the Creation* (1730), Matthew Tindal refuted the Christian mysteries from a deistic point of view. Human reason is perfectly sufficient for appreciating the existence and attributes of God; neither revelation nor any other mysterious means are necessary.

The new natural science was also used in support of religion. Richard Bentley had argued, with Newton's approval, that the Newtonian world picture is proof of the existence of a Universal Creator. John Ray and William Derham evolved similar physico-theological views, amongst others on a biological basis.[24] The Deists' criticism of traditional Christianity initiated a lengthy discussion within British philosophy and theology about the reality of miracles, in which philosophers such as Samuel Clarke and William Wollaston participated;[25] the debate culminated in Hume's famous essay 'Of Miracles' in his *Enquiry concerning Human Understanding* (1748).[26]

In 1705, Mandeville had published a short poem entitled 'The Grumbling Hive: Or, Knaves turn'd Honest', which was republished in 1714, with the addition of copious notes, under the title *The Fable of the Bees: Or Private Vices, Publick Benefits*. In this fable, Mandeville not only drew attention to immorality and depravity as constituting the preconditions for the growth and prosperity of a society but also attacked Shaftesbury, whose moral and aesthetic writings had been republished in 1711 as a collected edition entitled *Characteristicks of Men, Manners, Opinions, Times*. In this, Shaftesbury had turned against moral hedonism, finding the origin of the distinction between good and evil in man's social nature; man has a moral sense for what serves the benefit of the community – that is, for actions that harmonise with the interests of society. This view of man seems to presuppose an innate benevolence towards one's fellows, whereas Mandeville's view compelled him to negate the existence of such benevolence.

Later, Hutcheson defended the moral sense theory against Mandeville's criticism: moral sense arouses pleasure in connection with actions useful to oneself and others, and this pleasure is independent either of cold rationality or of desire. In *An Inquiry into the Original of Our Ideas of Beauty and Virtue* (1725) and *An Essay on the Nature and Conduct of the Passions and Affections* (1728), Hutcheson refuted Hobbes's and Mandeville's scheming, rational egoism as well as Locke's hedonism and Clarke's moral rationalism. In *A Discourse Concerning the Unchangeable Obligations of Natural Religion* (1706), Clarke had tried to realise Locke's notion of a demonstrable morality, a notion that can be traced to Locke's study of Pufendorf. Inspired by Clarke, Richard Price turned against the moral sense theory in *A Review of the Principal Questions in Morals* (1758): the notions of good and evil do not stem from a special sense, as Hutcheson had thought, but are simple ideas, intuitively perceived by reason and denoting traits in actions that are independent of time, place, and the observer. Thus, moral statements are either necessarily true or necessarily false. Shaftesbury's moral sense theory was also attacked by Joseph Butler in his *Fifteen Sermons* (1726). Moral judgement and action do not spring from benevolence but from cool and constant self-love, and they are governed by the conscience. Butler thereby avoids identifying self-love with egoism.

Thus, British moral philosophy before Hume was divided into three schools: the moral sense school, which bases morality on emotion; moral rationalism, which equates morality with reason; and moral realism, which finds the principle for moral action and judgement in cool and constant self-love. Hume subsequently examined these three alternatives in his moral philosophy. For Shaftesbury, a precondition for the moral value of an action was its harmony with society as a whole. In Shaftesbury's Platonic-Plotinian aesthetics, harmony – or unity in multiplicity – is likewise a precondition for the experience of beauty. Like moral sense, the aesthetic sense, or taste, is a sense of harmony. Whereas seventeenth-century aesthetics was based on formal rules, the eighteenth century was the century of taste. In *The Spectator*, Joseph Addison wrote a number of articles on 'The Pleasures of the Imagination', in which he sketched a sensualist aesthetics of taste. The themes he dealt with were taken up again and again in eighteenth-century British aesthetics.

Hume's 'dead-born' *Treatise* was later converted into *An Enquiry concerning Human Understanding* (1748) and *An Enquiry concerning the Principles of Morals* (1751). It was these works, together with a number of essays on aesthetic, philosophical, and political themes, that made Hume famous all over Europe. During the period 1754–62, he published *The History of England*, a six-volume work in which he dismissed both the Whig and the Tory appeals to history in support of their respective politics. Hume's *Dialogues concerning Natural Religion*, in which he refuted deism and physico-theology and thereby also the Newtonian attempt to reconcile religion with natural science, was published posthumously in 1779.

Hume attempted in his philosophy to base the general laws of science and morality on human emotion: man was guided not by reason but by feeling. An experience of regularity makes us believe that we shall also come to experience a similar regularity in the future, and our moral judgements are to a great extent determined by human sympathy, which for Hume was not an emotion but an ability to share the emotions of others. According to the *Treatise*'s subtitle, Hume is making 'An Attempt to Introduce the Experimental Method of Reasoning into Moral Subjects' – in other words, to elaborate an anthropology which, like Newton's physics, is based on observation. Thus Hume imagined moral philosophy to be a science based on laws. He stresses in particular the 'principles of association' to which the human mind is subject. The importance of moral science was for Hume its political use in the attempt to balance the forces in society, and thus it contributed towards creating a stable and peaceful society. It is this conviction, amongst others, that makes Hume a typical philosopher of the Enlightenment.

In *The Theory of Moral Sentiments* (1759), Adam Smith inspired by Hume's moral philosophy, devised a model for describing and explaining moral judgements. Just as Newton justified his theory of gravitation by demonstrating that it allows us to link up and explain diverse physical phenomena, Adam Smith justified his model by demonstrating its ability to link up and explain moral judgements. Later, in *The Wealth of Nations* (1776), Adam Smith elaborated a model for man's economic behaviour, which made Smith the most important economist of the eighteenth century and a leading protagonist of liberalism.

According to Locke's theory of ideas, the mind perceives ideas and not, for example, physical objects. Hume accepted this theory of ideas, but his ensuing phenomenalism was opposed by a number of Scottish philosophers belonging to the Scottish Common Sense school – the only true philosophical school in eighteenth-century British philosophy. In 1764, Thomas Reid, the school's leading light, published his *Inquiry into the Human Mind on the Principles of Common Sense*, in which he rejected both Locke's and Berkeley's, as well as Hume's, Cartesian 'ideal theory'. Ideas, in the British empiricist sense of the word, do not exist, according to Reid, since the mind does not perceive ideas of itself and of external objects but perceives itself and external objects directly. Fundamental principles, such as the principle of causality, which according to Hume had no rational foundation, and which is a principle underlying all thought and science, do not require any justification because their validity is generally accepted. Reid called principles of this type 'principles of common sense'. In *An Examination of Dr. Reid's Inquiry into the Human Mind on the Principles of Common Sense*, Joseph Priestley attacked the philosophy of common sense. According to Priestley, Reid's principles of common sense should be derived from the laws of association. As a materialist, Priestley regarded these laws as natural laws pertaining to the function of the brain.

James Oswald, together with James Beattie, whom Hume called 'that bigotted silly Fellow', turned against Hume and criticised in particular his philosophy of religion on the basis of common sense. Dugald Stewart, who became famous in Europe as a lecturer, followed suit, though without applying the epithet 'common sense' to his philosophy.[27] Hume, Adam Smith, and the Common Sense school form part of the Scottish Enlightenment, which also included such philosophers as Henry Home (Lord Kames), James Burnett (Lord Monboddo), Adam Ferguson, and John Millar. Ferguson and Millar described the development and organisation of human society on a purely naturalistic basis as chapters in the natural history of mankind, and Monboddo accounted for the societal preconditions for the origin and development of language.[28]

Hutcheson, Hume, and Adam Smith all agreed that actions that are useful evoke pleasure and may therefore be regarded as morally good. In preferring the action which, in a given situation, provides the greatest possible happiness for the greatest possible number of people, we are guided, wrote Hutcheson, by our moral sense. The Italian jurist Cesare Beccaria took over this utilitarian principle from Hutcheson and, inspired by Beccaria, Jeremy Bentham reintroduced it in *An Introduction to the Principles of Morals and Legislations* (1789) as the foundation of morality and legislation.[29] Some years previously, in his *Principles of Moral and Political Philosophy* (1785), William Paley had argued in favour of a theological utilitarianism, in which virtue was defined as '*the doing good to mankind, in obedience to the will of God, and for the sake of everlasting happiness*'.[30] Paley's work became widely read, and possibly inspired Bentham to formulate his secular utilitarianism. Bentham's concern was to elaborate a jurisprudence founded on utilitarian principles capable of forming the basis of a reform of civil and criminal law. During the first half of the nineteenth century, a school arose which based its work both theoretically and practically on Bentham's ideas – the school of utilitarianism or philosophical radicalism. Whereas Hume and the Common Sense philosophers came to influence especially German and French philosophy, Bentham was to characterise British thought far into the nineteenth century. Thus, British philosophy of the Enlightenment developed from epistemology and metaphysics via moral science into social science. More than anything else, it was Hume's philosophical oeuvre that brought about this development.

The last half of the eighteenth century was a fruitful period for British sense-based aesthetics. Lord Kames published his systematic *Elements of Criticism* (1762–5); Burke reintroduced the sublime as an aesthetic category in *A Philosophical Enquiry into the Origin of Our Ideas of the Sublime and Beautiful* (1757); and Alexander Gerard, a member of the Scottish Common Sense school, described in *An Essay on Genius* (1774) how the strong feelings of the genius generate a wealth of ideas in his mind and thereby provide him with abundant material for his art. In 1742, Edward Young, in *The Complaint, or: Night Thoughts on Life, Death and Immortality*, posed the question, 'Are passions, then, the pagans of the soul? Reason alone baptized?' (IV.v, 629). In eighteenth-century British philosophy, emotions were certainly baptised.

III. EIGHTEENTH-CENTURY FRENCH PHILOSOPHY

At the beginning of the eighteenth century, French philosophy and science were influenced by Cartesianism. Below the surface circulated a clandestine literature, which criticised both Christianity and the government. Typical of this literature was the priest Jean Mesliers's manuscript of over 300 pages, *Memoire*, often known as Mesliers's testament, in which he attacked ecclesiastical institutions and the Christian faith from a materialistic, atheist point of view. The French Enlighteners later used Mesliers's arguments as ammunition. The manuscript exists in several versions, and a selection was published by Voltaire in 1762.[31] In 1726, Voltaire had been banished to England, where he became acquainted with Locke's philosophy and Newton's physics. With his *Lettres philosophiques* (1734) and *Eléments de la philosophie de Newton* (1738), Voltaire introduced British philosophers to French readers. Apart from those of Locke and Newton, Voltaire also studied the philosophical works of Mandeville. In British scientific circles, Newton was regarded by his contemporaries as a mathematician, but Voltaire described him as an empiricist and an experimentalist. And it was in this capacity that he inspired the eighteenth-century French philosophers and natural scientists to revolt against Descartes's physics and philosophy and the Cartesian conception of science.

Locke had written in his *Essay* that there is nothing contradictory in presuming that matter should be capable of thinking, even though he himself repudiated the idea (IV.iii.6). Voltaire quoted Locke's remark in his *Lettres*, and French philosophers turned this to account in favour of a philosophical materialism. In 1746, Condillac published his *Essai sur l'origine des connaissances humaines*, in which he attempted to derive all the faculties of the mind from sensation and all knowledge from sense impressions. Locke had maintained that there are two sources of human knowledge: sensation and reflection. Henry Lee, one of his earliest critics, had protested in his *Anti-Scepticism* (1702) that Locke's ideas of reflection seemed to be derivable from those of sensation, and so his theory of ideas provided no grounds for assuming the existence of a spiritual substance. Lee thought this showed that religious scepticism was one of the many refutable consequences of Locke's empiricism. Condillac likewise elaborated a consistent empiricism, but since he adopted Malebranche's theory of mind, he nevertheless maintained the Cartesian dualism. On the other hand, he dismissed Descartes's statement that man has in his mind an original and intuitive idea of his own ego that precedes any other idea. According to Condillac, this idea does not develop until he comes to distinguish between his mind and the external world, and this distinction arises by virtue of the sense of touch. It follows from this that the idea of a material external world is prior to man's idea of his own mind.[32] In *Traité des sistêmes* (1749), Condillac criticised the eighteenth-century rationalist systems. He had learnt from Locke and Newton that knowledge can only be attained through experience and that any attempt to penetrate behind observable reality is in vain. Condillac's theory of science was representative of the anti-metaphysical and positivist manner of thinking that characterised French science and philosophy from the middle of the eighteenth century until the beginning of the nineteenth.

If man's knowledge about himself and the external world is conditioned by sensations, and his mind from birth is like a piece of 'white paper', as Locke said,[33] the progress of humanity depends on the exposure of the individual to influences favourable to his mental development. Therefore the key to the future lies in education, and Helvétius accordingly maintained, in *De l'homme*, that education makes man what he is. Man is a plastic being, capable of being moulded into any shape. Contemporary society being what it is, however, it is impossible to educate people to become perfect beings. The clash of interests in a hierarchical society hinders this and so is also a threat to the future of mankind. Thus Helvétius's own ideas of education developed into social criticism.

The year after Condillac's *Essai* came out, La Mettrie published *L'homme machine* (1747), in which he outlined a crude form of materialism and psychological hedonism that aroused attention and disgust all over Europe. He regarded man as a machine whose behaviour was determined by his endeavours to gratify his lust, but his materialism was not a physical materialism; he made a distinction between self-organised and self-correcting organic matter and inert physical matter. Underlying this distinction was the Swiss physiologist Albrecht von Haller's demonstration of the inherent irritability of muscle fibres.[34] Diderot likewise evolved a materialist view of man and nature. In *De l'interpretation de la nature* (1753), he drew attention to the weak point in La Mettrie's materialism, namely, the distinction between organic and physical matter.

The most consistent version of French materialism during the Age of Enlightenment was elaborated by Holbach in his anonymously published work *Système de la nature* (1770), which has often been called the bible of materialism and atheism. Philosophy was for Holbach a fight against prejudice and against the way in which those in power seek – entirely for their own interests and with the aid of religion and the clergy – to sustain the prejudices of the citizens and thus to enslave them. This 'conspiracy theory' was the radical French Enlighteners' simple explanation of the political structure of society.

Helvétius, Holbach, and La Mettrie belonged to the group of liberal-minded French *beaux-esprits* and scientists known as *les philosophes*. They constituted a movement rather than a school, and none were original thinkers. They were epigones – propagandists rather than philosophers – and their most prominent trait was their radicalism. In contrast with most Enlightenment thinkers, they were atheists and materialists, who advocated the supremacy of reason and enlightenment over religion and tradition. They had a positivist view of science, which was modelled on the empirical sciences and biology in particular. They ascribed to science and philosophy a political potential; enlightenment and knowledge would assure mankind of a happy future. They confronted the static society of French absolutism with the idea of a dynamic society based on scientific insight into human nature and motivation.

Although in many respects a *philosophe*, Diderot is now seen to have been a creative and original thinker. He was also the creator of the great *Encyclopédie*, the focus for so much of both radical and conservative Enlightenment thought. Along with others, Diderot found support for the belief in evolution and progress also in the natural sciences. In 1749, George Louis Leclere Buffon had outlined a theory for the development of the solar system, and in *De l'interpretation de la nature* Diderot arguably anticipated the theory of biological evolution, though this is disputed. History has shown that culture and society undergo a development, and in the biological world the individual undergoes a similar development. Is it not then feasible that the genera and species into which the Swedish naturalist Carl von Linné had divided the biological world, and which he regarded as constant, develop likewise?[35] The French Enlighteners replaced the static conception of society and nature with a dynamic one.

Outside the circle of the encyclopedists was the somewhat older Montesquieu, who in 1748 had published *De l'esprit des lois*, in which he tried to show that man's character as well as the society in which he lives is determined by the climate, the soil, the vegetation, and the fauna. Montesquieu also argued that the freedom of the individual within the framework of society can only be safeguarded if the different powers of the state are separated and balanced. With *De l'esprit des lois*, Montesquieu became one of the founders of sociology, anthropology, and social psychology, at the same time carrying on the liberalistic tradition from Locke.

The optimistic belief in science and in a future free society that characterised French philosophy around the middle of the eighteenth century was challenged by Rousseau, who turned against *les philosophes* in his *Discours sur les sciences et les arts* (1750). Rousseau rejected the idea that the development of culture and science helped to improve public morals and make men happy, basing this rejection partly on the organisation of society and partly on human selfishness. In *Discours sur l'origine et les fondements de l'inégalité parmi les hommes* (1755), Rousseau showed that differences in rank and class are not inherent in nature but are the result of a disastrous development caused in particular by the introduction of private property, whereupon, in *Du contrat social ou Principes du droit politique* (1762), he outlined the conditions for a society that did not have the same fatal consequences as the class-divided and absolutist French state. In a society in which the general will – in other words, the sheer will to survive – legislates, man is subordinate to his own will and therefore free. Rousseau himself doubted whether such a society was possible, but his idea of a society governed by law and not by individuals, in which the citizen is free, came to enter the ideology underlying the French revolution.

In the same year as the *Contrat social*, Rousseau also published his main pedagogical work, *Émile ou De l'éducation* (1762), in which he, in line with Diderot, criticised the French Enlighteners' tendency to lay sole weight on the human intellect and to underestimate human feelings. The task of the teacher is not only to develop the child's powers of reasoning but to produce a whole and harmonious human being. The goal of education is humaneness – to turn individuals into unaffected and unselfish natural human beings. One of Rousseau's most important pedagogical ideas in *Émile* is that children are not just small adults – that childhood is not simply preliminary to adulthood but an independent stage in human development.

In the shadow of the guillotine, one of the last representatives of radical Enlightenment critique, the mathematician and philosopher Marie Jean Antoine

Condorcet, wrote his *Esquisse d'un tableau historique des progrès de l'esprit humain* (1795), in which he repeated the French Enlighteners' optimistic belief in the future. The future would see the elimination of inequality among nations, would create equality between people, and witness the perfection of man. Rousseau had defined man as a perfectible being capable of adapting himself to all conditions. In this definition is founded the belief in the future and the developmental function of education as an instrument in social reform. Condorcet went one step further: the future would be able to produce the perfect human being.

IV. EIGHTEENTH-CENTURY GERMAN PHILOSOPHY

The German Enlightenment, like the Scottish, was a far more academic affair than either the English or the French but had, for all that, no less influence. Unlike the English and especially the French, it acquired a firm hold on the universities and schools, and generations of teachers and clerics were instrumental in disseminating it. This was partly due to the fact that the German Enlightenment was not as critical of society or as hostile towards religion as the French, and was professionalised to a greater extent than the English. In England, the great philosophers were men of letters; in Germany, as in Scotland, they were university professors.

The early German Enlightenment is characterised by two schools, one issuing from Thomasius and the other, the predominating school, from Wolff. Whereas Thomasius was a realist and an empiricist and regarded science as a social process, Wolff was an idealist and an intellectualist and maintained that science could in principle be advanced a priori as a logical-deductive system. While Thomasius considered logic to be psychology of knowledge rather than formal science, Wolff defined it as an a priori science. Both of them place human reason on a pedestal, but whereas Thomasius regarded reason as historically determined, Wolff saw reason as timeless and ahistorical. Both of them wrote in German; Thomasius was one of the first to lecture in his native tongue, and both set out to communicate useful knowledge in a pedagogically appropriate manner.

The Thomasian Enlightenment, which had many adherents, especially from 1700 until around 1720, had close connections with German Pietism and was antagonistic towards the more secularly oriented Wolffianism, which reigned almost supreme in German academic philosophy from about 1720. Thus, a number of Wolffianism's strongest critics, such as Joachim Lange and Andreas Rüdiger, were pupils of Thomasius. In 1723, Wolff himself was banished from Halle, the seat of Pietism, because of a speech, *Oratio de Sinarum philosophica practica* (On the Practical Philosophy of the Chinese) (1721), which he gave as chancellor of the university. In it, he drew attention to the morality of

Confucianism as secular because of its independence of religion. Wolffianism was later also criticised by Christian August Crusius, who opposed its outspoken intellectualism. Contrary to Wolff, Crusius stressed the failings of reason and also, like Kant, its limitations. Crusius, too, had close connections with Pietism.[36]

Wolff's philosophy was already termed 'Leibnizo-Wolffian' by his contemporary critics, though he himself rejected the term, although not denying that Leibniz's theory of fundamental logical and metaphysical principles had greatly influenced his thought. In many ways, Wolff's philosophy may be seen as a well-conceived though banal version of Leibniz's metaphysics, though some scholars see it as more original and independent of Leibniz.[37] *Vernünfftige Gedanken von den Kräfften des menschlichen Verstandes*, the first textbook in Wolff's system, was published in 1713. It was followed by works on metaphysics, ethics, political philosophy, physics, and natural teleology, all with titles starting with the words 'Rational thoughts'. Wolff used the axiomatic-deductive method of geometry as his model, and the separate works are built up like deductive systems founded on definitions and axioms. Twelve years after the publication of *Logic*, Wolff completed his so-called German system, which became normative for countless textbooks throughout the century. In 1728, he started publishing his system in Latin. It eventually comprised twenty-five huge volumes.

Wolff's system springs from a scholastic system-building urge combined with the need for textbooks. It is founded on a rationalist idea of human knowledge. The relation between cause and effect is identified with the relation between antecedent and consequence in a logical implication. Since Wolff's aim was to communicate certain and useful knowledge, he tried to show that experience and history can form just as secure a foundation for knowledge as mathematics. He did not, however, succeed in clarifying the relation between the a priori knowledge of logic and mathematics and the a posteriori knowledge of the empirical sciences, for which he was later criticised by Johann Heinrich Lambert, who drew the attention of Wolffians to the problem regarding the foundation of the empirical sciences. Logic and mathematics, Lambert said, can justify deductions from the truth of one proposition to that of others, but it is impossible to determine the actual truth of the propositions concerned a priori.[38] Lambert did not, however, solve the problem of the relation between a priori and a posteriori knowledge. Kant's solution, which first appeared in full in *Kritik der reinen Vernunft* (1781), totally altered the philosophical landscape.

In accordance with seventeenth-century rationalism, Wolff regarded impressions and emotions as indistinct and imperfect knowledge, which the mind must either dismiss or elaborate and replace with clear and distinct concepts. That man senses and feels pain and pleasure is a direct consequence of his imperfection.[39] In an attempt to create an aesthetics, Wolff's theory of sensation and feeling was challenged by a number of his pupils. He had defined beauty according to the degree of pleasure an object is capable of producing in the observer; the experience of beauty thereby became part of the indistinct contents of the mind.[40] Wolff did not himself produce any theory of the fine arts, but in 1730 Gottsched, one of his most faithful disciples and at that time a literary arbiter of taste, published his *Versuch einer critischen Dichtkunst*, in which he conventionally stressed the classical demands that art should be didactic and imitative of nature.

In Alexander Baumgarten's *Aesthetica* (1750–8), beauty is defined as sensuous perfection, where perfection represents a unity of order, expression, and content. Johann Georg Sulzer severed the connection between aesthetics and the theory of sense impressions by introducing the feeling of pleasure and pain as a faculty of the mind on a par with reason and will and by correlating the experience of perfection with the feeling of pleasure. Later on, Moses Mendelssohn defined aesthetic experience as perfect sense impressions, whereby aesthetic qualities were no longer viewed as properties of objects but exclusively as qualities of experience.[41] This development was instrumental in establishing aesthetics as an independent philosophical science, but at the same time the possibility of communicating aesthetic experience and the validity of aesthetic statements became problematic.

Leibnizo-Wolffian philosophy became subject not only to internal but also to external criticism. Lessing, for example, rejected the notion that the science of history could attain the same degree of certainty as mathematics.[42] Wolffian intellectualism also came under fire. Friedrich Heinrich Jacobi, influenced by Hume, identified reason with the ability to believe, a faculty he regarded as underlying all the other faculties of the mind, while Johann Georg Hamann, influenced by Hume's theory of belief, also said that the existence of the macrocosm as well as our own microcosm is only given to belief. In this reason plays no part, since belief is no more founded on reason than are the senses of touch or sight.[43] Jacobi and Hamann opened up a world of existence and belief totally different from the world populated by Wolff and the Wolffians.

Herder, too, turned against the German Enlightenment's cult of reason. In *Ideen zur Philosophie der Geschichte der Menschheit* (1784–91), he rejected the conception of history as a constant progression. The belief in progress current in the Enlightenment led to the present being regarded as a rung on the ladder, understandable and explicable only on the basis of the future. It is correct, Herder thought, that every new age represents a stage in the development of mankind, but each stage is independent and must be understood according to its own premises and not according to future events. Man is both a biological and a historical being, and history, like nature, is subject to laws determining its progress. In his philosophy of history, Herder approximated the viewpoints Vico had advanced in his *Principi di una scienza nuova* (*The New Science*) (1725, rev. 1744); here man is defined as a being of unbridled selfishness whose consciousness is determined by history. The logic of history – or 'Providence', as Vico called it – is nevertheless immanent and forces man against his will to curb his selfishness and to form communities.

In the second half of the eighteenth century, the influence of British philosophy in Germany was extraordinarily great; this applies both to Hume and to the Common Sense school.[44] When reestablishing the Berlin Academy in 1744, the Francophile Frederick II of Prussia had somewhat artificially attempted to further the influence of the French Enlighteners on German intellectual life by summoning, amongst others, Voltaire, La Mettrie, and d'Alembert to Berlin. In his youth, Frederick had been a follower of Wolff, but Voltaire soon convinced him of the impossibility of metaphysics. The French philosophers and *beaux-esprits* had only slight influence on well-established academic philosophy in Germany, but they – and above all Diderot – had a significant impact on the important nonacademic thinkers, such as Herder, Lessing, and Mendelssohn.[45]

In eighteenth-century British and German philosophy, questions were raised as to the validity of the empirically founded natural sciences and the possibility of moral science and aesthetics. These problems received a comprehensive treatment in Kant's criticism. Kant was educated in the Leibnizo-Wolffian school, but, as he subsequently said, it was the reading of Hume that aroused him from his 'dogmatic slumbers'.[46] The Common Sense school, as well as British moral philosophy and aesthetics, also influenced his thought. It was precisely because he attempted to combine eighteenth-century British empiricism with Leibniz's idealism that his philosophy can be regarded as a synthesis of empiricism and rationalism.

Kant advanced his theory of knowledge in *Kritik der reinen Vernunft* (1781); in this he concedes, to empiricism on the one hand, that sensation is the precondition for all knowledge and, to rationalism on the other, that real and not formal a priori knowledge of the world of experience exists. Knowledge is only possible, Kant maintains, if the unity of the self is maintained throughout time, and this presupposes the synthesis of the sensory content of the mind. Thus all knowledge results from syntheses, and since knowledge – such as Newtonian physics – is universally valid, the synthesis-creating function of the mind must be governed by rules, and these rules must therefore express the preconditions for the possibility of knowledge. Kant called the deduction from concrete knowledge to the preconditions making it possible 'transcendental deduction', and so his philosophy is often called transcendental philosophy.

The rules for forming a synthesis of what is given to the senses must be rediscovered in the finished product as general traits of the world of experience;

that is, as laws whose a priori validity is thereby proved. The law of causality and the law of conservation of matter are examples of such a priori valid natural laws, but precisely because their validity is proved by way of a transcendental argument, their a priori validity is only proved in relation to the world of experience. They are valid for us as cognitive subjects but cannot be proved as possessing validity for what cannot be an object of possible experience. The field of certain knowledge is thereby restricted in comparison with the area to which classical metaphysics had laid claim.

In *Kritik der praktischen Vernunft* (1788), Kant presented his solution to the problem of the possibility of morality. Hume and Adam Smith had made it depend on man's natural sympathy for his fellows: sympathy enables us to act for the benefit of others and not solely in our own interests. Kant's solution was analogous to this, but his anthropology was different. If the will is determined by reason, which is universal, and not by inclinations, which are determined by man's sensual nature, the resulting action is morally good. As a sensory being, man is subject to the universal laws of nature; as a being whose will can be determined by reason, he is free. Underlying Kant's concept of a rational will is Rousseau's concept of the general will and his doctrine that the individual who is bound by his own will is free. After Hume, it was Rousseau who most influenced Kant. Finally, in *Kritik der Urtheilskraft* (1790), Kant concerned himself with the possibility of aesthetics. In this work, he defines the aesthetic pleasure underlying aesthetic propositions as disinterested pleasure, as pleasure devoid of desire. Precisely because man, as an aesthetically discerning being, can disregard his own interests, aesthetic experience can be communicated and become the object of discussion.

Kant's criticism constituted an epoch in philosophy in the same way as Descartes's idealism had constituted an epoch during the previous century. In British empiricism, Cartesian idealism had petered out into scepticism and subjectivism, views which, according to Kant, conflicted with the fact that man is indeed capable of communicating and discussing matters relating to knowledge, morality, and aesthetics. Kant tried to find the conditions for the possibility of this fact and formulated them as a priori valid propositions.

Kant acquired both disciples and opponents. Small Kantian schools developed towards the end of the eighteenth century and at the beginning of the nineteenth. Decisive for the further development of philosophy was the fact that philosophers such as Johann Gottlieb Fichte, Friedrich Wilhelm Joseph Schelling, and Georg Wilhelm Friedrich Hegel tried, each in his own way, to transcend the boundaries of human knowledge drawn up by Kant. Fichte, and especially Schelling, became the great philosophers of German Romanticism; Hegel, who converted Kant's knowing and acting rational being into an individual whose mind is subordinate to historical and social conditions, had a tremendous influence on the development of philosophy in the first half of the nineteenth century. The Kantian rational being was superior to nature and fell outside the dimension of time; he was in fact ahistorical. Hegelian man is incorporated in history and in socially created reality. In Kant, the reason that determines human knowledge and action became individualised; in Hegel, it became the immanent logic of history.

NOTES

1 Charles Pinot Duclos, *Considerations sur les mœurs de ce siècle* (Paris, 1751), ch. 2, 38.
2 Claude-Adrien Helvétius, *De l'homme, de ses facultés intellectuelles et de son education*, in *Oeuvres complètes*, 5 vols. (London, in fact, Amsterdam, 1781), vol. 5, Bk. XI, ch. 1, pp. 1, 3.
3 Jean le Rond d'Alembert, *Essai sur les éléments de philosophie ou sur les principes des connaissances humaines*, ed. C. Kintzler (Paris, 1986), 10.
4 Alexander Pope, *An Essay on Man*, Epistle II.i, v. 1–2, in Pope, *Poetical Works*, ed. H. Davis (Oxford, 1966), 250.
5 Pierre Charron, *De la sagesse* (Geneva, 1777), Bk. I, ch. 1, p. 2: 'la vraye science & la vray estude de l'homme, c'est l'homme.'
6 François-Marie Arouet de Voltaire, *Lettres philosophiques ou Lettres sur les Anglais*, ed. G. Lanson, rev. edn., ed. A.-M. Rousseau, 2 vols. (Paris, 1964), ltr. 13, 1: 83.
7 John Locke, *An Essay Concerning Human Understanding*, 10.
8 Francis Bacon, *Essayes or Counsels, Civill and Morall* (1625) in *Works*, eds. J. Spedding, R. L. Ellis, and D. D. Heath, 14 vols. (London, 1857–74), 6: 413; Bacon, *New Atlantis*, in *Works*, 3: 121–66.
9 Thomas Sprat, *History of the Royal Society* (London, 1667), 429.
10 Blaise Pascal, *Les pensées*, ed. P. Sellier (Paris, 1991), fr. 680; translated as *Pensées and Other Writings*, trans. H. Levi, ed. A. Levi (Oxford, 1995), 158.
11 Hermann Samuel Reimarus, *Allgemeine Betrachtungen über die Triebe der Thiere, hauptsächlich über ihre Kunsttrieb* (Hamburg, 1760).
12 Known posthumously as *Discours sur le bonheur*; see the edition by J. F. Falvey (Banbury, 1975).
13 See E. M. Wilkinson, *Johann Elias Schlegel: A German Pioneer in Aesthetics*, 2nd edn. (Darmstadt, 1973), 62, 64 ff.
14 Jean-Jacques Rousseau, *Émile ou De l'éducation*, in *Oeuvres*, 4: 600.
15 Johann Nicolas Tetens, *Philosophische Versuche über die menschliche Natur und ihre Entwicklung*, in *Die Philosophischen Werke*, 2 vols. (Leipzig, 1777), vols. 1–2.
16 Étienne Bonnot de Condillac, *Essai sur l'origine des connaissances humaines* (Paris, 1746); Rousseau, *Essai sur l'origine des langues*, in *Traités sur la musique* (Geneva, 1781). See also Rousseau, *Essai sur l'origine des langues où il est parlé de la mélodie et de l'imitiation musicale*, ed. J. Starobinski (Paris, 1990); Pierre-Louis Moreau de Maupertuis, *Réflexions philosophiques sur l'origine des langues, et la signification des mots* (Paris, 1748); Tetens, *Über den Ursprung der Sprache und der Schrift* (Berlin, 1772); Johann Gottfried Herder, *Abhandlung über den Ursprung der Sprache* (Berlin, 1772); Giambattista Vico, *Princípi di scienza nuova d'intorno alla comune natura delle nazioni* (Naples, 1747).
17 Edward Gibbon, *Essai sur l'étude de littérature* (London, 1762), art. 1, p. 1.
18 David Hume, *The Philosophical Works*, eds. T. H. Green and T. H. Grose, 4 vols. (London 1882), 3: 2.

19 Nicolas Malebranche, *De la recherche de la vérité*, in *Oeuvres complètes*, ed. A. Robinet, 20 vols. (Paris 1958–84), vol. 2, ed. G. Rodis-Lewis (1962), Bk. 3, ch. 2, 433–47.

20 Pierre Bayle, *Dictionnaire historique et critique*, 5th edn., 5 vols. (Amsterdam, 1734), 'Pyrrhon', 4: 669–74; translated as *Historical and Critical Dictionary: Selections*, trans. and ed. R. H. Popkin (Indianapolis, IN, 1965), 194–209.

21 Locke, *Examination of P. Malebranche's Opinion of Seeing All Things in God*, in *Works*, 10 vols. (London, 1823), 9: 211–55. See C. J. McCracken, *Malebranche and British Philosophy* (Oxford, 1983) and A. A. Luce, *Berkeley and Malebranche: A Study in the Origin of Berkeley's Thought*, 2nd edn. (Oxford, 1967).

22 Thomas Reid, *Essays on the Intellectual Powers of Man*, eds. D. R. Brookes and K. Haakonssen (Edinburgh, 2002), II.7, 104–12.

23 Locke, *The Reasonableness of Christianity, as delivered in the Scriptures* (London, 1695).

24 Richard Bentley, *A Confutation of Atheism from the Origin and Frame of the World* (London, 1692). See also Isaac Newton, *Four Letters from Sir Isaac Newton to Doctor Bentley containing some Arguments in Proof of a Deity* (London, 1756); John Ray, *The Wisdom of God Manifested in the Works of Creation* (London, 1691); William Derham, *Physico-Theology: or a Demonstration of the Being and Attributes of God, from the Works of Creation* (London, 1713).

25 Samuel Clarke, *A Discourse concerning the Being and Attributes of God, the Obligations of Natural Religion, and the Truth and Certainty of the Christian Revelation* (London, 1706); William Wollaston, *The Religion of Nature Delineated* (London, 1722). See R. M. Burns, *The Great Debate on Miracles: From Joseph Glanvill to David Hume* (Lewisburg, PA, and London, 1981).

26 Hume, *An Enquiry concerning Human Understanding*, ed. T. L. Beauchamp, in *Works* (2000), 10.1–2, SBN 109–31.

27 James Oswald, *An Appeal to Common Sense in Behalf of Religion*, 2 vols. (Edinburgh, 1766–72); James Beattie, *An Essay on the Nature and Immutability of Truth, in Opposition to Sophistry and Scepticism* (Edinburgh, 1776); Dugald Stewart, *Elements of the Philosophy of the Human Mind*, I–III (Edinburgh, 1792–1827). See also *The Letters of David Hume*, ed. J. Y. T. Greig, 2 vols. (Oxford, 1932), 2: 301.

28 Adam Ferguson, *An Essay on the History of Civil Society* (Edinburgh, 1767); Ferguson, *Principles of Moral and Political Science*, 2 vols. (Edinburgh, 1792); John Millar, *The Origin of the Distinction of Ranks; or An Inquiry into the Circumstances which give rise to Influence and Authority, in the Different Members of Society* (Edinburgh, 1771); James Burnett (Lord Monboddo), *Of the Origin and Progress of Language*, 3 vols. (Edinburgh, 1773–6). For an overview of the Scottish Enlightenment, see Richard B. Sher, *Church and University in the Scottish Enlightenment: The Moderate Literati of Edinburgh* (Edinburgh, 1985).

29 Cesare Beccaria, *On Crimes and Punishments and other Writings*, ed. R. Bellamy (Cambridge, 1995), 7; Jeremy Bentham, *An Introduction to the Principles of Morals and Legislation*, eds. J. H. Burns and H. L. A. Hart (London, 1970), 11–12.

30 William Paley, *The Principles of Moral and Political Philosophy*, ed. D. L. Le Mahieu (Indianapolis, IN, 2002), 25.

31 Jean Meslier, *Oeuvres complètes*, eds. J. Deprun, R. Desné, and A. Soboul, 3 vols. (Paris, 1970–2); [Voltaire], *Extrait des sentimens de Jean Meslier* (Geneva, 1762).

32 Condillac, *Traité des sensations* (Paris, 1754), in *Oeuvres complètes*, ed. A. F. Théry, 12 vols. (Paris, 1821–2), vol. 3, Bk. 4, ch. 8, 295–306.

33 Locke, *Essay*, II.i.2.

34 Albrecht von Haller, *Primae lineae physiologiae* (Göttingen, 1747), translated as *Elemens de physiologie*, trans. P. Tarin (Paris, 1752).

35 Carl von Linné (Linnaeus), *Systema naturæ* (Leiden, 1735).

36 Christian August Crusius, *Entwurf der nothwendigen Vernunft-Wahrheiten, wiefern sie den zufälligen entgegen gesetzet werden* (Leipzig, 1745). See Lewis White Beck, *Early German Philosophy: Kant and His Predecessors* (Cambridge, MA, 1969), 394–402.

37 See Manfred Kuehn, Chapter 14, this volume.

38 Johann Heinrich Lambert, '*Abhandlung vom Criterium veritatis*', ed. K. Bopp, in *Kantstudien*, Ergänzungshefte 36 (Berlin, 1915), see, for instance, §§3, 28, and 45, pp. 9–10, 19–20, 27.

39 Christian Wolff, *Psychologia rationalis* (Frankfurt and Leipzig, 1740), in *Werke*, II.6: §516, p. 434.

40 Wolff, *Psychologia rationalis*, §544, pp. 465–6.

41 Johann Georg Sulzer, *Allgemeine Theorie der schönen Künste*, 2 vols. (Leipzig, 1771–4); Moses Mendelssohn, *Briefe über die Empfindungen* (Berlin, 1755). See Beck, *Early German Philosophy*, 287–8, 326–9.

42 Gotthold Ephraim Lessing, *Über den Beweis des Geistes und der Kraft* (Braunschweig, 1777).

43 Friedrich Heinrich Jacobi, *David Hume über den Glauben, oder Idealismus und Realismus* (Breslau, 1787); Johann Georg Hamann, *Sokratische Denkwürdigkeiten* (Amsterdam, in fact Königsberg, 1759), in *Sokratische Denkwürdigkeiten: Aesthetica in nuce*, ed. S.-A. Jørgensen (Stuttgart, 1968), 51.

44 See Manfred Kuehn, *Scottish Common Sense in Germany, 1768–1800: A Contribution to the History of Critical Philosophy* (Kingston and Montreal, 1987); Günther Gawlick and Lothar Kreimendahl, *Hume in der deutschen Aufklärung. Umrisse einer Rezeptionsgeschichte* (Stuttgart-Bad Cannstatt, 1987); N. Waszek, *The Scottish Enlightenment and Hegel's Account of 'Civil Society'* (Dordrecht, 1988).

45 See Roland Mortier, *Diderot en Allemagne* (Geneva and Paris, 1986).

46 Immanuel Kant, *Prolegomena zu einer jeden künftigen Metaphysik, die als Wissenschaft wird auftreten können* (Riga, 1783), Ak 4: 260.

4

THE INSTITUTIONALISATION OF PHILOSOPHY IN CONTINENTAL EUROPE

T. J. HOCHSTRASSER

I. INTRODUCTION

Although the historiography of this subject is large, it is also remorselessly particularist in focus, rarely venturing beyond the study of individual institutions to discern broader national or European trends and developments. Any overview must therefore begin with a few cautionary and defensive words defining the limits to be placed on the meaning of institutionalised philosophy during this period. Next we shall consider some generalisations that are relevant to the teaching of philosophy across all the many and varied European institutions of learning where it was officially taught. Then we shall examine separately the phenomenon of the learned academy as it matured in this era. Finally, some brief but more detailed remarks will be offered on developments in France and Germany. These countries are chosen partly for their intellectual and geopolitical dominance but also because they illustrate respectively the two contrasting patterns of change that philosophy experienced as a discipline. In France, philosophy is subdivided and taught as a series of new specialisms whereas in Germany, its remit is substantially extended from an introductory to the foundational role. This division is symbolised at the end of the period by the respective dominance of two differing concepts of institutionalised philosophy that in France owed much to Condillac and in Germany to Kant.[1]

The most obvious difficulty we have is how broadly to interpret the category of philosophy itself: a minimalist approach would restrict coverage to those courses at universities and colleges that are explicitly designated as philosophical according to the eighteenth century's own subdivision of the subject, but at the other end of the spectrum it may equally be argued that this investigation should comprehend those subdivisions of the discipline that are recognised *today* irrespective of the faculty or course where they were taught and located in the eighteenth century. The loss of historical precision and nuance attendant upon this last approach, however, surely outweighs the gains in accessibility and 'relevance' that the adoption of a twentieth-century framework would bring.

There is no escaping from the canon of textbooks and curricula that were pre-scribed and that significantly changed in the course of the century. However, this does not mean, for example, that the teaching and organisation of exper-imental and theoretical science can be neglected – indeed one of the major themes of any survey of the period must be the way in which the content and range of 'natural philosophy' are first increased, then gradually bracketed off, and ultimately separated from the study of logic, metaphysics, and ethics over the period 1680–1820.

We must also assess whether the teaching of philosophy is best studied in comparative, cosmopolitan terms (on the assumption that useful generalisations can be formed across the 'Republic of Letters') or whether institutional prac-tices are so divergent that the national context remains the only meaningful framework for discussion. Further scepticism can be introduced also about this level of inquiry, arguing that a national context distorts the real relationship be-tween universities and their political context in early modern European history by positing a uniformity of educational theory and pedagogic practice, which investigation of individual cases soon shows to be erroneous.[2] Commonsense historical practice would suggest that all these approaches have valid claims on our attention so long as it can be shown that there are instances of contempo-rary teachers, reformers, and administrators on occasion adopting, for whatever motives, these modes of analysis. The growth of review periodicals with an in-ternational audience, the increasing practice of translation of notable texts from one language to another, the international network of correspondence built up by university professors such as Jean Barbeyrac, and the development of text-books such as Brucker's *Historia critica philosophiae* (1742), which are accepted across national boundaries, all indicate that it does on occasion make sense to talk of the institutionalisation of philosophy across Europe as a whole.

Similarly, the increasing interest taken by many European governments in fostering self-consciously 'useful' courses of a (normally) cameralist kind that would train both pastors and bureaucrats for the service of the state gives legit-imacy to the national context of analysis: as the introductory course in almost all cases, philosophy was close to the centre of attention in all these efforts to coordinate and maximise state resources and itself moulded and was moulded by such initiatives. However, it was only in Catholic countries that cameralism was actually incorporated as part of the philosophy curriculum; in Protestant universities the cameralist focus on the household as a model for the state led to intellectual association with the law faculty instead.[3] Even in a state such as France, where no such concerted policy was pursued, the continuing dom-inance of the Church in Parisian universities and provincial colleges ensured that coordination of orthodox belief and censorship practice was in line with government policy.[4]

So, just as in the case of sixteenth-century Italy, where it is meaningful to generalise across a geographical unit larger than the individual component city-states, it is possible to discuss university and collegiate developments within the framework of contemporary state formations. Yet if we are to increase our knowledge of the topic of institutionalisation at *all* levels, ultimately this can only be done through the creation of a series of specific studies of pedagogic practice within individual universities and of the ways in which those practices filtered, rejected, or incorporated the results of the Enlightenment of which they were both part and observers. Only then shall we have a secure base of evidence from which to proceed to well-informed generalisations at other levels.

This prospect is complicated by the fact that this same issue of how to identify the sources and locus of change – on the cosmopolitan, national, or local levels – is itself a central bone of contention in the historiography that has defined and continues to redefine the eighteenth-century Enlightenment itself. The question of how to define a *philosophe* could be answered in each of these three ways – the cosmopolitan, the national, and the local – and for this reason alone it is peculiarly difficult to address the problem of how to relate the Enlightenment satisfactorily to the teaching of philosophy at universities.

Thirty-five years ago, when the Enlightenment was still considered primarily a French phenomenon among Anglophone historians, it was possible for it to be conceptualised with relative ease (it is perhaps no coincidence that the last major single-author survey of the Enlightenment – by Peter Gay – dates from this era and has had no successor). Thus it was easy to analyse the relationship between the French Enlightenment and French universities and colleges, which were generally perceived to be obscurantist and irrelevant to intellectual progress. Indeed, the anti-clerical focus of so much of the polemic produced by the *philosophes* seemed particularly damning in this context when the bulk of university and college-based education was indeed in the hands of the clergy. Although many of the direct attacks focused more narrowly on the theologians of the Sorbonne and their role in censorship, episodes such as the debacle of the Abbé de Prades's doctoral thesis served to distribute the obloquy more widely across French higher education. In his *Philosophical Dictionary*, Voltaire had dismissed the past achievements of philosophy and hailed human intelligence as sufficient for an understanding of philosophy: 'Centuries were needed to become acquainted with a part of the laws of nature. One day is enough for a wise man to get to know the duties of man.'[5] As long as this same definition of a *philosophe* was taken to be the general test for Enlightenment, the institutionalisation of philosophy was not likely to be considered a felicitous subject for research.

However, in the last two decades, numerous studies of the Enlightenment in a variety of national contexts have somewhat redressed the balance in favour of the official channels of higher education as an integral part of the manifold project of Enlightenment. This trend has been well summarised by a historian of the Scottish Enlightenment, the context where this symbiosis is at its most evident:

If the Enlightenment in France developed outside of, and sometimes in opposition to, the clergy and the schools, the Enlightenment in Scotland, along with less spectacular instances in parts of Germany and other Protestant countries, was largely an ecclesiastical and academic phenomenon.[6]

Yet the historiography of this field is still generally underdeveloped in at least two very important respects: first, we have very little work to guide us on the question of the contribution made by extra-institutional activities, such as *salons*, reading clubs, and 'patriotic' societies, and the penumbra of semi-clandestine philosophical discussion associated with early eighteenth-century Freemasonry. Chartier, Darnton, Roche, and others of the recent generation of historians of the French pre-Revolution have made us aware of the extent to which more or less sophisticated versions of dissident-enlightened thought percolated a newly broadened reading public, but the contribution of such groups to the achievement of eighteenth-century philosophy and their involvement in the institutional side of the enterprise remain largely unexamined and unexplored.[7]

Second, there is relatively little scholarship devoted to the work of the religious orders within colleges and learned societies (as opposed to universities), where the Jesuits, in particular, remained crucial. It would be very useful to know how far their courses on philosophy were drawn from existing courses at universities or were more directly influenced by other, less orthodox intellectual currents.[8] Many of the most interesting questions raised by the institutionalisation of philosophy – such as the varying degrees of separation achieved between the disciplines of theology and philosophy, the role of philosophy in assisting the formation of state ideology, the state's interest in the content of university courses, and the eclectic use made of dissident thought within church-sponsored education – are highlighted in the context of the debate over the merits or demerits of Jesuit training. This debate was experienced in a personal sense by many of the *philosophes* who had themselves been educated in Jesuit establishments. Similarly, to follow, for example, the history of the Berlin Academy of Sciences from its foundation by Leibniz to its role as an element of Frederick the Great's model of enlightened despotism is to express and experience the scope and limits of state-sponsored philosophical enquiry. Such institutions, lying outside conventional frameworks and with a fresh intellectual agenda, often mediate more clearly than traditional universities the changing perceptions of the social role of philosophical enquiry in the eighteenth century.

Finally, it is difficult to identify any effective synthesis on the practical side of teaching, including such subjects as the canon of authors, choice of textbooks, teaching methods (lectures and/or disputations), and changes in the taxonomy of subdivisions of the subject of philosophy. Although we have a patchy knowledge of a number of these different topics, there is no map offering a general picture, whether comparative or analytical, of the development of philosophy within the orthodox European channels. It is this issue above all that historians of philosophy should begin to address. One explanation of this deficiency is that philosophers and historians have very different views on the analysis of how universities contribute to intellectual life, with historians focusing on outcomes and organisation – emphasising the later occupational priorities of students and the development of the relevant faculties – and philosophers focusing more narrowly on those universities that produced identifiable schools with a discrete contribution to the subject itself.[9]

II. PHILOSOPHY AT UNIVERSITIES AND COLLEGES

If one takes first the issue of what was taught in European universities, then one has to remark that the eighteenth century sees a gradual regression from the neo-scholastic syllabus and teaching methods. This occurs at different rates according to the national context upon which one focuses. The crucial variables that determine the rate of such regression often include the interests of particular secular patrons, which manifest themselves typically in new foundations that can define their own definitions of the subject afresh; the development of teaching in the national language rather than in Latin; and above all the incorporation of Cartesian and Lockean epistemology into the older scholastic subject definitions, which allows the old fabric to be patched up with new materials. For much of the century, it is therefore a process of assimilation of new ideas that is at work, together with a smaller number of newer establishments blazing a fresh trail. For our purposes, it is a question of defining how readily older institutions absorbed enlightened ideas and how much influence was exerted by the newer bodies. Notwithstanding these changes, we still have to conclude that it was only after the institutional destruction brought about by the French Revolution and the Napoleonic Wars that the content of the philosophy course in French and German higher education could be comprehensively remodelled.[10]

According to the old scholastic definitions, philosophy, together with theology, law, and medicine, was categorised as one of the four major sciences that offered a causal explanation of the world.[11] However, its particular character was propaedeutic, providing the basic skills needed for progress in the other disciplines, except that it had been established that a Master of Arts degree was not a necessary precondition for the study of law. The principal subdivisions of philosophy throughout this period were still logic, ethics, physics, and metaphysics, each of which was seen as a way of preparing a student for study in the other senior sciences (ethics for law, physics for medicine, and metaphysics for theology), with logic considered to be of general relevance.[12]

Of the four subdivisions, metaphysics, as the most abstract, was judged in theory to be the most significant, but as the century progressed it became clear that physics and logic were the most important branches of the course. L. W. B. Brockliss has, for example, suggested that at the University of Paris, physics formed the main part of the second-year course and was the basis of most of the theses submitted. Moreover, in the course of the eighteenth century, the physics course itself became more and more mathematical, which further reduced the number of topics, even in physics, that could be covered in the time available.[13] This is strong evidence in favour of the willingness of even the most orthodox channels of higher education to adapt to intellectual trends that impinged upon them from outside, for much of the physics taught reflected the latest developments in the field. A classic case of a trade-off between orthodox religion (in this case Calvinism) and the new science took place in the Dutch universities, where a compromise was arranged that lasted for much of the eighteenth century, in itself helping to explain the relative insulation of the Dutch *Verlichting* from French religious scepticism and materialism.[14]

However, in the older institutions in France and Germany, the methods of teaching philosophy generally varied little from traditional scholastic practice; a logically linked sequence of topics was divided up into *quaestiones* and approached through the traditional tripartite formula of argument (*dico*, *objicio*, and *respondeo*). This tired methodology did at least ensure that the history of major disagreements around core philosophical topics was conveyed to students, and of course there was, as always, scope for the teacher to skew the presentation to suit his own particular enthusiasms. But this hardly encouraged independent thought; nor was an adequate historical overview of the subject provided as context (although Thomasius at least sought to remedy this in the recent foundation at Halle by offering the history of philosophy as a *compulsory* preliminary course).

Procedures in the classroom were no more advanced, with the academic lecture (often based on a textbook written by the professor himself) forming the basis of instruction. Lectures were often no more than a detailed commentary on the positions set out in the textbook, which the students then added to their copies of the core text. This is as much true of Hegel's *Grundlinien der Philosophie des Rechts* (1821) as of the multi-volume series of works by Christian Wolff written in both Latin and German in the first half of the eighteenth century. As Keith Tribe has pointed out, university life in the eighteenth century was still in a real sense an oral culture, where what was written was composed with an eye for its success as material to be read out loud, and with recourse to the full resources of the classical arts of rhetoric or to a formal mathematical mode of exposition also geared to oral presentation.[15] In France, too, professors still dictated to their classes in the eighteenth century, and the only textbooks in regular use seem, for obvious reasons, to have been devoted to mathematics, which would indeed have been impossible to teach without them.[16]

Again, it was only in physics that there was a major departure from existing teaching methods, as some experimental work was admitted, by way of illustration, into the lecture hall. This was tacked onto the end of the course and was often open to visitors as well. By the end of the eighteenth century, the presence of *cabinets de physique* was widespread in French universities and colleges, and a course of this kind was commonplace at the *collèges de plein exercice* (the equivalent of public grammar schools which offered a basic set of lectures on philosophy).[17] But this observation serves to emphasise how the teaching of philosophy had been decentralised: while there were some 180 universities in Europe in the eighteenth century, as opposed to 60 in 1500, the length of courses had contracted and the profession of academic teaching was challenged by rival collegiate institutions that stood outside the university framework. As an index of this development, a course in philosophy could be taken at over 100 institutions in France, only 20 of which were universities. And if one is seeking to explain why the structures of French higher education remained relatively open to enlightened scientific thought, then one important factor was certainly that the balance of scientific teaching activity took place outside official structures.

By 1750, there had been some moves towards teaching and publishing in the vernacular, but these proceeded at varying rates. The earliest steps were taken in Germany by Thomasius, who led the way at Leipzig in 1687, and others who pioneered new foundations, notably G. A. von Münchhausen at the new university at Göttingen. For a period in the 1710s and 1720s, parallel editions of texts were still published in Latin and German, but the publication of Christian Wolff's major series of tomes in German represented a crucial watershed and an example to other philosophers writing in German. Indeed it may be argued that Wolff's devising of a systematic philosophical vocabulary of concepts in German was an important factor in making the critical philosophy of Kant possible. If one seeks reasons apart from the initiative of individuals to explain this phenomenon, they may be found in three factors: the decline in the proportion of the population speaking Latin after the Thirty Years War, the role of Pietism within the educational system as a whole, and the increasing intervention of the state in university affairs, insisting that courses be made more relevant to clerical and bureaucratic careers. Pietism stressed the need to read sacred texts in the vernacular, arguing that the task of spiritual illumination (*erleuchten*) involved extending access to knowledge as much as providing new knowledge. And behind the involvement of the state lay mercantilist fears that without such flexibility students would be lured away to foreign universities, where vernacular courses would be available.[18]

However, in France it was not until the late eighteenth century that the vernacular became the undoubted medium for teaching and discussion, as opposed to the language of textbook publication: once 'scientific' philosophy became more mathematical and complex, the pressure to teach physics in French became irresistible. By the time of the Revolution, a trend had developed for physics to be seen as a near relation of mathematics rather than of logic and ethics, with whose principles it was linked in the traditional schema. The reforms of the Revolution only made manifest what was already implicit in pedagogic practice. The origins of what is usually seen as a nineteenth-century phenomenon – the emergence of sciences based on mathematical training and humanities subjects based on the traditional disciplines of logic – can already be observed. Indeed it is already schematically present in the proposals for educational reform put forward at the beginning of the Revolution by Condorcet. As a further example, one may cite the restructuring of the curriculum at the University of Salamanca in the 1770s.

Given that some states, such as Denmark and Hungary, retained Latin as the chief language of academic discourse, one must ask why Germany and France made some moves towards the teaching of philosophy in the vernacular while retaining Latin for other disciplines.[19] Despite the dangers involved in arguments associated with the emergence of nationhood, it cannot be denied that these moves are at least contemporaneous with attempts at patriotic self-assertion: instead of remaining part of the 'private' sphere of various provincial cultures, philosophy in both Germany and France had, by the end of the eighteenth century, become part of the national 'public' sphere, just as the universities themselves had become part of the national culture – in the French case through government intervention and in Germany by the creation of a specific cultural definition of nationhood based on a desire to transcend cultural subjugation both to French taste and to Protestant-scholastic restrictions on the definition of the legitimate subject matter of philosophy. If Germany could not be a political nation, it could at least offer a mature philosophical language as part of its claim to be a *Kulturnation*.

Even to pose the question of whether philosophy in the university and collegiate world was part of the public or the private sphere quickly isolates the uneasy transitional nature of higher education during this period: on the one hand, control by the state or government becomes ever more pressing as the century progresses; on the other, the bulk of teaching in philosophy in Germany still takes place in the unregulated form of private enterprise in the house of the professor, who often provides bed and board for his students as well. As ever, circumstances vary from one country to another.

If one is seeking to provide a general framework for developments in European philosophical institutions during the period 1690–1810 (without necessarily wanting to set the argument in terms of rigid Kuhnian paradigms), then the following subdivisions could broadly be said to obtain: the period 1690–1730 is distinguished by a gradual reshaping of the social context of universities, with significant changes taking place in the aspirations both of students and of their teachers (more emphasis on 'manners' and a 'polite' general education suited to future courtiers and bureaucrats); there is also a new interest taken by the state in ensuring that universities produced graduates suitable for appointment to the government, church, or primary education system.[20] The one exception here is France, where, as we shall see, the impact of the *Unigenitus* debate ensured that the institutional separation of ethics and theology that was taking place elsewhere was inhibited, limiting curricular change before the French Revolution to tactical accommodations between Cartesianism and experimental science.

The period 1730 – 89 represents another discrete phase, in which there is further expansion in the role of the universities in shaping citizens for participation in an enlightened culture. More practical courses are devised that confer priority upon history, geography, and rhetoric while stigmatising the old scholastic learning as 'monkish' and old-fashioned. Locke's writings on the appropriate education for the sons of gentlemen gain a wide currency, and Ferguson and Iselin stand out as representative types of institutional philosophers.[21] This is the heyday of the University of Göttingen as a propaedeutic finishing school, taking in mainly very young students whose skills would later be refined outside a university framework by participation in the 'Republic of Letters'. There is a greater sense now of the different audiences for philosophy, both within and outside and in opposition to official academe. Of course, it is far from clear that these moves towards a greater professionalism in teaching and standardisation of the course benefited the discipline internally, for a system which encouraged its best students to prepare for a different career outside the university ensured that fewer good academics stayed on to teach and write – perhaps helping to explain the high level of competence but absence of great names among the German philosophers of this period. The same *cursus* can be observed in France, where most professors sought ultimately to pursue a career in the church. Here, of course, it is traditional practice rather than the state's policies of social engineering that is responsible.

The importance of this phase is that it effectively constitutes the end of the time when a common and agreed set of philosophical references could be said to support both the assumptions and the practice of theology, law, medicine, and the natural sciences. Until this time, the flexible and adaptable categories of humanist exegesis and Aristotelian verbal logic had offered a common metaphysics and method for the pursuit of knowledge. Yet once physics hived itself off as an empirical and specialised mathematical discipline, fragmentation and specialisation within the university teaching system were brought much nearer, whereby the new models of mathematical logic and empirical method could be given wider application. This tendency was reinforced from another direction by the threat that new academies posed to the universities' traditional monopoly of useful learning. It was the academicians who led the way in demonstrating to the professors that Cartesian physics could not be defended against Newton's attractionism and prompted the universities of mainland Europe to install the new orthodoxy. Of course, this process of curricular reform was further accelerated by the gradual removal of the Jesuit order, in the 1760s and 1770s, from a role in higher education. From here, it was a short step to the opening up of the universities to forms of materialism and early utilitarianism in ethics and to vitalism and mechanism in medicine.[22]

One of the important preconditions of the rapid change that was to follow in the next decades had therefore already been met: the universities no longer had a monopoly on knowledge and would have to adapt to the priorities of new disciplines if they were ever to regain it. Moreover, it was clear from internal developments that the creation of a more mathematical physics had produced an overloaded syllabus which would need to be subdivided into separate specialisms. Given that governments for their own reasons remained committed to the greater integration of university courses into a specified range of professional career options, the imposition and subsequent export of revolutionary reforms on exactly those lines ensured lasting changes to the place of philosophy in the curriculum of European universities.

A final phase is represented by the era 1789–1810, bounded by the beginning of revolutionary change and the creation of the University of Berlin during the Humboldt reform period. The impact of the French Revolution helped to promote the inclusion of new subjects such as political economy, mathematics, and languages within a wider range of European courses on philosophy. But institutionally, the key change (pioneered in France) was the creation of separate faculties of arts and sciences after 1808, an innovation which was to be imitated in Belgium, Holland, Spain, and Italy before 1848. Under the combined pressure of an increasingly overloaded syllabus and successive governments in desperate need of an increased number of trained professionals, it was necessary to set up a course in moral sciences as preparatory for law and theology and a course in natural science as a propaedeutic for medicine. In Germany philosophy remained a unified discipline and during the preponderant influence of the Critical Philosophy established itself as *the* repository of truth over and above the state rather than a merely preparatory study. But in a period of political disruption that saw many universities either abolished or temporarily closed, the initiative passed to private academies whose practical emphases and priorities gained them more support from governments during the Napoleonic era than the traditional teaching universities. If the research university was the main innovation of the nineteenth century, then the academies were its real precursors – for example, they certainly influenced the institutional development of Humboldt's ideas in Berlin. Yet despite the recovery of an institutionalised role for philosophy, by 1810 it had lost its traditional role as a linking discipline, although the best efforts of Kant had been devoted to providing a new formula. But it was no longer possible to assert that universities operated under the umbrella of a united metaphysics.

III. THE GROWTH OF ACADEMIES

If one examines the article 'Académie' in the first volume of Diderot and d'Alembert's *Encyclopédie*, one can see how the author views academies as part of a continuum initiated in the seventeenth century. The purpose of an academy is defined as 'a society or company of men of letters, established for the cultivation and advancement of the Arts or the Sciences'. However, the function of academies is here one of general improvement rather than instrumental teaching: 'an Academy is not destined to teach or profess any Art, whatever it may be, but to achieve its perfection'.[23] It was the further development of the art or skill concerned that mattered here, for these were of essential interest to the state that provided the patronage.

But in actual fact one needs to distinguish the famous academies founded in the seventeenth century (such as the Académie Française, Académie Royale des Sciences, and Académie des Inscriptions in France and the Royal Society in England) from their eighteenth-century successors, which were tied by their founders to a much more specific and narrow set of aims and functions. Thus

the remit of the Académie des Sciences, founded in 1666, was never strictly defined but covered both theoretical and practical science, public education, and
invention of new technology. The predominance of one or another definition
of utility often depended on royal or ministerial wishes rather than the internal
priorities of the Académie, which partly explains why so many of its projects
were often inconclusive.[24] The focus of such institutions as the Royal Prussian
Academy and those like it at Göttingen and Munich, the *Ritterakademien*, and the
many provincial French academies was usually limited to practical knowledge
rather than theoretical subjects, but this had the beneficial result of encouraging an eclectic and open approach to modern enlightened philosophy as it
developed outside university systems. Moreover, the success of these institutions
undoubtedly helped the cause of those reformers who sought to reinvigorate
the older seats of learning – it is difficult, for example, to imagine Thomasius's
success in propagating a practical *aulic* philosophy for pastors, teachers, and bureaucrats without the example of the academies pioneered by his friend A. H.
Francke and other Pietists. Likewise, the career *cursus* for pastors and civil servants recommended by the cameralists also assisted the success of new university
foundations, such as Göttingen, in breaking away from the traditional concepts
of philosophical curricula.

Despite the example of the Royal Society, academy culture on the European
pattern did not flourish in Britain (the dissenting academies must surely be
discounted in this context). The crucial factor underlying the success of
the academies in Europe was patronage, whether from local provincial elites in
the French case or from the state in the cases of Germany and Russia, where the
academies were associated with the state-building process from their inception.
The case of the Russian Royal Academy of Sciences (1724) is a particularly
interesting example of government patronage determining the priorities and
scope of academicians' work: the absence of other institutions of higher education in Russia ensured that the royal patrons required the academy and its
members to perform many of the functions of a university. It provided training
for future academicians and a translation service for foreign publications. Also,
and crucially, foreign members of the Academy were paid retainers to lobby on
its behalf and to pass on information about important new books and inventions
to Russia as soon as possible.

Even if it is difficult to generalise across the European academies of France,
Germany, Italy, and Russia (because at many points their activities seem to overlap with and shade into the activities of literary societies, patriotic clubs, and
salons), nevertheless some common traits are clearly discernible. While they varied greatly in the definitions of their categories of membership, most academies
were arranged in four sections – mathematics and natural philosophy, historical

researches, the study of the structure and history of languages, and medicine. All these subjects were poorly represented at the universities and promised relevant practical applications. Academies only rarely met collectively for the reading of papers and presentation of prizes. Otherwise, administration tended to lie in the hands of the secretary and other officials, while the core membership was encouraged to pursue private research which would then be published in the house journal run by the academy, thus giving a wider circulation and seal of approval to the finished product and boosting the prestige of the academy itself. Other ways of raising the profile of the academy were to publish large bodies of inscriptions and other necessary tools of historical research and to sponsor lectures and competitions. This was particularly a feature of French provincial academies, hoping somewhat disingenuously to encourage the outbreak of a literary *affaire* on their own territory.[25]

In the case of French provincial academies, one should not look there for depth of philosophical enquiry: they were explicitly elitist organisations, administered chiefly by the *honoraires* (honorary members), who were for the most part local notables. Nevertheless, the essay competitions they organised contributed a significant stimulus to enlightened opinion, of which Rousseau's two encounters with the Académie de Dijon are only the most famous examples. The different fortunes of Rousseau's two discourses illustrate the precise limits of enlightened opinion within the world of the French academy: the victory of the first discourse on the progress of the arts and sciences may be explained by the *éclat* of its wrongheadedness rather than because the sentiments it contained met with approval; the defeat of the second discourse may be attributed not only to the breaking of the conditions of anonymity but also to the discourse's searching critique of contemporary enlightenment, which could not easily be brushed off as a provoking attempt to play devil's advocate. It was also perfectly possible for the same author to win two prizes in different competitions by arguing two opposing points of view.[26]

These academic contests served the valuable purpose of bringing into the circle of enlightened discussion many middle-class professionals in the provinces who would otherwise not have participated at any level. On practical topics, such as agricultural reform and the social problems of how to improve the education and condition of the poor – where a precise set of local benefits could be discerned – daring proposals for change were often put forward.[27] Nor should one underestimate the success of these local academies in disseminating the discussion of more abstract scientific ideas emanating from the metropolitan academies in Paris. One example that serves to illustrate the point is the academy of Châlons-sur-Marne, which was elevated from a literary society to a full academy in 1775 with the motto of *L'utilité*. Its researches were essentially devoted to the improvement and better use of the resources of the province (Champagne), and while one quarter of all the papers presented at its meetings were on scientific topics, a great many others were given over to historical and economic subjects.[28] This was the true face of practical philosophy in provincial France, showing both how far the social profile of philosophy should extend and where it should stop.[29]

The article, 'Académie', from the *Encyclopédie*, to which we have referred, adds that there are more academies to be found in Italy than in any other European country, and given the divisiveness of Italian political life and the absence there of many strong governmental patrons, this phenomenon deserves further investigation. The very fragmentation of Italy led – as in the case of the Holy Roman Empire – to attempts by petty princes to assert themselves culturally instead of militarily, and the creation of an academy thus became as much part of the court furniture as other projections of royal propaganda. But there was usually more to it than this, as in the case of the Accademia di Medinaceli, which was founded by the Neapolitan government in 1690 to help create a loyal intellectual elite independent of the Catholic Church in anticipation of political troubles once the last of the Spanish Habsburg rulers had died. We see the same attempt by a government to replace an intellectual elite with one more malleable in Kaunitz's creation of an Imperial and Royal Academy of Sciences and Literature in Belgium in 1772 to counterbalance the University of Leuven. The idea of the academy as a social space that could balance the influence of the Church was the original motive for the creation by Gravina of the *Arcadia*, an academy to embrace writers across the whole of Italy, and also for Muratori's later proposal for a 'Republic of Letters' in five provinces, which offered an alternative form of civil association for philosophers.[30] As the eighteenth century progressed, these grand schemes gave way to the creation of smaller groupings, often very informal, such as the tongue-in-cheek Accademia dei Pugni, comprising the circle surrounding Beccaria. Academies in Italy therefore came to serve another important purpose in simultaneously concealing and admitting the perceived relative decline of Italian culture in relation to France, Germany, and England: they offered ways of filtering the latest ideas and fashions into Italian intellectual circles while preserving the *appearance* of Italian initiative in the same areas. More significantly, the local academies provided excellent training for the administrators of Habsburg Italy, who were very successful in the later part of the century in implementing reforms whose intellectual pedigree lay elsewhere, particularly in France.[31]

The bulk of European academies represented a transitional form of intellectual affiliation. They were popular while different forms of state and church patronage competed with one another. Philosophers (broadly defined) began to move from being university professors or court retainers to the status of employees of an impersonal state bureaucratic structure; or they became authors in the public sphere outside the private world of universities and courts and had a direct relationship to a public subscribing to journals and underwriting the production of books. The academy offered a new form of social space free from the traditional constraints that existed elsewhere.[32] Critical to this evocation of a forum for the free exchange of ideas was the exemption of an academy's publications from the laws of censorship that operated in many states. It mattered much less that the membership of academies was often still dominated by the social elite, for the members of that elite could usually ensure protection against the punitive actions of the government and its agents. This was particularly the case in France, where academicians used their institutions as much as mouthpieces of opposition as in support of government reform projects, especially during the ministries associated with the ideas of the physiocrats. Once freedom from censorship was guaranteed, the reputation of the relevant academy was enhanced abroad, in turn raising sales of its published (and uncensored) proceedings and increasing its sources of revenue. These were vital to funding its activities – monarchs proving less reliable with funds than they were with privileges and exemptions – and to further increasing independence.

Paradoxically, it was the reliance of the academies on government guarantees of freedom of expression that ensured their ultimate loyalty to the state because the freedom most academicians sought was from the impositions and restrictions of the church, not from the government, which was often viewed as a natural protector. Once this right was secured, the academies were unlikely to push their dissent very far. This was partly because their independence of the church and universities had been secured, but also because the preponderance of members drawn from the ruling elite ensured a degree of self-censorship. The really sensitive political issues of the day were thus sidestepped or struck off the agenda (one sees the process in operation in the Berlin Academy of Sciences, where Frederick II's guarantees were always interpreted with circumspection). The one exception is for the period 1750–70, an era when, as Franco Venturi has shown, many more members of the elite, including academicians, were tempted to participate in reform movements by proposing truly controversial matters for debate (for example, in 1770 the Berlin Academy set an essay on the topic of whether it is right for a ruler to deceive his people – a deliberate acceptance of the challenge laid down by Frederick II's *Anti-Machiavel* [1740]). It is instructive to examine briefly how the Berlin Academy, founded by Gottfried Wilhelm Leibniz in 1700, negotiated these reefs successfully.

Leibniz was a natural figure to act as the founder of the Berlin Academy, for his belief in the unity of knowledge, the need for European reconciliation to be led by a unified intellectual elite, and the possibility of a universal scholarly language were all goals that were most naturally addressed within the institutionalised format of an academy.[33] Berlin represented a strategic site for the Academy because there was no rival university established there. Nor did Leibniz seek to imitate one, as the practical imperatives of the Academy were always uppermost in his considerations:

The purpose [would be] to combine theory with practice and to improve not only the arts and sciences but also the country and the people, agriculture, manufacturing and commerce and, in a word, food. Also, to make discoveries which redound profusely to the Glory of God and assist in the perception of His miracles, and thus in the implantation and dissemination of the Christian religion, strong government, stability and morality among peoples partly heathen, partly still ignorant, even barbaric.[34]

Leibniz's concern to see knowledge applied practically bore early fruit in the publication of a journal under the auspices of the academy, the *Miscellanea Berolinensia* (1710), which gained a wide following. After a period of enforced specialisation on military topics under Frederick William I, the Berlin Academy reached its apogee in the period 1740–70 when reconstituted by Frederick II. It aimed to cover the whole gamut of disciplines, which were divided into four classes: fine arts, mathematics (including modern physics), speculative philosophy (embracing ethics, logic, and metaphysics), and experimental philosophy (devoted essentially to chemistry, anatomy, and botany). There were sixteen stipendiary members, each of whom submitted two papers a year, which were read at regular meetings and subsequently published. Equally important were corresponding members in other countries whose contacts with the indefatigable secretary of the Academy, J. H. S. Formey, helped to keep alive the notion of a 'Republic of Letters' long after it had receded to the status of a faded aspiration in other European countries. It is no coincidence that many of the members in both categories were French or Swiss Protestants who had both linguistic flexibility and – by reason of their position as Huguenots – no rival overriding national affiliations. Although part of the *Aufklärung*, the Berlin Academy gained its reputation because its proceedings and so many of its personnel were French and thus well placed to mediate in a truly cosmopolitan fashion between states. Its essay competitions on such topical subjects as 'Is it useful to deceive the people?' and an invitation to discuss the oversimplified Leibnizian principle of 'Everything is for the best' attracted contributions from many different countries. The Academy lost impetus in the later years of Frederick II's reign, as the king himself became more reactionary. Leaders of enlightened opinion in Berlin gravitated instead to the *Mittwochsgesellschaft* and the *Montagsclub*, while those who were Jews were in any case excluded from Academy membership.[35]

But the Academy nevertheless survived to make a contribution to the curricula of the nineteenth-century University of Berlin.

It was above all the focus on experimental scientific inquiry that separated the academies of the eighteenth century from their predecessors. The famous French academies of the seventeenth century had turned their attention mainly to exercises in compilation or categorisation, and while these were not neglected, it increasingly was experimental science with practical application to agriculture and industry that secured the attention and financial patronage of academicians across eighteenth-century Europe.[36] The needs of the state were more and more defined in terms of gaining economic advantage over competitor countries, and so the added strength of state patronage was accorded to local initiatives until ultimately the universities were able to regain effective institutional control of scientific research in the mid-nineteenth century.

But while such organisations played an important role in the infrastructure of the Enlightenment, it would be wrong to regard them as being at the fore-front of new discovery in experimental science. It was in most cases a matter of observation, collection, and commentary upon natural curiosities. A typical academician would in this sense have been Buffon, the French classifier of species, and a representative academy, the Leopoldina, founded originally in 1652, granted the status of Imperial Academy in 1687, and still in existence today. As van Dülmen has argued, what mattered in this case was not the methodological innovations of its practice, but 'the emergence of a community spirit under the protection of the Emperor'.[37] It was as a new form of intellectual association free from external controls (other than the usually flexible requirements of the immediate patron) that the academy made its major contribution to eighteenth-century intellectual life. Membership of an academy was a valued honour to which all those who were interested above all in the new sciences – whether bureaucrats, doctors, clergy, or professors – could aspire on terms of equal status. Contacts were facilitated and affinities strengthened among those who were already predisposed to prefer new ideas to older orthodoxies, but in a more formal context than in the contemporary Masonic lodges. Nor should one forget that the academies also played a minor role in teaching. In funding chemistry courses, for example, the academies met a need that was blocked in traditional universities by the restrictions imposed by the faculties of medicine.[38]

IV. INSTITUTIONALISATION OF PHILOSOPHY IN FRANCE

Outside the sphere of natural philosophy, the teaching of philosophy in France in the traditional areas of logic, ethics, and metaphysics did not undergo major changes during the eighteenth century. It was, as Brockliss remarks, 'a history of stasis'.[39] Each area of the discipline of philosophy was permeated to a different extent by Cartesian influences, but these were *least* apparent in the field of ethics, where Descartes himself had made no specific contribution. Moreover, the combined political influence of the Crown and the Catholic Church ensured that doctrinal conservatism prevailed in ethics, a key point in the eyes of the government because most students were subsequently trained as lawyers and clerics and therefore required an orthodox education from the earliest stage. Similar conservatism prevailed in logic, where the set text essentially remained Aristotle's *Organon*, with the syllogism as the main unit of analysis. Instead of the innovative exegesis of the humanist civil lawyers of the Renaissance, there was in general a tired imitation of old models. Aquinas and his commentators retained an immovable dominance. It was figures outside the institutional framework, such as Descartes, Malebranche, Fontenelle, Domat, and the *philosophes*, who set the intellectual pace. Assimilation accommodated only doctrines that did not touch traditional dogmas such as transubstantiation. Cartesian dualism may have been embraced, but only on the condition that the essence of mind and matter remained beyond the scope of human knowledge. The French universities and colleges did not provide within their ethics courses anything that approached the teaching of politics and economics within German cameralism for those who would go on to serve the state; nevertheless, the combined effect of imbibing the political and religious prejudices of the humanities course, followed by the forensic and analytical skills gained from the courses on logic and metaphysics, produced much the same result – a professional elite equipped and prepared to defend traditional positions with more respectable skills and modern knowledge.

Although this system was changed rapidly in the years after 1789, it is striking how successful official institutions of learning had been in insulating themselves from the really significant philosophical developments taking place around them. 'Modern' natural law theory as mediated by Barbeyrac eluded them, and the influence of Lockean thought was restricted to epistemology, and then only in an attenuated form. In general, the ideas and theories of foreign authors had to wait until the era of the *Encyclopédie* before they gained any widespread acceptance. Hitherto any dissident movement in French intellectual life, such as Jansenism, had represented a disagreement within official, orthodox Catholic circles rather than an intellectual departure from the effectively sealed world of institutionalised French thought.

Part of the problem lay in the domination of the University of Paris by the Sorbonne, the senior faculty for the study of theology in Europe. Behind the Sorbonne lay the considerable authority of the Archbishop of Paris, vested not only in the powers of appointment and patronage at his disposal but also in the statutes of the university. The realities of the subjugation of philosophy in the French capital were thus correctly identified by Rousseau in his letter of protest to M. de Beaumont on the suppression of *Émile* and *Du contrat social* (1762). The scope for innovation in the philosophy faculty was further constrained by the dispute between Jesuit and Jansenist factions that continued to simmer after the publication of *Unigenitus*, with the Jansenist academics taking strongly Cartesian positions. In the wake of these tensions, it was never likely that government would move against the Jesuit control of the *collèges*. This meant in turn that outside Paris, and rather against expectations, the situation offered little more variety.[40]

One should not underestimate the role of boundary disputes and academic infighting in the eighteenth-century controversies that periodically affected the University of Paris. Although the theological infractions involved in both the Abbé de Prades's thesis and extrapolations of Cartesian epistemology were minor issues, they were treated as major threats because the Sorbonne interpreted them as much as threats to its authority as to doctrine and used them as an excuse to extend its control over the Faculty of Arts. Likewise, the theologians refused to be reconciled to the popular success of physics at the expense of the three other sciences: logic, metaphysics, and ethics. In 1704, the university had to remind the professoriat that they were under an obligation to teach the whole course. But, according to Brockliss, this had little effect in practice: '[T]he small space devoted to the other three sciences in the Paris theses sustained after 1720 would seem to suggest that physics in the eighteenth century was the only part of the course that really captured the interest of professor and student'.[41] In 1752, a separate physics course was ultimately made available by the creation of a chair in experimental physics at the Collège de Navarre.

During the Revolutionary and Napoleonic administrations, philosophy was in essence deconstructed and broken up into a number of discrete subjects. In the *écoles centrales*, created in 1795, the new curriculum paid its debt to empiricism in the form of a foundation course in botany and drawing which was intended to show the students how to use the senses and owed a great deal to Condillac. From this basis, they learned the natural sciences, which taught them how to use their minds, and finally they graduated to ethics and civics, which conferred a training in practical reasoning. What followed in lieu of a university degree was specific vocational training in a special school devoted to a particular profession. While this system was displaced by Napoleon's *lycées* in 1802, the emphasis on practical civic outcomes remained, and the professional schools retained their status under the grand scheme of a *Université impériale*, which was introduced in 1808.[42]

V. THE INSTITUTIONALISATION OF PHILOSOPHY IN GERMANY

Before we can offer generalisations about institutionalised philosophy in Germany, we need to be very clear about the kinds of comparisons that may be drawn across the different polities within the Reich. Geographical distinctions between northern or southern eastern or western locations were not recognised by contemporaries. Nor is it helpful to make comparisons on a confessional basis given the decline in direct polemical confrontation between Protestants and Catholics, the corresponding rise of theological conflicts *within* confessions, and the sharing of common textbooks across confessional boundaries that was in place even before the abolition of the Jesuits.

Rather, it is more helpful to isolate the political sovereignty that lay behind the creation of university policy. It was, for example, Prussian policy making, enacted in the Ministry of Justice and the so-called Spiritual Ministry (covering Lutheran church affairs, schools, and universities) that provided the common link explaining the development of the study of philosophy at Halle, Jena, Königsberg, and Frankfurt (Oder). Likewise, it was Hanoverian policy, shaped by the political link to Great Britain, that was the decisive influence in determining the priorities of the new University of Göttingen, which in turn became the object of imitation in both Catholic and Protestant universities across Germany. Sovereign affiliation was the distinguishing mark of universities recognised by contemporaries.

These political facts help to throw light upon the relative lack of confrontation between official philosophy and the *Aufklärung* and the generally smooth incorporation of philosophy into the business of providing a practical education for state servants. The subordinate position of philosophy in relation to the three other faculties and its role as a foundation discipline made it more open to curricular reform at the behest of rulers than the other faculties. In Protestant universities, this reform tended to take the form of intruding elements of so-called aulic philosophy or training in court etiquette, whereas in Catholic states, as we have seen, the philosophy course was used as the best framework for teaching cameralist science. A common feature was the determination of the rulers that the philosophy faculty should be independent of the theology faculty and therefore basically answerable to a government department alone. The independence of the philosophy faculty from the theology faculty had been established at Halle and Jena – both new foundations at the end of the seventeenth century – and then widely imitated elsewhere. And so the scope for confrontation between the forces of religious orthodoxy and enlightened thought (on the model of the French Enlightenment) was substantially reduced. This applied equally at the University of Vienna, where the success of Justi and

Sonnenfels owed much to the support of the government, who blocked Cardinal Migazzi's attempts to regulate and confine cameralist science.[43] A corollary of this is the untroubled participation of professors in late seventeenth-century and early eighteenth-century journalism: journals such as the *Acta Eruditorum* and *Göttingische Anzeigen von Gelehrten Sachen* operated free from official intervention and attracted a large audience well before the proliferation of periodicals in Germany during the second half of the century.[44]

The University of Halle, founded in 1694 at the instigation of Elector Frederick III of Prussia, was particularly well suited to promoting the training of servants of the state because the two driving forces behind it during its early years, Christian Thomasius and A. H. Francke, both placed a high value on the beneficent role of practical knowledge. Christian Thomasius had found protection within Prussian territory from the Protestant Aristotelians of Leipzig, who had expelled him for lecturing in the vernacular and challenging the authority of the theology faculty to determine the content of teaching in ethics, whereas A. H. Francke was devoted to the creation of a Pietist educational infrastructure stretching from basic schooling to university level. This Pietist commitment to providing education for the children of the poor at the expense of the community produced a university with a relative lack of social exclusivity and a willingness to act as a conduit for limited social mobility into the lower ranks of the clergy and bureaucracy. This was not sustained in the later eighteenth century, when the priority of governments, and therefore of the universities also shifted to one of stabilising social contours and thus restricting the access of the lower orders to higher education.[45]

It should perhaps be stressed that the most characteristically enlightened thought that evolved from Halle derived from the law faculty rather than from philosophy. The concept of *libertas philosophandi* applied first and foremost to jurisprudence and moral philosophy, where the battle was most intense between the opponents and defenders of Samuel Pufendorf. This contest was the analogue of the dispute within French higher education over the introduction of Newtonian mathematical physics in that it contained an intellectual dispute of substance alongside an important challenge to the traditional structure of university teaching. If mathematical logic and experimental principles shattered the unified metaphysics and shared methodological assumptions of French universities, then Pufendorf's voluntarist natural law theories had a similarly destabilising effect on the synthesis of Lutheran and Aristotelian natural law originally assembled by Melanchthon. Moreover, just as physics emerged as the cuckoo in the nest of French Cartesianism, so the new prominence of the law faculty that emerged from these polemics destabilised the traditional balance between the faculties. Without the focus on the history of public law that Thomasius initiated at the Halle faculty of law, it is difficult to see how Göttingen could later have made its rapid progress in using Roman and German legal codes to reinterpret the constitutional history of the Reich. The projected synthesis of history and its underlying sociological principles worked on by Gatterer, Schlözer, and Iselin still owes a lot to these pioneering efforts to relate natural law and history.[46]

Despite the association between Halle and Thomasius, it should not be forgotten how much was contributed to the institutional development of Halle by Christian Wolff. His insistence that philosophy alone possessed a rational deductive method of demonstration is often dismissed as no more than a sophisticated throwback to scholasticism. But this is to miss the central claim behind his system, which was that the unique ability of philosophy to aspire to the status of mathematical certainty should entitle it to lead the other faculties. This was bound to cause strife at a time when many of the professors of philosophy were also professors in the other faculties, and although the pretext for his expulsion by Frederick William I in 1723 was a charge of impiety, in fact the real reason lay in Wolff's attempt to further free the faculty of philosophy from the influence of theologians and assert its right to an independence and predominance that anticipates the claims of Kant's *Der Streit der Fakultäten*.[47]

The foundation of the University of Göttingen in 1737 could not have been brought about without the prior settling of these earlier disputes and represents an opportunity to incorporate their lessons. For example, the theology faculty was prevented from interfering in the activities of the other faculties, and although philosophy was retained in its traditional 'gatekeeper' role, new subjects were added to those taught within it – such as empirical psychology, natural law, natural history, pure and applied mathematics, and history, with its related disciplines of geography and diplomacy.[48] The direct interference of both lay and clerical sources of authority was effectively excluded by locating the university some distance away from Hanover's seat of government and by restricting the scope of theological disputation to a purely academic plane. Thus, the best features of the *Ritterakademien* and the old universities were attractively combined within one university, which through its connections with Britain was also well placed to act as a conduit for the most recent literary developments taking place abroad. This link influenced the university's emerging priorities in classical philology, the history of public law, and *Statistik* (comparative study of politics).[49]

The newer German universities such as Halle, Jena, and Göttingen enjoyed success in attracting students from outside the states in which they were located, and this, in turn, contributed to an increasing tendency in the late eighteenth century for professors to write their own textbooks, a development which acted as a form of advertisement for both the university itself and for the professor's own course. This trend also served the mercantilist tendencies of the state as it sought to attract students rather than to export them and strove to avoid reliance on the purchase of foreign textbooks – which also indicated a form of cultural subservience to other countries. These textbooks often provided much-needed extra income for academic philosophers, who mostly subsisted – even in Kant's time – by taking on an inordinate amount of teaching. Indeed, if one follows the career paths of successful German philosophers, it is striking how often they move from the philosophy faculty to posts in the law or theology faculties which were rather better paid.

Although it is true that in southern Catholic Germany there was ready access to Protestant texts by Wolff and Feder from the 1740s onwards, it is important to note that the main features of institutional reform – such as the rivalry between the Jesuits and the Academy of Sciences in Munich and the later abolition of the Jesuit order – are strongly correlated with the main changes in the philosophical syllabus. In this regard, the major change came after the removal of Jesuit influence when Wolff's textbooks on logic and metaphysics were made an integral part of the philosophy course.[50] These works, with their attempt to reconcile the powers of divine and human reason, were quite acceptable to the Thomist traditions in which Catholic German universities still operated. This had important consequences for the swift spread of idealism throughout the German university system in the last decade of the century. Not only was the removal of the ban on textbooks from a rival confession a necessary precondition for the free circulation of the ideas of a new philosophical school, but the preexisting focus on the works of Wolff ensured that there was a larger audience for an author such as Kant, who was in one sense responding specifically to the kind of rationalism embodied in Wolff's textbooks.

With the publication and subsequent dissemination of Kant's *Kritik der reinen Vernunft* in 1781, the teaching of philosophy in German universities entered a new phase, whose institutional aspect was summarised by Kant himself, somewhat tongue-in-cheek, in his later work *Der Streit der Fakultäten*. Here he suggests that philosophy's value is expressly non-utilitarian because it pursues truth rather than usefulness. While the government must regulate the so-called higher faculties because their work directly affects the people, it has no role in regulating philosophy, where reason rules. Philosophy is in fact the institutional correlate of Kant's bounded concept of free speech: its private pursuit of pure scholarship entitles it to judge and pronounce upon the activities of the other faculties. The humblest faculty is in fact the only one that can generate a unifying abstract metaphysics that can unite and underpin the whole project of a university and recover – in ethics and aesthetics at least – some of the ground lost to fissiparous empiricism and the relativism that flowed from it.

Kant's high notion of the role of philosophy – 'gatekeeper' turned poacher – spread quickly among the Protestant universities of Germany, partly because of shrewd and skilful action by his pupils but also because it met a perceived need to reintegrate the spectrum of subjects and subdivisions of knowledge pursued at university level and unite Newtonianism with a concept of divine order. But a further important reason for its success was the series of university reforms introduced by Kant's patron, Karl Abraham Freiherr von Zedlitz, the dedicatee of the *Kritik der reinen Vernunft* and the minister responsible for Prussian higher education from 1771 to 1788.[51]

The social policy devised by Frederick the Great during the period of 'Reconstruction' after the end of the Seven Years War emphasised conservative cameralism. What was desired was *Gleichgewicht*, which has been defined as 'a balance of productive forces' or consolidation of every class, corporation, and professional group within the state, thus maximising the state's efficiency and economic output.[52] In the field of education, this meant that everyone should have the education appropriate for their social background, with compulsory primary schooling for all but a university education reserved for those from propertied or professional backgrounds. This view was clearly articulated by Zedlitz in an essay published in the *Berlinische Monatschrift* in 1778:

[I]t is madness to provide a future tailor, cabinetmaker or shopkeeper with the same education as a future school rector or consistory official. The peasant must be educated differently from the future artisan, who must in turn have an education different from the future scholar, or youth destined for higher office.[53]

Educational policy was seen as a crucial mechanism for enforcing social equilibrium so that the bourgeoisie would not wish to acquire noble estates, the nobles would not seek to buy up peasant plots of land or participate in bourgeois professions, and peasants would not need to migrate to cities.[54]

School reform was tackled first in the 1760s, and then in the next decade Zedlitz applied himself to the four Prussian universities, seeking first of all to restrict matriculation to those whom the government considered suitable to receive higher education. Then he worked to ensure that lectures and textbooks were directed precisely at professional targets, purging Pietist influence wherever possible (as a distraction from professional formation) and holding up the worldly intellectual flexibility of Göttingen as an ideal for emulation. These measures were driven home with special vigour at Halle, of which Zedlitz was an alumnus. They were, of course, aimed particularly at the three 'higher' faculties and left space for Kant to project his superficially modest but in fact grandly ambitious unifying role for philosophy. The intellectually francophile Frederick the Great had pursued a policy that proposed a final social consolidation of the alliance between Crown, titled property, and service bureaucracy, yet indirectly he had nevertheless offered a unique opportunity for German philosophy to reassert its position within the microcosm of university structures under the protective umbrella offered by the state.

NOTES

1 The author is grateful to Dr. L. W. B. Brockliss, Dr. H. Klemme, and the editor for extremely helpful guidance, criticism, and comment on an earlier draft of this chapter. An important point of departure for the study of philosophy at the early modern university in Europe is provided by *A History of the University in Europe*, ed. W. Rüegg, vol. 2: *Universities in Early Modern Europe*, ed. H. de Ridder-Symoens (Cambridge, 1996). The chapters by Wilhelm Schmidt-Biggemann, Lawrence Brockliss, and Notker Hammerstein are of special relevance.

2 Such criticisms may be made, for example, of *The Enlightenment in National Context*, eds. R. Porter and M. Teich (Cambridge, 1981), and its subdivision of Germany in particular.

3 See Notker Hammerstein, *Ius und Historie: Ein Beitrag zur Geschichte des historischen Denkens an deutschen Universitäten im späten 17. und im 18. Jahrhundert* (Göttingen, 1972); Charles E. McClelland, *State, Society, and University in Germany, 1700–1914* (Cambridge, 1980); James Van Horn Melton, *Absolutism and the Eighteenth-Century Origins of Compulsory Schooling in Prussia and Austria* (Cambridge, 1988); Anthony J. La Vopa, *Grace, Talent and Merit: Poor Students, Clerical Careers and Professional Ideology in Eighteenth-Century Germany* (Cambridge, 1988).

4 See the article 'Collège' in Denis Diderot and Jean le Rond d'Alembert, *Encyclopédie ou Dictionnaire raisonné des sciences, des arts et des métiers*, reduced facsim. of original 35 vol. edn. (Paris and Amsterdam, 1751–80), 5 vols. (New York, NY, 1969), 3: 632–8. The arguments presented here suggest the existence of a debate on this issue.

5 François-Marie Arouet de Voltaire, *Dictionnaire philosophique*, eds. J. Benda and P. Naves (Paris, 1954), 'Philosophe', 342. This dismissive view reflects a widespread contention among the *philosophes* that ethics was not accorded a sufficiently important place in the university course in philosophy.

6 Richard B. Sher, *Church and University in the Scottish Enlightenment: The Moderate Literati of Edinburgh* (Edinburgh, 1985), 151.

7 But see Ann Thomson, Chapter 6, this volume.

8 Two works that do confront the issue of the contribution of the religious orders are Jean de Viguerie, *Une Oeuvre d'éducation sous l'Ancien Régime: les Pères de la doctrine chrétienne en France et en Italie 1592–1792* (Paris, 1976), and Rudolf Stichweh, *Der frühmoderne Staat und die europäische Universität: Zur Interaktion von Politik und Erziehungssystem im Prozess ihrer Ausdifferenzierung (16.–18. Jahrhundert)* (Frankfurt am Main, 1991), ch. 4, 232–84.

9 For an example that attempts to combine these approaches in a general account for the nineteenth century, see U. J. Schneider, 'The Teaching of Philosophy at German Universities in the Nineteenth Century', *History of Universities*, 12 (1993): 197–338.

10 The best account for this whole period is now L. W. B. Brockliss, *French Higher Education in the Seventeenth and Eighteenth Centuries: A Cultural History* (Oxford, 1987). Although the author focuses exclusively on France, many of his ideas (particularly his account of the openness of the old order to new ideas and the relative separation of natural philosophy from other branches of philosophy) are more widely suggestive. See also the same author's 'Philosophy Teaching in France 1600–1740', *History of Universities*, 1 (1981): 131–68, and 'Curricula', in *Universities in Early Modern Europe*, ed. H. de Ridder-Symoens, 565–620.

11 Brockliss, *French Higher Education*, 1.

12 Brockliss, *French Higher Education*, 186. One of the consequences of the introductory role of philosophy was that the students taking the subject tended to be very young, which was itself a factor in determining the level and ambition of the teaching offered to them.

13 Brockliss, *French Higher Education*, 188 and note 13, and 381–90.

14 See Wijnand W. Mijnhardt, 'The Dutch Enlightenment: Humanism, Nationalism and Decline', in *The Dutch Republic in the Eighteenth Century: Decline, Enlightenment, and Revolution*, eds. M. C. Jacob and W. W. Mijnhardt (Ithaca, NY, 1992), 197–223.

15 See Keith Tribe, *Governing Economy: The Reformation of German Economic Discourse 1750–1840* (Cambridge, 1988), 12–13, 16. He shows how little has changed since the classroom world of the sixteenth century, as described in Charles B. Schmitt, 'The Rise of the Philosophical Textbook', in *The Cambridge History of Renaissance Philosophy*, eds. C. B. Schmitt, Q. Skinner, and Eckhard Kessler (Cambridge, 1988), 792–804.

16 For a vivid evocation of classroom practice, see Brockliss, *French Higher Education*, 56–61, and for the evolution of textbooks in mathematics, 381–90.

17 Brockliss, *French Higher Education*, 190.

18 It should, however, be remembered that Kant's lectures were still in many cases a German commentary upon an existing text written in Latin. He did not write his own textbooks (with the exception of a textbook for physical geography).

19 However, there remain many interesting anomalies, such as the *écoles militaires*, which were run by the Benedictines but may well have used the vernacular in teaching.

20 For a typical instance, see Petra Blettermann, *Die Universitätspolitik August des Starken 1694–1733* (Cologne, 1990).

21 For a study of how Scottish writings of this era are creatively interpreted within German universities and among a wider public, see Fania Oz-Salzberger, *Translating the Enlightenment: Scottish Civic Discourse in Eighteenth-Century Germany* (Oxford, 1995).

22 Brockliss gives a compelling account of this process of corrosion and replacement from within in *French Higher Education*, chaps. 6–8, 277–440. He also emphasises that Newton's impact on the teaching of physics – as opposed to his longer-term impact on the place of physics within university structures – may have been less revolutionary than is often supposed when his physics was presented without its mathematical apparatus. See also the following case study of Leuven: G. Vanpaemel, *Echo's van een wetenschappelijke revolutie: De mecanistische natuurwetenschap aan de Leuvense Artesfaculteit (1650–1797)* (Brussels, 1986).

23 *Encyclopédie*, eds. Diderot and D'Alembert, 1: 51–7 at 52.

24 See Robin Briggs, 'The Académie Royale des Sciences and the Pursuit of Utility', *Past and Present*, 131 (1991): 38–88.

25 There are really only two major comparative surveys available on the academies of the eighteenth century: James E. McClellan III, *Science Reorganized: Scientific Societies in the Eighteenth Century* (New York, NY, 1985), and Ludwig Hammermayer, 'Akademiebewegung und Wissenschaftsorganisation – Formen, Tendenzen und Wandel in Europa während der zweiten Hälfte des 18. Jahrhunderts', in *Wissenschaftspolitik in Mittel- und Osteuropa. Wissenschaftliche Gesellschaften, Akademien und Hochschulen im 18. und beginnenden 19. Jahrhundert*, eds. E. Amburger, M. Ciesla, and L. Sziklay (Berlin, 1976), 1–84. See also Olaf Pedersen, 'Tradition and Innovation', in *Universities in Early Modern Europe*, ed. H. de Ridder-Symoens, 480–7. For France, see Daniel Roche, *Le siècle des lumières en province: Académies et académiciens provinciaux, 1680–1789*, 2 vols. (Paris, 1978); for Germany, see Andreas Kraus, 'Die Bedeutung der deutschen Akademien des 18. Jahrhunderts für die historische und naturwissenschaftliche Forschung', in *Der Akademiegedanke im 17. und 18. Jahrhundert*, eds. F. Hartmann and R. Vierhaus (Bremen and Wolfenbüttel, 1977), 139–70.

26 For an example stemming from the debate over physiocratic relaxation of the price controls on corn, see Janis Spurlock on Jean Baptiste Bizet in her 'What Price Economic Prosperity? Public Attitudes to Physiocracy in the Reign of Louis XVI', *British Journal for Eighteenth Century Studies*, 9 (1986): 183–96 at 186–7.

27 Interest in reform of local education seems to have grown as the century progressed, if one follows the total of academy essay contests organised as an index. See Harvey Chisick, *The Limits of Reform in the Enlightenment: Attitudes toward the Education of the Lower Classes in Eighteenth-Century France* (Princeton, NJ, 1981), 43–4.

28 See Daniel Roche, 'La diffusion des lumières. Un exemple: l'Académie de Châlons-sur Marne', *Annales: Économies, Sociétés, Civilisations*, 19 (1964): 887–922.

29 See Derek Beales, 'Social Forces and Enlightened Policies', in *Enlightened Absolutism: Reform and Reformers in Later Eighteenth Century Europe*, ed. H. M. Scott (London, 1990), 37–53.

30 It would be wrong to discern any proto-nationalist programme behind these proposals, which differ in kind from Herder's genuinely nationalist scheme of 1788 for a patriotic academy covering several provinces of Germany.

31 See, for example, Eric W. Cochrane, *Tradition and Enlightenment in the Tuscan Academies 1690–1800* (Chicago, IL, 1961), for a positive review of the importance of academies in the implementation of the Leopoldine reforms in Tuscany in the second half of the century.

32 See J. Voss, 'Die Akademien als Organisationsträger der Wissenschaften im 18. Jahrhundert', *Historische Zeitschrift*, 231 (1980): 43–74. However, the case of the Bavarian Academy of Science, founded in 1759, shows how in the circumstances of southern Germany the monasteries, which dominated the world of learning, could cooperate with the secular authority in founding an academy working to diminish the influence of the Jesuits over the education system. The initiatives undertaken by the Academy in support of historical research and its welcome of Wolffian philosophy and the new science were deliberate attempts to counterbalance the revamped scholasticism of the Bavarian Jesuits. See Ludwig Hammermayer, *Geschichte der Bayerischen Akademie der Wissenschaften 1759–1807*, 2 vols. (Munich, 1983).

33 For Leibniz's role in founding the Berlin Academy and his general involvement in the institutionalisation of philosophy, see, for example, Wilhelm Totok, 'Leibniz als Wissenschaftsorganisator', in *Leibniz – sein Leben – sein Wirken – seine Welt*, eds. W. Totok and C. Haase (Hanover, 1966), 293–320; Werner Schneiders, 'Gottesreich und gelehrte Gesellschaft: Zwei politische Modelle bei G. W. Leibniz', in Hartmann and Vierhaus, eds., *Der Akademiegedanke*, 47–61.

34 Gottfried Wilhelm Leibniz, 'Denkschrift über den Zweck und Nutzen einer zu gründenden Sozietät der Wissenschaften zu Berlin', in his *Politische Schriften*, ed. H. H. Holz, 2 vols. (Frankfurt am Main, 1966–7), 2: 86–9, as translated in Richard van Dülmen, *The Society of the Enlightenment: The Rise of the Middle Class and Enlightenment Culture in Germany*, trans. A. Williams (Cambridge, 1992), 27.

35 See Horst Möller, 'Enlightened Societies in the Metropolis: The Case of Berlin,' in *The Transformation of Political Culture: England and Germany in the Late Eighteenth Century*, ed. E. Hellmuth (Oxford, 1990), 219–33.

36 In the seventeenth century, the Académie des Sciences had devoted much of its effort to the compilation of a full description of French crafts and trades and to botanical classifications. See Alice Stroup, *A Company of Scientists: Botany, Patronage and Community at the Seventeenth-Century Parisian Royal Academy of Sciences* (Berkeley, CA, 1990).

37 See van Dülmen, *Society of the Enlightenment*, 20–3.

38 See C. Meinel, '*Artibus Academicis Inserenda*: Chemistry's Place in Eighteenth and Early Nineteenth Century Universities', *History of Universities*, 7 (1988): 89–115.

39 Brockliss, *French Higher Education*, 441.

40 See Jacques M. Gres-Gayer, *Théologie et pouvoir en Sorbonne: La faculté de théologie de Paris et la bulle Unigenitus 1714–1721* (Paris, 1991).

41 Brockliss, *French Higher Education*, 188.

42 See L. W. B. Brockliss, 'The European University in the Age of Revolution 1789–1850', in *The History of Oxford University*, ed. T. H. Aston, vol. 6: *Nineteenth Century Oxford*, Pt. I, eds. M. G. Brock and M. C. Curthoys (Oxford, 1997), 77–133.

43 See Notker Hammerstein, 'Die Universitätsgründungen im Zeichen der Aufklärung', in *Beiträge zu Problemen deutscher Universitätsgründungen der frühen Neuzeit*, eds. P. Baumgart and N. Hammerstein (Nendeln and Liechtenstein, 1978), 263–98.

44 See Hans Erich Bödeker, 'Journals and Public Opinion: The Politicization of the German Enlightenment in the Second Half of the Eighteenth Century', in *The Transformation of Political Culture*, ed. E. Hellmuth, 423–45.

45 See La Vopa, *Grace, Talent and Merit*, ch. 5, 137–64.

46 For the institutional impact of the Pufendorf polemics, see Hammerstein, *Ius und Historie*.

47 Immanuel Kant, *Der Streit der Fakultäten* (1798), Ak 7.

48 For more information on Göttingen's innovations, see McClelland, *State, Society, and University*, 42–3, and Notker Hammerstein, 'Göttingen, eine deutsche Universität im Zeitalter der Aufklärung', in *Die Universität in Alteuropa*, eds. A. Patschovsky and H. Rabe (Konstanz, 1994), 169–82. The decision to found Göttingen took place against a sombre background of falling student enrolment in what were perceived to be too many rather than too few German universities.

49 For Göttingen's receptivity to British thought, see Oz-Salzberger, *Translating the Enlightenment*, ch. 10, 229–56.

50 The first works of Wolff that had been received favourably in southern Germany were those devoted to ethics or politics, which like those of Thomasius offered a natural jurisprudential account of sovereignty that proved to be highly congenial to the local princes. See Notker Hammerstein, *Aufklärung und katholisches Reich: Untersuchungen zur Universitätsreform und Politik katholischer Territorien des Heiligen Römischen Reichs deutscher Nation im 18. Jahrhundert* (Berlin, 1977), 255–7.

51 Zedlitz is hardly mentioned in accounts of Prussian 'reconstruction' in English. See Peter Baumgart, 'Karl Abraham Freiherr von Zedlitz', in *Berlinische Lebensbilder: Wissenschaftspolitik in Berlin*, ed. W. Ribbe (Berlin, 1987), 33–46; Conrad Rethwisch, *Der Staatsminister Freiherr v. Zedlitz und Preussens höheres Schulwesen im Zeitalter Friedrich des Grossen*, 2nd edn. (Berlin, 1886).

52 Van Horn Melton, *Absolutism and Compulsory Schooling*, 119.

53 Karl Abraham Freiherr von Zedlitz, 'Vorschläge zur Verbesserung des Schulwesens in den Königlichen Landen', *Berlinische Monatsschrift*, 2 (1778): 97–115. (Quoted in Van Horn Melton, *Absolutism and Compulsory Schooling*, 182–3, note 41.)

54 For a survey that sets the new institutional primacy of philosophy in a wider enlightened context, see Wilhelm Schmidt-Biggemann, 'New Structures of Knowledge', in *Universities in Early Modern Europe*, ed. H. de Ridder-Symoens, 489–529. The discussion of Kant and Zedlitz derives from the material elaborated in my *Natural Law Theories in the Early Enlightenment* (Cambridge, 2000), 189–97.

5

THE CURRICULUM IN BRITAIN, IRELAND, AND THE COLONIES

M. A. STEWART

Philosophy, which once dominated the arts curriculum, still had a significant place in it in the eighteenth century. Many entered on a course intending to go into the Church or to become schoolteachers; for others, their studies were preparatory to training in law or medicine. Philosophy in its full extent included logic, metaphysics (primarily ontology), pneumatology (the philosophy of mind and spirits, and natural theology), moral philosophy (ethics, natural jurisprudence, and politics), and natural philosophy. Institutions and teachers differed over the balance, content, and separability of these elements. Philosophy was supplemented with studies in Latin, which was universally the language of instruction at the start of the century, and often in Greek and mathematics. A new service subject, history, had a shaky start in some institutions, being aimed at the sons of aristocratic and landed families who might not attend the full course. Before the century's end, additional studies were emerging as autonomous offshoots from philosophy, such as rhetoric and political economy. Of the three foundational subjects in the medieval *trivium*, only logic kept its place. Grammar and rhetoric became the preserve of either the Latin or the logic teacher. By the end of the eighteenth century, however, the art of public persuasion was the specialism of law and divinity students. In the arts programme, rhetoric had been appropriated to the written rather than the spoken word and to the study of literary criticism.

The traditional structure of the curriculum was most conspicuous in the Scottish universities, alongside some of the more marked advances in content. Elsewhere, Latin and Greek literature had generally been upgraded, so that philosophical and classical studies were more in balance. Virtually all universities and colleges had Church ties, the only significant exception being Gresham College, London, which had been a pioneering centre for experimental studies in the previous century. While continuing as a scientific institution, Gresham College provided teaching in the liberal arts and had a distinguished polymath in the professor of rhetoric and lay Dissenter John Ward,[1] but it was not empowered to confer degrees. All teachers and students in higher education in this period were male.

I. ENGLISH AND IRISH UNIVERSITIES

The Anglican institutions of the period – the medieval foundations of Oxford and Cambridge and the Elizabethan foundation in Dublin – were collegiate in structure, but Dublin never extended beyond one college. At Oxford and Cambridge there was a kind of dual curriculum and an inbuilt tension. Examinations were conducted and degrees conferred at the university level, but teaching rested with autonomous colleges where students worked mostly under a single tutor. There would be no regular chairholders in philosophy for another century, despite the mock antiquity of the names of some later Oxford chairs. The salary earmarked for a moral philosophy professor at Oxford was spent on the proctors; the Knightbridge chair at Cambridge was still nominally a chair in moral theology, but Edmund Law developed the position as a platform for philosophical instruction. At all three universities, teaching was in varying degrees still circumscribed by legislation of the sixteenth and seventeenth centuries. Archbishop Laud in the 1630s had a particularly repressive impact on Oxford, of which he had been chancellor; this was seen in the retention of a scholastic curriculum late into the eighteenth century, a retention reinforced by a prevailing political and theological conservatism. Tutors were predominantly, if not exclusively, unmarried clergy – at any rate, they were unmarried for the duration of their fellowships, and if not trained in law or medicine they were normally on their way to parish livings or other Church preferments. This affected their interests and the orientation of their teaching. No philosopher of eminence taught at Oxford in the eighteenth century.

Oxford students seeking to qualify for degrees had to engage in disputation, a process governed by formalised question and answer procedures and the rules of syllogism, and to attend an oral examination for which they had been nominally prepared by courses of public lectures.[2] Since lectures were both optional and subject to fees, and students needed leave from their colleges to attend them, the system was inefficient. Students were examined on Latin and Greek, logic and ethics, and geometry, the philosophical elements occupying the middle years of the curriculum. The learning that was tested was both conventional and traditional. On the philosophical side, it was largely Aristotelian, though only the *Poetics* and *Rhetoric* were much studied in their Aristotelian originals. Much effort went into memorising rehearsed 'strings' of answer and argument, even to the point of maintaining theses that were obsolete. Specimen strings published in the press with withering criticism as late as 1780 show that the examination system was unreformed and that even invalid syllogisms could pass muster in a disputation.[3] Candidates for masters' degrees repeated the ritual in moral and natural philosophy.

Insofar as Oxford provided an education, not just an examination routine, this was in the hands of the colleges, where training was offered not merely towards the examinations but in metaphysics and natural philosophy, as well as in theology and other subjects. There were competent natural philosophers around, and textbooks by second-generation Newtonians were among the recommended reading; but most tutors lacked the mathematical expertise to make Newtonianism an effective part of the training. A few reading lists and question sheets both from the colleges and from the examination schools survive and show some topics – a minority – that bear on recent philosophical and scientific controversies. There was early opposition to Locke's *Essay concerning Human Understanding* (1690) from High Church heads of houses, ostensibly because his approach to logic failed to equip students for the disputations, or 'hogshearing', that he condemned.[4] Jean Le Clerc of Amsterdam was also targeted, so the underlying ground of opposition may have been theological. One tutor, John Wynne, published a successful abridgement of the *Essay* in 1696 that was often reprinted, but Book I, a theologically sensitive debate on whether there was an innate sense of deity or morals, was expunged. Locke's work never had the ascendancy at Oxford that it had elsewhere.

Some tutors might issue advice about recent writers but not about those they did not wish students to read. Edward Bentham (1707–76) of Oriel, the principal Oxford writer on logic for much of the century, endorsed Locke's criticisms of the verbal extravagance into which formalised disputation had degenerated and welcomed his useful contributions to 'the natural history of man' (the psychology of thinking); but he considered them largely independent of logical study and tried to bring respectability back into the traditional curriculum.[5] So a convention grew up, reinforced by textbooks from outside, of trying to synthesise Aristotelian logic with Locke's epistemology. Watts's and Duncan's logics were popular.[6] That the topics of discussion overlapped those discussed by recent thinkers, however, more often shows that these sometimes took on board traditional questions and could be made parties to an artificial debate than that students came to the questions abreast of the latest ideas. To be preparing students to debate, for instance, in the 1770s whether 'a simple apprehension is capable of being false' or 'moral certainty in some things is the equal of demonstrative knowledge' – stock questions even then in Bentham's and others' lists – was still to be talking and thinking in pre-Lockean mode. Bentham's *Introduction to Logick* was published after he had become professor of divinity, at a time when James Beattie's bombastic *Essay on the Nature and Immutability of Truth* was temporarily in fashion and had just earned Beattie an Oxford doctorate. Aspects of Beattie's 'common-sense' defence of testimony are reflected in Bentham's updated treatment of the kinds of evidence and assent. He must have known it was targeted at David Hume, but he never suggested that students read and appraise the target themselves. He thought even Beattie might be beyond them:

> It is not everyone's good fortune to meet with, and digest such a sovereign antidote against the false reasonings of modern sceptics as hath been lately published by the spirited and judicious *Dr. Beattie*, nor may they know how to apply it.[7]

Bentham's primary debt remained, as it had throughout his life, to John Wilkins's influential *Principles and Duties of Natural Religion* of a century earlier. This was a standard source for the old concept of 'moral' certainty that had been rejected by Locke. It was popular among writers on natural and revealed religion and was part of the armoury of early probability theory.

A similar tension between new and old characterises Bentham's *Introduction to Moral Philosophy* (1745), which reviewed British ethical writing up to Francis Hutcheson, John Balguy, and George Turnbull;[8] this time he wanted to recommend the moral psychology of Joseph Butler but considered it too difficult for most students. However, the main narrative of Bentham's *Introduction to Moral Philosophy*, despite a deference to recent ideas and an attempt to document in an appendix where modern writers addressed relevant topics, still has its roots in traditional psychological notions and offers basic moral instruction with relatively little theoretical foundation. It was intended to reflect 'the Plan usually received in the Schools' and to be equally serviceable to those following the concepts and principles of traditional textbooks.[9] Those with scholarly inclinations and a good classical competence were urged to read Aristotle and Cicero, while Locke was commended not for his problematic advocacy of a demonstrative ethic but for recognising that the Gospel offers the student a better 'Body of Ethics' than human reason has yet devised, something Bentham painstakingly documents in his reading list.

> [A]s a *Moral Agent* (i.e. as a person sincerely desirous to secure his main happiness) it will be requisite for him to examine what the Holy Scripture has declared upon each article: and for this purpose it may be adviseable for him as he goes along to turn to the parallel heads in Bishop *Gastrel*'s Christian Institutes; a book which, I suppose, is, or which at least deserves to be in every one's hand.[10]

Across the whole curriculum, however, the important question is how the sources were used, on which we have too little information, and how much of their thought survived after it had been scrambled and syllogised.

Dublin in the eighteenth century responded more quickly to new ideas, while still constrained by traditional modes of teaching and examination.[11] A temporary partnership of the leading academics and physicians of the city in the short-lived Dublin Philosophical Society ensured that Newtonian and Lockean ideas got an early purchase,[12] but only with the development of mathematical teaching late in the eighteenth century did scientific study make much headway at Trinity College. Locke's philosophy, which was the latest of several seventeenth-century philosophies under debate when George Berkeley was a student, was more consistently studied in Dublin than at Oxford, but Berkeley's own revolutionary philosophy was not. By the mid-century, Locke, Boyle, and something of Newton were staples of the curriculum. Logic was built round seventeenth-century Dutch texts, of which the most progressive was Le Clerc's. Traditional metaphysics centred on the work of Robert Baron, a seventeenth-century Scots episcopalian. Ethics teaching initially combined Pufendorf's *De officio hominis et civis* with the scholastic Eustachius, but in the second half of the century they followed Burlamaqui and Locke's *Two Treatises of Government*. By the 1790s, a more conservative regime was coming back. A student (John Burk) was expelled in 1794 for trying to discuss the views of David Hume, Edward Gibbon, Joseph Priestley, and Richard Price. Two decades later, Locke was considered unsafe and was replaced in the syllabus by Joseph Butler's *Analogy of Religion*.

At Cambridge, the balance was different.[13] There the mathematical sciences largely displaced the discredited logic as the focal point of the degree examination and as the best way to satisfy the statutory requirement for training in sound reasoning. Where logic survived, it was through the use of Duncan's compromise textbook; and provided one avoided Locke's more hazardous ventures in theology, his philosophy was largely approved.[14] Disputation was retained, but students had better guidance on suitable reading for a substantive debate.

The ultimate influence here was plainly Newton, but Newton's supporters were able to make the headway they did because Cambridge had become a centre of latitudinarian theology. This openness to a new kind of undogmatic theology was an openness also to those scientific enquiries that tended to support natural religion, though there were still limits on freedom of thought: William Whiston's heterodox theology was too progressive for 1710, but Conyers Middleton's later rational theology, based like Samuel Clarke's on formidable historical scholarship, was tolerated. Even orthodox divines like Daniel Waterland of Magdalene College, a fierce critic both of Clarke's theology and of his metaphysical apriorism, saw much of the instruction within the context set by Locke and Newton. Waterland's *Advice to a Young Student*, prepared prior to 1710, assumed that philosophy in a broad sense should constitute one third of the college's supervision but that, of this one third, two thirds would be devoted to mathematics and natural philosophy. It required planned concentration, and students should not get ahead of the tutor's instruction. 'Set aside your Mornings and Evenings for Philosophy, when you begin to understand it; leaving your Afternoons for Classicks. The former is a Study which requires a cool clear Head, and therefore Mornings especially are the fittest Time for it.'[15]

Waterland proposed starting the first year with Burgersdijk's scholastic *Institutiones logicae* to teach the 'Terms of Art' but recommended unnamed recent work and Locke's *Of the Conduct of the Understanding* for the true 'Art of Reasoning'; in the second year, Locke's *Essay* was advised, 'however faulty the Author may have been in other writings', and George Cheyne's *Philosophical Principles of Religion, Natural and Revealed* (1715), which from its date must have been added later. In the third year, he recommended Daniel Whitby's seventeenth-century *Ethices compendium*, 'the latest and best System you will meet with', augmented with the natural-law theory of Grotius and Pufendorf; and in the final year, Baron's traditional metaphysics, supplemented with Malebranche and John Norris. Norris was previously recommended as theological reading, 'except in what relates to his *World of Ideas*, where he sometimes trifles'. Cicero's philosophical writing was included in the classical diet, together with Stoic moralists for those not reading theology. A similar subject balance but different structure was adopted by Robert Green of Clare College in 1707. In providing for limited philosophical study in the second year only, his main divergence from Waterland lay in dropping Whitby and adding '*Templer* against *Hobbs*'.[16]

When a posthumous 'corrected' edition of Waterland's *Advice* was published at Oxford in 1755, Burgersdijk was replaced with John Wallis as the source of 'Terms of Art'; Whitby's compendium remained, but its role as 'the latest and best System' was taken by Hutcheson's and Fordyce's ethics. The fourth-year metaphysicians were dropped in favour of Hutcheson. Butler and Wollaston were added to the theological diet. Some of these 'corrections' cannot have been Waterland's own, since Hutcheson's *Synopsis metaphysicae* (1744) and Fordyce's *Elements of Moral Philosophy* (1754) postdate his death. A liberalising hand may have operated in Oxford, but some see here the influence of Waterland's Cambridge friend Edmund Law, who was at the centre of a group of younger dons who sought to contain the growing dominance of mathematics and open up the discussion of Locke and Clarke as well as of the new generation of English moralists.[17] Law himself provided reading aids in contemporary metaphysics and moral philosophy through a succession of annotations to his translation of William King's *De origine mali* which became increasingly distant from King's own intentions.[18] In his preface to the fifth (1781) edition, he put his commentary in the context of discontents about the Cambridge curriculum both early and later in his life. Pedagogically, however, the most interesting product of this group is Thomas Johnson's *Quaestiones philosophicae*.[19] Johnson (d. 1737), a younger fellow of Magdalene who made his name as a writer on ethics and against deism, was still preparing students for disputations, since he reproduced the rules published a century earlier by Adriaan Heereboord of Leiden. The first eight chapters of *Quaestiones* are devoted to natural philosophy in all its branches, only the first addressing theoretical questions arising within the new science. The ninth, tenth, and eleventh chapters turn to logic, metaphysics (including pneumatology and natural religion), and ethics. Every question has a separate bibliography, which more often than not includes readings on both the affirmative and negative sides. Locke is matched against his critics, including Berkeley. In preparing to dispute whether the immateriality of the soul can be demonstrated, students must consult the opposite side in the leading freethinkers. There is an exceptionally full list on both sides of the debate as to whether God's existence can be demonstrated a priori, and likewise for the a posteriori argument and on the more metaphysical attributes of deity; free will also receives full treatment, acknowledging the freethinkers' position. Sometimes students are referred unspecifically to a whole author or school or to a whole work, but more often to a chapter, section, or page, which could lead them to ignore its context in the author's thought.

It is in Thomas Rutherforth's *Institutes of Natural Law* and William Paley's *Principles of Moral and Political Philosophy* later in the century that we come closest to a course of Cambridge lectures in this period.[20] Paley, who was active in social reform, shows a more marked utilitarian shift that goes beyond anything taught earlier in the century, although he was still indebted to the Lockean tradition in theology and epistemology. Ethics lectures of Thomas Balguy in the mid-century and John Hey in the third quarter of the century survive in manuscript,[21] but Hey is better known for his later divinity lectures.[22] He was to be significant for encouraging open debate on obnoxious opinions and for having Hume's *Dialogues concerning Natural Religion* on his syllabus immediately after its publication.

II. SCOTTISH UNIVERSITIES

There were three pre-Reformation universities in Scotland (St. Andrews, Glasgow, and King's College, Aberdeen) and two post-Reformation ones (Edinburgh and Marischal College, Aberdeen). After irregular seesawing between presbytery and episcopacy since the Reformation, presbyterianism was accorded the ascendancy by William III in 1689 and the universities fell into line. Like their English counterparts, they trained clergy and schoolteachers, but they attracted and educated a broader cross section of the population. They aimed to develop a sense of sound morals, responsible citizenship, and true religion, but their theological supervision was less constricting than that of the presbyteries beyond their bounds, and students as distinct from staff were not subject to sectarian tests. Scottish universities did not restrict the pool of teaching talent to unmarried clerics and could attract career academics. Teaching and examining were not subject to different administrations, and much of the examination was conducted on a daily or weekly basis in class. Over the course of the century, all the other Scottish institutions came to follow the lead of Edinburgh in abandoning the tutor or 'regent' system in favour of the Dutch practice of specialised professorial appointments in the separate elements of the curriculum, thereby securing the place of logic and metaphysics, moral philosophy, and natural philosophy for the foreseeable future. Although the traditional branches of the discipline were preserved, the boundaries between them were determined only by consensus, and there was no detailed supervision of the syllabus.[23] In the 1730s at Glasgow, Hutcheson instituted lectures in the vernacular, and within a decade the practice was widespread across the arts faculties of Scotland. This was not the forward-looking revolution it has seemed to later commentators but a prudential move to ensure that Hutcheson's teaching on sensitive subjects could not be subject to the same kind of career-destroying misconstrual that his divinity teacher, John Simson, faced immediately prior to Hutcheson's appointment.[24] Latin remained important for understanding key texts and for formal occasions including examinations, but abandoning it as the primary medium of instruction made it easier to abandon antiquated elements in the curriculum and to discuss the latest non-Latin literature.

So long as the regent system lasted, different students entering the same institution in successive years could read different syllabuses, one conservative and one progressive. Regents tended to retain their individual syllabuses once they had written them out, so the main source of innovation was the arrival of a new, younger regent. The practical consequences can be seen in Hume's student career at Edinburgh (1721–5), where his professors were former regents. Edinburgh University in the 1708 reform of the professoriate assigned the first two years of the arts course to Latin and Greek, leaving only the final two years for students to complete the three branches of philosophy, a logistical problem that was solved by making moral philosophy optional until it became clear in the late 1730s that the system was not working. Hume's memory of his student days eight years after finishing college was not of any philosophy but that his time had been dominated by the languages. There is circumstantial evidence that he made good use of his year of natural philosophy under Robert Steuart[25] but that his disrespect for the logic of 'our scholastic head-pieces and logicians'

(*A Treatise of Human Nature*, 1.3.15.11, SBN 175) reflected the instruction he received in logic and metaphysics from a professor, Colin Drummond, who was an unregenerate scholastic. On the other hand, the professor of moral philosophy, William Law, who conducted an optional course that Hume may never have heard, had already been abreast of Cartesian logic and Descartes's psychology of the passions, fifteen years before, and even knew some Locke, but he had no responsibility for logic by Hume's time.[26]

By the 1730s, metaphysics in the traditional sense was in decline. John Stevenson at Edinburgh advertised his lectures in the press: 'in place of the Systems of Metaphysicks commonly taught', he would 'Prelect upon an Abridgement of Mr Lock's Essay on Human Understanding'. As the years went by, he would take up other fashionable authors, such as Berkeley, Baxter, and eventually Reid. Topical authors likewise featured in the syllabus at Aberdeen, where discussion of Berkeley is found at Marischal College by 1719, Shaftesbury by 1720, and where Hume's philosophy was being debated in one or other of the colleges by at least the late 1750s.[27] Disputation died out in Scotland long before it did in England, and by the middle of the century logic was moving increasingly into epistemology. By the later part of the century, enquiries into the operations of the human mind, the laws of investigation, and the nature of evidence were commonplace.

In natural philosophy at the start of the century, some regents, particularly at Glasgow, were still coming to terms with Cartesianism, but most were at least acquainted with the early work of the Royal Society. All universities had provision for experimental work, but they made headway here only with the institution of the fixed professorships. Even then, the professor of natural philosophy needed to be suitably equipped. He might also show interest in the metaphysical side of Newton's work and in some of the popularisations of Newton's system put out by his English followers. But the professors of mathematics carried the burden of expounding the Newtonian system, which they did only to specialist students, in the first half of the century.

It was in moral philosophy that the Scottish universities made their most distinctive mark in the eighteenth century. Carmichael at Glasgow distinguished himself as an independent-minded commentator on Pufendorf and the natural-law tradition.[28] The professorial system came to Glasgow too late for Carmichael to benefit from it; for all but two years of his career, he was one of the regents who taught all the parts of philosophy in sequence. Elsewhere, others in the early part of the century were less independent, perhaps, but took their inspiration from the same source. When William Scott at Edinburgh transferred from Greek to moral philosophy in 1730, he lectured to the general class on Grotius, on whose work he had previously published a student guide,[29] and to a special class on Pufendorf. When John Pringle was appointed joint professor in 1734, he undertook the class on Pufendorf, adding a year later 'a Supplement from Lord Bacon, of the *Doctrina Civilis*' – presumably the treatment of ethics and civil law in *The Advancement of Learning* – which at some stage he taught with a historical overview of the rise of political institutions, and when the public class was restored to the fixed curriculum after 1737, he lectured on the relatively conventional syllabus of Cicero's *De officiis* and natural religion.[30] Reading in the ancient moralists, particularly the Stoics, provided a common framework for the teaching of moral philosophy throughout most of Scotland. Hutcheson and others of his generation came to this tradition, and themselves transmitted it, in part through its revival in the work of Shaftesbury and Molesworth; but their lasting impact lay in the importance they attached to pneumatology, including both natural religion and the study of moral psychology. By the second half of the century, tensions were starting to show between the presentation of moral philosophy as an accredited 'science', based upon and integrated with a study of human nature and the history of civil society, and its more traditional role as the motivator of virtuous action.[31] *The Elements of Moral Philosophy*, the popular text-book by David Fordyce (1711–51) of Marischal College, combined both aims.[32] No other university could match the record established at Glasgow after 1730, where Hutcheson, Adam Smith, and Thomas Reid successively dominated the scene, not just by their lectures but by recasting those lectures as comprehensive treatises for the educated public that reached a learned readership beyond the classroom and beyond the national boundaries. Adam Ferguson's lectures on politics and Dugald Stewart's on pneumatology and political economy would have a similar impact beyond the walls of Edinburgh University.

A bold structural change, portrayed as the rehabilitation of Stoic ideals but largely indebted to the theoretical writings of Bacon, Molesworth, and their own George Turnbull, was introduced into the curriculum in both Aberdeen colleges in the 1750s. The traditional sequence – logic, metaphysics, moral philosophy, natural philosophy – was abandoned. 'The only basis of Knowledge is now acknowledged to be an accurate and extensive history of nature, exhibiting an exact view of the various phaenomena for which Philosophy is to account, and on which it is to found its reasonings.'[33] So students were to start with natural history, within which was contained civil history. This would lead naturally to geography, chronology, and mathematics, and that to natural philosophy. Only after experiment and observation upon durable bodies were students in the final year to enter upon the more elusive study of the transient phenomena of the mind, which they were to apply to 'Morals, Politics, Logic and Metaphysics', in that order.[34] Thus the 'philosophy' of human nature was reached by way of the 'natural history' of human understanding. Logic was no longer the *organon*, and traditional logic, which was fit only for disputation, was dropped, its place taken by a retrospect on the different 'kinds of evidence' and a 'critical review of the sciences'. Metaphysics completed the scientific overview by becoming the study of final causes.

In spite of their acknowledged debt to the classics of antiquity and the seventeenth century, what distinguished the leading Scottish teachers of the eighteenth century was their engagement with the immediately previous generation and with their own contemporaries. Philosophy was a living instead of a dead subject and was pursued by teachers who were simultaneously establishing their own niche in the discipline.

III. DISSENTING ACADEMIES

Dissenting academies were small, run from and often in the local manse, frequently reliant on the tutor's personal library, and rarely lasting for more than one or two generations. They were associated with the three main traditions of English Dissent – Presbyterian, Independent, and Baptist. There were a few also in Wales and Ireland, the home ground respectively of Richard Price and of Hutcheson. All three denominations were Calvinist in origin and exemplify the tendency of the Calvinist tradition to fragment over theological subtleties; they had developed their identities prior to the English Civil War of the 1640s and continued to preserve them after the restoration of episcopacy in 1660 in reaction to the failure of Puritanism to maintain its ascendancy in the Church of England. The aim of the academies was partly to train Dissenting ministers, partly to educate lay persons who were unwilling to subscribe the Anglican Articles. By the eighteenth century, they divided between institutions that were theologically strict, where the whole emphasis was on preparation for the ministry, and those that offered to a mixed clientele a full educational curriculum in which theology was only one component. The latter group aimed to simulate a university course, and this is where we should look for philosophy teaching.[35] Baptists played a smaller part than the others, judging salvation to be more urgent than educated polish. The Dissenting institutions were neither as reactionary as Oxford nor as scientifically advanced as Cambridge. It was common in Ireland, and not unknown in England, for Dissenters who could not obtain adequate instruction in mathematics or natural philosophy to complete their studies in Scotland, from which they could then emerge with university degrees. The natural alliance of the academies was therefore with the presbyterian institutions of Scotland, from which many of their tutors, regardless of theological orientation, received earned or honorary degrees. But because Dissenters had restricted access to the professions, some of the academies also had a practical bent, offering training in modern as well as ancient languages, and in commerce, shorthand, anatomy, and other vocational skills. They might also provide cultural courses, developing rhetoric into grammar and *belles lettres* and adding the performing arts.

The teachers in these institutions were mostly orthodox ministers of their respective denominations, but the general ethos they cultivated was one of free enquiry and the recognition of alternative points of view. Locke, as the apostle of toleration, had a head start over any other contemporary writing, so that his epistemology and theology also received a sympathetic but not uncritical hearing, either directly or through the study of Watts's and other texts. The English presbyterians imposed fewer theological constraints, particularly those who after the Salters' Hall conference of 1719 opted not to enforce subscription to the Westminster Confession, so that some individual tutors and students by the second half of the century were moving to Unitarianism.[36] The tolerance of diversity characteristic of the more famous academies was not always perceived as educationally sound; it would be represented as a threat to efficient teaching by hidebound members of the Church establishment when the admission of Dissenters to Oxford and Cambridge became a live issue in the next century.[37]

Important for the dissemination of philosophy were the academies at Hoxton Square, London (where the most significant figure was Joshua Oldfield), Taunton (Henry Grove, Thomas Amory), Tewkesbury (Samuel Jones, whose famous students included Joseph Butler), Findern (Ebenezer Latham), Kibworth (John Jennings), Dublin (Francis Hutcheson), Northampton (Philip Doddridge), Kendal (Caleb Rotheram), Warrington (John Seddon, John Taylor, Joseph Priestley, and others), and Hackney (Richard Price, Thomas Belsham).[38] Oldfield's conversion of Locke's philosophy into a programme of practical instruction was detailed in his *Essay towards the Improvement of Reason*.[39] It was one of many near-contemporary readings recommended by Jennings (1687–1723), who published his own logic course.[40] Jennings gave schematic presentation to a rearrangement of Locke's *Essay* (without the contentious critique of innate knowledge) and his *Conduct of the Understanding*, presented as a discipline of signs. A mathematical theory of the weighting of testimony was substituted for Locke's account of probability. Ethics was taught as a rational discipline, acknowledging the importance of Grotius and Pufendorf. Students were deliberately exposed to the challenge of Shaftesbury.

Jennings's grounding of his course in a clear understanding of mathematical method, and his exposition of natural theology, were particularly admired by Philip Doddridge (1702–51), his best-known pupil, who developed his own method and syllabus at the Northampton academy out of his experience under Jennings.[41] Doddridge conducted classes in logic, metaphysics, natural philosophy, anatomy, and civil and sacred history, but the most important part of the philosophical instruction, that on pneumatology and morals, was integrated into the three-year divinity course that formed the core of his curriculum.[42] His syllabus proceeds systematically, each topic amply documented, from the existence and properties of the human mind to those of the divine mind, the nature and branches of moral virtue, the precepts of natural law, the divine sanctions by which it is enforced and the evidence of immortality, the degeneration of the world, and the need and evidence of revelation. In the text that has come down to us, John Toland and Matthew Tindal are employed as devil's advocates in a number of contexts; and although the deist critiques of the Christian evidences and of the doctrine of immortality are more fully documented through their opponents, there is independent evidence that Doddridge set his students to read the deists themselves.[43] Even in 1763, however, the bibliographical information had been adjusted by his editor, as it was by later editors up to 1803–4, each repackaging the work to suit his own educational agenda. Doddridge's authorities appear to incorporate most of Jennings's, with Locke this time moderated by Watts (for instance, on personal identity), and everything of significance published in Doddridge's lifetime except perhaps the work of Hume. The status of a reference to Hume's *Enquiry concerning Human Understanding* (his '*Philosophical Essays*' of 1748) early in Part II, lecture 23, is uncertain. It is cited for the sceptical principle, 'The Non-existence of any Being, without Exception, is as clear and distinct an Idea as its Existence.' If Doddridge himself was aware of the work, it is surprising that he did not address its challenge on more substantial topics in natural theology. His *Lectures* nevertheless constitute the most comprehensive textbook of the eighteenth century, exploring in detail the debates opened up by such writers as Clarke, Berkeley, and Hutcheson.

The lectures of Henry Grove (1684–1738) on moral philosophy, recast as a posthumous *System of Moral Philosophy* (1749), are another published resource. He has the reputation of being the first significant Dissenter to recognise ethics as a discipline autonomous from theology, although Hutcheson was actually in print earlier. Grove's Locke was less the epistemologist (except in defending the supremacy of reason) than the author of *The Reasonableness of Christianity*. Whether we have knowledge of Hutcheson's curriculum is more speculative. He taught logic and metaphysics only in his Dublin academy days, so the Latin textbooks that were published later may partly reflect his Dublin teaching. They show a conservative approach to both subjects.[44] His moral compend, published in Latin during his lifetime and in English by another hand posthumously, appears to have been kept more up-to-date;[45] it is a textbook of pneumatology, ethics, natural jurisprudence, and politics, in which he famously taught the right of rebellion. The philosophy for which he was best known outside the classroom – the philosophy of his popular English works on beauty, virtue, and the passions – plays a relatively subordinate role, but it was developed during his Dublin period and it is difficult to believe it did not impact on his teaching at that time. The English works were used elsewhere as textbooks, in both Britain and the colonies.

In the second half of the century, Warrington was the first attempt to build an academy on the scale of a university college, but it failed through overambition and other causes. Among its teachers, John Seddon, a student of Hutcheson, taught a Hutchesonian philosophy, and John Taylor (1694–1761), a follower of Wollaston, opposed it.[46] John Aikin, a former colleague of Doddridge, was an enthusiast for Turnbull. Priestley's role at Warrington was to teach both the theory and practice of history, where to some extent he too recreated the views of Turnbull: history was a subject that had an impact on life by strengthening the sentiments of virtue and giving the citizen a knowledge of public affairs.[47] Priestley also stressed the role of cause and effect in history and considered that it gave students an insight into economics that had political and moral applications.

IV. COLONIAL COLLEGES

As in the British Isles, the American colleges represented different religious interests that generated similar internal tensions. As long as these interests dominated, philosophy, including natural philosophy, rarely occupied more than a quarter of the curriculum. Harvard College, founded to train ministers in 1641, had its roots in English Puritanism and was initially as much a centre for Reformed scholasticism as any institution of its age. By the early eighteenth century, its library had become dated, the latest purely philosophical text in the catalogue of 1723 being a forty-year-old synthesis of scholastic and Cartesian learning by the Irish Dissenter Thomas Gowan.[48] This is consistent with evidence that the seventeenth-century Dutch debate on the relative compatibility of the Aristotelian and Cartesian philosophies with Christianity, centred on the textbooks of Heereboord, was well established at Harvard.[49] By the 1690s, the compromise evolved in Old World Cambridge reached New World Cambridge when the mellow Puritanism of Henry More's Christian ethics gained a hold at Harvard, while Charles Morton, formerly head of an English academy, brought across the Atlantic a knowledge of natural philosophy to the time of Boyle; his colleague William Brattle introduced Cartesian logic.[50] Outside the college, Cotton Mather (1663–1728) preached the reconciliation of the new Newtonianism with natural theology in the early years of the new century but criticised the move away from a biblical ethic.[51] It was not until after 1737, under the presidency of Edward Holyoke (1689–1769), that the place of Newtonian natural philosophy and Lockean philosophy was fully assured. When George Whitefield, the English evangelist, visited Harvard in 1745, he was shocked to find them teaching the liberal religion of Tillotson and Clarke. Holyoke later introduced Fordyce's ethics, which was used for many years. In 1767, professorial chairs were instituted on the Scottish model, a single professor taking responsibility for logic, metaphysics, and ethics.[52] There was a degree of political radicalism among the students in the eighteenth century, but this is traceable less to the content of the teaching than to discontent with authoritarian structures within the college.[53]

Yale College, founded in 1701, again to train ministers, initially set out to recover the earlier rigidity of the Harvard programme. Samuel Johnson (1696–1772), of Guilford, Connecticut, recorded the scant philosophy taught at Yale soon after its founding. He learned Ptolemaic cosmology and, for the rest, 'it was nothing but the cobwebs of a few little English and Dutch systems that would hardly now be taken up in the street, some of Ramus and Alstad's works was considered as the highest attainments.'[54] On graduating in 1714, he was cautioned against the new learning of Descartes, Boyle, Locke, and Newton because it would 'soon bring in a new divinity and corrupt the pure religion of the country', but by the end of that decade Yale, too, was shifting. Thanks to an active colonial agent in London, Yale almost from the outset had a more up-to-date library than Harvard. Johnson, promoted to the teaching staff, began to master and teach the recently forbidden writers but soon abandoned both Yale and Calvinism. More's ethics was in use by 1720; Clarke's edition of Rohault – a Cartesian natural philosophy text with Newtonian annotation – by 1726, and 'sGravesande's textbook of Newtonianism and Locke's *Essay* by the mid-century.[55] Natural philosophy came in the third year of study and the rest of philosophy in the fourth, after two and a half years of classical languages and mathematics. Yale remained nevertheless the more conservative institution, and Thomas Clap (1703–67), rector in the middle of the century, wrote his own religious ethics, castigating what he considered the insecure foundations of natural-law, rationalist, and moral-sense systems from Cumberland to Hutcheson.[56] But there are some interesting extrapolations to make from his account of the college in 1766. He notes that the library had 'not many Authors who have wrote within these 30 Years', but it did have the great benefit of Berkeley's gift of almost a thousand volumes in 1730, 'including his own Works' to that time. 'This College will always retain a most grateful Sense of his Generosity and Merits; and probably, a favourable Opinion of his Idea of *material Substance*; as not consisting in an unknown and inconceivable *Substratum*, but in a *stated Union and Combination of sensible Ideas*, excited from without, by some *Intelligent Being*.'[57]

Clap personally prepared a catalogue of the library as it existed in 1743, organising the subjects in a systematic progression to match the curriculum. Berkeley he classified as a natural philosopher, and the ethics was solidly seventeenth century; in the scheme of study set out in his 'Advertisement. To the Students of Yale-College', he drew no attention to the heavy concentration of works on history, civil and sacred, which he placed between metaphysics and morals.

The *Introduction to Philosophy* will give you a *General Idea* or *Scheme* of all the Arts and Sciences and the several things which are to be known and learnt: and this *Catalogue* will direct you to many of the best Books to be read in order to obtain the Knowlege of them. And I would advise you, my Pupils, to pursue a *Regular Course of Academical Studies* in some Measure according to the *Order* of this *Catalogue*. And in the *First Year* to Study principally the *Tongues, Arithmetic* and *Algebra*; the *Second*, *Logic*, *Rhetoric* and *Geometry*; the *Third*, *Mathematics* and *Natural Philosophy*; and the *Fourth*, *Ethics* and *Divinity*. Other less principal Studies may be occasionally intermix't with these. Above all have an Eye to the great End of all your Studies, which is to obtain the *Clearest Conceptions of Divine Things* and to lead you to a *Saving Knowlege of* GOD in his Son JESUS CHRIST.[58]

Harvard and Yale Colleges were Congregationalist in their orientation. The College of New Jersey (later Princeton University), founded in 1746 by orthodox Presbyterians, had early links with Doddridge (though an Independent) and other English Dissenters.[59] It sought to give students a strong classical grounding before introducing them to natural philosophy. Watts's work was prescribed for philosophical instruction in the college's early years,[60] to be later replaced by Locke. Joseph Periam, a tutor in the 1760s, introduced Berkeley's metaphysics. During the same period, the professoriate was reorganised. One tutor was assigned to teach rhetoric and metaphysics, another languages and logic; mathematics was understandably paired with natural philosophy, and moral philosophy was put under the professor of theology. When John Witherspoon (1723–94) crossed the Atlantic to become president of the college in 1768, his first important moves were to expand the library and ensure the development of the post in natural philosophy, while he himself assumed the position in divinity and moral philosophy. Even in Scotland, Witherspoon had begun to adopt a stance akin to the developing 'common sense' philosophy, which in 1764 received its first classic exposition in Reid's *Inquiry into the Human Mind*, and he moved quickly to establish the new philosophy at Princeton to see off the Berkeleyan competition. Only after the Revolution and the publication of Reid's and others' later works did this philosophy become a significant force in other states. Witherspoon's lectures on moral philosophy have not been adequately preserved,[61] but what does survive shows him to have steered a middle course through the competing traditions of eighteenth-century philosophy. He was a firm believer in the power of conscience, but those familiar with his role in the Revolution will look in vain for distinctively revolutionary sentiments in his lectures on civil society, government, and war, which follow the natural-law mainstream.

The College of William and Mary, established at Williamsburg, Virginia, in 1693 as a missionary college to train Anglican clergy and teach the Indians, did not begin college-level instruction until about the time that Berkeley set sail from Britain for Rhode Island in 1728 with similar ambitions. It was intended to have both a philosophy school and a divinity school, each contributing a two-year programme. The statutes of 1727, recognising that 'Aristotle's *Logick* and *Physicks*' were outdated, stipulated that there should be two philosophy masters, one for 'rhetorick, logick, and ethicks', the other 'physicks, metaphysicks, and mathematicks', to teach in consultation with the senior officers 'what systems ... they think fit in their schools'. Details are sparse, but James Blair, the first president, intended this to mean Locke and Newton after the Cambridge model.[62] In Thomas Jefferson's student days (1760–1) there was only one effective philosophy professor, William Small (1734–75). Small had studied under Francis Skene, William Duncan, and Alexander Gerard at Marischal College, Aberdeen, just as the new professorial system was being instituted, and seems to have felt the influence of Duncan's and Gerard's new third- and fourth-year curriculum. Jefferson first studied mathematics with him and learned something of the progress of science; a year later, Small established the first 'regular lectures in Ethics, Rhetoric & Belles Lettres'.[63] Small was already acquiring the reputation as a natural philosopher that would be confirmed after he returned to Britain, where he qualified in medicine and set up practice in Birmingham, becoming friendly with Erasmus Darwin and other members of the Lunar Society.

What syllabus Berkeley would have taught if his own project had been successful, whether in Bermuda or Rhode Island, is unknown beyond a commitment to religion, morals (aided by history), practical mathematics, and other useful learning as he considered it; but when Samuel Johnson informed him of the plans for the Anglican King's College (the future Columbia University) in 1749, Berkeley stressed the importance of Greek and Latin classics and the inculcation of sound morals.[64] Johnson modelled his plans on the educational philosophy of David Fordyce's *Dialogues concerning Education* (1745–8), classical texts being chosen to support religion and morals in a broadly Christian Stoic tradition that extolled reason and public service. After a grounding in Duncan's logic, he introduced students to Locke but taught basic ethics through Latin texts from Cicero to Pufendorf. The middle years of the course were assigned to mathematics and natural philosophy, but there was no adequate teacher of these subjects for more than half of Johnson's seven years as president; the institution also lacked any initial library beyond Johnson's extensive personal collection. In the final year's course, Johnson taught more advanced metaphysics, divinity, and ethics through his own *Elementa Philosophica*, a work dedicated to Berkeley just before the latter's death.[65] Although greatly beholden to Berkeley's metaphysics, and carrying further the Neoplatonism of Berkeley's *Siris*, it is an eclectic work that involves a natural history of the mind, a Lockean logic, and a fully fledged ethic of duty, set in the context of a detailed natural theology but founded ultimately in revelation. Johnson's conservative successor, Myles Cooper (1737–85) from Oxford, increased the weight of the classics and restored Aristotelian logic and ethics, publishing his own Latin textbook modelled on Whitby.[66] He did, however, encourage students to acquaint themselves with later ethical writers from Grotius to Hutcheson.

Two years after Johnson's college opened in 1754, the College of Philadelphia (the future University of Pennsylvania) developed out of a preparatory academy in which two Scots-trained tutors, Francis Alison (1705–79) and William Smith (1727–1803), had already begun to teach philosophy. The new institution was under largely Anglican management but without formal denominational ties. Smith became provost and Alison his deputy. Alison drew upon modern sources from Descartes to Hutcheson in his metaphysics teaching. He brought over from Scotland a strong attachment to the 'moral sense' philosophy and expounded Hutcheson's *Short Introduction* with modifications.[67] Smith had had a brief career as a Scottish schoolteacher, defending the unsuccessful political campaign to raise teachers' salaries in the early 1750s with arguments about the indispensable need to form the taste and manners of the rising generation by teaching them to regulate their passions and grow up 'reasonable and social creatures'.[68] The same philosophy guided him when he landed in New York as a family tutor in 1751. Within two years, he had published two educational tracts,[69] the second being a utopian blueprint for King's College which had some influence with Johnson; it secured Smith a probationary position at Philadelphia, where he turned his vision into concrete plans for the new college. A 'Scheme of a Liberal Education' was drawn up which shows a significant use of Scottish sources (Duncan, Fordyce, Hutcheson), and it follows the Scottish pattern in creating a curriculum round the idea of a 'philosophy school', broadly conceived. Philosophy in the narrow sense would alternate with linguistic exercises and classical literature and criticism as one half of a curriculum in which mathematics and natural philosophy constituted the other half. After early trials, it was recast as a programme in instrumental philosophy (languages, mathematics, logic and rhetoric, metaphysics) to take up the first year and a half, with private reading recommended in Watts, Locke, Hutcheson, Law's edition of King, and Samuel Johnson. This training was intended to 'strengthen the inventive faculties'. The second year and a half were devoted to moral philosophy (including natural and civil law, civil history, government, trade and commerce) and natural philosophy, running in parallel – subjects that 'require riper judgment' and are 'more immediately concerned with the main business of life'. In moral philosophy, reading was expected in Hutcheson, in English political writers such as Hooker, Harrington, Sidney, and Locke, and in classical and late-Latin sources in morals and jurisprudence from Seneca to Pufendorf. In natural philosophy, the standard works of the second-generation Newtonians were prescribed, together with those textbooks of the life sciences that supported natural religion, in preparation for a final year of biblical study, based on the recognition that when human science has reached its limits, revelation remains essential.[70] Throughout their course of study, students must 'every day converse with some one of the ancients' to develop skills in composition and criticism, using texts that would 'illustrate that branch of philosophy or science, to which the other hours of the day are devoted'. Hutcheson's place in the ethics training has led to speculation that here, too, the curriculum might have provided a special breeding ground for the Revolution, but this cannot be documented.

Rhode Island College, the future Brown University, was founded in 1764, and Queen's College, the future Rutgers University, in 1766. Queen's College was created by settlers belonging to the Dutch Reformed Church who wanted their own 'Seminary of True Philosophy'. An initial attempt to share philosophical instruction with the College of New Jersey failed, and the only surviving evidence of early teaching in philosophy relates to some unidentified natural philosophy.[71] Rhode Island College, succeeding on ground where Berkeley's enterprise was stillborn, was founded by Baptists without any narrow sectarian mandate and aimed to provide a less exclusively academic education and practically useful studies; but even here the syllabus seems to have been as conventional as it was modest. The first year was devoted to languages and rhetoric. Philosophy was taught, on a small scale, during the following three years, built round Watts's and Duncan's logics, and in the final year Locke's *Essay*. Between these came 'ethics', where the president's (James Manning's) lectures 'contained a compact, clear, though rather superficial, résumé of the more important doctrines of psychology, intellectual and moral philosophy, ontology and natural theology' based on some of Hutcheson's texts and the *Lectures* of Doddridge.[72] More of a rarity was the inclusion of Kames's *Elements of Criticism*. A small amount of scientific apparatus was secured, the students being active in raising subscriptions, but there was no adequate library until after the Revolution.

All the colleges of the colonial period kept up the Old World practice of scholastic disputation with varying degrees of strictness; hence the continuation of the tradition of Latin and syllogistic training. The more progressive experimented, however, with forensic debate and declamation in the vernacular and other forms of verbal exercise.

NOTES

1 Wilbur S. Howell, *Eighteenth-Century British Logic and Rhetoric* (Princeton, NJ, 1971), 83–124.

2 On Oxford in this period, see A. D. Godley, *Oxford in the Eighteenth Century* (London, 1908), chs. 3, 7; *The History of the University of Oxford*, 8 vols. (Oxford, 1984–2000), vol. 5: *The Eighteenth Century*, eds. L. S. Sutherland and L. G. Mitchell (1986), chs. 15, 20; David Womersley, *Gibbon and the 'Watchmen of the Holy City': The Historian and his Reputation, 1776–1815* (Oxford, 2002), ch. 8.

3 'Observations on the University of Oxford', *Gentleman's Magazine*, 50 (1780): 119–20, 277–8. Guidance for disputants can be found in Richard Newton's *Rules and Statutes for the Government of Hertford College, in the University of Oxford. With observations on Particular Parts of them, Shewing the Reasonableness thereof* (London, 1747). Edward Tatham's *The Chart and Scale of Truth*, 2 vols. (Oxford, 1790), was the first outright advocacy at Oxford of the methods of Bacon and Locke in preference to the traditional curriculum.

4 *The Correspondence of John Locke*, ed. E. S. de Beer, 9 vols. (Oxford, 1976–), 8: letters 3467, 3470, 3477, 3511.

5 Edward Bentham, *Reflections upon the Nature and Usefulness of Logick* (Oxford, 1740; 2nd edn., retitled *Reflexions upon Logick*, 1755), and *An Introduction to Logick, Scholastick and Rational* (Oxford, 1773).

6 Isaac Watts, *Logick, or The Right Use of Reason in the Enquiry after Truth* (London, 1725); William Duncan, *Elements of Logick* (London, 1748), previously published in Robert Dodsley's tutorial manual, *The Preceptor*, 2 vols. (London, 1748), 2: 2–194. See Howell, *Eighteenth-Century British Logic and Rhetoric*, 307, 331–61.

7 Bentham, *Introduction to Logick*, ii.

8 Edward Bentham, *An Introduction to Moral Philosophy* (Oxford, 1745; 2nd edn., 1746).

9 One such textbook still in use, known to us from lists at Christ Church, was that of the late scholastic Eustachius.

10 Bentham, *Introduction to Moral Philosophy*, preface, citing Francis Gastrell, *The Christian Institutes: or, The Sincere Word of God* (London, 1707).

11 Constantia Maxwell, *A History of Trinity College Dublin, 1591–1892* (Dublin, 1946), 148–54; R. B. McDowell and D. A. Webb, *Trinity College Dublin, 1592–1952: An Academic History* (Cambridge, 1982), 30–32, 44–9, 69–73.

12 K. T. Hoppen, *The Common Scientist in the Seventeenth Century: A Study of the Dublin Philosophical Society 1683–1708* (London, 1970).

13 John Gascoigne, *Cambridge in the Age of the Enlightenment* (Cambridge, 1989). Some otherwise inaccessible documentation is preserved in Christopher Wordsworth, *Scholae Academicae: Some Account of Studies at the English Universities in the Eighteenth Century* (Cambridge, 1877).

14 Henry Lee, author of *Anti-Scepticism: or, Notes Upon each Chapter of Mr. Lock's Essay Concerning Humane Understanding* (London, 1702), had left Cambridge by the time his critique of Locke appeared.

15 [Daniel Waterland], *Advice to a Young Student, with a Method of Study for the Four First Years*, 2nd edn. (London and Cambridge, 1730). The first, unauthorised edition had appeared in *The Present State of the Republick of Letters*, 4 (1729): 412–43. The second edition was later reset as a third edition (Cambridge, 1760; n.p., 1761), to counter the revisionist trends in a 'Second edition Corrected' (Oxford, 1755), later assimilated into Waterland's *Works*,

ed. W. Van Mildert, 10 vols. in 11 (Oxford, 1823), vol. 6. A partial collation of the second edition with the 'Second edition Corrected' is in Wordsworth, *Scholae Academicae*, 330–7.

16 Wordsworth, *Scholae Academicae*, 338–42. Templer was John Templer, *Idea theologiae Leviathanis* (London, 1673).

17 Isabel Rivers, *Reason, Grace, and Sentiment: A Study of the Language of Religion and Ethics in England 1660–1780*, 2 vols. (Cambridge, 1991–2000), 2: 195–7. On Law and his circle, see further John Stephens, 'Edmund Law and his Circle at Cambridge', in *The Philosophical Canon in the 17th and 18th Centuries*, eds. G. A. J. Rogers and S. Tomaselli (Rochester, NY, 1996), 163–73; B. W. Young, *Religion and Enlightenment in Eighteenth-Century England: Theological Debate from Locke to Burke* (Oxford, 1998), 99–112.

18 William King, *De origine mali* (Dublin, 1702), translated as *An Essay on the Origin of Evil* by Edmund Law (Cambridge, 1731; revised editions with updated commentary, 1732, 1739, 1758, 1781); see Marina Frasca-Spada, 'Compendious Footnotes', in *Books and the Sciences in History*, eds. M. Frasca-Spada and N. Jardine (Cambridge, 2000), 171–99.

19 Thomas Johnson, *Quaestiones philosophicae* (Cambridge, 1734; 2nd edn. 1735; posthumous 3rd edn. 1741). Though he published a commentary on Pufendorf's *De officio hominis et civis* (Cambridge, 1735), he referred students in his textbook to the full text of *De jure naturae et gentium*.

20 Thomas Rutherforth, *Institutes of Natural Law*, 2 vols. (Cambridge, 1754–6); William Paley, *The Principles of Moral and Political Philosophy* (London, 1785).

21 Gascoigne, *Cambridge in the Age of the Enlightenment*, 126–7, 245–6.

22 John Hey, *Heads of a Course of Lectures in Divinity* (Cambridge, 1783); *Lectures in Divinity* (Cambridge, 1796).

23 Regulations for the Edinburgh moral philosophy chair in 1734 were politically motivated. The regulations that ensued reflected what was perceived to be current best practice; but once set down, it is doubtful whether they were consulted again. For details, see Richard B. Sher, 'Professors of Virtue', in *Studies in the Philosophy of the Scottish Enlightenment*, ed. M. A. Stewart (Oxford, 1990), 87–126. For a broader review of the Edinburgh curriculum, see Alexander Grant, *The Story of the University of Edinburgh during its First Three Hundred Years*, 2 vols. (London, 1884), especially vol. 2, appendix R.

24 Anne Skoczylas, *Mr. Simson's Knotty Case* (Montreal, 2001).

25 Michael Barfoot, 'Hume and the Culture of Science in the Early Eighteenth Century', in Stewart, *Studies*, 151–90. Besides detailing Steuart's syllabus, Barfoot shows the significance of the class library catalogue as a pedagogical aid.

26 Drummond and Law dictates, National Library of Scotland, MSS 3938, 183. See M. A. Stewart, 'Hume's Intellectual Development', in *Impressions of Hume*, eds. M. Frasca-Spada and P. Kail (Oxford, 2005).

27 On the Aberdeen colleges, see Paul B. Wood, *The Aberdeen Enlightenment: The Arts Curriculum in the Eighteenth Century* (Aberdeen, 1993); M. A. Stewart, 'Rational Religion and Common Sense', in *Thomas Reid: Context, Influence, and Significance*, ed. J. Houston (Edinburgh, 2004), 123–60.

28 Carmichael's edition of Pufendorf's *De officio hominis et civis, juxta legem naturalem, libri duo* (Glasgow, 1718) contained an extensive section of 'supplements and observations'. For invaluable information both on Carmichael's total curriculum and on his distinctive slant in ethics, see *Natural Rights on the Threshold of the Scottish Enlightenment: The Writings of Gershom Carmichael*, trans. M. Silverthorne, eds. J. Moore and M. Silverthorne (Indianapolis, IN, 2002). The most comprehensive set of Carmichael's lecture dictates on metaphysics, pneumatology, and natural theology is in the New College collection at Dr. Williams's Library, London.

29 William Scott, *Hugonis Grotii De jure belli ac pacis librorum III compendium, annotationibus et commentariis selectis illustratum* (Edinburgh, 1707).

30 Information from contemporary press notices and from lecture dictates in Edinburgh University Library.

31 Sher, 'Professors of Virtue'; P. B. Wood, 'Science and the Pursuit of Virtue in the Aberdeen Enlightenment', in Stewart, *Studies*, 127–49.

32 David Fordyce, *The Elements of Moral Philosophy* (London, 1754). Like his colleague Duncan's *Logick*, this first appeared in Dodsley's *Preceptor*, 2: 239–380, and was abridged in the first edition of the *Encyclopaedia Britannica*, 3 vols. (Edinburgh, 1771).

33 [Alexander Gerard], *Plan of Education in the Marischal College and University of Aberdeen, with the Reasons of it* (Aberdeen, 1755), 5.

34 Hence Beattie's designation, on the title page of *An Essay on the Nature and Immutability of Truth, in Opposition to Sophistry and Scepticism* (Edinburgh, 1770), as 'Professor of Moral Philosophy and Logic'.

35 By the same token, Catholic seminaries, which were reestablished both in the north of England and in Ireland by the end of the century, have been excluded from this survey. They did not offer a general higher education.

36 C. G. Bolam and others, *The English Presbyterians: From Elizabethan Puritanism to Modern Unitarianism* (London, 1968), especially ch. 4.

37 Thomas Turton, *Thoughts on the Admission of Persons without Regard to their Religious Opinions to Certain Degrees in the Universities of England* (Cambridge, 1834; 2nd edn., 1835).

38 H. McLachlan, *English Education under the Test Acts* (Manchester, 1931); J. W. Ashley Smith, *The Birth of Modern Education: The Contribution of the Dissenting Academies, 1660–1800* (London, 1954). See also Alan P. F. Sell, *Philosophy, Dissent and Nonconformity 1689–1920* (Cambridge, 2004), chs. 2–3; M. A. Stewart, *Independency of the Mind in Early Dissent* (London, 2004); David L. Wykes, 'The Contribution of the Dissenting Academy to the Emergence of Rational Dissent', in *Enlightenment and Religion: Rational Dissent in Eighteenth-Century Britain*, ed. K. Haakonssen (Cambridge, 1996), 99–139, and articles against individual names in *The Dictionary of Eighteenth-Century British Philosophers*, eds. J. W. Yolton, J. V. Price, and J. Stephens, 2 vols. (Bristol, 1999).

39 Joshua Oldfield, *An Essay towards the Improvement of Reason in the Pursuit of Learning, and Conduct of Life* (London, 1707); see Smith, *Birth of Modern Education*, 124–6.

40 John Jennings, *Logica in usum juventutis academicae* (Northampton, 1721).

41 For a more precise analysis of the relationship, see Isabel Rivers, *The Defence of Truth through the Knowledge of Error: Philip Doddridge's Academy Lectures* (London, 2003).

42 Philip Doddridge, *A Course of Lectures on the Principal Subjects in Pneumatology, Ethics, and Divinity* (London, 1763).

43 Rivers, *The Defence of Truth*. For a contemporary account, see Job Orton, *Memoirs of the Life, Character and Writings of the late Reverend Philip Doddridge, DD* (Shrewsbury, 1766).

44 [Francis Hutcheson], *Metaphysicae synopsis* (unauthorized, Glasgow, 1742), replaced by *Synopsis metaphysicae* (Glasgow, 1744); *Logicae compendium* (posthumous, Glasgow, 1756). Both works appeared anonymously.

45 Francis Hutcheson, *Philosophiae moralis institutio compendiaria, ethices et jurisprudentiae naturalis elementa complectens, libris III* (Glasgow, 1742; 2nd edn., 1744); *A Short Introduction to Moral Philosophy* (Glasgow, 1747).

46 Taylor published *An Examination of the Scheme of Morality Advanced by Dr. Hutcheson* (London, 1759) and *A Sketch of Moral Philosophy: or, An essay to demonstrate the principles of virtue and religion, upon a new, natural, and easy plan* (London, 1760).

47 Joseph Priestley, *An Essay on a Course of Liberal Education for Civil and Active Life* (London, 1765).

48 Thomas Gowan (Goveanus), *Ars sciendi, sive Logica novo methodo disposita et novis praeceptis aucta* (London, 1681); see *Catalogus librorum bibliothecae collegii Harvardini* (Boston, MA, 1723).

49 Norman Fiering, *Moral Philosophy in Seventeenth Century Harvard: A Discipline in Transition* (Chapel Hill, NC, 1981), 96–102. Fiering notes that Heereboord was also used in the English academies in the late seventeenth century.

50 Henry More, *Enchiridion ethicum, praecipua moralis philosophiae rudimenta complectens* (London and Cambridge, 1667); Charles Morton, *Compendium Physicae* [1687] (Boston, MA, 1940); *Aristotelian Cartesian Logic at Harvard*, ed. Rick Kennedy (Boston, MA, 1995). On Morton's role in the Newington Green academy, see McLachlan, *English Education*, 76–80; Ashley Smith, *Birth of Modern Education*, 56–61; Wykes, 'Contribution of the Dissenting Academy'.

51 Cotton Mather, *The Christian Philosopher* (London, 1721); *Manuductio ad Ministerium: Directions for a Candidate of the Ministry* (Boston, MA, 1726). The latter work was answered from England by Henry Grove. Grove's posthumous *System of Moral Philosophy* (2 vols., London, 1749) circulated in New England and may have induced the reintroduction of an ethics section into Harvard's commencement exercises after 1751. See Fiering, *Moral Philosophy*, 40n. Fiering notes that ethics had retained a presence under other guises.

52 S. E. Morison, *Three Centuries of Harvard 1636–1936* (Cambridge, MA, 1937), 89–92.

53 Seymour Martin Lipset and David Riesman, *Education and Politics at Harvard* (New York, NY, 1975), Pt. I, ch. 5. For the topicality of political themes discussed in student theses, both at Harvard and elsewhere, see David W. Robson, *Educating Republicans* (Westport, CT, 1985), ch. 3.

54 *Samuel Johnson, President of King's College: His Career and Writings*, eds. H. Schneider and C. Schneider, 4 vols. (New York, NY, 1929), 2: 6. 'Alstad' was the early seventeenth-century Calvinist eclectic Johann Heinrich Alsted, a prolific textbook writer.

55 B. M. Kelley, *Yale: A History* (New Haven, CT, 1974), 78–80.

56 Thomas Clap, *An Essay on the Nature and Foundation of Moral Virtue and Obligation: Being a Short Introduction to the Study of Ethics, for the Use of the Students of Yale-College* (New Haven, CT, 1765). This was still in use after the American Revolution. For a full and sympathetic account of the Clap era, see Louis T. Tucker, *Puritan Protagonist: President Thomas Clap of Yale College* (Chapel Hill, NC, 1962).

57 Thomas Clap, *The Annals or History of Yale-College, in New-Haven, in the Colony of Connecticut, from the First Founding thereof, in the Year 1700, to the Year 1766* (New Haven, CT, 1766), 58, 86, 97.

58 *A Catalogue of the Library of Yale-College in New-Haven* (New London, CT, 1743), sig. A2v.

59 For a summary view, see T. J. Wertenbaker, *Princeton 1746–1896* (Princeton, NJ, 1946). There is useful information on eighteenth-century Princeton in Mark A. Noll, *Princeton and the Republic 1768–1822* (Princeton, NJ, 1989). Princeton's pioneers built upon the experience of small Presbyterian academies that had developed in Pennsylvania. On the readiness of this evangelical movement to confront new thinking, see Nina Reid-Maroney, *Philadelphia's Enlightenment 1740–1800* (Westport, CT, 2001).

60 John MacLean, *History of the College of New Jersey*, 2 vols. (Philadelphia, PA, 1877), 1: 140–2.

61 A manuscript synopsis that had passed among students was published by Ashbel Green in volume three of Witherspoon's *Works*, 4 vols. (Philadelphia, PA, 1800–1), and later reissued as a single work entitled *Lectures on Moral Philosophy*. It was re-edited by V. L. Collins (Princeton, NJ, 1912). The text is now available in *The Selected Writings of John Witherspoon*, ed. T. Miller (Carbondale and Edwardsville, IL, 1990).

62 *American Higher Education: A Documentary History*, eds. R. Hofstadter and W. Smith, 2 vols. (Chicago, IL, 1961), 1: 44; Susan H. Godson and others, *The College of William and Mary: A History*, 2 vols. (Williamsburg, VA, 1993), 1: 65–7.

63 Thomas Jefferson, *Writings* (New York, NY, 1984), 4, 276; Jenny Uglow, *The Lunar Men: The Friends who Made the Future* (London, 2002), 81–4 et al.; P. J. Anderson, *Fasti academiae Mariscallanae Aberdonensis*, 3 vols. (Aberdeen, 1889–98), 2: 122, 323, 592. At Aberdeen, Small was a fellow student with James Macpherson, the fabricator of Ossian.

64 George Berkeley, *Works*, 7: 347–8; 8: 127, 302.

65 Samuel Johnson, *Elementa Philosophica: Containing chiefly Noetica, or Things relating to the Mind or Understanding: and Ethica, or Things relating to Moral Behaviour* (Philadelphia, PA, 1752). The second part was a revised edition of Johnson's 'system' of morality, *Ethices Elementa* (1746). An edition of *Elementa* for the London market (1754) contained unauthorised revisions by its editor, William Smith, soon to be installed at the College of Philadelphia. For an account of Johnson's thought, see Elizabeth Flower and Murray G. Murphey, *A History of Philosophy in America*, 2 vols. (New York, NY, 1977), 1: 81–99. On the King's College curriculum, see further *A History of Columbia University 1754–1904* (New York, NY, 1904), appendix B; Johnson to East Apthorp, 1 December 1759, in Johnson, *Writings*, eds. H. Schneider and C. Schneider, 4: 54–7; David C. Humphrey, *From King's College to Columbia, 1746–1800* (New York, NY, 1976), ch. 10.

66 Myles Cooper, *Ethices compendium, in usum collegiorum Americanorum, emendatius editum; cui accedit Methodus argumentandi Aristotelica* (New York, NY, 1774).

67 David Fate Norton, 'Francis Hutcheson in America', *Studies on Voltaire and the Eighteenth Century*, 151–5 (1976): 1547–68.

68 William Smith and Thomas Peirson, 'Some reflexions on education, with a modest scheme for augmenting schoolmasters livings. Humbly offered to the impartial consideration of the publick', *Scots Magazine* (Oct. 1750), 488–92. On Smith, see Albert F. Gegenheimer, *William Smith: Educator and Churchman 1727–1803* (Philadelphia, PA, 1943); Edward Potts Cheyney, *History of the University of Pennsylvania, 1740–1940* (Philadelphia, PA, 1940).

69 [William Smith], 'Philomathes', *Some Thoughts on Education: With reasons for Erecting a College in this Province, and Fixing the Same in the City of New-York* (New York, NY, 1752); *A General Idea of the College of Mirania: With a Sketch of the Method of Teaching Science and Religion, in the Several Classes* (New York, NY, 1753).

70 Smith expounded the rationale for his scheme in the press in 1757, in his first commencement address, and in the 'Account of the College, Academy and Charitable School of Philadelphia in Pennsylvania' published in his *Discourses on Several Public Occasions* (Philadelphia, PA, 1759). See T. H. Montgomery, *A History of the University of Pennsylvania from its Foundation to AD 1779* (Philadelphia, PA, 1900), 236–9, 253; Ann Dexter Gordon, *The College of Philadelphia, 1749–1779: Impact of an Institution* (dissertation, University of Wisconsin-Madison, 1975), ch. 6. Smith's 'Account' was revised for the second edition of his *Discourses* (1762) and reissued, edited by Thomas R. Adams with commentary by Thomas Woody (Philadelphia, PA, 1951). Quotations are from p. 25 of Adams's edition.

71 W. H. S. Demarest, *A History of Rutgers College, 1766–1924* (New Brunswick, NJ, 1924), 36, 66, 133–7.

72 W. C. Bronson, *The History of Brown University* (Providence, RI, 1914), 102–10; quotation from 106.

6

INFORMAL NETWORKS

ANN THOMSON

The question of the informal circulation of philosophy in the eighteenth century is one which, by its very nature, is open to debate and surrounded by uncertainty. The subject – of which only the most important aspects can be treated in this survey – takes in private correspondence, groups of thinkers meeting in *salons* or other informal groupings, and the more or less clandestine networks distributing prohibited works, which often overlapped with journalistic circles. Journals were of course important throughout the century in informing readers of the main content of works, including those expressing heterodox ideas, often through the technique of apparent criticism. They were to some extent the visible expression of the Republic of Letters, supported by information networks which depended on personal contacts. Although the circles I am referring to generally avoided politically dangerous topics,[1] any questioning of established religious doctrines was inevitably seen as dangerous for society. Such ideas therefore circulated in underground networks. Information is consequently difficult to come by and is frequently misleading or open to misinterpretation, and although recent research has started to uncover much new knowledge, large areas of darkness remain. These networks, however, clearly constituted an important channel for the circulation of ideas and information, particularly concerning heterodox thinkers or discussions of theories which cast doubt on religious doctrines.[2]

The existence of a considerable body of mainly eighteenth-century philosophical manuscripts in a large number of libraries throughout Europe, but particularly in France, was first studied in the early years of this century. The most recent list contains around 150 separate items, some of them to be found in many different libraries.[3] These manuscripts, many of which also exist in semi-clandestine published editions, are the tangible evidence of the circulation of ideas in parallel and undercover networks throughout much of Europe during this period. They raise numerous problems concerning their authorship, distribution, and readership, which remain generally unsolved. They also give rise to questions about the circulation of ideas in general during this period and the reasons necessitating this sort of distribution.

Clandestine treatises, which circulated alongside erotic or alchemical texts, are mainly concerned with questions of religion. Large numbers of them link philosophical arguments to biblical erudition with the aim of criticising all organised religion, in particular, the official church and its doctrines, usually from the point of view of natural religion and belief in a benevolent God. Some develop materialistic arguments, which on occasion go as far as the espousal of atheism. Their inspiration is varied, with diverse doctrines often coexisting uneasily in the same text, and the argumentation can be simplistic. Nevertheless, they provided a vehicle for the circulation of theories and ideas that could not be expressed openly and seem to have played an important role in making certain philosophers known. Most intellectuals were probably aware of their existence, several made collections of them, and certain thinkers who form part of the mainstream of philosophical thought may have been influenced by them.

A particular characteristic of these clandestine works is that although some are known to be by a particular author or are copies of printed works or translations of foreign treatises, many seem to be the result of some kind of collective elaboration; they frequently incorporate long extracts from a wide variety of works and serve as vehicles for the circulation of extracts from books that might not otherwise have been known. In addition, in the course of their circulation they were rewritten, added to, reorganised, and even partially re-used in new works in an ongoing effort of collaboration. Both their origin and their diffusion are the result of the existence of groups of thinkers curious about new ideas and concerned to propagate them.

Who were these thinkers, and what were these circles? They formed a series of loosely linked networks covering several countries in Europe, but it is most convenient to begin with England, as the political and religious debates in that country were undoubtedly important in stimulating this movement of ideas. Heterodox thought in England continued a tradition of the period of the Civil War with its outburst of political and religious free thought, and Unitarian trends within the church also fuelled this more or less underground speculation. It was in part restricted to private discussions but also gave rise to publications and controversies. The numerous denunciations of deists or freethinkers found in a series of early eighteenth-century publications indicate that there was felt to be some sort of organised group of thinkers intent on undermining religion.[4] Figures such as John Toland or Anthony Collins do seem to have been the centre of circles which met in London in the Grecian Coffee House or in certain free-thinking clubs which have as yet been little studied. They were in contact with free-thinkers on the continent, in part through Huguenot exiles such as Pierre Des Maizeaux, who settled in London in 1699 and who officiated at the Rainbow Coffee House. He conducted an extensive correspondence and collaborated on French-language journals published in Holland, such as the *Journal littéraire*, the *Bibliothèque britannique*, or the *Bibliothèque raisonnée*, which were important vehicles for the circulation of ideas.[5] Collins himself also travelled to Holland to supervise the French edition of his *Discourse of Free-Thinking*, which followed immediately upon the English edition.[6] Exiled Huguenots in England and Holland were important in circulating information and works, both inside and outside France. Although they were by no means all irreligious thinkers, their hostility towards the Catholic Church led them to welcome arguments criticising its hierarchy, its intolerance, and many of its doctrines. The example of Pierre Bayle and the immense influence of his *Dictionnaire* in providing information on heterodox thought and 'enlightened' ideas is proof enough of this tendency; many references to Spinoza or other writers were taken directly from Bayle and imply no direct knowledge of the author concerned.[7] One of Bayle's friends was the Quaker Benjamin Furly, a friend likewise of Locke, who founded in the early years of the century, in Rotterdam where he had settled, a society called the Lantern, where free-thinkers met to discuss philosophy. Furly's extensive library, containing large numbers of subversive works, was used by many of his circle.

These groups in Holland and the journals they published, in particular the *Nouvelles de la République des Lettres*, helped to make known in France the works not only of Locke and Newton but also of deists such as Toland and Collins. Toland himself, a writer of political pamphlets for various leading 'Country' Whigs and editor of seventeenth-century political works, who also circulated Giordano Bruno's *Spaccio della bestia triomphante* (1584), travelled widely in Europe and was involved with free-thinking circles. The most important of these was the one centred around Des Maizeaux's rival Prosper Marchand at the Hague, a publisher, journalist (editor of the *Journal littéraire*), and sort of literary agent, who played a vital role in the circulation of clandestine philosophy. He was involved in the third edition of Bayle's *Dictionnaire* and seems to have been responsible if not for the fabrication then at least certainly for the diffusion of a number of clandestine philosophical works, in particular the *Traité des trois imposteurs* and *L'examen de la religion*, two of the most important texts. These Huguenot exiles around Marchand formed some sort of drinking and possibly philosophical society in The Hague, although its exact character is under dispute and claims that it was an early Masonic group remain unconvincing.[8] However, one of those on the fringes of this group in the 1730s, the exiled Piedmontese count Alberto Radicati di Passerano – author of irreligious works, some of which circulated in manuscript form, and who was arrested in London after the publication of his atheistic and materialistic *Philosophical Dissertation upon Death* (*Dissertation sur la mort*) in 1732 and then went to The Hague – was possibly a Freemason and certainly had Masonic connections.[9] His translator, arrested with him, was Joseph Morgan, a writer and translator of books on Islam and North Africa and editor of a collection of Civil War tracts in which he proclaims his Masonic connections.[10] He and Radicati are examples of members of the obscure networks of writers and thinkers linking England, Holland, and France in the first half of the eighteenth century.

The Huguenot exiles in particular benefitted from extensive connections in France which enabled them to send their manuscripts and publications for clandestine diffusion, often by means of peddlers. These networks of Protestants or crypto-protestants inside France seem to have played an as yet undefined role in the elaboration of heterodox works, as can be seen from the example of Gaultier of Niort, author of a materialistic work which circulated in both printed and manuscript form.[11] Huguenot exiles in many countries in Europe provided a ready-made network which enabled ideas to circulate. The Huguenot circles in Prussia, in particular Berlin, were part of this Europe-wide link, and there is evidence that some of them collected and circulated irreligious works, although they were not necessarily irreligious themselves.[12] The indefatigable secretary of the Berlin Academy of Sciences, the Huguenot pastor J. H. S. Formey, conducted a vast private correspondence in French and English in addition to that concerned with Academy business. In his as yet largely unpublished correspondence with pastors, intellectuals, and publishers in many different countries, we find discussions of philosophical publications and expositions of new theories. One of his more curious correspondents, for example, was a certain Cuentz, the Swiss author of the long *Essai d'un système nouveau concernant la nature des êtres spirituels* (1742), in which he defends Locke's philosophy against the accusation of materialism. Formey was also responsible, thanks to his translations, for helping to circulate the ideas of Wolff and Hume. Thanks likewise to his intensive journalistic activity (in addition to editing his own journals in Berlin, he collaborated on Dutch journals such as the *Nouvelle Bibliothèque germanique*), he kept his readers informed of the latest publications.[13] Although Formey was an enemy of irreligious thinkers, his curiosity and the network he maintained undoubtedly helped in the circulation of heterodox thought.

In addition to these extended networks, the existence of smaller groups of free-thinkers is well known. There were those, such as Nicolas Boindin, who met in coffeehouses in Paris such as the Procope and, despite police spies, discussed the existence of God or the immortality of the soul. In the 1720s, until it was closed down by the government, the famous Entresol club provided a meeting place for writers, statesmen, and officials, although their discussions seem to have been more directly political. But there were also more discreet circles meeting in the homes of more elevated members of society. Count Boulainvilliers is known to have formed part of such an informal grouping in the early years of the century; members of this 'private academy' included the immensely erudite Nicolas Fréret, perpetual secretary of the Académie des Inscriptions. Boulainvilliers wrote an analysis of the philosophy of Spinoza, which circulated secretly in manuscript form before being published after his death, in 1731, and a sympathetic life of the Prophet Mohammed which was a vehicle for criticising Christianity from a vaguely deist standpoint. This work was published at the same time in England after circulating in manuscript form.[14] Fréret is believed to have been the author of a number of irreligious philosophical works that circulated clandestinely in both manuscript and printed form, although the exact attribution of works to both Boulainvilliers and Fréret is still uncertain. Associated with this group was César Chesneau Du Marsais, who wrote grammatical articles for the *Encyclopédie* but is also generally credited with being the author of certain clandestine works, mainly *Le philosophe*, although here again attributions are open to debate.[15] This group has been said to constitute an organised centre for irreligious propaganda, although that too remains unproven.[16] They were, however, in correspondence with provincial friends whom they informed of the most recent works reserved for a restricted circle of intellectuals and for whom they obtained copies of these works. The diary and correspondence of the Paris intellectual Matthieu Marais or the letters of Benoît de Maillet, the former consul in Egypt and author of the clandestine treatise *Telliamed*,[17] provide ample evidence of such networks. There were probably, throughout the century, other similar informal groups of thinkers, often associated with journals, who published and distributed heterodox works, but this activity is still insufficiently known.

Another centre of similar activity which is better documented was constituted by Voltaire and Mme. du Châtelet at Cirey in the 1740s, when they studied Leibniz and helped in the spread of anti-religious works by publishing clandestine editions of some of them. They possibly even wrote some themselves. Voltaire is known to have published versions of the notorious *Mémoire* of the curé Meslier and of *L'examen de la religion*, although in both cases he removed the atheistic or materialistic developments.[18] His huge correspondence, itself a vehicle for the circulation of heterodox ideas, gives abundant details of such activity. During his subsequent stay at Frederick II's palace in Potsdam – inhabited also by free-thinkers such as d'Argens and La Mettrie, the most outspoken and scandalous of the eighteenth-century materialists, who had been forced to leave Holland – the French group at Sans-Souci was the centre of philosophical discussions separate from those of the Prussian Academy of Sciences of which they were members. It is probable that French clandestine philosophical works circulated within this group, as the royal libraries contained some copies, and it is from this period that La Mettrie's interest in *L'examen de la religion* dates. The marquis d'Argens in particular, who had long been in contact with Prosper Marchand, was probably involved with the diffusion of heterodox works. It is noteworthy that the first reference to *L'examen de la religion* occurs in one of his books.[19] His own popular semi-journalistic writings, such as *Lettres juives*, discussed current issues and expounded the ideas of Locke and Spinoza, among others, and undoubtedly played a role in the popularisation of philosophical discussions.[20] In general, the existence of clandestine French philosophical works in numerous libraries in Germany and throughout Eastern Europe is evidence of their widespread circulation, although it is difficult to pinpoint at what period this took place, as they continued to circulate and be copied untill the end of the century. It is known, however, that in the first half of the century, Prince Eugene of Savoy, who built up a large library in Vienna and employed agents to obtain books for him, had a collection of such works, and his court may have constituted another centre of clandestine diffusion. It was there that the Italian free-thinker Pietro Giannone came into contact with them and with English free thought.[21]

The presence in Prussia of the group of French *philosophes* assembled by Frederick II, and in particular of La Mettrie, who was at Sans-Souci in 1748–51, when several of his works were published and even translated into German, seems to have helped to bring their ideas to the attention of German intellectuals. During this period, certain French clandestine works, such as *L'esprit de Spinosa*, appear to have circulated in Germany, as did works by English deists and German free-thinkers, and Lessing in particular is known to have read some of them.[22] At the same time, knowledge of Spinoza developed with the first translation of the *Ethics* in 1744. The first to take a position openly in favour of Spinoza was Johann Christian Edelmann, who came across the *Tractatus theologico-politicus* in 1740. He had been influenced earlier by radical Pietism and had spent several years in Berleburg, where tolerance had encouraged an influx of different religious sectarians in the 1730s. He, too, was in contact with Huguenot circles in Amsterdam, from whom he claims to have received information concerning authorship of the clandestine treatise *L'examen de la religion* and a manuscript continuation of it by La Varenne, another journalist living in Holland.[23]

The importance of journalists in disseminating both works and information continued throughout the century. In the second half of the century, for example, the publisher and journalist Friedrich Nicolai in Berlin was important in spreading new ideas with *Briefe, die neueste Litteratur betreffend* (on which both Lessing and Moses Mendelssohn collaborated), followed by the *Allgemeine Deutsche Bibliothek*.[24] The Milan school around Verri and Beccaria, influenced by the French *philosophes*, published *Il Caffè* from 1764 to 1766 with the same aim, which was continued by the exiled de Felice's *Estratto della letteratura europea*.

Informal networks not only existed among journalists or in cafés but extended to the upper reaches of society. In France, among academicians who are suspected of having encouraged the clandestine circulation of philosophic ideas is Fontenelle, the influential secretary of the Académie des Sciences, who is even thought to have written some clandestine treatises himself.[25] He also frequented the *salons*, which were an important institution for much of the century in France. Among those *salons* particularly known to have encouraged philosophical discussion were those of Mme. de Tencin, Mme. Lambert, and Mme. Doublet in the early eighteenth century and, later, that of Julie de l'Espinasse, the friend of d'Alembert, who appears in Diderot's *Le rêve de d'Alembert*. Another *salon*, that of Mme. Geoffrin, was considered to be the meeting place of deist philosophers; the aged Fontenelle long reigned over it. It is otherwise difficult to know exactly what was discussed, despite references to particular events or individuals or anecdotes found in memoirs and letters.[26] What is certain is that these informal gatherings, which were regular meeting places for certain groups of thinkers, provided a fertile ground for discussions not only of current affairs or literature but also of philosophical questions, although frequently the tone was light-hearted. It is interesting that Thémiseul de Saint-Hyacinthe, a journalist and populariser of anti-religious philosophy and an associate of Des Maizeaux in London and Marchand in Holland, frequented several Paris *salons* in the 1730s.[27] Montesquieu, Diderot, d'Alembert, Helvétius, Condorcet, and many others are known to have frequented them, and certain works probably originated in these discussions; this is no doubt particularly the case with Diderot. The collective enterprise of the *Encyclopédie*, undertaken by a 'group of men of letters', is to some extent an extension of the same spirit. Such gatherings continued throughout the century; during the French Revolution, Mme. Helvétius's *salon* at Auteuil was an important meeting place for the Idéologues, although this group of thinkers, which included Destutt de Tracy, Cabanis, and Volney, also contributed to the creation of the new formal institutions which emerged from the revolutionary years.

The *salons* also welcomed visiting foreigners and were important arenas for establishing international links. When Hume visited Paris, he was introduced into such circles, including the *salons* of both Mme. Suard and the baron d'Holbach (also visited by Edward Gibbon), where he undoubtedly came into contact with irreligious philosophical speculation. Hume of course also frequented similar groups in his native Scotland, where clubs and societies were very important in helping new ideas to circulate and be discussed. In addition to the large number of student societies, the most radical of which met in taverns, the intellectual and social elite founded the 'Select Society' of Edinburgh, which lasted from 1754 to 1764.

Particular mention should be made of the gatherings at d'Holbach's home, where many intellectuals congregated twice a week, including a large number of those who contributed to the *Encyclopédie*. This coterie has generally been seen as a nest of free-thinkers and atheists, but recent research has tended to tone down this impression by showing that membership was more eclectic.[28] What is certain is that a hard core of members of the group around d'Holbach, including in particular Diderot, were responsible for the publication of a number of atheistic works, some of which had been circulating clandestinely in manuscript form for much of the century, as well as other collective compositions such as the *Système de la nature* (1770).[29] By this time, heterodox speculation had become more aggressively polemical and more clearly political than the daring speculations of philosophers in the secrecy of their study in the earlier part of the century. There was now a more self-conscious philosophical party conducting a concerted campaign against certain institutions, whereas earlier speculation had remained covert and reserved for fewer thinkers, many of whom were loath to publish their opinions for fear of undermining the social order. Nevertheless, the irreligious and atheistic works published by d'Holbach appeared anonymously or pseudonymously and continued to circulate in underground networks. At the same time, the manuscript *Correspondance littéraire*, begun by d'Holbach's friend Friedrich Melchior Grimm (a German like d'Holbach) and continued by Meister (a Swiss), which was sent to selected subscribers all over Europe, was an important vehicle for the distribution of many works, in particular of unpublished philosophical works by Diderot.[30] Diderot, of course, is an example of a thinker who frequented *salons* and remained outside official institutions. He was a member neither of the French Académie nor of the Royal Society, where he was blackballed, and even when he travelled to the court of Catherine the Great (having refused invitations to go to Frederick II's court at Potsdam), he took little part in the activities of the official Academy, whose members were generally hostile, resented his presence, and opposed his philosophy.[31]

Another form of sociability that probably played an important role in providing a forum for philosophical speculation, at least in the latter part of the century, was Freemasonry, although the famous Seven Sisters Lodge in Paris, to which Voltaire, Condorcet, and Franklin belonged, is considered something of an exception. It seems likely that several contributors to the *Encyclopédie* were Freemasons, but it is difficult to know how much should be made of this.[32] At the end of the century, lodges and other mystical orders were associated with the illuminism of Saint-Martin and others, but Nicolas de Bonneville's anti-clerical Cercle Social, at the time of the Revolution, was also inspired by Masonic ideals.[33] The proliferation of Masonic lodges throughout Europe beginning in the 1730s undoubtedly provided an important network for the circulation of ideas. In Italy, the lodges founded by English Masons in Tuscany contributed to the spread of new ideas, leading to a reaction on the part of the ecclesiastical and political authorities. Free-thinking intellectuals nevertheless continued to meet in the 1740s in the *salon* of Lady Walpole.[34] In Germany, Masonic lodges intersected with other societies of intellectuals such as the reading societies based on the British model. Particularly important in this respect were the radical Illuminati, founded in Bavaria by Weishaupt, an organisation which spread through Germany in the late 1770s and 1780s until it was banned after pressure from the churches. Informal groups of intellectuals had existed in Germany throughout the century, particularly in Berlin, where enlightened groups and *salons* existed separately from the Royal Academy of Sciences. The Society of Alethophiles was founded in 1736 with the aim of making known the philosophy of Wolff and Leibniz, and the Montagsclub, founded in 1749, counted Lessing among its members. The most important in the late eighteenth century was the Berliner Mittwochsgesellschaft, formed by members of the elite and including both journalists such as Nicolai (who was also a Mason) and government ministers. They met in secret but publicised some of their discussions in the *Berlinische Monatsschrift*, which published replies to the question 'What is Enlightenment?', including those of Kant and Moses Mendelssohn, who was a member. Although philosophical speculation formed part of their programme, they seem to have been generally more concerned with practical reform, particularly in the political sphere. Similar groups existed and were influential throughout Eastern Europe.[35]

It is difficult to know how far such groups influenced the circulation of more radical philosophical ideas and discussions, although they adhered to a broadly enlightened programme. Most relevant to the present theme are ideas that, because of their reputedly subversive nature, could not find a place within official institutions and were aired in the clandestine treatises whose circulation depended on the networks we have been discussing. An indication of their content, some of their main themes, and their relationship with mainstream philosophical writings will help to explain the necessity for their underground distribution. The clandestine literature's main thrust was anti-religious, or at least anti-church, and it drew on a variety of sources, including biblical criticism, Jewish writings, studies of other religions, in particular Islam, works of theologians, and part of the English debate derived from arguments within the Church of England. Certain texts are merely a patchwork of quotations.[36] Several use works from the Italian Renaissance or by seventeenth-century *libertins*, or claim to be part of the notorious mid-seventeenth-century Latin work *Theophrastus redivivus*. We also find translations from English writers such as Toland, Tindal, or Collins, or direct references to them, as in the title of a famous short collection of writings, the *Nouvelles libertés de penser* (1743). The philosophical inspiration was varied, and while these works played an important role in the diffusion of certain philosophies, they were also responsible for the deformed understanding of them. This is obviously the case for Spinoza, as deformation and faithful representation of his philosophy coexisted to an extent that has not always been realised.

Particularly important here is the work known variously as the *Traité des trois imposteurs* or *L'esprit de Spinosa*, one of the most widely distributed of the clandestine treatises, which seems to date from the late seventeenth century and was published in 1719 and 1721 by Prosper Marchand and his friends and again several times later in the century.[37] It is the result of a series of additions to an original text and mixes elements from the *libertin* tradition, from Vanini, Charron, or Naudé, and passages from Hobbes with authentic extracts from Spinoza, for it provides the first French translation of the appendix to the first part of Spinoza's *Ethics*. The original version, *L'esprit de Spinosa*, has recently been attributed to Jan Vroesen, a Dutch diplomat in contact with Furly (perhaps a member of his free-thinking club) and with the group around Marchand.[38] We see again the importance of Dutch circles, where French and English exiles and Dutch intellectuals met, in providing a forum for discussion and a network for the diffusion of ideas. The existence of manuscript copies of *L'esprit* in libraries all over Europe is a clear indication of its wide distribution. It probably helped to make known Spinoza's criticism of false conceptions of God and final causes, but this criticism is associated with denunciations of religions and their founders as impostors that come from the *libertin* tradition, and with a material conception of the fiery soul that is derived from the Paduan school. This conception is developed in a passage from a work called *Discours anatomiques* (1675) by the Epicurean doctor Guillaume Lamy;[39] this extract is also found in several other clandestine treatises, including *L'âme matérielle*, and was reproduced in La Mettrie's *Histoire naturelle de l'âme* in 1745.[40] Otherwise the *Traité des trois imposteurs* presents an essentially materialistic alternative to Christianity that denies the existence of an immaterial God distinct from nature and of an immortal soul; humans' behaviour and ideas are seen as being determined by their bodily states. The *Traité* therefore contributed to a vague conception of Spinozism as the equivalent of materialism, which became common in the eighteenth century. Despite the fact that Toland was associated with the groups in Holland responsible for the circulation of the *Traité*, we find little influence of his pantheism in this work.[41] His *Letters to Serena* (1704), which present Spinoza's ideas and claim to criticise them by insisting that motion is essential to matter, were translated by d'Holbach in 1768; in the earlier part of the century, however, they were little known, although Toland's *Pantheisticon* was translated and circulated in manuscript form. Materialism circulated under the name of 'Spinozism', absorbing, in addition to aspects of Spinoza's philosophy, elements of the Epicurean tradition, as found in the works of Gassendi and others.[42] This sort of circulation must therefore be separated from the diffusion of Spinoza's actual writings or works summarising them, such as Boulainvilliers's, which was published posthumously in 1730 by Lenglet Dufresnoy, one of the obscure figures who circulated among different groups in Europe and at one time was agent to Prince Eugene of Savoy, obtaining works for his library.[43]

The clandestine treatises were clearly important not only for attacking the churches and their doctrines but also for the circulation of materialistic themes. They were able to discuss the existence of the soul and an afterlife in a way that was impossible in officially published books. Indeed, the titles of several works indicate that they deal with the question of the soul, even if it is merely a presentation of the opinions of the ancients, including the Church fathers, in order to demonstrate that the immortality of the soul is a recent invention. Some go further and present materialistic interpretations of the human mind, as well as references to Locke's thinking-matter hypothesis;[44] note that the original version of Voltaire's thirteenth *Lettre philosophique*, the 'Letter on Locke', which discusses this hypothesis, seems to have circulated in manuscript form under the title of *Lettre sur l'âme*. Rejections of belief in an immortal soul to be found in clandestine treatises can be divided into two main groups. Many arguments taken from the Epicurean tradition posit the existence of a material soul, a very subtle substance found both in humans and in animals, whereas others explain thought in humans, like instinct in animals, as the result of the organisation of the brain.[45] This is often linked to a form of atomism emphasising the innate mobility of matter. Discussion of these questions is found in a number of clandestine works whose inspiration is eclectic, and numerous references to or extracts from writers such as Malebranche are used to suggest, in a coded way understood only by the initiated, materialistic conclusions. An interesting example is the *Parité de la vie et de la mort*, a reworking of a book published in 1714 by A. Gaultier, a provincial Protestant doctor who had spent some time in refugee circles and collaborated on journals in Holland before returning to France and converting to Catholicism. It incorporates elements from divergent philosophical traditions, mainly drawn from Bayle's *Dictionnaire* or from journalistic excerpts and discussions of recent scientific discoveries, in order to elaborate a materialistic view of 'man'.[46] Such discussions, however confused or incoherent, probably played an important role in spreading materialism among the intellectual elite who made up the networks distributing these works. It is known, for example, that La Mettrie was interested in such clandestine treatises, some of which he mentions. His works, presenting an uncompromising monist philosophy that explains intellectual functions by the workings of the brain but admits ignorance as to the nature of matter, adopt a position in some ways close to that of the *Parité de la vie et de la mort*. He draws on both the Scholastic tradition and the philosophy of Locke, and he also claims to be merely developing Descartes's theory of animal-machines. La Mettrie's insistence on physical determinism and his final refusal of all absolute moral values seem likewise to owe something to *L'examen de la religion*.[47] In many ways, La Mettrie, who was strongly influenced by Epicureanism and the *libertin* tradition, forms part of the philosophical underground, as his books were all distributed secretly and manuscript copies of his most notorious work, *L'homme machine*, also circulated.

During the latter part of the century, in France at least, materialism developed more openly and abandoned the masks it had adopted earlier. This led to franker discussions and to a strong counter-attack.[48] As the *Encyclopédie* got under way, a more self-conscious group of *philosophes* emerged and, as we have seen, d'Holbach's coterie was responsible for publishing and distributing both the earlier clandestine treatises and translations of Hobbes and Toland. The works they distributed were more aggressively materialist, in particular the collective *Système de la nature*, which relaunched the discussion on materialism in the 1770s. This work, which betrays the influence of Toland's *Letters to Serena*,[49] affirms that movement is essential to matter and develops an uncompromising atheism. Diderot, who probably participated in its writing, also explored the questions of matter, generation, and the origin of thought in such works as *Le rêve de d'Alembert* and *Principes philosophiques sur la matière et le mouvement*,[50] or in comments on Helvétius, whose *L'esprit* and *L'homme* expounded a theory of humans as totally determined by external factors.[51] Many aspects of his materialism, like d'Holbach's, are close to that of La Mettrie, although both writers rejected any association with La Mettrie's amoral conclusions. None of these daring philosophical speculations that, unlike the *Encyclopédie*, abandoned the coded language of most early eighteenth-century writing, were published during Diderot's lifetime, and they circulated only among a small group of friends. They were attempting to build a philosophical party providing an alternative to religion as a basis for society and no longer saw themselves as part of a small elite of like-minded intellectuals among whom truths inappropriate for the mass of the population could circulate. Their aim was the propagation of enlightenment in a more practical way, and in this project informal gatherings such as the *salons* seem to have been indispensable for the development of philosophical discussions that could not take place within institutional structures.

One English visitor, who attended these gatherings in 1774 and was shocked by the irreligious opinions he heard expressed and the number of atheists he met, was Joseph Priestley. At the same time, his reading of the *Système de la nature* convinced him of the need to counter their arguments and led him to develop, mainly in his *Disquisitions relating to Matter and Spirit*, a form of materialism presented as true Christianity, rejecting dualism and the existence of the soul and explaining that matter possesses the capacity for sensation and thought.[52] Priestley, whose voluminous writings covered many aspects of philosophy, theology, politics, and science, was a member of a very different informal circle of Unitarian thinkers concerned with political reform as well as philosophy. This group, whose members included aristocrats such as Shelburne and Grafton as well as Price and Priestley, was centred around the Unitarian Church, founded in London by Theophilius Lindsey in 1774, which became a centre for the discussion and diffusion of radical ideas.[53] Although Priestley's unorthodox philosophy was not accepted by other members of this group, they were at one in their radical political beliefs and later supported the French Revolution.[54] This final example indicates the existence of a variety of informal groups and the numerous ways in which they were interconnected. It also emphasises the more politically radical attitudes found towards the end of the century. For the earlier years, however, the link with political radicalism is more doubtful. In the present state of our knowledge, and given the discretion that inevitably surrounded these clandestine activities and works, their precise impact remains to some extent a matter for speculation. It is to be hoped that the research currently under way will also throw more light on the wider implications of this philosophical underground.[55]

NOTES

1 Margaret C. Jacob, *The Radical Enlightenment: Pantheists, Freemasons and Republicans* (London, 1981; revised edn., New York, NY, 2003), insists on their political radicalism, which cannot, however, be claimed for all clandestine networks.

2 See in general Anne Goldgar, *Impolite Learning: Conduct and Community in the Republic of Letters* (New Haven, CT, and London, 1995); *Scepticism and Irreligion in the Seventeenth and Eighteenth Centuries*, eds. R. H. Popkin and A. Vanderjagt (Leiden and New York, NY, 1993); John S. Spink, *French Free Thought from Gassendi to Voltaire* (London, 1960); Franco Venturi, *Utopia and Reform in the Enlightenment* (Cambridge, 1970). Ira O. Wade, *The Clandestine Organization and Diffusion of Philosophic Ideas in France from 1700 to 1750* (Princeton, NJ, 1938).

3 Miguel Benitez, 'Matériaux pour un inventaire des manuscrits philosophiques clandestins des XVIIe et XVIIIe siècles', *Rivista di storia della filosofia*, 3 (1988): 501–31. See also Benitez, *La face cachée des Lumières: Recherches sur les manuscripts philosophiques clandestines de l'âge classique* (Oxford and Paris, 1994); *La Lettre clandestine: Bulletin d'information sur la literature philosophique clandestine de l'âge classique*, 1 (1992); *La literature clandestine*, ed. A. McKenna (Oxford and Paris, 1996); A. Thomson, 'La literature clandestine et la circulation des idées antireligieuses dans la première moitié du XVIIIe siècle', in *L'encyclopédie, Diderot, l'esthétique: Mélanges en homage à Jacques Chouillet*, eds. S. Auroux, D. Bourel, and C. Porset (Paris, 1991), 297–304.

4 In particular, John Leland, *A View of the Principal Deistical Writers that have Appeared in England in the last and present Century*, 2 vols. and suppl. (London, 1754–6). On the subject in general,

see Justin Champion, *The Pillars of Priestcraft Shaken: The Church of England and its Enemies, 1660–1730* (Cambridge, 1992).

5 See Joseph Almagor, *Pierre Des Maizeaux (1673–1745), Journalist and English Correspondent for Franco-Dutch Periodicals, 1700–1720* (Amsterdam and Maarssens, 1989).

6 [Anthony Collins] *A Discourse of Free-Thinking, occasion'd by the Rise and Growth of a Sect call'd Free-Thinkers* (London, 1713). See James O'Higgins, *Anthony Collins: The Man and his Works* (The Hague, 1970), 79.

7 Pierre Bayle, *Dictionnaire historique et critique*, 2 vols. (Rotterdam, 1697). See Pierre Rétat, *Le Dictionnaire de Bayle et la lutte philosophique au XVIIIe siècle* (Paris, 1971).

8 This claim has mainly been made by Jacob (see her *Radical Enlightenment*); for opposing views, see Christine Berkvens-Stevelinck, *Prosper Marchand: la vie et l'oeuvre 1678–1756* (Leiden, 1987), and Silvia Berti, 'The First Edition of the *Traité des trois imposteurs* and Its Debt to Spinoza's *Ethics*', in *Atheism from the Reformation to the Enlightenment*, eds. M. Hunter and D. Wootton (Oxford, 1992), 183–220.

9 Alberto Radicati, conte di Passerano, *A Philosophical Dissertation upon Death: Composed for the Consolation of the Unhappy*, trans. J. Morgan (London, 1732). See Franco Venturi, *Saggi sull' Europa illuminista 1: Alberto Radicati di Passerano* (Turin, 1954).

10 See Ann Thomson, 'Joseph Morgan et le monde islamique', *Dix-huitème Siècle*, 27 (1995): 349–63.

11 *Parité de la vie et de la mort: La 'Réponse' du médecin Gaultier*, ed. O. Bloch (Paris and Oxford, 1993).

12 See Jens Häseler, 'Réfugiés français à Berlin lecteurs de manuscrits clandestins', in *Filosofia e religione nella letteratura clandestina*, ed. G. Canzoni (Milan, 1994), 373–85.

13 See the article on Formey in the *Dictionnaire des Journalistes*, ed. J. Sgard (Paris, 1999).

14 See Henri de Boulainvilliers, *Oeuvres complètes*, ed. R. Simon, 2 vols. (The Hague, 1973–5).

15 [César Chesneau Du Marsais], *Le Philosophe*, in *Nouvelles libertés de penser* (Amsterdam and Paris, 1743). See Du Marsais, *Examen de la religion ou Doutes sur la religion dont on cherche l'éclaircissement de bonne foi*, ed. G. Mori (Oxford, 1998); Herbert Dieckmann, *Le Philosophe: Texts and Interpretation*, ed. H. Dieckmann (St. Louis, MO, 1948); Gianluca Mori, 'Per l'attribuzione a Du Marsais dell' 'Examen de la religion', *Atti e Memorie dell' Academia Toscana di Scienze e Lettere La Colombaria*, 48 (1993): 257–333.

16 Stefano Brogi, *Il cerchio dell'universo: Libertinismo, Spinozismo e filosofia della natura in Boulainvilliers* (Florence, 1993).

17 Matthieu Marais, *Journal et Mémoires*, ed. M. de Lescure, 4 vols. (Paris, 1863–8). See M. Benitez, 'Eléments d'une sociologie de la littérature clandestine: lecteurs et éditeurs de *Telliamed*', in *De bonne main: La communication manuscrite au XVIIIe siècle*, ed. F. Moureau (Paris, 1993), 71–96.

18 Jean Meslier, *Mémoire des pensées et des sentiments*, in *Oeuvres complètes*, eds. J. Deprun, R. Desné, and A. Soboul, 3 vols. (Paris, 1970–2).

19 See *Le Marquis d'Argens*, ed. J. L. Vissière (Aix-en-Provence, 1990), in particular A. McKenna, 'Le Marquis d'Argens et les manuscrits clandestins', 111–40; *Correspondance entre Prosper Marchand et le marquis d'Argens*, ed. S. Larkin (Oxford, 1984).

20 Jean Baptiste de Boyer, Marquis d'Argens, *Lettres juives* (The Hague, 1738); see also his *Mémoires secrets de la république des Lettres* (Amsterdam, 1738).

21 G. Ricuperati, *L'esperienza civile e religiosa di Pietro Giannone* (Milan, 1970).

22 See M. Fontius, 'Littérature clandestine et pensée allemande', in *Le matérialisme du XVIIIe siècle et la littérature clandestine*, ed. O. Bloch (Paris, 1982), 251–62; W. Schröder, *Spinoza in der deutschen Frühaufklärung* (Würzburg, 1987); and his 'Spinoza im Untergrund: Zur Rezeption

seines Werkes in der 'littérature clandestine'', in *Spinoza in der europäischen Geistesgeschichte*, eds. A. Delf, J. H. Schoeps, and M. Walther (Berlin, 1994), 142–61.

23 Johann Christian Edelmann, *Sämtliche Schriften in Einzelausgaben*, ed. W. Grossmann (Stuttgart, 1969–), vol. 10 (1974), 125–31.

24 See Horst Möller, *Aufklärung in Preussen: Der Verleger, Publizist und Geschichtsschreiber Friedrich Nicolai* (Berlin, 1974).

25 For the most recent discussion of this question, see A. Niderst, 'Fontenelle et la littérature clandestine', in *Filosofia e religione*, ed. G. Canzoni (Milan, 1994), 161–73.

26 See in particular Dominique-Joseph Garat, *Mémoires historiques sur la vie de M. Suard sur ses écrits, et sur le XVIIIe siècle* (Paris, 1820).

27 See Elisabeth Carayol, *Thémiseul de Saint-Hyacinthe, 1684–1746* (Oxford, 1984).

28 See Alan C. Kors, *D'Holbach's Coterie: An Enlightenment in Paris* (Princeton, NJ, 1976).

29 Paul-Henri Thiry, baron d'Holbach, *Système de la nature, ou Des Lois du monde physique et du monde moral*, 2 vols. (London, 1770).

30 Friedrich Melchior Grimm et al., *Correspondance littéraire, philosophique et critique*, ed. M. Tourneux, 16 vols. (Paris, 1877–82).

31 See Georges Dulac, 'Un nouveau La Mettrie à Pétersbourg: Diderot vu par l'Académie impériale des Sciences', *Recherches sur Diderot et sur l'Encyclopédie*, 16 (1994), 19–44.

32 See Robert Shackleton, 'The *Encyclopédie* and Freemasonry', in *The Age of Enlightenment: Studies presented to Theodore Bestermann*, eds. W. H. Barber et al. (Edinburgh and London, 1967), 223–37.

33 See Gary Kates, *The Cercle Social, the Girondins and the French Revolution* (Princeton, NJ, 1985).

34 See Franco Venturi, *Settecento riformatore* (Turin, 1969–), vol. 1: *Da Muratori a Beccaria* (1969), 54–8; Mario Rosa, '*Encyclopédie*, 'Lumieres' et tradition au 18e siècle en Italie', *Dix-huitième Siècle*, 4 (1972): 109–68.

35 See *Was ist Aufklärung? Beiträge aus der Berlinischen Monatsschrift*, ed. N. Hinske (Darmstadt, 1990); *What is Enlightenment? Eighteenth-Century Answers and Twentieth-Century Questions*, ed. J. Schmidt (Berkeley, CA, 1996); Eva H. Balázs et al., *Beförderer der Aufklärung in Mittel- und Osteuropa: Freimaurer, Gesellschaften, Clubs* (Berlin, 1979).

36 See, for example, *L'âme matérielle: ouvrage anonyme*, ed. A. Niderst (Paris, 1969).

37 Abraham Anderson, *The Treatise of the Three Impostors and the Problem of the Enlightenment: A New Translation of the Traité des trois Imposteurs* (Lanham, MD, 1997).

38 On this work, its authorship, and different versions, see Berti, 'The First Edition', and Françoise Charles-Daubert, 'Les *Traités des trois imposteurs aux XVIIe et XVIIIe siècles*', in *Filosofia e religione*, ed. G. Canzoni (Milan, 1994), 291–336.

39 Guillaume Lamy, *Discours anatomique: Explication méchanique et physique des functions de l'âme sensitive*, ed. A. M. Belgrado (Oxford and Paris, 1996).

40 Subsequently revised as *Traité de l'âme* (1750), modern edition edited by T. Verbeek (Utrecht, 1988).

41 See in general Robert E. Sullivan, *John Toland and the Deist Controversy* (Cambridge, MA, 1982).

42 See *Spinoza au XVIIIe siècle*, ed. O. Bloch (Paris, 1990).

43 Geraldine Sheridan, *Nicolas Lenglet Dufresnoy and the Literary Underworld of the Ancien Régime* (Oxford, 1989), 133–41.

44 John W. Yolton, *Locke and French Materialism* (Oxford, 1991); and his *Thinking Matter: Materialism in Eighteenth-Century Britain* (Minneapolis, MN, 1983).

45 See Aram Vartanian, 'Quelques réflexions sur le concept d'âme dans la littérature clandestine', in *Le matérialisme*, ed. O. Bloch, 149–65.

46 See note 11.
47 See Thomson, 'La Mettrie et la littérature clandestine', in *Le matérialisme*, ed. O. Bloch, 235–44.
48 *Dix-huitième siècle*, 24 (1992): issue devoted to 'Le matérialisme des Lumières'.
49 London, 1704.
50 Diderot, *Le rêve de d'Alembert* (1769), and *Principes philosophiques sur la matière et le mouvement* (written circa 1770, publ. 1792), both in *Oeuvres philosophiques*, ed. P. Vernière (Paris, 1964), 257–385 and 393–400, respectively.
51 Claude-Adrien Helvétius, *De l'esprit* (Paris, 1758); *De l'homme, de ses facultés intellectuelles et de son education* (1772).
52 Joseph Priestley, *Disquisitions relating to Matter and Spirit* (London, 1777).
53 M. Fitzpatrick, 'Heretical Religion and Radical Political Ideas in late Eighteenth-Century England', in *The Transformation of Political Culture: England and Germany in the Late Eighteenth Century*, ed. E. Hellmuth (Oxford, 1990), 339–72.
54 Priestley's unorthodox views continued to inspire clandestine radicalism in Britain past the turn of the century; see Iain McCalman, 'New Jerusalems: Prophecy, Dissent and Radical Culture in England, 1786–1830', in *Enlightenment and Religion: Rational Dissent in Eighteenth-Century Britain*, ed. K. Haakonssen (Cambridge, 1996), 312–35.
55 In addition to the literature referred to above, see also Jonathan I. Israel, *Radical Enlightenment: Philosophy and the Making of Modernity 1650–1750* (Oxford, 2001); and Martin Mulsow, *Moderne aus dem Untergrund: Radikale Frühaufklärung in Deutschland 1680–1720* (Hamburg, 2002).

II

THE SCIENCE OF HUMAN NATURE

7

PHILOSOPHICAL METHODS

REINHARD BRANDT

I. BACKGROUND

Eighteenth-century philosophical methodology is a loose collection of divergent theories which can be put together only retrospectively. Our clue must be the word 'method' and the associated conceptual tradition, not the interpreter's particular preconception. The very meaning of *methodos* – the path of investigation – indicates the relevance of four problem areas. First, how does one ascertain and secure the origins of knowledge? Secondly, how do origins relate to outcomes – in ascending or descending order, by induction or deduction, by analysis or synthesis? Thirdly, how does one avoid arbitrary gaps so that the acquisition, foundation, or presentation of knowledge is a continuous process – a *scala intellectus*, incremental and certain?[1] Finally, apart from this question of coherence, every consideration of method raises the question of how there can be correspondence between the knowledge claims and reality and of how such correspondence can be known.

Eighteenth-century methodological reflection and adoption of particular methods drew heavily upon the more fertile contributions of the seventeenth century, which saw a fundamental redefinition of traditional theories of procedure in logic, rhetoric, mnemonics, medicine, philosophy, and mathematics.[2] In seventeenth-century rationalistic philosophy, especially in Descartes and Leibniz, we find two different approaches to the issue of how scientific knowledge is possible, the *mos geometricus* and the *mathesis universalis*.[3] The former method stems from Euclid and seeks, through *resolutio*, analysis, to reduce given problems or propositions to indubitable axioms or simple elements, and, going in the opposite direction, through synthesis – as practiced by Euclid himself, according to Descartes – to give the solution of the problem or the proof of the proposition. Analysis and synthesis are linguistically formulated, generally in syllogistic form, and intuitively controlled. The *mos geometricus* is, in other words, a procedure for decision-making and exposition. The *mathesis universalis*, on the other hand, is an *ars inveniendi* of new scientific knowledge. It is algebraic calculation using

artificial symbols and set rules of conversion – in short, a purely formal procedure but for the achievement of materially new knowledge in any given field.
Only what is quantifiable counts as an object of knowledge. Because of this
similarity in their objects, *mathesis universalis* was soon confused with geometry
and arithmetic by many authors. *Mathesis universalis* presupposes that the content of knowledge can be quantified, but it can neither provide nor control
this quantification itself, and this makes it useless in the empirical sciences. The
more colloquial *mos geometricus*, on the other hand, can be used as a model for
the building (*ordo*) of philosophical systems, as seen in the works of Spinoza and
the early works of Christian Wolff.

In his programmatic *Novum organum* (1620), Francis Bacon suggested a
methodology for new empirical science. His recursive methodology connects
increasingly refined observations and experiments with a progressive determination of those forms that constitute the basis of all natural phenomena.[4] John
Locke, in *An Essay Concerning Human Understanding*, renounced such methodological innovations and constructed an epistemology roughly along the lines of
the Aristotelian *Organon*: concepts were to be derived from sense data (Book II),
and propositions were to be constructed from the comparison of concepts (Book
IV), while the theory of inference as a mere method of exposition carried no
weight. In the Introduction, Locke says: 'I shall imagine I have not wholly
misemploy'd my self in the Thoughts I shall have on this Occasion, if, in this
Historical, plain Method, I can give any Account of the Ways, whereby our
Understandings come to attain those Notions of Things we have'.[5] The methodology chosen is that of 'following Nature in its ordinary Method', more concretely, in the reconstruction of the 'true *History of the first beginnings of Humane
Knowledge*', and the further 'progress of our Minds' (II.xi.14–15, II.xii.8). The
method supposedly follows its object, the human mind; it is not the other way
around, as in the *mathesis universalis*, where nothing is considered an object unless
it fits the one and only method. Isaac Newton also had a powerful influence on
eighteenth-century methodology through his few pronouncements on scientific procedure, especially the 'hypotheses non fingo': '[I]f natural Philosophy in
all its Parts, by pursuing this Method, shall at length be perfected, the Bounds
of Moral Philosophy will also be enlarged'.[6]

A further head start on eighteenth-century methodological discussion was
provided by the *Port-Royal Logic*, which followed Hobbes and Gassendi in building up a logic in four parts.[7] The traditional division of logic into concepts,
judgements, and inferences is followed by a methodology for the right use of
the preceding logic. In general, eclecticism flourished in the last quarter of the
century and provided the eighteenth century with the most important alternatives, but its reception varied from country to country.

In the English-speaking world, and in France after the publication of Voltaire's *Lettres philosophiques* in 1734,[8] the genetic or historical method from Locke's *Essay* dominated. Instead of geometry and algebra, Newton's natural philosophy and methodological ideas were prominent, and the works of Bacon set the programmatic goal of experimental reasoning. In Germany, the *mathesis universalis* made a last appearance with Johann Heinrich Lambert, while the *mos geometricus* became the architectonic principle for Wolff's systems, and a particular variant of syllogistic served as the basis for Andreas Rüdiger's method. Whereas in England the role of mathematics as the methodological ideal for philosophy came to an end already with Locke, in Germany this thought first broke through with Wolff and was only finally established with Kant, whose own system was cast according to new organising principles. Finally, in Italy, Giambattista Vico transferred Bacon's method of natural philosophy to his attempt at founding a science of history.

Together with these standpoints, the eighteenth century also inherited some unsolved problems. In all discussions of method, the distinction between analytic and synthetic was dominant, yet there was no agreement on the relationship between the two concepts. Descartes, for example, defined the two companions differently from Pappus, the ancient commentator on Euclid. According to Pappus, the analysis of a proposition leads either to agreement or disagreement with other propositions that are already known to be true. According to Descartes, analysis is aimed at disclosing the presuppositions of a proposition that already is accepted as true (for example, *cogito ergo sum*) in order thus to acquire further true propositions: 'In the former case, the procedure is from the unknown to the known, it is a formula for proving further propositions; in the latter case, the procedure is from the known to the unknown in accordance with the Aristotelian notion that knowledge concerns the grounds of that which is given in experience.'[9] However, in the relevant primary sources, there are no explicit discussions of this difference.

Another legacy from seventeenth-century epistemology and methodology was equally problematic. The criteria of *clare et distincte* (and the opposites *obscurum et confusum*), which derive from Aristotle's *Physics* I.1, were by Descartes endowed with universal validity across all subject matter. The aim of methodical knowledge of concepts, as opposed to propositions, was said to be clarification and certain apprehension of obscure and confused notions.[10] The words *clare et distincte*, however, were used differently, even contradictorily, in different contexts. Locke, for example, writes:

As a *clear Idea* is that whereof the Mind has such a full and evident perception, as it does receive from an outward Object operating duly on a well-disposed Organ, so a *distinct*

Idea is that wherein the Mind perceives a difference from all other; and a *confused Idea* is such an one, as is not sufficiently distinguishable from another, from which it ought to be different. (*Essay*, II.xxix.4, 364; compare II.i.7, 107)

Quite different is the tradition to which Kant still belongs: 'When we can *distinguish* one object from another in our ideas, we have CLEAR consciousness of them. But if the *composition* of our ideas is also clear, our consciousness of them is DISTINCT. Only when our ideas are distinct does a collection of them become *knowledge*.'[11] In this tradition, clear ideas can emerge from unclear and unconscious ones; in contrast, Locke and his Anglo-Saxon successors develop no standpoint on the unconscious. The starting point for Locke's model of knowledge was the simple ideas perceived by internal or external senses that the human mind could put together to create complex ideas (*Essay*, II). Judgement and thus knowledge arise from the comparison of such independent ideas (IV.i.1–2). Leibniz and his followers, on the other hand, start from the composite idea. At first obscure, it may become perceptibly clear and thus distinguishable from other ideas, though it remains confused in itself; and such ideas are analysed in their context by the understanding and made clear. In other words, the understanding finds the sought-after predicates *in* the concept of the subject; propositional knowledge is analytic; and philosophy consists in analysing and clarifying confused ideas or concepts. Clear knowledge becomes sufficient when analysis has captured all the previously confused ideas.

Whereas the method of Descartes and his followers was directed towards the acquisition of clear and hence certain and objectively valid, or real, concepts, methodology in the eighteenth century, especially its second half, was concerned with judgement. The quest for the certainty of concepts gave way to the search for the necessity and universal validity of judgements and laws.

Another legacy of methodological importance was the distinction between mathematical and moral certainty, deriving in particular from Aristotle's *Nicomachean Ethics* (1094b11–1095a4). Eighteenth-century methodology emancipated itself from Cartesian monism by maintaining a moral certainty that was not subject to the Cartesian criteria.

The relationship between philosophy and methodology, including methodical knowledge, remained unclear. Generally, however, the concept of philosophy was used to encompass both the method and the knowledge resulting from it. In one perspective, philosophy thus became the theory or methodology of science; in another, it became science itself with its new confidence.

II. BRITAIN

David Hume's *Treatise of Human Nature* is, according to its subtitle, 'An Attempt to Introduce the Experimental Method of Reasoning into Moral Subjects', and the *Enquiry concerning Human Understanding* (I.9) posits Newtonian physics as the methodological model for philosophy.[12] However, it is necessary to distinguish between, on the one hand, Hume's actual practice in the acquisition of knowledge, reminiscent of Aristotle's *De Anima*, and his procedure of literary presentation, and, on the other hand, the modern scientific programme that he declares. Let us begin with his actual practice. In the fourth section of the first part of the *Treatise*'s Book 1, Hume refers to 'the elements of this philosophy', which consist of two classes, first the constituent parts, namely the perceptions (impressions and ideas), and secondly the *dynamic* relations between these parts, namely the principles of association (1.1.4.7). They are taken as self-evident at the start of the *Treatise*, and they are reaffirmed in the construction of the system as a whole. The system of philosophy is thus congruent with the system of nature, but in contrast to Locke it is not conceived genetically but as a dynamic whole which transforms the impressions (of inexplicable origins) into ideas and makes associative connections between impressions and ideas. The human mind, or 'human nature' as there represented, is the object of this coherent philosophical system whose truth is confirmed by explaining the phenomena of 'moral subjects' and by founding the sciences, according to Hume's programme in the Introduction. Thus, Locke's 'labour of thought' becomes Hume's mental organism without any self in which ideas are formed and succeed each other according to fixed dynamic laws. The same epistemic structure is exhibited in the *First Enquiry*. But regardless of this general naturalistic view of the mind, Hume distinguished between, on the one hand, statements about relations of ideas which have an intuitive and, hence, demonstrative necessity, and, on the other hand, statements of matters of fact in nature which are purely inductive and probable (especially *First Enquiry*, 5.1).

Hume's literary mode of presentation caught attention both with the posthumous *Dialogues concerning Natural Religion* and the *Enquiry concerning the Principles of Morals*.[13] The artful composition of the *Second Enquiry* is clear already from the titles of its nine sections. Whereas Sections 1–4 and 6–8 (Section 9 is the Conclusion) begin with 'Of', Section 5 is singled out by the title 'Why utility pleases'. By showing the paradoxical coincidence of utility and pleasures, Section 5 concludes the preceding sections, and the following sections serve to deepen and confirm this central thesis of Hume's moral thought. The literary composition of the four essays on philosophical schools shows that the philosopher types form a methodic unity that inevitably concludes with the sceptic. The three or four possibilities arise from reflection upon the ways of living; the essays constitute one answer to the old question 'Quod sectabor vitae iter?' (Which way in life should I follow?), or, as Locke saw the matter, the quest for the summum bonum.[14]

Hume's methodological programme for philosophy is to transfer the successful experimental method from the natural to the human sciences and thus indeed make the latter into the foundation of all knowledge (*Treatise*, Intro. 6–8, SBN xvi–xvii). He does, however, appreciate the specific difficulties of making real experiments in the human sciences and generally emphasises observation, and he cannot be said to point the way towards mathematisation.[15] The discussion of mathematics as part of his own 'science of man' varies. In the *Treatise*, arithmetic and algebra are said to be the only sciences in which, despite long chains of proof, 'a perfect exactness and certainty' is maintained. Geometry, on the other hand, is the science of perceptual space and, as such, subject to empirical uncertainty (1.3.1.4–6, SBN 70–2). In the *First Enquiry*, however, geometry has the same epistemic status as arithmetic and algebra because it is not concerned with matters of fact but purely with relations of ideas (4.1.1, SBN 25). Still, when pure geometry is related to actual space, the difficulties mentioned in the *Treatise* recur. In sum, Hume has not made good his claim to found all sciences on the 'science of man' through the methodological ideal of natural science, and the discussion of the methodological basis for the sciences was continued in the nineteenth century at the point where Hume had left it.

In his early *Lectures on Rhetoric and Belles Lettres*, Adam Smith characterises as the 'Newtonian method' the procedure whereby a science, 'whether of Moralls or of Naturall Philosophy', posits one or a few principles as initial hypotheses that can explain multiple rules or phenomena. The contrasting Aristotelian method begins by positing the things that are to be explained and then seeks suitable principles from which to derive them.[16] Smith's *Theory of Moral Sentiments* is a clear example of Newton's hypothetico-deductive method. It begins with the principle of sympathy with the happiness or unhappiness of others and interprets all moral phenomena by means of this familiar idea. Unusual phenomena cause unease in observers, and the sciences in general attempt to subsume such phenomena under familiar principles and thus to explain them by integrating them into the known picture of the world. This psychological motivation behind the sciences does, however, lead to superstition under disorganised social conditions and only in a settled social order to scientific research.[17] Science connects with the experience of ordinary life and its self-correcting explanations – for example, when moral rules are established by induction of the understanding on the basis of our experiences of pleasure or displeasure.[18] Science can, however, abandon ordinary experience in favour of artificially constructed hypotheses, producing a break between the two (as in the case of the Copernican system). Hypotheses must be confirmed through their powers of prediction and allow for correction in the light of contradictory experience. Philosophy is therefore both in its theoretical and its practical aspects an empirical science of given facts and cannot possibly follow the mathematical method; but at the same time explanation must satisfy our 'wonder and surprise' at new facts by integrating them into what is already known, thus making coherence a central scientific virtue.[19]

Thomas Reid saw himself as a strict Newtonian in his methodology. Newton's successful empirical and inductive procedure with external nature applies equally to the human mind, which was Reid's object of study, for the human mind itself is so constituted that it only can acquire knowledge in the following manner. First, observation and experiment must analyse individual phenomena; secondly, '[I]n the solution of natural phænomena, all the length that the human faculties can carry us, is only this, that from particular phænomena, we may, by induction, trace out general phænomena, of which all the particular ones are necessary consequences. And when we have arrived at the most general phænomena we can reach, there we must stop.'[20] We are, in other words, urged, 'from real facts ascertained by observation and experiment, to collect by just induction the laws of Nature, and to apply the laws so discovered, to account for the phænomena of Nature.'[21] Here the constancy of nature and the general law of causation are presupposed as beyond doubt, and this is asserted against Hume with reference to Newton's principle that '*Effectuum naturalium ejusdem generis easdem esse causas*'.[22] No actual powers of nature are presupposed: 'As philosophy advances, life and activity in natural objects retires, and leaves them dead and inactive.... It must have been by the observation and reasoning of the speculative few, that those objects were to be discovered to be inanimate and inactive, to which the many ascribed life and activity'.[23] Only language, which also scientists must use, suggests the existence of hidden natural forces. With warmth and sharpness, Reid defended God-fearing empiricism against earlier, especially Cartesian, apriorism, which set the idols of the human mind – theories, hypotheses, and conjectures – up against God's creation. And again he invoked Newton's '*hypotheses non fingo*'.[24] In contrast, it is more under the influence of Bacon than of Newton that David Fordyce writes:

Moral Philosophy has this in common with Natural Philosophy, that it appeals to Nature or Fact; depends on Observation, and builds its Reasonings on plain uncontroverted Experiments.... [W]e must collect the Phænomena, or Appearances of Nature in any given Instance; trace these to some General Principles, or Laws of Operation; and then apply these Principles or Laws to the explaining of other Phænomena.[25]

Locke's battle cry, to follow the method of nature, was adopted by Edmund Burke in his *Reflections on the Revolution in France* and used against the violently unnatural events in Paris and, in general, against the abstract theories of the Enlightenment: 'Thus, by preserving the method of nature in the conduct of the state, in what we improve, we are never wholly new; in what we retain we are never wholly obsolete'. Burke urges us to hold fast to 'the same plan of a conformity to nature in our artificial institutions', thus reclaiming nature for his conservative, anti-revolutionary politics with the same animus against theories as that displayed by Hume and Reid.[26]

III. FRANCE

Jean-Jacques Rousseau's *Discours sur l'origine et les fondements de l'inégalité parmi les hommes* follows Locke's directions to trace human ideas 'in their rise, progress, and gradual improvements' (*Essay*, II.xi.14, 161). The human race replaces the individual as the subject of inquiry, and this change is connected with a further revision of a basic principle in Locke's theory: General ideas are no longer conceived as extra-linguistic, mental entities but can only be formed and communicated in language and, therefore, in society. Locke had only dealt with language in Book III, after the Book 'Of Ideas'. But for Rousseau the formation of general ideas is a socio-historical phenomenon, not a matter for an abstract individual, and it requires sentences or propositions, not isolated words or names: '[G]eneral ideas can enter the Mind only with the help of words, and the understanding grasps them only by means of propositions.'[27] Closely following Locke, the *Discours* shows the history of the development of the human mind in each phase of social reproduction in which different ideas can be formed, such as the idea of morals, which is totally absent from the first state of nature, the idea of property, and so on generally.[28] The 'historical plain method' historicises the human mind when applied not to the ahistorical abstract individual, as in Locke himself, but to humanity in its stages of development as determined by the conditions of production. Just as Locke does not explain how the method of nature is found, so Rousseau leaves open the question of how to recognise the historically invariant categories in terms of which the development of human self-consciousness is to be understood. A further methodological peculiarity of the *Discours* is the hypothetical approach, which has two fundamentally different aspects that Rousseau himself, like most commentators, barely differentiates. On the one hand, he follows Buffon, among others, in juxtaposing his history with the biblical account understood as purely hypothetical:

Let us therefore begin by setting aside all the facts, for they do not affect the question. The Inquiries that may be pursued regarding this Subject ought not to be taken for historical truths, but only for hypothetical and conditional reasonings.... [Religion] does not forbid us to form conjectures based solely on the nature of man and of the Beings that surround him.[29]

This must be distinguished from the introduction of hypotheses *within* the hypothetical account tolerated by contemporary theology; it is this type of conjecture that is most frequently used.[30] With this second hypothetical method, Rousseau provides a conjectural history and thus a programme of research for filling gaps and confirming or refuting conjectures. The methodology of this conjectural history, which was also practiced by Vico and the Scottish thinkers, was first articulated by Dugald Stewart in *Dissertation Exhibiting the Progress of Metaphysical, Ethical and Political Philosophy since the Revival of Letters in Europe*.[31]

The theme of the *Contrat social* implies a different method.[32] To begin with, dichotomies are applied to possible social forms, a move for which no reason is given but which is implied by the claim to completeness. Society can either be natural or artificial; the former can derive from natural descent or from natural power, the latter from a contract of subjection or of association. Of these four forms of association, the first three do not satisfy the conditions of rightfulness, thus leaving the last, whose actual possibility and practical necessity are shown in detail in the work.

IV. ITALY

Giambattista Vico writes in his *Princípi di scienza nuova*:

But in the night of thick darkness enveloping the earliest antiquity, so remote from ourselves, there shines the eternal and never failing light of a truth beyond all question: that the world of civil society has certainly been made by men, and that its principles are therefore to be found within the modifications of our own human mind.[33]

Opposing scepticism and Descartes's methodological devaluation of history, Vico, in order to place history above science, uses the Cartesian principle that the human mind knows itself best. An 'ideal eternal history' lies behind and shapes the individual cycles of history, though not with causal necessity. It is a story of development which takes place in individual nations just as in individual persons, though not in the human race as a whole. When no data are available, the historian may suggest hypotheses about how things must have happened: 'The decisive sort of proof in our Science is therefore this: that ... the course of the institutions of the nations had to be, must now be, and will have to be such as our Science demonstrates ...' (I.iv.348). The Bacon-inspired procedure is neither purely inductive nor purely deductive. Vico has apparently not noticed the danger of circular argument in his 'ideal eternal history'.

V. GERMANY

Insofar as the German Enlightenment is not traced back to English and French impulses but considered to have an original national source, it is Christian

Thomasius who is invoked. Before his temporary religious derangement after 1693, when he wanted to found physics on the Old Testament, he argued that the *philosophia eclectica* was preferable to all others. Especially in his *Introductio ad philosophiam aulicam* (1688), he suggested that eclecticism replaced authorities, sects, and schools with independent thought and opened up for selection what was best in each argument. In his eclectic method, Thomasius followed ideas which Johann Christoph Sturm had suggested in his *Physica conciliatrix* (1684) and was to develop into an independent scientific method in his *Philosophia eclectica* (1686) and *Physica electiva sive hypothetica* (vol. 1, 1697). Sturm's preface contains 'the most considered explanation of an eclectic scientific method'.[34]

Eclecticism with its motto of '*nullius in verba*' was an inspiration in the seventeenth century within English empirical philosophy in the tradition of Bacon. But by the eighteenth century it had become a side issue of no consequence and was replaced by an idea which had already been promoted by eclecticism, namely, that of a freedom or independence of thought that is yet compatible with having a system, whether one's own or an adopted one.[35] Andreas Rüdiger criticised the earlier scientific method that took its lead from syllogistic as fundamentally mistaken. One could not interpret the syllogism analytically, reading a proposition as the conclusion from its middle terms and thus, working backwards prosyllogistically, reach particular premises. Instead, one had to proceed synthetically from a definition whose truth had been ascertained empirically through the infallible *sensio*, both *sensio externa* and, especially, *interna*. On this basis, one could achieve divisions into subjects in accordance with the relevant sensory basis for the definition and then form axioms and deduce all their possible truths (*consectaria*) as the basic laws of a discipline, and from these true propositions one could then choose those that were useful.[36]

Christian Wolff, in his early phase, turned against the supposedly Aristotelian idea of syllogistic acquisition of knowledge and held up Euclidean geometry as the ideal for philosophical and scientific method.[37] After an intervention by Leibniz in a letter of 21 February 1705, Wolff changed his position as follows. Geometry, whose object is the relationship of imaginary dimensions, and philosophy, which seeks causes or grounds to explain all that is possible, have common foundations in being (ontology) and in the human mind (psychology).[38] Of Euclid it may further be said, in the words of Wolff's most important methodological work, 'the method which Euclid holds is not derived from its subject-matter but is deduced from the general notion of the very nature of entities and of the human mind'.[39]

Wolff's systematic philosophy dissolves the eclectic method by adopting it, as it were. The principle of selectivity is fully accepted, but the criterion of selection is that the ideas chosen make up a system – in other words, coherence is the criterion: 'Qui intellectu systematico praediti sunt, ab autoritatis praejudicio immunes, et eclecticos agere apti sunt'.[40]

Philosophy is concerned with the totality of *possible* truths among which *actual* truths about reality can be found only by supplementary conditions. Scientific theories begin with definitions from which axioms and postulates are derived '*immediately*' or '*per intuitum*'. Here we see that for the mature Wolff philosophy and mathematics by no means proceed in the same manner. Of course, once sure definitions have been established in philosophy, these can serve in the same manner, as in Euclidean geometry, as the basis for synthetic presentation and proof of philosophical knowledge. But first the philosophical definitions must be gained through analysis of the empirically given, not by arbitrary stipulation. Concepts and definitions are first acquired through reflection on perception, then by abstracting differences between the first concepts, and thirdly through the varying of determinants. The analytic method used here corresponds to the presentation of truths, 'as they were discovered or at least might have been discovered'.[41] On the other hand, Wolff also taught that nominal definitions un-ambiguously identify objects; that is to say, they do not simply stipulate language norms without truth value, like Locke's 'nominal essence', but give knowledge of reality.[42] Nominal definitions do not prove existence, as is required of real definitions, but for philosophy as the science of the possible, nominal knowledge suffices. Such knowledge is, however, beyond methodical control, as Wolff's op-ponents would point out. Meanwhile, the master and his many disciples wrote textbooks that are models of strict methodological *ordo* while a contemporary, Johann Heinrich Zedler, chronicled the discussion of method from antiquity to the early Enlightenment and provided a comprehensive bibliography.[43]

Johann Heinrich Lambert and Immanuel Kant appreciated the methodi-cal structure of the Wolffian philosophy but recognised a need for revision. Both thought that Wolff had failed to secure his basic concepts and principles methodologically. The relevant works of Lambert published in his lifetime are the *Neues Organon* (1764), which develops from what was called *Vernunftlehre*, and the *Architectonik* (1771), which develops from metaphysics and turns it into a methodology. Lambert's criticisms of Descartes and Wolff and the rudimentary methodology of his early 'Abhandlung vom Criterium veritatis' were published posthumously.[44] According to Lambert, the earlier metaphysics' demand for the *clare et distincte* was no longer tenable. Complicated truths could not be clear and distinct; moreover, these criteria were dependent upon the different edu-cation of people. Wolff's initial definitions could neither guarantee the alleged isomorphy between concept and possible object nor justify the presupposed dif-ference between essential attributes and those selected (out of infinitely many).

Lambert tried to solve the problem of the foundation of knowledge through a novel way of forming basic concepts. On the one hand, such concepts stem from experience: 'Basic concepts are derived from immediately verifiable experiences' and are the mind's window on reality. On the other hand, they are defined as the indubitable elements of basic principles: 'Basic principles depend on basic concepts. The latter must be such that one affirms them when denying them.'[45] The indubitable basic concepts with real referents are understood in a semiotic that is immune from the vicissitudes of natural languages. Lambert moved beyond Wolff in the area of relational concepts, which he divided into logical and metaphysical, the former being analytic and given with the terms, the latter being synthetic opening up for a heuristic, as in the case of the concept of causation. The combination of basic and relational concepts led Lambert to an *ars inveniendi*, but he failed to make a persuasive connection to existing science.

Lambert's deductive programme worked against the tendency of Wolff to turn logic into ontology and psychology, both tendencies present in the doctrine of the three operations of the mind. The demonstration of the rules of logic is to be sought in ontology; individual steps in proof, on the other hand, are conceived as mental acts. And it was the psychological version alone that dominated with Johann Georg Heinrich Feder, whom Lambert criticised in an anonymous review.[46]

In his first published work, *Gedanken von der wahren Schätzung der lebendigen Kräfte*, Kant declared, 'In a word, this whole treatise is to be thought of exclusively as a product of this method', and this 'our method' was a critical and negative one.[47] It referred to existing doctrines and was the art of 'considering the presuppositions and estimating whether a particular form of proof contains sufficient and complete principles to allow the conclusion. In this way we will perceive whether there is an error in it even though we cannot at first see it' (*Gedanken*, 96). This method is to be recommended because proofs often conceal their errors and thus 'deceive' the understanding; either they are only discovered accidentally or they are deliberately sought out when one already is certain that they exist. The important thing here is the reversal of the usual sequence and thus the precedence of the 'that' over the 'what' or 'wherein' (*Gedanken*, 93, 95, 98, 151). The allegedly novel way of testing proofs is used in this work on the problem of the magnitude of constant velocities, which Kant thought unresolved. Is the quantity mv or $\frac{mv^2}{2}$?[48] In Kant's view, the former (the Cartesian) measure is correct for what he calls dead movements, which are only transferred from one body to another, whereas the latter applies to the quantities promoted by the Leibnizians, which Kant called the living inner natural force of bodies. Because of their purely mathematical method of proof – their *modus cognoscendi* (*Gedanken*, 60) – the Leibnizians were basically unable to grasp living forces and therefore remained in thrall to Cartesianism and the mathematical definition of purely geometrical bodies and dead forces. The *vis viva* of natural bodies can only be conceived through a metaphysical knowledge of nature. This shows the force to be an internal property of bodies that maintains their motion (the law of inertia) but which also (in infringement of this very law!) generates and accelerates movement in a condition of rest. Through these principles, Kant wanted to make it possible that 'the very first movements in this world . . . may have come about through the action of matter at rest' (*Gedanken*, 62). Thus, no God is needed to give the first impulse to movement – pace Newton and, in Kant's view, Leibniz. Put in methodological terms, the principles of nature are conceived in such a way that human reason has the widest possible field of operation. This methodological principle is determining for the cosmological work of 1755, which corrects Newton, and for the whole of Kant's later methodology.

The diagnosis that a certain *modus cognoscendi* proves inadequate for understanding reality is made again later by Kant. Leibniz's purely conceptual grasp of the world is incapable of discerning the difference between right- and left-oriented bodies.[49] This failure of pure conceptualism led Kant to the recognition in 1770 of a pure a priori intuition of space and time as two complementary pillars of human knowledge.

The presentation and assessment of contrasting doctrines is another method of philosophical instruction that Kant cultivated. In an announcement of lectures for the summer semester of 1758, we read: 'In classes on Wednesdays and Saturdays I shall consider previously treated themes polemically, which I feel is one of the best ways of acquiring basic insights'. The announcement for the winter semester of 1765–6 states:

> The method of instruction, peculiar to philosophy, is *zetetic*. . . . The philosophical writer, for example, upon whom one bases one's instruction, is not to be regarded as the paradigm of judgement. He ought rather to be taken as the occasion for forming one's own judgement about him, and even, indeed, for passing judgement against him. What the pupil is really looking for is proficiency in the method of reflecting and drawing inferences *for himself.*[50]

Kant's most important precritical writing on method is the *Untersuchung über die Deutlichkeit der Grundsätze der natürlichen Theologie und Moral* (1764). Whereas mathematics begins with definitions and then progresses synthetically, philosophy, or metaphysics, has to analyse the confused concepts that are given in order to reach fundamental concepts and propositions that cannot be analysed further which then, in turn, make possible correct definitions and associated synthesis.

Often, certain insights of the analysis itself are of immediate importance on their own and require no definition. The criterion for an immediately certain, particular insight in metaphysics is described as follows:

> Likewise in metaphysics: by means of certain inner experience, that is to say, by means of an immediate and self-evident inner consciousness, seek out those characteristic marks which are certainly to be found in the concept of any general property. And even if you are not acquainted with the complete essence of the thing, you can still safely employ those characteristic marks to infer a great deal from them about the thing in question.[51]

In other words, Kant wants in a halfhearted way to establish metaphysics on an empirical basis – halfhearted because we are not told what a universal 'inner experience' is.

Kant's main opponent is contemporary metaphysics, especially Wolff's system ('. . . how mistaken the practice of philosophers is'). That which only can be the outcome of lengthy philosophical analysis is 'in all schools of philosophy' falsely presented at the beginning in the form of ontology: 'The most abstracted concepts, at which the understanding naturally arrives last of all, constitute their starting point, and the reason is that the method of the mathematicians, which they wish to imitate throughout, is firmly fixed in their minds'.[52] Kant arrives at a new idea of the 'two cultures'. On the one side is mathematics, with a synthetic method forced upon it by its subject matter; on the other side is metaphysics, with theology and ethics, which have to proceed in the opposite direction. Descartes's methodological monism has been dissolved.[53]

As in contemporary works on logic, Kant's inaugural dissertation, *De mundi sensibilis atque intelligibilis forma et principiis* (1770), concludes with a methodology: 'Section V. On method in metaphysics concerning what is sensitive and what belongs to the understanding'. At the beginning (§23), it was maintained that in the sciences and mathematics method followed science: 'use gives the method'. In metaphysics, on the contrary, 'method precedes all science' – another typically Kantian figure of reversing the usual sequence.[54] In the former, method is thus descriptive, whereas in the latter it is prescriptive, a distinction that is hardly to be found in the rest of the eighteenth century's methodological reflections. The last paragraph (30) lists three principles of nature that do not have their origins in natural science itself but that arise from the 'harmony' (*covenientia*) of the free and wide exercise of human understanding. The three 'principles of harmony' state that everything in the universe happens in accordance with laws of nature, that the principles of knowledge should not be unnecessarily increased, and that matter neither arises nor disappears.[55] These principles cannot be proved as constitutive laws of nature but are regulative laws for a possible and greatest possible *use* of the understanding. In the development after 1770, rules of this type are ranked as transcendental (and not just logical or heuristic) regulative principles.[56]

Critical or transcendental philosophy will here be presented from four points of view with regard to its methodology. First, is the new definition of the concept of 'system'.[57] Wolff, in his *Logic*, distinguished the *compilator*, who forces selected material into unjustified coherence, from the *conditor systematis*, who assembles and combines truths from other authors. Wolff saw his own logic as of the latter kind.[58] In preparing his *Kritik der reinen Vernunft*, Kant develops a different concept of system. He rejects the eclectic procedure for the discovery of truths and turns to the idea of the whole, which is reflected in the order and completeness of the system. His theory of systems is set out in the 'Doctrine of Method' in the *Kritik*: 'I understand by a system, however, the unity of the manifold cognitions under one idea' (A 832). In idea, the form of the whole and the relative arrangement of the parts are determined a priori; the *Kritik* was, in Kant's eyes, such a whole, even if not quite complete. On the one hand, it is a 'treatise on method' (B xxii; compare A 83), and on the other it is in itself a methodically organised whole which from an idea determines the totality of its parts a priori – a 'rational cognition from concepts' (A 713, 724, 837).

In accordance with the idea, the *Kritik der reinen Vernunft* forms a systematic whole but also owes something to the isolation of particular areas (A 22). In *Grundlegung zur Metaphysik der Sitten*, after referring to the fruitfulness of the division of labour, Kant asks, 'whether the nature of science does not require that the empirical part always be carefully separated from the rational part'.[59] Kant's notion of the division of labour does not stem from political economy and Adam Smith alone but goes back to Descartes's second 'précepte' of knowledge in his *Discours de la méthode*: 'to divide each of the difficulties I examined into as many parts as possible and as may be required in order to resolve them better'.[60] Later, Fichte, Schelling, and Hegel aimed at highlighting the idea of system; they turned against Kant's own philosophy because they did not find in it the development of a closed deductive or dialectic whole but rather a concern with contingent factors, such as the given forms of intuition, and even a use of the method of isolating and distinguishing problems. This ran counter to the holism of the idealists.

In the second point of view, the decisive heuristic factor is the 'sceptical method', which Kant also uses in the antinomial conception of the world by pure reason. This method 'can point to the [transcendental] dialectic as an example of the great utility of letting the arguments of reason confront one another in the most complete freedom' (A 507; compare A 423–5). Kant here adopts not Descartes's methodical doubt but the procedure of Pyrrhonist scepticism that already had served as the model of zetetic teaching. The sceptical method is limited in the *Kritik* to give arguments for and against in certain problem areas of 'rational cognition from concepts'. If there is antinomial equilibrium, we can infer that the basis for the conflict is a natural illusion of human reason. The conflict that the sceptical method presents as an antinomy in the concept of the world stems from the illusion that appearances are things in themselves. But if one adopts the transcendental aesthetic's insight that appearance and thing in itself must be distinguished, then reason's quarrel with itself is resolved. When this premise already is known to be true, neither of the two positions, or both of them, will prove to be true. In this way, the 'transcendental dialectic' in the manner of an experiment confirms the 'transcendental aesthetic', even though the latter is in need of no confirmation (A 46). This method, says Kant in his Preface to the second edition, is 'imitated from the method of those who study nature' (B xviii, note).

In the third point of view, Kant talks of 'transcendental procedures' (B 666) but not of the 'transcendental method' subsequently attributed to him.[61] The latter, according to Hermann Cohen, suggests that 'experience is given [in positive 'pure science'] and the task is to discover the conditions that make it possible. If the conditions are found that make possible a given experience in such a way that this experience can be regarded as a priori valid, then these conditions must be counted as the constitutive characteristics of the concept of experience.'[62] Kant avoids a circular argument of this sort. In the *Prolegomena zu einer jeden künftigen Metaphysik, die als Wissenschaft wird auftreten können*, he proceeds analytically, thus providing a model for the 'transcendental method', but he does so only as a method of presentation. The *Kritik der reinen Vernunft* forms the philosophical basis for this presentation and is 'written in the synthetic mode', as the *Prolegomena* retrospectively declares.[63] In the *Kritik*, the conditions of the possibility of experience are acquired independently of experience in the form of intuition in the formal logic.

Kritik der praktischen Vernunft, too, is developed and presented analytically. It posits at the outset consciousness of the categorical imperative in the form of a synthetic a priori proposition as a 'fact of pure reason'.[64] Reversing the sequence of the *Kritik der reinen Vernunft*, it then proceeds from this basic principle to the concepts of good and bad and to aesthetics in the form of the theory of incentives.

Finally, in the Preface to the second edition of the *Kritik der reinen Vernunft*, Kant turns the question of method into a problem of our mode of thinking, referring to 'what we assume as the altered method of our way of thinking' (B xviii; compare xix) and declaring: 'In this Preface I propose the transformation in our way of thinking presented in criticism merely as a hypothesis' (B xxii, note). The *Kritik* itself lays down in another context what is to be understood by 'mode of thought', namely the moral rather than purely empirical character of the mode of perception (A 551). True and false methods are conceived in terms of a figure of reversing the sequence and the conditioning: We cannot understand human action in terms of an inference from cause to effect but must begin from action as an effect and then accept it as a moral event conditioned by that which cannot be thought of in causal terms, the free will. Analogously, radical evil is later (1793) conceived as a tendency in man to proceed in accordance with the wrong method, namely, a 'reversal of incentives through a human being's maxim': 'The human being (even the best) is evil only because he reverses the moral order of his incentives in incorporating them into his maxims.'[65] A connection between philosophical method and moral mode of thought was still foreign to Kant in 1781, but when he wrote the Preface to the second edition of the *Kritik* (1787) he approached this idea by seeing his own critical turn in metaphysics as a 'revolution in the way of thinking' (B xi) and this was soon taken up by German Jacobins and 'left-Kantians' to forge a link between the political revolution in France and the *Kritik*'s revolution in thought.

The connection between epistemic method and morality was explicitly drawn up by Johann Gottlieb Fichte in his 'provisional investigation of method in science', where he followed Kant's Preface from 1787. The philosophical triad in the acquisition of knowledge, proceeding through thesis, antithesis, and synthesis, was developed by Fichte in his *Grundlage der gesammten Wissenschaftslehre*. Fichte stands in the Cartesian tradition of seeking ultimate certainty in a *clare et distincte* insight, and to this purpose he posits three basic principles concerning the I for itself, the I in distinction from the not-I, and the synthesis in self-knowledge. He states the most important methodological consideration:

Before embarking on our course let us meditate briefly upon it. We have established only three logical principles: that of *identity* which is the foundation of all the others, and then the two which are reciprocally based upon it, the principle of opposites and the *grounding* principle. It is the latter two which first make possible the process of synthesis in general, by establishing and grounding its form. We need nothing more therefore, to assure us of the formal validity of our method of reflection.[66]

Such reflection, as pure analysis, is concerned with the triadic unity of I, non-I, and their synthesis, and according to Fichte it proves the validity of the method of presentation in his science of knowledge. Method is thus again a fourth factor added to the dialectic triad.[67] Friedrich Wilhelm Joseph Schelling took up Fichte's suggestion but stressed that it is only a reflection. Philosophy could have only one method. 'What has recently been called the synthetic method is certainly a true representation of this absolute method but it has been distorted through reflection. For what the synthetic method presents as a procedure and

156 *Reinhard Brandt*

divides into thesis, anti-thesis and synthesis, is the true method and in every genuine philosophical construction one and together'.[68] A year later, Schelling called a variant of this method 'dialectic' and formulated it as an ontological principle or, in other words, a dialectics of reality,[69] while Hegel made dialectic the centre of his philosophy by taking it to be a principle shared by method and object, by logic and metaphysics.

NOTES

1 This postulate was already formulated by Plato, though without use of '*methodos*'; see *Philebus* 17a; *The Sophist* 253d.
2 See Rudolph Goclenius, *Lexicon philosophicum* (Frankfurt, 1613), 'Methodus', cols. 683–6.
3 See Hans Werner Arndt, *Methodo scientifica pertractatum: Mos geometricus und Kalkülbegriff in der philosophischen Theoriebildung des 17. und 18. Jahrhunderts* (Berlin, 1971).
4 See Antonio Pérez-Ramos, *Francis Bacon's Idea of Science and the Maker's Knowledge Tradition* (Oxford, 1988).
5 John Locke, *An Essay Concerning Human Understanding*, ed. P. H. Nidditch in the *Clarendon Edition* (1975), I.i.2.
6 Isaac Newton, *Opticks: or, A Treatise of the Reflections, Refractions, Inflections and Colours of Light*, 4th edn. (London, 1730), 381. See also *The Methodological Heritage of Newton*, ed. R. E. Butts and J. W. Davis (Oxford, 1970).
7 Antoine Arnauld and Pierre Nicole, *Logic, or the Art of Thinking,* trans. and ed. J. V. Buroker (Cambridge, 1996).
8 François-Marie Arouet de Voltaire, *Lettres philosophiques ou Lettres sur les Anglais*, ed. G. Lanson, 2 vols. (Paris, 1915). An English version preceded the French one in 1733. For a modern translation, see *Letters on England*, trans. L. Tannock (Harmondsworth, 1980).
9 Arndt, *Methodo scientifica pertractatum*, 57.
10 See, for example, Johann Heinrich Lambert, *Neues Organon, oder Gedanken über die Erforschung und Bezeichnung des Wahren und dessen Unterscheidung vom Irrtum und Schein*, 2 vols. (Leipzig, 1764), 1: §8.
11 Immanuel Kant, *Anthropologie in pragmatischer Hinsicht*, Ak 7:117–415 at 137–8. Translated as *Anthropology from a Pragmatic Point of View*, trans. and ed. M. J. Gregor (The Hague, 1974), 18.
12 David Hume, *A Treatise of Human Nature: Being an Attempt to Introduce the Experimental Method of Reasoning into Moral Subjects*, eds. D. F. Norton and M. J. Norton, in *Works* (2000), *An Enquiry Concerning Human Understanding (First Enquiry)*, ed. T. L. Beauchamp in *Works* (2000).
13 David Hume, *Dialogues Concerning Natural Religion* (1779), ed. J. V. Price, in *The Natural History of Religion and Dialogues Concerning Natural Religion*, eds. A. W. Colver and J. V. Price (Oxford, 1976); *An Inquiry Concerning the Principles of Morals* (1751), ed. T. L. Beauchamp, in *Works* (1988).
14 David Hume, *Essays: Moral, Political, and Literary*, ed. E. F. Miller (Indianapolis, IN, 1987), 138–80. Locke, *Essay*, II.xxi.55. Concerning Hume's method of presentation, see Reinhard Brandt, 'Beobachtungen zur gedanklichen und formalen Architektonik Humescher Schriften', *Archiv für Geschichte der Philosophie*, 72 (1990): 47–62.
15 See James Noxon, *Hume's Philosophical Development: A Study of his Methods* (Oxford, 1973), especially 108–23, and John Laird, *Hume's Philosophy of Human Nature* (London, 1932), 139–43.

16 Adam Smith, *Lectures on Rhetoric and Belles Lettres*, ed. J. C. Bryce, in *Works* (1983), 146. On the errors of ancient moral philosophy, see his *An Inquiry into the Nature and Causes of the Wealth of Nations*, eds. R. H. Campbell, A. S. Skinner, and W. B. Todd, 2 vols. (Oxford, 1976), I.iii.2. See also T. D. Campbell, *Adam Smith's Science of Morals* (London, 1971), 26–52.

17 See Campbell, *Smith's Science of Morals*, 33, with reference to Locke, *Essay*, II.xxi.29–60.

18 Smith, *The Theory of Moral Sentiments*, eds. D. D. Raphael and A. L. Macfie, in *Works* (1976), VII.iii.2.6, 319.

19 See A. S. Skinner, *A System of Social Science: Papers Relating to Adam Smith* (Oxford, 1979), ch. 2.

20 Thomas Reid, *An Inquiry into the Human Mind on the Principles of Common Sense*, ed. D. R. Brookes (Edinburgh, 1997), ch. 6, §13, 132.

21 Reid, *Essays on the Intellectual Powers of Man*, eds. D. R. Brookes and K. Haakonssen (Edinburgh, 2002), II.8, 121.

22 Reid, *Intellectual Powers*, VI.5, 489–90. '[T]he causes assigned to natural effects of the same kind must be...the same'. Isaac Newton, *The Mathematical Principles of Natural Philosophy*, trans. I. B. Cohen and A. Whitman (Berkeley, CA, 1999), Bk. 3, rule 2, 795.

23 Reid, *Essays on the Active Powers of Man*, in *Philosophical Works*, ed. W. Hamilton, 2 vols. in 1 (Edinburgh, 1895), vol. 2, IV.3, 605b.

24 *Intellectual Powers*, I.3, 52. 'I do not feign hypotheses'. Newton, *Mathematical Principles*, General Scholium, 943. See *Inquiry*, ch. 1, sect. 1, 12. Contrast Newton's own use of hypothesis; see Alexandre Koyré, 'Hypothèse et expérience chez Newton', *Bulletin de la Societé française de philosophie*, 50 (1956): 59–79.

25 David Fordyce, *The Elements of Moral Philosophy* (London, 1754), 7–8. See Paul B. Wood, 'Science and the Pursuit of Virtue in the Aberdeen Enlightenment', in *Studies in the Philosophy of the Scottish Enlightenment*, ed. M. A. Stewart (Oxford, 1990), 127–49; and Roger L. Emerson, 'Science and Moral Philosophy in the Scottish Enlightenment', also in *Studies*, ed. Stewart, 11–36 at 26.

26 Edmund Burke, *Reflections on the Revolution in France*, ed. J. G. A. Pocock (Indianapolis, IN, 1987), 30.

27 Jean-Jacques Rousseau, *Discours sur l'origine et les fondements de l'inégalité parmi les hommes*, in *Oeuvres*, 3: 149 (Première Partie); translated as *The 'Discourses' and Other Early Political Writings*, trans. and ed. V. Gourevitch (Cambridge, 1997), 148. Translation page numbers hereafter appear after the slash: 149/148.

28 *Discours*, 153, 165 ff., and 132/151, 161 ff., and 131–2.

29 *Discours*, 132–3/132. See Buffon's letter of 12 March 1751 to the Faculty of Theology at the Sorbonne, in Georges-Louis Leclerc, comte de Buffon, *Oeuvres philosophiques* ed. J. Piveteau (Paris, 1954), 108.

30 See, for example, *Discours*, 172/166: 'It is very difficult to conjecture...'; and 166/163: 'This is how men might imperceptibly have acquired some crude idea...'.

31 See Hans Medick, *Naturzustand und Naturgeschichte der bürgerlichen Gesellschaft: Die Ursprünge der bürgerlichen Sozialtheorie als Geschichtsphilosophie und Sozialwissenschaft bei Samuel Pufendorf, John Locke und Adam Smith* (Göttingen, 1973), 305–13.

32 Rousseau, *Du contrat social ou Principes du droit politique* (Amsterdam, 1762).

33 Giambattista Vico, *Princípi di una scienza nuova d'intorno alla comune natura delle nazioni* (Naples, 1725; 3rd edn. 1744), here quoted from *The New Science*, rev. trans. of 3rd edn. (1744) by T. G. Bergin and M. H. Fisch (Ithaca, NY, 1970), I.iii.331.

34 Michael Albrecht, *Eklektik: Eine Begriffsgeschichte mit Hinweisen auf die Philosophie- und Wissenschaftsgeschichte* (Stuttgart-Bad Cannstatt, 1994), 336.

35 See Albrecht, *Eklektik*, 539ff.

36 See especially Andreas Rüdiger, *Institutiones eruditionis, seu philosophia synthetica* (1711).
   See Heinrich Schepers, 'Andreas Rüdigers Methodologie und ihre Voraussetzungen. Ein
   Beitrag zur Geschichte der deutschen Schulphilosophie im 18. Jahrhundert', *Kantstudien
   Ergänzungsheft*, 78 (1959): 117–25.

37 See Ferdinando L. Marcolungo, 'Wolff e il problema del metodo', in *Nuovi studi sul pensiero
   di Christian Wolff* (*Werke*, III.31), eds. S. Carboncini and L. C. Madonna (Hildesheim, 1992),
   11–37 at 12–13.

38 See Gottfried Wilhelm Leibniz, *Briefwechsel zwischen Leibniz und Christian Wolff*, ed. C. I.
   Gerhardt (Halle, 1860), 18. Concerning the difference between mathematics and philosophy,
   see Wolff, *Philosophia rationalis sive logica*, in *Werke*, II.1, 'Discursus praeliminaris de philosophia
   in genere' (Frankfurt and Leipzig, 1728), ch. 1, §§1–28.

39 Wolff, 'De differentia intellectus systematici et nonsystematici', in *Horae subsecivae Marbur-
   genses*, in *Werke*, II.34.1–3: §11.

40 Wolff, 'De differentia', §16, 149. See Albrecht, *Eklektik*, 532–8.

41 Wolff, *Philosophia rationalis*, pt. III, §885, in *Werke*, II.1.3: 633. See Hans-Jürgen Engfer,
   'Zur Bedeutung Wolffs für die Methodendiskussion der deutschen Aufklärungsphilosophie',
   in *Christian Wolff, 1679–1754: Interpretationen zu seiner Philosophie und deren Wirkung*, ed.
   W. Schneiders (Hamburg, 1983), 48–65 at 56–9; and Cornelis Anthonie van Peursen,
   'Ars inveniendi im Rahmen der Metaphysik Christian Wolffs', in Schneiders, 66–88 at
   69–76.

42 Wolff, *Vernünftige Gedanken von den Kräfften des menschlichen Verstandes und ihrem richtigen
   Gebrauche in Erkänntnis der Wahrheit* (Deutsche Logik), ed. H. W. Arndt, in *Werke*, I.1.1:
   143–4.

43 Johann Heinrich Zedler, *Grosses vollständiges Universal-Lexikon aller Wissenschaften und Künsten*,
   art. 'Methode', 64 vols. (Halle and Leipzig, 1732–50), 20: 1292–1339.

44 Johann Heinrich Lambert, *Neues Organon, oder Gedanken über die Erforschung und Bezeichnung
   des Wahren und dessen Unterscheidung vom Irrtum und Schein*, 2 vols. (Leipzig, 1764), vol. 1;
   same, *Anlage zur Architectonik, oder Theorie des Einfachen und des Ersten in der philosophischen und
   mathematischen Erkenntniss*, 2 vols. (Riga, 1771); same, 'Abhandlung vom Criterium veritatis'
   (1761), ed. K. Bopp, in *Kantstudien Ergänzungshefte*, 36 (Berlin, 1915). See Gereon Wolters,
   *Basis und Deduktion: Studien zur Entstehung und Bedeutung der Theorie der axiomatischen Methode
   bei J. H. Lambert (1728–1777)* (Berlin, 1980); and Fabio Todesco, *Riforma della metafisica e sapere
   scientifico: Saggio zu J. H. Lambert (1728–1777)* (Milan, 1987).

45 Lambert, 'Über die Methode die Metaphysik, Theologie und Moral richtiger zu beweisen'
   (written 1762), in *Kantstudien Ergänzungshefte*, 42 (Berlin, 1918): 9.

46 Wolff, *Philosophia rationalis*, §89, in *Werke*, II.1.1: 39–40. Wolters, *Basis und Deduktion*, 108–9
   and note 40.

47 Immanuel Kant, *Gedanken von der wahren Schätzung der lebendigen Kräften*, (1747) Ak 1: 1–181
   at 94, 98.

48 See Erich Adickes, *Kant als Naturforscher*, 2 vols. (Berlin, 1924–5), 1: 65–144.

49 Kant, *Von dem ersten Grunde des Unterschieds der Gegenden im Raume* (1768), Ak 2: 375–83,
   translated as *Concerning the Ultimate Foundation of the Distinction of Directions in Space*, in *Works/
   Theoretical Philosophy, 1755–1770*, trans. D. Walford and R. Meerbote (1992).

50 Kant, *Neuer Lehrbegriff der Bewegung und Ruhe*, Ak 2: 13–25 at 25; Kant, *Vorlesungs-
   ankündigungen für das Wintersemester 1765–1766*, Ak 2: 303–13 at 307, translated in *Works/
   Theoretical Philosophy, 1755–1770*.

51 Kant, Ak 2: 273–301 at 286, translated as *Inquiry concerning the Distinctness of the Principles of
   Natural Theology and Morality*, in *Works/Theoretical Philosophy, 1755–1770*.

52 Ak 2: 289.

53 See Engfer, 'Zur Bedeutung Wolffs', and Giorgio Tonelli, 'Der Streit über die mathematische Methode in der Philosophie in der ersten Hälfte des 18. Jahrhunderts und die Entstehung von Kants Schrift über die "Deutlichkeit"', *Archiv für Philosophie*, 9 (1959): 37–66.

54 Ak 2: 385–419 at 410–11; translated as *Concerning the Form and Principles of the Sensible and Intelligible World*, in *Works / Theoretical Philosophy, 1755–1770*.

55 Ak 2: 418.

56 See *Kritik der reinen Vernunft* (1781; 2nd edn. 1787), Ak 3 (A) and Ak 4 (B), 'Anhang zur transzendentalen Dialektik. Von dem regulativen Gebrauche der Ideen der reinen Vernunft', A 642–68, translated as *Works/Critique of Pure Reason*, trans. and eds. P. Guyer and A. W. Wood (1998), 'Appendix to the transcendental dialectic: On the regulative use of the ideas of pure reason'. Subsequent references will be to the pages of the first (A) and second (B) editions; these are given in the margins of the translation.

57 See Ralf Selbach, *Staat, Universität und Kirche: Die Institutionen- und Systemtheorie Immanuel Kants* (Frankfurt, 1993), 39–91.

58 Wolff, *Philosophia rationalis*, Pt. III, §889, in *Werke*, II.1.3: 635.

59 Kant, *Grundlegung zur Metaphysik der Sitten*, Ak 4: 385–463 at 388, translated as *Groundwork of The Metaphysics of Morals*, in *Works / Practical Philosophy*, trans. and ed. M. J. Gregor (1996).

60 René Descartes, *Discours de la méthode pour bien conduire sa raison, et chercher la vérité dans les sciences*, 2éme Partie, in *Oeuvres*, eds. C. Adam and P. Tannery, 11 vols. (Paris, 1897–1910), 6: 18, translated as *Discourse on the Method of Rightly conducting one's Reason and seeking the Truth in the Sciences*, in *The Philosophical Writings of Descartes*, trans. J. Cottingham, R. Stoothoff, and D. Murdoch, 3 vols. (Cambridge, 1984–91), 1: 120. See Arnauld and Nicole, *Logic*, Pt. IV, ch. 2, 233.

61 See Manfred Baum, 'Methode, transzendentale', in *Historisches Wörterbuch der Philosophie*, eds. J. Ritter et al., 11 vols. (Basel and Darmstadt, 1971–), 5: 1375–8.

62 Hermann Cohen, *Kants Begründung der Ethik* (Berlin, 1877), 24.

63 Kant, *Prolegomena zu einer jeden künftigen Metaphysik, die als Wissenschaft wird auftreten können*, Ak 4: 253–383 at 263, see also 274–5, translated as *Prolegomena to Any Future Metaphysics that Will Be Able to Come Forward as a Science*, trans. G. Hatfield, in *Works/Theoretical Philosophy after 1781* (2002).

64 Kant, *Kritik der praktischen Vernunft*, Ak 5: 1–163 at 31, translated as *Critique of Practical Reason*, in *Works/Practical Philosophy*.

65 Kant, *Die Religion innerhalb der Grenzen der bloßen Vernunft*, Ak 6:1–202 at 36, translated as *Religion within the Boundaries of mere Reason*, in *Works/Religion and Rational Theology*, trans. and eds. A. Wood and G. di Giovanni (1996).

66 Johann Gottlieb Fichte, *Grundlage der gesammten Wissenschaftslehre als Handschrift für seine Zuhörer*, in *Gesamtausgabe*, I.2: 173–457 at 283; trans. in J. G. Fichte, *Science of Knowledge, with the First and Second Introductions*, trans. and eds. P. Heath and J. Lachs (Cambridge, 1982), 120.

67 See note 9 and Reinhard Brandt, *D'Artagnan und die Urteilstafel: Über ein Ordnungsprinzip der europäischen Kulturgeschichte* (Munich, 1998), 129–77.

68 Friedrich Wilhelm Joseph Schelling, *Fernere Darstellungen aus dem System der Philosophie*, in his *Werke*, ed. M. Schröter, 12 vols. (Munich, 1927–59), 1: 385–575 at 451.

69 Schelling, *Vorlesungen über die Methode des akademischen Studiums*, in *Werke*, 3: 229–374 at 289; see Kurt Röttgers, 'Dialektik IV: Die Dialektik von Kant bis zur Gegenwart', *Historisches Wörterbuch der Philosophie*, vol. 2, ed. J. Ritter (Darmstadt, 1972), cols. 184–9.

8

HUMAN NATURE

AARON GARRETT

I. INTRODUCTION

'Human nature' in eighteenth-century philosophy is linked to the idea of surveying, analyzing, and discussing human beings, practices, social arrangements and behaviors in their variety and particularity. The great thinkers we associate with the Enlightenment, such as Hume, Montesquieu, Diderot, Herder, and Kant, and the great collaborative projects, such as the *Encyclopédie*, offer accounts of man centered on four common theses: (1) that the scientific analysis of man is crucial to the success both of science as such and enlightenment; (2) that human activities and human creations are central to the analysis of man; (3) that the human sciences are systematic in intent and universal in scope; (4) and that human nature is everywhere uniform and unites humankind both as objects of study by the sciences and as subjects capable of enlightenment. Often these theses were presented within a 'Newtonian' philosophy that meant little more than a vague scientism. Although there are many exceptions, this is the common Enlightenment ideal of how to account for man. It is well captured by Mme. Lambert: '[T]he highest science is the science of man ... [and] as nothing is more equivocal than the actions of men one must continuously return to principles if one wishes to understand him'.[1]

Yet, in text after text, as soon as these restrictive theses are stated, they are violated – particularly the fourth. In the works of Hume, Diderot, Montesquieu, Kant, and many lesser lights, men do not seem terribly uniform but are divided up into sexes, races, national characters, the sighted and the blind, and many other categories. Furthermore, the divisions between men and other beings, particularly animals, are far more complicated and important for the 'human sciences' than they first appear. This was recognized by many eighteenth-century philosophers. In the words of the Scottish conjectural historian James Dunbar, human nature is 'in some respects ... so various and fluctuating; so altered, or so disguised by external things, that its independent character has become dark and problematical'.[2] Diderot's famous exclamation, 'What contrasts in the ways and mores of *man*!'³ is perhaps as much a gasp of horror as a breath of exultation at man's riotous diversity. The interest of many eighteenth-century philosophers in wild children, orangutans, and other 'prodigies' further muddies the mix, casting doubt over the border between man and animal and, by extension, over the very object of the sciences of man.

In this chapter, I will discuss human nature, as presented by a variety of eighteenth-century philosophers, through considerations of animals, the sexes, race, wild children, and the blind. Many of these categories overlap: for example, the article 'L'Homme (Morale)' in the *Encyclopédie* (by the pioneering animal ethologist George Le Roy) begins with an analysis of the minimal differences between men and animals and ends with a consideration of female education. Similarly, Catharine Macaulay's important work on 'the women question', *Letters on Education,* opens with an extended defense of the animal afterlife and includes discussions of slavery – a common point of comparison for feminists in the age of the French Revolution. The categories are also very different – women are for the most part considered human but intrinsically different from men, the non-white races are often considered barely human (although their humanity is a central point of debate), and animals are considered to be not human. Thus, considerations of women, animals, the non-white races, and other categories draw out different aspects of theories of human nature. The categories are too extensive for exhaustive treatment, but examination of notable authors and trends provides an insight into eighteenth-century philosophers' complex attitudes toward human nature and questions the idea of an 'Enlightenment science of human nature'.⁴

II. ANIMALS

The eighteenth century saw enormous growth in the life sciences and with it the discussion of animals and their relation to humans. Yet, despite this great novelty, problems, attitudes, and vocabularies from the seventeenth century remained of great importance.

In his article 'Rorarius' in the *Dictionnaire historique et critique*, Pierre Bayle summarized and criticized some of the main seventeenth-century arguments about the differences between man and beast.⁵ The writer Hieronymus Rorarius, following the sceptical line of Montaigne, had argued that animals were often more rational and virtuous than humans. Bayle used a discussion of Rorarius as a launching pad from which to criticize and appraise the Aristotelians, Leibniz (at length), Locke (briefly),⁶ and Descartes, each of whom viewed the differences between man and beast as important themes in their moral and psychological theories. Bayle's criticism inspired numerous eighteenth-century proponents and critics of these positions.

Cartesians emphasized that bodies, animal and human, were thoughtless, extended machines, while human minds were thinking, rational, and free. All animal behavior, as well as the workings of the human body, had to be explained mechanically without recourse to thought or intention, making animals 'beast-machines'. Cartesian mechanistic physiology, which built on this claim, remained influential in Europe throughout the eighteenth century in the works of the iatromechanist Hermann Boerhaave, who was venerated by philosopher-doctors as diverse as his student La Mettrie (who translated him into French), von Haller (who annotated Boerhaave's *Institutiones medicae*), and William Cullen (who translated Boerhaave into English). One of the most influential exponents of the Cartesian dualistic anthropology and mechanist natural science was the natural philosopher Buffon.[7]

Descartes's beast-machine was morally suspect. The distinction between beast-machines and 'man-machines' seemed metaphysically tenuous and a slippery slope, as already noted by Descartes's contemporaries. If fabricants such as Jacques de Vaucanson were able to make uncannily lifelike mechanical musicians, was life perhaps just matter in motion? If material sense was sufficient to explain the dispositional similarities between men and animals, why not among men as well? It was not difficult to find a secret materialism in the Cartesian discussion of animals, and this seemed to imply immoralism, libertinism, or worse.

Furthermore, many found the idea of the beast-machine ethically repugnant. Cartesians, Malebranche, and the Port-Royal vivisectionists were sometimes seen to legitimate indiscriminate cruelty toward animals (such as in experimentation) and to violate elementary humanity because they denied that animals could feel pain.[8] Scientists such as Robert Boyle, Robert Whytt, and William Harvey reasoned that although animals suffered, vivisection was excusable insofar as it helped us understand God's creation,[9] and other options, such as experimenting on criminals, were even more reprehensible. Even if they cared little about animal misery, there seemed a notable difference between that and sanctioning wanton and purposeful cruelty.

Unlike Descartes, Leibniz's rationalist psychology implied continuity between animal and human minds, as the variances between them were due to features they shared – monadic organization and relative distinctness of perception. However, Leibniz added to this metaphysical and psychological continuity a more fundamental moral distinction arising from the uniquely human reflective awareness of divine punishment and reward that allowed men to be 'citizens in the Republic of God'.[10] Animals' incapacity for self-reflection and apperception was the metaphysical and psychological basis for a fundamental moral distinction, and conversely man's reflective capacity distinguished him as a conscious being capable of following or transgressing the teleological laws of divine justice.

The eighteenth-century responses to Leibniz's version of the animal and human distinction thus differed from the responses to Descartes, given the former's emphasis on psychological continuity but moral difference. Kant is the most well-known philosopher to follow Leibniz in emphasizing the centrality of our moral reflexive awareness and how it engenders a moral community, but Leibniz's great advocate Christian Wolff is perhaps a more instructive example of how eighteenth-century concerns with human/animal relations modified seventeenth-century psychology and anthropology by relating them to the passions and moral psychology.

Wolff followed Leibniz's account of the psychological distinctions between human and animal souls to a great extent,[11] but he modified it to take account of our relations to animals *due to* our capacity to represent brutes as subject to passions. Wolff combined a comprehensive theory of the affections – which expanded Leibniz's rationalist psychology to include our passionate relations to other beings of all sorts – with a Leibnizian emphasis on man's capacity for representation (*vis repraesentiva*) and reflection. Although our relations with brutes are structured by our reflective capacities, which animals lack, still, insofar as we have passions, if we love them we must pity them when they show sadness, just as we pity humans we love.[12] Even if animals are not reflective, we represent them to ourselves as beings we love and empathize with as if they were reflective, and our love and empathy are real and manifest themselves accordingly. Thus, Wolff accommodates Leibniz to empirical affective psychology. As we will see, animals were often linked to sentiment, but sentiment no longer considered as a passive, brute condition. For Wolff, brute affection has a legitimate claim on the more rarefied Leibnizian psychology.

Unlike Descartes and Leibniz, Locke stressed empirical similarities between men and animals and accounted for human understanding (in part) through its observable (as opposed to metaphysical) continuity with and divergence from animals. For Locke, we share some of our mental capacities, such as perception and memory, with animals as lowly as oysters and birds. Other capacities, such as abstraction, are distinctive to human minds. As animals and humans both have senses, and as human knowledge is ultimately derived from the senses, to deny any contiguity between human and animal minds is intuitively and empirically as implausible as to assert their identity. Locke by no means wished to maintain the sceptical thesis that animals are equal or superior to humans – he thought animals were cognitively limited and lacking in reason. Nor did he wish to deny man a spiritual nature. Rather, Locke attempted to explore the faculties common to men and animals and to use the empirical divergences as a key to human nature.

For Locke's eighteenth-century readers, this was an invitation to explore human psychology through animals and glimpse in them the origin of the mind and its functions, as well as to centralize different faculties. In the *Traité des animaux*, Condillac criticized Buffon's distinction between material and spiritual sense, arguing that if beasts feel, they feel as we do.[13] But, Condillac argued, animal understanding is still far more restricted than that of humans because of animals' limitations in communicating their ideas. Each animal, however social, begins anew and responds to experience no faster than previous generations, unable to learn from the species's mistakes and successes through a common storehouse of language. Man, on the other hand, accumulates reflective knowledge, which, although derived from the senses, is able through language to expand and progress into an open-ended future.

Condillac's discussion went far beyond that of Locke in emphasizing the centrality of language to human diversity, community, and invention. He in fact criticized Locke for concentrating on faculty psychology and ignoring the nature of signs.[14] Thus, for Condillac, the comparison of human and animal sensitive, imaginative, and intellectual capacities resulted in a language-centered account of human nature that supplemented the subject-oriented psychology of earlier authors with an intersubjective social and historical medium. For Condillac, like Locke, the higher animals are continuous with man when considered solely in terms of our respective psychological faculties, but man and animal diverge radically when viewed historically via man's capacity for artificial language and his resultant self-advancement.

Thomas Reid took the Lockean legacy in a substantially different direction from Condillac, prompted by Berkeley's combination of phenomenalism and providentialism and his own concern with finding methodological positions capable of refuting Hume's sceptical appropriation of Locke. For Reid, our difference from the animals lay not so much in *what* we create (as it did for Condillac) as in the particular intellectual capacity for reflecting on thoughts and actions and judging them (namely the *capacity* to create such essential human institutions as language). This intellectual power to reflect is also the origin of our moral reasoning and moral judgment and thus the fundamental source of our discovery of those moral principles by and through which we govern our moral communities.

Because animals do not have this capacity, they 'are stimulated to various passions by their instincts, by their appetites, by their passions', whereas man 'is capable of acting from motives of a higher nature', given his capacity for reflective judgment.[15] When we examine activities we *seem* to share with animals, it always turns out that in us they arise from complex principles of action and choices built on reflective judgments, whereas animals unreflectively follow their brute instincts.

The emphasis on principles and motivations makes the gap between humans and animals far more radical for Reid than for Locke. How, then, does Reid make sense of Locke's argument that there are similarities between the powers of animal and human minds? The complexity and reflexivity of human ideas and the distinctive (moral) motivation of human action mean that Lockean continuity between human and animal minds must be understood as a reflective and organizing principle that arises in the human mind. *We* separate the 'animal' from the 'noble' elements that are mixed together in our actions, and we do so in accordance with Locke's model of continuity. It is this capacity to distinguish and arrange hierarchically that makes us radically different from animals who cannot worry about such things. Reid thus makes the continuity that Locke grounded on empirical knowledge into a principle arising from human consciousness and used to evaluate empirical knowledge.[16] Sceptics seeking to deflate man's capacities fail to realize that the very capacity to deflate makes man something very different from instinctual beings.

Condillac's and Reid's ways of thinking about the human/animal distinction thus provide us with radically different appropriations of Locke: Condillac emphasized human historical and societal inventions and intersubjective, communal institutions, and Reid emphasized the systematic examination of rational, intellectual powers as they arise within the mind of the individual subject. This contrast also points to an important pitfall in discussing human nature through the animal. Although writing forty years after Condillac, Reid presented the Lockean legacy as a contest about faculties, ideas, and epistemological issues, which became dominant in the nineteenth century, especially when coupled with the similar Kantian legacy. This was a consequence of Reid's desire to refute epistemological scepticism and to view the history of philosophy in terms of this issue. But scepticism was often of a rather different sort than Reid sought to combat. Condillac was no sceptic, but he did not view the animal/human distinction and the Lockean legacy in such limited terms. Animals were not just animal minds and actions deriving from such minds but rather scrambling, mute, and creating beings.

Condillac, Reid, Wolff, and Buffon are influential examples of how the philosophers Bayle had discussed were drawn in surprising directions by their partisans. The most surprising, though, was materialism, which radically minimized the differences between human and animal nature. Locke had refused to deny the possibility of sentient matter and was taken both by critical divines and approving materialists as a crypto-materialist and secret Hobbist.[17] Locke's position was further disseminated by Voltaire in the influential 'Lettre XIII' in *Lettres sur les Anglais*, in which he outlined the controversies over thinking matter.[18] Voltaire praised Locke, criticized the frenzied divines, and pointed to the possible consequences of thinking matter for man, beast, and machine. As with Cartesianism, it was a quick move from agnosticism about thinking matter to a materialist account of man. Even those sympathetic to Locke, such as Isaac Watts and Henry Lee, were uncomfortable with the possibility that what 'we call Thoughts . . . are only the Operations of Matter, qualified with the knack of thinking'.[19]

French and British materialists of the eighteenth century responded very differently to the notion of thinking matter. Locke's friend the freethinker Anthony Collins, and more mainstream Protestants such as John Gay, contributed to a distinctively British and religious materialist philosophy of mind, of which the most renowned exponents were David Hartley and his and Collins's unceasing advocate, Joseph Priestley. Hartley's *Observations on Man, his Frame, his Duty, and his Expectations* provided an astonishing synthesis of materialist physiological explanations of mental dispositions, associationist psychology, universalist theology, moral sense theory, rational self-interest, benevolence, and a vision of human integration through the passions – most of which was taken up by Priestley, who considered Hartley the discoverer of the 'science of human nature'.[20]

Neither Hartley nor Priestley derived their materialisms from Epicureanism, that is, from arguments that all features of living beings could be explained on the basis of the chance organization of their atomic constituents without recourse to a transcendent cause and consequent self-interest. This last, 'the mechanical principle of self-interest',[21] was the issue on which William Hazlitt distinguished Hartley from Helvétius. Priestley's aversion to any form of Epicureanism included Hume, Gibbon, and d'Holbach, who were all criticized together in the *Letters to a Philosophical Unbeliever*.[22] Despite their differences, Priestley felt all the 'unbelievers' denied the existence of a 'cause of causes', which for British materialists was the necessary precondition of all beings, imparting powers in matter and arranging the powers according to its omniscient knowledge of physical laws.

Although Priestley, Hartley, and Collins all advocated necessitarianism, it was a compatibilist necessitarianism consistent with the moral and rational powers we recognized in ourselves before we knew ourselves to be necessitated. All saw material necessity as consistent with true Christianity, as they denied the notion of the separable soul and centralized the miracle of the bodily resurrection and the integration of the whole human being. Unsurprisingly, they also adhered, to varying degrees, to Locke's emphasis on the physical and psychological continuity of men and animals. Admittedly, Hartley did not think animals, small children, and some adults to be rational, Collins accepted a strong dose of Montaigneian scepticism, and Priestley thought animal intelligence and even the animal afterlife likely; but they all thought it important to see ourselves thoroughly linked to brute creation.

In Collins's words:

> *Sheep*, for example, are supposed to be *necessary agents*, when . . . they are fickle or stedfast in their amours; when they take more or less care of their young. . . . And why should man be deemed *free* in the performance of the same or like actions? He has indeed more knowledge than sheep. . . . He is also subject to more vain fears, more mistakes and wrong actions. . . . But these large powers and larger weaknesses which are of the same kind with the powers and weaknesses of sheep, cannot contain liberty in them, and plainly make no perceivable difference between them and men, as to the general causes of action.[23]

Collins has taken over the sceptical claims of Montaigne and used them as an argument against the free will – most influentially in his polemics with Samuel Clarke. Hartley and Priestley, having little irony, combined the unsystematic new arguments of the freethinkers with more mainstream sources into a 'science of human nature' as a material analysis of man and creation. When we recognize ourselves as continuous with animal nature, we recognize the community of all beings and their dependence on the 'cause of causes' that imbues them with powers by which they recognize themselves and others. The similarity of their material organization results in common dispositions and a belief in the universality of reason as arising from the universality of necessitated, organized matter.

The great French materialists, Diderot, Helvétius, La Mettrie, and d'Holbach pursued a modernized Epicurean and Lucretian materialism that subverted the 'cause of causes' and all rigid hierarchies. Drawing on natural scientific research (notably Abraham Trembley's discovery of a water polyp each piece of which was capable of reproducing a complete polyp), Diderot built his natural philosophy upon the interrelated principles of the productive power of matter and the unceasing metamorphosis of all natural beings. Living beings were everywhere. Each organ in an animal or human being was an independent species of animal functioning within a whole and was itself in turn filled with microscopic animals. Matter itself was alive and continuously transforming, through digestion, fertilization, and procreation, into more or less organized life. For Diderot, men were animal in an even more literal sense than for the British materialists: they were cooperative efforts of numerous animals forming organized wholes that in turn formed other organized beings.

Diderot did not blur the line entirely; men also differed meaningfully from the animals that composed and surrounded them. Among the animals, man is like Titian among the painters, inferior to many when one appraises each individual faculty distinct from the others, 'superior to all when the faculties are taken together'.[24] His 'perfectibility is born from the failure of the other senses, none of which are able to dominate the organ of reason; if man had a dog's nose he would always smell, if he had the eagle's eye he would never stop using it'. As no one sense dominates human reason, all the senses can take center stage, allowing man the unprecedented ability to respond to his environment and to change it and himself materially. Diderot thus accounts for man's distinction from the animals through the balance of man's senses, which when unsettled, as in the case of the blind, would lead to a different experiential and moral world and a different nature.

Helvétius saw the distinction between men and other animals in similar but starker terms. *De l'esprit* opens with a discussion of the causes of 'the inferiority of animal souls'[25] in order to isolate the human 'spirit'. The difference between man and other animals has a material basis: unlike men, who have hands and feet, animals have only feet of little deftness, clumsy hoofs, and claws. Due to this lack of subtlety of touch and manual dexterity, animals are unable to use, much less invent, tools. If we had hoofs, according to Helvétius, we would have to hide in the forests. As it is, we dominate the earth. Helvétius recognized the limitations of this explanation and supplemented it with a series of additional material factors. Animals have shorter lives in which to learn, their limited desires need less invention, and, most interestingly, they spend much of their limited time hiding from man, who makes weapons with his hands. Thus, Helvétius argues, once man triumphs on the earth, there is no turning back; the triumph leads to *ennui,* and this in turn becomes another fundamental difference between man and beast.

Before Diderot and Helvétius, and likely influencing Diderot,[26] the infamous La Mettrie argued that the only difference between men and animals is their relative complexity of organization. Although Diderot, d'Holbach, and Helvétius all discussed the difference between man and animal in terms of organization, none developed it to the extreme that La Mettrie did. He saw his philosophy as drawing out the Epicurean elements in Cartesian physics and physiology, and the work of Boerhaave, through the idea of the 'man-machine' – thus creating a non-dualistic 'Epicuro-Cartesianism'. No transcendent causes were allowed, natural law, providence, and teleology were denied, nature was 'governed' by chance, and morals were reduced to the health and vitality of individual organisms. Men were no less machines than animals, and conversely, if men were more than machines, so were animals, due to their similar organizations.

Before La Mettrie, Fontenelle had inverted Descartes's reasoning to show that whatever had a mechanical explanation in animals ought to have the same explanation in man, and conversely, whatever was not mechanistically explainable in man could not be so in animals.[27] La Mettrie, however, drew much more radical consequences. Little could be said of man that cannot be said of animals, or even plants, and conversely we can learn about everything 'human', even morals, from less organized creatures. 'Men' and 'animals' are ultimately groups of individuals, each of which is comparable to many others irrespective of their categorizations. This did not mean for La Mettrie that one should necessarily overthrow or invert governing social mores, as advocated by the Marquis de Sade (who, however, merely inverted mores, whereas La Mettrie undermined their basis, namely dualism). However, if one's nature is a result of material organization, a criminal can no more be blamed for having a depraved nature than a lion can for being bloodthirsty. Conversely, there can be no blame for criminals who pursue health in a way conducive to their organism 'as long as they are able to be criminals without remorse'.[28] La Mettrie incarnated the worst fears of the critics of Descartes, Locke, the freethinkers, and all those who were taken as undermining the borderline between man and beast.

La Mettrie's Epicurean take on Descartes's 'beast-machine' showed that man could be viewed as part of the natural order without a transcendent explanation. The moral consequences, for La Mettrie, were a radical combination of moral conventionalism, self-interest, and amoralism. But this was an almost unique response to the Cartesian discussion of animals – particularly its moral consequences. Mainstream reactions can be seen in the entry titled 'Animal Souls' in the *Encyclopédie*, which discussed and summarized two well-known French philosophers, David Boullier and Guillaume-Hyacinthe Bougeant.

The issue of 'animal souls' combined moral and epistemological questions with topics in natural law, theology, and providence. To ask whether animals had souls was to ask how to treat them if they were like us and whether they would have an afterlife. Very few philosophers argued that animals had morals. Bougeant, in his *Amusement philosophique sur le langage des bestes,* followed the popular seventeenth-century Jesuit critiques of Cartesianism by Ignace Pardies and Gabriel David in arguing that man and beasts are susceptible to the same passions, mores, and, by extension, morals.[29] Flirting with heresy by implying an afterlife, morals, justice, and punishment for beasts, Bougeant argued that the beasts around us are animated by demons subjected to the indignities of brute bodies while awaiting Judgment Day! This explains the similarities between man and beast and why beasts are often so bestial and vicious; they are in fact immoral, and their suffering is thus righteous. The popular, much translated, and very funny book also included a dictionary of animal language and descriptions of animal mores and love.

Although linked with Bougeant through the influential *Encyclopédie* article, Boullier's writings on animal souls contained little humor and less scepticism and were unfortunately far more paradigmatic. Boullier was a minister in Amsterdam and later London, who trenchantly criticized Voltaire's 'Lettre XIII' and Cartesianism. Against materialism he argued that although we differ from animals and our automatic bodily functions are necessary for our soul's operations, mechanical bodies are an insufficient explanation for human and animal actions. Against the Cartesians Boullier argued that since animal actions appear like human actions, if God created animals to appear like us, then He deceived us into thinking they have souls, contradicting Descartes's argument against a deceiving God.

However, one could not dispense with the Cartesian explanation of animals so simply since Malebranche had provided a further important argument.[30] If animals were not machines incapable of understanding natural or revealed moral law, then God would be unjust in allowing them to suffer, as 'under a just God, one would not be allowed to be miserable without having merited the misery'.[31] Hence animals must be machines.

Malebranche's argument, unlike Descartes's, ingeniously brought together mechanism and morality in a way that attempted to preserve divine justice while accusing those who by allowing feelings and thoughts to animals undermined it. To counter Malebranche's argument, Boullier invoked the 'great chain of being', the oft-invoked image of a hierarchical chain stretching from inanimate life godwards and ranking all in between. Every creature was a link in the chain, with a station appropriate to it, and united with the whole in expressing and manifesting God's purpose. Boullier argued that if the bodies of beings lower on the chain are used for the spiritual happiness of beings higher up (by virtue of the latter's reason), then lower beings are happy in some measure to serve the utility of higher beings. Their ignominious deaths are sometimes necessary to promote the greatest happiness in a created hierarchical world through universal divine justice, but this excuses only purposive cruelty, not wanton cruelty.[32]

Boullier employed the chain in a fairly conventional manner to preserve the status quo and to see all as providentially guided by a just, if in some ways unknowable, ruler, and he bolstered it by providentialist considerations of utility. All of creation was guided by natural justice, and this legitimated human treatment of those beneath. In so doing, Boullier tried to explain an inherent tension between the continuity between creatures and the singularity of man pointing to man's great difference from other creatures. The tension was well stated by Dugald Stewart, who argued that animals and humans differ not only by degree in constitution but in kind with respect to 'moral and intellectual principles'. Stewart concluded that 'perhaps, this is the single instance, in which that regular gradation which we, everywhere else, observe in the universe, fails entirely'.[33]

A radical response to accounts such as Boullier's is to be found in the writings of the great Swiss naturalist Charles Bonnet. Bonnet attempted to overcome the tension by arguing that the chain of being would likely be preserved in the afterlife. Man differs from all other beings on the chain by his perfectibility, which allows him to realize himself in a manner unavailable to other creatures. Although man differs from animals in kind, the faculties of *all* creatures will be enlarged and unfolded in the afterlife and the continuity of the chain preserved. Consequently, although man will far exceed other creatures in his perfection in the next life, perhaps some animals will be wiser than many of us were in this life.[34]

This influences the moral standing of animals in a somewhat different direction than in the works of Boullier. The idea that the chain of being extended beyond this world should, according to Bonnet, promote an ethic of kindness toward all creatures. Although animals lack understanding and morality in this life, perhaps they will gain them in the next, and we should behave toward all living creatures as if they were possible moral beings. The gnat we torture may become sage after passing through Saint Peter's gate, and we will be more tormented by our cruelty toward it when we become more perfect. A similar (although less extreme) position was maintained by the curate Richard Dean, who also invoked the great chain of being and the future life on behalf of brute creatures:

Must there not be a huge Chasm, and a vast Defect in the Universe, if all Nature is to be radically Destroyed below Man? Must there not be wanting, on this Hypothesis, Myriads of Creatures to testify the Excellence of the Divinity? What can exhibit... [i]nfinite Goodness but the Gift of all possible Degrees of Happiness?[35]

However, there is another problem brought out by Boullier's treatment. The early utilitarian Soame Jenyns took a providentialist theory of this kind, specifically the account of the great chain of being laid out by Pope in *An Essay on Man*, to imply that there likely are beings above us who think about their utility in relation to our own much as we do in relation to the animals. Our need to cause animal pain for our pleasure shows that in the chain of being pain and pleasure are almost always connected and complementary. But this does not necessarily imply that those in pain are much inferior to those who gain pleasure from this pain or that brutalizing them is necessarily a mark of superiority.[36] Furthermore, as pain and pleasure are always connected, and as the great chain spreads above and below us, our pains must serve for higher beings who 'destroy us, for the ends only of their own pleasure or utility' (*Free Inquiry*, 67).

Jenyns's recognition that man's feeling of superiority in creation was a pretense transformed the chain of being into an economy of pain and pleasure spreading heavenwards. We are among many middle-ranked beings, in Samuel Johnson's famous rendition of Jenyns's views, morally smug and cruel toward our inferiors while beings 'are hovering about us . . . torturing us to madness . . . sometimes breaking a traveller's bones, to try how he will get home; sometimes wasting a man to a skeleton, and sometimes killing him fat, for the greater elegance of his hide'.[37] Yet Johnson's criticisms are somewhat off target. Jenyns did not wish to legitimate an inverted chain of being, according to which one *ought* to be cruel to one's 'inferiors'. Rather, one *ought not* rationalize away the real sufferings of others that are the necessary condition of our pleasure, as we are for other beings: pain and pleasure go hand in hand.

Boullier, Bonnet, and Jenyns thus gave three distinct responses to the problem of animal souls and the conflicts inherent in the great chain of being. Boullier and Bonnet both relied on a Leibnizian form of providentialism that emphasized that this is the best of all possible worlds, but they differed on what this meant and what the consequences of it were. Jenyns rejected the optimism inherent in such a view of providence and provided a stepping-stone in the development of utilitarianism: providence is what we and others make right through our choices of pain and pleasure. Obviously, the different resolutions of this problem result in radically different accounts of human nature.

Jenyns's emphasis on the utility of pain in bringing about pleasure and his rejection of any optimistic providentialism is a variant on Bernard Mandeville's famous motto 'Private Vices Publick Benefits', the subtitle to the *Fable of the Bees*. Perhaps the most well-known, oft responded to, and reviled sceptic of the early part of the eighteenth century, Mandeville combined scepticism and Hobbesian self-interest (although of a very rich and complicated sort) with the burgeoning theory of the affects. Explorations of animal psychology had been put to a sceptical use under the influence of the animal fables of La Fontaine and Montaigne's 'Apologie de Raimond Sebond'. The *Fable of the Bees* and the poem 'The Grumbling Hive' with which it began were derived from Mandeville's early verse translations of La Fontaine and their expansion to include Mandeville's own fables in *Aesop Dress'd*.[38] But whereas La Fontaine had used such fables to undress and instruct human vanity, Mandeville (like Bougeant and Collins) had a rather different attitude, namely, to see vanity naked and dressed as equally essential to human nature.

Whereas Locke, Leibniz, Descartes, and some of their heirs focused on the *cognitive* similarities and differences between humans and animals (though as the basis for a moral distinction in, for instance, Leibniz and Reid), Mandeville emphasized our *affective* similarities and relations to animals and their explanatory power. Consequently, animal psychology should not be identified with epistemology, and the two often offered opposing visions of human nature. Hume, Montaigne, and Mandeville were all acute psychologists who used their analyses to argue that man's affective similarities to animals far outweighed any cognitive dissimilarities and that the affections, as opposed to cognitive faculties, were constitutive of human nature. For Mandeville, perhaps man's greatest difference from the animals was his vain desire for concealment – for the emperor's new clothes.

This combination of scepticism and affective explanation is well illustrated by a dialogue between a man and a lion in the *Fable of the Bees*. A shipwrecked Roman and his slave come across a multilingual lion of the Aesopian variety. The slave wisely climbs a tree, but the merchant attempts to reason with the lion, arguing that as the human species is 'of a more exalted nature' the lion should spare his life. The hungry lion undercuts this logic derived from the great chain of being stating 'Tis only Man, mischievous Man, that can make Death a Sport', and only man is able to eat vegetables but chooses out of love of novelties to make creatures suffer and eat meat. This repudiates Mandeville's own earlier Cartesianism:

When a creature has given such convincing and undeniable Proofs of the terrors upon him, and the Pains and Agonies he feels, is there a follower of Descartes so inur'd to Blood, as not to refute, by his Commiseration, the Philosophy of that vain Reasoner.

While admitting that the lion may be overstating the case a little, Mandeville allows the unconvinced lion to follow his strictly carnivorous nature and dine.[39]

But Mandeville went further than this, again following Montaigne. Human arrogance is not the result of providence but stubborn human custom; otherwise

Men of any tolerable Good-nature could never be reconcil'd to the killing of so many Animals for their daily Food ... in such perfect Animals as Sheep and Oxen, in whom the Heart, the Brain and Nerves differ so little from ours.... I can't imagine how a Man not hardened in Blood and Massacre, is able to see a violent Death, and the Pangs of it, without Concern. (*Fable of the Bees*, 173)

But whereas Montaigne's purpose in remarks similar to this was to show that human nature was worse than bestial, Mandeville used the stubbornness of custom and the analysis of actual human practices to overthrow any theory of human nature, including sceptical ones, which oversimplified it. As with Jenyns, both wanton cruelty and pity are part of humanity, and just as all human beings are crueler than they might admit, so those who deny pity are denying their humanity. Human nature ought neither to be demonized nor elevated but understood and explained in terms of its numerous affects and beliefs which do not necessarily form a logical, coherent whole. This was noted by Rousseau, who commented (albeit critically) on the importance of pity in Mandeville's philosophy.[40]

The combination of Mandeville's sceptical account of our affective relations to other creatures and of the structuring power of our beliefs with Locke's empirical account of our cognitive and psychological continuity led to the best-known eighteenth-century theory of the passions and affects, that of David Hume. Hume went far past Locke's discussion of the cognitive similarities between men and animals and undermined it by asserting (with a sceptical flair) that 'no truth appears to me more evident, than that beasts are endow'd with thought and reason as well as men'.[41] Hume used this assumption to employ animals as an experimental court by which to judge the adequacy of philosophical systems in explaining human nature. Much like Mandeville's lion, if a philosopher's explanation of human nature or of a particular human behavior is too subtle or grandiose to apply to animals, the 'brute court' will show the doctrine to be inadequate. Thus animals and their similarities to us provide a check on flights of philosophical fancy. By interpreting Locke's empirical psychology through a sceptical critique of human vanity and undermining our cognitive superiority to animals through emphasizing our similarities, the tables were turned on Descartes, Leibniz, and even Locke himself. For Hume, it applies for the greatest part of our lives (if not for the brief moments we spend philosophizing) that whither animals thither men.

As in Mandeville, our most important continuity with animals is in our passions and reasons. Men vainly think that their motivations and minds are unique, whereas they share most faculties, passions, and reason itself with animals; the differences are primarily in the subtlety of their employment. Animals lack morals and humans have them, but this is not because we differ radically from animals and have a unique divine gift or reflective power. Rather, animals fail to attain the critical mass of certain passions and the subtlety of moral feelings about their world that result in stable characters and moral actions. Yet, although we differ from them, we still share a sympathetic, passionate, and even rational world, differing only in subtlety: we recognize the pride of the peacock as pride, and insofar as we share peacock passions we ought to make gentle use of them.

Hume's discussion of animals is an ideal fulcrum for tracing the divergences from his supposed progenitor, Hutcheson. Whereas for Hume, Mandeville, and Collins our relations to animals arose from shared passions, sympathies, conventions, and customs, Hutcheson took a remarkably different tack. Although the natural lawyers had denied rights to animals, insofar as animals are incapable of understanding the natural law and thus cannot understand the obligations entailed by a right, Hutcheson argued for a set of animal rights.

When rights did come up in the eighteenth century in relation to animals, it was most commonly our rights *to* animals as property. Perhaps the most interesting discussion of this was provided by William Paley in *The Principles of Moral and Political Philosophy*. Paley reviewed the claims made for our right to eat animals, most importantly that animals prey on each other and so we also have a right to prey on them, and concluded that all arguments by analogy between animals and man are 'extremely lame; since brutes have no power to support life by any other means, and since we have'.[42] It was crucial for Paley to maintain this since a right grounded in the actions of birds of prey might conceivably lead to natural-right legitimations of all sorts of difficult behavior. But although one might argue rationally for a right to eat nonsentient vegetables, the fact that we can live without flesh means there can be little support for flesh-eating solely through natural reason. One must have recourse to Scripture and God's grant to Noah that 'every moving thing shall be meat'. Yet the fact that man is given animals by divine dispensation, as opposed to natural right, protects animals from 'wanton, and what is worse, studied cruelty', as none of this is granted to Noah, and as God's gift of animals to man should not be wasted (*Principles of Moral Philosophy*, 65). Consequently, Paley gave divine protection to animals while legitimating our eating of them by refusing to anchor our suppers in natural right.

Hutcheson was far more radical in attempting to found animal rights within precisely the sort of natural-law theory that Paley criticized. He did this by treating animals' status as intermediate between property and servants and by emphasizing that the superiority of man to the rest of brute creation entailed duties to inferiors. We form an evolving, providentially governed community with animals, and our relations and responsibilities to them vary with the needs of the superior members of the community: men. In times of scarcity and crisis, we owe animals nothing. In better times, we should defend the tamer species who in turn work for us and thus 'by human dominion over the brutes, when prudently and mercifully exercised, the tameable kinds are much happier, and human life exceedingly improved'.[43]

Like Boullier, Hutcheson suggests that we have a right to eat animals, as it is in 'the interest of the animal system that the nobler kinds should be increased, tho' it diminished the numbers of the lower' – a point that Paley specifically questioned. But, as all of creation aspires to happiness, and is governed accordingly, animals too have a right to happiness and

a right that no useless pain or misery should be inflicted on them. . . . 'Tis plainly inhuman and immoral to create to brutes any useless torment, or to deprive them of any such natural enjoyments as do not interfere with the interests of men. 'Tis true brutes have no notion of right or of moral qualities: but infants are in the same case. . . . Not to mention that frequent cruelty to brutes may produce such a bad habit of mind as may break out in like treatment of our fellows.[44]

This final reason was a traditional one later made famous by Kant. He took the radical mental and moral distinction between man and beast as obvious, given that animals are incapable of self-consciousness and freedom. Yet, Kant argued for the importance of not being cruel to animals. We have no direct duties toward animals, but when we 'stifle the instinct of humanness within us and make ourselves devoid of feeling' it is 'an indirect violation of humanity in our own persons'.[45] Thus Kant used this old argument for decent behavior towards animals as being consistent with a radical distinction between animals and men that in Cartesianism had legitimated wanton cruelty towards animals.

But the claim that animals had rights to happiness grounded in natural law, although they themselves had no notion of right, was more original, as was Hutcheson's notion of a providentially guided moral community between men and domestic animals who have needs for community. In arguing for moral community, Hutcheson extended the reach of the natural law and the ideas of right and obligation. Later, Reid followed Hutcheson but reconceptualized Hutcheson's animal rights as economic rights and claims: 'Even the Brutest animals who serve at this entertainment must not be neglected. They must have their Entertainment and their Wages for the Services they do us'.[46]

In Hutcheson's wake, more and more authors espoused the rights of animals in the latter part of the eighteenth century. Some, such as Humphrey Primatt, relied on a Hutchesonian 'right to happiness'. John Hildrop, in a commentary on Bougeant's *Amusement*, based an animal rights argument on a concept of natural justice due to all beings with souls. By the late eighteenth century, the clamor was sufficient to warrant a parody by Thomas Taylor. The founding of organizations for animal protection soon followed in the early nineteenth century.[47]

Hutcheson's paternalistic view of man as helping to shepherd providentially governed creation toward happiness had little in common with Hume's and Mandeville's vision of a community of sympathy governed internally by stubborn customs, passions, self-interest, and the multitude of associations and powers making up human and animal nature. For Hutcheson, men, in contrast to animals, have a moral sense that makes us *imago dei* and that differs in kind from animal senses. Hutcheson's moral sense providentially associates us with others in a community that is guided by the public and moral senses, and animals thus have rights insofar as they share in community but are subordinated to us insofar as they lack the moral sense. In contrast, Hume's community lacks providence and rights, and our obligations toward animals (and humans) are grounded not in natural law but in the varying degrees of sentiment and affection engendered by spheres of association. As with Mandeville, we are inhumane when we act barbarously toward beings with whom we have natural attachments. A synthesis of the sceptical tradition and Hutcheson is perhaps achieved by shifting the role of providence to general utility, as Jeremy Bentham did. In a famous footnote in *An Introduction to Principles of Morals and Legislation*,[48] he asserted that the utilitarian calculus of pains and pleasures also necessarily must be applied to animals in view of the clear similarity between their pains and pleasures and ours.

Toward the end of the century, we see these lines of argument mixing. The Jacobin atheist John Oswald's scathing arguments in *The Cry of Nature* are consonant with Mandeville when he argues that our distance from the act of slaughter leads to our cruelty to animals, for 'within us there exists a rooted repugnance which yields only to custom, and which even the most inveterate customs can never entirely overcome'.[49] 'Sympathetic affection for every animal' arises both from the similarities between our passions and animal passions and from a native pity that is part of human nature (30). But man has been estranged from his pity and his original Edenic and vegetarian state by the interrelated evils of scientism and superstition. (Oswald had picked up vegetarian philosophy on his travels in India.) The religious sacrifices of animals led to a scientific attitude towards brute creation, sanctioning vivisectionists to 'interrogate trembling nature, plunge into her maternal bosom the butcher knife', as animals were made for humans and they must submit to men (32). All this led further to war, inequality, the destruction of nature, and self-destruction. Thus, Oswald related animal persecution to the philosophy of history and to Rousseau's account of man's fall from the state of nature into history, civil society, and self-estrangement.

III. ORANGUTANS AND BEAVERS, WILD CHILDREN, THE BLIND, AND THE DEAF

In presenting the history of cruelty toward animals as a history of human alienation, Oswald implicitly drew on a central Rousseauian concept: *perfectibility*. While many thinkers in the second half of the eighteenth century used this term to mean humanity's providentially given and guided capacity for perfecting itself and progressing in a way that realized the God-given capacities separating it from the stationary nature of brutes, Rousseau used it quite differently in the second *Discourse*.

Rousseau adopted Buffon's distinction between *l'homme physique* and *l'homme morale* and, like him, used it to separate man from beast, claiming that *l'homme physique* tells us little about human nature. It is *l'homme morale* that differs significantly from animal nature, due primarily to perfectibility. Whereas animals are 'ingenious machines', subordinated to deterministic laws, man has free will, which allows him to create society, language, and history where 'nature is silent'.[50]

Unlike Buffon, and following Condillac, Rousseau paradoxically allowed a similarity of sense between man and beasts, although the latter lack general ideas due to their lack of language. But Rousseau's difference from both Condillac and Buffon was more pronounced than the similarity. Perhaps the most common way of distinguishing humans from animals was and is the distinction between reason and instinct. Animals are part of nature and as such are guided by instinct that is subject to the immutable laws governing animal behavior. Man's reason places him above nature and allows him variously to create an artificial world or second nature, to take part in the spiritual world beyond the physical, and to learn and transform himself on the basis of this learning. The distinction between reason and instinct, vague as it is, was taken up in a great variety of ways. Many agreed that man had instincts. Some, such as Hume and John Hunter, argued that reason was an instinct and that the very distinction was meaningless.

Rousseau replaced the dichotomy between 'reason and instinct' with 'perfectibility and instinct'. Man is instinctless, or, at most, his faculties cooperate in a quasi-instinctual manner to preserve him in the state of nature. Whereas the nature of animals is governed by instinct, and their senses and ideas respond to and merely follow the natural order, humans are governed by perfectibility. Through it they wax and wane with circumstances, they have free wills, they can create and learn through history, they recognize their inherent spirituality, and, perhaps most importantly, they are a continuing project of becoming.

In giving precedence to perfectibility and deriving reason, history, and language from it, Rousseau broke with the Cartesian and Lockean psychologies that either centralized reason and thought, or perceptual and cognitive faculties, from which or in relation to which all else was derived. By giving primacy to moral and historical perfectibility, the human world was viewed primarily as moral and historical and only derivatively as rational and cognitive. Whereas for Condillac the transformative and historical power of language ultimately arose from perception and our particular cognitive powers, for Rousseau the very powers were derivative of, and morally and historically tinged by, perfectibility.

Yet the concept was rarely used as Rousseau intended. Characteristic examples of its widespread employment and deformation by thinkers other than Rousseau can be found in the works of Adam Ferguson and Johann Gottfried Herder. Ferguson's *An Essay on the History of Civil Society* is in part a polemic against Rousseau's mythic state of nature, arguing *contra* Rousseau that man always belonged to an evolving and changing society and cannot be imagined ever to have stepped from the state of nature into civil society. However, when Ferguson has to say what it is that allows man to transcend animal sensibility, he points to 'a principle of progression, and a desire of perfection'.[51] By expressing it as a 'desire of perfection', Ferguson presents his own principle of perfectibility within the scope of the teleological providentialism of the more conservative, and dominant, aspects of the Enlightenment. But this principle also, much like

Rousseau's perfectibility, makes man distinct from brute nature and gives him the ability to wax and wane with his surroundings. It is the root of language, social change, and history.

In *Ideen zur Philosophie der Geschichte der Menschheit*, Herder situated the natural world within human history through an eclectic and far-ranging synthesis of the scientific, historical, and philosophical knowledge of the later eighteenth century. Animals exhibit varying degrees of physical and neurological organization, with regard to both their complexity and their vertical orientation. Rousseau, Blumenbach, and Buffon had all emphasized man's uprightness as differentiating him from animals, and, in particular, from orangutans, the eighteenth-century term for the higher primates. Herder used this to argue further that man's face, his bodily organization, and even the structure of his brain represent a vertical triumph over the horizontal brute creation. Man is the only being upright enough to gaze not only at the earth but at the unending expanses before and above him.

As much as Herder's theory seems a strange physical epigenecism, it is his use of Rousseau's concept of perfectibility that transforms it into something quite different. Drawing on Condillac and Bonnet, Herder viewed all of nature as reflecting successive stages, each reaching its apogee and mimetic summation in man, the 'most perfect form, in which the features of all are collected in the most exquisite summary'.[52] This can perhaps best be seen in the development of the human embryo, which changes from fish to dog to monkey to man in nine months. But the specific character of human beings as opposed to the rest of the creation, whose perfection is epigenetically presented in human beings, is Rousseauian: 'Born without instinct, we are formed to manhood only by the practice of a whole life, and both the perfectibility and corruptibility of our species depend on it'. But despite the fact that our lack of instinct and our free ability to transform ourselves and nature divide *l'homme physique* from *l'homme morale* – the animal and natural from the human – the former is reflected in the life of the latter insofar as it is through human perfectibility that all of nature and *l'homme physique* are gathered together and united in human life and history.

Given Herder's emphasis on nature and spirit being united in man, it is not surprising that he would diverge from Rousseau when considering the orangutan. For Herder, Rousseau, and many others, the orangutan was a difficult cipher posed between man and animal, between *l'homme physique* and *l'homme morale*. What are we to make of those higher primates that were mainly known through travel narratives and tales and looked so much like us on the surface? The debate about orangutans was brought to the fore when the great naturalist Carl von Linné (Linnaeus) placed man among the quadrupeds, seemingly denying any important empirical distinction between man and the higher apes and thus problematizing the border between man and beast. As his *Systema Naturae* progressed through its numerous editions, Linné expanded the genus *homo* to include the orangutan (*homo sylvestris*), the wild man (*homo ferus*), and the cave-dwelling troglodyte (*homo nocturnus*). For Linné, this did not mean that man and beast were the same, or even that the difference between man and beast was not based on our having an immortal soul. Rather, Linné implied that neither the soul nor any other differentiating characteristic was to be given in terms of external and descriptive criteria and thus, viewed scientifically, man was a near ape.

William Tyson, Nicolas Tulp, and later the influential Dutch physiologist Peter Camper dissected higher primates and found them anatomically similar to humans but with important differences. (Camper particularly emphasized the differences between orangutan and human larynxes and their abilities to modulate speech.) Following Tyson, Buffon argued that the evidence of physical similarity did not imply any spiritual similarity, and Herder followed in his own way.

Rousseau, and following him Lord Monboddo, took the extreme and much mocked position that the differences between man and orangutan were no greater than that found between many humans. For example, Monboddo noted that it was empirically verifiable that humans were occasionally born with tails, an observation vigorously denied by the racist great-chain-of-being thinker Charles White, as it conflicted with the strict gradation of nature.[53]

Rousseau and Monboddo did not assert men were apes, although they were taken as believing this by a chorus of mocking philosophers; rather, apes were uncultivated men. They had an unlikely ally in La Mettrie, who thought that the anatomical similarities between men and apes implied that the latter could be taught sign language as easily as people deaf from birth. Given proper medical techniques, apes could likely even speak.[54] But where La Mettrie took our consanguinity with the orangutan as confirming the organizational similarities among all living beings, and thus as part of his project to undermine any chain of being, Monboddo and Rousseau separated the orangutan from our far remoter simian kin and argued that the orangutan alone was human. Monboddo declared: 'Though I hold the Orang Outang to be of our species, it must not be supposed that I think the monkey, or ape, with or without a tail, participates of our nature, on the contrary, I maintain, that, however much his form may resemble ours, yet he is, as Linnaous [sic] says of the Troglodyte, nec nostri generis, nec sanguis'.[55] Monboddo also took great care to distinguish between orangutans, troglodytes (whom both he and Buffon thought 'white negroes' and not a different species), and other pretenders to humanity, while criticizing any fundamental distinctions between humans, all of whom ought to belong not only to the same genus but the same species.

Both Monboddo and Rousseau note that our judgments on the humanity of orangutans are on a par with our judgments about the humanity of indigenous peoples whose languages we cannot properly understand and about 'wild children', all of whom were discussed together in the famous tenth footnote of Rousseau's *Discours sur l'inégalité*. To deny humanity to orangutans, given our limited information, and confine the fraternity of man, would be empirically unsound. Those who, like White, simply ruled out the possibility, ignored the empirical evidence and were, pace Harry Bracken, the anti-empiricists.[56] Allowing the possibility of humanity to the orangutan is the science of human nature at its most open-minded and empirical: given the great variety of the human species, it is possible that 'various animals similar to men, which travelers have without much observation taken for Beasts... [might] indeed be genuine Savage men'.[57]

In addition, discussions of orangutans and wild children gave entry to man's linguistic and political nature. Rousseau and Monboddo argued that the speechlessness of orangutans should not lead us to discount their humanity. Language is a product of civilization, and the capacity for language is specific to man *qua* his perfectibility. But even though speech differentiates socialized men from animals, a speechless being could just as well be a perfectible *homo sylvestris* who is not yet speaking as it might be an animal incapable of speech – only further experimentation would determine this. Thus, by seeing perfectibility as underlying language and as a feature (if not the defining one) of humanity, creatures could be deemed human insofar as they were perfectible but still solitary and pre-linguistic.

Wild children were an even more popular object of speculation concerning language. In his *Essai sur l'origine des connaissances humaines*, Condillac discussed a child who had been reared by bears and had difficulty learning conventional language. The child uttered only accidental signs, since animals lack conventional signs, and the natural signs of bears are unsuited to human natural expressions due to the particularity of ursine physical organization.[58] La Mettrie had previously discussed the example and drew a rather different moral from it, namely that the child's lack of appropriate sensory stimulation proved that all ideas arise from the senses. The bear children (of which three were reported) and numerous other examples gained wide circulation through Linné (who, as we have seen, made wild men a taxonomic category and thus an object of scientific discussion), Fontenelle, Leibniz, Rousseau, Buffon, Blumenbach, Condillac, and others.

Before Condillac, La Mettrie considered the bear boy along with examples of the blind and deaf, including a deaf man from Chartres whose hearing was awakened by the sound of church bells ('a man without ideas of morals') and a man blind from birth whose cataracts were surgically removed by William Cheselden. This last example was made famous by Voltaire in *Eléments de la philosophie de Newton*, where Cheselden's operation was taken as empirical support for Locke's and Berkeley's negative answers to Molyneux's question: that if a man born blind was given vision, he would be unable at that moment to distinguish a cube from a sphere through sight alone.[59] For late seventeenth-century and early eighteenth-century authors, Molyneux's question concerned the nature of perception, the interrelations among the senses, and the origin of our ideas. For later eighteenth-century thinkers, the question became more and more complex. Condillac demonstrated the enormous practical difficulties involved in the experiment.[60]

Diderot took up the question in his famous *Lettre sur les aveugles* and considered Molyneux's question in relation to the blind genius Saunderson. Like La Mettrie in his analysis of the young deaf mute from Chartres (a case derived from Fontenelle), who, when he could hear and speak, was found to lack ideas of God and morals, Diderot argued that the blind have different sensations than the sighted and consequently different morals (for example, they consider theft a far more serious crime than adultery). Even blind genius is different.[61] For Diderot, a proper analysis of Molyneux's question demanded an anthropology of the world of the blind. Given the variety of human sense experience and its constitutive role for human nature, the conclusion was that morals *qua* sensation situated within an experienced life world are relative.

At the end of the eighteenth century, Jean Itard wrote the most famous of all case studies of wild children, *De l'éducation d'un homme sauvage; ou, Des premiers développemens physiques et moraux du jeune sauvage de l'Aveyron*. Itard opened the work with an invocation of Condillac's thought experiment of the two deserted children and closed with the claim of having provided 'a material proof of the most important truths . . . for the discovery of which Locke and Condillac were indebted merely to the force of their genius, and the depth of their reflections'.[62] The 'truths' were that in the state of nature man is inferior to many animals, that man's moral superiority is due to convention and civilization, that with society comes a multiplication of ideas and wants, and finally that progress in natural science is important for understanding the human species and aiding it.

If Itard's and Condillac's analyses of wild children functioned as an empirical confirmation of the origin of language and mind, and La Mettrie's and Diderot's invocations of the blind and deaf helped to question the absolute nature of morals, then Rousseau's and Monboddo's discussions of the orangutan differed in pointing toward political life. Monboddo took travel narratives describing the gentle and sociable life of orangutans and beavers, and tales about Kamchatkan sea-cats who are 'as brave as any Spartan',[63] as proof that political society existed before language, thus removing 'Mons. Rousseau's chief difficulty concerning the invention of language, by shewing that society, and even the political life, which he judges rightly to be necessary for the invention of language, may exist without language' (426). With this, he seemed to refute the criticisms of Ferguson and others that Rousseau's solitary man was impossible. In a similarly Rousseauian vein, he emphasized the orangutan's use of tools, which implied reason and a progressive and perfectible nature different from creatures of pure instinct (410–11).[64] The orangutan was thus viewed as an exhibition of original human nature, a living demonstration that society of a noble sort existed before language and property, although Monboddo did note that even the orangutan was already one step removed from the origin of man.

But what sort of society and nobility? Where Rousseau's orangutans in-sofar as they were natural men might be imagined as egalitarian and demo-cratic, Monboddo's monkey men were quite different. Although an admirer of Rousseau's criticisms of the moderns, Monboddo was an advocate of ancient meritocracy and saw in the orangutan a natural gentleman emerging from the undifferentiated herd to which democrats like Rousseau would return us. The orangutan was a sort of Greek hero, faster than Achilles, naturally noble, and manifesting the virtues of both servant and master.

The orangutan was not unique in providing an image of the state of nature from which to derive an ideal politics or to bemoan its loss. Many eighteenth-century authors discussed animal societies, including insect societies (particu-larly in France). But if orangutans according to Monboddo and Rousseau were human, then their passions and actions must bear some resemblance to ours, however removed. Thus, even if we cannot return to the original orangutan state, we can allow orangutan political arrangement as an ideal toward which we might aspire (for Monboddo if not Rousseau). But as William Smellie, natu-ralist, critic of Monboddo, and compiler of the *Encyclopaedia Brittanica*, pointed out, the same cannot be said of beavers, as their political successes arise from the fact that they are decidedly not human:

The society of beavers is a society of peace and of affection. They never quarrel or injure one another, but live together . . . in the most perfect harmony. The principle of their union is neither monarchical nor despotic. . . . [They] seem to acknowledge no chief or leader whatever. Their association presents to our observation a model of a pure and perfect republic, the only basis of which is mutual and unequivocal attachment. They have no law but the law of love and of parental affection. Humanity prompts us to wish that it were possible to establish republics of this kind among men. But the dispositions of men have little affinity to those of the beavers.[65]

IV. RACE AND NATURAL CHARACTER

In a discussion of goats in his *Histoire naturelle*, Buffon noted that 'the same species occasionally has two races, the one masculine and the other feminine'.[66] This is evidence of the fact that the word 'race' had quite different meanings to different eighteenth-century philosophers and naturalists. For Buffon, race was a methodological distinction to divide up the more basic unit of species. Kant's follower Christoph Girtanner discussed races of plants and animals. Smellie defined race in the *Encyclopaedia Britannica* as 'in genealogy, a lineage or extraction continued from father to son'.[67] For Kant, race primarily referred to skin color; for Kames, to a people's way of life. At least one historic law case hung on the vagueness of 'race' and racial designations such as 'negre'.[68] Yet despite this enormous variety of definitions, some consensus emerged during the century on what to consider in discussions of race, namely those essential qualities of humans that divided them into broad groups beyond civil society (although there were numerous counterexamples).

Unsurprisingly, then, race and its cognates intersected with concepts such as 'national character', 'Volscharakter', 'mores', and 'l'esprit des nations'. Different groups of individuals were viewed more or less in terms of race or national character. Most Western and Central Europeans were viewed as having national characters (or the like) and sharing a race ('white', 'European', 'Caucasian'), with the French and English normally meriting the most distinct, nuanced, and often strongly opposed character types. Some, such as Africans, American Indians, and Lapps, had race but rarely national characters and were viewed as amorphous entities with little internal differentiation (although many counterexamples will be given). Then, as now, the primary objects of interest in racial theories were Africans, with American Indians and Lapps of lesser but still great importance. The centrality of Africans in discussions of race was, of course, connected with the slave trade and the rise of abolitionism. Some groups, such as North Africans, Russians, Poles, Gypsies, Jews, and Turks, were indeterminate and difficult to classify for different reasons: Jews, and to a lesser extent Turks, fell under religious distinctions, North Africans were liminal,[69] as were Eastern Europeans and Gypsies, who were difficult to discuss within climatological theories. Race mostly involved physiognomic distinctions, character distinctions of mores, conventions, and culture (even if these were ultimately reducible to physical causes). Even for those authors who used 'national character' and 'race' interchangeably, there were troubles where the two met.[70]

Prior to the eighteenth century, many European racial theories were grounded in, or tacitly referred to, the story of Noah's three sons, particularly the identification of the cursed Ham and his son Cush with dark skin color and slavery. Each of Noah's sons formed an unchanging group with specific racial or religious features. By the mid-eighteenth century, many philosophers dismissed or derided this explanation,[71] although arguments that all humans descended from one original pair agreed with *Genesis in abstractu*. For the most part, though, racial discussions in the eighteenth century revolved less around Scripture and more around foundational questions in the new sciences of man: Which differences between peoples were 'natural' and physical? Which involved mutable 'artificial' qualities and mores? Did mankind descend from an original pair or did people from different regions descend from different pairs? Who and where were the original humans and how were human beings disseminated over the globe? What were the differences among the peoples of different climes and regions, and what effect did the differences have upon them and their societies? What distinguishes races?

As to distinctions between races, the eighteenth century's dubious contribution to the discussion of race was the centralization of physiognomic distinctions. Which distinctions, as well as which races, were important varied over the course of the century. But one consistent pattern was to locate between three and six races, two of which were invariably white Europeans and black Africans, to argue that there were basic differences between the races chosen (whether mutable or immutable), and that these races were, if not the only races, the most fundamental ones. 'Races' beyond the fundamental ones were viewed as mixtures derivative of more basic racial categories.

The eighteenth-century fascination with racial typologies goes back to François Bernier (1620–89) and earlier, but was popularized in works such as Linné's *Systema naturae* (1735). Linné presented four fundamental races – American, European, Asiatic, and African – and, as mentioned, various monstrous humans, wild men, and troglodytes. In addition to distinguishing the races through descriptions of their physiognomy and character, Linné also provided general claims about their social organizations: Africans were governed by caprice, Asians by opinions, Americans by customs, and Europeans by laws. Linné's distinctions between races accorded with his descriptive realism in natural philosophy in general, so he presented no connection between the political systems, characters, and physiognomies of the races he set forth in his stark typology.

Early in the century, there was relatively little discussion of race by philosophers and naturalists in comparison with the latter half of the century. Linné added the discussion of different types of men in later editions of the *Systema naturae* and expanded it until 1758–9. There was a great variety of travel literature, as well as numerous discussions of non-European cultures. But the philosophical discussions of other cultures were often a means of evaluating Europe and Europeans. Montesquieu's *Lettres persanes* (1721) used the seraglio as a means to criticize authoritarian societies and had as much to do with Persian life as Mandeville's *Fable* had to do with bees. Diderot wrote the *Supplément au Voyage de Bougainville* (posthumous, 1796) to criticize French sexual mores and the monkish virtues promoted by the clergy and, like Montesquieu, had the exotics describe Europeans in order to criticize French social arrangements. Even philosophical ethnographers, such as the renowned Lafitau, had European agendas. His *Moeurs des sauvages ameriquains comparées aux moeurs des premiers temps* (1724) set out to show that American Indians, like the ancient Greeks, believed in God and had a simple religion with vestigial trinitarianism that only later was corrupted by heathen nations, finally to be redeemed by Christianity. Lafitau was deflating the atheistic potential in cross-cultural comparison by arguing that all peoples had religions consistent with Christianity or had perverted them.

The non-Europeans who were perhaps taken most seriously, especially in Germany and France in the first half of the eighteenth century, were the Chinese, particularly Confucius and Confucians. Leibniz wrote about Confucianism knowledgeably and approvingly and compared Chinese and Christian natural theology.[72] Christian Wolff also wrote about Chinese philosophy, particularly moral philosophy, and his sinophilia led to accusations of atheism, controversy with Joachim Lange, and his expulsion from Halle.[73] Voltaire promoted the idea of the 'nation of sages' ceaselessly, seeing China as an ordered, tolerant alternative to a Jesuit-dominated France, while conveniently ignoring the fact that it was Jesuit missionaries who had supplied Europe with the Confucian idyll. Voltaire was particularly drawn to the perceived universalism and deism of Confucius and the fact that Chinese society functioned effectively with such a philosophical religion; he idealized Chinese justice, law, and government as a weapon against the Church. Others were somewhat less adulatory, particularly Montesquieu, who saw China as a despotic opposite to European freedom.[74] Hume viewed China as an example of how well-established and extensive government can result in uniform mores irrespective of great climatic differences, but with little scientific progress, as opposed to the individualistic English.[75]

China worship saw a serious decline in the second half of the eighteenth century. Ferguson followed Montesquieu in emphasizing China's political despotism,[76] while Smith noted that the stationary nature of the Chinese society and economy resulted in abominably low wages and great poverty for laborers, although enough to maintain a consistent population.[77] Mably, Raynal, Rousseau, Diderot, and Helvétius all criticized the slavishness of Chinese society and the Chinese people.[78] With the rise of scientific accounts of race, China was treated additionally as a racial type, Mongolian, Hun, or Asian, and in the work of authors such as Christoff Meiners became the depraved moral and racial opposite of European culture.

The other group that fascinated Voltaire and stood as a sort of opposite to the sagacious Chinese were the Jews. For the most part, the Jews were not central to discussions of race in the eighteenth century (despite pervasive anti-Semitism and political discrimination), as Jews were still part of a religious worldview. Some racial theorists, such as Charles White, used Jews as well as Gypsies as examples to show that climate did not have a great impact on human diversity. Others, such as the Spanish Benedictine Benito Jerónimo Feijoo y Montenegro, used the diversity of Jews to argue the opposite. But, for the most part, Jews were treated via older religious distinctions.

Voltaire discussed Jews in many places throughout his *Oeuvres*, making remarks so vitriolic as to startle even a hardened twenty-first-century reader.[79] As with his discussions of China, much of the impetus behind his attacks on the Jews was to criticize the corrupt origins of Christianity and the poverty of the doctrines shared by Christians and Jews in an, unfortunately, socially acceptable way. In Jews, Voltaire found an ideal target for his sarcasm and vitriol, a tone also present in his remarks about blacks and, of course, priests.

The most important responses to Voltaire were Isaac de Pinto's *Apologie pour la nation Juive* and Antoine Guénée's popular *Lettres de quelques juifs portugais et allemands à M. de Voltaire* (which went into new editions well into the second half of the nineteenth century).[80] De Pinto, an important economic theorist and critic of Hume and Mandeville on luxury, was noted by Voltaire but had little effect on him. Antoine Guénée's work purported to be a series of letters and commentaries by a diverse group of European Jews. Guénée defended the character of the Jews, the Old Testament, and by extension Christianity against Voltaire, pointing out countless interpretive errors along the way as well as the similarities between Voltaire's beloved Quakers and the Jews.

Voltaire responded to Guénée with *Le Viellard du mont caucase aux juifs por- tuguais, allemands, et polonais*, later titled *Un chrétien contre six juifs*. Beginning with anti-Jewish remarks from St. Jerome as license, but asking the pardon of de Pinto, whom Voltaire noted was 'greatly esteemed by Christians', Voltaire defended his picture of the Jews point by point, admitting that Guénée was intelligent if as 'wily as a monkey'.[81] However, it is difficult to view this as a controversy about race insofar as it primarily concerned Christianity, not to mention that biological definitions of Jews were not given. Jews stood as proxy, whipping boy, and defendant to Voltaire's prosecution.

In mid-century, other more important philosophers and naturalists discussed race in greater detail, particularly in Germany, England, and France. These theories were quite different from Voltaire's accounts of Chinese or Jews. Even Voltaire's polygenecism, as disturbing and bigoted as it was, mocked the vanity of the unity of mankind more than it attempted to provide a real explanation, and later writers agreed that 'he was equally a wretched philosopher and a brilliant wit' when writing about race.[82] Instead, as the century moved on, racial classifications were given natural scientific, causal explanations. Climate was emphasized, and races were primarily distinguished in terms of color, as well as hair and other external physical attributes such as size. In the last quarter of the century, there was a growing emphasis on distinguishing races through skull types and other 'immutable' skeletal and anatomical features, although some, such as Samuel Stanhope Smith, argued for skeletal mutability.

Writers of the early and middle eighteenth century, such as Voltaire, Maupertuis, Buffon, Le Cat, Feijoo, and many others, were particularly fascinated by the origin of dark skin color and 'white negroes' or albinos. The *Encyclopédie* listed 'Negre' and divided the article into 'Negre (*Hist. nat.*),' 'Negres Blancs (*Hist. nat.*),' 'Negres (Commerce.)', 'Negres (considérés comme esclaves dans les colonies de l'Amérique)'; the first two discussed skin color at length, the latter two slavery. Similarly, the first edition of Smellie's *Encyclopaedia Britannica* devoted four paragraphs to 'negroes,' two concerning skin color and two slavery.

The most popular climatological theory of race was that presented in Buffon's *Histoire naturelle*. Buffon argued that all human beings descended from the same germ, and although various human groups had different traits, they all shared an 'inner form' that differed radically from the form of animals and all other living beings. From the perspective of Buffon's philosophy of nature, humans formed a species, as all humans were capable of creating viable and fertile offspring, regardless of the physiognomic variances of different populations. These physiognomic variances distinguished races, and races, in turn, marked divergences within a species.

Buffon distinguished human races by various markers with different causes. Skin, eye, and hair color were produced by the most important cause, climate, while other traits such as size and hair texture arose from a region's food and even *moeurs*, by which Buffon understood a people's practical way of life. Given their many causes, races for Buffon were something impermanent and mutable. As populations moved and their climates changed, so, in theory, did their races, although to prove it, Buffon admitted, one would have to transplant Ethiopians to Denmark and wait to see what happened.[83] On the rare occasions when Buffon spoke of 'black' and 'white' races, he noted that Africa had a greater variety of skin color, size, hair, and other features than any other continent.[84]

These descriptive aspects of Buffon's racial anthropology were explained via a general theory of the observed variation. All races descended from an original pair of whites; additional qualities found in non-white races were caused by the climate. To explain the diversity of flora and fauna between continents, Buffon developed a theory of degeneration that was tacitly applied to humanity, particularly to American Indians.[85] American Indians were stunted, like all the flora and fauna of the New World, lacking in 'ardor', and hairless. Their lack of ardor perhaps contributed to the meager human population of the New World, which was insufficient to produce any civilization, leaving its inhabitants 'all equally stupid, equally ignorant, equally devoid of art and industry'.[86] Although the theory of degeneration was not systematically employed by Buffon to explain race, it was objected to by many, perhaps most famously by Jefferson, who argued both that the American landscape supported animals and plants as large as or larger than their European counterparts and that American Indians had sufficient ardor and were capable of oratorical genius.[87]

Buffon's ordering of races with reference to a white archetype was combined with aestheticization and the identification of beauty with good mores and ugliness with repellent mores.[88] The combination of a theory of degeneracy that was not obviously reversible, a climatology making racial differences gradual and mutable, and an aestheticization of race and mores made for a somewhat confusing combination, as pointed out by a number of critics. These tensions are characteristic of a great deal of racial literature.

A far more extreme attitude was found in Cornelius de Pauw's popular and controversial *Recherches philosophiques sur les Américains* (1768–69). De Pauw, like Buffon (who criticized him), argued for the climatic degeneration of the New World, but in far more extreme terms. The climate of the New World degraded all who entered it – human, plant, or animal. Native Americans were the source of venereal disease, had little regard for life, death, or the sufferings of others, and had most known vices. Still, de Pauw harshly criticized the destruction of the New World and saw its human inhabitants, although 'barely beyond the level of the quadrupeds, and of other animals abandoned to their instinct', as depraved, untutored children, not nearly as objectionable as the 'wretched Asiatics' who were conscious of their vices.[89]

De Pauw also saw the climate of the New World as further damaging Africans, whose intellects had already been enfeebled by 'the fire of their natal climate'(*Recherches philosophiques*, 182). The New World caused them, like all of its inhabitants, to lose their ardor and made the continuous importation of slaves necessary, a status for which de Pauw thought Africans particularly well-suited (28–9, 182). This led him to claim that species distinctions between whites and blacks ought not to be based on skin color or facial features but on intelligence (189). Still, despite the racism inherent in this remark, de Pauw's theory is staunchly climatological and looks back toward Buffon and the sarcastic tone of Voltaire far more than forward toward the technical language and immutable physiological qualities in racial theories of the 1770s.

There was another important strand of climate theory, which emphasized the importance of air, sometimes in conjunction with climate and sometimes distinct from it. John Arbuthnot had argued that air formed the 'Manners of Mankind, which are found to vary much in different Countries and Climates'.[90] The influential aesthetician the Abbé Du Bos had argued that the artistic genius of different nations was due in a great part to air and climate. Du Bos minimized the importance of *les causes morales* and argued that *les causes physiques,* particularly changes in air quality, were able to explain the variations of genius in the history of a people. Air also provided the basis for the analysis of national character.[91] Neither Du Bos nor Arbuthnot was particularly interested in race, but the previously mentioned Feijoo argued in 'Color etiópico' that sun and temperature were insufficient as an explanation of race; air must be added to provide an adequate explanation (in a world before Priestley's discovery of dephlogisticated air). As with Buffon, the theory implied skin color changing with climate.[92]

A central question in the discussion of climate and race that seems quite peculiar today was the status of 'white negroes', the inhabitants of the 'torrid zone' who had not turned black. Buffon saw them as Africans (or Indians, as he noted the existence of albinism on other continents) who had further degenerated, but it is not clear what sort of explanation, given his emphasis on climate in explaining skin color in general,[93] he could give for what he considered singular and individual mutations. De Pauw wrote a lengthy chapter on it.[94] The proximate and remote source of their interests, and the interest of many *philosophes*, was a young albino boy, of African-American extraction, who had been displayed in Paris at the Académie des Sciences and was considered by Voltaire, Maupertuis, and Fontenelle.

Voltaire discussed albinism in a number of works (most notably the *Essai sur les moeurs*), arguing that albinos were an independent race inferior even to Hottentots, with a different origin, a theory derided even by de Pauw.[95] Maupertuis's analysis, on which the *Encyclopédie* article was based, was taken far more seriously. Albinos were an essential test of his embryology, as any theory of generation and gestation must explain why light-skinned children are occasionally born to dark-skinned parents. Thus Maupertuis assumed, *contra* Voltaire, that albinos did not form a race unto themselves – although the myth of a tribe of white Africans persisted late into the eighteenth century.

Maupertuis argued that women's eggs and men's seminal animalcules usually combine along established lines, but there are occasional deviations and white children are born from black parents (as well as the entire spectrum between). But why then are black children not commonly born from white parents? Maupertuis saw the prevalence of white albinos as demonstrating that all men had common white ancestors, although it was entirely possible that white families could become black. Unlike Voltaire, Maupertuis thus emphasized races as various possibilities of human beings in general, and, unlike Buffon, as innate dispositions arising from combination. One possible consequence of this theory, noted with interest by Kant, was breeding for desired qualities, or eugenics.[96]

A third and very influential explanation was given by Nicolas Le Cat. Le Cat saw dark skin as having its basis in the color of the nerve fluid specific to blacks, although blacks and whites were anatomically similar in most other respects. Le Cat conjectured that white negroes were to blacks as pink-eyed white rabbits were to black rabbits, a mutation specific to one of the three basic colors of human beings (black, white, and copper). Le Cat also analyzed how whites could become black, arguing it had a cause quite different from albinism, namely skin disease.[97] Later, Benjamin Rush used a similar analysis to explain how the original white humans had become black, emphasizing that blackness was merely skin deep.[98]

As the century went on, however, more authors concentrated on anatomical features beneath the skin. For example, in *An Account of the Regular Gradation in Man* (1799), Charles White assumed that all living things were continuously, hierarchically graded, and as the inferiority of Africans and their proximity to orangutans was scientifically demonstrable, so it was clear that Africans were the link between whites and orangutans and that whites and blacks were species with different origins.[99] In order to demonstrate this, White employed charts, measurements (particularly of skulls; he was trained by the famous surgeon and naturalist John Hunter, whose skull collection provided White's initial insight about the gradations of man), scientific names, scholarly references, samples of the population of London, and other pseudo-scientific trappings, all of which were vociferously and effectively attacked by his critics, who also attacked his conflicting claims that blacks both were and were not human.[100] Finally, White ordained that the divergences among humans showed immutable differences in the nature of men, pointing to the diverse origins of different groups of men as opposed to the unity of the human species in a shared descent from an original pair.

Whereas Buffon's account of race was part of a more general philosophy of nature, of which the description of the natural history of mankind was only a part, White localized race as *the* central question upon which tools of the sciences were brought to bear. Conversely, for White, 'science' was able to discover permanent features of the races that caused particular features of character, something neither Buffon nor Blumenbach would allow. To do this, White drew on those thinkers from the second half of the eighteenth century who had focused on racial features other than color. The influential Peter Camper had shown that the races could be 'ranked' via facial angles, although Camper's analysis was intended only as a tool for making more accurate drawings of the human figure.[101] John Hunter had theorized similarly about cheekbone angles.[102] Samuel Thomas Soemmering had concluded, based on comparative anatomical studies, that the nerves at the base of the brain were larger in blacks than whites, and thus they were a different, intellectually inferior race.[103]

All of these thinkers, unlike White, asserted that blacks, even if they formed a race different from whites, were human and radically different from the higher apes: they assumed the fundamental unity of the human species even if some of its members were less human. White alone took the next step of arguing 'scientifically' what had previously been asserted by crude racists such as Edward Long, that blacks stood in between whites and higher apes, although White's account was deeply incoherent on the issue of whether blacks were part of the human species or not. But White and the others were united in following the great zoological classifications of Buffon and Linné and the growth in comparative anatomy (particularly Tyson's influential anatomical comparison between man and orangutan).[104] 'Comparative anatomy' compared animals, or animals and humans (human anatomy was not comparative but anatomy as such). White and others applied it, however misguidedly, to the search for the origin of human nature in the structure of the human body itself, with the underlying assumption that it would reveal which peoples were more or less human.

The celebrated anatomist and naturalist Johann Friedrich Blumenbach opposed the definitions of species by Soemmering and Camper, but particularly that of Buffon. Buffon's criterion, namely the ability to create fertile offspring, was rejected, as it had the unfortunate consequence that all dogs, from Great Dane to Pekinese, belonged to the same species! Blumenbach replaced it with a definition emphasizing those similarities of formal features intransigent through climate and inexplicable by it.[105] This definition, unlike that of Buffon but like that of Camper and others, stressed anatomical comparison and played an important role in moving accounts of race away from external description to structural comparisons. But unlike White and Soemmering (both of whom cited him to legitimate their arguments), Blumenbach employed comparative anatomy to argue against the chain of being, for the unity and structural similarity of the races, and for the relative unimportance of climatic differences in comparison with man's unique capacity for artificial self-cultivation. Like Buffon, Blumenbach stressed the great variety of Africans, and humans in general, as opposed to strict racial typology, and strongly emphasized their full mental and physical equality.[106]

Blumenbach also analyzed race through skulls. Ethiopians and Mongolians each had their own extreme skull features, with Caucasians providing the perfect symmetrical balance in between. Notably, though, Blumenbach emphasized skull diversity as being primarily the product of art and modes of life. Thus he seemed to anchor Buffon's equation between mores and physiognomy beneath the skin while giving an un-Buffonian primacy to mores and their ability to degenerate the body 'into a second nature' (*De generis humani varietate nativa*, 121). These remarks would later be taken up by Samuel Stanhope Smith.

Given his arguments for the fundamental unity of mankind, one would expect Blumenbach to condemn the slave trade and White to defend it. Surprisingly,

White closes *An Account of the Regular Gradation in Man* with a liberal plea for abolition, arguing that intelligence ought not to be the guarantor of civic rights. Similar apparent contradictions, between virulent denigrations of blacks as hardly or not at all human and vigorous attacks on the slave trade in the name of humanity, can be found in the works of Franklin, Raynal, Hume, Voltaire, Forster, and many others. Jefferson, after praising the virtue of American Indians *contra* Buffon, attacked the intelligence and character of the American Negro while at the same time arguing against slavery and invoking the necessity of separating whites and blacks after emancipation so that blacks could 'be removed beyond the reach of mixture', all the while admitting that the inferiority of blacks is 'a suspicion only'.[107]

Smellie's *Encyclopaedia Britannica* article is more the norm in this regard than the *Encyclopédie* articles on 'Negres'. The latter attempted to humanize Africans in order to highlight the brutality of the slave trade, as did much popular literature in France and England, such as the various *Oronooko* plays, showing the nobility of Africans and the turpitude of traders.[108] But philosophers, like Smellie, tended to separate race from slavery, which in many cases made a great deal of argumentative sense. The condemnation of slavery as an economic institution by Adam Smith and John Millar held irrespective of any particular features of the slave, as it did for Hume and Mirabeau, and derived its argumentative force from minimal, universal features of men arrived at through the empirical analysis of history and economic practices. Smith argued that slavery arose from an unsavory, but unfortunately universal, aspect of human nature, that 'the pride of man makes him love to domineer', which manifested itself in societies where there were no countervailing forces.[109] Both Smith and Millar argued that slavery was far less economically productive than competitive labor markets.[110]

Although few important philosophers were actively involved in the antislavery movement, philosophical arguments found their way into anti-slavery pamphlets (as well as those of advocates of slavery such as Edward Long). Granville Sharp, one of the architects of the demise of slavery in England, argued against the 'just war' defense of slavery, notorious in Locke's works and often used as a legitimation of slavery a century later. Sharp reasoned that the just war argument could only justify public slavery (as in public jails), not private slavery.[111] Sharp drew heavily on Hutcheson's important arguments against just war and hereditary slavery and the Scottish jurist George Wallace's even stronger claims that slavery had no place in Scottish law.[112] Hutcheson was also used to justify the arguments of Anthony Benezet, who, with John Woolman, spearheaded the Quaker abolitionist movement, ran a school in Philadelphia for free blacks, and compiled the earliest volume of anti-slavery literature.[113]

Condorcet was an important exception to the general rule that philosophers were not involved in the practical business of abolition; Paley was another. Condorcet's writings and actions accorded with what one might have expected of an Enlightenment intellectual. In *Réflexions sur l'esclavage des nègres*, a lengthy pamphlet for the *Société des amis des noires*, he asserted that blacks 'had the same mind, the same reason and the same virtues' as European whites but ought not to be insulted by being compared with the whites of the colonies: 'if one wants to find a man [*homme*] in the American Isles, he won't be found among white-skinned folk [*gens*]'.[114]

Condorcet provided a detailed plan to remedy slavery, providing for slaves' autonomy, economic stability, and self-esteem. He attacked the economics of slavery as well as its brutality and racism, but the fundamental argument was political and moral (*Réflexions*, §5). Even if it were the case that slavery was essential to the success of the colonies, this could never legitimate it. Slavery was a criminal act depriving a man not only of his property and means of acquiring it 'but of the property of his time, of his force, of all that which nature has given him to conserve his life or satisfy his desires. . . . Either there are no morals, or they must admit this principle' (§1). In denying fundamental rights to men, the legislator committed a criminal act violating the contract on which political society was based and the rights it was erected to preserve.

The implicit presupposition of Condorcet's liberalism was that men everywhere are the same and have fundamentally the same desires, which are to be served by a liberal civil order. In order to claim this, he denied a crucial Montesquieuian proposition, stating 'it is neither climate, nor terrain, nor constitution, nor national spirit to which the laziness of certain peoples ought to be attributed; it is the bad laws that govern them' (§6, 18).

Condorcet's implied criticism pointed to conflicts between the desire for scientific explanation of differences in national character and the universal application of good laws to human nature. Throughout Europe, the fifteenth chapter of Montesquieu's *De l'esprit de lois* was taken as a definitive attack on slavery. Yet, when viewed in context, serious conflicts arose between discussions of national character and discussions of slavery. Montesquieu condemned slavery in Europe as destructive of both the slave and the slaver (XV.1), mocked the rationales of the advocates of slavery with crushing irony (XV.5), attacked the economic arguments for slavery (XV.8), and identified slavery with bad laws and despotic government (XV.6). But he also provided a second despotic origin of slavery, that 'there are some countries where heat enervates the body and weakens the courage so greatly that men can only be induced to perform unpleasant duties by fear of punishment' (XV.7). In such despotic climates, slavery is still against nature, but it is founded on 'natural reason' and therefore deserves less blanket condemnation than in Europe. While against any slavery in Europe, in the colonies Montesquieu emphasized better treatment for the slaves.

In Book XIV, Montesquieu had argued that laws ought to be relevant to the differences in characters and passions caused by different climates. Thus, in hot climates laws ought to induce people to labor, and the laws already established in those climates will reflect the needs of particular temperaments resulting from the action of the climate on the senses and passions. This climatology would seem to conflict with the equality of men, resulting in the legitimation of practices and laws in one climate due to needs that bring national characters and the universality of reason into conflict. In other nations, such institutions would be pointless, intolerable, or altered due to the action of climate on character (XIV.15, XVII.5). However, Montesquieu is not arguing for simple climatological determinism, as is made clear in many passages emphasizing the importance of moral causes. The difficulty in Montesquieu, and the source of Condorcet's remark, seems to arise from the conflict between immutable natural causes (such as the impact of physiology or climate) and their mutable practices (such as mores), with national laws and their spirit perching precariously between.

A related problem arises in Hume's essay 'Of National Characters' (1748). Hume took the divergences between national characters as important, if often overstated. In 'The Rise and Progress of the Arts and Sciences' (1742), he explored the complicated and mutually supportive relations between nation, character, mores, and government, focusing on France and England. In 'Of National Characters', he continued the discussion more generally, following Du Bos in distinguishing between 'physical causes', such as climate, and 'moral causes', such as general rules, manners, or a nation's situation with regard to its government and neighbors, which communicate like a contagion 'through the whole club or knot of companions'.[115] Hume argued, *contra* Du Bos, that the latter almost wholly explained national characters.

This emphasis on moral causes, although not the norm, was shared by philosophers such as Helvétius, Diderot, and Rousseau, each of whom would use it to emphasize, in quite different ways, the fundamental mutability of man through education, irrespective of physical conditions. Hume asserted that men owe nothing 'of their temper or genius to the air, food, or climate' and emphasized instead the power of mores and manners. These are sometimes as difficult to change as the climate, and their intransigence and power arise from belief, which, in Hume's moral psychology, gave mores a stubborn character foreign to Helvétius's sensationalism.

Yet Hume's apparently thoroughgoing emphasis on moral causes does not hold for blacks,[116] who according to Hume differ so uniformly and consistently from whites that nature must have 'made an original distinction between these breeds of men' (*Of National Characters*, 86n). Although Hume admitted that whites also had rude origins, even then they had a dignity lacking in non-whites. Hume countered the possible objection that there were learned blacks by claiming that they were 'admired for slender accomplishments, like a parrot, who speaks a few words plainly' (86n).

James Beattie ferociously attacked Hume for reverting to a modern version of Aristotle's 'natural slave argument' in arguing for the inferiority of blacks. Associating Hume with slavery was not fair, as Hume's 'Of the Populousness of Ancient Nations' was an important source of anti-slavery arguments and was cited approvingly by anti-slavery advocates. But Beattie compellingly argued that Hume dangerously confused the capacities of a people and their condition as slaves, showing a troubling lack of ability to understand the devastation of slavery.[117] Lord Monboddo noted against Hume that the ancient Egyptians were the source of Greek learning and an African people unequaled by modern Europeans. To the objection that sub-Saharan Africans have 'thicker' features, Monboddo remarked, 'I hope the reader will not believe that the qualities of the mind depend on the features of the face, any more than upon the colour of the skin or the nature of the hair.'[118]

Both Beattie and Monboddo were interested in confuting far more than Hume's racism. They were attempting Christian revivals of ancient philosophy and saw Hume's scepticism as irreligious and immoral, with the footnote to 'Of National Characters' as a particularly satanic implication. Others praised Hume, such as the racist Edward Long and, more surprisingly, Kant, who in the concluding section of *Beobachtungen über das Gefühl des Schönen und Erhabenen* provided an aesthetic turn on Hume's 'Of National Characters', contrasting different national characters in terms of their varied aesthetic feelings.[119] Kant reduplicated Hume's natural distinction between whites and non-whites and cited Hume's footnote with great approval while adding his own scathing remarks about blacks.

It would be absurd to take these isolated remarks as the whole of Hume and Kant. But Hume's footnote in particular points to conflicts between nature and artifice in his thinking about human nature. If it is the case that 'such a uniform and constant difference could not happen, in so many countries and ages, if nature had not made an original distinction betwixt these breeds of men',[120] does it then follow that uniform differences that hold over a variety of different circumstances point to natural distinctions? Furthermore, why do moral causes not hold in these humans set apart by nature? Do they, like animals, lack sufficient refinement to have an aesthetic or moral sense and therefore to be alert to the aesthetic and moral contagions informing the higher humans?[121] Must the artificial be anchored in inviolable, natural distinctions? Like Montesquieu, for whom the conflict between the natural and the artificial manifested itself in the two natural origins of slavery, for Hume certain mores had to be separated from humanity in order to preserve the plausibility and stability of 'our' conventional world.

Unlike Hume, Kant modified his views on race dramatically, arguing from 1775 onward that all races derived from an original white-skinned, brown-haired root (*Stammgattung*) and gained persistent skin coloration due to their interactions with the climates to which they emigrated, a feature that did not disappear upon transplantation.[122] Color was the ultimate marker of race, as no other physiognomic feature, when crossed with another, resulted in a consistent mixture. Four colors – white, black, copper-red, and olive-yellow – were sufficient to generate all other racial half-breeds, functioning as constitutive racial categories with white and black as *Grundrassen*.[123] Kant provided a theoretical twist on the color-based racial categorizations prevalent in the mid-eighteenth century.

After 1775, Kant distinguished between character, temperament, and race in order to avoid biological determinism. Race was a purely physical designation, centered on color. Temperament had both bodily and psychological aspects, the bodily constitution perhaps mysteriously influencing psychological qualities, such as the sanguine, the phlegmatic, and so forth. A character, in contradistinction to temperament, was the set of practical principles that an individual prescribed to herself or himself through reason. This could be good or bad, and Kant notes that we generally admire a bad character over a good temperament without character.[124]

But when Kant discussed a nation or a people, difficulties appeared. Kant variously claimed in his *Anthropologie in Pragmatischer Hinsicht* (1798) that Poles had had character but lost it, Russians had not yet developed any character, and European Turks 'never have had the character of a people, nor will ever attain one' (319). Clearly, Kant saw the periphery of Europe as being relatively characterless. But as Kant viewed the character of a people as being distinct from government or climate and, in opposition to Hume, thought that there was a very close connection between national character and the characters of the individuals who made up the nation, it is unclear how one might deny the capacity for character to a whole people – and whether by doing so one also denied them the capacities as individuals. Furthermore, by diminishing the importance of race and emphasizing the moral potential of the human 'race' as a whole, irrespective of the failures of individuals or groups, Kant created a new problem with *Volkscharakter* – although very tentatively.

The two possibilities such a theory could take are exemplified by Kant's student Christoph Girtanner and Kant's sometime critic Christoph Meiners. Kant wrote little about race and instead suggested that readers consult Girtanner's 'development of his principles' (*Anthropologie*, 320). Girtanner's *Über das Kantische Prinzip für die Naturgeschichte* (1796) follows Kant's theory of color and mixtures and broadens it to take in a vast amount of anthropological observation and the latest developments in racial discussions, particularly those of Blumenbach.[125] Following the Kantian distinction between natural history and natural description, Girtanner set out to provide a history of man as exhaustive as E. A. Zimmermann's monumental description of man's geographical diversity – *Geographische Geschichte des Menschen* (1778–83).[126] Girtanner's work in fact shows how cosmopolitan racial discussions had become by the end of the century, as he easily moved back and forth between different languages and vastly different theories. Meiners, on the other hand, developed the distinction between good and bad characters in a way Kant could not approve of: by ranking the races according to their various moral potentials and viewing them all on a scale with white Europeans and Mongols as the respective good and bad extremes.[127] In his early works, Meiners saw these differences as being environmentally conditioned, but in a later effort, he suggested that the ranking was inherent.[128]

Kant's own racial theory was criticized by Georg Forster and Kant's student Johann Gottfried Herder. Forster had a subtle and firsthand understanding of the great variations of human society from his education in England, Russia, and Germany and from his part in Captain Cook's second expedition, about which he wrote in *Voyage Round the World*.[129] Unsurprisingly, Forster attacked Kant's emphasis on color, his reduction of color to a fourfold typology, and the theoretical attitude that governed this reduction. His empirical criticisms of Kant led Forster to attack Kant's monogenism, arguing that the best empirical hypothesis was different origins for different races in the different climates to which they were suited. Polygenism demanded no extraneous theorizing about common ancestors.

Following the work of his friend Soemmering, who had argued that black brains had larger nerves than those of whites and were thus mentally inferior, Forster claimed that blacks formed a race different from Europeans. Given this difference, and given the fact that color was changeable through the mixing of races, how did races maintain their consistent features? Forster concluded that each race had an innate instinct that prevented it from intermixing with other races, preserving distinct groups within a whole, and supplemented his empirical polygenism with an argument against 'repellent' (*Ekel*) racial mixing.[130]

This obviously conflicted with Forster's Jacobinism, his belief in the fundamental equality of humankind, and his Leibnizian holistic and gradualist vision of the interconnections of the entirety of nature.[131] Unlike earlier philosophers, such as Voltaire, whose sarcastic polygenism insulted non-Europeans and claimed the divergent origins of blacks, Asians, and other races in order to undercut the biblical account,[132] Forster's was a seriously weighed and deeply conflicted union of misguided empiricism and a political and metaphysical universalism. Forster's example, like White's internal confusion about whether blacks were human or not, goes a long way toward showing how various strands of the eighteenth-century sciences of man came into deep conflict: political universalism, comparative anatomy, geographic diversity, and the search for origins combine into a confused and fascinating mixture. The same can be said, if less extremely and *without* the important ingredient of comparative anatomy, about Kant, Hume, and Montesquieu.

Comparing Forster with Lord Kames and Herder demonstrates even further the difficulty of discussing late eighteenth-century theories of the diverse origins of the human species under one rubric such as polygenism, and it also shows that there were important exceptions to the general shift to biological accounts of race. Unlike the much younger Forster, Lord Kames was a Christian, who attempted to reconcile polygenism with the Mosaic account. Like Forster, Kames thought polygenism to be an obvious consequence of the empirical study of man, but unlike Soemmering, White, Camper, and others, his arguments were primarily based on history and ethnography – not comparative anatomy (although he thought human biological organization differed among the species of men). His 'polygenism' was more akin to the work of the so-called conjectural historians[133] and to the proto-Romantic Herder, as his Christianity led him to emphasize the unity of all men of whatever species.

In order to bolster his arguments, Kames, like Blumenbach, criticized Buffon's claim that all dogs belonged to one species. As Darwin's finches would in the nineteenth century, dogs offered an analogy for human variety and descent. Did dogs descend from one common ancestor or a mixture of jackals, wolves, and more? Were the great variations in dog-kind due to climate?[134] Kames argued that if dogs were shown not to belong to one species, then, by analogy, 'there are different species of men as well as of dogs: a mastiff differs not more from a spaniel, than a white man from a negro, or a Laplander from a Dane'.[135] In order to allow for this, Kames posited a multiplicity of Adams and Eves that 'were fitted by nature for different climates' (*Sketches of the History of Man*, I: 23). All the species were human, made in the image of God, and their variations were due to God-given qualities for coping with their original climates. Despite his criticisms of Buffon, for Kames climate had an effect when groups suited to one region migrated to a new region, resulting in degeneration from the original place to which they were suited. Kames took the climatic degeneration of non-whites as proof of polygenism; it was not only whites who found it hard to cope with a new climate.

Groups also had different internal dispositions, or national characters, and these were as important as, if not more important than, physical characteristics in identifying a race. Kames saw the enormous variety of racial characters, in similar stages of society, as proof that theories of history such as Ferguson's or Robertson's were empirically false because they viewed all men as having a similar sort of character at the simplest stages of society (I: 44–5).[136] This was also assumed to hold for other conjectural histories: if man was diverse in his first stage, the history of mankind was irremediably sketchy and conjectures had to proceed along very general lines. Progress was intermittent and complicated. Like Buffon, though, Kames vacillated between the idea of considering race as a totally local concept and the idea of a few fundamental races derived from their respective Adams and Eves.

Although Kames's polygenism seems particularly benign and he emphasized climate to a far greater degree than the comparative anatomist polygenecists, he still had difficulties discussing Africans. Kames remarked that 'the colour of the Negroes, as above observed, affords a strong presumption of their being a different species from the Whites; And I once thought that the presumption was supported by inferiority of understanding in the former'. But now Kames claimed that insofar as the African continent is so luxuriant that the inhabitants have little need to use their intellect, and Africans abroad are mostly slaves, there is not sufficient evidence on which to judge them inferior. Yet Kames immediately equivocated, 'yet, after all, there seems to be some original difference' as Hindus live in a similarly idyllic climate but have made great intellectual advances (I: 64–5).

Comparing Kames with the arch-monogenecist Herder complicates matters still further. Herder essentially denied the meaningfulness of race and emphasized instead the centrality of culture in the constitution of distinct human groups, views criticized by Kant in a famous review.[137] For Herder, all men were equally instinctless, malleable, adaptive, and perfectible until they entered society, where the specific customs and traditions of a people were transmitted to them and allowed them to cope with their surroundings and express their natures. Man was both radically diverse and radically united: each individual was a unique expressive world, a part of a family, a community, a nation, and psychically one with the rest of mankind.

Unsurprisingly, Herder showed a remarkable and unusual relativism toward other cultures, exemplified by his well-known remarks about Africans:

It is but just, when we proceed to the country of the blacks, that we lay aside our proud prejudices, and consider the organization of this quarter of the Globe with as much impartiality, as if there were no other. Since whiteness is a mark of degeneracy in many animals near the pole, the negro has as much right to term his savage robbers albinoes and white devils, degenerated through the weakness of nature, as we have to deem him the emblem of evil, and a descendent of Ham, branded by his father's curse. I, might he say, I, the black, am the original man. I have taken the deepest draughts from the source of life, the Sun.[138]

Although Herder ranked the relative progress of peoples, an anarchistic and relativistic strain is evident throughout his early work, drawing him to emphasize the unique genius of almost every people, except the Gypsies.[139] By subordinating the influence of nature to human adaptation, sociability, and language, Herder was able to consider the characters of human groups as the unique expressions of their particular customs and situations, all of which joined the unity of human experience and genius.

But in many ways the racial theories that Herder approaches most closely are those of his polygenecist contemporaries Forster and, particularly, Kames. His criticisms of Kant were quite similar to those of Forster. His emphasis on culture as essential to 'racial' identity, on the importance of custom as a means of transmitting this identity, on the relative virtues of a multiplicity of cultures within a generally progressivist scheme, and on man's situatedness in nature and relation to the rest of nature by analogy while at the same time being a sociable, instinctless, perfectible, and radically distinct being – all these features are similar to those of Kames, perhaps a consequence of their common indebtedness to the ever-present Rousseau. The comparison shows that perhaps the rubrics 'polygenist' and 'monogenist,' though useful, are less important than how thinkers conceptualized race within broader political, natural historical, and social theories and the contradictions arising in relation to these different ways of presenting it.

It is appropriate to conclude with a 'monogenist' who fuses together different strands of eighteenth-century discussions as interestingly as did Kames, the American Samuel Stanhope Smith. The first edition of his *An Essay on the Causes of the Variety of Complexion and Figure in the Human Species* (1787) was a reasonably straightforward Christian, monogenist, climatological critique of polygenists, particularly Kames. But by the time the second edition appeared in 1810, Smith had been deeply influenced by Blumenbach and angered at the appropriation of Blumenbach's work by White, Soemmering, and others (he used 'the respectable naturalist' Forster's relativistic remarks in *A Voyage* to bolster his claims, unaware of Forster's racism).[140]

Emphasizing Blumenbach's arguments for skeletal mutability through climate and his comparative anatomical revision of Buffon's species definition, Stanhope Smith argued that climate operates in proportion to the savageness of a society

(93). As society advances, climate can be warded off, diet improved, marriages cultivated for a particular notion of beauty, manners and taste inculcated, and both mind and body transformed! Thus Stanhope Smith links a progressivist Scottish account of the transformative power of society and manners to a climatological racial theory, arriving at the power of climate to cause degeneration and of society to cultivate and transform.

What will the result be for the American blacks? In his 'Animadversions on Certain Remarks Made on the First Edition of This Essay, By Mr. Charles White', Smith argued that the American blacks are generally whitening in their new climate and, *contra* Jefferson, White, and others, that the deformities of their skulls were the product of climate, barbarism, and the wretched condition of slavery (151–64). Given Smith's principles, one might reasonably expect them to become 'white' in body and mind. Thus the peculiar result of Smith's monogenism was the gradual 'whitening' of the human race through civilizing, with race as the forgotten marker of savagery. The physical and anatomical nature of race, and the animal in general, could be transcended through the unifying power of European culture. But note the remark of Smith's anonymous, and mostly approving, reviewer:

He affirms, that the native blacks in America *mend* in their *colour, features*, and *hair*, in every generation. This would be controverted, no doubt, by a negro critic, who would certainly object to the word *mend*; which however, perhaps, he would candidly consider as an error of the press, & shortly say 'for *mend* read *degenerate*:' and 'for *hair*, read *wool*.[141]

V. WOMEN, MARRIAGE, AND FEMALE EDUCATION

Antoine-Léonard Thomas, when weighing the relative intellectual and moral merits of women and men in his popular book *Essai sur le caractère, les moeurs et l'esprit des femmes dans les différens siecles* (1772), lamented that the philosophers of 'the seventeenth century, the most brilliant of epochs, which had created and asked this question' had much more compelling things to say about it, and more interest in it, than his contemporaries.[142] It is not surprising that Thomas came to this conclusion. Although there were countless considerations of the sexes in poetry, novels, educational manuals, conduct literature, satires, and so forth, philosophers seemed to say little new on behalf of the equality of the sexes in the middle years of the eighteenth century. In the late seventeenth century and early eighteenth century, Poulain de la Barre, Mandeville, Judith Drake, Mary Astell, and others argued for the (relative) equality of male and female minds and against the hypocrisy of women's exclusion from education. In the late eighteenth century, Olympe de Gouges, Catharine Macaulay, Mary Wollstonecraft, Mary Hays, Condorcet, and others explicated contradictions in the expansion of political rights for 'men' while denying them to some 'men' – that is, women.[143] But for Thomas both 1789 and de la Barre, whom Thomas thought the most impressive of the seventeenth-century thinkers on women, were remote.[144]

Thomas's comment is also somewhat misleading. The sexes, and their differences, were a major topic of discussion in the eighteenth century, but the ways in which the sexes were considered often bore little similarity to de la Barre's arguments that 'L'Esprit n'a point de Sexe'[145] – that the merely physiological differences between women and men had little effect on their intellectual capacities. Thomas's own writings were in fact characteristic of mid-eighteenth-century attitudes towards what would later be called the 'woman question', despite his ingrained nostalgia for the seventeenth century. In opposition to de la Barre, he denied women the capacity for logical and philosophical reasoning and for action in the political sphere. Women rather excel in religion (de la Barre had also emphasized religious virtues), in the domestic virtues, and in some aspects of the social virtues, a verdict heavily influenced by Rousseau. But more importantly, an age that respects women and their virtues is a moral age and one that benefits from the tempering effect of the female moral virtues.[146] Thus women are idealized within the spheres of religion, the home, and polite society, while considered inferior in philosophy and politics, and the recognition of their ideal status reflects on the importance of morality and *tendresse* in a given period. A few, notably Mme. D'Epinay, criticized Thomas on the grounds that there were no decisive differences between male and female virtues.[147] But Thomas's idea of the differences between the male and female, with women characterized not by their intellect but by their morality, were of a piece with diverse notable views such as Burke's argument that Marie Antoinette provided a feminine ideal to be worshipped, Bentham's discussion of women as intellectually weaker but stronger in morals, sensibility, and religion, Rousseau's account of Sophie in *Émile* (clearly the major influence on Thomas), and even Diderot's *Sur les femmes*, which portrays women as creatures given to moral extremes, in criticism of Thomas's idealizations.[148]

As with race, the questions and assumptions underlying these arguments will be explored, as will those of other advocates of the sciences of man, such as the authors of the *Encyclopédie* articles 'L'Homme (morale)' and 'Femme'. Whereas animals were mostly considered not human and non-white peoples liminally human, there was no question for most authors that women were human (although in 'Femme (anthropologie)' an anonymous author was cited who had argued that 'women are not part of the human genus *mulieres homines non esse*').[149] However, this makes the discussion of women as broad, diverse, and chaotic as the consideration of human nature itself. 'Femme' demonstrates the great diversity of ways in which the 'woman question' was considered. Mallet's 'Femme (anthropologie)' discusses, and rejects, the idea that women are *un homme manque*, the different ways in which political systems have prejudiced people into thinking that men are superior to women and encouraged domestic servitude and polygamy, and the question of what sort of access to education women ought to have, all after having set aside physiognomy and anatomy as topics of discussion. This is followed by further articles – Jaucourt's 'Femme (Droit nat.)', Desmahis's 'Femme (morale)', and 'Femme (Jurisp.)', each offering a multitude of often contradictory perspectives. Desmahis found this equivocation to be inherent in the subject matter: 'Who is able to define women? Every truth speaks in them, but in an equivocal language'.[150] The feminist Mary Hays found this equivocation less endemic to women and more to men's portrayal of them: 'Of all the systems – if indeed a bundle of contradictions and absurdities may be called a system – which human nature in its moments of intoxication has produced; that which men have contrived with a view to forming the minds, and regulating the conduct of women, is perhaps the most completely absurd'.[151]

Even Mary Hays might allow, however, that for better or worse there were a few important and prominent issues concerning women in eighteenth-century philosophical discussions that overlap and intersect within different areas of philosophy and are instructive if not exhaustive of the topic. Three questions arose frequently: (1) What are the moral differences between men and women? (2) Should women be educated and how? (3) What is the lot of women in other times and societies, particularly in regard to marriage, and what does it tell us more generally?

Perhaps the most characteristic eighteenth-century way of answering the first question was to distinguish between the male and female virtues. For many, such as Hume, Montesquieu, and Rousseau, respect for the female virtues of moderation, *pudeur*, chastity, delicacy, and others was an essential index of the progressiveness of a given society. The female virtues were often seen as inherently destructible and tied to female weakness and fragility. Burke, for example, in *A Philosophical Enquiry into the Origin of Our Ideas of the Sublime and Beautiful*, identified beauty as a social passion, the highest object of which is the beauty of women. The emphasis on women as objects of aesthetic judgment and aesthetic pleasure was (and is) quite common; note Desmahis's remark in Femme (morale): 'There are three things, said a gay spirit, that I have always loved and never understood, painting, music, and women.'[152] But men (or, for

Burke, 'we') do not find women beautiful insofar as they are perfect or regularly proportioned; rather beauty,

> where it is highest in the female sex, almost always carries with it an idea of weakness and imperfection. Women are very sensible of this; for which reason they learn to lisp, to totter in their walk, to counterfeit weakness, and even sickness. In all this they are guided by nature. Beauty in distress is much the most affecting beauty.[153]

A mannered society is therefore needed to cultivate and foster beauty and to guard the correspondent female qualities or virtues, with the woman exhibiting moderation and submission in turn.

The female virtues were not always viewed so approvingly or paternalistically. Some authors saw the supposed weakness of the female virtues as part of women's desire to dominate. The second of Pope's *Epistles to Several Persons* (also known as *Moral Essays*) (1731–5), 'To a Lady – Of the Characters of Women', is both characteristic and influential. Pope claimed, if somewhat tongue in cheek, that the particular characters of women were far more variable than those of men, as

> Nothing so true as what you once let fall
> Most Women have no Characters at all.
> Matter too soft a lasting mark to bear,
> And best distinguish'd by black, brown, or fair.[154]

This statement was singled out for criticism by Mary Hays, who argued that such weakness did not arise from the hand of nature but rather from men's tyrannical molding of women.[155] For Pope, though, women were weak and amorphous, like Aristotelian matter, like Eve made from lesser stuff, inconstant and difficult to explain. Yet, although more variable in the particular, women are less so in general, as

> In Men, we various Ruling Passions find,
> In Women, two, almost divide the kind;
> Those, only fix'd, they first or last obey,
> The love of Pleasure, and the Love of Sway
> (Epistles, ll. 207–10).

And the latter amorphousness and supposed weakness fuel Hobbesian and Epicurean tendencies.

These were not the only available pictures of the female virtues. A few years before Pope's *Epistles*, the influential Madame Lambert in her *Avis d'une mère à son fils* and *D'avis d'une mère à sa fille* argued that men and women each had particular virtues that were to be cultivated, ultimately coming together in marriage.[156] But the female virtues, anchored by *pudeur*, were not hothouse qualities but rather the constituents of a different temperament more guided by the heart

than by the mind (although they were sometimes quite intellectually capable)
and equally important for any society. Thus, corresponding to Lambert's neo-
Stoic *honnête-homme*, the noble, confident man exhibiting virtue to all around
him, self-sufficient but useful to others, was an equally neo-Stoic woman: chaste,
honest, kind, pleasing, but not servile. Lambert's defense of the female virtues
comes out most strongly in her brief *Réflexions nouvelles sur les femmes*, where
she responds to various misogynist wags who blame the degradation of society
on women. Lambert's advocacy of women defends female virtue, in particular
taste and aesthetic judgment, against the mores of the times, which are the work
of men.[157]

But despite her defense of women, Lambert *Réflexions* were remote from de
la Barre's arguments that there was no real difference between men and women
in either their capacity for virtue or in the content of their virtues (just as
she was far from the later arguments of Wollstonecraft and others).[158] Lambert
has greater proximity to Kant, who argued (under the influence of Burke) in
his early *Beobachtungen über das Gefühl des Schönen und Erhabenen* that the ideal
of the female sex is the beautiful and the male the sublime, that women have
a greater understanding of the beautiful in their persons but seek nobility in
the male and vice versa, and together the married couple forms a mutually
perfecting, beautifying, and ennobling association built both on their aesthetic
temperaments and their desires. This sexualization of aesthetics is notably absent
from the later *Kritik der Urtheilskraft*, although in the *Anthropologie* Kant strongly
distinguishes between male and female virtues in a Popean vein and, like Pope,
emphasizes women's natural desire for dominion.[159]

Some of the most extreme claims that women were 'all Machiavellians'[160]
were to be found in Diderot's *Sur les Femmes*. Initially begun as a review of
Thomas's *Essai* and its portrayal of the female virtues, which Diderot called
a 'hermaphroditic' work manifesting 'neither male nerve nor female softness'
(251), the work evolved into a remarkable – if paradoxical – distillation of a
number of ways of considering the differences between men and women. First,
Diderot emphasized that many of the ways in which women acted derived from
the fact that men treated them like 'idiot children' and constrained and governed
their sexuality to an unnatural degree.

The negative consequences of the constraint of female sexuality were a major
preoccupation of Diderot's in the novel *La religieuse*, where he explored the disastrous effect that religious and sexual constraint had in magnifying sexuality and
viciousness (much like Laclos's *Les liaisons dangereuses*).[161] Diderot also explored
this somewhat more benignly, if equally scandalously, in the *Supplément au Voyage de Bougainville*.[162] In the Tahitian paradise described by Diderot, artificial
modesty was unknown and the only laws that dictated sexual mores were desire

and fertility. Natural virtue was equated with productivity and lack of constraint, as opposed to the crippling mores of civilized Europe dictated by unnatural religious celibates. These mores led to a war between the sexes, as opposed to the relatively egalitarian and undifferentiated social order of Tahiti. Furthermore, sexual mores were, Diderot argued, independent of morals, and both sexual mores and morals were independent of a society's technological progress.

Diderot's critique of constraint was combined with an emphasis on materialism and the productive and natural. This is present in the *Supplément* via the Tahitians' 'natural' morality, which emphasizes natural productivity over the artificial. It underlies Diderot's novel *Les bijoux indiscrets*, where female genitals speak truth.[163] In *Sur les Femmes*, Diderot stressed the physiognomical basis for the differences between the male and female characters and virtues. Women are capable of extremes in desire and action – now timid, now heroic, now sweet, now capable of hysterical and 'epidemic' ferocity – as they have 'inside them an organ prone to terrible spasms' that induces all their extreme ideas. Their physiognomical difference from men, whose 'organ is more indulgent', makes them almost like another race. In Diderot's words, 'the general symbol of women is Apocalypse, on the brow of which is written: MYSTERY' (255, 252, 260).

Diderot's most celebrated discussion of the physiognomical distinction between men and women pointed in a rather different direction. In *Le rêve de d'Alembert*, Diderot asserted, through the character of Madame L'Espinasse, that perhaps 'man is the monster of woman, and woman the monster of man'.[164] By this Diderot meant that the parallels between male and female anatomy opened up the possibility that males and females were mutations, each of the other. These physiognomical arguments, as well as the critique of constraint, were pushed to more paradoxical extremes by the Marquis de Sade (although *Le rêve de d'Alembert* was not published until 1831). In Sade's world, the libertine is the one who recognizes the inherent mutability and monstrousness of all of nature and chooses vice or individual happiness over the social and religious control of virtue. The sisters Juliette and Justine, one virtuous and one vicious, show the changeability and reversibility of all of nature, that all is a continuously changing *tableau vivante*, mutating with no fixed law. The role of the libertine and the 'sodomite' is to overturn a false and restrictive providence by continuously acting against nature, partly through the denial of all supposedly natural sexual roles. In their place Sade embraces the truly 'natural' – desire and individual fulfillment. But in other places Sade made grossly misogynistic claims that undercut his emphasis on sexual mutability and the interrogation of nature *contra naturam*[165] (although Sade is sufficiently paradoxical that these, too, can be read as a critique of Thomas's and Rousseau's view of women as the moral sex).

Diderot, like Rousseau and others (even Sade), built the case for the difference between male and female characters and virtues in relation to the distinction between the natural and the artificial, arguing for the precedence of nature over artifice. 'Nature over artifice' was a sort of mantra in the later seventeenth century and the eighteenth century, intoned by nearly everyone, whether emphasizing the dangers of women falling into coquettery and artificiality or men becoming fops and 'Beaus'. The exponents of the 'artificial' were those, such as Mandeville, Hume, and Millar, who argued for 'luxury' as against spartan simplicity and natural virtue and for modern luxury against antiquity. The consequences for 'natural virtue' were notorious: '[T]here is nothing so perfectly Good in Creatures, that it cannot be hurtful to any one of the Society, nor anything so entirely Evil, but it may prove beneficial'.[166] It is not surprising that a radical step toward the artificial was taken in Mandeville's discussion of the female virtues, especially chastity. Mandeville argued:

> Young Girls are taught to hate a Whore, before they know what the Word means; and when they grow up, they find their worldly Interest entirely depending upon the Reputation of their Chastity. This sense of Honour and Interest, is what we may call artificial Chastity; and it is upon this Compound of natural and artificial Chastity, that every Woman's real actual Chastity depends.[167]

Mandeville not only emphasized the artificiality of chastity, but also that female chastity was a two-place predicate, that it depended on men. For Mandeville, women were, like men, sexual and desiring beings, and chastity was a virtue whose hold was continuously made more and more tenuous by both men and women. Insofar as chastity involves a relation between two people, Mandeville argued that the legalization of prostitution, and its policing, would provide a successful means for maintaining this chastity, as men would spend less of their time attempting to overcome the chastity of their female equals when there was well-organized sex for hire. This argument was combined with empathy for the women who become prostitutes due to poverty, maintaining that by bringing prostitution aboveboard their lots would be improved.

Mandeville also provided an acute analysis of the psychology of vice, explaining why unchaste women are likely to fall into vices. This was due neither to the inherent viciousness of prostitution nor to modesty as the essential anchor of female virtue, according to Mandeville, but rather to the fact that the criminalization of prostitution pushed it toward the margins of society and allowed it to meld more easily with other vices. Thus *pudeur* was an anchor of the female virtues not due to its inherent importance or because it is the essence of woman but because of its perceived importance, especially in social perceptions of women. Most crucially, chastity is central in women's social self-understanding. The desire to appear to have this artificial virtue is often so great that it can curb natural desire and this is, according to Mandeville, the source of many of the virtues and can even negate a woman's maternal instincts and lead to infanticide (which, Mandeville noted by way of proof, was less prevalent among prostitutes, as they did not lose social standing by having a bastard child).

Mandeville's account of female virtue was certainly not the norm. But he was important and original in maintaining that a supposedly 'natural' virtue was in fact the end result of socialization and education, thereby both calling the idea of natural virtue and a natural God-given frame into question and questioning the role of the 'natural' in maintaining a coercive state of affairs. Mandeville's most attendant pupil on this issue, as on many others, was David Hume. Unlike Mandeville, Hume emphasized the natural differences between the sexes. But chastity was an artificial virtue also for him, although it was more specific to the 'fair sex' and had clearer social utility than for Mandeville. Due to the respective physiologies of men and women, which Hume sees as the origin of 'that vast difference betwixt the education and duties of the two sexes',[168] women always know whether a child is theirs, whereas men never really do. Thus it is necessary that chastity be reinforced as a strong general rule in order that men know that they are bringing up their own progeny. The rules do not apply nearly as strictly to men, as there is far less utility in their chastity.

Many of these discussions of distinctive virtues and vices presupposed a vague consensus that there is a common human 'frame' or a group of basic dispositions, faculties, passions, inclinations, and so forth, and that the role of the philosopher is to ferret out these regularities. The idea of a common human nature as an object of study was cultivated by numerous philosophers of the seventeenth century, most influentially Hobbes, Grotius, Locke, Pufendorf, and Malebranche. There were also in the eighteenth century many fundamental disagreements as to the content of the human frame and its structure. But a common approach was to argue that one or more basic principles (self-interest, sociability, the moral sense, conscience, the capacity for abstraction, the understanding, judgment, reflection, and so on) made the specific difference or essential characteristic of human beings (as opposed to the animals), from which a host of other inclinations, passions, virtues, and so forth could be derived. In Pope's words, 'The science of Human Nature is, like all other sciences, reduced to a few clear points'.[169] Thus Hobbes and Mandeville were often considered to view all virtues as derivable from 'selfish interest', Hume from two principles of self-interest and benevolence, Butler from three, and so on. This was also the source of many familiar debates, such as between the benevolent (Shaftesbury, Hutcheson) and selfish (Mandeville, Hobbes, Helvétius) systems.

This sort of reductivism, going back to Descartes and Grotius (but often associated with Newtonianism) and the search for basic principles that distinguish humanity from both animals and angels are not obviously reconcilable with the numerous claims about thoroughgoing differences between male and female principles. One could argue, if not fully coherently, for the general regularity of human nature and its particular diversity. Thus Pope viewed women as lesser beings motivated by fewer principles (but principles shared with men) in an attempt to fit his account within the reductivist language of 'springs' and uniformity of frame. This approach might be considered 'Lockean' or 'Newtonian', with its emphasis on the empirical search for the constituents of the frame, but only in a vague sense, as there was little consensus on what qualified as an important object of study, as evidence, or as empirical study.

The problem was that male and female virtues, characters, dispositions, and so forth may ultimately have the same source, but they also seem fundamentally and unchangeably different. As with race and national character, if the sexes were fundamentally different in morals and in character, how could this difference be reconciled with physical, intellectual, or social explanations for the divergence? And if the principles in men and women were shared at the broadest level by 'human nature' as such, how could the differences and their significance be explained? As was so often the case, Rousseau stated it most sharply. In the opening of Book V of *Émile*, he noted that men and women are the same in every way *except* their sex and that women are not just deficient men. However, the 'male is male only at certain moments. The female is female her whole life or at least during her whole youth';[170] women *are* their sex and thus thoroughly different from men. Rousseau is particularly extreme, but the basic idea of an essentially female divergence both from man and 'human nature' in general is a theme we have already witnessed in Pope, Diderot, Thomas, and others.

One common way to explain this mysterious, necessary difference was, as noted, in terms of providentialist presuppositions that the union and complementarity of the two sexes were essential for the teleological course of nature, society, and so forth: that '[w]ith regards to natural outlines, men and women are the same. . . . Nature, however, intending them for mates, has given them dispositions different but concordant, so as to produce together delicious harmony'.[171] But the 'delicious harmony', and its importance, could be interpreted in manifold ways – whether William Nicholls's argument that marital unity depended on the submission of naturally inferior women to naturally superior men or Astell's claim in opposition to Nicholls that '[t]he Relation between the two Sexes is mutual, and the Dependence Reciprocal, both of them Depending intirely upon God, and upon him only; which one wou'd think no great Argument of the natural Inferiority of either Sex'.[172]

The reciprocal relations between the two sexes and the legitimacy or illegitimacy of man's dominion over woman were often discussed in the context of marriage and the history of women. The historicization of the relations between men and women as part of the 'moral' history of man complemented Thomas's consideration of the male and female virtues. This moral history was developed, often within a natural law framework, by Hume, Montesquieu, Adam Smith, John Millar, and others, most of whom treated it both comparatively and historically. An exception was Montesquieu, who greatly influenced the authors who followed after him, but whose primary interest was the comparative treatment of women's status. In the section on domestic servitude in *L'esprit des lois*, Montesquieu considered the 'natural inequality of the sexes' to be found in hot, southern countries, an issue central to the drama and turmoil of his earlier *Lettres persanes*. Unlike Hume in 'The Rise and Progress', the natural difference between men and women and the natural superiority of male over female were primarily conditioned and altered by physical causes, inflaming the passions and heating the natural affections between the sexes. Unlike Diderot, Montesquieu did not consider this physiologically or medically but rather within the broad framework of climate that we discussed in connection with race.

As a consequence of the natural power of climate, according to Montesquieu, women in southern climes are marriageable at a younger age than their northern sisters, and their looks decay before they become rational. Thus they are cast away for another wife in a polygamous harem without ever gaining proper control over their husbands. This gives the rude nations of the south a character very different from those in the north and explains their propensity for polygamous marriages and absolutist governments, which go hand in hand.[173]

Marriage, including polygamy, and divorce were intertwined with issues of sexual difference for many eighteenth-century philosophers and were often considered within a natural-law framework of the contracts and duties of marriage. Pufendorf had argued, in the early 1670s, that the contractual structure of marriage and its obligations, both the mutual duties of the partners and the duties of marriage as such to the human race, could be discovered and analyzed. In Pufendorf's scheme, the superiority of the husband in marriage was 'in keeping with the natural condition of the sexes', although there was no natural mandate for tyranny within the marriage bond.[174] This relation was, in a tradition derived from Aristotle, one of the three fundamental roles anchoring the duties and obligations derived from natural law and providing the moral structure of (male) human nature. But as opposed to the Aristotelian tradition, Pufendorf's 'natural condition of the sexes' made few, if any, assumptions about nature as such and understood human nature primarily in terms of social roles and how given human natures fit them. Locke drew on a similar scheme in his famous analysis of marriage in the second of his *Two Treatises of Government*, showing that husband and wife each had a demarcated sphere in marriage and both were necessary to fulfill the parental obligations to the child. Locke thus gave to maternity a stronger role than Pufendorf had and de-emphasized the idea that the science of morals is knowledge of man's (not women's) duties.[175]

Pufendorf argued against polygamy by pointing out the superior utility and appropriateness of monogamy and the tendency of polygamy to violate the roles of the marriage contractors (*Duty of Man and Citizen*, II.2.10). 'Utility' and 'appropriateness' were vague and begged to be taken up in drastically different ways. Hutcheson emphasized that polygamy was unsuitable to the natural qualities of the sexes and therefore ruled out the viability of the communistic experiment of Plato's *Republic*.[176] Adam Smith criticized polygamy for thwarting the formation of an aristocracy that historically had been the counterweight to monarchs and a necessary step in the history of liberty.[177] Lord Kames took over the Montesquieuian emphasis on climate but framed by a sketch of the history of women in savage times.[178] William Smellie, and others, went even further back than rude times to show the legitimacy of monogamy. Following Buffon's arguments against domestication in *Histoire naturelle*, Smellie averred that the simplicity and naturalness of love are destroyed by human institutions and artificial distinctions among the ranks. The latter leads beautiful women to marry 'puny', wealthy men and creates 'debilitated races' and 'universal degeneration'.[179] One can see how natural monogamy falls into artificial polygamy by looking toward the animal world: 'The dunghill cock and hen, in a natural state, pair. In a domestic state, however, the cock is a jealous tyrant, and the hen a prostitute' (278). Domestication therefore is the likely cause of men's and women's infelicities, divorce, and human polygamy.

This diversity of response shows also that the 'superiority of male to female' and the 'roles of the marriage contractors' were vague notions that allowed many different interpretations of the nature of the monogamous bond and of the means to discredit polygamy. Despite his belief in the differences in the moral and intellectual natures of the sexes, Bentham saw male superiority purely as a consequence of strength and expediency: superior male strength and the need to adjudicate between marriage contractors meant that disaster would ensue if the stronger was not given final right of adjucation, although he granted 'that on the principle of utility the interests of both ought alike to be consulted: since in two persons, taken together, more happiness is producible than in one'.[180]

However, the Pufendorfian legacy could also be taken as undermining the fixedness of 'natural inequality'. In this way, Hutcheson questioned the notion of 'natural inequality' between the sexes within the contractarian account and, by extension, the religious overtones of the sin of Eve and the stewardship of Adam implicit in orthodox ways of looking at marriage. According to Hutcheson, the marriage contract assumed no natural difference between the sexes and minimal natural roles, and it stipulated equality as one of the fundamental rules of the marital contract since 'nature shews no foundation for any proper jurisdiction or right of commanding in this relation'.[181] The argument was empirical; even if we grant that men are generally 'superior in strength of body and mind . . . this does not give any perfect right of government in any society' for 'it does not at all hold universally'. Marriages will vary due to the characters of the contractors, and if a preponderance of marriages are governed by the man (who generally has a stronger mind and body), this does not mean that all should be. Thus, in an extension of Pufendorf, 'natural' came to mean 'appropriate to a role'.

Unlike Pufendorf, Hutcheson's fundamental unit of analysis for the marriage was not the duty of the husband but rather the marriage contract itself, within which roles could vary. But, as with Pufendorf, the existence and importance of the roles is given – even if they don't always take on the same character. This was a necessity given the teleological and providentialist assumptions that Hutcheson entertained. Marital roles, when united with the moral sense shared by men and women, lead to the differentiated, providentially associated whole of human society, and their union is a necessary precondition of the moral perfection of this society.

A more bare-bones picture was offered by Kant in his *Metaphysik der Sitten*. Kant discussed marriage in terms of contractual rights and distinguished between 'marriage right' and 'parental right'. A marriage contract is primarily the lawful and reciprocal right to exclusive use of sexual organs and capacities initiated by conjugal sexual intercourse. Although the natural end of marriage is childbearing and child rearing, as a marriage does not end when a couple stops having children, this cannot be the basis of marital right. This reciprocal equality of possession rules out polygamy, as polygamy is not equal and it assumes no particular qualities of the contractors nor dominion *qua* right.[182] This does not rule out that one might give an anthropological analysis of the natural suitability of certain people to certain roles, just that this anthropological analysis is not to be derived from a contract.

Hume was notably different on this question. Unlike Hutcheson, Locke, Kant, or Bentham, Hume minimized the contractual basis of marriage itself and max-imized the passions, viewing the relations between the sexes as responding both to natural inequality and to natural affections and sentiments of benevolence. The latter provide a 'natural' equality between the sexes through the benevo-lent institutions holding between them. This natural equality is not a political right, nor does it result from a contract, nor is it, as for Hutcheson, the basis for a natural, providential association. It is rather predicated on the differences between the sexes and their passions, the affections between men and women, and the institutions arising from these differences. 'Natural' equality is a kind of artificial corrective to central productive differences in human nature, and greater equality is a sign of manners prevailing over violence and the despotism of the harem.

Consequently, sexual difference is both artificial and doubly natural: artificial insofar as countless institutions arise from it, and natural both insofar as it signals a transhistorical and transcultural set of differences in the power of mind and body and insofar as its abuses necessitate a corrective that allows the natural passions between the sexes to prosper. But even though sexual difference is transhistorical and transcultural, its artificial character makes it a key historical index, moving the discussions of women and marriage from ahistorical and permanent relations to changing bonds. Man's desire (in the best of cases) 'to alleviate that superiority, as much as possible, by the generosity of behaviour, and by a studied deference and complaisance for all her inclinations and opinions'[183] is the motor of these changing bonds. The consequent politeness and refinement of manners provide the crucial index of enlightenment: barbarous nations reduced women to domestic slavery insofar as their authority was based on physical violence ('The ancient Muscovites wedded their wives with a whip instead of a ring'), whereas in civilized nations men act with studied deference but no less ultimate authority. This refinement of manners and mores in turn has tempered monarchy, as the mannered wife has tempered the husband, and given modern, as opposed to ancient, art its signature politeness.

The science of human nature that takes appraisal of these bonds is consequently a historical analysis of the ways in which fixed differences lead to and manifest themselves in vastly different manners. In John Millar's words:

> Of all our passions, it should seem that those which unite the sexes are most easily affected by the peculiar circumstances in which we are placed, and most liable to be influenced by the power of habit and education. Upon this account they exhibit the most wonderful variety of appearances, and, in different ages and countries, have produced the greatest diversity of manners and customs.[184]

The historical consideration of the woman question was taken up by later British thinkers such as Millar and Smith. The former provided the most extended and impressive discussion in his *Origin of the Distinction of Ranks*, which opens with the quotation just cited. Millar took over the idea from Hume and Smith that the history of women is a primary index of progress. Whereas Hutcheson and Pufendorf had discussed these relations in terms of *duties*, Millar transformed it into a question of *authority*, a change already apparent in Hume and Montesquieu. However, whereas Montesquieu and Hume viewed the problem as primarily one of *our* authority (civilized Europeans) and *their* authority (absolutist barbarians), Millar considered the issue through the sharp lens of his teacher Adam Smith.

Smith discussed marriage *qua* rights, but 'rights' understood neither as pre-social grants from God nor as formally contracted bases for performing duties as in Kant, but as social and historical claims arising spontaneously from the interaction of spectators, interactions that could vary historically and culturally.[185] In the *Origin of the Distinction of Ranks*, Millar combined this approach with an emphasis on the problem of authority. This leads to a multiple-stage history of the status of women. No difference in human nature between men and women is assumed other than a difference in strength and suitability for 'martial employments' (33). The relations between the sexes are structured by distinctions between social ranks, luxury, private property, and the accessibility of the sexes to each other. Men in barbaric times (whether Iliadic warriors or Native Americans) had little regard for modesty, chastity, and women in general because of the proximity and accessibility of women for sex, the harshness of the climate (and consequent lack of leisure), the general martial tenor of these societies, and the concentration of authority in the hands of men with no legal or societal checks.

Women did gain authority in barbaric societies occasionally, through the power of maternal authority, in particular in countries and times where there were no marital bonds and children had little acquaintance with their fathers. This led to 'this unusual kind of polygamy', polyandry, which although antithetical to 'the views and manners of a civilized nation' is entertained by Millar as a real historical possibility (54–5). But Millar's account of polygamy reveals best the depths of his innovations in historical analysis. He replicates Montesquieu's analysis but then remarks in the footnote: 'What is here said with respect to polygamy is only applicable to ... opulent and luxurious nations; for in barbarous countries, where it is introduced ... from motives of conveniency, and where it is accomplished with little or no jealousy, it cannot have the same consequences' (102–3n). Thus polygamy and its consequences are only analyzable within their particular historical settings, and polygamy does not function as a simple aberration of human nature.

As society became more complex, wealthy, and leisurely and the borders between clans and the sexes more pronounced, the passions between the sexes were amplified and women were prized and idolized. With even further differentiation between ranks, women were 'valued upon account of their useful talents and accomplishments' (97). Finally, after passing through pastoral and agricultural stages where property became fixed and the polite arts began to flourish, society paradoxically moved closer and closer to that 'same free communication between the sexes as in the ages of rudeness and barbarism'

(101). But in this case it was due not to women's lack of station but rather to 'those agreeable qualities which they possess, and the rank and dignity in which they hold as members of society' (101). However, in contrast with the rudest times, free sexual commerce became objectionable because of its tendency to undermine the far more complex and differentiated modern societies (as may be seen in the dissipation of the French and the Italians) (107).

All the authors just discussed assumed that monogamous marriage was a reasonably uncontroversial institution in modern, progressive societies. Marriage was rarely rejected outright. However, William Godwin, riding his enthusiasm for the French Revolution, criticized the conservatism of those, such as Hume, who assumed the legitimacy of property, laws, and marriage as institutions. Laws enchain humans and goad them into violence and self-destruction. Property similarly pens and limits individuals, and marriage is a particularly repressive consequence of our attitudes toward both property and law. As all laws and property must eventually go, so also the marital bonds are repressive and destroy spontaneity, affection, love, and human growth.[186] But Godwin's position was anomalous.

A more influential and much earlier critique of marriage was offered by Mary Astell, who, unlike Godwin, was no friend of revolution. Astell argued that marriage was a necessary and important institution for society but criticized its all too common tyrannical reality, most famously in the anti-Lockean claim, 'If *all Men are born free*, how is it that all Women are born slaves?'[187] Men such as Locke who attacked Tory assertions of divine-right monarchy were perfectly happy to exploit their divine right on the hearth. Astell pointedly used such lines of reasoning against the contractarian analogy between marriage and civil government in the work of Hobbes and Locke. Yet she claimed that although marriage was a necessity – and always to be obeyed once entered into – this did not pardon its abuse. But neither did the abuse legitimate divorce. The right to revolution held for Astell as little in the family as in the state, and she saw much hypocrisy in its invocation.[188]

Astell was criticized in numerous places, including Addison and Steele's *Tatler*, and applauded by some whom Astell certainly would have had little truck with, namely Daniel Defoe and Mandeville.[189] The latter wrote for a journal called the *Female Tatler*, which argued against many of Steele and company's (Swift, Addison, Pope) derogations of women. Mandeville consistently argued for the equality of male and female minds and women's equal capacity for virtue. Like Astell, he made no claims for their political emancipation or rights (*Essays in the Female Tatler*, 188–91); unlike Astell, he ignored High Church piety and the necessity of female submission in marriage (55). And in his contemporaneous work *The Virgin Unmask'd*, Mandeville emphasised the sufferings women incur in discharging the duties of marriage, in particular childbirth.[190]

Both Astell and Mandeville (as well as Lambert, Diderot, and others) agreed that the heart of the problem of women's status in marriage was the lack of female educational opportunities and the ways in which society considered women as naturally inferior, as 'idiot children', and then blamed them for their inferiority. Astell was particularly critical of the enfeebling of women via the poverty of their education and proposed a female Christian educational retreat as an emetic, '[f]or since GOD has given Women as well as Men intelligent Souls, why should they be forbidden to improve them?'[191] For Astell, this was likely the better side of a disjunction – either submit to the offices of marriage willingly or retreat from the world of sexual commerce entirely – although she also argued for the education of married women (167–8).

Considerations of the education of women were perhaps the most common way of debating the social and intellectual standing of women throughout the eighteenth century. In France, toward the end of the eighteenth century but before the Revolution, there were numerous essay prizes given on the question of women's education, some of the famous contestants included Mme. Genlis, Mme. D'Epinay, and Laclos, who produced his famous 'Des Femmes et de Leur Éducation' for a contest given by L'Académie de Châlons-sur-Marne. In the mid-eighteenth century, the need for change in women's education had become a consensus among many Enlightenment thinkers, irrespective of their other attitudes toward women. Discussions of education were, of course, enormously popular throughout the century, and educational manuals and advice books, already a popular genre in the sixteenth and seventeenth centuries, flourished. The works of two late seventeenth-century authors were continuous touchstones in educational discussions throughout the eighteenth century: François de Salignac de la Mothe-Fénelon's *Les Aventures de Télémaque* (1699) and *De l'éducation des filles* (1687) and Locke's *Some Thoughts Concerning Education*. The works were quite different in substance, although they were sometimes bundled together.[192] Both argued broadly for a 'natural' education, emphasizing the importance of the child's own experience of things.

Locke's *Some Thoughts Concerning Education* was written in response to requests for educational advice by his friend Edward Clarke and Clarke's wife. It is one of Locke's key works, providing an anti-authoritarian, experientially motivated, and liberal theory of education for those who 'dare venture to consult their own Reason, in the Education of their Children, rather than wholly to rely upon Old Custom.'[193] Locke hardly spoke of girls, but many of his educational lessons could be taken to apply to both sexes. Locke's account of the centrality of learning by trial and error, and not the least of loose clothing and fresh air, influenced many, including Wollstonecraft, Genlis, and Rousseau.

Archbishop Fénelon of Cambrai composed *Télémaque* as part of the education of his student the Duc de Bourgogne, Louis XIV's grandson. It was one of the most popular works of the eighteenth century, going through over 150 editions and 80 translations.[194] Through it, Fénelon became a touchstone for virtue well into the late eighteenth century by writers as opposed as Catharine Macaulay and Edmund Burke.[195]

Télémaque provided a narrative of the spiritual and moral development of Telemachus and his education by his tutor Mentor. The device allowed Fénelon to present his emphasis on natural education and virtues in a classical guise. *Télémaque* is the guide throughout Sophie's education in *Émile*, her favorite book, which Émile should read in order to understand her, while Telemachus is her ideal man by whom she measures Émile. As part of his moral development, Telemachus must choose among different women to love, culminating in a mature love for Antiope, and the catalog of Sophie's virtues is much like those of Antiope.

In his earlier work, *De l'éducation des filles*, Fénelon presented a fairly liberal account of women's education that spoke to particular female duties – above all, those of the household and the need to educate young children – and corrected vices such as vanity, jealousy, timidity, and coquettishness. The curriculum included basic reading, writing, and math, and even a little Latin if the girl was modest, but never licentious Italian or Spanish – a common refrain in the female education genre.[196] But girls had to be strictly supervised as they 'always risk going to extremes in everything'.[197] Fénelon's style was replicated in many works, including Madame Lambert's far more liberal *D'Avis d'une mère à sa fille*, which Fénelon admired.

Works on female education took countless other forms. Some were religious works such as Cotton Mather's *Ornaments of the Daughters of Zion, Or the Character and Happiness of a Vertuous Woman* (1691), Richard Allestree's (the author of the extremely popular Christian work *The Whole Duty of Man*) *The Ladies Calling* (1673), or William Kenrick's *The Whole Duty of Woman* (1753). Some took an epistolary form, including Catharine Macaulay's *Letters on Education* (1790), the reactionary Hester Chapone's very popular *Letters on the Improvement of the Mind* (1773), and Madame Genlis's *Adèle et Théodore, ou Lettres sur l'éducation* (1782). Some, such as Lambert's two *Avis*, Wollstonecraft's *Thoughts on the Education of Daughters* (1787), Lady Sarah Pennington's *An Unfortunate Mother's Advice to her Absent Daughters* (1761), and John Gregory's *A Father's Legacy to his Daughters* (1774), were shaped as parental advice. Many were conduct manuals, such as Defoe's *Family Instructor* (1715) and *Conjugal Lewdness: Or, Matrimonial*

Whoredom (1727). Still others were in dialogue or narrative form, such as Fénelon's *Télémaque*, Rousseau's *Émile*, and Madame D'Epinay's *Les Conversations d'Émilie* (1773).[198] The dialogue genre was popular enough to warrant parodies, such as Sade's *La philosophie dans le boudoir* (1795).

Rousseau's *Émile* was one of the most influential philosophical works of the second half of the eighteenth century, although not as popular as its literary counterpart on the consequences of bad marriage, *Julie ou la Nouvelle Héloïse* (1761). Rousseau took over from Locke and Fénelon the emphasis on 'natural' education, although for Rousseau this meant a private, experientially based education for independence of mind and self-perfection without corruption through artifice. He criticized Locke for his excessive rationalism and refusal to consider children as children, not little adults,[199] and instead emphasized an education with lessons suited to man's natural, changing stages of growth. Rousseau's education was primarily a moral education centered on sensibility and the gentle and attractive passions such as sympathy. Women have two fundamental roles in this education, as mothers and as wives. With regard to the former, Rousseau stressed the importance of maternity to an unusual degree. But whereas Diderot equated maternity with material productivity, Rousseau stressed maternal love, natural affection, and, through this, moral regeneration. This aspect of *Émile* was very influential, to the point of engendering a fad for the public nursing of children in Parisian society.[200] It also was a common theme in French Revolution accounts of the social role of women.

It was through the other role, as wives, that Rousseau emphasized the differences between the sexes as fundamental and moral, conditioned by differences of sex (whether physiological or not). 'From this diversity arises the first assignable difference in the moral relations of the two sexes. One ought to be active and strong, the other passive and weak. One must necessarily will and be able; it suffices that the other put up little resistance.' From this, Rousseau derived the 'law of nature' that 'woman is made specially to please man', despite her natural 'cunning' and her excessive passions moderated by modesty, the recurrent Popean picture of women, which Rousseau also emphasized.[201]

But the law of nature, that woman was made for man's delight, became the primary basis for the education of Émile's future wife, although in such a way as to emphasize modesty, gentleness, willing submission to injustice, simple beauty, practical reasoning, and other natural female virtues, and to curb female vanity and cunning. The final goal of the education was to make for man an ideal partner, entrenched in the sphere of the household and hidden from public life. But in Rousseau's eyes these limitations on women only strengthened their power over men, for the differences between men and women, especially female sway, were the source of their mutual attraction, and ultimately this sway was a moral influence on men and, through them, on society and history.

Surprisingly, more men than women criticized Rousseau's education of Sophie in France in the first few decades after the publication of *Émile*, while many of the advocates of Sophie's education were women.[202] But some important woman intellectuals did confront the picture of Sophie, albeit often circuitously. Madame Genlis, the celebrated writer and governess of the Dauphin, was often highly critical of Rousseau, but her own emphasis on preserving women's office of pleasing men and women's traditional duties, while providing them a great deal more education than Sophie, had a Rousseauian flavor at numerous points.[203] Despite describing Rousseau's *Émile* as 'the most boring book she had ever read,'[204] she published an expurgated version of it. Rousseau's patron Madame D'Epinay, with whom Rousseau had a falling out and then attacked in *The Confessions*, wrote *Les Conversations d'Émilie* in response to her many discussions with her granddaughter Emilie. The work is remarkably naturalistic in describing the particular difficulties of women as it deals with Émilie's education and growth through various stages of womanhood. Although Epinay did not attack Rousseau directly, she argued for a far broader and deeper education for Émilie than Rousseau gave to Sophie. This was in accordance with a neo-Stoic resolve concerning women's place in society and with an emphasis on moderation reminiscent of Madame Lambert.[205] An important exception to such subtle criticism was Madame de Staël, who was a staunch advocate of Émile's education and highly critical of that of Sophie.[206]

It may seem at first surprising that feminists of the era of the French Revolution, such as Etta Palm and Olympe de Gouges, did not attack Rousseau. But de Gouges, for example, took great succor from Rousseau's analysis of class and adopted Rousseauian language, despite her very different position on women and her opposition to many of the elements of the Revolution that took *Émile* as a touchstone.[207] The Rousseauian theme, that one can transform a society by educating its citizens, was a gripping one, irrespective of Rousseau's particular discussions of women. And there is no need to assume that feminists such as de Gouges evoked Rousseau ironically: who better than women of the lower and middle classes could understand Rousseau's picture of the smothering nature of class and how rank destroys natural talent, even if Rousseau himself perhaps could not understand how it might apply to women. Thus Rousseau resonated far more with women than Helvétius's account of the transformation of society through education because the former emphasized society's victims to a far greater degree.

Thus, one could view the Rousseauian tale of man's self-alienation from his own nature independently of Rousseau's particular attempts to explain the division of human nature into male and female. It is this theme of the education of society in order to free it from its own self-alienating and self-applied bonds that resonates in the works of de Gouges. Like Condorcet, she was a victim of the revolution and, like him, a ferocious abolitionist, who wrote the remarkable 'Déclaration des Droits de la Femme' a year before Wollstonecraft's *Vindication of the Rights of Woman* appeared. Claiming 'that ignorance, neglect, or contempt of the rights of woman, are the sole causes of public misfortunes and the corruption of governments', de Gouges 'resolved to set forth in a solemn declaration, the natural, inalienable, and sacred rights of woman'.[208] De Gouges had moved the discussion of the status and education of women from the arena of comparative virtue to rights, demanding equality of rights both by and under the law – in her ironic words, 'woman has the right to mount the scaffold; she should equally have the right to mount the Tribune' (105/383). The corruption of society was a consequence of its self-alienating misogyny, and the only way for both men and women to become virtuous was through repudiation and education.

This demand for equality of rights had also been maintained in the previous year by Condorcet, who attacked the various arguments that the differences be-tween female and male virtues legitimated 'depriving half of the human race of the right of taking part in the formation of laws'.[209] Both de Gouges and Con-dorcet had far more optimistic, 'liberal', and Enlightenment pictures of history than Rousseau, but though no Rousseauian, Condorcet shared Jean-Jacques's preoccupation with victims. Condorcet argued that most differences between men and women are the results of socialization, and as to maternal virtues, 'Why should individuals exposed to pregnancies and other passing indispositions be unable to exercise rights which no one has dreamed of withholding from per-sons who have the gout all winter or catch a cold quickly?' (98). In a rhetorical flourish, Condorcet claimed that the British would be much better represented by Catharine Macaulay than by Burke and Pitt, and the French better by Mme. Lambert (99).

In contrast with the French feminists, who rarely criticized Sophie, the impor-tant British historian and feminist Catharine Macaulay saw herself as belonging to a line of authors from Fénelon and Locke to Rousseau and Genlis, of whom she was also critical.[210] Unlike Fénelon, Rousseau, and Genlis, she emphasized that women and men had the same capacities, deserved the same extremely broad and deep education, and even boys should be taught 'some handicraft business' (65). She went much further though in criticizing Pope and asserting that Rousseau's discussion of Sophie 'has lowered the man of genius to the licen-tious pedant' (206). The supposed characteristic difference between the sexes is only the result of the superior strength of the male over the female, and only as arose because men in barbarous ages destroyed 'all the natural rights of the female species, and reduced them to a state of abject slavery' (206). Educating women, à la Rousseau, to please men is a moral corruption to coquettishness and intrigue, whereas true virtue in one sex must be equally so in the other (201). As to chastity, it is equally useful to both sexes but a necessity for women primarily because of social expectations, the constant pressure of 'male rakes', and women's precarious historical situation.

Macaulay's argument for human education and human virtues, as opposed to the sex-specific education and the difference between male and female virtues, has many similarities with that of Poulain de la Barre, although her epistemological commitments were Lockean and not Cartesian. Nevertheless, unlike de la Barre, Macaulay discussed the education of women as a part of education in general, which in turn was part of the discussion of political education, the familiar Rousseauian themes of the conflict between private and public education, and the (historical) relation between virtuous citizens and governments.

The best-known eighteenth-century exponent of the rational and political equality of men and women, Mary Wollstonecraft, was deeply influenced by Macaulay. For Wollstonecraft, and increasingly for others, the success or failure of the 'education of mankind' was crucial to any understanding of the Enlightenment, or at least the part of it that centered on the promise of the French Revolution. Following her own *Vindication of the Rights of Men*, Wollstonecraft provided a critique of the often reactionary practice legitimated by the doctrines of the rights of man from within. The claim, that 'there are rights which men inherit at their birth, as rational creatures, who were raised above the brute creation by their improvable faculties, and that in receiving these, not from their forefathers but, from God, prescription can never undermine natural rights',[211] showed that such rights must be universal and necessarily extend to all rational creatures, women not excepted.

Wollstonecraft developed this argument for women's rights within a thorough critique of a great deal of the literature on women and their education, with extended discussions of Rousseau, Fordyce, and Gregory, as well as briefer criticisms of Genlis, Pope, Staël, and many others. Unlike de Gouges and Condorcet, Wollstonecraft was an advocate of the French Revolution through all its stages (including the Terror) and very influenced by Richard Price and the Rational Dissenters. Like Price and Priestley, she saw a core of political virtues – honesty, simplicity, and sobriety of mind – as crucial to the transformation of society and equally basic to both men and women. In a manner consistent with Rational Dissent, she criticized the two primary eighteenth-century ideas of women, 'as moral beings, or so weak that they must be entirely subjected to the superior faculties of men' (134). Each portrayal of women was a pathology, perpetuated by both women and men, that enfeebled society and resulted in political servitude for both.

Wollstonecraft's originality can be glimpsed in her treatment of modesty and female duties. She claimed, perhaps surprisingly, that modesty was 'the pale moon-beam that renders more interesting every virtue it softens, giving mild grandeur to the contracted horizon' (262). But modesty was not specific to women; rather, it 'must be equally cultivated by both sexes, or it will ever remain a sickly hot-house plant' (258). All humans must be modest for that virtue to flourish. Even if women are temperamentally more chaste and modesty is the result of chastity, the virtue cannot exist successfully as a natural dispensation but only as a common social virtue (256). Therefore, modesty is not a sexual virtue; even if women 'have different duties to fulfil . . . they are human duties', not female duties (165). All duties and virtues differentiate humans and must be understood as part of the duty of man as a whole.

In this discussion, Wollstonecraft follows Rousseau and resembles de Gouges and Condorcet. She draws together the main questions considered here. The history of women, the tyranny possible within marriage, women's supposed moral difference from men, and their education are thoroughly interrelated through women's historical estrangement, including self-estrangement, and its alleviation. Accordingly, common human nature becomes a basis for political right and social duty, as opposed to an independent object of empirical study whose faults could be remedied outside of a social whole.

But radicals were not the only ones who took up Rousseau's ideas about women. In *Loose Hints Upon Education* (1781) and the *Sketches*, Kames combined Rousseau's account of Sophie with a conservative emphasis on natural ranks and duties and a vague republicanism. A similar influence can be seen in John Gregory's popular *A Father's Legacy to his Daughters*. Rousseau's emphasis on social duty is also present in one of Wollstonecraft's critics, Thomas Gisborne, who seems an appropriate figure with whom to conclude. Gisborne followed his *An Enquiry into the Duties of Men in the Higher and Middle Classes of Society in Great Britain* with *An Enquiry into the Duties of the Female Sex*.[212] He was a religious utilitarian, whose *Enquiries* belonged to a moderate line of 'sober' Christian thinkers including Hannah More and Hester Chapone. Chapone's *Letters on the Improvement of the Mind* advocated a fairly broad education for girls that was anchored in religion, emphasizing domestic oeconomy, politeness, moral philosophy, literature, history, and other accomplishments proper to 'sex, character, and station' (i.e., virtues 'of a private and domestic kind'[213]), including kindness to inferiors while avoiding all intimacy. Gisborne emphasized, in his *Enquiry into the Duties of the Female Sex*, that women, like barristers and physicians, have duties that change according to their age and association (married or unmarried). As in Rousseau, the performance of duties is essential for a happy and orderly society, and female duties in particular, since women provide comfort, effect the improvement of manners and conduct through association with men and by example, and educate the young. At the same time, women ought to be forthright and never hide their intellects, even though women are normally weaker of mind. Unsupported women of the lower ranks might perhaps even enter the public sphere as shopkeepers (263–7, 319). While women are different from men by nature, it is their social roles and duties, as opposed to their allurements, charms, and biology, that are of primary importance.

NOTES

1 Anne-Thérèse de Marguenat de Courcelles, marquise de Lambert, *Avis d'une mère à son fils*, in *Oeuvres*, ed. R. Granderoute (Paris, 1990), 43–94. Lambert's advice may echo Pope's famous dictum, 'The proper study of Mankind is Man'.

2 James Dunbar, *Essays on the History of Mankind in Rude and Cultivated Ages*, 2nd edn. (London, 1781), Essay 1.

3 The *Encyclopédie* article 'Homme (Hist. nat.)', in Denis Diderot, *Oeuvres complètes*, eds. H. Dieckmann et al. (Paris, 1975–), 7: 417.

4 Although separating philosophers from the rest of cultured knowledge in the eighteenth century is arbitrary, I will limit myself (very roughly) to the views of those deigned philosophers in the twenty-first century.

5 Pierre Bayle, *Dictionnaire historique et critique*, 2 vols. (Rotterdam, 1697; 4th edn., 4 vols., Amsterdam, 1730), translated as *The Dictionary Historical and Critical*, 5 vols. (London, 1734–8).

6 For Locke's response, see Letters 3495 and 3498, in *The Correspondence of John Locke*, ed. E. S. De Beer (Oxford, 1976–), vol. 8 (1989), 249–50, 253–6.

7 Georges-Louis Leclerc, comte de Buffon, *Histoire naturelle, générale et particulière*, 36 vols. (Paris, 1749–1804). References are to the selections in *Oeuvres philosophiques*, ed. J. Piveteau (Paris, 1954), 297, 323, 337–50.

8 See Jean Raoul Carré, *La philosophie de Fontenelle ou Le sourire de la raison* (Paris, 1932), 71.

9 See Andreas-Holger Maehle, *Kritik und Verteidigung des Tierversuchs: Die Anfänge der Diskussion im 17. und 18. Jahrhundert* (Stuttgart, 1992), 89.

10 Gottfried Wilhelm Leibniz, 'Epistola ad Wagnerum, De Vi activa Corporis, de Animâ, de Animâ Brutorum', in *Opera omnia: Nunc primum collecta, in classes distributa*, ed. L. Dutens, 6 vols. (Geneva, 1768), 2: 229.

11 See Ludwig Philipp Thümmig, *Institutiones philosophiae Wolfianae* (1725–6), §§291–8, in Christian Wolff, *Werke*, III.19:1.

12 Christian Wolff, *Psychologia Empirica*, §701 in *Werke*, II.5.

13 Étienne Bonnot de Condillac, *Traité des animaux* (1755), in *Oeuvres philosophiques*, ed. G. Le Roy, 3 vols. (Paris, 1947–51), 1: I.iii.

14 Condillac, *Essai sur l'origine des connaissances humaines*, in *Oeuvres philosophiques*, 1: 4. See Chapter 14, this volume.

15 Thomas Reid, 'Introduction', in *Essays on the Active Powers of Man*, in *Philosophical Works*, ed. W. Hamilton, 2 vols. in 1 (Edinburgh, 1895), vol. 2.

16 Reid, *Essays on the Intellectual Powers of Man*, eds. D. R. Brookes and K. Haakonssen (Edinburgh, 2002), I.5.

17 See John W. Yolton, *Thinking Matter: Materialism in Eighteenth-Century Britain* (Minneapolis, MN, 1983), 29–48.

18 François-Marie Arouet de Voltaire, *Lettres philosophiques, ou Lettres sur les Anglais* (1734), ed. G. Lanson, 2 vols. (Paris, 1915); rev. edn. A.-M. Rousseau, 2 vols. (Paris, 1964).

19 Henry Lee, *Anti-Scepticism: or, Notes Upon each Chapter of Mr. Lock's Essay Concerning Humane Understanding, With an Explication of all the Particulars of which he Treats, and in the same Order* (London, 1702), 246–7. See also 60–1, 122–3.

20 David Hartley, *Observations on Man, his Frame, his Duty, and his Expectations* (London, 1810). See Richard C. Allen, *David Hartley on Human Nature* (Albany, NY, 1999).

21 William Hazlitt, *An Essay on the Principles of Human Action: Being an Argument in Favour of the Natural Disinterestedness of the Human Mind. To Which are Added, Some Remarks on the Systems of Hartley and Helvetius* (London, 1805), 143.

22 Joseph Priestley, *Letters to a Philosophical Unbeliever*, Pt. 1 (Bath and London, 1780), 2nd edn. (Birmingham and London, 1787); Pt. 2 (Birmingham and London, 1787).

23 Anthony Collins, *A Philosophical Inquiry concerning Human Liberty*, ed. Joseph Priestley (Birmingham, 1790), from the 3rd edn. of 1735, 37–8.

24 See note 3.

25 Claude-Adrien Helvétius, *De l'esprit* (Paris, 1758), Essay I, ch. 1, esp. n.1.

26 The *philosophes* reacted very strongly to La Mettrie, especially Diderot and Voltaire (see Julien Offray de La Mettrie, *Discours sur le bonheur*, ed. J. F. Falvey (Banbury, 1975), 91–8). In spite of this, there are deep similarities between La Mettrie's and Diderot's materialisms, but great differences in their attitudes toward its social and moral consequences. See Ann Thomson, *Materialism and Society in the Mid-Eighteenth Century: La Mettrie's Discours Preliminaire* (Geneva and Paris, 1981), 181–6.

27 Bernard le Bovier de Fontenelle, 'Sur l'instinct', in *Oeuvres de Fontenelle* (Paris, 1790–2), 5: 416. Quoted in Carré, *La philosophie de Fontenelle*, 88.

28 La Mettrie, *Discours sur le bonheur*, §167.

29 Guillaume-Hyacinthe Bougeant, *Amusement philosophique sur le langage des bestes* (Paris, 1739).

30 Nicholas Malebranche, *De la recherche de la Verité*, in *Oeuvres*, ed. G. Rodis-Lewis, 22 vols. (Paris, 1979), 1: 467 (IV.11).

31 *Encyclopédie*, I:350. This was the most popular expression of Boullier's arguments; see also David Renaud Boullier, *Essai philosophique sur l'âme des bêtes* (1728) (Amsterdam, 1737).

32 Boullier, *Essai philosophique*, II.14.

33 Dugald Stewart, *Outlines of Moral Philosophy* (Edinburgh, 1793), 72.

34 Charles Bonnet, *La palingénésie philosophique, ou Idées sur l'état passé et sur l'état futur des etres vivants* (Geneva, 1769), 203.

35 Richard Dean, *An Essay on the Future Life of Brute Creatures*, 2 vols. (London, 1768), 2: 116.

36 Soame Jenyns, 'Letter III: On Natural Evils', in *A Free Inquiry Into the Nature and Origin of Evil*, 2nd edn. (London, 1757), 69.

37 Samuel Johnson, *A Review of Soame Jenyns, A Free Enquiry into the Nature and Origin of Evil*, in *The Works of Samuel Johnson*, 11 vols. (Oxford and London, 1825), 6: 47–76 at 66.

38 Bernard Mandeville, *Aesop Dress'd: or A Collection of Fables Writ in Familiar Verse* (London, 1704).

39 Mandeville, *The Fable of the Bees: or, Private Vices, Publick Benefits*, ed. F. B. Kaye, 2 vols. (Oxford, 1924), 1: 178 and 181.

40 Jean-Jacques Rousseau, *Discours sur l'origine et les fondements de l'inégalité parmi les hommes*, in *Oeuvres*, vol. 3; translated as *Discourse on Inequality*, in *The Discourses and other Early Political Writings*, trans. and ed. V. Gourevitch (Cambridge, 1997), 152.

41 David Hume, *A Treatise of Human Nature*, 1.3.16.1, SBN 176.

42 William Paley, *The Principles of Moral and Political Philosophy* (1785), 4th edn. (Dublin, 1788), II.11, p. 64.

43 Francis Hutcheson, *A System of Moral Philosophy* (London, 1755), 1: 313. See Knud Haakonssen, *Natural Law and Moral Philosophy: From Grotius to the Scottish Enlightenment* (Cambridge, 1996), ch. 2, particularly 78–9.

44 Hutcheson, *System*, I: 316 and 314. Paley, *Principles*, II.11, p. 64.

45 Immanuel Kant, *Lectures on Ethics*, trans. P. Heath, eds. P. Heath and J. B. Schneewind, in *Works* (Cambridge, 1997), 434–5.

46 Reid, *Practical Ethics: Being Lectures and Papers on Natural Religion, Self-Government, Natural Jurisprudence, and the Law of Nations*, ed. K. Haakonssen (Princeton, NJ, 1990), 205. See the editor's commentary, 378–9.

47 Humphrey Primatt, *A Dissertation on the Mercy and Sin of Cruelty to Brute Animals* (London, 1776); John Hildrop, *Free Thoughts upon the Brute-Creation: In Two Letters to a Lady*, in *The Miscellaneous Works of John Hildrop*, 2 vols. (London, 1754), vol. 1.

48 Jeremy Bentham, *An Introduction to the Principles of Morals and Legislation*, eds. J. H. Burns and H. L. A. Hart (London, 1970), ch. 17, §1n.

49 John Oswald, *The Cry of Nature; or, an appeal to Mercy and Justice, on behalf of the persecuted animals* (London, 1791), 29.

50 Rousseau, *Discours sur l'origine*; trans., 140.

51 Adam Ferguson, *An Essay on the History of Civil Society*, ed. F. Oz-Salzberger (Cambridge, 1995), 14; see also Ferguson, *Principles of Moral and Political Science: Being Chiefly a Retrospect of Lectures Delivered in the College of Edinburgh*, 2 vols. (Edinburgh, 1792), 1: 4.

52 Johann Gottfried Herder, *Ideen zur Philosophie der Geschichte der Menschheit*, 4 vols. (Riga and Leipzig, 1784–91), 2: 3, translated as *Outlines of a Philosophy of the History of Man*, trans. T. O. Churchill (London, 1800).

53 James Burnett (Lord Monboddo), *Of the Origin and Progress of Language*, 2nd edn., 6 vols. (Edinburgh, 1774–92), 1: 262n. Charles White, *An Account of the Regular Gradation in Man, and in Different Animals and Vegetables; and from the Former to the Latter* (London, 1799), 24n.

54 Julien Offray de La Mettrie, *L'homme machine*, in *Oeuvres philosophiques*, 2 vols. (Berlin, 1774), 1: 302–3. See also *Traité de l'âme*, in *Oeuvres*, 1: 180.

55 Burnett, *Origin*, 311.

56 See Harry M. Bracken, 'Philosophy and Racism', in *Philosophia*, 8 (1978): 241–60.

57 Rousseau, *Discourse on Inequality*, 'Note 10', 205.

58 Condillac, *Essai*, I.iv.23–5.

59 Voltaire, *Eléments de la philosophie de Newton* (London [i.e., Paris]; Amsterdam, 1738), II: 7.

60 Condillac, *Essai*, I.vi.

61 Diderot, *Pensées philosophiques. Addition aux Pensées philosophiques. Lettre sur Les aveugles. Additions à la Lettre sur les aveugles. Supplément au Voyage de Bougainville*, ed. A. Adam (Paris, 1972), 83–6.

62 Jean Itard, *De l'éducation d'un homme sauvage; ou, Des premiers développemens physiques et moraux du jeune sauvage de l'Aveyron* (Paris, 1801); translation in L. Malson and J. Itard, *Wolf Children. The Wild Boy of Aveyron*, trans. E. Fawcett, P. Ayrton, and J. White (London, 1972), 138.

63 Burnett, *Origin*, 1: 424.

64 See also 'Lord Monboddo to Sir John Pringle, June 16, 1773', in *Lord Monboddo and Some of His Contemporaries*, ed. W. A. Knight (London, 1900), 84–5.

65 William Smellie, *The Philosophy of Natural History*, 2 vols. (Edinburgh, 1790–9), 1: 419–20.

66 Buffon, *Histoire naturelle, générale et particulière*, in *Oeuvres philosophiques*, 384.

67 *Encyclopaedia Britannica or, a Dictionary of Arts and Sciences, Compiled upon a New Plan*, ed. W. Smellie, 3 vols. (Edinburgh, 1771), 3: 525.

68 See Sue Peabody, *'There Are No Slaves in France': The Political Culture of Race and Slavery in the Ancien Régime* (Oxford, 1996), ch. 4.

69 See Ann Thomson, *Barbary and Enlightenment: European Attitudes towards the Maghreb in the 18th Century* (Leiden and New York, NY, 1987).

70 From this point on, I will use race to designate the cluster of race-related terms and character to designate the character-related terms, on occasion substituting others when the specific usage merits or for variety.

71 For examples, see Claude Nicolas Le Cat, *Traité de la couleur de la peau humaine en général et de celle des nègres en particulier, et de la métamorphose d'une de ces couleurs en l'autre, soit de naissance, soit accidentellement* (Amsterdam, 1765), I.2; Georg Forster, 'Leitfaden zu einer künftigen Geschichte der Menschheit', in *Werke: sämtliche Schriften, Tagesbücher, Briefe* (Berlin, 1958–), vol. 8, ed. S. Scheibe (1972), 193; Benito Gerónimo Feijoo, "Color etiópico", in *Teatro crítico universal, ò Discursos varios en todo género de materias, para desengaño de errores comunes,* 9 vols. (Madrid, 1726–40), vol. 7, 3, §§3–5 (originally published 1736).

72 Especially *Novissima Sinica* (1697); translated with other pieces in Gottfried Wilhelm Leibniz, *Writings on China*, trans. D. J. Cook and J. H. Rosemont (Chicago and La Salle, IL, 1994).

73 Christian Wolff, *Oratio de Sinarum philosophia practica / Rede über die praktische Philosophie der Chinesen*, trans. and ed. M. Albrecht (Hamburg, 1985), ix–lxxxix.

74 Charles de Secondat de Montesquieu, *L'esprit des lois* (1748), XVII.6.

75 Hume, 'Of the Rise and Progress of the Arts and Sciences' and 'Of National Characters', in *Political Essays*, ed. K. Haakonssen (Cambridge, 1994), 66, 83.

76 Ferguson, *An Essay on the History of Civil Society*, Pt. 5, §4; Pt. 6, §5.

77 Adam Smith, *An Inquiry into the Nature and Causes of the Wealth of Nations*, eds. R. H. Campbell, A. S. Skinner, and W. B. Todd, 2 vols., in *Works* (1976), I.viii.24–5.

78 On the rise and fall of China worship in France, and the criticisms of the authors mentioned, see Henry Vyverberg, *Human Nature, Cultural Diversity, and the French Enlightenment* (Oxford, 1989), 121–35.

79 See 'Anthropophages', in *Voltaire, Les Oeuvres complètes / The Complete works*, ed. T. Besterman (Geneva, Toronto, and Oxford, 1968–), vol. 35: *Dictionaire philosophique*, ed. C. Mervaud, 349.

80 Isaac de Pinto, *Apologie pour la nation Juive: Réflexions critiques sur le premier chapitre du viie tome des oeuvres de M. Voltaire* (Amsterdam, 1762), included in Antoine Guénée, *Lettres de quelques Juifs portugais et allemands à M. Voltaire avec des réflexions critiques* (Lisbon [in fact, Paris], 1769), translated as *Letters of certain Jews to Monsieur Voltaire*, trans. P. Lafanu (Dublin, 1777).

81 Voltaire, *Un chrétien contre six juifs ou Réfutation d'un livre intitulé, Lettres de Quelques Juifs Portuguais, Allemands, et Polonais*, in *Oeuvres complètes*, 8: 503.

82 Samuel Stanhope Smith, *An Essay on the Causes of the Variety of Complexion and Figure in the Human Species. To which are added, animadversions on certain remarks made on the first edition of this essay, by Mr. Charles White . . . Also, strictures on Lord Kaim's discourse on the original diversity of mankind.* [1782] 2nd edn. (New Brunswick, NJ, 1810). Here after the modern edition by W. Jordan (Cambridge, 1965). See also my discussion of Johann Gottfried Blumenbach later in the present chapter.

83 Buffon, *Histoire naturelle*, in *Oeuvres philosophiques*, 395.

84 Buffon, *Oeuvres complètes*, ed. M. le comte de Lacepède, 26 vols. (Paris, 1825–8), 13: 510.

85 Buffon, *Histoire naturelle*, 395; see Phillip Sloan, 'The Idea of Racial Degeneracy in Buffon's *Histoire Naturelle*', in *Studies in Eighteenth Century Culture: Racism in the Eighteenth Century*, ed. H. Pagliaro (Cleveland, OH, 1973), 293–321.

86 Buffon, *Oeuvres complètes*, 13: 481.

87 Thomas Jefferson, *Notes on the State of Virginia* (1787), ed. W. Peden (Chapel Hill, NC, 1955), 62.

88 For the equation of beauty and good mores, see Buffon's account of the Bengals in *Oeuvres complètes*, 13: 395–6, on ugliness and impoverished mores see the discussion of the Lapps at p. 350 in the same work. See also Jacques Roger, *Buffon: Un philosophe au Jardin du Roi* (Paris, 1989), 238.

89 Cornelius de Pauw, *Recherches philosophiques sur les Américains ou Mémoires intéressant pour servir à l'histoire de l'espèce humaine*, 3 vols. (London, 1771), I: 121 and 126.

90 John Arbuthnot, *An Essay Concerning the Effects of Air on Human Bodies* (1733) (London, 1751), VI:14.

91 Jean-Baptiste, Abbé Du Bos, *Réflexions critiques sur la poësie et sur la peinture* (1719), 7th edn., 3 vols. (Paris, 1770), 2: 13–20.

92 Feijoo, 'Color etiópico', VII.3, §§10–11, 39–40, 53.

93 Buffon, *Oeuvres complètes*, 493–4, 519–20.

94 De Pauw, *Recherches philosophiques*, II.2.

95 Voltaire, *Essai sur les moeurs et l'esprit des nations*, I.2 in *Oeuvres*, vol. 11 (the 'Introduction', including the passage on albinism, was originally published in 1765); de Pauw, *Recherches philosophiques*, 2: 14. See P. Emeka Abanime, 'Voltaire as an Anthropologist: The Case of the Albino', in *Studies on Voltaire and the Eighteenth Century*, 143 (1975): 85–104.

96 Pierre-Louis Moreau de Maupertuis, *Dissertation physique a l'occasion du negre blanc* (Leiden, 1744); *Vénus physique* (The Hague, 1745); and *Système de la nature* (Berlin, 1754). Kant, 'Von den verschiedenen Racen der Menschen' (1775), in Ak II: 427–43 at 431.

97 Le Cat, *Traité de la couleur de la peau humaine*, III.1 and 4.

98 Benjamin Rush, 'Observations Intended to Favour a Supposition that the Black Color (As it is Called) of the Negroes is Derived from the Leprosy', in *American Philosophical Society Transactions*, 4 (1799): 289–97.

99 White, *An Account of the Regular Gradation in Man*.

100 See Samuel Stanhope Smith, 'Remarks on Certain Strictures by Charles White', in *Essay*, 151–86; Anonymous, 'On Charles White's Account of the Regular Gradation in Man', *Monthly Review*, 33 (1800): 360–4.

101 Pierre Camper, *Dissertation physique. Sur les différences réelles que présentent les traits du visage chez les hommes de différents pays et de différents âges; Sur le beau qui caractérise les statues antiques et les pierres gravées. Suivie de la proposition d'une nouvelle méthode pour déssiner toutes sortes de têtes humaines avec la plus grande sûreté*, trans. D. B. Q. D'Isjonval (Utrecht, 1791), 8 (originally published in Dutch, 1790).

102 John Hunter, *Essays and Observations on Natural History, Anatomy, Physiology, and Geology*, 2 vols. (London, 1861), I:45.

103 Samuel Thomas Soemmering, *Ueber die körperliche Verschiedenheit des Negers vom Europäer* (Frankfurt am Main, 1785).

104 Edward Tyson, *The Anatomy of a Pygmy Compared with that of a Monkey, an Ape, and a Man. With an Essay concerning the Pygmies . . . of the Antients* (London, 1751), 2nd edn. (originally published 1699 in Latin as *Orang-outang, sive homo sylvestris*), 92–4.

105 Johann Gottfried Blumenbach, *De generis humani varietate nativa* (1770), 3rd edn. (Göttingen, 1795), II.23.

106 Blumenbach, *De generis humani*, II.87, and his *Beyträge zur Naturgeschichte*, 2 vols. (Göttingen, 1806–11), I.13.

107 Jefferson, *Notes on the State of Virginia*, 143.

108 J. R. Oldfield, *Popular Politics and British Anti-Slavery: The Mobilisation of Public Opinion Against the Slave Trade 1787–1807* (Manchester, 1995), chs. 1–2.

109 Adam Smith, *Wealth of Nations*, III.ii.10. See Knud Haakonssen, *The Science of a Legislator: The Natural Jurisprudence of David Hume and Adam Smith* (Cambridge, 1981), 140–1.

110 Smith, *Wealth of Nations* III.ii.10; John Millar, *The Origin of the Distinction of Ranks; or, An Inquiry into the Circumstances which give rise to Influence and Authority, in the Different Members of Society*, 3rd edn. (London, 1781), VI.4.

111 Granville Sharp, *Extract from a Representation of the Injustice and Dangerous Tendency of Tolerating Slavery, or Admitting the least Claim of private Property in the Persons of Men in England* (London, 1769), 31–5.

112 Sharp, *Injustice*, 40–2; Hutcheson, *System*, III:3; George Wallace, *A System of the Principles of the Law of Scotland* (Edinburgh, 1760), I: 88–98. Sharp reprints the same texts as Anthony Benezet, from whom he seems to have derived them, as well as extracts from James Foster.

113 On Hutcheson, see Anthony Benezet, *A Short Account of that Part of Africa, Inhabited by the Negroes* (Philadelphia, PA, 1762).

114 Jean-Antoine-Nicolas de Caritat, marquis de Condorcet, *Réflexions sur l'esclavage des nègres*, 2nd edn. (Paris, 1788), ii (published under the pseudonym Schwartz!).

115 Hume, 'Of the Rise and Progress of the Arts and Sciences' and 'Of National Characters', in *Political Essays*, 58–77 and 82.

116 By the 1777 edition, Hume had revised the more general attack on non-whites in the 1753 edition, restricting it to just blacks.

117 James Beattie, *An Essay on the Nature and Immutability of Truth, in Opposition to Sophistry and Scepticism* (1770), ed. J. Fieser (Bristol, 2000), III.2, 228–30.

118 James Burnett, *Antient Metaphysics. Volume Third Containing the History and Philosophy of Men* (London, 1784), 185n.

119 Kant, *Beobachtungen über das Gefühl des Schönen und Erhabenen*, Ak 2: 243–56.

120 Hume, 'Of National Characters', 86n.

121 For a hint of this, see 91.

122 Kant, 'Von den verschiedenen Racen der Menschen', Ak 2: 427–443.

123 Kant, 'Von den verschiedenen Racen der Menschen', Ak 2: 433, 441.

124 Kant, *Anthropologie in pragmatischer Hinsicht*, Ak 7: 293.

125 Christoph Girtanner, *Über das Kantische Prinzip für Naturgeschichte: Ein Versuch diese Wissenschaft philosophisch zu behandeln* (Göttingen, 1796).

126 Eberhard August Wilhelm von Zimmermann, *Geographische Geschichte des Menschen, und der allgemein verbreiteten vierfüssigen Thiere: nebst einer hieher gehörigen zoologischen Weltcharte* (Leipzig, 1778–83).

127 Christoph Meiners, *Grundriss der Geschichte der Menschheit* (Lemgo, 1785), 43.

128 Meiners, *Untersuchungen über die Verschiedenheiten der Menschennaturen*, 3 vols. (Tübingen, 1811–15).

129 Georg Forster, *A Voyage round the World*, 2 vols. (London, 1777).

130 Georg Forster, 'Noch etwas über die Menschenraßen', in *Werke*, 8: 144 (originally published 1786).

131 See Thomas Strack, 'Philosophical Anthropology on the Eve of Biological Determinism: Immanuel Kant and Georg Forster on the Moral Qualities and Biological Characteristics of the Human Race', in *Central European History*, 29 (1996): 285–308.

132 See Voltaire, *Traité de metaphysique* [1734], ed. H. A. Temple Patterson (Manchester, 1937), I.1.

133 See Paul B. Wood, 'The Natural History of Man in the Scottish Enlightenment', *History of Science*, 27 (1989): 89–123.

134 See particularly 'Canis', in the *Encyclopaedia Brittanica*.

135 Lord Kames (Henry Home), *Sketches of the History of Man* [1774], 4 vols. (Edinburgh, 1788), 1: 20.
136 See Adam Ferguson, *An Essay on the History of Civil Society*, II.1–2; William Robertson, *History of America*, in *Works*, 8 vols. (London, 1827), 6: 248–9.
137 Kant, *Recensionen von I. G Herders Ideen zur Philosophie der Geschichte der Menschheit*, Ak 8: 43–66.
138 Herder, *Ideen zur Philosophie der Geschichte der Menschheit*, VI, ch. 4. Trans. from *Outlines*.
139 Herder, *Ideen*, XVI, ch. 5. See also, in the same chapter, Herder's remarkable discussion of the Jews.
140 Samuel Stanhope Smith, *Essay*, 103. See also Jordan's invaluable 'Introduction', vi–lvii.
141 Anonymous, rev. of Samuel Stanhope Smith's AN ESSAY ON THE CAUSES OF THE VARIETY, *Monthly Review*, 80 (1789): 184–5; in *Race: The Origins of An Idea*, ed. H. F. Augstein (Bristol, 1996), 57.
142 Antoine-Léonard Thomas, *Essai sur le caractère, les moeurs et l'esprit des femmes dans les différens siècles* (Paris, 1772), 117.
143 De la Barre had actually argued that women were capable of social and political authority, but not in relation to rights and democracy – rather, Queen Elisabeth, Queen Christina, and others were far more recent memories. See François Poulain de la Barre, *De l'égalité des deux sexes* (Paris, 1984), 80–4 (originally published 1673). It was translated into English shortly after publication, but reappeared in mid-century under the pseudonym 'Sophia'.
144 There were, however, some writers continuing the line of de la Barre, such as the Abbé Dinouart. See P. D. Jimack, 'The Paradox of Sophie and Julie: Contemporary Response to Rousseau's Ideal Wife and Ideal Mother', in *Woman and Society in Eighteenth-Century France: Essays in Honour of John Stephenson Spink*, eds. E. Jacobs et al. (London, 1979), 152–65 at 154.
145 De la Barre, *De l'égalité des deux sexes*, 59.
146 Both the genre of the catalog of female virtues and the history of women go back well before the eighteenth century. See, for example, John Shirley, *The Illustrious History of Women, or, A Compendium of the Many Virtues that Adorn the Fair Sex* (London, 1686).
147 Lieselotte Steinbrügge, *The Moral Sex: Woman's Nature in the French Enlightenment*, trans. P. E. Selwyn (Oxford, 1995), 104. I am indebted to Steinbrügge in my discussion of the French Enlightenment, although I do not agree with her on many particulars, such as Thomas.
148 Edmund Burke, *Reflections on the Revolution in France*, ed. C. C. O'Brien (New York, NY, 1986), 169–71; Bentham, *Principles of Morals and Legislations*, ch. 6, §35; Rousseau, *Émile ou de l'éducation*, in *Oeuvres*, vol. 4; Diderot, *Sur les femmes*, in *Oeuvres complètes*, eds. J. Assézat and M. Tourneux, 20 vols. (Paris, 1875–7), 2: 251–62.
149 *Encyclopédie*, 6: 470–1.
150 *Encyclopédie*, 6: 472.
151 Mary Hays, *Appeal to the Men of Great Britain in Behalf of Women* (London, 1798), 31–2, 47.
152 *Encyclopédie*, 6: 472.
153 Edmund Burke, *A Philosophical Enquiry Into the Origin of Our Ideas of the Sublime and Beautiful*, 2nd edn. (London, 1759), III.9.
154 Alexander Pope, 'Epistle II: To a Lady: Of the Character of Women', in Alexander Pope, *Epistles to Several Persons (Moral Essays)*, ed. F. W. Bateson (New Haven, CT, 1951), ll. 1–4, p. 45.
155 Hays, *Appeal to the Men of Great Britain*, 31–2.

156 Anne-Thérèse de Marguenat de Courcelles, marquise de Lambert, *Avis d'une mère à son fils* (1728), *D'Avis d'une mère à sa fille* (1726), in *Oeuvres*, ed. R. Granderoute (Paris, 1990), 43–94 and 95–150.

157 Lambert, *Reflexions nouvelles sur les femmes* (1728), in *Oeuvres*, 213–37.

158 De la Barre, *De l'égalité des deux sexes*, 94–106.

159 Kant, *Kritik der Urtheilskraft* (1790), Ak 5; *Anthropologie in pragmatischer Hinsicht*, Ak 7: 239–43.

160 Diderot, *Sur les femmes*, in *Oeuvres*, 2: 261.

161 Choderlos de Laclos, *Les liaisons dangereuses, ou Lettres recueillies dans une société et publiées pour l'instruction de quelques autres*, 4 vols. in 2 (Amsterdam, 1782); Diderot, *La religieuse* (1780), in *Oeuvres complètes*, vol. 5.

162 Diderot, *Supplément au Voyage de Bougainville* (1798), in *Oeuvres philosophiques*.

163 Diderot, *Les bijoux indiscrets* (1748) in *Oeuvres complètes*, vol. 4.

164 Diderot, *Le rêve de d'Alembert* (written 1769), in *Oeuvres philosophiques*, 328.

165 See, for one example, Donatien Alphonse François, marquis de Sade, 'Cent onze notes pour la Nouvelle Justine', in *Oeuvres complètes*, eds. A. Le Brun and J.-J. Pauvert, 15 vols. (Paris, 1986–91), 3: 593.

166 Mandeville, *Fable of the Bees*, I:367.

167 [Mandeville], *A Modest Defence of Publick Stews: or, An Essay Upon Whoring as it is now Practis'd in These Kingdoms* (1724), ed. R. I. Cook (Los Angeles, CA, 1973), 42.

168 Hume, *Treatise*, 3.2.12.3, SBN 571.

169 Pope, *An Essay on Man: The Design*, in *The Poems of Alexander Pope*, ed. M. Mack (New Haven, CT, 1952), III.1, 52.

170 Rousseau, *Émile*, 697; as translated in *Émile or On Education*, trans. A. Bloom (New York, NY, 1979), 361.

171 John Adams, *Curious Thoughts on the History of Man; Chiefly Abridged from the Celebrated Works of Lord Kames, Lord Monboddo, Dr Dunbar and the Immortal Montesquieu* (London, 1789), 93–5. This popular work gives an excellent summary of standard eighteenth-century philosophical opinions on a wide array of subjects.

172 Mary Astell, *Reflections upon Marriage*, in *Political Writings*, ed. P. Springborg (Cambridge, 1996), 13, and, on William Nicholls's neo-Filmerian *The Duty of Inferiours towards their Superiours, in Five Practical Discourses* (London, 1701), see Springborg's discussions at 5, 12n11, 243–4.

173 Montesquieu, *L'esprit de lois*, XVI.9.

174 Samuel Pufendorf, *On the Duty of Man and Citizen according to Natural Law*, ed. J. Tully, trans. M. Silverthorne (Cambridge, 1991), Bk. II, ch. 2, §5.

175 Locke, *Second Treatise*, paras. 52–3 and 77–83; compare *First Treatise*, paras. 61–7.

176 Hutcheson, *System*, 2: 185.

177 Adam Smith, *Lectures on Jurisprudence*, eds. R. L. Meek, D. D. Raphael, and P. G. Stein, in *Works* (1978), 157.

178 Kames, *Sketches*, II.26.

179 Smellie, *Natural History*, 1: 271–2.

180 Bentham, Principles of Morals and Legislation, ch. XVI, §44n and §51.

181 Hutcheson, *System*, 2: 164.

182 See Kant, *Metaphysik der Sitten*, Ak 6: 277–80; cf. *Anthropologie*, Ak VII: 303–11. See also Kant's odd remarks about the 'cannabilistic' nature of sexual intercourse, Ak 6: 359–60.

183 Hume, 'Of the Rise and Progress of the Arts and Sciences', 74.

184 Millar, *The Origin of the Distinction of Ranks*, 14.

185 Haakonssen, *Natural Law and Moral Philosophy*, 134–5.

186 William Godwin, *An Enquiry Concerning Political Justice*, in *Political and Philosophical Writings of William Godwin*, ed. M. Philp, 7 vols. (London, 1993), 3: VIII.6, pp. 161–284.

187 Astell, *Reflections upon Marriage* (1700, 3rd edn. 1706), in *Political Writings*, ed. P. Springborg (Cambrige, 1996), 18. On Astell's criticisms of Locke, see Springborg's Introduction, xix–xxv.

188 See Astell's remarks on Milton's defense of divorce in *Reflections upon Marriage*, 46–7.

189 See Springborg, Introduction, xiv–xv. Astell's *A Fair Way with the Dissenters and their Patrons* (London, 1704) was a response to Daniel Defoe's *More Short-Ways with the Dissenters* (London, 1704). See also Mandeville, *By a Society of Ladies: Essays in The Female Tatler*, ed. M. M. Goldsmith (Bristol, 1999), 54–5.

190 Mandeville, *The Virgin Unmask'd: or Female Dialogues Betwixt an Elderly Maiden Lady and her Niece on Several Diverting Discourses on Love Marriage, Memoirs and Morals of the Times* (London, 1709), 31–5, 112–23, 127. The work is cited and discussed in Mandeville's *By a Society of Ladies*, 28–9.

191 Astell, *A Serious Proposal to the Ladies for the Advancement of their True and Greatest Interest*, in *The First English Feminist: Reflections Upon Marriage and other writings by Mary Astell*, ed. B. Hill (New York, NY, 1986), Pt. 1, p. 153 (reprint of the 3rd edn. of 1696).

192 See *Herrn Johann Locks Unterricht von Erziehung der Kinder, aus dem Englischen: nebst Herrn von Fénelon . . . Gedancken von Erziehung der Töchter, aus dem Frantzösischen übersetzet*, trans. G. Olearius (Leipzig, 1708).

193 Locke, *Some Thoughts Concerning Education*, eds. J. W. Yolton and J. S. Yolton (Oxford, 1989), 265.

194 James Herbert Davis, *Fénelon* (Boston, MA, 1979), 108–9.

195 Catharine Macaulay (Graham), *Letters on Education with Observations on Religious and Metaphysical Subjects* (London, 1790), 21; Burke, *Reflections on the Revolution in France*, 253.

196 Madame Lambert noted that 'Les Auteurs Italiens sont peu châties', in *Avis d'une mère à son fils*, 144.

197 François de Salignac de la Mothe-Fénelon, *De l'éducation des filles*, in *Oeuvres*, ed. J. Le Brun, 2 vols. (Paris, 1983–97), 1: 156.

198 On the breadth of the genre, see Janet Todd, 'Introduction', in *Female Education in the Age of Enlightenment*, 6 vols. (London, 1996), 1: viii–xxiii. See also *Women in the Eighteenth Century*, ed. V. Jones (London, 1990), ch. 3.

199 Rousseau, *Émile*, 317–20.

200 See Jimack, 'The Paradox of Sophie and Julie', 161–2. On Rousseau's impact on issues of maternity, see Jean H. Bloch, 'Women and the Reform of the Nation', in *Women and Society in Eighteenth-Century France*, eds. E. Jacobs et al., 16.

201 Rousseau, *Émile*, 693; trans. 358.

202 Jean H. Bloch, *Rousseauism and Education in Eighteenth-Century France* (Oxford, 1995), 215–16; Colette Piau-Gillot, 'Le discours de Jean-Jacques Rousseau sur les femmes, et sa réception critique', in *Dix-Huitième Siècle*, 13 (1981): 317–33.

203 Stéphanie Félicité Genlis, *Adèle et Théodore, ou Lettres sur l'éducation* (Paris, 1782), Letters IX–X.

204 Mary Trouille, 'Eighteenth-Century Amazons of the Pen: Stephanie de Genlis & Olympe de Gouges', in *Femmes savantes et femmes d'esprit: Women Intellectuals of the French Eighteenth Century*, eds. R. Bonnel and C. Rubinger (New York, NY 1994), 341–70 at 349.

205 See Madame D'Epinay, *Les Conversations d'Émilie* (1773), ed. R. Davis (Oxford, 1996), 1–26; Mary Trouille, 'La Femme Mal Mariée: Mme. D'Epinay's Challenge to Julie and Émile', in *Eighteenth-Century Life*, 20 (1996): 42–66; Steinbrügge, *The Moral Sex*, 103–4.

206 Germaine de Staël, *Lettres sur les écrits et le caractère de J.-J. Rousseau* (1788), in *Oeuvres complètes*, 17 vols. (Paris, 1820–1), Lettre III, 1: 55–6.

207 Trouille, 'Eighteenth-Century Amazons of the Pen', 343–6.

208 Olympe de Gouges, 'Déclaration des Droits de la Femme, Dédiée à la Reine', in *Oeuvres*, ed. B. Groult (Paris, 1986), 1031, as translated in Mary Wollstonecraft, *A Vindication of the Rights of Men, and A Vindication of the Rights of Woman*, eds. D. L. Macdonald and K. Scherf (Peterborough, Ont., 1997), 381.

209 Marie-Jean-Antoine-Nicolas de Caritat Condorcet, 'Sur l'admission des femmes au droit de cité' (1790), in *Oeuvres*, eds. A. C. O'Connor and F. Arago, 12 vols. (Paris, 1847–9), vol. 10, here as translated in *Selected Writings*, ed. K. M. Baker (Indianapolis, IN, 1976), 97.

210 Macaulay, *Letters on Education*, 21–2.

211 Wollstonecraft, *A Vindication*, 43.

212 Thomas Gisborne, Gisborne, *An Enquiry into the Duties of Men in the Higher and Middle Classes of Society in Great Britain* (London, 1794); Gisborne, *An Enquiry into the Duties of the Female Sex* (London, 1797).

213 Hester Chapone, *Letters on the Improvement of the Mind* (Brookfield, VT, 1996), 121.

9

PERCEPTION AND IDEAS, JUDGEMENT

KENNETH P. WINKLER

I. PERCEPTION AND IDEAS

1. Perception and understanding: a general introduction

'The Word "Idea" is one of those that are so clear that they cannot be explained by others, because none is more clear and simple.' So say Antoine Arnauld and Pierre Nicole, the authors of *La logique, ou L'art de penser* (1662), better known as the *Port-Royal Logic*, a seventeenth-century handbook of logic widely used in Europe throughout the eighteenth century.[1] John Locke, whose *Essay Concerning Human Understanding* (1689) was treated as a 'logic' by many of the thinkers who followed in his wake, defined an idea as 'whatsoever is the Object of the Understanding when a Man thinks', a convenient vehicle, he went on to explain, 'to express whatever is meant by Phantasm, Notion, Species, or whatever it is, which the Mind can be employ'd about in thinking' (I.i.8). Locke resisted demands for further clarification. One natural question, raised by some of the first responses to the *Essay*, is whether ideas are substances ('thing'-like entities capable of separate existence) or modes (determinate states or aspects of substances). To this, Locke's reply was 'let them be what they will. When they are classified as modes or substances,' he explained, 'I am no more instructed in their nature, than when I am told they are perceptions, such as I find them'.[2] Yet despite the confidence of Locke and the authors of the *Port-Royal Logic*, the eighteenth century was riddled with disagreement and confusion about ideas – about their origin and composition, their role in judgement, their relation to the will, their intrinsic nature, and even their very existence. The opening section of this chapter traces these disagreements and confusions and examines their influence on a range of topics in the theory of knowledge. The second section turns from ideas to theories of the judgements or propositions in which they figured. The confusion and disagreement about ideas did not escape notice in the eighteenth century itself. In Voltaire's entry on 'Idea' in the *Dictionnaire philosophique portatif* (1764), for example, two voices – one sceptical from the start, the other sceptical by the dialogue's end – debate the nature of ideas. 'It's very sad to have so many ideas and not to know precisely the nature of ideas', the first concludes. 'I admit it', says the second, 'but it's much sadder and much more foolish to think we know what we don't know'.[3] In his *Essays on the Intellectual Powers of Man* (1785), Thomas Reid delivered much the same verdict with less amusement. 'Philosophers', he wrote, 'notwithstanding their unanimity as to the existence of ideas, hardly agree in any one thing else concerning them. If ideas be not a mere fiction, they must be, of all objects of human knowledge, the things we have best access to know, and to be acquainted with; yet there is nothing about which men differ so much.'[4]

The main eighteenth-century theories of perception were self-consciously 'modern'. Those who followed the 'way of ideas' (as it was called by Locke's critic Edward Stillingfleet)[5] were united in their opposition to scholastic theories of sense perception – or to scholastic theories as they understood them. In the view of their critics, these theories were closely tied to a metaphysics portraying bodies as material substrata informed by what we (following the critics) now call 'qualities'.[6] Bodies were held to be *causes* of perception,[7] and their causal power was traced to the transmission of 'forms' or 'species' capable of existing (though in 'diverse Manners', as the late seventeenth-century scholastic John Sergeant explained) in both body and mind.[8] When a form exists 'materially' in a body, it invests the body with a quality or feature. When the same form exists 'immaterially' in a mind, it invests the mind with perception or knowledge of the body so qualified. The philosophers to be examined here repudiated all forms or species leading a double life in the knower and the known. John Locke, whose response to scholasticism was both influential and typical, replaced forms and species (as the marginal annotation to *Essay* II.viii.8 bluntly indicates) with 'Ideas *in the Mind, Qualities in Bodies*'. He abandoned transmission as a causal mechanism, appealing first to *impulse* or *impact* (the action of one body as it pushes against another), which explains how external objects stimulate the sense organs and how this sensory stimulation or disturbance is conveyed through the body to the brain and then to *God*, whose omnipotent will picks up the process where impulse or impact leaves off, 'annexing' ideas or perceptions to motions in the brain. Some eighteenth-century philosophers (notably Berkeley) abandoned impulse or impact as an authentic causal mechanism, as Malebranche had in the seventeenth century; others (d'Holbach and Priestley, for example) explained – or dreamed of explaining – everything in terms of it. But no follower of the way of ideas contemplated a return to transmission as a causal mechanism. They viewed it as an unintelligible hypothesis that left the scholastic philosophers with no way of understanding how forms or species voyage from the body to the mind, no account of the manner in which their immaterial or intentional

existence differs from their actual embodiment, and no way of explaining how a
form or species survives, its identity intact, in hosts as different as mind and body.

For the most part, eighteenth-century philosophers viewed the understanding as one of several 'faculties' or *powers* of the human mind; *perception* (or one
of its cognates) was their preferred label for its characteristic or most basic act or
operation. In this they followed the example set by Descartes, Malebranche, and
Locke. (The word 'perception' was also used, however, as a synonym for 'idea' –
that is, as a label for the *object* of an act of understanding, as opposed to the act
itself.)[9] At the same time, eighteenth-century philosophers generally honoured
a long-standing distinction, reinforced by the standard logic textbooks of the
seventeenth and eighteenth centuries, among three more specific acts or operations of the understanding: *apprehension* or *conception*, the bare representation
of an object; *judgement*, the formation of a belief concerning the object apprehended or 'thought of'; and *reasoning*, the act of eliciting conclusions from
judgements taken as premises. Part I of the *Port-Royal Logic*, for example, had
been devoted to 'the first action of the mind, which is called conceiving' (I.25).
Part II was concerned with 'Judgments', in which the terms or ideas discussed
in Part I are joined together to form propositions (II.73). Part III was 'On reasoning', in which judgements are ordered into syllogisms (III.135). The first or
theoretical part of Christian Wolff's *Philosophia rationalis sive logica, Pars II* (1728),
for example, follows the same general plan. It opens with a general discussion of
the three operations of the mind, and the succeeding chapters take them up in
the usual order, as do the chapters of Francis Hutcheson's much briefer *Logicae
compendium* (1756), which is, in this respect, typical of the many logic hand-
books published in Britain during the eighteenth century. Though Condillac,
in his *Essai sur l'origine des connaissances humaines* (1746), jumbles the order of the
textbooks, all the powers enumerated in his definition of the understanding can
be placed, as my bracketed additions indicate, under one of the three standard
headings:

Here is what characterizes the understanding: to perceive or to be conscious, to pay
attention, to recognize, to imagine, to remember, to reflect, to distinguish ideas [all forms
of apprehension], to abstract them, compare them, compose them, decompose them,
to analyze [forms of apprehension, or, perhaps, in some cases of judgment], [to] affirm,
deny, judge [forms of judgment], reason [reasoning], and to conceive [apprehension
again, or, perhaps, a catch-all for all the preceding].[10]

David Hartley, in his *Observations on Man* (1749), defines the understanding as
'that faculty, by which we contemplate mere sensations and ideas, pursue truth,
and assent to, or dissent from, propositions'.[11] Like Condillac, Hartley neglects
the textbook order but respects its classification: contemplation is *apprehension*;

assent and dissent are the forms of *judgement*; and the pursuit of truth is, in part at least, the exercise of *reasoning*.

Some philosophers (most conspicuously Kant) withdrew reasoning from the scope of the understanding, assigning it to a separate faculty of reason.[12] But, for others, understanding and reason were one and the same. Locke, for example, defined 'reason' (in one of its several senses) as 'That Faculty, whereby Man is supposed to be distinguished from Beasts, and wherein it is evident he much surpasses them' (*Essay*, IV.xvii.1). It therefore coincided with the understanding, whose scope and limits were the subject matter of the *Essay*. Dugald Stewart objected to those who confined the label 'reason' to the illative or discursive faculty. He criticised Samuel Johnson, for example, for giving this meaning of the word first place in his *Dictionary of the English Language* (1755). Reason, according to Johnson, is 'the power by which man deduces one proposition from another, or proceeds from premises to consequences'.[13] Although the 'affinity' between 'reason' and 'reasoning' accounts for this narrowing, Stewart thought it was obvious on 'the slightest reflection' that '*reasoning* only expresses *one* of the various functions or operations of *reason*'.[14]

Apprehension, the 'first' or most basic act of the understanding, was sometimes distinguished, at least implicitly, from comprehension or 'adequate' understanding, though, in their struggle to make the distinction clear, many philosophers found themselves appealing to metaphor. Descartes, for example, had written that although I do not 'grasp' or comprehend the infinite, I am nonetheless able to 'touch' it in my thought, just as 'we can touch a mountain with our hands but we cannot put our arms around it as we could put them around a tree or something else not too large for them'.[15] Whether the understanding can touch or reach what it does not comprehend depends in part on whether, in order for the understanding to 'touch' an object, it must know the object to be the object that it is, as opposed to something else. If the answer is yes, and if the standards for such knowledge are exacting enough, there may be no *apprehension* apart from something that looks very much like *comprehension*. This form of argument was used throughout the eighteenth century by philosophers, among them Berkeley, Hume, and Kant, willing to deny that we apprehend (or in any way conceive of) some of the central objects in the metaphysical schemes of their predecessors.

A further distinction among the *forms* or *manners* of apprehension was also commonplace. It was standardly suggested that some objects are brought to the mind's attention via *sensation*, some are reproduced by *memory*, others are formed by the *imagination* from material provided by sensation and stored in memory, and still others are intuited by *pure intellect*. Some philosophers, many of them materialists, denied the existence of pure intellect; all our ideas, they contended, are

ideas of sense, or ideas concocted by a sense-based memory and imagination with
the power to recall ideas of sense and combine them in new ways. *Reflection* –
the mind's apprehension of its own acts and operations (and even, according
to some, of its own essence) – was another widely acknowledged channel of
apprehension, but its relationship with the trichotomy of sensation, memory
or imagination (two faculties which were closely linked and sometimes even
identified), and intellect was understood in strikingly divergent ways. Some
philosophers assimilated reflection to sensation. For them, reflection became an
'inner' sense, something that could fairly be described as a form or aspect of
experience. Others saw reflection as the work of the pure or abstract intellect
and treated its existence as an argument for purely intellectual ideas representing
objects other than the mind and its operations (objects in nature, for example,
or in the mind of God, or in some third, abstract realm).

The views of Gottfried Wilhelm Leibniz show how complex, and how varied
in their influence, eighteenth-century accounts of the forms of apprehension
could be. The basic entities in Leibniz's metaphysical scheme were immaterial
'monads' or 'entelechies' characterised by powers of perception and 'appetition'.
(In *Leibniz's Monadologie* (1714), appetition is defined as 'the internal principle
which brings about change or the passage from one perception to another'.)[16]
Each of these simple substances perceives (or expresses or represents) the entire
universe. As Leibniz explains in the *Principes de la nature et de la grâce* (1714), each
one 'is a living mirror . . . and . . . represents the universe according to its point
of view and is regulated as completely as is the universe itself'.[17] Representation
or expression does not require consciousness; as Leibniz explained in his *Correspondence avec Arnauld*, 'one thing expresses another, in my usage, when there is
a constant and regular relation between what can be said about one and about
the other'.[18] But monads express the universe with more or less clarity and distinctness. When one perception enjoys enough 'contrast and distinction' with
those that are received along with it, it 'may amount to *sensation*, that is to say, to
a perception accompanied by *memory* – a perception of which there remains a
kind of echo for a long time which makes itself heard on occasion' (*Principes*, §4;
1035). The memorability of a sensation seems to be a consequence of its greater
distinctness.[19] The intrinsic difference between a mere perception and a sensation is therefore a matter of degree, and a difference of degree is all that separates
a sensation or sensible idea, considered in itself, from an intellectual one. 'Confused thoughts' are not 'entirely different in kind from distinct ones', Leibniz
claimed in a 1702 reply to objections made by Pierre Bayle. Confused thoughts,
he explained, are 'merely less distinguishable and less developed because of their
multiplicity'.[20] 'The soul itself does not know the things which it perceives until
it has perceptions which are distinct and heightened. And it has perfection in

proportion to the distinctions of its perception. Each soul knows the infinite, knows everything but confusedly.'[21] The line of thought just reviewed led to the 'one-faculty' theory of Christian Wolff.[22]

According to Wolff, the cognitive powers of the human soul are all expressions of one basic power – a unitary *vis repraesentativa* (representative power or representative faculty) that is responsible for sensations when its representations are confused and for concepts when its representations are clear and distinct.[23] In his *De mundi sensibilis* (1770), Kant derided 'the illustrious WOLFF' for thereby abolishing, 'to the great detriment of philosophy', the very 'distinction between what is sensitive and what belongs to the understanding'.[24] Wolff's distinction, Kant complained, was merely 'logical'. '[S]ensitive representations can be very distinct', Kant wrote, 'and representations which belong to the understanding can be extremely confused' (§7). Kant repeated the complaint in his *Kritik der reinen Vernunft* (1781), where he targeted not only Wolff but Leibniz. The difference between sensible and intelligible representations, he wrote there, 'does not concern merely the . . . form, of distintness or indistinctness, but its origin and content' (A 44/B 61–2). For Leibniz, Kant wrote, sensibility was 'only a confused kind of representation . . . and not a special source of representations' (A 270/B 326). Hence Leibniz 'intellectualised the appearances', which in the end brought him close to Locke, who 'sensitivized the concepts of understanding' by treating them 'as nothing but empirical or abstracted concepts of reflection'. These opposite mistakes, committed by philosophers with very different starting points, left them (in Kant's view) in much the same place. Neither Leibniz nor Locke saw that 'understanding and sensibility' are 'two entirely different sources of representation' which can 'judge about things with objective validity *only in conjunction*' (A 271/B 327).

A somewhat different account of the dividing line between the sensible and the intelligible emerges, however, in Leibniz's *Nouveaux essais sur l'entendement humain* (1765), a running commentary, in dialogue form, on Locke's *Essay*. Leibniz completed this work in 1704 but withheld it from publication because of Locke's death in that same year. The claim that sensations and intellectual representations differ in degree is undeniably to be found there,[25] but Leibniz also claims that intellectual representations differ in source from their counterparts in sensation, and he sometimes suggests – as he does in other works – that they differ in content as well. Theophilus, Leibniz's spokesman in the dialogue, points to a difference in source or origin in response to Philalethes' insistence that all ideas come from the senses:

Intellectual ideas, from which necessary truths arise, do not come from the senses; and you acknowledge that some ideas arise from the mind's reflection when it turns in on itself.... [T]ruths involving ideas which come from the senses are themselves at least partly dependent on the senses. But the ideas that come from the senses are confused; and so too, at least in part, are the truths which depend on them; whereas intellectual ideas, and the truths depending on them, are distinct, and neither ... originate in the senses. (81)

Even intellectual ideas of the external world have their source in the mind's reflection on itself:

[I]deas which are said to come from more than one sense – such as those of space, figure, motion, rest – come rather from the common sense, that is, from the mind itself; for they are ideas of the pure understanding (though ones which relate to the external world and which the senses make us perceive). (128)

A difference in content is implied by Leibniz's contrast between ideas and images. But Leibniz's understanding of images, at least in the *Nouveaux essais*, is not entirely stable. In some places, he suggests that images are not ideas at all (see pp. 261 and 487, for example); elsewhere he suggests that they are ideas of a restricted kind (451). Leibniz's test for the presence of a clear and distinct idea – the ability to give a priori proofs of many truths about the corresponding thing (219) – suggests that having a clear and distinct idea at least is fundamentally different in character from the mere registration of an impression or image. Having an idea seems to be a functional capacity, one not so different from the capacities for the assembly or 'synthesis' of representations that Kant himself associates with concepts of the understanding.[26]

Eighteenth-century philosophers used a variety of names for the objects of apprehension. They were spoken of simply as *objects*, as *notions, concepts, phantasms, species*, or *representations*, and even as things themselves. But for most of the century, at least in Britain and France, the word 'idea' (*idée*), as it was used in the previous century by Descartes, Gassendi, Locke, and the authors of the *Port-Royal Logic*, was by far the most popular choice. In Germany, philosophers followed Wolff and Kant in speaking more often of representations (*Vorstellungen*). As we have seen, Locke's use of the word was deliberately broad. 'Idea' was an umbrella term, and collected beneath it were a host of more specific ones, their shades of difference holding little interest for Locke and many of the philosophers he influenced. Berkeley's *Essay Towards a New Theory of Vision* (1709) testifies to the growing influence – and the self-consciously 'modern' tone – of this broad conception of ideas. He writes that 'when I speak of tangible ideas, I take the word idea for the immediate object of sense or understanding, in which large signification it is commonly used by the moderns'.[27]

Yet there were those, among them Berkeley himself in subsequent works, who were unwilling to speak of *all* objects of the understanding as ideas.[28]

Berkeley believed that all representative ideas are images: they represent their objects only because they resemble them. On this basis, he argued that there can be no ideas of the mind and its operations. These are essentially active, and wholly unlike the passive and inert ideas that are supposed by some to represent them. We have, Berkeley proposed, *notions* of the mind's acts and operations, but we do not – we cannot – have ideas of them. Berkeley's use of the word *notion* was influenced by his predecessors, who (despite their broad understanding of 'idea') often used 'notion' for objects of apprehension other than those passively received through the senses. Locke, for example, speaking of the mind's power to join ideas 'without examining whether they [or rather their objects] exist so together in Nature', writes that 'these *Ideas* are called *Notions*: as if they had their Original, and constant Existence, more in the Thoughts of Men, than in the reality of things' (*Essay*, II.xxii.2). Several of Berkeley's contemporaries followed his lead. Samuel Johnson, whose *Elementa philosophica* was published in Philadelphia in 1752, takes note of the broad use of the word 'idea' but recommends that the word be used more narrowly. The word 'idea', he explains, 'has been commonly defined and used by the Moderns' to signify 'any immediate Object of the Mind in Thinking, whether sensible or intellectual, and so is, in Effect, synonymous with the word *Thought*, which comprehends both'. He continues, 'It may be best', however, 'to confine the Word *Idea* to the immediate Objects of Sense and Imagination, which was the original Meaning of it; and to use the Word *Notion* or *Conception*, to signify the Objects of Consciousness and pure Intellect'.[29] Christian Wolff proposed a different distinction, between an idea [*idea*] as a representation of a particular thing, and a notion [*notio*] as a representation of a universal (such as a species or genus) shared by many things.[30] Wolff's proposal was perpetuated by Georg Friedrich Meier, who distinguished between an 'abstract concept', or *notio* – a representation of many things – and a 'singular concept', or *idea*.[31]

In *An Enquiry concerning Human Understanding* (1748), Hume took exception to what Berkeley and Johnson called the 'modern' way of speaking, but for a different reason. He complained that the word idea is 'commonly taken in a very loose sense, by LOCKE and others; as standing for any of our perceptions, our sensations and passions, as well as thoughts'.[32] Hume himself divided all the mind's objects (which he called *perceptions*) into impressions (the more forcible and lively perceptions) and ideas (the less forcible and lively). Hence sensations and passions are not ideas but *impressions*. (Locke had used the word 'impression' primarily for the direct effect of external bodies on our sense organs.) Hartley also excluded sensations from the class of ideas. He defined sensations as internal feelings arising from impressions made by external objects on the body.[33] Ideas, he said, are all *other* internal feelings.

Kant was influenced more than most of his contemporaries by the Platonic affiliations of idea. 'Plato', he wrote in the *Kritik der reinen Vernunft* (A 313/ B 370), 'made use of the expression "idea" in such a way as quite evidently to have meant by it something which not only can never be borrowed from the senses but far surpasses even the concepts of understanding . . . inasmuch as in experience nothing is ever to be met with that is coincident with it'. Kant used the word *Vorstellung* (representation) where Hume used 'perception' and Locke and Descartes used 'idea'. A 'representation with consciousness' is a perception, and a perception of an object is either an *Anschauung* (intuition) or a *Begriff* (concept). 'The former relates immediately to the object and is single, the latter refers to it mediately by means of a feature which several things may have in common' (A 320/B 377). A pure concept of the understanding, or 'category', is a general representation which, instead of being derived from experience, makes experience (or 'empirical knowledge') possible. These concepts are *transcendental* because they are *enabling* of empirical knowledge; their employment, though it is neither owed to experience nor justified by it, is nonetheless confined to the objects of experience. A pure concept, 'in so far as it has its origin in the under- standing alone', is a notion (A 320/B 377). An idea (*idée*) or 'concept of reason' is, like the ideas of Plato, 'a concept formed from notions and transcending the possibility of experience'.

Ideas were commonly regarded as the immediate signification of words, and the communication of ideas was often portrayed as the chief (if not the sole) end of language. Ideas and words therefore served as the foundation of analo- gous structures: ideas corresponded to single words or expressions; judgements to whole propositions or sentences; and inferences to syllogisms or larger 'dis- courses'. Locke had announced that ideas are the primary and immediate signi- fication of words, but even he recognised exceptions: 'negative Names' such as barrenness and 'particles' such as 'is' and 'is not'.[34] Berkeley argued that many words do not excite ideas, and that their meaningfulness is in no way compro- mised by this. Language has, he suggested, many uses besides the communication of ideas – the raising of passion, for example, and the guiding of action. Words without ideas can be meaningful if they are part of a system of signs with a bearing on practice. Expressions such as 'force', 'the square root of negative one', and 'the grace of God' are examples.[35] David Hartley expanded on this theme. Some words, he contended, have definitions but no ideas. His examples include algebraic roots, scientific terms of art, and indeed 'most abstract general terms'. Others – such as the, of, to, for, and but – have neither.[36]

Whether all ideas are objects of conscious awareness was a topic of active disagreement. In his attack on innate ideas in Book I of the *Essay*, Locke asserted that the mind must be conscious of any idea in it. (As his critics were quick to point out, this makes a mystery of memory. They used memory as evidence that ideas may be present in the mind – or present to it – even at birth, waiting to be drawn into the light of consciousness.)[37] In the *Nouveaux essais*, Leibniz called Locke's view into question and proposed a distinction between perception and being aware (or 'apperception', as Leibniz was the first to call it). 'A perception of light or colour of which we are aware', his spokesman Theophilus explains, is 'made up of many minute perceptions [*petites perceptions*] of which we are unaware' (134). 'To give a clearer idea of these minute perceptions', Leibniz explained in the Preface to the *Nouveaux essais*,

I like to use the example of the roaring noise of the sea which impresses itself on us when we are standing on the shore. To hear this noise as we do, we must hear the parts which make up this whole, that is the noise of each wave, although each of these little noises makes itself known only when combined confusedly with all the others, and would not be noticed if the wave which made it were by itself. (54)

In the *Nouveaux essais*, Leibniz speaks of apperceiving external things as well as what is in ourselves, but in the *Principes de la nature et de la grâce*, apperception is defined as a 'consciousness or the reflective knowledge of [an] inner state ... which is not given to all souls or to any soul all the time'.[38] In the *Monadologie*, perception is distinguished 'from apperception or from consciousness': an apperception is apparently a perception that is itself perceived – a perception of which we are conscious or aware. The exact interpretation of Leibniz's developing views on apperception is a matter of controversy, but apperception – reflective awareness or consciousness – is perhaps another feature separating intellectual ideas from sensible ones. Apperception may be a kind of attention or focused reflection that makes it possible for the mind to achieve the a priori proofs mentioned above.[39]

The Leibnizian distinction between perception (the act by which an object is represented to the mind) and apperception (the act by which the mind is conscious of what is represented) was codified by Wolff in his textbooks. The alternative Lockean position was emphatically endorsed by Condillac. He compared saying that we perceive without being conscious to saying that we perceive without perceiving.[40]

2. The nature and existence of ideas

A. ACTS OR OBJECTS? In the seventeenth century, Arnauld and Malebranche debated both the nature of ideas and the proper interpretation of Descartes's account of their nature. Arnauld ascribed to Descartes what he himself took to be the true view: an idea is simply an act or modification of the mind by which the mind apprehends an object. Malebranche ascribed to Descartes what *he* took to be the true view: an idea is an object of the mind, distinct from the act by which it is apprehended. In Malebranche's view, ideas are in God, who vouchsafes glimpses to us. *Sensations* or *sentiments* are in us, but Malebranche rigorously distinguished them from the intelligible notions that are ideas strictly so called.[41] Descartes's own pronouncements on the nature of ideas are undeniably ambiguous.[42] Locke's official explanations of his understanding of 'idea' are less so – they lean unmistakably towards an 'objectual' interpretation, despite Locke's hostility to Malebranche's theory of ideas.[43] But Locke's *use* of the word is another matter.[44] As Joseph Butler wrote in the Preface to his *Fifteen Sermons*, philosophical notions 'never are in themselves determinate, but become so by the train of reasoning and the place they stand in'.[45] Many eighteenth-century philosophers, especially in France, stated their views very clearly, thanks perhaps to the light cast by the Arnauld/Malebranche debate. Their official formulations often aligned them with Arnauld, but their practice did not always comply with their formulations.

According to Condillac, for example, ideas are merely

the modes of existence of the soul. They exist so long as they modify the soul and they no longer exist when they cease to modify it. To search within the soul for ideas which I am not thinking of at all, is to seek them where they no longer are: to search for them in the body is to seek them where they never were. Where are they, then? Nowhere.[46]

Condillac compares the ideas of the soul to the sounds of a harpsichord, which vanish as soon as the playing ceases; both this comparison and the earlier formulation ally him with Arnauld. But elsewhere Condillac defines an idea in terms of the impression produced or occasioned in the mind by an object. An idea, he explains, is 'the notice we take' of this impression 'as an image'.[47] Here a modification – an impression in the mind – seems to function as an object, as something the mind 'notices' or contemplates. The idea, it seems, is something distinct from this modification: an act by which the impression is interpreted as an image or sign of a thing. This act can itself be regarded as a modification, but we are left with a view more complex than it seemed to be at first. We now have *two* modifications – an impression, and an act of interpretation by which the impression becomes an image – and one of them (the impression) *functions* as an object.

D'Holbach, in his *Système de la nature* of 1770, defines an idea as 'only an imperceptible modification of the brain'.[48] 'Every *sensation*', he explains, 'is nothing more, than the shock given to the organs; every *perception*, is this shock propagated to the brain: every idea, is the image of the object to which the sensation and the perception is to be ascribed' (I.i.8, p. 189). Like most other eighteenth-century materialists, d'Holbach makes a clear distinction between the physical modification of the brain, which is the *act*, and the object *in the world* towards which it is directed. But when he speaks of the act as an image, it begins to function as an object – as an intermediary triggered or occasioned by the external object to which the contemplating mind (or brain) 'ascribes' it.

In his *Meditationes de cognitione, veritate et ideis* (1684), to which he often referred in his late works, Leibniz also seemed to side with Arnauld, despite his evident sympathy for the doctrine of divine illumination he took Malebranche to represent. 'As to the controversy whether we see all things in God (an old opinion which, properly understood, is not to be rejected) or whether we have some ideas of our own', he writes,

it must be understood that, even if we saw all things in God, it would still be necessary to have our own ideas also, not in the sense of some kind of little copies, but as affections or modifications of our mind, corresponding to the very object we perceive in God. For whenever thoughts succeed each other, some change occurs in our mind.[49]

Here ideas seem to be identified with a person's occurrent thoughts. But in the *Nouveaux essais* Leibniz warns against this identification. Ideas 'are in us', Theophilus explains, '. . . before we actually think of them. . . . If anyone wants to take ideas to be men's actual thoughts, he may; but he will be gratuitously going against accepted ways of speaking.'[50] Elsewhere in the *Nouveaux essais*, Theophilus agrees – though only on certain conditions – with Philalethes's proposal that (quoting Locke's marginal summary of *Essay*, II.i.1) an idea is the object of thinking:

I agree about that, provided that you add that an idea is an immediate inner object, and that this object expresses the nature or qualities of things. If the idea were the *form* of the thought, it would come into and go out of existence with the actual thoughts which correspond to it, but since it is the *object* of thought it can exist before and after the thoughts. Sensible outer objects are only *mediate*, because they cannot act immediately on the soul. God is the only *immediate outer* object. One might say that the soul itself is its own immediate inner object; but that is only to the extent that it contains ideas, i.e. something corresponding to things. For the soul is a little world where distinct ideas represent God and confused ones represent the universe. (109)

Ideas, Theophilus later explains, are dispositions that remain as our thoughts come and go.[51] They are what might be described as content-conferring dispositions: its various ideas enable the mind to think one thing rather than another, and it is this content-conferring power Leibniz gestures towards when he speaks of ideas as the immediate inner objects of the mind. Ontologically considered, an idea is an 'affection' of the mind – a standing disposition as opposed to an occurrent thought. But it is at the same time an object of the mind, and an immediate one, because it is what enables the mind to think of the various mediate objects outside it.[52]

Other eighteenth-century philosophers who treat ideas as objects made no attempt to reduce them to the mind's modifications or affections. Berkeley, for example, speaks persistently of ideas as the immediate objects of thought. They are, he writes in *A Treatise concerning the Principles of Human Knowledge* (1710), in the mind 'not by way of *mode* or *attribute*, but only by way of *idea*' (§49, 61).[53] And they function as objects in, for example, his influential account of abstract thinking, which we will discuss. Hume's perceptions are also described as objects, and they function as objects in his account of abstract thinking (an elaboration of Berkeley's) and in his discussions of scepticism.[54]

Classifying ideas as objects gives rise to many questions. Perhaps the most basic is whether ideas are what might be described as ordinary objects – that is, objects that must exist in order to serve as objects – or what we now call *intentional* objects – objects that are merely the content (or some aspect of the content) of our perceptual acts. Berkeley's ideas are non-intentional or 'ordinary' objects, as are Hume's perceptions. Thomas Reid contended in *Philosophical Orations* that ideas or perceptions so understood are a 'fictitious hypothesis of philosophers, favorable to the views of skeptics but an impediment to sane or useful knowledge'.[55] Reid's own account of the objects of thought begins with a clear distinction between act and object:

> [W]e must distinguish between that act or operation of the mind, which we call conceiving an object, and the object which we conceive. When we conceive any thing, there is a real act or operation of the mind, of this we are conscious, and can have no doubt of its existence. But every such act must have an object; for he that conceives, must conceive something. (*Essays on the Intellectual Powers*, p. 311)

But this object, he adds, need not exist. 'The powers of sensation, of perception, of memory, and of consciousness, are all employed solely about objects that do exist, or have existed', Reid concedes (311). But the objects of imagination do not exist. They are creatures, he explains, that 'never [were] created' (311). It follows that the object that an act of thought *must* have, just because it is an act of thought, is not 'ordinary' but intentional.

Reid believed that all his most famous predecessors – Descartes, Malebranche, Locke, Berkeley, and Hume – treated ideas as 'ordinary' objects. He argued that this drew them into scepticism. If the immediate objects of perception are ideas, he argued (following Berkeley and Hume) that there is then no way of establishing the existence of a world beyond our ideas. Reid's assessment is controversial.[56] In his *Lectures on the Philosophy of the Human Mind* (1820), Thomas

Brown writes that, with the exception of Berkeley and Malebranche, 'who had peculiar and very erroneous notions on the subject', all the philosophers Reid opposes 'would, if they had been questioned by him, have admitted, before they heard a single argument on his part, that their opinions, with respect to ideas were precisely the same as his own'.[57]

Many eighteenth-century philosophers claimed that all ideas are images. Others emphatically denied it. The claim was understood in a wide variety of ways. It was sometimes taken to mean that ideas are representations, and in this sense it was accepted by almost everyone.[58] But it was also taken to mean that all ideas are derived from sensation, and this claim, as our earlier discussion of Leibniz and his influence indicated, was highly controversial. Note that an idea can be an image in this narrower sense whether it is an act of the mind, an 'ordinary' object, or an intentional one. This is because it is possible, on any one of the three understandings, to give sense to the claim that an idea (or its representational content) is derived from sensation.

B. THE EXISTENCE OF IDEAS In Berkeley's *Three Dialogues between Hylas and Philonous* (1713), the existence of ideas (as the immediate, yet non-intentional, objects of perception) is defended by a series of arguments from perceptual relativity. According to these arguments, the immediate objects of perception must be something other than physical objects themselves because *what we immediately perceive* (what we see or hear) changes as *we* change, even though the objects remain the same. Hume offered a concise statement of the argument, one that Reid later examined in some detail. According to Hume,

The table, which we see, seems to diminish, as we remove farther from it: but the real table, which exists independent of us, suffers no alteration: it was, therefore, nothing but its image, which was present to the mind. These are the obvious dictates of reason; and no man, who reflects, ever doubted, that the existences, which we consider, when we say, *this house* and *that tree*, are nothing but perceptions in the mind, and fleeting copies or representations of other existences, which remain uniform and independent.[59]

Reid's criticism of Hume's argument borrows a distinction between visible or apparent magnitude and tangible or *real* magnitude from Berkeley's theory of vision. Reid summarises Hume's argument as follows:

[T]he table we see seems to diminish as we remove farther from it; that is, its apparent magnitude is diminished; but the real table suffers no alteration, to wit, in its real magnitude; therefore it is not the real table we see. (*Intellectual Powers*, II.14, 182)

His response is to grant both premises but deny the conclusion:

The syllogism has what the Logicians call two middle terms: Apparent magnitude is the middle term in the first premise; real magnitude in the second. Therefore, according to the rules of logic, the conclusion is not justly drawn from the premises. (182)

Reid goes on to examine the argument further 'by the light of common sense'. He points out that the real table *must* seem to diminish as we remove farther from it. 'Mr HUME's argument not only has no strength to support his conclusion, but . . . leads to the contrary conclusion' because the observed changes in apparent magnitude are 'demonstrable' given the existence of the table (183).

Reid might have said that the external existence of a table with a stable real magnitude is the best explanation of the observed changes in apparent magnitude. Such a response would have been more faithful to the original setting of many of the arguments from perceptual relativity (in Hobbes and Locke, for example). These were not attempts to establish the existence of ideas by linear argument. They were attempts to show that nonscholastic theories of perception – theories that dispensed with the transmission of forms – offered more promising explanations of a range of familiar facts (why a bucket of lukewarm water, for example, feels warm to a cool hand and cold to a warm one) than their Aristotelian competitors. If Reid had chosen to put his argument in these terms, it would perhaps have raised even more fruitful questions about the aim of theories of perception. Is it the aim of such theories to explain why an act of mind is 'of' a certain object? Reid himself disavowed such a hope, but it was one to which many of the philosophers he criticised remained attached. If a philosopher hopes to do more than record the fact that a given act is 'of' a given (nonmental) object, it is natural to assume we are faced with a mental object – an immediate object whose apprehension by the mind is unproblematic – with the power to represent it. Both Berkeley and Hume argue against this view, in part by attacking the distinction between direct and indirect perception which underlies it. Berkeley argues, for example, that there is no relation between the direct object and the indirect object that can be used to explain how one represents the other. But Berkeley in his theory of vision does make positive use of a distinction between direct and indirect perception.

Reid traced the theory of ideas partly to the prejudice that 'in all the operations of understanding, there must be an object of thought, which really exists while we think of it; or, as some philosophers have expressed it, that which is not cannot be intelligible' (*Intellectual Powers*, IV.2, 312). To this he replied that we can easily have 'a distinct conception of things which never existed' (313). We can, for example, conceive of a centaur, even though no centaur has ever existed.

Reid imagines that the defender of ideas will say that 'the idea is an image of the animal, and is the immediate object of my conception, and that the animal is the mediate or remote object' (321). But, Reid plausibly replies, it is one thing to conceive of an animal and another to conceive of its image.

C. THE ORIGIN OF IDEAS Any account of eighteenth-century debate concerning the origin of ideas must begin with Locke, whose attack on innate ideas was revered by some and viewed with puzzlement or alarm by others. Lockean empiricism was especially influential in France and Britain. Condillac, Voltaire (in his *Lettres philosophiques ou Lettres sur les Anglais*, 1733), and d'Alembert (in his *Discours préliminaire de l'Encyclopédie*, 1751) were among those in France who promoted the Lockean thesis that all ideas are derived from experience – that no idea is innate. They praised Locke partly by deriding Descartes, who, according to Condillac, 'knew neither the origin nor the generation of our ideas'.[60] Condillac's *Essai sur l'origine des connaissances humaines* was an attempt to extend Locke's achievement in the *Essay*. 'We must ascend to the origin of our ideas, reveal how they are generated, trace them to the limits that nature has set for them, and thereby determine the extent and limits of our knowledge and invest human understanding with new life' (*Essai*, 5). To advance in knowledge is to connect ideas, but their connection, at least in its upper reaches, depends on the arbitrary signs connected with them. These arbitrary signs – words are the most conspicuous examples – enable us to analyse our ideas, and this analysis enables us to combine ideas into judgements that possess more clarity, scope, and certainty than the confused judgements we make (without reflection or deliberation) when jumbles of undiscriminated ideas impress themselves upon us.

'All our direct knowledge', writes d'Alembert, 'can be reduced to what we receive through our senses; whence it follows that we owe all our ideas to our sensations'. D'Alembert, like Condillac, emphasises the importance of connecting ideas. The difference between the person of genius (*ingenium* or wit) and others is the ease with which the first connects ideas.[61]

The major British philosophers had a more complicated relationship to Locke's empiricism.[62] Berkeley agreed that all *ideas* are derived from experience, but whether notions are so derived is less clear. Hume claimed to be puzzled by Locke's attack on nativism:

It is probable that no more was meant by those, who denied innate ideas than that all ideas were copies of our impressions; though it must be confessed, that the terms, which they employed, were not chosen with such caution, nor so exactly defined, as to prevent all mistakes about their doctrine. For what is meant by *innate*? If 'innate' be equivalent to 'natural', then all the perceptions and ideas of the mind must be allowed to be innate or natural, in whatever sense we take the latter word. . . . If by *innate* be meant, *contemporary to our birth*, the dispute seems to be frivolous.... I should desire to know, what can be meant by asserting, that self-love, or resentment of injuries, or the passion between the sexes is not innate?[63]

Reid was leery of the word 'innate', but the instinctive tendencies he attributes to the mind are undeniably innate, and the conceptions to which they give rise, because they are *prompted* by experience rather than derived from it, are arguably innate as well.

Some British philosophers tried to escape the limitations they saw in Lockean empiricism by claiming that there were senses Locke had neglected. Francis Hutcheson, for example, made a case for the existence of a moral sense. He conceived of it as a tendency to respond (with moral approbation or disapprobation) to circumstances brought to its attention by reason, as it infers benevolent motivation or its contrary from the deliverances of other senses.[64] In his exposition of Hutcheson's views, Adam Smith distinguished between a direct or antecedent sense and a reflex or consequent one. A *direct* sense does not presuppose the antecedent perception of any other sense; a *reflex* sense does.[65] This distinction cuts across the distinction between an internal sense and an external one: the stimulus of an *internal* sense is within the mind, and the stimulus of an *external* sense is without it. The moral sense, Smith suggests, is an internal reflex sense. Lockean reflection (as Hutcheson and Smith interpret it) is internal and direct.

Hutcheson seemed to accept Locke's attack on nativism. Yet he warned that too much had been made of it, and Hutcheson's moral sense seems to deliver ideas that cannot be derived from the senses in the ways allowed by Locke.[66] Hutcheson said that all ideas 'take rise' (*oriuntur*) from experience, but he did not expect the idea derived from an experience to be a *copy* of it, or to be intelligibly related to it in any other way. To say an idea is derived from experience is simply to say that in the ordinary course of things, experience prompts it. This reflects a change in the eighteenth-century understanding of causation, a general movement away from the very demanding standards of (for example) Spinoza and Malebranche, for whom the causal relation must be intelligible or comprehensible, towards the less demanding view most clearly illustrated by Hume, for whom a cause, considered objectively, is merely an event constantly conjoined with another.

In eighteenth-century Britain, there were two very different ways of remaining faithful to Locke. Hutcheson's way was to reinterpret derivation to allow for a wider variety of senses. This tendency was most pronounced in Scotland, where it led to the plethora of senses or instinctive principles that Joseph Priestley, for example, found it 'really tiresome' to enumerate.[67] The second way was to accept only the Lockean senses, and to appeal to association to account for the objects of thought that others traced to senses or principles Locke did not recognise. (This is discussed in the following section, on the association of ideas.)

The first way of being faithful to Locke was characteristic of the philosophers of common sense. According to James Oswald, although Hutcheson 'thought that he had made a discovery of a new faculty of the human mind, which he was intitled to call by a new name', this 'acute philosopher' had in fact 'only got a view, and but a partial view of common sense'.[68] Common sense was construed (by Reid, Oswald, and those they influenced) as an internal reflex sense that leads, without deliberation or choice, to both conception and belief. As James Beattie wrote, common sense is

that power of the mind which perceives truth, or commands belief, not by progressive argumentation, but by an instantaneous, instinctive, and irresistible impulse; derived . . . from nature; acting independently on our will . . . according to an established law, and therefore not improperly called *Sense*.[69]

Earlier in the century, the French philosopher Claude Buffier had defined common sense in a strikingly similar way. It is, he wrote,

that disposition or quality which Nature has placed in all men, or . . . in the far greater number of them, . . . to form a common and uniform judgment with respect to objects different from the internal sentiment of their own perception, and which judgment is not the consequence of any anterior principle.[70]

According to the common-sense philosophers, experience *prompts* the formation of certain ideas or conceptions (the ideas or conceptions that figure in the judgements of which both Beattie and Buffier speak), but these ideas or conceptions are not derived from experience. Lockean empiricism had made many objects of the mind problematic. If the self, for example, does not fall within the scope of experience, an empiricist must either explain how to construct an idea of the self (the *first path* of development) or admit that we have no idea of the self at all (the *second path*). Other problematic objects were the infinite, God, space and time, and virtue and vice; for some, notably Berkeley and Hume, even physical objects became problematic. The second path quickly arrives at the deepest form of scepticism, one that denies our ability to form the conceptions implicated in the beliefs that more modest sceptics doubt. But the empiricist who travels the first path will have to specify routines of conception-construction, and these routines cannot call for much in the way of creativity. If they do, the empiricist will have to wonder whether the ideas do in fact come from experience, instead of being imposed upon it, a priori, by the creative mind.

What becomes, then, of the empirical criticism of conceptions? At the very least, it loses much of the authority it had for Locke, Berkeley, and Hume. There is no longer a possibility of appraising a conception's implicit claim to content by comparing it with the experience that gives rise to it. The experience may have prompted the conception, but it was not necessarily the source of its content or significance. Disputes about the genuineness of content are therefore likely to end in stalemate: one party claims to have a conception (it *seems* as if we have it, they may say), whereas the other party is doubtful that anyone *really* has it because they cannot see where the content of the conception comes from. The second party may confess that they seem to themselves to have the conception but that they suffer, like the other party, from an illusion of understanding.

In the second half of the eighteenth century, Germany remained a stronghold of belief in ideas or conceptions independent of experience, despite Locke's influence on J. H. Lambert, J. N. Tetens, and others there.[71] Locke had argued that the belief in innate notions is either plainly false (as when it is taken to mean that there are principles commanding an actual, universal assent) or trivially true (as when it is taken to mean that the mind is able to understand and assent to them). Leibniz, seeking an intermediate interpretation, compared the soul to 'a veined block of marble', as opposed to a homogeneous block or blank tablet (*tabula rasa*) (*Nouveaux essais*, 52). 'If there were veins in the block which marked out the shape of Hercules rather than other shapes', he explained,

then that block would be more determined to that shape and Hercules would be innate in it, in a way, even though labour would be required to expose the veins and to polish them into clarity, removing everything that prevents their being seen. This is how ideas and truths are innate in us – as inclinations, dispositions, tendencies, or natural potentialities, and not as actions; although these potentialities are always accompanied by certain actions, often insensible ones, which correspond to them. (42)

Leibniz observed that Locke's system 'is closer to Aristotle and mine to Plato' (47). Kant saw things in the same way:

In respect of the origin of the modes of 'knowledge through pure reason', the question is as to whether they are derived from experience, or whether in independence of experience they have their origin in reason. *Aristotle* may be regarded as the chief of the *empiricists*, and *Plato* as the chief of the *noologists. Locke*, who in modern times followed Aristotle, and *Leibniz*, who followed Plato (although in considerable disagreement with his mystical system), have not been able to bring this conflict to any definitive conclusion. (*Kritik*, A 854/B 882)

In Karl Leonhard Reinhold's view, the conflict was brought closer to resolution by Kant. According to Reinhold's elaboration of Kant's narrative, the 'theories on the origin of representations' developed by Locke and Leibniz had put the finishing touches on the systems Reinhold named empiricism and rationalism. 'The two philosophers laid down, one in the simple representations drawn from experience and the other in innate representations . . . the only foundation of

philosophical knowledge possible for the empiricists . . . and the rationalists. . . .'
Then came Hume, who, 'being more consistent than Locke', showed that neither system can prove 'any real conformity of representations to their objects'.
Kant, 'putting together whatever truth there is in Locke's empiricism and in
Leibniz's rationalism', set philosophical knowledge on a new foundation, one
able to 'rise above all the objections offered by Hume's skepticism, and satisfy
its rigorous but fair requirements'.[72]

According to Kant, there are both pure intuitions and pure concepts. A representation is pure if it contains 'no admixture of anything empirical' (*Kritik*, B 3).
Kant argued that neither pure intuitions (the singular representations of space
and time) nor pure concepts (general representations of such things as substance and accident or cause and effect) can be derived from experience because they are necessary conditions of its very possibility. As the century closed,
German philosophers were by no means united behind Reinhold's assessment of
Kant's achievement,[73] but most agreed with Reinhold that the origin of representations was crucially relevant to the question posed so crisply by Johann
Gottlieb Fichte: 'What is the connection between our representations and their
objects?'[74]

Disagreements about the origin of ideas or representations were often linked,
especially early in the century, with disagreements about their causation. In 1696,
Leibniz had distinguished three ways of understanding the 'communication'
between mind and body.[75] He argued that we should reject the 'way of influence' because 'it is impossible to conceive of material particles or of species or
immaterial qualities which can pass from one of these substances into the other'
(*Philosophical Papers*, vol. 2, 751). The 'way of assistance', which he attributed
to the 'system of occasional causes', is also unacceptable because 'it makes a
deus ex machina intervene in a natural and ordinary matter where reason requires
that God should help only in the way in which he concurs in all other natural
things' (751). The way of assistance was defended in the eighteenth century by
French philosophers such as David R. Boullier and Cardinal Giacinto Sigis-
mondo Gerdil. They saw Locke as an advocate of the way of influence and argued that an occasionalist view was more consonant with mind/body dualism.[76]
Leibniz himself preferred the 'way of pre-established harmony', which holds that
'God has made each of the two substances from the beginning in such a way
that, though each follows only its own laws which it has received with its being, each agrees throughout with the other, entirely as if they were mutually
influenced or as if God were always putting forth his hand, beyond his general
concurrence' (751). In his *Psychologica rationalis*, Christian Wolff, after evaluating
all three systems in detail, sided with Leibniz. Interest in the competition diminished as the century progressed, partly because of changing conceptions of

causation, partly because of doubts about occasionalism and pre-established harmony as metaphysical schemes, and partly because philosophers came to believe
that epistemological claims – even claims about origin – could to some extent
be freed of causal import. Thus Condillac claims that objects are the causes or
occasions of sensations and Hume distinguishes between impressions and ideas
on phenomenological rather than causal grounds.

3. *The association of ideas*

The 'association of ideas' was named by Locke, who made use of it only to
explain pathological or disordered thought. For Locke, the train of thought
should, ideally, be *content-driven* or *truth-sensitive*: one thought should follow
another because the content of the first demands it. Besides this content-driven
connection of ideas, he explained, 'there is another Connexion of *Ideas* wholly
owing to Chance or Custom; *Ideas* that in themselves are not at all of kin, come
to be so united in some Mens Minds, that 'tis very hard to separate them' (*Essay*,
II.xxxiii.5). No sooner does one idea enter the mind 'but its Associate appears
with it; and if they are more than two which are thus united, the whole gang
always inseparable shew themselves together'. The upshot, Locke explains, is
the joining of ideas 'not ally'd by Nature' (II.xxxiii.6).

Berkeley was the first eighteenth-century philosopher to assign a significant
positive role to the association of ideas, though he spoke of 'suggestion' rather
than association. Berkeley used association to explain the visual perception of the
distance, size, and situation of objects. Distance, he assumed, is not immediately
perceived by the sight. We see it only because certain visible ideas come, by
means of experience, to suggest certain tangible ideas – ideas by which distance
is immediately perceived. Experience, in other words, invests ideas of sight
with a tangible or distance 'meaning'.[77] Experience can have this effect, of
course, only because it activates potentialities latent in the mind. Berkeley did
not explain how these potentialities were embodied there. Later associationists,
such as Hartley and Priestley, who unlike the immaterialist Berkeley were able
to give embodiment a physical interpretation, could at least point in a general
direction.

Hume gave the association of ideas a central role in both *A Treatise of Human
Nature* (1739–40) and *An Enquiry concerning Human Understanding*. In Hume's
theory, association carries out two tasks, though the distinction between them
was made explicit only later, by Hartley. The first task is to account for the formation of complex ideas. This is the result of what Hartley called 'synchronous'
association, and the universal principles defining it – principles that hold sway
across national or linguistic boundaries – explain, for example, why words in one

language so often have equivalents in another.[78] The second task is to account for the twists and turns taken by the train of thought. Here Hume appealed to what Hartley later called 'successive' association.

Hume identified three principles of association, whether synchronous or successive: contiguity, resemblance, and cause and effect. 'A picture', for example, 'leads our thoughts to the original' – an instance of association by resemblance. 'The mention of one apartment in a building naturally introduces an enquiry or discourse concerning the others' – an instance of association by contiguity. 'If we think of a wound, we can scarcely forbear reflecting on the pain which follows it' – an instance of association by cause and effect. Hume claims that this enumeration is complete; his defence is to ask the reader for counterexamples and to suggest that 'the more instances we examine, and the more care we employ, the more assurance shall we acquire, that the enumeration . . . is complete and entire' (*Enquiry*, 3.3, SBN 24).

Hartley makes no reference to Hume. He says it was John Gay who first proposed that 'all our intellectual pleasures and pains' could be explained by association (*Observations*, iii). In his brief essay on moral virtue, Gay explained how association can give rise, for example, to a desire for money, even though money is not inherently desirable. Hartley tried to complete Gay's project. He appealed to association to explain both the train of ideas and the constitution of complex ideas. According to one of his central principles, if sensation A occurs along with sensations B, C, and D, the sensation gains the power to excite ideas corresponding to the sensations usually in its company. (A sensation has an intrinsic ability to excite the idea that corresponds to it.) This principle is explained in turn by Hartley's doctrine of vibrations, an account of disturbances in the medullary substance triggered by bodily impressions. Every sensation leaves a bodily trace; the trace is more permanent, and the corresponding idea more resilient, if the sensation occurs repeatedly. But beliefs about the physical basis of association were highly controversial. Condillac, for example, was careful to say that 'the sense organs are only the occasional cause of the impressions which objects make upon us',[79] perhaps because the system of physical (or natural) influence was associated, at least in France, with scholasticism and materialism.

Voltaire and Condillac (in France), Priestley (in Britain), and Tetens (in Germany) were among the many others who made significant use of the association of ideas. They moved away from Locke's depiction of association as 'a sort of Madness' towards the conviction that the principles of association could explain many of the normal (and perfectly respectable) ways in which ideas are brought together. Voltaire began his influential exposition of Newtonian mechanics with a sketch of Berkeley's associationist theory of vision.[80] Tetens appealed to association to explain, among other things, our belief in external objects, but he claimed that others, such as Condillac and Hartley, made too much of association, and gave too little recognition to the mind's active powers.[81]

The aim of the more ambitious associationists, such as Hartley and Priestley, was to save Lockean empiricism and keep innate or instinctive principles down to a minimum. For them, Locke's condemnation of association was unduly influenced by his lingering rationalism – his assumption that in the conduct of argument, one idea should follow another not because they are associated but because content or truth demands it. Even in the case of mathematical demonstration, of course, it needs to be explained how content or truth plays this guiding role. Locke invokes our ability to intuit connections among ideas, and here, perhaps, custom would be an unworthy guide. But it is difficult to see how association can be condemned when we turn to the justification of empirical beliefs. Here it seems that mere content is by itself no guide – if it were, the truths in question would be a priori or non-empirical. If truth is to be our guide in this case, it seems it can guide us only through experience.

4. Memory and imagination

Memory was generally understood as a power to reproduce earlier ideas or representations. It was often described as a faculty of recalling sensations and the ideas derived from them – one that preserves the combination or order they had when they entered the mind. In Hartley, for example, traces of sensations and ideas are recalled 'in the same order and proportion, accurately or nearly' (*Observations*, iii). Like others who offered this standard definition, Hartley did not ask whether memory is a faculty that somehow aspires to accuracy or one that achieves it by definition.

Hume explained that when an impression makes a second appearance as an idea, it does so in one of two ways: either it retains a considerable share of its former vivacity (and 'is somewhat intermediate betwixt an impression and an idea') or 'it entirely loses that vivacity, and is a perfect idea' (*Treatise*, 1.1.3.1, SBN 8). The faculty by which we repeat impressions in the first way is memory; in the second, it is imagination. Imagination, then, is merely 'the faculty, by which we form our fainter ideas' (1.3.9.19n, SBN 118 fn). Yet 'the chief exercise of the memory is not to preserve the simple ideas, but their order and position' (1.1.3.3, SBN 9).

Condillac's account of memory was notable for two reasons: it assigned a central role to signs; and it abandoned the widespread assumption that the idea called up by the memory is typically at least a roughly accurate reproduction of the idea remembered. Condillac distinguished between perceptions 'that we remember at least the next moment', and those 'we forget as soon as we have had them' (*Essai*, I.ii.2.§6, 21). Perhaps the best example is the letters we see in reading (§9, 23). We remember the words but not the letters. We are conscious of perceptions when we have them, but we forget them the next moment. Reminiscence is Condillac's label for our recognition that we have had certain perceptions before. Without reminiscence, each moment of our life would seem the first of our existence, and our knowledge would never extend beyond a first perception (§15, 25).

When we remember, instead of reviving the idea we had before, we revive 'various circumstances, or some general idea' in its stead (§20, 28):

Let us think, for example, of a flower with a familiar scent; we recall the name, remember the circumstances in which we have seen it, and represent the fragrance as the general idea of a perception that affects the sense of smell; but we cannot reawaken the perception itself. (§18, 27)

Specific revival is by no means impossible, though it is often beyond our power. But artificial signs are essential to memory (though not, presumably, to reminiscence), whether or not it takes the form of faithful revival:

[W]e cannot recall a thing unless it is at some point connected with some of those things that we control. For a man who has only accidental signs and natural signs has none that is at his command. Thus his needs can cause only the exercise of his imagination, and by that token we will be without memory. (I.ii.4,§39, 37)

Here Condillac contrasts the passive mind that is confined to reminiscence with the active, potentially knowing mind that exploits artificial or arbitrary signs. Linguistic mediation was a recurring theme in eighteenth-century theories of ideas; it played an important role in theories of abstraction and judgement.

According to Leibniz, the mind is able to retain both innate ideas and ideas derived from the senses. Ideas of either kind are dispositions or tendencies, and since there are no 'bare "powers" or "faculties"', they must be realised in something actual – presumably the mind's insensible perceptions (*Nouveaux essais*, 140). 'There are dispositions which are the remains of past impressions', Theophilus tells Philalethes, 'in the soul as well as in the body, but which we are unaware of except when the memory has a use for them. If nothing were left of past thoughts the moment we ceased to think of them, it would be impossible to explain how we could keep the memory of them; to resort to a bare faculty to do the work' – as Leibniz thought Locke had done – 'is to talk unintelligibly' (140).

Imagination and memory were closely allied in eighteenth-century accounts of the understanding. According to the standard view, codified in Locke's *Essay*, memory supplies the material for imagination, which combines the elements of memories in new and unexpected ways. This 'combinatorial' imagination works within limits that could, given an inventory of the available elements, be defined a priori, as all permissible combinations of the elements. Thus, Hume writes:

[N]othing, at first view, may seem more unbounded than the thought of man.... What never was seen, or heard of, may yet be conceived; nor is any thing beyond the power of thought, except what implies an absolute contradiction. But though our thought seems to possess this unbounded liberty, we shall find, upon a nearer examination, that it is really confined within very narrow limits, and that all this creative power of the mind amounts to more than the faculty of compounding, transposing, augmenting, or diminishing the materials afforded us by the senses and experience. (*Enquiry*, 2.4–5, SBN 18–9)

Vico, who observes that the *immaginare* of ordinary Italian is equivalent to the *memorare* of the Latins, accepts the same view in an early work.[82] The Greeks were right, he suggests, to hand down the tradition 'that the Muses, forms of imagination, were the daughters of Memory'.

Hume's account of imagination rests on a Lockean distinction between simple and complex ideas. This distinction is essential to Hume's empiricism: all ideas, he argues, are copies of precedent impressions, but this is not because every idea is a direct copy of an earlier impression. Every *simple* idea is a direct copy, but complex ideas sometimes are and sometimes are not. The distinction was used in the same way by many other empiricists influenced by Locke, such as Condillac. Berkeley, however, was suspicious of it because he had trouble finding a convincing example of a simple idea. Locke seemed to treat specific shades of colour as simple ideas, but Berkeley suggested that even scarlet colour is complex. The proof is that it falls into distinct resemblance classes: the class of all colours and the class of all shades of red.[83] Hume was aware that shades of colour present at least a technical problem for his empiricism. He invites us to imagine someone who has experienced all the colours except one, a certain shade of blue, and asks whether he may be able, in spite of this, to frame an idea of the missing shade. Hume answers yes and treats the case as evidence that simple ideas are not always derived from corresponding impressions. Yet the instance is 'so singular', he thinks, that it does not call for the amendment of his empiricist maxim.[84] It is odd that Hume did not consider the possibility that shades of colour are not simple and that the idea of the missing shade could be formed by mixing simpler elements in the shades that flank it in the spectrum.[85]

Is the combinatorial imagination genuinely creative? Dugald Stewart, in his *Outlines of Moral Philosophy* (1793), writes that

the province of Imagination is to select qualities and circumstances from a variety of different objects; and, by combining and disposing these, to form a new creation of its own. In this appropriated sense of the word, it coincides with what some authors have called *Creative* or *Poetical Imagination*.[86]

Many writers shared Stewart's view. D'Alembert writes in the *Discours préliminaire* that

we do not take imagination here to be the ability to represent objects to oneself, since that faculty is simply the memory itself of sensible objects, a memory which would be continually in action if it were not assisted and relieved by the invention of signs. We take imagination in a more noble and precise sense, as the talent of creating by imitating. (*Encyclopédie*, 1: xvi; trans. 50)

This is the imagination Coleridge described in 1795: 'to imitate Creativeness by combination [is] our most exalted and self-satisfying Delight'.[87] Coleridge went on to develop a more ambitious theory of a more radically creative imagination, whose creative freedom goes beyond the limits imposed by sense.

Kant, who influenced Coleridge's later views, distinguished between *productive* imagination, which engages in fiction, *reproductive* imagination, which engages in recall, and *creative* imagination, which is 'capable of producing a presentation of sense that was never before given to our power of sense', although the material employed *is* given.[88] In other places, Kant assigns to imagination more exalted roles: it assists the understanding in the very constitution of experience and interprets the ideals of reason.[89]

Imagination played a central role in eighteenth-century accounts of dreaming and madness. Hartley writes that 'dreams are nothing but the imaginations, fancies, or reveries of a sleeping man' (*Observations*, I.iii.5, 384). This was the standard view.[90] Dreams are to be explained, Hartley adds, by the impressions and ideas lately received (in particular, those of the previous day); by the state of the body, especially the stomach and brain; and by association.

Malebranche, Locke, and Leibniz all attributed madness, in at least some of its forms, to an excess of imagination. Locke denied that madness is a defect of reason in the strict sense. It is the product of a too violent imagination, causing madmen to 'put wrong *Ideas* together, and so make wrong Propositions, but argue and reason right from them' (*Essay*, II.xi.13). Hume linked imagination with madness in the *Treatise* (1.4.4.1, SBN 225–6), where he compared the way in which custom 'infixes and inlivens' an idea with the way in which whatever it is produces the obsessiveness of a person 'tormented he knows not why, with the apprehension of spectres in the dark'. Again there is no defect of reason, in the strict sense in which reason is opposed to apprehension and judgement. The person afraid of the dark 'may, perhaps, be said to reason, and to reason naturally too'.

There was a long tradition attributing mental disorders to bodily causes – to imbalances in the bodily humours, for example. But how the body contributed to mental disorder was a matter of dispute. La Mettrie wrote that although the causes of insanity are not obvious, 'the defects of their brains are not always hidden from our investigations'.[91] Both Hartley and Kant developed elaborate taxonomies of mental disorder. Hartley explained that melancholy, for example, passes into madness 'strictly so called' when absurd desires, hopes, and fears, instead of being resisted, are wholeheartedly embraced. Hartley commented (as Leibniz had) on the selectivity of madness: 'mad persons often speak rationally and consistently upon the subjects that occur, provided that single one which most affects them, be kept out of view' (*Observations*, I.iii.4, 400–1). This suggests that madness is not a defect of reason. Kant assigned the imagination a central role in *Wahnsinn*, or 'dementia', where it constructs, wholesale, a false representation, and in *Wahnwitz*, or 'insania', where it causes the understanding to assimilate two very different things. These disorders are distinguished from (for example) *Aberwitz*, or 'vesania', which is a disturbance of reason.[92]

5. *Abstract and general ideas*

Abstraction is one of the most tangled topics in eighteenth-century theories of the understanding. The *process* of abstraction is one of separation or 'precision'. Ideas become general, Locke explained, 'by separating from them the circum-stances of Time, and Place, and any other *Ideas*, that may determine them to this or that particular Existence. By this way of abstraction they are made capable of representing more Individuals than one' (*Essay*, III.iii.6). In much the same way, Kant identified abstraction as the 'negative' condition of universal representa-tions. Its 'positive' counterparts are comparison and reflection. Comparing a spruce, willow, and linden, I see that they differ. But I then reflect on what they have in common, and by abstracting this from their differences – the figures of the leaves, for example – I arrive at the concept of a tree (an 'empirical' concept because it is derived from experience).[93] The *product* of abstraction – the general idea or universal concept – can be described as 'abstract', but the label was also applied to ideas of pure intellect (ideas 'separate' from matter or sense) owing nothing to the *process* of abstraction.

Our reliance on abstraction was widely viewed as a mark of our imperfection. God, who is able to survey all particulars in an instant, was thought to have no need of it. Empiricists used abstraction to account for ideas that others traced to pure intellect. But the empiricist Berkeley made an influential case against it. He argued that if everything that exists is particular, as Locke himself admitted, then ideas too must be particular. And if they are, then no idea can satisfy Locke's description of the general idea of a triangle, which is, according to *Essay*, IV.vii.9, 'neither Oblique, nor Rectangle, neither Equilateral, Equicrural, nor Scalenon;

but all and none of these at once'. Though this fragment may not convey it, Locke's point is not that the idea is both equilateral and scalene. He is saying that the idea is indeterminate, and therefore fit to represent triangles of either kind. Berkeley's reply is that if an indeterminate triangle is impossible, so is an indeterminate idea of a triangle. 'It is, I think, a receiv'd Axiom', he wrote, 'that an Impossibility cannot be conceiv'd. For what created Intelligence will pretend to conceive, that which God cannot cause to be?'[94]

Berkeley supposed that Locke's abstract ideas were abbreviated objects of thought. But a closer look at the *Essay* suggests that they are acts of thought with general content. Their content is general because the mind is capable of 'partial Consideration' or selective attention: it can concentrate on certain features of fully determinate ideas while ignoring others. Berkeley cannot in fairness object to this because he appeals to selective attention in his own account of general thinking. 'It must be acknowledged', he writes, 'that a man may consider a figure merely as triangular, without attending to the particular qualities of the angles, or relations of the sides. So far he may abstract: but this will never prove, that he can frame an abstract general inconsistent idea of a triangle' (Introduction to the *Principles*, §16, 35).

Does Berkeley's criticism, then, leave everything as it was? I do not think so because Berkeley went on to argue that significant names need not stand for ideas and to suggest that a name owes its generality not to a private object of thought but to the word's public role. Locke had said that words become general when they are made the signs of general ideas; Berkeley suggests that ideas become general when general words are made to signify them. The generality of words is, in turn, a matter of what is now called their 'functional role'. Closely related suggestions were made by Hume and Condillac. 'Abstract ideas', says Condillac, 'are only denominations' (*Logic*, 247). If we had no words, we would have no abstract ideas (249). 'All general ideas', Hume wrote, 'are nothing but particular ones, annexed to a certain term, which gives them a more extensive signification, and makes them recall upon occasion other individuals, which are similar to them' (*Treatise*, 1.1.7.1, SBN 17).

II. JUDGEMENT

1. Introduction

The most striking developments in eighteenth-century theories of judgement were challenges to the textbook portrayal of judgement as an act of mind resting on prior acts of bare perception or apprehension. (For a sketch of the textbook view, see Section I.1.) This section surveys several such challenges; two were especially noteworthy.

The first challenge was laid down by philosophers who proposed that judgement is, at bottom, nothing but sensation, or the work of the sensitive faculty. Condillac, inspired by Locke's definition of knowledge as 'the perception of the connexion and agreement, or disagreement and repugnancy of any of our Ideas' (*Essay*, IV.i.2), insisted that judgement, however complex it may seem, 'is still only sensations' (*Logic*, 135). Hume, in an attempt to account for judgement or belief naturalistically, argued that it is 'more properly an act of the sensitive, than of the cogitative part of our natures' (*Treatise*, 1.4.1.8, SBN 183). Hume's suggestion drew support from the increased reliance on the association of ideas as an explanatory principle. Association was used by Hume and others not only to explain the construction and succession of ideas but to account for the generation of expectation and the fixation of belief. These beliefs and expectations were not (as they had been for Descartes) the achievements of a will free to say yes or no to propositions placed before it by the understanding.[95] They were the non-voluntary upshot of the laws of mental life. Berkeley had used the association of ideas much as Hume did, to explain expectation or belief. He spoke, for example, of explaining 'sudden judgments' of size and distance, yet he was able to write that

To perceive is one thing; to judge is another. So likewise, to be suggested is one thing, and to be inferred another. Things are suggested and perceived by sense. We make judgments and inferences by the understanding. What we immediately and properly perceive by sight is its primary object, light and colours. What is suggested or perceived by mediation thereof, are tangible ideas which may be considered as secondary and improper objects of sight.[96]

Despite what he says here, Berkeley's suggestion generates what Thomas Reid was later to call 'a determination with regard to truth and falsehood' – a judgement or belief. So Berkeley, in spite of himself, contributes to what might be described as the 'sentimentalising' of judgement – a blurring of the boundary between judgement on the one hand and sensation or sentiment on the other. The blurring was explicit not only in Hume but in the common-sense philosophers who were his critics. As we saw in Section 1c, philosophers regularly defined common sense as a power productive of belief or judgement. For Buffier, for example, it is a disposition or quality 'to form a common and uniform *judgment*' (my emphasis, see note 70). For Beattie, it is a power by which the mind 'perceives truth, or commands belief', a power properly called sense because it is 'instantaneous, instinctive, and irresistible' (see note 69). And for Reid, common sense is a body of 'original and natural judgments' (*Inquiry*, 215).

'We are under a necessity to take [them] for granted in the common concerns of life', Reid observes, 'without being able to give a reason for them' (*Inquiry*, ch. 2, §6, 33).

The second challenge to the textbook tradition came from a different direction. According to the textbook trichotomy of the powers of the understanding, simple apprehension is the first or most basic act of the understanding, and in many eighteenth-century compendia, the chief example of simple apprehension was sensation. According to both Reid and Kant, however, sensation is far more complex than the textbooks suggest. For Reid, a judgement or belief is part of every sensation. For Kant, the kind of mental activity characteristic of judgement – the combination or 'synthesis' of representations – is presupposed by every sensation. On either view, sensation incorporates a level of mental activity that the textbooks ignore.

The influence of the textbooks persisted, of course, and this section ends by examining the traditional table of the forms of judgement and some of the questions it raised for eighteenth-century philosophers. I consider the use Kant made of the table and briefly discuss his influential distinctions between analytic and synthetic and a priori and a posteriori judgements.

Before turning to the major developments I have outlined, it will be helpful to dwell briefly on a more modest development along the same lines. The textbook tradition suggests that ideas are both prior to judgements and independent of them – that an idea is what it is *before* it enters into judgement. As the expression 'enters into' itself suggests, we begin with an idea – an idea whose identity has already been firmly and irrevocably established – and carry it into a judgement. But this priority thesis was called into question even by Locke, who observed (*Essay*, II.ix.8) that ideas are often '*alter'd by the Judgment*, without our taking notice of it'. A round globe, for example, is seen as a three-dimensional solid, even though the idea imprinted on our mind is 'of a flat Circle variously shadow'd, with several degrees of Light and Brightness coming to our Eyes'. Theophilus, Leibniz's spokesman in the *Nouveaux essais*, says that this is 'perfectly true' and that it explains 'how a painting can deceive us, by means of an artful use of perspective' (135).

The altering of ideas by judgement (or, more precisely, by suggestion) is a main theme of Berkeley's theory of vision. When one idea comes to suggest another, we can arrive at the second idea without even noticing the first. Reid made use of the same principle, which resembles Leibniz's doctrine of minute perceptions, in suggesting that some perceptions are unnoticed or at the very least not attended to. One difference between Leibnizian minute perceptions and the unnoticed perceptions or alterations of Berkeley and Reid (and presumably of Locke) is that originally the latter were conscious. And this is perhaps why the unnoticed perceptions of Berkeley and Reid can more easily be retrieved into consciousness despite Leibniz's assurance that we can 'in fact become thoroughly aware of them [our minute perceptions] and reflect on them' (*Nouveaux essais*, 134). According to Berkeley and Reid, we are capable of misinterpreting our ideas and seeing them as they are given to us. We can rid them of associations and see them afresh, as they really are. We are faced, therefore, with a *modification* or *amendment* of the priority thesis rather than a wholesale rejection of it. The idea is there, and its nature is independent of our judgement; it is simply that judgement or habit may cause us to neglect it. We can remedy the neglect, however, because what we are neglecting is there in our experience, waiting to be recovered. The challenges to tradition examined later in this chapter were more radical.

The altering of ideas by judgement was denied by Condillac, who was un-willing to accept Locke's notion of an unconscious judgement. Our initial idea of the globe, he says, is richer than Locke allows. Locke is right to suppose that the image impressed on the eye is 'merely a flat circle, illuminated and colored differently', but he is wrong to think that 'the impression that is con-sequently made on the mind gives only the perception of this circle' (*Essai*, I.vi.2, 102). The idea contains more, in effect, than its proximate physical occasion.

2. Theories of judgement: The perceptual model versus the verdictive model

There were two influential models of judgement in the eighteenth century: the perceptual and the verdictive. According to the first, judgement is akin to perceiving. It is a matter of seeing, with the eye of the mind, that something is the case. According to the second, judgement is a matter of considering a proposition (along, perhaps, with the evidence for and against it) and then, in a separate act, arriving at or issuing a verdict. Descartes's account of judgement is an extreme case of the verdictive model: according to this, the understanding exhibits a proposition to the will, which is free – absolutely free – to affirm or deny it. When the proposition is clear and distinct, the will's assent is inevitable, but affirmation remains an operation of the will. On either model, a judgement can be described as an 'act' of the mind, in one venerable sense of that word. An act in that sense is simply the exercise of a psychological capacity – the actualisation of a mental power. Even simple apprehension is an act in this sense. Judgement, on either model, is equally an act in this sense, though it could perhaps be said that it involves more activity on the verdictive model because arriving at a verdict calls upon a larger number of powers. In another sense of the word 'act', an act essentially involves will. Berkeley understands it in this way in the *Three Dialogues between Hylas and Philonous* (1713), where his spokesman Philonous argues that we are passive in sense perception. Hylas agrees that the mind is active 'when it produces, puts an end to, or changes any thing', and Philonous argues that it can work such changes only by 'an act of the will'. 'The mind . . . is to be accounted active in its perceptions', he concludes, 'so far forth' – and, it seems, *only* so far forth – 'as volition is included in them'. In sensory perception, therefore, 'I am altogether passive'.[97] In this sense of the word, judgement will count as an act on the verdictive model if the verdict is an act of will, and it will count as an act on the perceptual model if perception is taken to involve will.

For Locke, the mind 'has two Faculties, conversant about Truth and Falshood' (*Essay*, IV.xiv.4), or two faculties of assent. In *knowledge*, the mind perceives the agreement or disagreement of ideas, either immediately, as in *intuitive* knowledge, or by means of intervening ideas, as in *demonstrative* knowledge. In what Locke calls *judgement*, the 'Agreement or Disagreement is not perceived, but presumed' to obtain (IV.xiv.4). In judgement, he explains, 'the Mind takes its *Ideas* to agree, or disagree; or which is the same, any Proposition to be true, or false, without perceiving a demonstrative Evidence in the Proofs' (IV.xiv.3). 'If it so unites, or separates them, as in Reality Things are', he says, 'it is *right Judgment*'; otherwise, it is false or mistaken (IV.xiv.4). Locke's strongly perceptual model of judgement in knowledge was embraced by the eighteenth-century logician William Duncan, who wrote that judgement is the perception of a relation 'immediately discoverable by the bare Inspection of the Mind', upon the 'joint View' of two ideas.[98] Locke's portrayal of probable judgement was clearly more verdictive than his portrayal of judgement in knowledge; in probable judgement, the mind *presumes* ideas to agree, without seeing (by intuition or demonstration) that they do.

Henry Aldrich's *Artis logicae compendium* (1691), published the year after the first edition of Locke's *Essay*, was highly influential in eighteenth-century Britain.[99] Much of Hutcheson's *Logicae compendium*, for example, is cribbed from it (or from a common source), sometimes almost verbatim. Aldrich presents a strongly verdictive conception of judgement that contrasts strikingly with the Lockean perceptual model of judgement in knowledge. In judgement, Aldrich explains, the mind does not merely perceive objects. Instead, ideas stand before the mind 'as if before a tribunal', and the judging mind signifies 'by declaration' that the objects it perceives agree or disagree (I.i.2, 1). Both Gershom Carmichael and Francis Hutcheson also present verdictive definitions. According to Hutcheson, for example, judgement is an act of the mind in which two ideas are connected in a verdict (*sententia*).[100] 'Sententia' is practically a synonym of 'judicium'. Hutcheson's resort to it is a mark of his distance from the Lockean perceptual model, though his logic is indebted to Locke's *Essay* on many other counts.

In the *Nouveaux essais*, Leibniz favours a verdictive model. In response to Locke's definition of knowledge (summarised by Philalethes, on p. 355), Theophilus suggests that questions 'can be said to be midway between an idea [viewed as a component of a proposition] and a proposition'. Some questions, he explains,

ask only for a Yes or a No, and these are the closest to propositions; but there are others which ask how, and ask for details, and so on, and more must be added to these if they are to become propositions. (356)

According to Theophilus, propositions incorporate or otherwise depend on determinate contents capable of truth or falsehood, but they are unlike even yes-or-no questions (which are presumably equally determinate) in incorporating the verdicts those questions invite.

Many authors were influenced by both models. According to Christian Wolff, we judge when we observe (*spectamus*) that one thing does (or does not) pertain to another. This definition is strongly perceptual, but Wolff goes on to explain that judgement is an act of mind in which one thing is assigned to another or taken away from it.[101] In judgement, as he explains in another place, 'two notions are conjoined or separated' (*Logicae*, §40). These characterisations are more verdictive. For Wolff, a judgement is an act of mind, whereas a proposition or enunciation is a linguistic entity. The constituents of judgements were ideas, notions, or concepts; the constituents of propositions were words or terms. The distinction between a judgement (a mental act) and a proposition (the linguistic sign expressive of it) was a standard one. Hutcheson, for example, explains that the sign of a judgement is 'proposition or enunciation, which is a form of speech in which one thing is affirmed or denied of something else'.[102] Despite the distinction, the close association between judgement and proposition may explain why some philosophers who accept the perceptual model stray toward the verdictive one. The *expression* of a judgement involves more activity than the mere *making* of one.[103]

Reid's account of judgement contains both perceptual and verdictive elements. In judgement, he explains,

there must be two objects of thoughts compared, and some agreement or disagreement, or, in general, some relation discerned between them; in consequence of which, there is an opinion or belief of that relation which we discern. This operation is expressed in speech by a proposition. (*Intellectual Powers*, I.7, 65)

Here we have a relation discerned (*perception*), a consequent opinion (a *verdict*), and an expression in speech (a *proposition*). These are familiar elements.

Edward Bentham offers a similar analysis in *An Introduction to Logick, Scholastick and Rational* (1773). He defines judgement as 'that act of the mind whereby we *acknowledge* the relation of agreement or disagreement between ideas' (emphasis added).[104] He explains that he uses the word 'acknowledge' rather than 'perceive' because 'all assent to the truth of a proposition is an act of Judgment, whether the ground of that assent lye in our deference to the authority of some intelligent person, or in our own immediate perception'. However, Reid breaks new ground when he defines judgement elsewhere as any 'determination of the mind concerning what is true or what is false' (*Intellectual Powers*, VI.1, 411). This opens the door to more pragmatic conceptions of belief – conceptions that define belief not as a mental state whose object is a proposition, but as a state with a certain bearing on our behaviour. David Hartley, for example, makes a distinction between *rational assent* and *practical assent*. Rational assent is a readiness to affirm as true (see, *Observations*, I.iii.2, 324–5). Practical assent is a readiness to act as the frequent and vivid recurrence of rational assent disposes us to act. In Hartley's account, the two kinds of assent are closely linked, in part because the behavioural indications of practical assent are defined in terms of rational assent. (Hartley accordingly noted that practical assent is the 'natural and necessary consequence' of rational assent (325).) But the distinction raises the possibility of a kind of assent that does not require us to entertain a proposition.

Kant's remarks on what he regarded as the received view of judgement are an implicit repudiation of the perceptual model. According to that account, a judgement is 'the representation of a relation between two concepts' (*die Vorstellung eines Verhältnisses zwischen zwei Begriffen*) (*Kritik*, B 140). This is the account provided by Meier in his *Auszug aus der Vernunftlehre* (1752), a handbook used by Kant's logic students for more than forty years.[105] Meier defines a judgement as 'a representation of a logical relation' (*eine Vorstellung eines logischen Verhältnisses*) among concepts. He adds (much as Locke had before him) that the relation is one of agreement or disagreement, but this does not satisfy Kant, who asks, in effect, what this 'agreement' (or 'disagreement') is. What is intended (to put the question another way) by the copula 'is' (*das Verhältnisswörtchen 'ist'*)? Meier's unhelpful answer had been that the copula (*Verbindungsbegriff*) is a representation of agreement. Kant's own view is that to say 'the body is heavy' is not merely saying that the two representations are 'found together in perception', but that they are 'combined in the object, i.e., regardless of any difference in the condition of the subject' (*Kritik*, B 142). It is hard to see how Meier's account or the perceptual model can distinguish between a mere conjunction of representations in my perception (a 'judgement of perception', as Kant calls it in the *Prolegomena zu einer jeden künftigen Metaphysik*), and their conjunction or combination in the object (what the *Prolegomena* calls a 'judgement of experience').[106] A

Lockean may say that in knowledge two ideas or representations are not merely conjoined but are seen to agree. But if the agreement is not internal to the representations, how can even the most persistent inspection disclose it? Locke would not be unhappy with this result because his account of knowledge is not an account of judgement (or even true judgement) in general. But Kant is especially interested in judgements whose truth is not internal to the representations involved.[107] How, he wonders, does the claim of objective validity enter into *them*? We return to this question in II.5.

Kant's distinction between judgement and proposition is another implicit repudiation of the perceptual model. '*Judgment* and *proposition*', Kant explains, are 'actually distinct as to usage', a point we have already encountered in the works of Wolff, Hutcheson, and Reid. But Kant develops the point in a new way. When the logicians say that a 'proposition is a judgment clothed in words', he complains, 'that means nothing, and this definition is worth nothing at all. For how will they be able to think judgments without words?'[108]

Thus we prefer to say that a judgement considers the relation of two concepts insofar as it is problematic, whereas by propositions we understand an assertoric judgement. In judgement I test my proposition; I judge before I maintain. In the case of a proposition, however, I posit and I assert something, and the proposition consists in just this assertion.

The perceptual model seems unable to distinguish between judging that two representations *may* be related and judging that they actually *are*. The perceptual model suggests that the difference should be open to view, but it is doubtful that the holding of a relation (as opposed to its mere possibility) is something that can be 'viewed' at all. 'In descriptions', Leibniz had said in the *Nouveaux essais*, 'there is a tacit assertion of possibility'.[109] In his *Lectures on Logic*, Kant proposes that every judgement is at least tacitly problematic and that full-fledged judgements – propositions – are also assertoric.[110] 'Before I have a proposition', he concludes, 'I must first judge'. 'In judgment', Kant explains, 'the relation of various representations to the unity of consciousness is thought merely as problematic, but in a proposition as assertoric' (605). Although Kant's account of assertion is not expressly verdictive, his understanding of judgement is obviously closer to the verdictive model than it is to the perceptual.

3. '*What thin partitions Sense from Thought divide*': The sentimentalising of judgement

We turn now to two ways of 'sentimentalising'[111] judgement, beginning with Condillac's very abrupt reduction of judgement to sensation. The reduction is motivated, at least in part, by Condillac's impatience with questions such as the following:

'whether judgment belongs to the understanding or to the will'; ... 'whether the will is capable of knowledge, or whether it is a blind faculty'; 'whether, finally, it controls the understanding or is itself guided and determined by the latter'? (*Essai*, I.v.10, 97)

If judgement is reduced to sensation, Condillac thinks, it becomes pointless to wonder what faculty of mind it belongs to. He arrives at his reduction by joining the perceptual model of judgement to his belief that all perception is sensation:

Immediately upon comparing two objects – or experiencing the two sensations, which they exclusively produce in us, as if they were alongside one another – we perceive whether they resemble each other or are different. Now to perceive resemblances or differences is to judge. Judgement, therefore, is still only sensations. (*Logic*, 135)

Condillac's reduction is only as secure as his premises. Unfortunately, he offers no account of the way in which a combination of sensations can play the functional role of a judgement.

Hume's more interesting effort to sentimentalise judgement rests on his distinction between relations of ideas and matters of fact. 'All the objects of human reason or enquiry', he writes, 'may naturally be divided into two kinds, to wit, *Relations of Ideas*, and *Matters of Fact*'. Relations of ideas include the sciences of geometry, algebra, and arithmetic – 'in short, every affirmation which is either intuitively or demonstratively certain'. The truth of these propositions is 'discoverable by the mere operation of thought, without dependence on what is anywhere existent in the universe'. 'The contrary of every matter of fact', on the other hand, 'is still possible; because it can never imply a contradiction' (*Enquiry*, 4.1.1–2, SBN 25).

Although Hume describes his theory of belief as an account of the 'whole nature of belief' (*Enquiry*, 5.2.11, SBN 48), it covers only beliefs in matters of fact.[112] He devotes particular attention to inductive expectations. We come to believe in the existence of y, for example, when we experience x after having experienced a constant conjunction of x and y. Because belief is merely a lively or vivacious conception of an object, the principles of association can be used to account for it. We know that associated ideas enliven conceptions. Association does not merely convey the mind to the associated idea; it endows the idea with more force and vigour (*Treatise*, 1.3.9.2, SBN 107). In the case of cause and effect, this enlivening can amount to belief. (The other principles of association are, according to Hume, unable to produce belief.) 'Thus all probable reasoning is nothing but a species of sensation' (1.3.8.12, SBN 103). As he writes later in the *Treatise*,

The mind can never exert itself in any action, which we may not comprehend under the term of *perception*; and consequently that term is no less applicable to those judgments, by which we distinguish moral good and evil, than to every other operation of the mind. (3.1.1.2, SBN 456)

From these claims (and others about reasoning) Hume draws the conclusion that the three acts of the understanding usually distinguished by logicians 'all resolve themselves into the first, and are nothing but particular ways of conceiving our objects' (1.3.7.5n, SBN 97 fn).

Hume's account of inductive expectations supports the conclusion that 'belief consists merely in a certain feeling or sentiment; in something, that depends not on the will, but must arise from certain determinate causes and principles, of which we are not masters' (App 2, SBN 624). '*Belief*', as he writes in Book 1, '*is more properly an act of the sensitive, than of the cogitative part of our natures*' (1.4.1.8, SBN 183). Does it follow that Hume's account of inductive judgements (or the similar account of his common-sense critics) conforms to the perceptual model? I do not think so. On the Humean or common-sense account, the mind does not 'see' a relation between ideas or objects, as it does in Locke's account of, say, mathematical knowledge. It responds instead by producing a certain sentiment – a sentiment of belief. If this is akin to perception, it is, at least for Hume, more akin to the perception of secondary qualities than it is to a mathematician's insight.

In evaluating the reductions proposed by Condillac and Hume, it is important to bear in mind that in early modern philosophical prose, a 'sentiment' is not always a sensation or passion. The word is frequently applied, by both French and English authors, to beliefs or opinions. Thus Joseph Butler was able to ask whether our faculty of moral approval and disapproval is 'a sentiment of the understanding' or 'a perception of the heart'.[113] But for Condillac and Hume, at least in the passages we have reviewed here, it is the link between 'sentiment' and sensation (or passion) that is uppermost in mind.

The sentimentalising of probable judgement reinforced the staying power of nativism, despite the prestige of Locke's arguments against it. As the eighteenth century progressed, it became increasingly clear that a large number of powers belong to the mind by nature. These powers could not all be traced to experience, if only because the ability to learn from experience is itself a power (or a varied set of powers). Even if a given idea or belief is not innate to the mind, the power to form the idea, or to acknowledge the belief (in word or in deed), may nonetheless be. The power to form inductive expectations, as it was understood by Hume and his common-sense critics, is innate in just this way. There was, however, no accepted way of understanding how such powers are realised in the mind. It was agreed that there are no *bare* or *brute* powers, in the mind or anywhere else. If something has the power (even a passive one) to contribute to a result or to achieve a state, there must be something, it was agreed, in which that power is realised. Consider our tendency to project past regularities into the future. Because it is a tendency that takes us from one belief to another, it is tempting to represent it as a proposition – a proposition which, in the presence of the first belief, supports (or even entails) the second. But once the tendency is represented in this way, an argument that the tendency is innate is likely to be confused with an argument that the proposition is innate. And if the proposition is innate, the ideas that figure in it must (as Locke himself insisted) be innate as well. The only compelling way to avoid these conclusions is to find non-propositional representations (or non-propositional 'embodiments') of belief-producing tendencies, but whether such representations can be found is even now a matter of debate.

4. Reid

Reid and Kant both disputed the priority of sensation to judgement or belief. For Reid, sensation *includes* judgement and belief (*Intellectual Powers*, IV.3, 326), which are excluded from simple apprehension. As he explains in one of the section headings in his *Inquiry*, 'Judgment and belief in some cases precede simple apprehension' (*Inquiry*, 29). The modern 'theory of ideas', in Reid's view, makes the same mistake as its textbook counterpart: it tells us that belief is always put on hold until we apprehend ideas, compare them, and perceive the relations between them.

Instead of saying that the belief or knowledge is obtained by putting together and comparing the simple apprehensions, we ought rather to say that the simple apprehension is performed by resolving and analysing a natural and original judgement. And it is with the operations of the mind, in this case, as with natural bodies, which are, indeed, compounded of simple principles or elements. Nature does not exhibit these elements separately, to be compounded by us; she exhibits them mixed and compounded in concrete bodies, and it is only by art and chemical analysis that they can be separated (see *Inquiry*, ch. 2, §4, 29–30).

When we sense a thing, in Reid's view, we judge that it exists.[114] It follows that simple apprehension, though it can still be called the simplest, is not the first operation of the understanding: '[I]nstead of saying that the more complex operations of the mind are formed by compounding simple apprehensions', as Condillac in effect had done, 'we ought rather to say, that simple apprehensions are got by analysing more complex operations' (*Intellectual Powers*, IV.3, 327). In general, simple ideas are the products of abstraction, as Berkeley had already suggested. 'In persons come to years of understanding, judgment necessarily accompanies all sensation, perception by the senses, consciousness, and memory' (*Intellectual Powers*, IV.1, 409). What Reid calls 'consciousness' – consciousness of self – involves a judgement, a determination concerning the truth of the proposition that I am (I.7, 66–7). The judgements that accompany sense and memory are gifts of nature. Reid calls them 'judgments of nature'. They are descendants of the natural judgements of Malebranche, who actually compares them to sensations. We make a judgement, for example, that the heat is in both our hand and the fire. 'This natural judgment is only a sensation', and according to Malebranche it may or may not be followed by a 'free judgment'.[115] '[W]e have no sensation of external objects that does not involve one or more false judgments' (*De la recherche de la vérité*, II.xiv.1, 67). We feel ourselves strongly inclined to judge that our sensations are in objects, but we should resist. Malebranche uses his doctrine of natural judgement to account for such things as our perception of Locke's cube. 'When we look at a cube...', he explains, 'it is certain that the sides of it that we see almost never project an image of equal size in the fundus of our eyes.... Nonetheless, we see them as equal, and we are not deceived.' This happens by a kind of judgement that we make, 'that the faces of the cube, that are farthest away and that are viewed obliquely should not form images on the fundus of the eye as big as those formed by the faces that are closer'. But since it is given to the senses only to sense and not to judge, this is in fact a 'compound sensation'. 'For the same reason, I see an approaching man as having always the same size' (I.vii.4, 34).

Something like sensation, then, comes in through the back door. Reid, an apparent defender of the activity of judgement, becomes an advocate of its *passivity*. But perhaps this is no surprise. Malebranche embraces a Cartesian account of judgement: for Malebranche, as for Descartes, a judgement is an act of the will – a voluntary act. Reid rejects the Cartesian account. He can therefore emphasise the mind's passivity, as Hume does, and yet refuse to reduce judgement to sensation. Beliefs arise involuntarily, Reid thinks, but they are not mere sensations. They are determinations with regard to truth and falsehood.

Reid criticises both Locke's theory of judgement and Hume's theory of belief. His criticisms of Hume are especially shrewd. He uses Hume's own appeal to observation against him:

The belief of a proposition is an operation of mind of which every man is conscious, and what it is he understands perfectly, though, on account of its simplicity, he cannot give a logical definition of it. If he compares it with strength or vivacity of his ideas, or with any modification of ideas, they are so far from appearing to be one and the same, that they have not the least similitude. (*Intellectual Powers*, III.7, 291–2)

Every proposition that can be the object of belief has a contrary one. But, according to Hume, the ideas of both are the same and differ only in degrees of vivacity.

Reid disapproved of Locke's theory partly because it involves the theory of ideas. One of his objections anticipates Kant's concern with the meaning of the copula: if the objects of thought are ideas, Reid argues, we cannot make judgements about things themselves. For both Reid and Kant, a judgement is (at least in part) a verdict, and they want to ensure that the verdict is correctly located – that it concerns real things rather than ideas or representations of things.

5. *Kant*

In judgement, Kant writes in the *Kritik der reinen Vernunft*, a representation is brought under another representation. 'In every judgment', he explains, 'there is a concept that holds of many, and that among this many also comprehends a given representation, which is then related immediately to the object.' A representation that is immediately related to its object is, as we saw in Section I.1, an *intuition*. 'So in the judgment, e.g., "All bodies are divisible," the concept of the divisible is related to various other concepts; among these, however, it is here particularly related to the concept of body, and this in turn is related to certain appearances' – that is, to certain intuitions – 'that come before us' (A 68/B 93).

As we saw in Section II.2, Kant holds that when we make a judgement, we assert that representations are combined 'in the object, i.e., regardless of any difference in the condition of the subject' (B 142). The role of the copula, in fact, is 'to distinguish the objective unity of . . . representations from the subjective' (B 142). 'Only in this way', Kant continues, 'does there arise from this relation *a judgment*, i.e., a relation which is *objectively valid*, and that is sufficiently distinguished from the relation of these same representations in which there would be only subjective validity, e.g., in accordance with laws of association' (B 142). What Kant calls objective validity is not objective truth but objective *bearing* – a *claim* or *allegation* of objective truth. His concern in the present context is not to explain what makes a judgement *true* of an object, but to explain how a judgement acquires what he elsewhere calls 'reference to' an object.[116]

According to Kant, a judgement makes a claim on the allegiance of every possible consciousness, or on the allegiance of consciousness as such.[117] Such a claim is possible, he argues, only if the intuition subsumed under a concept in judgement is also subsumed under what he calls a category, or pure concept of the understanding. The judgement that air is elastic, for example, makes a claim on every consciousness

because certain judgments occur beforehand, which subsume the intuition of the air under the concept of cause and effect, and thereby determine the perceptions [of air and its elasticity] not merely with respect to each in my subject, but with respect to the form of judging in general . . . and in this way make the empirical judgment universally valid.[118]

The judgement that the surrounding air is elastic, then, involves not only the two representations acknowledged by the received account (the intuition of the surrounding air and the concept of the elastic), but a third representation (the category of cause and effect), under which the intuition must be subsumed if it is to figure in judgement at all. It follows that even intuitions, so long as they are fit to play a role in judgement, involve an act of subsumption or synthesis that is characteristic of judgement. 'The same function that gives unity to the different representations *in a judgment*', Kant writes in the *Kritik*, 'also gives unity to the mere synthesis of different representations *in an intuition*' (A 79/B 104–5). This striking reversal of the textbook ordering of faculties compromises even some of Kant's own remarks on the difference between intuition and understanding. For example, in the *Kritik* he writes that

All intuitions, as sensible, rest on affections, concepts therefore on functions. By a function, however, I understand the unity of the action of ordering different representations under a common one. Concepts are therefore grounded on the spontaneity of thinking, as sensible intuitions are grounded on the receptivity of impressions. Now the understanding can make no other use of these concepts than that of judging by means of them. Since no representations pertains to the object immediately except intuition alone, a concept is thus never immediately related to an object, but is always related to some other representation of it (whether that be an intuition or itself already a concept). Judgment is therefore the mediate cognition of an object, hence the representation of a representation of it. (A 68/B 93)

Yet it follows from Kant's account of the objective bearing of judgement that even sensible intuitions rest on functions and therefore on the spontaneity of thought.

6. *Forms of judgement*

A. THE TRADITIONAL TABLE OF JUDGEMENTS Eighteenth-century philosophers inherited a standard table of the forms of judgement. The table's arrangement varies from author to author, but all of the distinctions made pre-date the eighteenth century. Most of them can in fact be traced to Aristotle.

The simplest judgements (or propositional expressions of judgement) were assigned both a subject and a predicate. As the authors of the *Port-Royal Logic* explain,

This judgment is also called a proposition, and it is easy to see that it must have two terms. One term, of which one affirms or denies something, is called the *subject*; the other term which is affirmed or denied, is called the *attribute* or *Prædicatum*.[119]

The copula is the word or expression that indicates the connection or separation between subject and predicate.[120] The resulting judgements differ first of all in quality: they can be either *affirmative* ('the stone is heavy') or *negative* ('the stone is not heavy'). They differ as well in quantity: they can be *universal* ('all stones are heavy', 'no stones are heavy'), *particular* ('some stones are heavy', and its negative counterpart 'some stones are not heavy'), or *singular* ('this stone is heavy', and its negative counterpart 'this stone is not heavy'). (Singular judgements were standardly viewed as limiting cases of universal judgements.) Judgements differ also in modality: besides the judgement (sometimes called *assertoric*) that the stone is actually heavy, there is the (*apodeictic*) judgement that it is heavy necessarily and the (*problematic*) judgement that it is possibly so. These are forms exemplified by simple categorical judgements, which enter into compound judgements such as 'if this stone is heavy, it will fall' (a *hypothetical* judgement), and 'either this stone is heavy or it will not fall' (a *disjunctive* one).

One issue raised by the traditional table concerns the depth of the distinction between categorical and hypothetical judgements. Christian Wolff defined a categorical proposition as one in which the predicate is attached to the subject absolutely, or without a condition (*Logicæ*, I.iii.1, §216). In a hypothetical proposition, the *antecedent* or 'if' clause posits a condition; the predicate of the *consequent* or 'then' clause is attached to the subject only on the hypothesis that the condition is met. The relation between subject and predicate was the central theme in the Leibnizian account of truth. Leibniz had proposed that for a judgement to be true, the predicate must be contained within the subject.[121] Wolff agreed that there had to be a sufficient reason for attaching the predicate to the subject, but he departed from Leibniz in thinking that it could be outside the subject as well as inside. If outside, it could be added to a categorical judgement as follows:

Judgement: (1) This stone is heavy.
   The same judgement with the condition specified: (2) The stone, being a material thing, is heavy.

The condition appears in (2) as a participial phrase. But (2), Wolff thought, can also be expressed hypothetically:

(3) If the stone is a material thing, it is heavy.

Kant objected that 'this will not do, because the two' — (1) and (3) — 'are wholly different from one another as to their nature'.

In categorical judgments, nothing is problematic — rather, everything is assertoric — but in hypotheticals only the *consequentia* is assertoric. There is an essential difference between the two propositions, 'All bodies are divisible', and, 'If all bodies are composite, then they are divisible'. In the former proposition, I maintain the thing directly, in the latter only under a condition expressed problematically.[122]

The traditional table of judgement assumes that every judgement includes two terms. (Valid syllogisms include three.) Both Berkeley and Hume questioned this. Berkeley attacked Locke's theory of judgement as part of his attack on the assumption that every significant name stands for an idea. 'It is said ... that a Proposition cannot otherwise be understood than by perceiving the Ideas marked by the terms ... of it.' But suppose 'I have the Idea of some one particular ... Dog to which I give the name Melampus and then frame this Proposition *Melampus* is an Animal'. Then

if a Man may be allow'd to know his own meaning I do declare that in my thoughts the Word Animal is neither supposed to stand for an Universal Nature nor yet for an Abstract Idea which to me is at least as absurd and incomprehensible as the other. Nor does it indeed in that Proposition stand for any Idea ... at all. All that I intend to signify thereby being only this. That the particular ... thing I call Melampus has a right to be called by the Name Animal ... I perceive it evidently ... that upon laying aside all thought of the Words *Melampus is an Animal* I have remaining in my Mind one only naked and bare Idea viz. that particular one to which I give the Name Melampus.[123]

Hume shared Berkeley's view that a judgement or belief need not always involve two terms or ideas, but he pointed to the example of existential propositions.

'Tis far from being true, that in every judgment, which we form, we unite two different ideas; since in that proposition, *God is*, or indeed any other, which regards existence, the idea of existence is no distinct idea, which we unite with that of the object, and which is capable of forming a compound idea by the union (*Treatise*, 1.3.7.5n, SBN 96 fn).

In the Appendix to the *Treatise*, Hume brings forward several considerations in support of these claims about existence. One is that because 'the mind has the command over all its ideas, and can separate, unite, mix, and vary them, as it pleases', it would be in our power to believe whatever we please, if belief consisted in a new idea (App 2, SBN 623–4).

B. KANT'S TABLE OF JUDGEMENTS The understanding, Kant contended, is a faculty of judgement. This is because it is (by definition) a faculty of thought, and because thought is knowledge by means of concepts, and concepts are predicates of possible judgements (*Kritik*, A 69/B 94). It follows that '[t]he functions of the understanding can . . . all be found together if one can exhaustively exhibit the functions of unity in judgments' (A 69/B 94). Kant finds a complete enumeration of these functions of unity in the traditional table of judgements.[124] Kant's table comprises 'four titles, each of which contains . . . three moments' (A 70/B 95):

Quantity of Judgements
Universal
Particular
Singular

Quality		*Relation*
Affirmative		Categorical
Negative		Hypothetical
Infinite		Disjunctive

Modality
Problematic
Assertoric
Apodeictic

There are two notable departures from the traditional table: singular judgements (such as 'Socrates is mortal') are set apart from universal ones; and infinite judgements (such as 'The soul is not mortal') are assigned a separate place under quality. In the latter case at least, Kant is looking ahead to the use he will later make of the table. Although he presents it here (A 70/B 95) as part of what he calls pure *general* logic, which 'abstracts from all contents . . . and difference of its objects, and has to do with nothing but the mere form of thinking' (B 78/A 54), when he insists on a separate place for infinite judgement, he in effect treats the table as a contribution to *transcendental* logic, which is concerned with 'a determinate content, namely that of pure *a priori* cognitions' (A 131/B 170), and is therefore obliged to consider 'the value or content of the logical affirmation' (A 72/B 97). Because general logic abstracts from the content of the predicate (A 72/B 97), 'The soul is not mortal' is (from that point of view) affirmative. But because the judgement does not determine the concept of the soul in an affirmative manner, it is, with respect to content, merely limitative.

It therefore deserves a separate place in a 'transcendental table of all moments of thinking in judgments, since the function of understanding that is hereby exercised may perhaps be important in the field of its pure *a priori* cognition' (A 73/B 98).[125] This moment of thought seems to be at work in creating the 'necessary' but merely *limiting* concept (A 255/B 310) of a *noumenon* – the concept of a thing '*insofar as it is not an object of our sensible intuition*' (B 307).

Kant insisted that his table of judgements is complete, a claim that Tetens, Reinhold, and Solomon Maimon met with scepticism.[126] Kant also claimed that because '[t]he same function that gives unity to the different representations *in a judgment* also gives unity to the mere synthesis of different representations *in an intuition*, which, expressed generally, is called the pure concept of understanding' (*Kritik*, A 79/B 105), the table of judgements yields a complete table of the pure concepts of the understanding, or at any rate the basic ones. The category of substance and accident, for example, is derived from the categorical judgement form; the category of cause and effect is derived from the hypothetical. Kant follows Aristotle in calling these concepts *categories* (A 80/B 105), but the completeness of Kant's table, because it is 'systematically generated from a common principle' (A 80–1/B 106), is allegedly guaranteed. Aristotle's catalogue of categories was assembled 'as he stumbled on them', and its completeness is uncertain because it is based on induction only (see A 81/B 106).

C. ANALYTIC AND SYNTHETIC JUDGEMENTS Kant put forward a second classification of judgements that has been of enduring influence. An analytic truth is a truth whose predicate is contained within its subject (*Kritik*, A 6–7/B 10). It is therefore a contradiction to deny it. A synthetic truth is one whose predicate is not contained within its subject. It can therefore be denied without contradiction. Kant combined this distinction with one between a priori truths (those that can be justified without appealing to experience; see A 2/B 2–3) and a posteriori truths (those that cannot be). There are four combinations of the four terms:

> analytic and a priori;
> analytic and a posteriori;
> synthetic and a priori;
> synthetic and a posteriori.

There are, however, no analytic a posteriori truths: if a truth is analytic, its truth can always be determined without consulting experience by making explicit what is contained in its subject. Analytic a priori truths coincide with Hume's relations of ideas, and synthetic a posteriori truths coincide with Hume's matters of fact. In dividing all the objects of reason into relations of ideas and matters of fact, Hume had in effect assumed, without argument, that there are no synthetic a priori truths. Kant thinks that there are, and explaining how they are possible is a central task of the *Kritik der reinen Vernunft*.

NOTES

1 Antoine Arnauld and Pierre Nicole, *La logique, ou l'art de penser* (Paris, 1662). Translated as *Logic, or The Art of Thinking*, trans. J. Ozell (London, 1717), 34. See also Antoine Arnauld and Pierre Nicole, *The Art of Thinking: Port-Royal Logic*, trans. J. J. Dickoff and P. P. James (Indianapolis, IN, 1964), Pt. 1, ch. 1, 31.

2 John Locke, *An Examination of P. Malebranche's Opinion of Seeing all Things in God*, in *Posthumous Works of Mr. John Locke*, 10 vols. (London, 1810), 9: 209–55 at 220. The question of whether ideas are modes or substances had been raised by John Norris in the second part of his *Christian Blessedness . . . To which are added, Reflections upon a late Essay concerning Human Understanding* (London, 1690).

3 François Marie Arouet de Voltaire, *Dictionnaire philosophique portatif* (London, i.e., Geneva, 1764). Translated as *Philosophical Dictionary*, trans. and ed. T. Besterman (Harmondsworth, 1971), 237: 'Idée: Idea'.

4 Thomas Reid, *Essays on the Intellectual Powers of Man*, eds. D. R. Brookes and K. Haakonssen (Edinburgh, 2002), II.14, 184.

5 Edward Stillingfleet, *The Bishop of Worcester's Answer to Mr. Locke's Letter* (London, 1697), facsim. in Stillingfleet, *Three Criticisms of Locke* (Hildesheim and New York, NY, 1987), 80 and elsewhere. Stillingfleet applied the label to Locke's account of reasoning, but historians of philosophy now use it more broadly, as a label for early modern theories of perception and knowledge.

6 For seventeenth-century portrayals of scholastic theories of perception, see Nicolas Malebranche, *De la recherche de la vérité* (1674–5), in *Oeuvres complètes*, ed. A. Robinet, 22 vols. (Paris, 1958–84), vol. 1, ed. G. Rodis-Lewis (1962), III.ii.2. Page citations refer to the translation, *The Search after Truth*, trans. T. M. Lennon and P. J. Olscamp (Columbus, OH, 1980), 220–1; Locke, *Examination of Malebranche*; and two texts included in Gottfried Wilhelm Leibniz, *Philosophical Papers and Letters*, trans. and ed. L. E. Loemker, 2 vols. (Chicago, IL, 1956): 'Second Explanation of the New System: Postscript of a letter to Basnage de Beauval, 1696', in 2: 750–2, and 'The Controversy between Leibniz and Clarke, 1715–16', 1095–1169.

7 On the scholastics as advocates of what Leibniz called 'the system of physical influence', see, for example, Christian Wolff, *Psychologica rationalis*, §563 ('*Aristotelico-Scholastici sunt Influxionistæ*'), in *Werke*, II.6: 483. See also the account of Jean-Henri Formey in John W. Yolton, *Locke and French Materialism* (Oxford, 1991), 10–12.

8 [John Sergeant] *The Method to Science* (London, 1696), 3.

9 This use was deplored by Christian Wolff, for example, who urged philosophers to distinguish between perception (an act of mind) and idea (the object of an act). See his *Psychologica empirica*, §§24 and 48 in *Werke*, II.5: 17 and 30).

10 Étienne Bonnot de Condillac, *Essai sur l'origine des connaissances humaines*, in *Oeuvres philosophiques*, ed. G. Le Roy, 3 vols. (Paris, 1947–51), I.ii.8, §73. Citations refer to the translation, *An Essay on the Origin of Human Knowledge*, trans. and ed. H. Aarsleff (Cambridge, 2001).

11 David Hartley, *Observations on Man: His Frame, his Duty, and his Expectations*, 2 vols. (London, 1801), Introduction, 1: iii.

12 Kant uses 'reason' in at least two ways. For a contrast between reason and understanding, see Immanuel Kant's *Kritik der reinen Vernunft*, in Ak vols. 3 and 4, hereafter B and A, respectively. Translated as *Works/Critique of Pure Reason*, trans. and eds. P. Guyer and A. W. Wood (Cambridge, 1998), A 303–4/B 360–1. For 'reason' as a label for all human cognitive capacities, see for example A vii and B vii.

13 Samuel Johnson, *A Dictionary of the English Language*, 2 vols. (London, 1755), vol. 2.

14 Dugald Stewart, *Elements of the Philosophy of the Human Mind* (1792), in his *Collected Works*, ed. W. Hamilton, 11 vols. (Edinburgh, 1854–60), vols. 2–4 at 3: 10.

15 René Descartes, Letter to Mersenne, 27 May 1630, AT I 152, in *The Philosophical Writings of Descartes*, eds. J. Cottingham, R. Stoothoff, and D. Murdoch, 3 vols. (Cambridge, 1984–91), 3: 25.

16 Leibniz, *Monadologie*, ed. É. Boutroux (Paris, 1970). Page citations refer to the translation, *Monadology*, in *Philosophical Papers*, vol. 2, §15, p. 1046.

17 Leibniz, *Principes de la nature et de la grâce fondés en raison*, in *Philosophischen Schriften*, vol. 6. Page citations refer to the translation; translated as *Principles of Nature and of Grace, Based on Reason* (1714), in *Philosophical Papers*, 2: 1033–43, here §3 at 1035.

18 Leibniz, *Discours de métaphysique et Correspondance avec Arnauld*, ed. G. Le Roy (Paris, 1970). Page citations refer to the translation, 'Letter to Arnauld', 9 October 1687, in *Philosophical Papers*, 1: 521.

19 See *Principes*, §4, and *Philosophical Papers*, 2: 1036, where Leibniz speaks of 'perceptions . . . not distinct enough so that they can be remembered'. See also §§19 and 20 of the *Monadologie*, in *Philosophical Papers*, 2: 1044–61 at 1047.

20 Leibniz, 'Reply to the Thoughts on the System of Pre-Established Harmony . . . in Bayle's Critical Dictionary', in *Philosophical Papers*, 2: 944.

21 Leibniz, *Principes*, §13, 1040.

22 I borrow this designation from Lewis White Beck, *Early German Philosophy: Kant and His Predecessors* (Cambridge, MA, 1969), 271–2. See also Frederick C. Beiser, *The Fate of Reason: German Philosophy from Kant to Fichte* (Cambridge, MA, 1987), 171.

23 See Beck, *Early German Philosophy*, 268.

24 Immanuel Kant, *De Mundi sensibilis atque intelligibilis forma et principis* (§7), Ak 2: 395, translated as *On the Form and Principles of the Sensible and the Intelligible World [Inaugural Dissertation]*, in *Works/Theoretical Philosophy, 1755–1770*, trans. and eds. D. Walford and R. Meerbote (1992).

25 See, for example, Leibniz, *Nouveaux essais sur l'entendement humain*, eds. A. Robinet and H. Schepers, in *Akademieausgabe*, VI6 (1962). Page citations refer to the translation, *New Essays on Human Understanding*, trans. and eds. P. Remnant and J. Bennett (Cambridge, 1981), 81, 254, 382, 487.

26 For further discussion of Leibniz's views, see Robert McRae, *Leibniz: Perception, Apperception, and Thought* (Toronto, 1976), especially ch. 5, 126–45.

27 George Berkeley, *An Essay Towards a New Theory of Vision*, §45 in *Works*, 1: 188.

28 See Berkeley, *A Treatise concerning the Principles of Human Knowledge*, §§27, 89, 140, and especially 142, in *Works*, 2: 52–3, 79–80, 105, 106. The *Treatise* was first published in 1710; the passages (§§89, 140, 142) contrasting ideas and notions were added in the second edition (1734).

29 Samuel Johnson, *The Elements of Philosophy*, 3rd edn. (London, 1754), Tract I, ch. 1, §4, pp. 21, 22.

30 Wolff, *Psychologica empirica*, I.ii.1, §§48, 49, pp. 30 ff.

31 Georg Friedrich Meier, *Vernunftlehre* (Halle, 1762), Pt. I, sect. 8, §293, p. 428. See his *Auszug aus der Vernunftlehre* (Halle, 1752), §260, 71. According to Meier, concepts are acquired in three ways: by experience (*Erfahrung*), by abstraction (*logische Abstraction*), and

by wilful combination (*willkürliche Verbindung*), Pt. 1, sect. 8, §288, §292, p. 416, p. 426, §299, p. 439.

32 David Hume, *An Enquiry concerning Human Understanding*, ed. T. L. Beauchamp, in *The Clarendon Edition* (2000), 2.9n, SBN 22.

33 David Hartley, *Observations* Pt. 1, Introduction, 1: i.

34 For Locke on particles, see *Essay*, III.vii; for negative names, see III.i.4.

35 See Berkeley's Introduction to the *Treatise*, §§19–20, in *Works*, 2: 37, and *Alciphron, or the Minute Philosopher* (1732), Dialogue VII in *Works*, 3: 286–329.

36 Hartley, *Observations*, I.iii.1, 278–9.

37 See, for example, Norris, Reflections upon a late Essay concerning Human Understanding, in *Christian blessedness*.

38 Leibniz, *Principes*, §4, 1036.

39 On the interpretation of Leibniz on apperception, see McRae, *Leibniz*; Mark Kulstad, *Leibniz on Apperception, Consciousness, and Reflection* (Munich, 1991); and Udo Thiel, 'Leibniz and the Concept of Apperception', *Archiv für Geschichte der Philosophie*, 76 (1994): 195–209.

40 Condillac, *Essai*, I.ii.2, §8, 22.

41 For accounts of Arnauld and Malebranche on the nature of ideas, see two books by Steven M. Nadler, *Arnauld and the Cartesian Philosophy of Ideas* (Manchester and Princeton, NJ, 1989), and *Malebranche and Ideas* (New York, NY, 1992), as well as Thomas M. Lennon, *The Battle of the Gods and Giants: The Legacies of Descartes and Gassendi, 1655–1715* (Princeton, NJ, 1993).

42 See, for example, the Third Meditation, in Descartes, *Philosophical Writings*, 2: 24–36 at 25–6. For commentary on Descartes's understanding of ideas, see John Yolton, *Perceptual Acquaintance from Descartes to Reid* (Minneapolis, MN, 1984), 18–41, and Vere Chappell, 'The Theory of Ideas', in *Essays on Descartes' Meditations*, ed. A. Oksenberg Rorty (Berkeley, CA, 1986), 177–98.

43 See, for example, Locke, *Essay*, I.i.8 and II.viii.8. For Locke's opinion of Malebranche, see his *Examination of Malebranche*, and Charles J. McCracken's commentary in *Malebranche and British Philosophy* (Oxford, 1983), ch. 4, 119–55.

44 On Locke, see the essays by Douglas Greenlee, Gunnar Aspelin, and H. E. Matthews in *Locke on Human Understanding*, ed. I. C. Tipton (Oxford, 1977); Yolton, *Perceptual Acquaintance*, 76–104; Michael Ayers, *Locke: Epistemology and Ontology*, 2 vols. (London, 1991), vol. 1, Pt. 1: Ideas; and Vere Chappell, 'Locke's Theory of Ideas', in *The Cambridge Companion to Locke*, ed. V. Chappell (Cambridge, 1994), 26–55.

45 Joseph Butler, *The Works of Joseph Butler*, ed. W. E. Gladstone, 2 vols. (Oxford, 1896), Preface to *Fifteen Sermons*, §3, vol. 2: 3. Butler was actually speaking of 'morals, considered as a science'.

46 Étienne Bonnot de Condillac, *La Logique – Logic* (1780), parallel text edn., trans. W. R. Albury (New York, NY, 1980), 169. See also 'Idée', in *Encyclopédie ou Dictionnaire raisonné des sciences, des arts et des métiers*, [with suppls.], eds. D. Diderot and J. le Rond d'Alembert, 35 vols. (Paris and Amsterdam, 1751–80), 8: 489.

47 Condillac, *Essai*, I.iii, §16, 76.

48 Paul-Henri Thiry d'Holbach, *Système de la nature, ou Des loix du monde physique et du monde moral*, ed. D. Diderot, 2 vols. (Paris, 1821). Page citations refer to the translation, *The System of Nature, or The Laws of the Moral and Physical World*, 2 vols. (London, 1817), I.i.11, 280. For d'Holbach, a human being is just 'a material being, organized after a peculiar manner', I.i.6, 138.

49 Leibniz, *Meditationes de cognitione, veritate et ideis*, in *Philosophischen Schriften*, 4: 422–6; page citations refer to the translation, *Meditations on Knowledge, Truth and Ideas*, in *Philosophical Papers*, 1: 448–54, at 454.

50 Leibniz, *New Essays*, 300.

51 See, for example, Leibniz, *New Essays*, 140. This understanding of Leibnizian ideas is developed by Nicholas Jolley in *The Light of the Soul: Theories of Ideas in Leibniz, Malebranche, and Descartes* (Oxford, 1990).

52 Leibniz believes these dispositions are grounded in something actual (see, for example, *New Essays*, 52). These must in the end be perceptions.

53 See, for example, Berkeley, *Philosophical Commentaries* (1707–8), 427a, 643, and 808, in *Works*, 1: 53, 79, 97; and *Treatise* §§1, 2, vol. 2, pp. 41–2. For discussion of Berkeley's understanding of ideas, see Yolton, *Perceptual Acquaintance*, 135–42 and 209–10; I. C. Tipton, 'Ideas in Berkeley and Arnauld', *History of European Ideas*, 7 (1986): 575–85; and Kenneth P. Winkler, *Berkeley: An Interpretation* (Oxford, 1989), 1–21 and 290–309.

54 For Hume on abstraction, see *A Treatise of Human Nature*, 1.1.7, SBN 17 ff. For Hume on scepticism, see *Treatise*, 1.4.2, and *Enquiry*, 12.1–3, SBN 149.

55 Thomas Reid, *The Philosophical Orations of Thomas Reid*, ed. D. D. Todd (Carbondale, IL, 1989), 74, where Reid also describes three perfectly acceptable meanings of the word 'idea'. See also the *Essays on the Intellectual Powers*, I.1, §10, 27–32.

56 As are my own interpretive claims about Descartes, Locke, Berkeley, and Hume.

57 Thomas Brown, *Lectures on the Philosophy of the Human Mind*, 2 vols. (Edinburgh, 1820), Lecture XXVI, vol. 2, 1–25 at 23–4. More recently, Yolton has argued, in *Perceptual Acquaintance*, that no important early modern philosopher thought of ideas as mental intermediaries.

58 Not, however, by Berkeley, who claimed that ideas of sense are real things rather than representations.

59 Hume, *Enquiry*, 12.1.9, SBN 152.

60 Condillac, *Essai*, 'Introduction', 4. 'Our Des Cartes', Voltaire wrote in his letter on Locke, was 'born not to discover the Errors of Antiquity, but to substitute his own in the Room of them' (in his *Lettres philosophiques ou Lettres sur les Anglais* (Amsterdam [Rouen], 1734). Page citations are from the translation, *Letters concerning the English Nation*, ed. N. Cronk (Oxford, 1994), 55.

61 Jean le Rond d'Alembert, 'Discours préliminaire', *Encyclopédie*, 1: i–xlv at ii and ix. Quoted from *Preliminary Discourse to the Encyclopedia of Diderot*, trans. R. N. Schwab and W. E. Rex (Indianapolis, In, 1963), 6 and 31.

62 Locke had his critics even in early eighteenth-century Britain, of course. Apart from Norris, the most notable were Henry Lee and Peter Browne.

63 Hume, *Enquiry*, 2.2.9n, SBN 22n.

64 Hutcheson defends this view in *An Inquiry into the Original of Our Ideas of Beauty and Virtue*, 4th edn. (London, 1738), and *An Essay on the Nature and Conduct of the Passions and Affections, with Illustrations on the Moral Sense* (1728), ed. A. Garrett (Indianapolis, IN, 2002).

65 Adam Smith, *The Theory of Moral Sentiments*, eds. D. D. Raphael and A. L. Macfie, in *Works* (1976), VII.iii.6, 322.

66 See, for example, Francis Hutcheson, *Inaugural Lecture on the Social Nature of Man*, §34, in *On Human Nature: Reflections on our Common Systems of Morality and On the Social Nature of Man*, ed. T. Mautner (Cambridge, 1993), 143–5. The quotation in the next section is from *Logicae compendium*, 19.

67 Joseph Priestley, *An Examination of Dr. Reid's Inquiry into the Human Mind on the Principles of Common Sense, Dr. Beattie's Essay on the Nature and Immutability of Truth and Dr. Oswald's Appeal to Common Sense in Behalf of Religion*, in *Theological and Miscellaneous Works*, ed. J. T. Rutt, 25 vols. in 26 (London, 1817–32), 3: 1–67 at 27.

68 James Oswald, *An Appeal to Common Sense in Behalf of Religion*, 2 vols. (Edinburgh, 1766–72), I.iii.3, 158.

69 James Beattie, *An Essay on the Nature and Immutability of Truth, in Opposition to Sophistry and Scepticism*, 4th edn. (London, 1773), Pt. 1, ch. 1, 45.

70 Claude Buffier, *Traité des premières véritéz et de la source de nos jugements ou l'on examine le sentiment des philosophes sur les premiers notions des choses* (Paris, 1724), no. 33, as translated in Louise Marcil-LaCoste, *Claude Buffier and Thomas Reid: Two Common-Sense Philosophers* (Kingston and Montreal, 1982), 21.

71 For Lambert and Tetens and their debt to Locke, see note 85, as well as Lewis White Beck's briefer essay 'From Leibniz to Kant', in *The Age of German Idealism*, eds. R. C. Solomon and K. M. Higgins (London, 1993), 5–39. For Locke's post-Kantian influence in Germany, see Frederick C. Beiser, *The Fate of Reason: German Philosophy from Kant to Fichte* (Cambridge, MA, 1987). On the influence of Scottish common-sense philosophy in Germany, see Manfred Kuehn, *Scottish Common Sense in Germany, 1768–1800: A Contribution to the History of Critical Philosophy* (Kingston and Montreal, 1987). Kuehn outlines Tetens's views on representation (and documents the influence of Reid) on 122–7.

72 Karl Leonhard Reinhold, *Über das Fundament des philosophischen Wissens [On the Foundation of Philosophical Knowledge]* (Jena, 1794), 44, 45, and 56, as translated in *Between Kant and Hegel: Texts in the Development of Post-Kantian Idealism*, trans. and eds. G. di Giovanni and H. S. Harris (Albany, NY, 1985), 56–7, 71. According to Reinhold's 'principle of consciousness', 'in consciousness representation is distinguished through the subject from both object and subject and is referred to both' (*Fundament des philosophischen Wissens*, 78; *Between Kant and Hegel*, 70).

73 See Beiser, *The Fate of Reason*.

74 Johann Gottlieb Fichte, *Vergleichung des vom Hrn Prof. Schmid aufgestellten Systems mit der Wissenschaftslehre* [Science of Knowledge], in *Gesamtausgabe*, I.1, §4, 247: 'Wie hangen unsere Vorstellungen mit ihren Objekten zusammen?'

75 See Leibniz, 'Second Explanation', in *Philosophical Papers*, 2: 750–2. Leibniz's influence in eighteenth-century France is discussed by Yolton in *Locke and French Materialism*.

76 See Yolton, *Locke and French Materialism*, 60–2 (on Gerdil) and 110–35 (on Boullier).

77 As Margaret Atherton explains in her exposition of Berkeley's theory, *Berkeley's Revolution in Vision* (Ithaca, NY, 1990).

78 Hartley, *Observations*, I.i.2, 65.

79 Condillac, *Logic*, 47.

80 Voltaire, *Eléments de la philosophie de Newton* (London [i.e. Paris]; Amsterdam, 1738). Translated as *The Elements of Sir Isaac Newton's Philosophy*, trans. J. Hanna (London, 1738).

81 See Beck, *Early German Philosophy*, 412–25.

82 Giambattista Vico, *De antiquissima italorum sapientia*, 3 vols, (Naples, 1710). Page citations refer to the translation, *On the Most Ancient Wisdom of the Italians*, trans. L. M. Palmer (Ithaca, NY, 1988), 96.

83 See Winkler, *Berkeley*, ch. 3, 53–75.

84 See Hume, *Enquiry*, 2.8, SBN 31, and *Treatise*, 1.1.1.10, SBN 6.

85 Lambert was among the other eighteenth-century philosophers puzzled by necessary connections among simple ideas or concepts. See Beck, *Early German Philosophy*, 406–7.

86 Dugald Stewart, *Outlines of Moral Philosophy*, Pt. 1, sect. 8, §66, in *Works*, 2: 26. (*Outlines*, Pt. 2, is prefixed to vol. 6 of *Works*.)

87 Quoted in *Imagination in Coleridge*, ed. J. S. Hill (London, 1978), 27; see 'Lecture on the Slave-Trade' (1795), in Samuel Taylor Coleridge, *Lectures 1795 on Politics and Religion*, eds. L. Patton and P. Mann (1971), in *Collected Works*, eds. K. Coburn and B. Winer (London, 1969–), 1:235.

88 See Immanuel Kant, *Anthropologie in pragmatischer Hinsicht*, I.i, §28, Ak 7: 167–8.

89 See Rudolf A. Makkreel, *Imagination and Interpretation in Kant: The Hermeneutical Import of the 'Critique of Judgment'* (Chicago, IL, 1990).

90 It is accepted by Kant, for example, in the *Kritik der Urtheilskraft* (1790), II.ii, §67, Ak 5: 380, translated as *Critique of the Power of Judgment*, trans. P. Guyer and E. Matthews, ed. P. Guyer, in *Works* (2000), Pt. II: 29.

91 Offray de la Mettrie, *Machine Man and Other Writings*, trans. and ed. A. Thomson (Cambridge, 1996), 10.

92 Kant, *Anthropologie* I.i, §52, Ak 7: 215–16.

93 Kant, *Jäsche Logik*, Ak 9: 1–150, notes 1–3 in §6 at 94–5; translated as *The Jäsche Logic* in *Lectures on Logic*, trans. and ed. J. M. Young, in *Works* (1992).

94 *George Berkeley's Manuscript Introduction*, ed. B. Belfrage (Oxford, 1987), §14, 75.

95 Descartes's account of judgement was very much a minority view. For an account of its fate in the eighteenth century, see Gabriel Nuchelmans, *Judgment and Proposition from Descartes to Kant* (Amsterdam, 1983).

96 See Berkeley, *An Essay Towards a New Theory of Vision*, §24, in *Works*, 1: 176; *The Theory of Vision . . . Vindicated and Explained* (1733), §42, in *Works*, 1: 265–6.

97 Berkeley, First Dialogue, in *Works*, 2: 196.

98 William Duncan, *Elements of Logick*, 5th edn. (London, 1764), Bk. 2, ch. 1, p. 145.

99 [Henry Aldrich] *Artis logicæ compendium* (Oxford, 1691).

100 Francis Hutcheson, *Logicae compendium* (Glasgow, 1756), 38–9. For 'sententia', see 16–17. Gershom Carmichael, *Breviuscula introductio ad logicam*, 2nd edn. (Edinburgh, 1722), 8, translated as *A Short Introduction to Logic*, in *Natural Rights on the Threshold of the Scottish Enlightenment: The Writings of Gershom Carmichael*, trans. and eds. J. Moore and M. Silverthorne (Indianapolis, IN, 2002), 289–317 at 298.

101 Christian Wolff, *Logicae* I.i.1, §39, in his *Philosophia rationalis sive logica*, ed. J. École, in *Werke*, II.1.1–3, at 1.2: 129.

102 Hutcheson, *Logicae*, 16–17. See note 100.

103 For more examples of the two models (and of views influenced by both), see Nuchelmans, *Judgment and Proposition*.

104 Edward Bentham, *An Introduction to Logick, Scholastick and Rational* (Oxford, 1773), Pt. II, §1, 35.

105 Meier, *Auszug aus der Vernunftlehre*, §§292, 293, p. 81; *Vernunftlehre* Pt. I, sect. 9, §§325–6, pp. 483–6. On Kant's use of Meier's *Auszug*, see Young's introduction to the *Lectures on Logic*, p. xxiii, and 'Biographical-bibliographical sketches', in Kant, *Theoretical Philosophy*, *1755–1770*, 510.

106 'Empirical judgments, insofar as they have objective validity, are *judgments of experience*; those, however, that are only subjectively valid I call mere *judgments of perception*.' See *Prolegomena zu einer jeden künftigen Metaphysik, die als Wissenschaft wird auftreten können*, II, §18, in Ak 4: 298, translated as *Prolegomena to Any Future Metaphysics that Will Be Able to Come Forward as Science*, trans. G. Hatfield, eds. H. Allison and P. Heath, in *Works / Theoretical Philosophy after 1781*.

107 Judgements whose truth is internal to the representations involved are *analytic*, according to Kant. See p. 278.

108 Kant, *Wiener Logik*, Ak 24: 787–940 at 934, translated as *The Vienna Logic*, in *Lectures on Logic*.

109 *Leibniz, New Essays*, 356. Hume makes a similar claim in *Treatise*, 1.2.2.8, SBN 32: '*whatever the mind clearly conceives includes the idea of possible existence*'.

110 In *Logik Blomberg* (Ak 24: 7–301), §301, Ak 24: 275–6 (translated as *The Blomberg Logic* in *Lectures on Logic*), and *Jäsche Logik*, §30, Ak 24: 108–9, Kant makes a distinction between

considering and positing a relation between two concepts. See also Kant's letter to Reinhold of 19 May 1789, where he distinguishes between 'judgments...as *problematic*' (what he calls 'mere judgments') and judgments 'as *assertoric*' ('propositions'); Kant, *Correspondence* in *Works*, trans. and ed. A. Zweig (1999), 308.

111 The quotation is from Alexander Pope, *Essay on Man* (1733), in *Poetical Works*, ed. H. Davis (Oxford,1966), Epistle I, l. 226.

112 Hume offers no account of beliefs in relations of ideas. The little he says suggests that the mind sees relations among ideas, but whether this is the judgement, or merely preparation for judgement, he does not say.

113 Butler, *Dissertation on Virtue*, §2, in *Works*, 1: 397–411 at 399.

114 In the *Treatise*, Hume made a similar suggestion, though it was couched in terms of his sentimentalising theory of belief. Belief or assent, he claimed there, always attends the perceptions of the senses: ''Tis merely the force and liveliness of the perception, which constitutes the first act of the judgment, and lays the foundation of that reasoning, which we build upon it, when we trace the relation of cause and effect' (1.3.5.7, SBN 86).

115 Malebranche, *De la recherche de la vérité*, I.x.6, 52.

116 For reference to an object, see Kant, *Prolegomena*, §§18 and 20, Ak 4: 297–8.

117 See, for example, *Prolegomena*, §18, Ak 4: 297–8.

118 Kant, *Prolegomena*, II.20, Ak 4: 301.

119 Arnauld and Nicole, *Logic*, Pt. 2, ch. 3, 82.

120 Wolff, *Logicae* I.iii.1, §201, in *Werke*, II.1.2: 217.

121 Leibniz: see, for example, 'First Truths', in *Philosophical Papers*, 1: 411–17 at 412, 'On Freedom', in *Philosophical Papers*, 1: 404–10 at 405; and his *Discours de métaphysique*, §13, in *Philosophischen Schriften*, vol. 4, translated as *Discourse on Metaphysics and Related Writings*, trans. and eds. R. N. D. Martin and S. Brown (Manchester, 1988), 50–2.

122 Kant, *Jäsche Logic*, note 2 in §25, Ak 9: 105–6.

123 Berkeley, *Manuscript Introduction*, §§33–4, pp. 101, 103.

124 Kant's revisions are, in fact, traditional, though the reasons behind them are not. For a discussion of Kant's sources, see H. J. de Vleeschauwer, *La déduction transcendentale dans l'oeuvre de Kant*, 2 vols. (Paris, 1934), 1: 244–50.

125 Kant, *Wiener Logik*, Ak 24: 930.

126 For a defence of Kant's claim to completeness, see Klaus Reich, *The Completeness of Kant's Table of Judgements*, trans. J. Kneller and M. Losonsky (Stanford, CA, 1992). See also Robert Greenberg, *Kant's Theory of A Priori Knowledge* (University Park, PA, 2001), Reinhard Brandt, *The Table of Judgments: Critique of Pure Reason A 67–76;B 92–101*, trans. Eric Watkins (Atascadero, CA, 1995), and Beatrice Longuenesse, *Kant and the Capacity to Judge*, trans. C. T. Wolfe (Princeton, NJ, 1997).

10

SELF–CONSCIOUSNESS AND PERSONAL IDENTITY

UDO THIEL

This chapter deals with a number of related issues concerning the human self. The first section examines the notion of consciousness and associated concepts, such as reflection, which were central to fundamental philosophical discussion in the eighteenth century. The second section is concerned with the issues of personal identity, in which the notion of consciousness plays a crucial role, and the nature of the mind. These two sections, for the most part, cover material from the early eighteenth century to the 1770s only. The third section is devoted to the most important development during the 1780s and 1790s: the notions of transcendental self-consciousness and self-identity in the works of Kant and Fichte, which play a central and systematic role in their respective systems of philosophy and which greatly influenced the development of German Idealism in the early nineteenth century.

I. RELATING TO THE SELF: CONSCIOUSNESS AND REFLECTION

What was meant by 'consciousness' and what was the function of this notion in eighteenth-century theoretical philosophy? In some contexts, consciousness was thought of as relating to *external* objects, but generally it was understood as a way of relating to *oneself*. This inner-directed consciousness is the main focus of this section. Now, to say that consciousness is a form of relating to the self is basically to say that it is to be understood as *self*-consciousness, but it remains to be explained what form of self-relation this was held to be and how it connected with other forms of relating to the self. There appears to be no general agreement among eighteenth-century philosophers as to precisely what kind of self-relation terms such as 'consciousness' or 'self-consciousness' denote. We shall see that the notion of *reflection* is of special importance to an understanding of what was meant by 'consciousness'.

I am grateful to Manfred Kuehn for valuable comments on an earlier version of this chapter.

There are very few explicit discussions of consciousness in the early part of the century: the issue was just one problem among many others. If it was raised at all, it was mostly discussed in broader, mostly epistemological contexts. It was not until the late 1720s that consciousness became an explicit object of more substantial philosophical inquiry. Most importantly, in 1728, an essay solely devoted to the notion of consciousness was published anonymously in London.[1] In Germany, Christian Wolff's empirical and rational psychologies of the 1720s and 1730s contain reflections on (self-) consciousness, and by the 1730s it had come to be regarded as a fundamental philosophical concept. For Wolff, for example, the issue of self-consciousness is central to his account of our knowledge of the external world: the problem of external objects cannot even be formulated without raising questions about our own self. Later, especially from the mid-1760s onwards, consciousness was discussed not only in the context of other philosophical debates but also in an increasing number of independent tracts devoted to consciousness itself. In 1778, Joseph Priestley could safely say that 'in all metaphysical subjects, there is a perpetual appeal made to *consciousness*'.[2] Priestley's remark indicates, however, that in addition to special tracts devoted to consciousness, the concept continued to be more widely discussed or 'appealed to', and philosophical discussion of consciousness reached its peak in the transcendental philosophies of Kant and especially Fichte towards the end of the century. By the 1780s and 1790s, the issue of self-consciousness had become absolutely fundamental to the philosophical enterprise as a whole. The problems connected with the self had moved from the periphery to the very centre of discussion: for Fichte, self-consciousness constitutes the highest principle of all philosophy. Before the *Essay on Consciousness* of 1728, however, there are, at best, only fragments of a theory of consciousness, remarks made in wider contexts that hint implicitly at the importance of various conceptual distinctions concerning the issue of relating to oneself.[3]

1. The Seventeenth-century background

Remarks made by various philosophers of the late seventeenth century suggest that for them 'consciousness' denotes a feeling or an immediate perception of one's own activities. The Cambridge Platonist Ralph Cudworth, for example, holds that consciousness 'makes a Being to be Present with it self';[4] Nicolas Malebranche suggests that 'conscience' denotes an immediate relation to the self by defining the term as *sentiment intérieur*;[5] and Louis de la Forge argues explicitly that the relation between consciousness and thought is characterised by immediacy: consciousness is not a separate mental act but an essential element of thought itself.[6]

This notion of consciousness is present also in John Locke's *Essay Concerning Human Understanding*. Locke, too, does not say very much about 'consciousness', but what he does say indicates that the notion is of central importance to his account of thought and must be distinguished from what he calls 'inward sense' or 'reflection'. He states that 'consciousness . . . is *inseparable* from thinking, and as it seems to me essential to it: It being impossible for any one to perceive, without perceiving, that he does perceive. When we see, hear, smell, taste, feel, meditate, or will any thing, we know that we do so. Thus it is always as to our present Sensations and Perceptions' (my emphasis).[7] For Locke, 'being conscious' denotes an immediate awareness that is an integral part of all acts of thinking: 'thinking consists in being conscious that one thinks' (II.i.19). He makes it quite clear that, unlike consciousness, 'reflection' is *not* an essential element of thought as such and is not characterised by immediacy. 'Reflection' or 'inner sense' requires special attention (II.i.24). In reflection, the mind relates to itself in the sense that it *observes* its own operations and produces *ideas* of them: Locke links reflection, but not consciousness, to contemplation (II.vi.1; II.i.4, 7, 8). There is a broader sense of 'consciousness' in Locke which includes memory (for example, in his discussion of personal identity[8]), but it is obvious that, in general, he does not equate consciousness with memory.

Étienne Bonnot de Condillac, Locke's influential follower in France, defines consciousness in Malebranche's terminology as *sentiment intérieur*, as a feeling 'of what is passing within us'.[9] In his *Essai sur l'origine des connaissances humaines* (1746), he states that 'everyone agrees that the mind has perceptions that are not there without its knowledge. The sentiment that produces this knowledge and that tells us at least partially what goes on in it I call 'consciousness.'[10] Condillac even holds that the terms 'perception' and 'consciousness' denote different aspects of the same operation: 'When it is looked upon as the impression made in the mind, we can keep the name 'perception.' When it makes its presence known to the mind, we can call it 'consciousness.''[11] Condillac differs from Locke in not regarding reflection as an independent and original source of ideas: through reflection we merely direct our attention towards various given ideas and compare them with one another.[12]

Locke's notion of ideas of reflection was also attacked by philosophers inspired by Malebranche, who had maintained that the *only* acquaintance we have with our own souls is through *conscience* or *sentiment intérieur*. He appears to rule out all other, mediate forms of relating to the self (such as reflection). This idea had a considerable impact on early eighteenth-century conceptions of consciousness. Berkeley, for example, claims that we are not able to acquire 'ideas' of our thoughts and souls through reflection.[13] Consciousness is the only mode of relating to oneself: 'There are two supreme classes of things, body and soul.

By the help of sense we know the extended thing... but the sentient, percipient, thinking thing we know by a certain internal consciousness' ('conscientia quadam interna').[14] This knowledge by consciousness is understood by Berkeley as an immediate or intuitive form of knowledge.[15] Occasionally he makes use of the term 'reflection', but this term does not denote a form of self-relation which differs from that of immediate consciousness.[16] Similar accounts of consciousness are present in the works of other British philosophers of the early eighteenth century. Malebranche's follower John Norris, for example, argues that we have 'no Ideal Knowledge of... [our] Soul' and its operations but merely an 'inward Sense and Consciousness of it'.[17] Likewise, Peter Browne holds that we have no representative '*Ideas of Reflection*' of the operations of our minds but only an immediate consciousness of them.[18]

2. *An Essay on Consciousness*

The anonymous author of the *Essay on Consciousness* expresses surprise that the various epistemological investigations by other philosophers had not led to examinations of consciousness, finding it 'not a little surprising that They, who have search'd and ransack'd every nook and corner of the Mind, for *Ideas*... should never once happen to *Stumble* upon *Consciousness*' (195).

According to this author '*Consciousness*... is that inward Sense and Knowledge which the Mind hath of its own Being and Existence, and of whatever passes within itself, in the Use and Exercise of any of its Faculties or Powers' (144–5). Several times the author emphasises the immediacy of consciousness (149–50, 175). Further, consciousness is characterised by the highest degree of certainty: It 'is indeed the Basis and Foundation of all Knowledge whatsoever' (147; see also 177). Despite its immediacy, however, consciousness is conceived of as an act of perception which is distinct from the act to which it relates: '*Thinking*, the *Consciousness* of it, and the *Perception* of This, tho' each of them be a several Act, and quite distinct from the other, are *simultaneous*' (214; see also 215). Yet the author, though regarding consciousness as a distinct mental act, distinguishes it from reflection: it does not require attention or application. Whereas consciousness necessarily accompanies all perceptions and is not 'capable of being exerted, as the Mind's other Faculties and Powers are' (173–4), this is not true of reflection: our acts of thinking are not automatically accompanied by reflection (that is, by an explicit relating to them), for that 'would be a Hindrance and Impediment to such Acts' (206).

One major problem arises from the position adopted by the anonymous author, namely that of an infinite regress of consciousness. This is an old problem in philosophy and had been discussed, in various forms, well before the eighteenth century; Hobbes had raised the issue in his objections to Descartes, and Leibniz in his critique of Locke. Our author explicitly addresses this issue, holding that we are conscious of all our mental acts and are always conscious of our consciousness of our mental acts but maintaining that it does not follow that there should be any further acts of consciousness beyond this second level: 'But farther than This, or beyond a *Sense* of *Consciousness*, there is no proceeding. For admitting a *Perception* of a *Sense* of *Consciousness*, that is, in other Words, a *Perception* of a *Perception*, of a *Perception* ... the Progress might as well be *in infinitum*; which therefore cannot be admitted, as being absurd and impossible' (165). The author realises that the notion of an infinite regress of acts of consciousness is not acceptable and therefore maintains that there are no further acts of consciousness beyond the consciousness of consciousness. However, the author does not *show* how, on the account of consciousness presented, the problem can be avoided. Since, on this view, consciousness is a separate mental act and acts of consciousness accompany all our mental acts, it follows that the consciousness of consciousness must in turn be accompanied by another act of consciousness, and so on, ad infinitum.

3. Hume, Reid, and Dugald Stewart

It is not known whether Hume read the *Essay on Consciousness*. In any case, he does not explicitly discuss consciousness at all. Yet the notion of consciousness which is implicit in his theoretical philosophy is basically the same as that of the anonymous *Essay*. At first, it seems that for Hume consciousness is a self-relation to be explained in terms of reflection. For example, in the *Treatise of Human Nature* (1739–40) he states that 'consciousness is nothing but a reflected thought or perception'.[19]

Yet several passages indicate that Hume has a notion of consciousness which is distinct from that of reflection. He characterises reflection as an explicit turning of the mind's attention to its own perceptions: it does not signify an immediate or automatic relation to the self. To reflect is to perceive or *observe* one's own perceptions (1.4.6, SBN 252). *Consciousness*, however, Hume often describes as an *immediate* relation of oneself to oneself. Through it, but not through reflection, the operations of the mind are 'most intimately present to us'.[20] It is clearly the immediacy of the self-relation through consciousness which Hume thinks is responsible for the fact that 'consciousness never deceives' but is absolutely certain.[21] Because of its immediacy and certainty, consciousness for him is apparently a basis for the distinctions which philosophical reflection draws (*Enquiry*, 1.13, SBN 14). Hume points out, however, that, despite the fact that our mental operations are immediately present to us through consciousness, to distinguish and examine them through reflection is not an easy task. Nor is mere consciousness of them of great help here:

It is remarkable concerning the operations of the mind, that, though most intimately present to us, yet, whenever they become the object of reflexion, they seem involved in obscurity; nor can the eye readily find those lines and boundaries, which discriminate and distinguish them. (*Enquiry*, 1.13, SBN 13)

Obviously, then, the absolute certainty which distinguishes the self-relation via consciousness does not, according to Hume, extend to other forms of self-relation such as reflection. It is also obvious that, in making these points, he implies a distinction between consciousness and reflection.[22]

Thomas Reid is very critical of Hume's philosophy of mind in general and of his account of personal identity in particular. Yet, despite these differences and some differences in terminology, his account of the nature of consciousness is basically the same as that of Hume. In *Essays on the Intellectual Powers of Man* (1785), Reid defines consciousness as 'that immediate knowledge which we have of our present thoughts and purposes, and, in general, of all the present operations of our minds'.[23] Reflection, by contrast, is said to be that act of the mind through which we make 'our own thoughts and passions, and the various operations of our minds' the objects of attention, 'either while they are present, or when they are recent and fresh in our memory' (I.2, 42; see also I.5, 58–9 and VI.1, 420–1). Whereas reflection is a voluntary act, consciousness is an 'immediate and intuitive' self-relation (VI.5, 470).

Although Reid holds that there is consciousness of one's own perceptions, he emphasises that a self beyond the perceptions cannot be an object of consciousness: 'The conception of a mind is neither an idea of sensation nor an idea of reflection; for it is neither like any of our sensations, nor like any thing we are conscious of'.[24] Unlike Hume, however, Reid sees no reason to be sceptical about the existence of a subject of the perceptions. We are conscious of ourselves only insofar as we think, feel, or act, but the existence of a thinking, feeling, and acting self does not have to be *inferred* from this consciousness. Rather, the consciousness of perceptions immediately suggests the existence of a subject of those perceptions: 'We are only conscious of the thoughts, yet when we reflect upon them there arises immediately and unavoidably a Notion of a thinking thing'.[25] To Reid, the existence of the self as a *res cogitans* is one of the fundamental principles of common sense. Reid maintains, then, that the consciousness of perceptions suggests the existence of a self to which the perceptions belong. Dugald Stewart argues that in the last analysis it is the consciousness of external objects which suggests to us the existence of a thinking and perceiving self:

> [O]ur own existence is not a direct or immediate object of consciousness.... We are conscious of sensation, thought, desire, volition; but we are not conscious of the existence of the mind itself; nor would it be possible for us to arrive at the knowledge of it ... if no impression were ever to be made on our external senses.[26]

4. The concept of apperception: Leibniz, Wolff, and empirical psychologists

Leibniz is generally recognised as having made a crucial and most influential contribution to the theory of consciousness. In particular, his famous distinction between *perception* and *apperception* is said, quite correctly, to have had an immense impact on subsequent philosophical and psychological thought about consciousness. He first introduced the term *l'apperception* in the *Nouveaux essais sur l'entendement humain* (1704). There is, however, no agreement among commentators as to how Leibniz's notion of apperception should be interpreted.

Some passages clearly suggest that Leibniz uses *l'apperception* synonymously with *la conscience*. For example, in a famous passage from section four of *Principes de la nature et de la grâce, fondés en raison* (1714), he defines 'perception' and 'apperception' as follows: '[I]t is well to distinguish between *perception*, which is the inner state of the monad representing external things, and *apperception*, which is *consciousness* [*conscience*], or the reflective knowledge of this inner state, and which is not given to all souls, nor at all times to the same soul'.[27] Here, *l'apperception* is explained in terms of *la conscience*; *la conscience* is understood as a 'knowledge' of inner states or perceptions; and this in turn is accounted for in terms of reflection or 'reflective knowledge'. This passage suggests, then, that 'apperception', 'reflection', and 'consciousness' all mean the same thing. In order to ascribe to Leibniz a distinction between consciousness/apperception on the one hand and reflection on the other, it is sometimes claimed that he intended the 'or' in 'consciousness or the reflective knowledge of this inner state' to be read in the exclusive sense, but there is no evidence to support this claim. Leibniz nowhere distinguishes explicitly between apperception and reflection; indeed there are passages which appear to preclude such a distinction. For example, in the Preface to the *Nouveaux essais*, he writes: '[A]t every moment there is in us an infinity of perceptions, unaccompanied by awareness [apperception] or reflection; *that is*, of alterations in the soul itself of which we are unaware' (my emphasis).[28] Further, it is often argued that, at an 'ontological level', Leibniz distinguishes between apperception in animal souls and apperception in rational souls, and only in the latter is apperception linked to reflection. But the precise nature of this link remains unclear. The texts indicate that Leibniz identifies apperception and reflection. Thus, although he points out the difference between unconscious perceptions and those perceptions which are apperceived, and although he employs numerous terms for relating to oneself (*l'apperception, la conscience,* and *la réflexion,* for example), he does not draw any clear distinctions among various types of relating to oneself.[29]

Christian Wolff takes over the notion of apperception from Leibniz and, like him, links it to consciousness (*Bewustseyn,* or *conscientia*). However, to Wolff, consciousness is broader than apperception: it can denote a relation to external objects as well as to one's own ideas or thoughts. Apperception, by contrast, always denotes a relation to our own perceptions, and Wolff holds that every thought involves both perception and apperception.[30] Like Leibniz, Wolff links (self-referential) consciousness to reflection (*Überdenken*) and attention.[31] He argues that to be conscious of an object is to *distinguish* it from other objects, and that, in distinguishing objects from one another, we become conscious of *ourselves* as distinct from the objects of which we are conscious: consciousness of objects necessarily involves *self*-consciousness since in being conscious of objects we are conscious of *our* mental act of distinguishing and thereby of our own self. Conversely, Wolff holds that without a consciousness of external things, we could not become conscious of ourselves; for without consciousness of objects, we could not distinguish ourselves from other things. It appears that the notion of self-consciousness invoked here is different from that of apperception: the latter is a consciousness of ideas or mental acts, whereas the former is likened to the consciousness of objects. We are conscious of our own self as a distinct entity or thing. Wolff suggests, then, that self-consciousness and consciousness of objects are mutually dependent on each other. He does not, however, explain this relation of mutual dependence in any detail. He concludes that reflection – understood not as Lockean inner sense but as the act of comparing a multiplicity of ideas – is required for consciousness to be possible. For to distinguish objects from one another, we have to compare them. Reflection is in turn linked to attention, for attention is the faculty of relating to particular thoughts in such a way that they become clearer than other thoughts. Lastly, Wolff points out that, in addition to reflection, memory is required for consciousness; in order to compare ideas, we must be able to remember them and know that we have had them before.

The Wolffian understanding of apperception was adopted and sometimes modified in many subsequent discussions of the topic. This is true even of the developing discipline of empirical psychology in the second half of the century. The writings of the influential Swiss psychologist Charles Bonnet, published in the middle of the century, were of paramount importance to the development of this discipline. Unlike Leibniz and Wolff, Bonnet locates most mental activities in the brain and not in the immaterial soul. Yet despite the physiology-based analysis, Bonnet's discussion of consciousness (which he equates with apperception) is similar to Wolff's account in explaining consciousness in terms of attention and reflection.[32] Johann Nicolas Tetens, too, in his *Philosophische Versuche* (1777), endorses a psychological approach to philosophical issues. Again, despite the emphasis on experience and terminological differences, the account of apperception and consciousness is very similar to Wolff's theory. Like Wolff, Tetens argues that attention and reflection are necessary to apperception.[33] To be conscious of an object is a mental state in which one feels an object or its representation as well as one's own *self*: consciousness is a feeling which combines the feeling of the object and the feeling of oneself.

There seem to be no explicit references to Leibniz's and Wolff's treatment of apperception in the writings of the materialist *philosophes* in France of the 1760s and 1770s. Yet even here, despite differences in questions concerning the ontological base of thought and consciousness, there are similarities to Wolffian ideas. D'Holbach, for example, in his *Système de la nature* (1770), explains consciousness as the capacity to *distinguish* impressions. He holds that consciousness of the existence of the self is dependent on consciousness of our ideas and on memory.[34] The idea that memory is a precondition of self-consciousness is also present in the earlier writings of Helvétius and Diderot.[35]

5. *Towards Kant: Self-Consciousness and the possibility of knowledge*

We have seen that for thinkers as diverse as Wolff and d'Holbach, consciousness of our own self depends on the consciousness of our perceptions or mental activity. Against this it was argued by some philosophers that consciousness of the self must be primary or 'original' for knowledge and thought in general to be possible. It was Kant who fully developed this notion as a central part of his transcendental epistemology. But there were philosophers prior to Kant who argued for the 'originality' of self-consciousness.

Wolff's critic Johann Bernhard Mérian, for example, insists that the consciousness of one's own existence is not derived from any kind of reflection but belongs to an 'original apperception' (*l'apperception primitive*) which is part of thought as such.[36] I always already know that it is I who think, see, remember, and so forth. The mental act of reflection *presupposes* a certain relation between the self and its thoughts – for if there were no such prior relation between the self and its thoughts, the self could not *turn* to its thoughts in the reflective mode. We apperceive our own existence immediately and intuitively: no thought could exist without the 'pre-existence of the *conscium sui*' (*Mémoire sur l'apperception*, 434).

Although Merian speaks of the 'pre-existence of the *conscium sui*', he says in some passages that the *conscium sui* is part of each particular thought: it is not clear whether he regards it as a separate mental act or as an element of all thoughts as such. Rousseau addresses precisely this question (without, however, referring to Merian or answering the question). His brief discussion of self-consciousness is in the 'Profession of Faith of the Savoyard Vicar' in Book IV of *Émile* (1762). The crucial passage is this:

I exist, and I have senses by which I am affected. This is the first truth that strikes me and to which I am forced to acquiesce. Do I have a particular sentiment of my existence, or do I sense it only through my sensations? This is my first doubt, which it is for the present impossible for me to resolve; for as I am continually affected by sensations, whether immediately or by memory, how can I know whether the sentiment of the *I* is something outside these same sensations and whether it can be independent of them?[37]

Rousseau clearly believes that the existence of the self is the first truth and immediately and absolutely certain. What is doubtful, in his view, is *how* I know the existence of the self. There are two possibilities: (a) there is a sentiment or feeling of the self which is separate from all my other feelings and sensations; (b) the feeling of my existence is an element inherent in each particular sensation. He says that it is difficult to decide whether (a) or (b) is true because we are in fact never without sensations, and we cannot tell whether or not 'the sentiment of the *I*' is something independent of them. He goes on to argue that the connection between our sensations is not perceived passively but is the result of the *activity* of the self. Only through our activity of combining or 'synthesising' (to use the Kantian term) is it possible for us 'to know that the body we touch and the object we see are the same'. It is the self or 'I' that brings about this synthesis and thereby constitutes knowledge of objects:

Let this or that name be given to this force of my mind which brings together and compares my sensations; let it be called *attention, meditation, reflection*, or whatever one wishes. It is still true that it is in me and not in things, that it is I alone who produce it, although I produce it only on the occasion of the impressions made on me by objects. (*Émile*, 271)

There is no detailed conceptual analysis of consciousness in the works of Johann Heinrich Lambert, but his remarks about consciousness in his *Neues Organon* (1764) are important because he argues that consciousness is a necessary condition of conceptual thought in general.[38] For Lambert, consciousness is a fundamental 'postulate' or principle: it is a postulate for thought in general because 'in thinking beings no clear sensation, representation, concept etc. would be possible' without it ('Alethiologie', I.ii.§70). Although this understanding of consciousness as an essential element of thought is not new (it is present in the works of Locke), Lambert's shift towards epistemological considerations is significant in the largely psychology-based context of the 1760s and 1770s in Germany.

As we shall see, Kant's notion of *transcendental* self-consciousness accompanies a new notion of self-identity. Even before Kant, though, the concept of consciousness was seen as crucial, not only to questions concerning the problem of knowledge in general but also to the special issue of personal identity.

II. THE NATURE OF THE MIND AND PERSONAL IDENTITY

The various answers to the question of what constitutes personal identity through time depend to a considerable extent on the views adopted about the nature of the human mind. Here, the battle between materialist and immaterialist philosophers of the mind is of central importance. Most immaterialist philosophers of the mind argue that personal identity consists in the identity of a mental substance and that the identity of a mental substance is a direct consequence of its immaterial nature; it is because of its immateriality that the mind is not subject to change and remains the same through time. There are two standard arguments in support of the immaterial nature of the mind or soul which are directly related to the question of personal identity. The first, from the unity of consciousness, argues that this is not compatible with the extension of matter and with a multiplicity of material particles. The second argument appeals directly to the issue of identity through time: identity of the self is necessary for just divine rewards or punishments in the afterlife. If the soul were not immaterial, this 'identity-condition' of immortality could not be satisfied (since matter constantly changes).[39]

The debates about personal identity are not, however, as clear-cut as the simple division between materialists and immaterialists might suggest. Thus, one might expect materialistically inclined philosophers to argue for the opposite view, that personal identity consists in the identity of the *material* substrate of thought. However, this is not the case. Rather, materialists and philosophers tending towards materialism typically place personal identity in consciousness or memory. The reason for this move seems to be that materialists basically accept the immaterialists' argument that identity through time cannot be ascribed to systems of matter because matter is subject to constant change. Since they reject the notion of an immaterial soul, they resort to consciousness or memory to account for personal identity.[40]

Further, although most immaterialist philosophers of the mind reject consciousness as a source of personal identity, there are a number of philosophers who accept the notion of an immaterial mental substance or soul and yet distinguish between the identity of the mental substance and *personal* identity, recognising, in various ways, the importance of consciousness or memory to the identity of the self as person; there are several ways of accounting for personal identity from within an immaterialist position. Lastly, some philosophers do not commit themselves to either the materialist or the immaterialist position, either, like most materialists, arguing for consciousness or memory as a source of personal identity, or, like some materialists, adopting a sceptical attitude towards the question of personal identity.[41]

1. Locke and reactions to him

Locke's account of personal identity, as put forward in the second edition of his *Essay* (1694), proved to be the most influential treatment of the topic during the eighteenth century. This is true not only of philosophers covered in this subsection who explicitly refer to Locke's treatment of the topic but also of most discussions of personal identity until at least the 1770s, even in cases where no reference at all is made to Locke. The influence of Locke's theory was not confined to philosophical disputes; summaries of Locke's theory appeared in some of the leading encyclopedias of the time, and Lockean ideas on identity had a considerable impact on eighteenth-century literature – for example, in Jonathan Swift and Laurence Sterne.

Two central features of this theory are particularly important in the eighteenth-century debates.[42] First, there is Locke's neutrality with respect to the nature of the thinking substance or mind; although he holds it to be the 'more probable Opinion' that thought is 'annexed' to an immaterial substance (*Essay*, II.xxvii.25), he explicitly states that he believes thinking *matter* to be possible (that is, to involve no contradiction).[43] Secondly, and closely related to the thinking matter suggestion, there is his account of personal identity in terms not of the identity of the thinking substance but of consciousness uniting thoughts and actions. These aspects of Locke's theory aroused much controversy as soon as it appeared in print late in the seventeenth century and were continually debated throughout the eighteenth century. Many philosophers mistook Locke's suggestion about thinking matter for an endorsement of materialism, and he was praised by materialists and attacked by immaterialists. As far as his own theory is concerned, our view about the nature of the thinking substance is irrelevant to the question of personal identity. The theory would in principle fit as easily into a materialist as into an immaterialist theory of the mind.

Locke's account of personal identity marks a decisive break with traditional accounts of the self. It differs from both the Cartesian and the scholastic positions, which identify either the soul or the man (or human being) with the person as a *res* whose individuality is constituted independently of, and prior to, consciousness. Locke, by contrast, distinguishes the unity of the person from both that of a soul, as substance, and that of life (man), for neither of these latter unities is coextensive with that of consciousness, and 'person' or 'personality' is the term for this unity of conscious thoughts and actions. Unlike both Cartesians and Scholastics, Locke holds that consciousness fulfils a constitutive function for personal identity: the unity and identity of the self as person exist only by virtue of its being constituted by consciousness. Further, it is in its relationship to the past that consciousness constitutes the identity of the person over time (*Essay*, II.xxvii.16): I am at present the same person as I was in the past not because I am the same living body, nor because the same substance thinks in me, but only because my present conscious experience is connected to my past conscious experiences: they belong to one conscious life and thus are part of one identical person.

Locke's theory aroused controversy very soon after its first publication in 1694, and it inspired critics and defenders throughout the eighteenth century. Some criticism related to its moral and legal implications, but most was based on metaphysical and theological arguments which assume that personal identity is the identity of an immaterial mental substance. One standard objection was the charge of circularity, urging that consciousness presupposes personal identity and therefore cannot constitute personal identity. This argument was first brought forward in the seventeenth century by John Sergeant; it was repeated many times in the eighteenth century, most famously by Bishop Joseph Butler.[44] However, it presupposes the very thing Locke challenged, namely that the person is an object, thing, or substance to which consciousness relates as to an already individuated being. In short, it ignores (or rejects) his crucial distinction between man and person.

Another standard immaterialist objection to Locke's theory was put forward by Samuel Clarke in 1708. Clarke argues (against Locke's follower Anthony Collins) that the consciousness of an action can be a consciousness that *I* performed the action only if the substance which performed the action is the same as the one which is now conscious of that action; genuine consciousness that *I* did an action requires the identity of my self as substance.[45] If the thinking substance is not the same, then my memory of an action is not the memory that *I* did the action but the memory of someone else's action and not genuine self-ascription.[46] Furthermore, the substance can only remain identical if it is immaterial and indivisible, for material beings constantly change. According to Clarke, then, we retain our personal identity through time because we are indivisible immaterial beings.[47] A genuine *problem* of personal identity does not arise for Clarke.

Within Berkeley's immaterialist metaphysics, too, a real problem of personal identity through time does not arise. According to Berkeley, the self is an immaterial spiritual substance.[48] His few explicit discussions of personal identity are brief and devoted to a critique of Locke's theory. The most original objection to Locke appears in Berkeley's *Alciphron* of 1732, wherein he argues that Locke's theory is inconsistent with the transitivity of the identity–relation. This point was taken up later in the century by Thomas Reid in his famous 'gallant-officer' story.[49] This concerns a general who remembers his actions as an officer but not what happened to him as a boy at school (where he was flogged 'for robbing an orchard'), although when an officer he had remembered this. Now, in Locke's theory, the officer is the same person as the boy and the general is the same person as the officer, but the general is not the same person as the boy because there is no link of consciousness here. However, Reid argues, it belongs to the logic of identity that, if the boy and the officer, and the officer and the general, are the same person, respectively, then the general and the boy are the same person, too. For Reid and Berkeley, Locke's theory, which bases personal identity on consciousness, must be rejected because identity is transitive, whereas consciousness is not transitive.

Throughout the eighteenth century, the critical voices were in the majority. But Locke had a considerable number of defenders; among the philosophically important ones were Anthony Collins (1708) and Edmund Law (1769). Collins appears to accept the standard anti-materialist argument that, if the self were a material substance, it would not have, qua substance, unity and identity through time. Yet he argues (against Clarke) that substantial unity and identity are not what matters for the identity of the self as person. Since personal identity is determined through consciousness, it can be retained through a change of that substance which is the bearer of consciousness: identity of person is consistent with change of substance.[50] Edmund Law focuses on the moral and legal aspects of Locke's theory, emphasising the importance of Locke's man–person distinction. He argues that 'person' refers to a Lockean 'mode': it denotes 'some such quality or modification in man as denominates him a moral agent, or an *accountable* creature', and, when we apply the term to an individual being, 'we do not treat of him absolutely, and in gross; but under a particular relation or precision'.[51] On this basis, Law explicitly defends Locke's theory against the charge of circularity.

In France, Condillac did not set out to defend Locke, but his account of personal identity is in similar terms. This is also true of Rousseau's brief remarks on the topic later in the century. Like Locke, Condillac distinguishes between the memory-based personal self and the mind or soul, whose essence is unknown. Using the image of a statue which progressively comes to life, he explicitly links memory to personality: 'If it [the statue] is able to say "I" ("*moi*") it can say it in all the states of its duration; and at each time its "I" will embrace all the moments of which it might have preserved recollection'.[52] However, behind this experiential or personal self is the mind or soul, whose essence remains unknown.[53]

2. *Leibniz and Wolff*

Locke's most important contemporary critic, Gottfried Wilhelm Leibniz, had worked out his own theory of self-identity independently of Locke and well before he wrote the *Nouveaux essais* (1704) criticising him. Although Leibniz emphasises in many places that, on his view, the self is never without a body,[54] it is clear that he regards the immaterial soul as the real self (II.xxvii.14, 239). The identity of the soul or self over time is secured a priori by its intrinsic nature or 'complete notion'; Leibniz maintains that everything that is to happen to the self 'is already included virtually in his nature or notion, just as the properties of a circle are included in its definition'.[55] Thus, 'there is in the soul of Alexander for all time traces of everything that happened to him, and marks of everything that will happen to him'.[56] Consciousness or 'my subjective experience' merely *convinces* me '*a posteriori* of this identity'.[57] Leibniz points out, against Locke, that consciousness of past states of the mind merely makes 'the real identity appear' (II.xx.14, 239).

But Leibniz does in a way ascribe to consciousness a constitutive function, for he says that consciousness constitutes the identity of the self as *person* or *moral entity*.[58] He distinguishes between the *metaphysical* identity of the self (as immaterial substance) and the *moral* identity of the self (as person), which is constituted by consciousness, 'for it is the memory and knowledge of this *me* that makes it liable to punishment and reward'.[59] However, he rejects Locke's idea that moral or personal identity is based *solely* on inner consciousness: the identity of the self as person can also be established by the testimony of others (II.xxvii.9, 237). The most fundamental difference between Leibniz and Locke is that for Locke personal identity without substantial identity, or in Leibniz's terminology, 'that this apparent identity could be preserved in the absence of any real identity', is a real possibility (II.xxvii.9, 236). To Leibniz, however, this 'would be a miracle' (II.xxvii.23, 245). According to the 'order of things', he argues, real identity must be presupposed by apparent identity (II.xxvii.18, 242). Thus, although he does not equate personal identity with substantial identity, he holds that the former depends on the latter. Whereas Locke argues for keeping personal and substantial identity separate, Leibniz maintains what was assumed by Cartesians, namely that the (personal) identity required for morality can be preserved only by the metaphysical identity of the self as immaterial soul.[60]

Leibnizian theory dominated philosophy at German universities until about the middle of the century through Christian Wolff, who had adopted a largely

Leibnizian account of the self. Wolff defines the human soul as a simple substance which is characterised by one unitary power, namely the power to represent the universe.[61] However, he also accounts for the soul in terms of consciousness, describing the soul as a thing or substance which is conscious of itself and of other things.[62] He argues that we are persons or moral beings through the consciousness or memory *of our identity through time*.[63] It is important to note that, despite its emphasis on consciousness and memory, Wolff's account is Leibnizian rather than Lockean. Locke's view is that consciousness of thoughts and actions constitutes personality and personal identity, but Wolff holds that the consciousness of identity makes us persons. Wolff, but not Locke, believes the identity of the soul, as mental substance, must be presupposed for there to be personal identity.

3. Hume and Scottish Common Sense

Like Locke's and Kant's discussions of identity, Hume's treatment of personal identity is still much discussed in current debates on the issue.[64] Hume rejects the traditional Cartesian view that we retain our personal identity through time because we are immaterial souls which are not subject to change. Hume also comments on what we *can* know about the self, person, or mind on the basis of inner experience or introspection, namely that inner experience reveals that the self or person is not identical through time. With inner experience or introspection, I can identify only a variety of distinct perceptions, thoughts, and feelings; there is no experiential evidence of a soul that remains the same through time (*Treatise*, 1.4.6.1–4, SBN 252). Thus, Hume maintains, all we can say on this basis is that the mind is 'nothing but a bundle or collection of different perceptions, which succeed each other with an inconceivable rapidity, and are in a perpetual flux and movement'.[65] He concludes that 'they are the successive perceptions only, that constitute the mind'; and that 'there is properly no *identity* [of the mind] . . . [at] different [times]'. He recognises, however, that we nevertheless do ascribe unity and identity to the self; indeed he claims that we have a 'natural propension' (1.4.6.4, SBN 253) to believe in personal identity. He proceeds to give a psychological account of how we come to have this belief in an identical self.

Hume argues that the idea of a unitary and identical mind is due to the imagination connecting successive ideas in such a way as to create the belief that there is an identical self to which all these ideas belong (1.4.6.16, SBN 260). He emphasises the importance of causality as a connecting principle here (1.4.6.19, SBN 261): it is the causal connection of our perceptions in particular which leads the imagination to construct the belief in a unitary and identical self. The notion of causality is, in turn, linked to memory. According to Hume, memory is a source of personal identity, first, because it alone acquaints us with the succession of our perceptions, and second, because without memory we would have no notion of causation, 'nor consequently of that chain of causes and effects, which constitute our self or person'. Having acquired the notion of causation through memory, we extend the chain of ideas, and that is the identity of our persons, 'beyond our memory' (1.4.6.20, SBN 262). Moreover, the causal connections among the perceptions lead the imagination to 'feign' an identical self to which those causally related perceptions belong. Thus Hume says, 'the identity, which we ascribe to the mind of man, is only a fictitious one' (1.4.6.15, SBN 259).

Further, Hume argues that 'we must distinguish betwixt personal identity, as it regards our thought or imagination, and as it regards our passions or the concern we take in ourselves' (1.4.6.5, SBN 253). He believes that the identity with regard to the passions strengthens the imagination in constructing the idea of an identical self because the former makes the causal relations between our perceptions apparent (1.4.6.19, SBN 261). In other words, the causal connections between our passions provide support for our belief in the causal connections between our perceptions in general, and they thereby 'corroborate' the fictitious identity of the imagination. The section on personal identity in Book I of Hume's *Treatise* deals only with personal identity as it regards the imagination. One would perhaps expect Hume to address personal identity 'as it regards our passions or the concern we take in ourselves' in Book II of the *Treatise*. But although the issue is of importance in Book II, as we shall see, there is no separate account of personal identity, or discussion of the issue there.

In the Appendix to the *Treatise*, published a year after the first two books had appeared, Hume reflects on his discussion of personal identity in Book I (App. 10–22, SBN 633–6). Here he says that that account is 'very defective' and, worse still, that he does not 'know how to correct' his 'former opinions'; he even concedes that 'this difficulty is too hard for my understanding'. He never again explicitly discusses the personal identity problem in any published writings. However, it is important to note that Hume does not reject everything he says about personal identity in Book I. Hume says the problem relates to his explanation of 'the principle of connexion', which binds the perceptions together 'and makes us attribute' identity to the mind. We saw that, according to Book I, this principle of connexion is causality. In the Appendix, Hume maintains that pointing to causal connexions among perceptions does not explain why we come up with the belief in an identical self. Perceptions for Hume are 'distinct existences', and such existences can of course be causally related to one another; but it is not clear why their causal connectedness should bring about the idea of a unitary and identical self to which they all belong. Perceptions that are part of the idea of my own self may be causally related to perceptions I do not attribute to myself at all. Nonetheless, other aspects of Hume's discussion are not targeted in the Appendix. Hume still holds all of the following: (1) the belief in an identical thinking substance cannot be justified; (2) inner experience and observation reveal only collections or 'bundles' of perceptions; (3) we neverthe-less have a 'natural propension' to ascribe identity to the self; (4) this commonly involves the fiction of a perfectly identical mind; and (5) we need in any case to distinguish between personal identity as it regards the imagination and personal identity 'as it regards our passions or the concern we take in ourselves'.

Most of Hume's early critics, such as the Scottish Common Sense philoso-phers, seem to realise that the 'bundle of perceptions' view of the mind or self is not affected by the argument in the Appendix, for that is the main target of their criticism. The Scottish Common Sense philosophers, such as Beattie, Reid, and Lord Kames, all deal with the personal identity problem. Roughly speaking, in their view there are certain fundamental principles which have to be taken for granted and accepted as true. These require no argument or proof; they are im-mediately and intuitively known and consented to by all humankind. They are part of human 'common sense'. Self-identity is said to be one of these common sense principles. It is not surprising, then, that the Common Sense philosophers reject both Locke's and Hume's theories of personal identity: James Beattie re-peats the charge of circularity against Locke and rejects Hume's 'bundle' theory of the self. According to Beattie, it is obvious that the thinking being in us remains identical through time: 'That the thinking principle, which we believe to be within us, continues the same through life, is equally self-evident, and equally agreeable to the universal consent of mankind'.[66] Thomas Reid, too, holds that one is immediately and 'irresistibly' convinced of one's own iden-tity. The identity of the thinking being is a principle which we have to accept without proof: 'I take it for granted, that all the thoughts I am conscious of, or remember, are the thoughts of one and the same thinking principle, which I call *myself* or my *mind*' (*Intellectual Powers*, I.2, §4, 42).

However, Beattie's critique of Hume at least is problematic. For Beattie seems to think that Hume makes an ontological claim. He holds that Hume reduces the self to perceptions and that he denies the existence of an essential self underlying the perceptions. Yet Hume does not deny the existence of an essential self. He says that the self, insofar as it is accessible through inner experience, consists of nothing but perceptions and that therefore any knowledge claims about the nature of the mind and its identity that go beyond the 'bundle of perceptions' view cannot be justified. This is not to deny an essential self. Hume adopts a sceptical position as far as an essential self is concerned: we cannot know anything about it (*Treatise*, Intro. 1, SBN xiii). But this sceptical attitude is not a denial of an essential self – in fact it would be inconsistent with such a denial.[67]

More important than Beattie in this context is Henry Home, Lord Kames. Kames was a friend and correspondent of Hume's. He deals with personal identity in a short section of his *Essays on the Principles of Morality and Natural Religion*, which first appeared in print in 1751.[68] There he refers to Hume, but like Beattie and others, he argues that there is 'a feeling of identity, which accompanies me through all my changes' (233–4). This would seem to contradict Hume's account. However, in 1746 Hume commented on what is probably an early manuscript version of Kames's treatment of personal identity. He wrote to Kames: 'I likt exceedingly your Method of explaining personal Identity as more satisfactory than any thing that had ever occur'd to me'.[69] Assuming that Hume is not merely being polite, this passage raises the question of what it is that Hume finds so attractive in Kames's discussion of identity. In the *Essays* Kames rejects both Locke's account and Hume's 'bundle' theory. To Kames, it is an undoubted truth that we have 'an original feeling, or consciousness' of our own selves (231). Moreover, he argues that 'it is by means of this perception [of self] that I consider myself to be the same person, in all varieties of fortune, and every change of circumstance' (233). This, he says, is a 'natural feeling'. Importantly, Kames's discussion is very much in terms of the practical aspects of selfhood, relating to the notion of self-concern in particular: He states that 'self-preservation is every one's duty; and the vivacity of this perception [i.e., of self] is necessary to make us attentive to our own interest, and particularly, to shun every appearance of danger' (232). Kames clearly appeals to a common sense evidence for personal identity, but he does so by emphasising that it is the very nature of concern that involves a feeling of our own self and its identity.

Hume agrees. Like Kames, he holds that the belief in personal identity is not to be derived from 'any argument or chain of reasoning' (Kames, *Essays*, 234). And in Book II of the *Treatise*, which deals with the 'passions or the concern we take in ourselves' Hume is clear that an immediate consciousness of our own self is involved in 'passions' such as pride and humility, for example. He appeals to this consciousness of self many times in Book II. Thus he speaks of the 'self or that identical person of whose thoughts, actions, and sensations we are intimately conscious' (2.2.1.2, SBN 329). According to Hume, we can account for passions such as pride only if we acknowledge that the consciousness of our own selves 'is always intimately present with us' (2.1.11.4, SBN 317). Like Kames, Hume emphasises that the nature of concern involves a consciousness of our own 'identical person' and that this consciousness is common to all humankind. Thus, although it had not 'occurred' to Hume explicitly to work out a position such as Kames's, much of what Kames says about personal identity is in fact compatible with Hume's account in the *Treatise*.

However, there are also important differences between Hume's position and the Common Sense view about personal identity. Kames, for example, says that 'natural feelings' (such as the feeling of identity) must be 'admitted as evidence of truth' (*Essays*, 234). That is to say, he assumes that natural beliefs are not only consented to by all humankind but also represent metaphysical truths, in this case that of personal identity. This view gains more prominence in the works of later Common Sense thinkers. Beattie, for example, points out both that personal identity is a 'dictate of common sense' and that it is an 'intuitive truth' (*Truth*, 88). On this view, the fact that common sense 'dictates' the belief in personal identity makes this belief a true one. Hume does not accept this. Although he does not deny the existence of an essential self, neither does he affirm it. There is a 'natural propension' to believe in personal identity, and this belief plays an important role in our everyday lives. But for Hume it does not follow that the belief is true. We do not know whether it is true or not. All we can do is try and explain how this belief arises and analyse its role in relation to the 'concern we take in ourselves'. Another important difference between Hume and the Common Sense thinkers is that the latter believe that the feelings of identity and so on are 'instinctive', whereas for Hume they develop through experience and are due to the imagination; in principle we can explain how the imagination arrives at these beliefs.[70]

4. Debates about materialist theories of the mind and personal identity

There were several debates about materialism in the late seventeenth and early eighteenth centuries. In many of these disputes, the problem of personal identity was not addressed at all. The issue was raised, as we saw, in the controversy between Anthony Collins and Samuel Clarke. But Collins did not explicitly commit himself to materialism, adopting the Lockean position that personal identity consists in consciousness, no matter what the nature of the mind may be. The materialist cause was strengthened in the middle of the century through the work of Charles Bonnet. Bonnet himself was not a materialist; he argued explicitly for the existence of an immaterial soul. What proved influential, however, was not his endorsement of the notion of an immaterial soul but his mechanist, physiological account of mental phenomena. This account, with its emphasis on the activity of 'fibres in the brain', certainly tends towards materialism. Bonnet's account of our mental life influenced many thinkers who were critical of the traditional philosophy of the mind. Later in the century, d'Holbach presented a complete materialist doctrine in his *Système de la nature*. Yet the French materialist *philosophes* did not concern themselves very much with the special problem of personal identity through time. Neither La Mettrie nor d'Holbach, for example, discussed the issue in any detail. In the writings of Diderot, there are only a few remarks on personal identity, which suggest that we remain the same person because memory connects our past and present sensations.[71]

However, Bonnet deals with the isssue at more length. In his *Essai analytique*, he draws a distinction between two kinds of personality: the first results from the connection which memory establishes between past and present mental states; the second consists in the *reflection* on the first kind of personality.[72] Furthermore, he distinguishes between personality as a composite entity which has appropriated to itself various sensations through memory and personality as considered from the standpoint of an omniscient being or god. With respect to the former, memory is essential to identity through time, and 'the total loss of *memory* would therefore bring about the destruction of *personality*'. On the other hand, from the point of view of an omniscient being or god, memory is not what matters; I may lose the feeling (*sentiment*) of my personality and yet remain the same person for the omniscient spirit who considers and judges me. Moreover, we do not have to have knowledge of what goes on in other people's minds in order to establish their identity: we can identify them by referring to their physical and moral characteristics.

As materialism became an increasingly powerful force, its connection with a physiology-based psychology led to renewed discussions of personal identity, which did not, however, produce any entirely new answers to the philosophical question of what constitutes personal identity. There was the Lockean answer in terms of consciousness or memory, and there was the sceptical position, reminiscent of Hume. Joseph Priestley, for example, criticises the standard immaterialist argument from the unity of consciousness: I have 'a feeling or perception of the *unity of my nature or being*; but all that can be inferred from this is, that I am only *one person, one sentient and thinking being*, and not two persons, or two sentient or thinking beings'.[73] One cannot infer from the feeling of unity that this sentient being cannot be divided or that it cannot be a material being. Priestley also argues that materialists are not committed to the absurd view, often ascribed to them, that the individual particles of which the brain consists are separately conscious, so that one would have to postulate as many distinct consciousnesses as material particles, for 'if the perception that we call *consciousness*, or that of any other *complex idea*, necessarily consists in, or depends upon, a very *complex vibration*, it cannot possibly belong to a single *atom*, but must belong to a *vibrating system*, of some extent' (87). Yet his account of personal identity through time is not in terms of the nervous system or brain. At one stage, he postulates what he, like others before him, calls 'stamina', meaning certain essential particles that belong to 'the *germ* of the organical body' (161). He claims that these essential particles are never destroyed or interchanged and guarantee the identity of the person. It is unclear, however, how serious Priestley is about this, for when challenged to provide some evidence for the existence of these particles, he does not attempt to defend this account, suggesting that for those who are not convinced by this hypothesis there is always the Lockean theory, which explains personal identity perfectly well. And so, like Locke, Priestley distinguishes between the identity of the person and the identity of the man. The self as man or material substance constantly changes, but it retains its identity as person through the continuity of consciousness. Consciousness-based personal identity is all that matters in regard to the self as moral being (157–9).

Other materialist thinkers of the time did not accept the Lockean answer. Michael Hissmann, for example, one of the most radical materialists in Germany, denied that there is such a thing as personal identity at all; a feeling of personal identity is simply 'physically impossible' because our soul is subject to constant change. In reality, there is no personal identity through time. Our common sense beliefs are, in this regard, simply false.[74] Similarly, Priestley's follower Thomas Cooper argues that 'strictly and philosophically speaking' there is no identity over time. At best, we have an 'approximation to identity', namely a 'high degree of similarity'. Not unlike Hume, Cooper argues that we are led to ascribe identity to the self because the changes perceived in our body or self are so gradual that the perceptions are thought to belong to the same self or body – the bearer of those perceptions.[75]

Priestley's critics, such as Richard Price and John Whitehead, appeal to the standard anti-materialist arguments already discussed.[76] In Germany, Tetens, too, rejects materialism. However, he differs from thinkers such as Price and Whitehead in arguing that the essence of the mind is not known to us. Nevertheless, he believes that we can at least know that both the brain and the immaterial soul belong to the whole self, which feels, thinks, and wills (Tetens, *Versuche*, II.169ff.). Our very *Selbstgefühl* (feeling of self), Tetens maintains, indicates that the self is more than a play of fibres in the brain, namely that it is a unitary entity, not a 'heap of several things' (II.178, 183). The self which sees is the same as that which tastes, thinks, wills, and so forth; there is one unitary entity involved in all mental operations. Tetens emphasises that the very act of forming judgements presupposes the unity of the self. In order to form even the most basic judgement, we need to synthesise or combine subject, predicate, and the relation between the two. This synthesis would not be possible if there were no unitary self to which these various thoughts belong (II.195). This idea, that a unitary and identical self is presupposed by our very activity of forming judgements or propositions, is further developed by Kant.

III. TRANSCENDENTAL SELF-CONSCIOUSNESS
AND SELF-IDENTITY: KANT AND THE BEGINNINGS
OF GERMAN IDEALISM

The notions of self-consciousness or apperception and self-identity play a cru-cial and systematic role in Kant's critical philosophy. They are introduced in the Transcendental Deduction of the Categories, the heart of his *Kritik der reinen Vernunft*, and are also central to his critique of rational psychology in the first part of the Transcendental Dialectic.[77] Kant was familiar with most of the con-ceptions of consciousness and identity we have discussed (in particular, those of Locke, Hume, Tetens, the Wolffian School, and the materialists).[78] His own approach is different in kind from previous examinations of those issues because he is not concerned with empirical self-consciousness and empirical personal identity. He comments on these empirical questions in some places but does so in the light of his important distinction between empirical and what he calls 'pure' or 'transcendental' self-consciousness or apperception.

Of empirical apperception, Kant says that it 'accompanies different represen-tations' and 'is by itself dispersed and without relation to the identity of the subject' (B 133). Empirical consciousness is the explicit awareness of a particular mental state; therefore, it cannot be precisely the same at different points of time.

Consciousness of oneself in accordance with the determinations of our state in internal perception is merely empirical, forever variable; it can provide no standing or abiding self in this stream of inner appearances, and is customarily called *inner sense*, or *empirical apperception*.[79]

Kant suggests that the notion of *pure* apperception can be expressed in the judgement or proposition 'I think'. He writes:

The *I think* must *be able* to accompany all my representations; for otherwise something would be represented in me that could not be thought at all, which is as much as to say that the representation would either be impossible, or else at least would be nothing for me. (B 131–2)

This 'I think' does not state anything about the content of my thought, but only that I am conscious of it (B 400). The 'I' in the proposition 'I think' is 'purely intellectual' because it belongs to 'thinking in general' (B 423). Unlike empirical apperception, pure apperception is empty of content and *is* in itself related 'to the identity of the subject'; the 'I think' is the same with regard to all particular thoughts (B 133). This is what Kant refers to as the identity or '*analytical unity of apperception*' (B 133). He argues that the 'identity of apperception' is 'original' because it 'precedes *a priori* all *my* determinate thinking' (B 134).

Kant distinguishes between the 'analytical unity of apperception' and 'some synthetic [unity]': pure self-consciousness or apperception is an 'original-synthetic unity of apperception' (B 131ff.). The notion of 'original-synthetic unity of apperception' refers to the possibility of combining (or 'synthesising') representations in one self-consciousness. Kant argues that the (analytical) unity of apperception is possible only by virtue of a synthesis or combination of representations: a multiplicity of representations can belong to the same *I* only if they are *combined* in one consciousness. 'I.e., the *analytical* unity of apperception is only possible under the presupposition of some *synthetic* one' (B 133). It is for this reason, then, that Kant believes that the 'necessary synthesis of representations' is the most fundamental a priori condition of knowledge, including the a priori 'employment of the understanding' (B 134–5). He attaches the label *transcendental* to the original-synthetic unity of consciousness precisely 'in order to designate the possibility of *a priori* cognition from it'.[80]

Kant's account of the nature and function of the transcendental self has consequences for his treatment of traditional rationalist metaphysics of the self or soul, known as 'rational psychology'. According to Kant, the project of rational psychology can be based only on the 'I think' of pure apperception; its aim is 'to know [no]thing about the soul beyond what, independently of all experience . . . can be inferred from this concept *I* insofar as it occurs in all thinking'.[81] Rational psychology aims to show by way of a priori reasoning that the soul is a simple substance, numerically identical at different points of time, and is 'in relation to *possible* objects in space' (A 344/B 402). Kant, however, holds that rational psychology fails to show this. For example, he argues that the substantiality of the soul cannot be inferred from the consciousness that I am the subject of all my thoughts (B 402ff.), for knowledge of objects, including knowledge of the self as object, requires *intuition* (B 406, 408). It follows that 'I cognize myself not by being conscious of myself as thinking, but only if I am conscious to myself of the intuition of myself as determined in regard to the function of thought' (B 406). In other words, theoretical self-knowledge is possible only in terms of *empirical* knowledge. The *transcendental* self of pure apperception is not 'determinable' as an object precisely because it is an a priori *condition* of any determination of objects: it is 'determining', but not 'determinable': '[The object] is not the consciousness of the *determining* self, but only that of the *determinable* self, i.e., of my inner intuition' (B 407).

Thus Kant believes he has undermined the very project of rational psychology: having shown that the 'I think' is its sole basis, he argues that rational psychology draws inferences from this basis which cannot be justified. And yet, although there can be no theoretical-speculative proof of the existence of the self as a simple unitary substance, he holds that there is more to be said about the self than what is involved in the empirical and transcendental aspects of it. Appealing to his general distinction between objects of experience (appearances or phenomena) and objects considered independently of the conditions of experience (things-in-themselves, or noumena), he distinguishes three aspects of the self: the self as empirical or 'psychological' self (or the self as 'phenomenon'), the transcendental self of pure apperception, and the self as 'thing-in-itself' (or noumenon) about whose nature we can have no theoretical knowledge whatsoever (B 157). Kant suggests that the fact that there is knowledge of my self as phenomenon or appearance means that I may be *considered* not only as phenomenon, but as noumenon. As noumenon, I am not an object of empirical knowledge. But certain things can be said about the self as noumenon simply on the basis of an *analysis* of the concept of self as noumenon. I know that, as noumenon, I do not exist under the conditions of space and time and that, consequently, as noumenon I cannot be affected by spatio-temporal determinations and in this sense am 'free' (B 567, 569). Within the framework of *theoretical* reason, I know of myself as noumenon only in a 'problematic' mode, meaning that I can make no synthetic judgements about the nature of my noumenal self, including the question of the reality of my freedom (B 310). However, in his moral philosophy, Kant attempts to show that the idea of *moral-practical freedom* has objective reality. Here, he distinguishes between moral and empirical personality; I do not acquire a moral personality through empirical self-consciousness but only by being *homo noumenon* – that is, a free being. I am a moral being by virtue of my noumenal self.[82]

The foundational function of consciousness was examined and developed further in the debates about Kant which took place in the late 1780s and 1790s. Karl Leonhard Reinhold is one of the most important thinkers of this period and an important link between Kant and German Idealism. I refer to his *Versuch einer neuen Theorie des menschlichen Vorstellungsvermögens* (Essay towards a New Theory of the Faculty of Representation) of 1789 and the piece *Über das Fundament des philosophischen Wissens* (On the Foundation of Philosophical Knowledge) of 1791.[83] In his account of the nature of representation, Reinhold argues that what he calls the 'principle of consciousness' (*Satz des Bewußtseins*) provides the foundation not only of knowledge in general but also of philosophy itself. He holds that this principle properly grounds Kantian transcendental philosophy.[84] Not surprisingly, Reinhold's *Versuch* is full of Kantian ideas and Kantian lines of thought. However, Frederick Beiser's comment that Reinhold's principle of consciousness is 'an attempt to develop or explicate Kant's principle of the unity of apperception' is not precise enough,[85] for Reinhold's foundational principle concerns 'consciousness in general' (*Bewußtsein überhaupt*), not self-consciousness. Self-consciousness is just one particular type of consciousness, and Reinhold does not deal with it until the third part of his *Versuch*.

He formulates the principle thus: '*[I]n consciousness representation is distinguished through the subject from both object and subject and is referred to both*'.[86] Reinhold insists that this principle is not a definition of representation and that it is not derived from any part of philosophy (if it were it could not fulfil its foundational role). Rather, the principle is 'drawn from the CONSCIOUSNESS of an *actual fact* [*Tatsache*]'(70). It expresses a pre-philosophical, pre-reflective fact of consciousness. There are many problems with Reinhold's account, for example with his claims that the principle is self-evident and that philosophy can be founded on this principle. These issues cannot be dealt with here. However, the principle plainly relates directly to the theme of this chapter. It states that a representation necessarily involves a subject (which has the representation) and an object, as well as the activity of distinguishing and that of referring (or relating) the representation to both subject and object.

Now, *self*-consciousness, Reinhold says, is the consciousness of the subject as that which is engaged in the activity of representing. This means that in self-consciousness the subject and the object of consciousness are identical (*Versuch*, 326, 335). It has been argued that this account of self-consciousness is inconsistent with Reinhold's principle of consciousness: whereas the former postulates the identity of the subject and the object of consciousness, the principle emphasises the distinctness of subject and object in *all* consciousness.[87] This type of critique usually continues with the demand for a non-representational account of self-consciousness and with an appeal to Fichte's understanding of the issue.

This critique, however, leads us back to the principle of consciousness itself. For the principle does postulate a self-relation that is both more fundamental than self-consciousness and not itself representational. The relating to the subject that is invoked by the principle of consciousness is something which, as Reinhold says, 'precedes' all particular representations and is present in all representations even though it is not itself represented (339). But to focus on the relating to the subject is to neglect a most important aspect of Reinhold's principle, for it says that representation in general involves an immediate relating not only to the self or subject but also to the object. The two relations are equally 'original' or fundamental, according to Reinhold. It is impossible, on this view, to ascribe priority to one relation over the other. In thinking (or representing) I am always already related to my own self as the subject of thought, but I am also always already related to an object. It is this double relation to subject and object that makes thought or representation possible.

Fichte developed his own transcendental philosophy independently but with explicit reference to Kant's published critical writings and to the debate surrounding his critical philosophy. In Fichte's system, (non-empirical) self-consciousness is the highest principle of all philosophy. He argues (against Reinhold) that representation or representational consciousness cannot be the highest principle of philosophy. For Fichte, representation or consciousness of objects involves or presupposes self-consciousness. 'Insofar as you are conscious of some object – for example, the wall in front of you – you are . . . conscious of your thinking of this wall, and a consciousness of the wall is possible only inso-far as you are conscious of your thinking. But in order to be conscious of your thinking, you must be conscious of yourself'.[88] Fichte argues (against Reinhold again) that self-consciousness itself does not have a representational structure, for if self-consciousness were a consciousness of the self as object, then, like the consciousness of the wall, it would presuppose consciousness of thinking and of oneself and so on, ad infinitum. This old problem of an infinite regress leads Fichte to search for an account of self-consciousness that is not in terms of the notion of representation.[89] It should be noted, however, that Fichte, in his critique of Reinhold, appears to ignore the non-representational relating to the self that is invoked by Reinhold's principle of consciousness.

Fichte accounts for the non-representational relation to the self in terms of the concept of *intellectual intuition* or *self-positing* of the subject. Intellectual intuition is an immediate relation to the self: it is 'that whereby it [that is, the presentation] is related to the subject, and becomes *my* presentation'.[90] All consciousness of objects is accompanied by a self-positing or intellectual intuition or immediate consciousness of the activity of consciousness or thought. Fichte links this intellectual intuition to Kant's pure apperception (*Zweite Einleitung*, §6, 471–9/44–52). Fichte's intellectual intuition, however, involves more than does Kant's pure and 'empty' apperception; it involves the positing of myself (in a non-representational mode) as activity. 'It is the immediate consciousness that I act, and what I enact: it is that whereby I know something because I do it' (§5, 463/38). The 'I' which is posited in intellectual intuition is neither the empirical self nor the self understood in terms of Kant's thing-in-itself; it is not a thing or substance at all. Fichte refers to it as the pure or *absolute* self.[91] The absolute self is the *I* as pure activity or *Tathandlung* (or self-positing or intellectual intuition).[92] In any particular thought, I implicitly posit myself as activity. Intellectual intuition is an intuition of 'sheer activity'.[93] As was indicated earlier by the 'consciousness of the wall' example, the positing of the absolute self is involved in whatever we do or think. This means that it fulfils a *transcendental* role: for it is 'a necessary factor whereby . . . [consciousness] first becomes possible'.[94] This positing of the self or *Tathandlung* is expressed in Fichte's *Grundlage der gesammten Wissenschaftslehre* (1794) as the principle 'I am I'. Things other than the self can be posited only under the presupposition of the absolute self. Self-consciousness is absolute because the question 'What was I, then, before I came to self-consciousness?' is an 'improper' question: we cannot assume a self without self-consciousness. 'The self exists only insofar as it is conscious of itself.' For 'you cannot think at all without subjoining in thought your self, as conscious of itself; from your self-consciousness you can never abstract'.[95]

At first, Schelling and Hegel adopted a positive attitude towards Fichte's idealism. But they soon distanced themselves from Fichte's philosophy and its emphasis on oppositions such as that between self and non-self. They pursued, in quite different ways, the project of overcoming Kantian and Fichtean 'dualisms' in philosophy. In their 'absolute idealism', the issues of relating to oneself and of personal identity through time are no longer a major concern. However, both Kantian and psychological examinations of consciousness and identity continued to appear simultaneously with the speculations of the idealists. Sometimes the psychological investigations were inspired or influenced by Kantian ideas (Schmid), whereas at other times they were opposed both to Kant and to absolute idealism (Schulze).

NOTES

1 Anonymous, *Two Dissertations concerning Sense, and the Imagination. With an Essay on Consciousness* (London, 1728). A recent edition of the *Essay, Pseudo-Mayne: Über das Bewusstsein 1728*, trans. and ed. R. Brandt (Hamburg, 1983), contains an important introduction and notes by the editor.

2 Joseph Priestley, *A Free Discussion of the Doctrines of Materialism and Philosophical Necessity . . . to which are added . . . Introduction . . . and Letters . . . on his Disquisitions Relating to Matter and Spirit* (London, 1778), 280.

3 The literature on self-consciousness in Kant and Fichte is vast, but there is comparatively little on earlier conceptions of (self-)consciousness. See, however, K. J. Grau, in *Die Entwicklung des Bewusstseinsbegriffs im XVII. und XVIII. Jahrhundert* (Halle, 1916); C. S. Lewis, *Studies in Words* (Cambridge, 1960), 181–213; Ben Lazare Mijuskovic, *The Achilles of Rationalist Arguments: The Simplicity, Unity and Identity of Thought and Soul from the Cambridge Platonists to Kant. A Study in the History of an Argument* (The Hague, 1974); Christopher Fox, *Locke and the Scriblerians: Identity and Consciousness in Early Eighteenth-Century Britain* (Berkeley, CA, 1988); Catherine Glyn Davies, 'Conscience' as Consciousness: The Idea of Self-Awareness in French Philosophical Writing from Descartes to Diderot* (Oxford, 1990); Ruth Lindemann, *Der Begriff der Conscience im französischen Denken* (Jena, 1938); Geneviève (Rodis-)Lewis, *Le Problème de l'inconscient et le Cartésianisme* (Paris, 1950); Udo Thiel, 'Hume's Notions of Consciousness and Reflection in Context', *British Journal for the History of Philosophy*, 2 (1994): 75–115.

4 Ralph Cudworth, *The True Intellectual System of the Universe* (London, 1678), Bk. I, ch. 3, §16, 159. See Thiel, 'Cudworth and Seventeenth-Century Theories of Consciousness', in *The Uses of Antiquity*, ed. S. Gaukroger (Dordrecht, 1991), 79–99.

5 Nicolas Malebranche, *De la recherche de la vérité* (1674), III.i.1 and III.ii.7, in *Oeuvres complètes*, ed. A. Robinet, 22 vols. (Paris, 1958–70), vol. 1, ed. G. Rodis-Lewis (1962), 382 and 451–3.

6 Louis de la Forge, *Traité de l'esprit de l'homme . . . suivant les principes de René Descartes* (Paris, 1666), ch. 6, 54.

7 John Locke, *An Essay Concerning Human Understanding*, ed. P. H. Nidditch, in *The Clarendon Edition* (1975), II.xxvii.9.

8 See, for example, *Essay*, II.xxvii.13. For a more detailed account of Locke's notion of consciousness, see Thiel, *Lockes Theorie der personalen Identität* (Bonn, 1983), 128–51, and Thiel, 'Hume's Notions of Consciousness', 102–5.

9 Étienne Bonnot de Condillac, *Oeuvres philosophiques*, ed. G. Le Roy, 3 vols. (Paris, 1947–51), 3: 143; *Traité des sensations*, IV.vii.4 (in *Oeuvres* 1: 309–10), translated as *Condillac's Treatise on the Sensations*, trans. G. Carr (London, 1930), 226.

10 Condillac, *Essai sur l'origine des connaissances humaines*, I.ii.1, §4 in *Oeuvres*, 1: 11, translated as *An Essay on the Origin of Human Knowledge*, trans. and ed. H. Aarsleff (Cambridge, 2001), 20. (Translation page numbers hereafter appear adjacent to original page numbers, separated by a slash.)

11 Condillac, *Essai*, I.ii.1, §13, 13/24.

12 Condillac, *Traité*, II.viii.14, 263–4/105–6.

13 George Berkeley, *A Treatise concerning the Principles of Human Knowledge* (1710), §135, in *Works*, 2: 1–113 at 103.

14 Berkeley, *De Motu*, §21, in *Works*, 4: 9–52 at 15–16 and 36. See A. C. Lloyd, 'The Self in Berkeley's Philosophy', in *Essays on Berkeley: A Tercentennial Celebration*, eds. J. Foster and H. Robinson (Oxford, 1985), 187–209, especially 199ff.

15 Berkeley, *Three Dialogues between Hylas and Philonous*, Third Dialogue, in *Works*, 2: 163–263 at 232: 'My own mind and my own ideas I have an immediate knowledge of'.

16 For Berkeley's use of the terminology of reflection, see, for example, *Principles*, §89 (*Works*, 2: 80): 'We comprehend our own existence by inward feeling or reflexion'. See also *Dialogues*, Third Dialogue, 232–3.

17 John Norris, *An Essay towards the Theory of the Ideal or Intelligible World*, 2 vols. (London, 1701), 2: 111.

18 Peter Browne, *The Procedure, Extent, and Limits of Human Understanding* (London, 1728), 64–72, 96–7, 222.

19 David Hume, *A Treatise of Human Nature*, eds. D. F. Norton and M. J. Norton, in *The Clarendon Edition* (2006), App. 20, SBN 635.

20 Hume, *An Enquiry concerning Human Understanding*, ed. T. L. Beauchamp, in *The Clarendon Edition* (2000), 1.13, SBN 13; see also *Treatise*, 1.4.2.47, SBN 212.

21 Hume, *Enquiry*, 7.1.13, SBN 66; see also *Treatise*, 1.4.2.7 and 47, SBN 190, 212.

22 For a more detailed account of Hume's concept of consciousness, see Thiel, 'Hume's Notions of Consciousness'.

23 Thomas Reid, *Essays on the Intellectual Powers of Man*, eds. D. R. Brookes and K. Haakonssen (Edinburgh, 2002), I.1.vii, 24.

24 Reid, *An Inquiry into the Human Mind on the Principles of Common Sense*, ed. D. R. Brookes (Edinburgh, 1997), 60.

25 Reid in a note from 1758, quoted from D. R. Brookes's edition of the *Inquiry*, 320, n. 15.

26 Dugald Stewart, *Collected Works*, ed. W. Hamilton, 11 vols. (Edinburgh and London, 1855), 5: 58.

27 Gottfried Wilhelm Leibniz, *Principes de la nature et de la grâce, fondés en raison*, §4, in *Die philosophischen Schriften*, ed. C. I. Gerhardt, 7 vols. (Berlin, 1875–90), 6: 598–606 at 600; in *Philosophical Writings*, trans. M. Morris and G. H. R. Parkinson, ed. G. H. R. Parkinson (London, 1973), 197.

28 Leibniz, *Nouveaux essais sur l'entendement humain*, eds. A. Robinet and H. Schepers, in Akademieausgabe, VI. 6 (1962), 53. The translation is from Leibniz, *New Essays on Human Understanding*, trans. and eds. P. Remnant and J. Bennett (Cambridge, 1981), which follows the same pagination.

29 For further discussion of Leibniz's understanding of apperception, see Robert McRae, *Leibniz: Perception, Apperception and Thought* (Toronto, 1976); Mark Kulstad, *Leibniz on Apperception, Consciousness, and Reflection* (Munich, 1991); Thiel, 'Leibniz and the Concept of Apperception', *Archiv für Geschichte der Philosophie*, 76 (1994): 195–209.

30 Christian Wolff, *Psychologia empirica* (1732), ed. J. École, in *Werke* II.5: §§25–6, pp. 17–18.

31 For the following argument, see Christian Wolff, *Vernünfftige Gedancken von Gott, der Welt und der Seele des Menschen, auch allen Dingen überhaupt*, ed. C. A. Corr, *Werke*, I.2: §§729–34, pp. 454–8. The first edition was dated 1720 but in fact appeared at the very end of 1719; see Corr's introduction.

32 Charles Bonnet, *Essai de psychologie* (London, 1755), ch. 38 at 129–32.

33 Johann Nicolas Tetens, *Philosophische Versuche über die menschliche Natur und ihre Entwicklung*, 2 vols. (Leipzig, 1777), 1: 281–5.

34 Paul-Henri Thiry, baron d'Holbach, *Système de la nature, ou Des loix du monde physique et du monde moral*, ed. D. Diderot, 2 vols. (Paris, 1821), 1: 131–2 and 196–7. For his definition of memory, see p. 138.

35 Claude-Adrien Helvétius, *De l'homme, de ses facultés intellectuelles et de sa éducation*, 2 vols. (London, 1773), 1: 85; trans. W. Hooper, *A Treatise on Man, his Intellectual Faculties and his Education*, 2 vols. (London, 1810), 1: 104, and Diderot's Commentary on Hemsterhuis in François Hemsterhuis, *Lettre sur l'homme et ses rapports avec le commentaire inedit de Diderot*, ed. G. May (New Haven, CT, 1964), 159.

36 Johann Bernhard Merian, 'Mémoire sur l'apperception de sa propre existence', in *Histoire de l'Académie Royale des Sciences et Belles Lettres*, Année 1749 (Berlin, 1751), 416–41 at 432–3. A German translation, 'Ueber die Apperzeption seiner eignen Existenz', appeared in *Magazin für die Philosophie und ihre Geschichte*, ed. M. Hissmann, 1 (1778): 89–132. For a more detailed discussion of Merian's theory, see Thiel, 'Between Wolff and Kant: Merian's Theory of Apperception', *Journal of the History of Philosophy*, 34 (1996): 213–32.

37 Jean-Jacques Rousseau, *Émile*, in *Oeuvres*, 4: 570–1, translated as *Émile or On Education*, trans. A. Bloom (Harmondsworth, 1991), 270.

38 Johann Heinrich Lambert, in his *Neues Organon, oder Gedanken über die Erforschung und Bezeichnung des Wahren und dessen Unterscheidung vom Irrtum und Schein*, 2 vols. (Leipzig, 1764), 'Dianoiologie', 1: i.§8.

39 For the notion of the identity-condition of immortality, see Roy W. Perrett, *Death and Immortality* (Dordrecht, 1987), 93–6.

40 Mijuskovic, in *Achilles of Rationalist Arguments* (105), claims that materialists tried to establish personal identity on a model of bodily identity but provides no evidence for this.

41 There are few general treatments of eighteenth-century theories of personal identity but see, for some aspects, the following: Mijuskovic, *Achilles of Rationalist Arguments*, ch. 4, 93–118; Jean A. Perkins, *The Concept of the Self in the French Enlightenment* (Geneva, 1969); Christian Hauser, *Selbstbewußtsein und personale Identität* (Stuttgart, 1994) (see my review in *Das Achtzehnte Jahrhundert*, 19.2 (1995): 243–5); *Individuation and Identity in Early Modern Philosophy: Descartes to Kant*, eds. K. F. Barber and J. J. E. Gracia (Albany, NY, 1994) (see my critical discussion: Thiel, ''Epistemologism' and Early Modern Debates about Individuation and Identity', *British Journal for the History of Philosophy*, 5 (1997): 353–72); Raymond Martin and John Barresi, *Naturalization of the Soul: Self and Personal Identity in the Eighteenth Century* (London and New York, NY, 2000). For the seventeenth-century background, see Thiel, 'Personal Identity', in *The Cambridge History of Seventeenth-Century Philosophy*, eds. D. Garber and M. Ayers (Cambridge, 1998), 868–912.

42 For more details and references to secondary sources, see Thiel, *Lockes Theorie der personalen Identität*, and 'Personal Identity'.

43 Locke, *Essay*, IV.iii.6. See John W. Yolton, *Thinking Matter: Materialism in Eighteenth-Century Britain* (Minneapolis, MN, 1983), and his *Locke and French Materialism* (Oxford, 1991).

44 John Sergeant, *Solid Philosophy Asserted . . . with Reflexions on Mr. Locke's Essay concerning Human Understanding* (London, 1697), Reflexions §14, 267; Joseph Butler, 'A Dissertation on Personal Identity', in *Works*, ed. W. E. Gladstone, 2 vols. (Oxford, 1896), 1: 317–25.

45 Samuel Clarke, *A Fourth Defense of an Argument made use of in a Letter to Mr. Dodwel, to prove the Immateriality and Natural Immortality of the Soul* (London, 1708), 56.

46 Clarke, *A Third Defense of an Argument made use of in a Letter to Mr. Dodwel, to prove the Immateriality and Natural Immortality of the Soul. In a Letter to the Author of the Reflexions on Mr. Clark's Second Defense* (London, 1708), 64.

47 See Clarke, *Third Defense*, 61f.

48 Berkeley, *Principles* §139, 104–5. See also §2, 41–2, and *Dialogues*, Third Dialogue, 231.

49 Berkeley, *Alciphron, or The Minute Philosopher*, Seventh Dialogue, §8 in *Works*, 3: 296–9; Reid, *Intellectual Powers*, III.6, 276.

50 Anthony Collins, *An Answer to Mr. Clark's Third Defence of his Letter to Mr. Dodwell* (London, 1708), 76.

51 Edmund Law, *A Defence of Mr. Locke's Opinion concerning Personal Identity* (Cambridge, 1769), 2. This pamphlet is reprinted in the 1823 edition of *The Works of John Locke*, vol. 3.

52 Condillac, *Traité*, I.vi.1, 238–9/43.

53 Condillac, *Traité*, IV.viii.6, 313/235–6. Elsewhere he argues that at least we know that the mind must be a simple unitary substance distinct from the body: *Essai*, I.i.1, §6, 7/13.

54 See, for example, *Nouveaux essais*, Preface, 58.

55 Leibniz, *Discours de métaphysique*, §13, in *Philosophischen Schriften*, 4: 437. The translation is from Leibniz, *Discourse on Metaphysics and Related Writings*, trans. and eds. R. N. D. Martin and S. Brown (Manchester, 1988), 51. (Translation page numbers hereafter appear adjacent to original page numbers: 437/51.)

56 Leibniz, *Discours*, §8, 433/46.

57 Leibniz, 'Remarques sur la lettre de M. Arnauld', in *Philosophischen Schriften*, 2: 43, translated in *The Leibniz-Arnauld Correspondence*, trans. and ed. H. T. Mason (Manchester, 1967), 46.

58 Leibniz, *Discours*, §36, 462/82. See also his letter to Arnauld, 9 October 1687 (*Philosophischen Schriften*, 2: 125/160).

59 Leibniz, *Discours*, §34, 460/80. See also *Nouveaux essais*, II.xxvii.9, 235. See Samuel Scheffler, 'Leibniz on Personal Identity and Moral Personality', *Studia Leibnitiana*, 8 (1976): 219–40.

60 See Margaret D. Wilson, 'Leibniz: Self-Consciousness and Immortality in the Paris Notes and After', *Archiv für Geschichte der Philosophie*, 58 (1976): 335–52; Edwin Curley, 'Leibniz on Locke on Personal Identity', in *Leibniz: Critical and Interpretive Essays*, ed. M. Hooker (Manchester, 1982), 302–26; Ezio Vailati, 'Leibniz's Theory of Personal Identity in the *New Essays*', *Studia Leibnitiana*, 17 (1985): 36–43; Nicholas Jolley, *Leibniz and Locke: A Study of the New Essays on Human Understanding* (Oxford, 1984), 136–9; Thiel, 'Personal Identity'; Marc Bobro, '*Self and Substance in Leibniz*' (Dordrecht and Boston, 2004).

61 Christian Wolff, *Psychologia rationalis*, in *Werke*, II.6: §63, p. 42; compare §53, p. 35. See also *Vernünfftige Gedancken von Gott*, §§744, 755–6, pp. 464, 469.

62 Wolff, *Vernünfftige Gedancken von Gott*, §§192–4, pp. 107–8; *Psychologia empirica*, §§11, 20–2, pp. 9, 15–16; *Psychologia rationalis*, §10, pp. 9–10.

63 Wolff, *Vernünfftige Gedancken von Gott*, §924, 570. See also *Psychologia rationalis*, §§741, 743, 660–1.

64 The literature on Hume's account of personal identity is vast. See, for example, Terence Penelhum, 'Hume on Personal Identity', *Philosophical Review*, 64 (1955): 571–89; Barry Stroud, *Hume* (London, 1977), 118–40; Jane L. McIntyre, 'Personal Identity and the Passions', *Journal of the History of Philosophy*, 27 (1989): 545–57; David Pears, *Hume's System: An Examination of the First Book of his Treatise* (Oxford, 1990), 120–51; Wayne Waxman, *Hume's Theory of Consciousness* (Cambridge, 1994), 203–37; Fred Wilson, 'Substance and Self in Locke and Hume', in *Individuation and Identity*, eds. Barber and Gracia, 155–99; Donald Ainslie, 'Scepticism about

Persons in Book II of the *Treatise*', *Journal of the History of Philosophy*, 37 (1999): 469–92; Kenneth P. Winkler: '"All is Revolution in Us"': Personal Identity in Shaftesbury and Hume', *Hume Studies*, 26 (2000): 3–40; Galen Strawson, 'Hume on Himself', in *Exploring Practical Philosophy: From Action to Values*, eds. D. Egonsson et al. (Aldershot, 2001), 69–94.

65 *Treatise*, 1.4.6.4, SBN 252. See also 1.4.6.4–5, SBN 253 and 1.4.2.39, SBN 207.

66 James Beattie, *An Essay on the Nature and Immutability of Truth, in Opposition to Sophistry and Scepticism* (Edinburgh, 1770), Pt. I, ch. 2, sect. iii at p. 79.

67 For other non-ontological readings of Hume's bundle theory, see Edward Craig, *The Mind of God and the Works of Man* (Oxford, 1987), 111–20, and Strawson, 'Hume on Himself', 71–4 and 78–80. Neither Craig nor Strawson, however, links Hume's account to that of Kames and other Scottish Common Sense philosophers.

68 See Henry Home, Lord Kames, *Essays on the Principles of Morality and Natural Religion* (Edinburgh, 1751), Part II, Essay 2, 'Of the Idea of Self and of Personal Identity', 231–6.

69 *New Letters of David Hume*, eds. R. Klibansky and E. C. Mossner (Oxford, 1954), 20.

70 For a different account, see Albert Tsugawa, 'David Hume and Lord Kames on Personal Identity', *Journal of the History of Ideas*, 22 (1961): 398–403.

71 Diderot's Commentary, in Hemsterhuis, *Lettre sur l'homme*, 159. See also Perkins, *Concept of the Self*, 124.

72 Charles Bonnet, *Essai analytique sur les facultés de l'âme* (Copenhagen, 1760), ch. 24, §§702–13. The quotation is from §706, p. 458.

73 Joseph Priestley, *Disquisitions relating to Matter and Spirit* (London, 1777), 86.

74 Michael Hissmann, *Psychologische Versuche* (Göttingen, 1777), 148–9. For Hissmann, see Thiel, 'Varieties of Inner Sense: Two Pre-Kantian Theories', *Archiv für Geschichte der Philosophie*, 79 (1997): 58–79.

75 Thomas Cooper, 'On Identity', in *Tracts Ethical, Theological and Political* (1789), in *Philosophical Writings of Thomas Cooper*, ed. U. Thiel, 3 vols. (Bristol 2001), 1: 305–464 at 356, 463. See Thiel, 'Locke and Eighteenth-Century Materialist Conceptions of Personal Identity', *The Locke Newsletter*, 29 (1998): 59–83; Thiel, 'Introduction', in *Philosophical Writings of Thomas Cooper*, 1: v–xix.

76 Richard Price, *A Free Discussion of the Doctrines of Materialism and Philosophical Necessity in a Correspondence between Dr. Price and Dr. Priestley* (London, 1778), 10. John Whitehead, *Materialism Philosophically Examined* (London, 1778), 77–88.

77 See Kant, *Kritik der reinen Vernunft*, in Ak, vols. 3 (2nd edn., Berlin 1904) and 4 (1st edn., Berlin, 1903), hereafter B and A, respectively, translated as *Critique of Pure Reason*, trans. and eds. P. Guyer and A. W. Wood (1998), in *Works*.

78 Kant refers to Priestley's materialism in the *Kritik*, A 745/B 773.

79 Kant, *Kritik*, A 107. See also Kant, *Anthropologie in pragmatischer Hinsicht*, Ak 7: 117–333 at 134. See *Anthropology from a Pragmatic Point of View*, trans. and ed. M. J. Gregor (The Hague, 1974), 15.

80 Kant, *Kritik* B132. Compare A 107, B 139, and A 341/B 399.

81 *Kritik*, A 342/B 400. Kant says on the same page that rational psychology is a 'putative science, which is built on the single proposition *I think*'. Compare also A 343/B 401, where he states that the '*I think* is . . . the sole text of rational psychology, from which it is to develop its entire wisdom'.

82 See Kant, *Metaphysik der Sitten*, Ak 6: 223, 239, 418, 429, 434f.; *The Metaphysics of Morals*, trans. M. J. Gregor, in *Works/Practical Philosophy* (1991). See Paul Guyer, 'Kant on Apperception and a priori Synthesis', *American Philosophical Quarterly*, 17 (1980): 205–12; Karl Ameriks, *Kant's Theory of Mind: An Analysis of the Paralogisms of Pure Reason* (Oxford, 1982); Werner Hinsch, *Erfahrung und Selbstbewusstsein: zur Kategoriendeduktion bei Kant* (Hamburg, 1986); Henry E. Allison, *Kant's Transcendental Idealism: An Interpretation and Defense* (New

Haven, CT, 1983), 255–93; Dieter Sturma, *Kant über Selbstbewusstsein: zum Zusammenhang von Erkenntniskritik und Theorie des Selbstbewusstseins* (Hildesheim, 1985); Dieter Henrich, 'The Identity of the Subject in the Transcendental Deduction', in *Reading Kant*, eds. E. Schaper and W. Vossenkuhl (Oxford, 1989), 250–80; C. Thomas Powell, *Kant's Theory of Self-Consciousness* (Oxford, 1990); Georg Mohr, *Das Sinnliche Ich: Innerer Sinn und Bewusstsein bei Kant* (Würzburg, 1991); Wayne Waxman, *Kant's Model of the Mind* (Oxford, 1991); Andrew Brook, *Kant and the Mind* (Cambridge, 1994); Heiner F. Klemme, *Kants Philosophie des Subjekts* (Hamburg, 1996); Pierre Keller, *Kant and the Demands of Self-Consciousness* (Cambridge, 1998); James van Cleve, *Problems from Kant* (Oxford, 1999); Thiel, 'Kant's Notion of Self-Consciousness in Context', in *Kant und die Berliner Aufklärung*, eds. V. Gerhardt, R. Horstmann, and R. Schumacher, 5 vols. (Berlin, 2001), 2: 468–76.

83 Karl Leonhard Reinhold, *Versuch einer neuen Theorie des menschlichen Vorstellungsvermögens* (Prague and Jena, 1789); *Über das Fundament des philosophischen Wissens* (Jena, 1791).

84 See A. Klemmt, *Karl Leonhard Reinholds Elementarphilosophie* (Hamburg, 1958); Frederick C. Beiser, *The Fate of Reason: German Philosophy from Kant to Fichte* (Cambridge, MA, 1987), 226–65; Manfred Frank, *'Unendliche Annäherung': Die Anfänge der philosophischen Frühromantik* (Frankfurt, 1997), 152–427; Karl Ameriks, *Kant and the Fate of Autonomy: Problems in the Appropriation of the Critical Philosophy* (Cambridge, 2000), 81–160.

85 Beiser, *The Fate of Reason*, 254.

86 'The Foundation of Philosophical Knowledge. By Karl Leonhard Reinhold', in *Between Kant and Hegel: Texts in the Development of Post-Kantian Idealism*, trans. G. di Giovanni, eds. G. di Giovanni and H. S. Harris (Albany, NY, 1985), 54–103 at 70.

87 See Dieter Henrich, 'Die Anfänge der Theorie des Subjekts (1789)', in *Zwischenbetrachtungen im Prozeß der Aufklärung. Jürgen Habermas zum 60. Geburtstag*, eds. A. Honneth, et al. (Frankfurt, 1989), 106–70 at 150–1; Jürgen Stolzenberg, 'Selbstbewußtsein: Ein Problem der Philosophie nach Kant. Zum Verhältnis Reinhold-Hölderlin-Fichte', *Revue internationale de philosophie*, 197 (1996): 461–82 at 466.

88 Johann Gottlieb Fichte, *Versuch einer neuen Darstellung der Wissenschaftslehre* (1797), in *Werke*, 1: 526. The translation is from Frederick Neuhouser, *Fichte's Theory of Subjectivity* (Cambridge, 1990), 73.

89 See Fichte, *Recension des Aenesidemus* (1792), in *Werke*, 1: 10.

90 Fichte, *Zweite Einleitung in die Wissenschaftslehre* (1797), in *Werke*, 1: 474. Translations are from Fichte, *Science of Knowledge, with the First and Second Introductions*, trans. and eds. P. Heath and J. Lachs (Cambridge, 1982), 47. (Hereafter page citations from the translation follow those of the original, separated by a slash.)

91 See Fichte, *Zweite Einleitung* §9, 501–4/71–4; and *Grundlage der gesammten Wissenschaftslehre* (1794), in *Werke*, 1: 264–5.

92 See Fichte, *Grundlage*, 96–8.

93 Fichte, *Zweite Einleitung*, 465/40.

94 Fichte, *Zweite Einleitung*, 473/47.

95 Fichte, *Grundlage*, 97–98. See Dieter Henrich, *Fichtes ursprüngliche Einsicht* (Frankfurt am Main, 1967); Ulrich Claesges, *Geschichte des Selbstbewusstseins: der Ursprung des spekulativen Problems in Fichtes Wissenschaftslehre von 1794–1795* (The Hague, 1974); Wilhelm Lütterfelds, 'Zum undialektischen Begriff des Selbstbewusstseins bei Kant und Fichte', *Wiener Jahrbuch für Philosophie*, 8 (1975): 7–38; John Taber, 'Fichte's Emendation of Kant', *Kant-Studien*, 75 (1984): 442–59; Robert B. Pippin, 'Fichte's Contribution', *Philosophical Forum*, 19 (1987–8): 74–96; Neuhouser, *Fichte's Theory of Subjectivity*; Jürgen Stolzenberg, *Fichtes Begriff der Intellektuellen Anschauung: die Entwicklung in der Wissenschaftslehre von 1793/94 bis 1801/2* (Stuttgart, 1986); Stolzenberg, 'Selbstbewußtsein'; Ameriks, *Kant and the Fate of Autonomy*, 163–264.

11

REASON

MICHEL MALHERBE

It might seem evident that the Age of Enlightenment, or *le siècle des Lumières* or *die Aufklärung*, is pre-eminently the Age of Reason. But, upon further consideration, this conclusion is not so clear. First, what precisely is meant by the term *reason*? The old sense of mathematical proportion, enlarged to the idea of abstract reasoning? The human faculty of knowledge, generally taken, or the faculty of thinking according to rules? The order of things such as it has been fixed up by the wisdom of God or the set of the first and innate truths? Secondly, are we to examine reason as a theoretical principle or as a moral and political foundation, as a formal rule or as a determining power? Thirdly, are we able to coordinate into a consistent whole the study of the relationship between reason and the senses, between reason and the understanding, reason and the passions, reason and morality, reason and faith, or reason and enthusiasm? Now, if we want to classify the different philosophies or systems of the eighteenth century, we should be able to answer these questions and give a definition of reason which, though complex, might nevertheless be determinate. As a matter of fact, though, such an attempt is hopeless. We cannot even say that one of the main features of the eighteenth century was rationalism. It was tormented from within by scepticism; it was beset from without by such issues as experience, liberty, evil, enthusiasm, and public policy. In England and Germany, it was a deeply religious century, and it engendered and bred the first beginnings of Romanticism. However, on the other hand, if it is true that a full conception of reason is not reached unless it goes through a criticism by which reason, by itself, can determine its power, its limits, and, generally speaking, its relationship to reality, undoubtedly the eighteenth century is the Age of Reason since it was a time when this principle or faculty tried to steady itself because it was losing its ontological or theological foundation. Therefore, it is worth giving an account of the story of this critical period, from the philosophies of Locke and Leibniz to the fully developed scepticism of Hume and Kant's *Kritik der reinen Vernunft*, and trying to disentangle the various threads that give this century its intellectual coherence.

How did eighteenth-century philosophy come to a critical conception of reason? Unhappily, we cannot start from what would be an unambiguously precritical and metaphysical concept of reason. But let us try at first to characterize the feeling of reason (so to speak) that more or less pervaded seventeenth-century thought, a feeling that blended the scholastic legacy with a renewed Stoïcism. In a way, reason is not to be defined since it is our own nature; it is the *lumen naturale* in which we think and act. We do not see the light itself but the things that are in the light, and we can apprehend our own mind, which lives in the light. The light can be corrupted by prejudices or obscured by passions, but in itself it is always true. Reason is a *recta ratio*. Besides, our nature is a part of the universal nature and has been created by God, who is the very Light from which we have received our intellectual and practical powers (that is, our own reason). Therefore, under the government of divine reason, our human reason is fitted to agree with the reason that is in the nature of things. Reason is the truth itself. But, in other respects, reason is also *logos*, both discourse and reasoning. A reasoning links up several *rationes*, or proportions, and goes from principles to consequences, from causes to effects (or the other way if it is analytical). But since effects or phenomena are best known for us (as Aristotle said), rational knowledge must discover the true and first principles or causes, which are best known by nature, before proceeding to the consequences by a deductive or synthetic way. From this point of view, reason is both the human faculty of reasoning and the set of first truths or common notions on which any real knowledge depends.

Locke breaks away from this prevailing conception by attacking its main postulate. When offering his own definition in contrast with the ancient notion, he draws a sharp distinction between reason itself and the object of reason, between the subjective or human faculty of reasoning and the objective nature of things.[1] Reason is not to be taken as *recta ratio* but only as *ratiocinatio*. Human reason does not naturally participate in a supposed universal and eternal nature that could be intuitively apprehended by the contemplation of innate ideas hidden in the mind and taken as the first principles of the truth of things; it is the specifically human faculty of reasoning. Hence there follow several consequences.

First, reason is no longer the very nature of man: it is a mere faculty. Or, more accurately, if the general faculty of knowing, both in its passive and active characters, is said to be the understanding, reason, as the reckoning or deduction of consequences from principles, is the higher form of judgment and knowledge.

Secondly, since Locke does not follow Hobbes in the way of nominalism, he immediately meets with a problem that he expresses himself. Of course, reasoning being a succession of reasons (that is, of *rationes* or proportions) by which the mind chains up conclusions with principles or given truths, it will not be confused with intuition or the perception of a truth by and in itself. But Locke retains the Cartesian conception of deduction, taken as a succession of intuitions, each intermediary step of the reasoning being the intuitive perception of the agreement or the disagreement of the two terms that are considered. And, in such a case, the knowledge of the inferential connection does not depend on the logical rules of a formal computation but on the ability of the human mind to see that two terms agree or disagree in themselves: as the mind *sees* the ideas that are its immediate objects, so it sees the connection between these ideas by an immediate apperception. Therefore, deduction is a kind of intuition delayed by interjected intuitions. Now, the difficulty is as follows: if the human mind is endowed with the empirical faculty of receiving, perceiving, and retaining ideas from sensation and reflection, and if, moreover, it owns the faculty of immediately perceiving whether two ideas agree or disagree, what room then is left for reasoning besides these two intuitive faculties – sensible and intellectual?

Locke's answer is congruent with the whole argument.

What need is there of Reason? Very much; both for the enlargement of our Knowledge, and regulating our Assent: For it hath to do, both in Knowledge and Opinion, and is necessary, and assisting to all our other intellectual Faculties, and indeed contains two of them, *viz*. *Sagacity and Illation*. (*Essay, Concerning Human Understanding* IV.xvii.2)

Consider two ideas about which I ask whether they agree or disagree. You can answer that you immediately perceive that they agree or disagree. But you may be wrong, and in this case you entertain a prejudice if it is not right that the two ideas are *immediately* comparable and if intermediate ideas are to be considered before an answer can be given concerning their agreement or disagreement. Therefore, reason is needed as the fitness of the mind for detecting when a reasoning (a succession of intuitions) is required and for discovering the intermediate ideas, their correct number, and the various links between their extremes. In these cases, an inference (an illation) must be substituted for the initial and unrefined intuitive perception. Moreover, at each step of the chain or in the argument taken as a whole and compared with another, the same certainty is not always to be expected. But, if reason is a power of analysis and distinction, it makes the mind able to appreciate the degree of assent that it must give to this or that conclusion: either full certainty or measured probability. Thus 'the Faculty which finds out the Means, and rightly applies them to discover Certainty in the one, and Probability in the other, is that which we call Reason' (*Essay,* IV.xvii.2).

One aspect of the definition of reason cited earlier is full of promise: the idea that reason as such is less the reasoning itself than the faculty of judging – of appraising the degree of assent to be given – less a faculty among other faculties than the means to rule and correct all the faculties of the human mind. Here one finds the main features of a critical reason chiefly concerned with the correct assent to be given to a proposition according to its degree of evidence. Moreover, Locke understands that this jurisdiction of reason is to be defined and that it cannot be defined unless reason is the only principle capable of founding any jurisdiction whatever, so he takes up again the old question of the relationship between reason and faith (*Essay*, IV.xviii) and tries to clear it up by means of three theses. The first one denies that any new simple idea (that is, ultimate matter of knowledge) can be communicated to anybody else: an original revelation from God is possible but cannot be conveyed to another mind, so any tradition or transmission is under the jurisdiction of reason, which alone can determine its valid conditions. The second thesis claims that the jurisdiction of reason depends on reason and that divine revelation cannot run counter to clear and distinct knowledge nor change its degree of certainty since faith is always more obscure than reason. The third thesis marks the boundaries of faith: revelation informs men's minds of facts or truths that are above reason and may determine our assent concerning uncertain propositions, but in both cases reason alone can judge whether a truth is a divine revelation. Revelation is a source of truths, but the judge of these truths is reason, this natural light that the Creator has given to His creatures. Whoever pretends that a proposition is true because it is present in his own mind and that this truth comes from nowhere but God himself is a liar or an enthusiast – enthusiasm being the exact opposite of reason since in the name of God (as a matter of fact, because of a too vivid imagination or the influence of passions) it intends to free any evidence from a critical appraisal.

This conception of reason seemed reasonable to many people, to philosophers, even to theologians. Locke offered a kind of map of human knowledge and a balanced criterion of truth. However, although his rationalism is not a violent one, there remains a large part of ambiguity. This fact can be confirmed by examining how his doctrine of the degrees of certainty was taken up by authors during the first part of the eighteenth century. On the one hand, deists used it as a war machine. John Toland, in his *Christianity not Mysterious* (1696), claims that there is nothing in the Gospel that could be not only contrary to reason but also above reason: mystery denotes either a thing that is intelligible in itself but has been made unintelligible by words or superstitions, or a thing that cannot be conceived in itself but will appear reasonable once it has been revealed.[2] In both cases, the content of the Bible, which is at our disposal, is rationally understandable. Later, Collins and others would work out a more analytical criticism, scrutinizing the Scriptures in fuller particulars but keeping the same Lockean line of argument that revelation is undoubtedly the word of God but, since it cannot be contrary to reason, it appears that its content, once purified from verbal ornaments and superstitious corruptions, perfectly agrees with pure reason. However, on the other hand, in order to prove that no natural objection can be raised against revelation, the same agreement of faith and reason is argued by Joseph Butler, a theologian who became a bishop, in his *Analogy of Religion, Natural and Revealed* (1736).[3] His method of analogy is based on Locke's theory of probable knowledge and critical assent to truth, but Butler gives it a practical turn. In the conduct of our life, we are under the obligation to act, and sometimes to act even upon the presumption of a low probability. Whereas reason collects the different relevant facts, ponders the various arguments, and measures the exact degree of theoretical assent, a decision cannot be divided, and once it has been taken, it is practically valid as if it were founded on full evidence. Thus, as philosophers are moved to frame likely hypotheses concerning the invisible causes of phenomena and, thanks to probable reasoning, to give the required assent, according to a critical appraisal, so a religious man, who surely cannot enter God's intentions, can nevertheless proceed, by the analogy of nature, which is an experienced object, to the supposition of God's moral dispensation and draw from his own experience of the present world a sufficient probability to confirm the religious assumption and to be obliged to make up his mind in favour of a moral and pious life. The course of nature, analogically taken, confirms not the reasons we believe but the act by which we assent to our faith and carry a moral resolution.

In a way, Butler underlines the practical and subjective side of Locke's conception of reason. For this critical reason that determines the degrees of assent according to the degrees of certainty is not governed by a set of logical laws but regulated by a kind of reasonable sense. Locke, like Descartes, assigns the discovery of truth to the power of the human mind. And since he dismisses syllogism (and any formal consideration) as being useless and burdensome, he takes reason as the legitimate practice of reasoning. He considers it not really an art, as a matter of fact, because he questions the possibility of making up such an art that could be taught, but rather human nature itself, rightly used. Finally, reason is the nature of the human mind when it is unbiased and, since the human mind is besieged with prejudices, lucid enough to check its own operations.

The comparison of Locke's text and Leibniz's response in the *Nouveaux essais* (written around 1700–4) easily shows the irreducible difference between the two philosophers' definitions of reason.[4] Whereas Locke contrasted his own definition with traditional ones, Leibniz systematically restores the old (and complex) meaning of reason and goes a step further. 'Reason is the known truth which being connected with another one, less known, makes us give the latter our assent' (*Nouveaux essais*, IV.xvii.1). We give our assent to consequent truths insofar as they are connected with antecedent truths, and the latter are the reasons of the former. Moreover, a reason is not only the cause of our assent to an inferred truth, but it is also especially the cause of truth itself. So, by considering the connection between two or more propositions independently of the act of perception by which the human mind seizes and understands it, we may speak of the reason of truth: reason is the cause that a truth, either derived or primary, is a truth. And, since the cause in things responds to the reason in truths, we can speak of the reason of a thing, whereby we mean the intelligible cause of the thing considered. Things or events have causes, and these causes are the intelligible reason for their being. Of course, such an objective or metaphysical rationality can be understood by the human mind, within its limits, so that by reason we also mean the capacity of our mind for entering the reasons of truths or the reasons of things and seizing the a priori connections that depend on necessary and universal truths. But human reason is then entirely ruled by objective laws that can be displayed in a logical form. Leibniz's notion of reason is still metaphysical, but it is also logical.

Since reason is at first a *ratio*, let us begin with the difference between the primary truths and the secondary truths. The former are identical truths that state the nature of a thing in itself. They are ruled by the law of identity, which is also, to some extent, the law of contradiction. The law of contradiction states that out of two contradictory propositions one is true and the other false. It is a formal principle that is the sine qua non condition of all thinking. But, by linking this law to the law of identity, Leibniz, faithful to Aristotle, subordinates logic to metaphysics. This principle, which forbids the mind to set forth two contradictory propositions concerning the same thing at the same time, also states that each thing remains what it is insofar as it is determined in its being by predicates or qualities that are identical to themselves.

As for the secondary truths, they are truths that can be reduced to the primary truths by the analysis of notions and the use of definitions. Thus, any demonstration is a kind of definition and aims at showing that the predicate is in the subject and, ultimately, that the proposition is identical since it is the same thing that is expressed by the subject and the predicate, reasoning being nothing else but the more or less intricate reduction to an identical proposition. So, to give the reason of something is to prove that the predicate is contained in the subject by a real and intelligible implication that means the identity of the two terms, and, metaphysically taken, rationality is the mere identity of a thing with itself – that is to say, its own and complete determination. Of course, such a reason is a priori, and, since propositions thus understood are ultimately analytical, it is entirely subordinated to logical rules that are set down by the study of syllogism and other forms of demonstration.

If we did not proceed further than this first distinction between the first and the second propositions, the only principle of reason would be for any truth whatever the law of identity or contradiction. Leibniz introduces a second distinction, that between necessary truths and contingent truths. Every predicate forms a part of the subject except existence, or, to put it in Leibnizian words, existence is a predicate that does not add anything to the determination or the essence of the thing. Essence without existence is still complete. To that extent, I can have (in principle, not in fact, except for abstract essences such as mathematical objects) an a priori knowledge of the essence of things, and this knowledge is made up of necessary truths governed by the law of contradiction and logically derived. Existence cannot be demonstrated except by God; thus, it is contingent and given to us by experience. And since our mind is empirical in three-quarters of its thoughts and actions, it is furnished with a lot of such existential truths for which the law of contradiction does not help much with respect to their contingency.

Therefore, contingent truths cannot be reduced to necessary truths, even by God's mind. And, since the mind cannot figure to itself a truth without a reason of its truth or an existence without a cause of its being, another principle of reason must be set forth next to the law of contradiction. Reason must be given for actual existences. Such is the office of the law of sufficient reason, which is made up of two parts. It says on the one hand that any existence must have a cause and on the other hand that for every existence being determined in such and such a way there must be a reason that it is so and so.

One must consider that there are two great principles in our reasonings. The one is the law of contradiction which imports that out of two contradictory propositions one is true and the other false; the other is the law of determining reason: it says that nothing happens without a cause, or at least a determining reason, that is to say something that can help to give an a priori reason why this thing is existing rather than not existing and why it is so rather than otherwise.[5]

This principle determines existences as the law of contradiction determines essences, but it is no less a priori than the latter.

What can the content of such a principle be since it concerns only actual existences, every qualitative or essential determination being governed by the law of identity or law of contradiction? Indeed, it introduces a kind of super-determination that is essentially final: it governs every existence by *le principe du meilleur*. It is better that something be rather than nothing; it is better that this existence be this, and that existence be that; it is better that the world in which we live be this one rather than another logically possible world; it is better that every being be singular and that there not be two leaves exactly the same in the gardens of German princesses; it is better that this actual world be the richest and the most abundant one and nevertheless be governed by the simplest laws and so on. This architectonic principle governs not only God's creation but also philosophy. The best philosophy is the most systematic one, which explains more things with fewer principles, which does not allow any void in a given explanation, which gives reasons that are all materially different although they are all formally identical, and so forth.

One can prefer Locke's philosophy because of its easiness and prudence, but one cannot help admiring the intelligent and aesthetic philosophy of Leibniz. It doubtless represents the acme of classical rationalism, where, so to say, reason and reality act in such narrow collusion with one another that reason is not yet the problematical property of man. And even if Leibniz's thought was imperfectly known during the eighteenth century, it shone like either a valuable reference or an impossible model that should be destroyed with regret. It was widely influential. In Germany, it was reworked by Christian Wolff, who was at the time a well-known professor and, as usual with professors, added material of his own and changed Leibniz's philosophy into a dogmatic and tightly systematic teaching from which no part of knowledge or action could escape. In England, it inspired Alexander Pope's poetry in an *An Essay on Man* (1733–4) by its aesthetic and religious aspects, but not without a peculiar blending of reason and sentiment or emotion.[6] In France, a country deeply permeated with Cartesian philosophy, the *philosophes* more and more clearly praised the genius of a philosopher with whom they agreed on certain points or from whom they borrowed some claims or trains of reasoning.

But besides technical difficulties, there were fundamental problems with this view of reason. Leibniz himself allowed that his system, clear and distinct as it was, contained two labyrinths, the labyrinth of continuity and the labyrinth of liberty and evil. The first one concerns the possibility of reaching ultimate or simplest elements and rests on the divorce between the logic of ideality, for which the division of a whole goes on ad infinitum, and the logic of reality, which requires that every complex reality be made up of unities or simple terms, or monads. It goes through mathematics, draws out dynamics between geometry and metaphysics, and disturbs monadology. The second labyrinth, much less sophisticated, affects the practical field and can be discerned easily. If everything in the world is rational and determined both by the law of contradiction and the law of sufficient reason, and if furthermore man is a part of the world, then we must conclude that all man's actions – past, present, and future – are included in the subjective position of his essence and respond to one or both principles. It was necessary that Caesar, being Caesar (and the world being this world), should become a dictator and be murdered by Brutus. Therefore, what room was left for human liberty in a world governed by necessity? And if such a necessity was anyway for the best, everything could be explained and justified, even evil. Therefore, we should say that God is accountable for the evil that is in the world. And, since God is the supreme reason, we must say that reason is responsible for the existence of evil, for evil does exist. Such a conclusion is unacceptable.

The first attack on this point had come from Bayle's *Dictionnaire historique et critique*, published in 1697.[7] This very influential dictionary (the second edition was released in 1702), in the article 'Rorarius', questioned Leibniz's pre-established harmony, one of the metaphysical and theological consequences of the principle of reason. And Leibniz answered Bayle's critique in his *Théodicée* in 1710. Generally speaking, Bayle was anxious in his dictionary to fight all the forms of dogmatism that, by reaction, are wont to generate the deepest scepticism in metaphysical and theological fields. Reason, given up to the demands of absolute coherence and perfect rationality, is led relentlessly to its own destruction. An excessive use of reason endangers our knowledge and our faith. But the debate between Bayle and Leibniz is mainly speculative. When, half a century later, Voltaire writes his *Candide* (1759), he is less concerned with theological and metaphysical discussions concerning God's relationship to the world and to human liberty than by the existence of evil.[8] Evil is not only unacceptable but unbearable. It is irrational at the core. And any attempt to try to justify it rationally is a kind of scandal and deserves to be derided. What is Leibniz's optimistic rationalism worth when it is applied to such a disaster as the Lisbon earthquake and when it persists in claiming 'that all is well when all goes wrong'?

In order to escape such a dramatic and, indeed, tragic dispute, Locke offered the modest, but effective, model of a reasonable reason. And this model prevailed throughout most of the eighteenth century since, thanks to its strength, speculative and practical Pyrrhonism could be defeated. Reason is this human faculty that can reign on the progress of sciences and the moral improvement of man and society if it is able to draw its own limits. It will give up the claim to the a priori knowledge of innate ideas and of primary principles; it will not try to know the essence of things but will rely on experience to determine general facts or laws; it will confine the understanding to those operations that can be applied to a matter received from the senses or from reflection and by which it can have clear and distinct ideas, such as discerning, comparing, and judging ; by a careful analysis and a judicious disposition, it will patiently spread the province of knowledge; and it will take a well-informed experience as the general and sufficient rule for the conduct of life.

Our Business here is not to know all things, but those which concern our Conduct. If we can find out those Measures, whereby a Rational creature put in that State, which Man is in, in this World, may, and ought to govern his Opinions, and Actions depending thereon, we need not be troubled, that some other things escape our Knowledge. (*Essay*, Intro., §6)

Therefore, everybody can exercise his own reason in order to follow the path of truth and make up his own mind freely. It is not unreasonable to think that such reasonable men will be able to live together peacefully, to organize a better society, and to secure a good education for the generations to come.

Let us consider, as the epitome of this concept of reason, Newton's famous rules of method, which, resting on the success of the new physics, are universally known as the very spirit of experimental philosophy.[9] There are four *regulae philosophandi*. The first one says that, nature doing nothing in vain, one must not admit any other causes but those that are necessary to the explanation of phenomena. This is a rule of economy and accurate determination. The second rule, the rule of uniformity, says that the same effects must be, as far as it is possible, ascribed to the same causes. The third rule, the rule of experience, explains what can be meant by the generality of a law or a property and states that it is by experience and by the analogy of nature that we can know the universal properties of bodies, which are to be observed to belong to every one of them and not by an a priori knowledge of the essence of matter; cautiously, Newton does not come to a decision whether gravity, although it is a universal phenomenon, must be counted as one of these properties. The last rule is a rule of epistemological prudence: propositions drawn from experience and inferred by induction are to be considered as true as long as they are not falsified or restricted by contrary facts. No other rational rules are needed, nor do they make up a logical doctrine (such as for instance Leibniz's essays towards a *mathesis universalis*).[10] As a matter of fact, Newton's four rules are nothing but a cautious conduct for the human mind when it is connected with experience.

Such a conception of an experimental reason, which is not deprived of greatness, does stand, provided it is not examined too closely. And we could say that the eighteenth century tells the story of the more or less perceptible fractures that will gradually break it up. Of course, Hume's bold attack on it will be repelled, with a seeming success, as proceeding from excessive metaphysics. But it is not difficult to find out that its own advocates, when they undertake its defense or illustration, are promoting ideas or values that do not agree with it.

One of the first critiques that did not come from the Cartesian party was expressed by the young George Berkeley in his *Treatise concerning the Principles of Human Knowledge* (1710) (§§101–10).[11] Experimental reason fosters scepticism.

It makes a virtue of the impossibility of knowing the essence of things, but thereby it owns that things cannot be known. Now, a phenomenal knowledge is not a real knowledge since it is satisfied with introducing some regularity or uniformity between phenomena: general connections that are laid down by it derive entirely from the various operations of the human mind on its own ideas and cannot be taken as the laws of nature. Of course, it is worth developing natural philosophy because it gives us a sense of generality (which is to be severely controlled) and it extends our prospect beyond what is present and near to us, thanks to analogies and agreements; but it cannot pretend to know real causes. Indeed, it proves, in spite of itself, that there are no efficient causes. The critique of essence is right insofar as it destroys the current opinion that everything includes within itself the cause of its properties, and it does not make sense to come back to the old Aristotelian physics or to tip into the Leibnizian metaphysics of identity. Thus, if we consider the relation between what we call a cause and what we call an effect, as long as we do not rise up to the true concept of causation, the concept of final causes, we have nothing else but two ideas or two terms, regularly connected, and as such we can say that the first one is for our mind the sign of the second one, which it does not explain but only indicates. Natural philosophers are grammarians. Natural science is a kind of language that does not give the reason of things but is very useful for the improvement of our understanding and the ordinary conduct of our lives. All this is of service to Berkeley's spiritualism since 'that [observations and experiments] are of use to mankind, and enable us to draw any general conclusions, is not the result of any immutable habitudes, or relations between things themselves, but only of God's goodness and kindness to men in the administration of the world' (*Principles*, §107). The whole argument looks backwards and forwards at the same time: on the one hand, it defines true reason as the ability to embrace final causes, whereas one of the most immediate effects of modern science had been to shake down the old Aristotelian superiority of final causes upon the other kinds of causation in scientific explanation; on the other hand, it shows that in experimental reason there are on the subjective side a mere empirical behaviour and, on the formal side, a nominalistic use of signs (warranted by God), which is the only foundation for the generality and necessity of the supposed efficient causes.

David Hume completes on a general scale and in a much more lucid way (as to the sceptical consequences) what Berkeley had begun to do. It is not easy to sum up his own conception of reason because his use of the term is unsteady, but such an ambiguity can be held as the sign that the common concept is broken to pieces by his scepticism: the various meanings of reason that previous authors held could still coexist with one another; now they are no longer reconcilable.

The first meaning, which is doubtless the most easily characterized, is reason as reasoning or demonstration.[12] All the objects of human understanding are relations, and the whole stock of relations may be divided into two kinds, the relations of ideas and matters of fact. Whereas the latter are known by experience and are mainly causal, the former, which bear on qualities or quantities and not on existences or events, are discoverable by mere inspection of the mind when it compares the given ideas. The agreement or disagreement of ideas can be perceived either by an immediate intuition or by demonstration. Reason will be this province of abstract and exact inference or pure knowledge ruled by the law of contradiction and, in this respect, will be mainly concerned with mathematics. On the contrary, any proposition concerning facts or phenomena must rely on experience. This great division between rational demonstration and experimental reasoning (which is founded on mere constant empirical conjunctions of phenomena) is quite fundamental because it draws a line between two kinds of knowledge in which the understanding does not act in the same way. And if it keeps mathematics safe from the problems surrounding causal inferences, it opens a gap that cannot be filled at the core of modern science for this science is mathematical *and* experimental: What relationship can be established between mathematical reasoning that bears on ideas or signs and that is governed only by logic and causal inferences, which rest on a mere regularity of phenomena? How is it possible to apply the logical necessity of reasoning to phenomena that are linked by a mere conjunction? How could the very same science be rational on the one hand and experimental (that is, nonrational) on the other?

But before considering causal inferences, let us examine abstract demonstrations (see Hume, *Treatise of Human Nature*, 1.4.1). Mathematical (and other forms of) reasoning is rational since, by comparing two or more ideas, we can say whether they are consistent or not and whether the second one is a necessary consequence of the first or can be substituted for it. But for us there are no grounds for such necessary relations other than the fact that we perceive them, either immediately or by following the various steps of reasoning. And if we say that demonstrative sciences are ruled by certain and infallible rules, we have to perceive and apply these rules. Thus reason can be said to be the faculty of the human understanding by which it seizes the truth of analytic relations. But when we perceive these relations or apply these rules, we may be mistaken without knowing that we are mistaken, chiefly in the complex reasoning of abstract sciences. Reason, as a human faculty, is the cause of truth, but the relationship between a cause and its effect is never perfect and therefore, even in pure knowledge, certainty degenerates into probability since we must constantly add a second judgment concerning our perception of relations to the judgment concerning the relations themselves. And if we want to check our actual reasoning by applying rules (for instance, by checking a reckoning by using another reckoning), we will control a probability by using another probability. Thus Locke's right reason loses its self-confidence. If we say that human reason is a natural power and that we have no other resources but to commit our reasoning to its good disposition, we correct our first judgment derived from the nature of the object by using another judgment derived from the nature of the understanding. But it is a general experience that the human mind does fall into error. Thus we introduce another uncertainty and so on. At the end, there would remain nothing of the original probability.

But it is worse if we turn to causal inferences (i.e., what makes up most of common sense or of the science of nature and informs us of existences and objects that are beyond our actual experience). Since a causal inference is not an a priori reasoning because its truth rests upon experience and not upon our perception of the agreement or disagreement of ideas, any cause being able to produce any effect whatever, we must allow that logical reason is not the ground of its truth. You can consider the idea of the cause and the idea of the effect by themselves and will never find out why the cause produces the effect. Therefore, let us examine whether experience offers a sufficient reason or rational foundation for deriving causal consequences. Causation imports the idea of a necessary connection between the two objects, which are said to be the cause and the effect. Only such a necessary and universal connection could be a sufficient foundation for all our predictions, for we can predict an existence of which we do not have actual experience or an event that has not yet happened if and only if it is necessary that such an existence should be produced and such an event should happen. Now, all that we know by experience is that the two objects are contiguous (that the one is prior to the other), and both of them can thus be conjoined into a constant experience. Still, never will such a constant conjunction be held as a necessary connection. In a word, neither by demonstration nor by experience can the principle of necessary connection be justified; therefore our causal inferences are deprived of rational justification. But we do infer causally. Therefore, our causal inferences are not rational: we cannot give any reason that it is '*necessary*, that every thing whose existence has a beginning, shou'd also have a cause' and why we may 'conclude, that such particular causes must *necessarily* have such particular effects' (*Treatise*, 1.3.2.14–15, SBN 78). Leibniz's principle of reason has lost its evidence.

But since it is impossible to demonstrate by a priori reasons or to infer from experience why a cause is always necessary for any existence or event and is always followed by the same effect, the only thing we can do is to inquire how we causally infer how our belief that the sun will rise tomorrow is produced and how a viable and consistent system of experience is gradually made up. Thereby, we can get an explanation of our experimental reasoning, but such an explanation is irrational and sceptical. It is irrational because it plainly falls into a vicious circle: causal inferences are causally explained; constant connection is the cause of our inference, but certainly not its reason, since we cannot draw from mere generality the necessity principle, which would be a sufficient foundation; our mind changes generality into necessity by the obscure effect of imagination applied to constant experience; and our inferences are habits. All that we can say is that causation is an unfathomable principle of the imagination. Hume's theory is also sceptical since the mind cannot have a rational insight into its own operations but only knows their internal causes by the experience that it gets from its theoretical practice. Of course, this practice may be said to be natural, but by nature we mean nothing but an original and incomprehensible fact. The old complicity between reason and nature has now disappeared, both on the objective and the subjective sides: reason is no longer the set of first principles that could be called natural because they were the principles of the real world itself, nor the clear and distinct power of the mind to infer and to conclude while justifying its inferences and conclusions. What becomes of reason when necessity and sufficiency are no longer paired?

All our demonstrations degenerate into probabilities (that is, into causal inferences) when we try to have the proof of their certainty; all our causal inferences are the product of the imagination and a habit that moves us to draw conclusions concerning existences and events of which we do not have an actual experience and to lay down laws of nature. But one must not infer from these claims that Hume's epistemology is irrational. First, as in every scepticism, his critique of reason and nature is rational right through. Secondly, as there is in his philosophy a positive doctrine or explanation of the experimental mind, so we can find an original and positive conception of reason.

It might appear that an empiricist and sceptical philosophy is unable to promote a theory of reason. However, such a philosophy (and this fact will be acknowledged by Kant) is far better equipped to delineate the problem of reason. It makes it impossible to deal with reason metaphysically and to mistake it for the law of nature, the order of things, or God's primitive reason and will. Therefore, reason is only the power of rules. But what is the foundation of this power? Whereas Locke thought that it was enough to say that reason is the nature of man, Hume has shown that this nature is effective, but irrational, since it is an instinct. He has also shown that there is no empirical conception of reason. Should we say with Kant that Hume asked a good question but was unable to give the answer? As a matter of fact, Hume gives an answer consonant with his explanation of causal inferences. The rules of reason cannot be rationally justified, but it can be explained how the human mind comes to frame and exert rules.

Consider inferences. The mind is unceasingly determined to infer effects from causes and to set laws, and we observe that common sense multiplies such laws and is usually more dogmatic than it should be. Where a conclusion should be taken as only probable or partial, common sense makes it general and even necessary. 'An Irishman cannot have wit, and a Frenchman cannot have solidity' (*Treatise*, 1.3.13.7, SBN 146). Carried away by the imagination (that is, by human nature), common sense is subject to errors of this kind. Nevertheless, men are able to form general rules strong enough to influence and correct their first judgments derived from habit and experience. Otherwise, there would be no difference between the grossest common sense and the most refined scientific or philosophical mind. Past experience, associated with imagination, leads the mind to belief. But belief is susceptible to several degrees of probability according to whether past experience is incomplete, contradictory, or more or less similar; besides, a causal reasoning may include many circumstances that may be more or less important for the production of the effect. Either naturally or by education, we may be heedful of these variations and disposed to be cautious in our reasoning. But, we can go further and, not satisfied with being prudent, we can form rules by a reflection on the operations of our own mind and declare that the human understanding must take into account the degree of perfection of past experience and accordingly proportionate its assent. These reflective rules can gradually gain influence if we are willing to delay our first judgments. But this influence on the imagination is not derived from principles other than those on which all judgments concerning causes and effects depend. Reflective rules are formed from experience and proceed by a natural determination or transition, just like other rules or laws. Accordingly, the opposition or the conflict is not between what would be a pure reason and a natural imagination but between two propensities of our mind, which are of the same nature but related in such a way that the second one regulates and corrects the first. In his *Enquiry Concerning Human Understanding*, Hume increases the power and enlarges the role of this critical reason (although it remains natural and not rational) so as to have it cut short metaphysical disputes on liberty and necessity, provide a methodology to weigh human testimony, fight against superstition, and narrow the sphere of human knowledge to abstract reasoning concerning quantity or number and experimental inferences concerning matters of fact and existence.[13]

One can imagine how such a paradoxical conception of reason was received by most of Hume's contemporaries. It appeared all the more scandalous as he claimed to offer a science of the human mind both so close to the principles that many philosophers were willing to accept it and yet so far from them in its sceptical consequences. Let us consider Hume's moral philosophy as a last example. Following Francis Hutcheson, who had confuted Locke's claim that moral propositions could be demonstrated, Hume asserts that morality is founded on a moral sense and that we do not know our duties by deducing them from rational principles or from a universal and eternal order. So far, he is adopting the prevailing doctrine of morals of his time. But, he takes this doctrine literally: not being a moral principle, reason is quite indifferent to morality. 'Tis not contrary to reason to prefer the destruction of the whole world to the scratching of my finger' (*Treatise*, 2.3.3.6, SBN 416). Being the mere faculty of knowing by demonstration or knowledge, it can say what is true or false but not what is right or wrong. 'Laudable or blameable, therefore, are not the same with reasonable or unreasonable' (3.1.1.10, SBN 458). Such a saying is not so easily heard. But, moreover, reason is not only indifferent but also morally powerless: it is not a motive for any action. Experience shows that reason is efficient only by the influence of our judgments upon our actions: thanks to reasoning, our passions can go from the ends to the means, extend from one object to another, and so forth, but reason does not have any direct power over our decisions, even if reflection and deliberation precede these decisions. The supposed conflict between passion and reason is a fancy raised by philosophers. 'Reason is, and ought only to be the slave of the passions, and can never pretend to any other office than to serve and obey them' (2.3.3.4, SBN 415). Of course, moralists will oppose such a statement and say that it may be true that reason is the slave of the passions (and moralists are used to beginning with this sad observation), but one cannot allow that reason ought to be the slave of the passions. At least, one will say, Hume grants that morals do rest upon a moral sense. But there is an ambiguity. By moral sense, one usually means both a natural determination to good conduct and conscience, in such a way that conscience, being the clear and distinct representation of our duties, appears to be the foundation, and one will say the rational foundation, of our inclination for what is right. Hume does not allow this kind of disguised rationalism: it is true that we naturally approve or blame men's actions, but we cannot know the reasons of our approval or blame. All that we can know by an empirical inquiry, by inferences derived from the observation of men's behavior, are the causes that make us approve or blame. For instance, to say that we approve certain actions because they are useful to ourselves or to others is to say that utility is the cause (known by experience) that makes us approve such actions and nothing more; a cause is not a reason.

The best opponents of this devastating scepticism tried to answer Hume's challenge by philosophical reasoning (and not by insults, as many did). The greatest of these philosophers was Thomas Reid, whose main argument, displayed in his *Inquiry into the Human Mind* (1764) and his two books, *Essays on the Intellectual Powers of Man* (1785) and *Essays on the Active Powers of Man* (1788), can be summarized as follows.[14] Hume's scepticism is the consequence of an excessive rationalism that requires every proposition to be founded on a reason (that is, on an antecedent proposition) and every principle to be rationally justified. There exist first principles that cannot be explained by reason except by saying that they depend on the primitive constitution of our nature or God's will – which is not a real explanation. But these principles are known by common sense. Any philosophical inquiry must accept being kept within certain limits and acknowledge that there are two distinct intellectual faculties: reason for deduced truths and common sense for primary truths.

> The defects and blemishes in the received philosophy concerning the mind, which have most exposed it to the contempt and ridicule of sensible men, have chiefly been owing to this: That the votaries of this Philosophy, from a natural prejudice in her favour, have endeavoured to extend her jurisdiction beyond its just limits, and to call to her bar the dictates of Common Sense. (*Inquiry*, 19)

Philosophy has to assign its legitimate province to each faculty and reconcile them. There is no steady reconciliation without subordination: reason (and therefore philosophy) is to be subordinated to common sense. Strictly speaking, common sense is the intuitive perception of first principles, which is common to all men. But although these principles can be perceived by everybody, not all of them have the same evidence. Besides, prejudices, education, and philosophical excess can obscure them. Moreover, it is one thing for the mind to live spontaneously in their evidence and another thing to reflect them and express them as propositions. It is the task of philosophy to make these clear principles distinct and give the criteria by which they can be recognized. To ensure this investigation, philosophy will turn to the experimental method: after a careful observation of facts and an accurate analysis of experiences, it will draw out general laws, the highest laws to be reached being the first principles of common sense.

One easily perceives the advantage offered by the experimental method: since principles are derived from experience, a rational foundation is not to be searched for them. Common sense is a general fact, and a fact is not to be discussed. But, just as easily, one may perceive the weakness of the whole argument: a general fact has no evidence other than being a fact, and such evidence is blind, even if it is certain. Now, common sense is here considered as intuitively evident. And it is difficult to make Reid's conception consistent: common sense is both the *terminus a quo* and the *terminus ad quem*, what is immediately and so clearly known by everybody that it makes the critique of every excessive rationalism possible, and what is inductively discovered by philosophy. Is the evidence of first principles naturally given or derived from experience? The primary truth of common sense seems to depend on the mixture of an a priori self-evidence and an a posteriori certainty. By a kind of reciprocal contamination, on the one hand, general laws, although they cannot be said to be self-evident since they are derived from experience, nevertheless are so since the mind constantly relies on their original certainty; and on the other hand, first principles, which are self-evident, nevertheless must be tested against some philosophers who want to give them a reason.

Even if it was not very coherent, Common Sense philosophy, which was mainly Scottish, was very influential because it offered a balanced and moderate solution to the problem of reason and, while opposing the sceptical threat, could get along with the new sensibility that was emerging. It reigned in Great Britain beyond the end of the eighteenth century; in France, it more or less easily mixed with the philosophy of the Idéologues, who were Condillac's heirs; and, in Germany, it became an important part of the intellectual environment and temporarily offered a kind of rival option to Kant's criticism.

That such a quiet and mixed rationalism could have been so influential means that the other European countries had followed a path similar to the intellectual evolution of Great Britain. Indeed, we find such an apparent but frail balance among the French philosophers and encyclopedists. As early as 1746, in his *Essai sur l'origine des connaissances humaines*, Condillac picks up Locke's teaching in a French context, marked by the Cartesian tradition of *l'art de penser*.[15] 'Reason . . . is nothing other than our knowledge of the manner in which we must govern the operations of the soul' (I.ii.11, §92) in the search for truth and the conduct of our life. And this knowledge is obtained through the careful study of our faculties and their proportionate objects. Thus understood, reason is less a distinct faculty than the harmonized and measured exercise of all the operations and actions of the mind or, so to say, the mind methodized. The evidence of reason that confirms abstract inference and rests upon the identity of terms or the substitution of identical terms must conspire with the evidence of fact that provides the mind with all its empirical materials and is fortified by the internal evidence of sentiment. Condillac's doctrine emphasizes the role of signs, linguistic or not, that are the greatest cause of our progress in the search for truth but also of our most lasting errors. Five years after Condillac's *Essai*, in his *Discours préliminaire de l'Encyclopédie*, d'Alembert offers the natural and methodical history of all the operations of the mind, a *généalogie* that goes from mere sensation to the most abstract science (algebra, which is a science applied to signs).[16] Reason is of course for d'Alembert, who is a mathematician, the faculty of reasoning, mainly employed in abstract physics and mathematics, but it is also the human mind, made coherent in its various operations, able to entertain the correct relationship with reality, adjusted to the progress of civilization or society, and providing the steady foundation that the *Encyclopédie* needs.[17]

If one looks more closely at this reasonable conception of reason, fractures are visible. For instance, deep differences can be found behind the seeming and official agreement between the two editors of the *Encyclopédie*, Diderot and d'Alembert, as early as their first collaboration. Whereas d'Alembert cautiously claims that it is possible to link all the moments and operations of the mind into a system, by a continuous chain that corresponds to the chain of beings, Diderot widens the gap between the mathematical sciences and the empirical sciences and brings to light what will be a deeper and deeper divorce between human reason and the being of things. Mathematical sciences can be certain and accurate because they operate upon signs, not upon things, and since there is no continuous way that could be laid out from things to signs by a correct abstraction or from signs to things by a lawful deduction, these sciences are merely formal and play with identical propositions: they will soon come to an end. On the contrary, as is explained by Diderot in *Pensées sur l'interprétation de la nature* (1753), the physical sciences that deal with nature need a new method better fitted to the infinite variety of things and using qualitative associations that men of genius (and no longer of reason) are able to catch, owing to an immediate and practical contact with nature.[18] Thus, Diderot joins an argument that Georges Buffon had developed in his *Discours sur la manière d'étudier et de traiter l'histoire naturelle* (1749) to defend the worthiness of his own science.[19]

Still more ambiguous is Rousseau's rationalism, where nature or conscience (*la voix de la nature*) and reason are now opposed, now reconciled. Reason is a natural power, but it develops, for better or for worse, through the education of individuals and the progress of society and civilization. Often, it serves passions, helps to create artificial and useless goods, and pretends to take hold of objects that are beyond its reach. Therefore, reason must be developed but controlled. Rousseau does not think that it is able to rule itself insofar as it cannot alone conduct our minds and our lives, being mainly a speculative faculty. Duties, but also truths, must be known, but they also must be assented by our heart. And this faculty of assent is *le sentiment intérieur* or, in the moral field, conscience. For instance, in religious matters, as le Vicaire savoyard explains in *Émile* (Book IV), there are truths concerning God's existence and nature and the origin of the world that can be decided only by an internal approval.[20] Thus, our *sentiment intérieur* directs us in matters that are beyond reason; it marks the limits of rational activity; it governs reason itself by assenting to the conclusions that are rationally proved; it informs us of our duties; and being both a love for order and a love for ourselves that is not corrupted, it is able to fight against the transports of passion and the excesses of reason. Rousseau is not an irrationalist: all that is contrary to reason must be rejected, but reason is subordinated to a more essential, more deeply rooted power – *la voix de la nature.*

As is usual in every study concerning the eighteenth century, it appears that so many things are common to so many philosophers that the actual differences among these philosophers are not always easily stated, as if they were counterbalanced by a kind of shared intellectual behaviour that makes such differences less important even when they are real. But this intellectual coherence and compactness is not systematic; you get the feeling of it when you go by association from an idea to another, from an argument to another, or from a value to another. It is Kant's greatness to have been able to recapture all these contents and to have tried to reorder them according to a new rational and systematic principle, thus being both faithful and unfaithful to the spirit of his time.

Kant's first act was to restore the right of pure reason: whatever the historical condition of philosophy may be, reason has the right to set up its tribunal and to declare its judgment, especially upon its own achievements. This means not only that reason can know itself but that it can govern and rule the human mind. Such a critical knowledge is entirely a priori and proceeds in such a way that reason is at the same time the author, the main object, and the means of the critique. Let us add that its right is also its duty.

Kant's second act was to appreciate the condition of knowledge, marked by the disorders of metaphysics, which are all the more disgraceful as the success of mathematics and physics is a patent fact. It appears that reason, carried away by its own power or its nature, which prompts it to pretend to an absolute knowledge of reality, has not worked out the critique of its own right to know: it dogmatically pronounces itself on matters that are beyond its limits, falls into contradictions, and by a violent reaction generates the most radical scepticism (Hume's philosophy). For reason, the present crisis of philosophy is the empirical proof of the necessity of a reflection on its own power: what are the a priori limits of all human knowledge? Such a rational appraisement is possible because, on the other hand, the mathematical and experimental science of the time proves the human mind can know and does know.

Kant's third act was to give a coherent answer to the various questions that had been raised and that endangered the rational unity of the understanding. For instance, the division between mathematics (Hume's relations of ideas) and experimental physics (causal inferences) could be overcome if, more generally, one tried to define the limits of human knowledge: we are able to know phenomena only, not things in themselves (that is, what is supposed to be at the foundation of phenomena) and apart from mere analytical judgments, which do not enlarge knowledge, any science whatever is made up of synthetic judgments, where the mind must get out of itself and rely on something else to establish truth. But, synthetic judgments are either a priori or a posteriori: the 'something else' is either space and time, which are the a priori forms of sensible intuition (the only intuition we can have), and then we have to deal with mathematics, or experience, and then we have to deal with physics.

The decisive question to be answered was Hume's question concerning causation, the Scottish philosopher arguing from the impossibility to found causal reasoning to conclude that most of the operations of the understanding are irrational. According to the right of reason, we must search the conditions of possibility of our experimental inferences. The matter of these inferences comes from experience and is made up of sense data. But their form, such as is expressed in the laws of nature, being universal and necessary, cannot be empirically derived. Thus, to satisfy reason, we must say that causation is a first and a priori principle of the understanding, founding the necessity of all synthetic and a posteriori judgments. And Kant, in the 'Transcendental Analytic' of the *Kritik der reinen Vernunft*, draws up the table of these first principles that are the formal conditions of every exercise of the understanding and the corresponding table of the first and a priori concepts or categories.[21] But there remains a difficulty over which Hume had stumbled: For if these categories or principles cannot be derived from experience, it is also true that they are mere logical requirements by themselves and that we are not allowed to make a transcendent use of them (that is, to consider that we get from them a real knowledge of things in themselves). Experience is needed. But how is it possible that a priori forms of the understanding could be related to the matter of fact? This is the core of the whole argument, what Kant called the transcendental deduction and what makes up the most difficult part of the *Kritik*, because reason has to explain rationally how, in intellectual judgments, it can relate to something that it is not: reality. Leibniz, by the law of identity and the law of reason, assumed that reason and reality were one and the same thing. But it was, according to Kant, a metaphysical postulate. Indeed, our knowledge is merely phenomenal: our understanding applies to sense data. And this is the mark of our finitude.

To think is to judge (that is, to join two terms according to a certain logical or rational form and pose this joining as existing). This is the task of the understanding, and Kantian critique determines the limits of knowledge by the possibility of experience. But judgments or propositions must in turn be connected within a theory or a systematic form; otherwise, all our judgments would remain scattered and would not make up a science. This requirement, inherited by Kant from Leibniz and Wolff, leads to a narrower conception of reason: reason is the faculty of thinking systematically. But just as the synthetic form of the understanding rests upon first concepts (the categories), the systematic form of reason depends on first and a priori notions or ideas that are the thought of the unity that can rule the systematic totality. There are three such ideas: the ideas of the self, of the world, and of God. They give rise to principles that govern the operations of the understanding. These rational ideas do not apply to things but to judgments; nevertheless, indirectly, they have to deal with reality and they are the notion of the totality of things. Therefore, they cannot be held to be mere logical functions and they have a transcendental meaning. But here no transcendental deduction is possible: the *Kritik* cannot show how the ideas apply to empirical matter, as it does for the categories. And, in the 'Transcendental Dialectic' of the *Kritik*, Kant strives to lay out a path between a pure logical reason, only concerned with the forms of deduction, and the dogmatic reason, which claims to know the first principles of things. Reason fixes up the limits of the understanding, but, according to the nature of every limit, can have a look above these limits; if it cannot lead to a metaphysical science of the self, of the world, or of God, it can nevertheless entertain the thought of such objects and regress in idea to the unconditioned. Such is the ambivalence of Kant's concept of speculative reason: it establishes the finitude of the human mind, but it makes it thinkable and in this respect goes beyond finitude.

Speculative reason is merely regulative: it is not able to draw out from itself the absolute truth of things in general. But this synthesis of reason and reality is achieved by practical reason. In the moral field, reason refers to its own legislation independently of any empirical condition since duty is a representation whose obligation cannot be subordinated to material considerations. By representing the universal and necessary form of moral law, practical reason objectively commands our sensible inclinations, gathers their particular objects in the rational idea of the *summum bonum* but in such a way that happiness is always subordinated to virtue, and, more generally, subjects human history to the duty of achieving the kingdom of ends. But, if it is to be allowed that practical reason is morally determining, a metaphysical condition must be granted. Of course, it can be said that, since I ought to do something, I can do it, but so far I only express the obligation where my will is to obey the moral law. But can I? Therefore, practical reason makes sense if, and only if, as Kant bluntly states at the beginning of the *Kritik der praktischen Vernunft*, the reciprocal and synthetic implication of moral law and liberty is posed.[22] By representing the moral law as conscience, practical reason, appealing to man's liberty, gives him the power to create a world conformable to the law of duty and respectful towards mankind, a world where, at last, happiness would get along with virtue.

Thus is defined a new concept of reason – critical reason. This concept means that human reason, from the very crisis in which it is immersed and that has been developing into an endless struggle between dogmatism and scepticism, is able to set itself as a tribunal of its own failures and to determine the conditions of its own relationship to the being of things. In so doing, human reason discovers its own finitude and marks its own limits; it says not only what they are but also what they ought to be. And it appears to be a ruling principle. Of course, the only thing that it can govern is itself, and, when determining the finitude of human nature, it is not able to change it. Since we know only phenomena, the possibility of metaphysical knowledge must be repudiated and science must be restricted to an experimental knowledge of nature. However, in the practical field, reason is not tied to such a limitation since morals command what we ought to do, and what we ought to do is independent of what we are; in the observation of duty, human reason is related to nothing except itself. The essence of moral laws is rationality. Therefore, men's actions are the true territory of reason, insofar as these actions ought to be conformable to the law. And there, its sovereignty is absolute. By extension, it will be widened to concrete individual human lives and even to collective human history.

This outstanding conception of reason spread out immediately and widely. But a closer consideration would show that it is not free of difficulties. Indeed, it was passionately opposed, discussed, or agreed to in Germany before and after 1800. Nonetheless, a new era was beginning. Now, if one looks backwards for a last survey of the eighteenth century, it seems that this many-sided story of reason tells how man, who was still at first a part of the world or of the Creation, the rationality of which he tried to discover with his own reason, gradually drew away from it and established a specifically human world, the world of history, morals, and politics. And this may happen if man understands that, thanks to reason, he has a power over nature whose efficiency is increased when its limitations are acknowledged, and that his real power is over himself and his own actions. Common Sense philosophy may mask this evolution. But at the end of the eighteenth century, and maybe still now, the alternative seems to be between a sceptical reason, conscious of its limits but attempting to manage a viable and comfortable world for mankind, and a practical reason attempting to draw out from itself a new moral and political order that could be substituted for nature.

NOTES

1 See John Locke, *An Essay Concerning Human Understanding* (1690), ed. P. H. Nidditch, in the *Clarendon Edition* (1975), IV.xvii; and *Essays on the Law of Nature* (written in 1663), trans. and ed. W. von Leyden (Oxford, 1954), ch. 4.
2 John Toland, *Christianity not Mysterious* (London, 1696).
3 Joseph Butler, *The Analogy of Religion, Natural and Revealed, to the Constitution and Course of Nature* (1736), in *Works*, ed. J. H. Bernard, 2 vols. (London, 1900), vol. 2.

4 Gottfried Wilhelm Leibniz, *Nouveaux essais sur l'entendement humain* [1704], eds. A. Robinet and H. Schepers, in *Sämtliche Schriften*, Reihe 6, Vol. 6.

5 Leibniz, *Essais de théodicée sur la bonté de Dieu, la liberté de l'homme et l'origine du mal* (1710), in *Philosophischen Schriften*, 6: 21–462, §44; see also his *Principes de la nature et de la grace fondés en raison et principes de la philosophie ou Monadologie*, ed. A. Robinet (Paris, 1954), §§31–6.

6 Alexander Pope, *An Essay on Man*, in *Poetical Works*, ed. H. Davis (Oxford, 1966).

7 Pierre Bayle, *Dictionnaire historique et critique*, 2 vols. (Rotterdam, 1697).

8 François Marie Arouet de Voltaire, *Candide ou L'optimisme* (Paris and Geneva, 1759).

9 Isaac Newton, *Philosophiae naturalis principia mathematica* (London, 1687; 3rd edn. 1726), Bk. 3.

10 Leibniz, *Opuscules et fragments inédits*, ed. L. Couturat (Paris, 1903).

11 George Berkeley, *A Treatise concerning the Principles of Human Knowledge,* in *Works*, eds. A. A. Luce and T. E. Jessop, 9 vols. (Edinburgh, 1948–57), vol. 2 (1949).

12 David Hume, *A Treatise of Human Nature* [1739–40], eds. D. F. Norton and M. J. Norton, in *The Clarendon Edition* (2000), 1.3.1.

13 Hume, *An Enquiry Concerning Human Understanding* [1748], ed. T. L. Beauchamp, in *The Clarendon Edition* (2000).

14 Thomas Reid, *An Inquiry into the Human Mind on the Principles of Common Sense*, ed. D. R. Brookes (Edinburgh, 1997); *Essays on the Intellectual Powers of Man*, eds. D. R. Brookes and K. Haakonssen (Edinburgh, 2002); *Essays on the Active Powers of Man*, in *Philosophical Works*, ed. W. Hamilton, 2 vols. in 1 (Edinburgh, 1895), vol. 2.

15 Étienne Bonnot de Condillac, *Essai sur l'origine des connaissances humaines*, in *Oeuvres philosophiques*, ed. G. Le Roy, 3 vols. (Paris, 1947–51), vol. 1, translated as *An Essay on the Origin of Human Knowledge*, trans. and ed. H. Aarsleff (Cambridge, 2001).

16 Jean le Rond d'Alembert, *Discours préliminaire de l'Encyclopédie* [1751], in *Oeuvres*, 5 vols. (Paris, 1821–2), vol. 1.

17 *Encyclopédie ou Dictionnaire raisonné des sciences, des arts et des métiers*, eds. D. Diderot and J. le Rond d'Alembert 35 vols. (Paris and Amsterdam, 1751–80).

18 Diderot, *Pensées sur l'interprétation de la nature* (Paris, 1753).

19 Georges Buffon, *Discours sur la manière d'étudier et de traiter l'histoire naturelle* (Paris, 1749).

20 Jean-Jacques Rousseau, *Émile ou De l'éducation* [1762], in *Oeuvres*, 4: 239–868.

21 Immanuel Kant, *Kritik der reinen Vernunft*, in Ak, vols. 3 and 4: A 65–292/B 90–349.

22 *Kritik der praktischen Vernunft*, in Ak 5: 1–163.

12

SUBSTANCES AND MODES, SPACE AND TIME

HEINER F. KLEMME

Discussion of the nature of substances, their relationships, and their interactions is at the heart of metaphysics. There seems to be no question of metaphysics which is not more or less obviously connected with the problem of substances: knowledge of the world, soul, and God, the relationship of body and soul, the freedom of the will and moral responsibility, the immortality of the soul, and the question of a first cause of being. Eighteenth-century conceptions of substances and modes and of space and time cannot be properly understood without an appreciation of the debates of the seventeenth century, particularly as they related to Descartes's philosophy.[1]

Starting from an Aristotelian definition, Descartes, in the *Meditationes de prima philosophia* (1641), understands substance as something existing for itself which cannot be expressed as a predicate of something else.[2] Assuming a methodically understood doubt, he finds in the *cogito* the epistemological basis of a *res cogitans*, an immaterial spiritual substance must be distinguished from the *res extensa*, which is understood as extensive and movable matter (31). Since all other substances can exist only with the assistance of God, the term 'substance' in its strict sense applies only to God, the eternal substance.[3] In the 'Third Meditation', even the certainty of the existence of the *res cogitans* is made to depend on the knowledge of God's existence.

With Descartes's new metaphysics, three basic questions are raised which came to dominate further debates concerning the nature and essence of substances. The first is how *res cogitans* and *res extensa* are interacting, the second refers to the religious and ethical consequences of the concept of substance, and the third relates to the growing success of physical theory and the experimental sciences, which seem to have no place for Descartes's theory of innate ideas. His dualism of incorporeal spiritual substance and material bodies was seen as particularly offensive in this respect, and both Thomas Hobbes and Baruch de Spinoza attempted to overcome Descartes's ontological dualism, albeit from two diametrically opposed viewpoints. Whereas Hobbes saw the concept of incorporeal substance as representing a *contradictio in adjecto*,[4] Spinoza, in his

Ethica ordine geometrico demonstrata, argued the pantheistic case. He there identifies the one substance – that is, God – with nature, so that knowledge of
nature is synonymous with knowledge of God. Thought and extension are thus
understood as attributes of one and the same substance.[5] In his first definitions, Spinoza understands substance as its own cause, he, too, falling back on
a definition of Aristotle.[6] Attributes represent that part of a substance 'which
the understanding recognises as belonging to its essence'. Modes, on the other
hand, are 'affections' caused by substance. In the end, God is the substance,
'consisting of infinite attributes, each of which expresses eternal and infinite
essence' (Pt. I, Prop. 11, p. 37). Only God, as a necessarily existing substance, is
free, since He alone acts according to the laws of His own nature (Pt. I, Prop. 17,
p. 44). 'God is the efficient cause, not only of the existence of things, but also
of their essence' (Pt. I, Prop. 25, p. 49). This theory seems to offend against
traditional theology and ethics. If human beings are mere modes of infinite
substance, then their free will is abolished and they cannot ultimately be held
responsible for their actions.

Spinoza's concept of God and nature as one self-causing substance obviously
negates a causal interaction between the objects of daily experience. Nicolas
Malebranche, in his *De la recherche de la vérité*, also denies an immanent effective
causality between substances, but his occasionalism derives causal interaction
between finite substances from an extramundane divine agency.[7]

John Locke, in *An Essay Concerning Human Understanding* (1690), deals with
substance as part of a critique of knowledge. Not only does he deny the widely
held doctrine of innate ideas, but in questioning the origin, certainty, and extent
of human knowledge,[8] he breaks with traditional metaphysics and its rationally
structured substance theory. No previous philosopher had so clearly shown the
way forward to the eighteenth century's concern with human cognitive capacity,
a concern of significant importance, not least for the development of empirical
psychology and anthropology.

Through Locke's analyses, the understanding, feeling, and acting person is
released from the burden of ontology and discovers himself as a being who
bases knowledge only upon ideas gained through experience. This immediately
establishes the impossibility of knowing real substances as carriers or causes of
ideas.[9] Substances are known only as nominal, not real, essences. One result of
this is a new understanding of the relationship between thinking and extended
substance, for if we cannot know the real nature of the objects of our experience,
then it is not impossible that God has granted matter the power to think.[10]

According to Locke, all our ideas originate in sensation or reflection and the
primary, as distinct from secondary, qualities 'are modifications of matter in the
Bodies that cause such Perceptions in us' (*Essay*, II.viii.7). Qualities are powers

of something which produces ideas in our mind. The secondary qualities which, like the primary ones, derive from sensation are engendered in us by specific forces in the substances. Thus bodies have the primary qualities of solidity, extension, figure, and mobility or rest, as well as number. Colours, sounds, and taste are secondary qualities (II.viii.9–10). Space and time represent simple ideas because there is a '*sensible Point*' (II.xv.9). Since a vacuum is conceivable, it is also possible (II.iv.3).

Although there is no idea of substance among our perceptions, an 'I know not what' understanding of substance must be regarded as proven since all our ideas need a bearer. Logic and psychology force us to accept coherent and uniform substances as bearers of our ideas though we cannot know them. Locke tries to deal with this fact through the concept of nominal essence, according to which we accept those qualities that appear together in our experience as belonging to one substance. Nominal substances, together with the ideas of modes and relations, are complex ideas.

The chief metaphysical opponent of Locke's empiricism was Gottfried Wilhelm Leibniz, according to whom the monad is a spontaneously active, simple substance with no extension or parts.[11] Against Locke's dictum that there are no perceptions without consciousness, Leibniz argues that there are also unconscious ideas of which the monads can become aware in empirical apperception. The alternative of conscious or unconscious ideas was among the most intensively debated theories throughout the eighteenth century.[12]

Leibniz's most influential follower was Christian Wolff, who undertook a momentous systematisation of metaphysics. He divides metaphysics into *metaphysica generalis*, or ontology, which treats being in general, and *metaphysica specialis*, which deals with world (cosmology), soul (rational and empirical psychology), and God (natural and revealed religion). Wolff also distinguishes between the theories of *influxus physicus*, occasionalism, and pre-established harmony as the only possible explanations of the interaction of substances[13] without, however, clearly adopting the Leibnizian position. In the end, Wolff believes that the doctrine of pre-established harmony is only the best hypothesis available to explain the relationship between body and mind (psycho-physical parallelism).[14]

In his *Ontologia*,[15] Wolff follows Leibniz's definition of simple substances: they are undivided, lack extension, are indivisible, and occupy no space (see §§673–9). He also deals in this work with the concepts of space and time. Unlike Kant's later theory of space and time as purely sensible forms of intuition, Wolff's theory makes no separation between space and time on the one hand and the concepts of the understanding in the narrower sense (causality, substance, and so on) on the other. The transition from sensibility to intellectual concepts is still seen as gradual.

According to Wolff, things that are simultaneous and external to us are separate from each other because different things cannot be understood as modalities of a single thing or substance (*Vernünfftige Gedanken von Gott,* §45). In his section on empirical psychology, he appeals to the basic and indubitable fact that we are conscious of ourselves and of many things as 'outside ourselves' (§§1, 45). Things are conceived of as existing outside ourselves because we are conscious of them as objects existing separately from ourselves. Wolff does not mean by this that the possibility and reality of substances depend on an act of knowledge by the self-conscious subject. Rather, the thinking self encounters substances as parts of the world.

The idea of the separateness of objects leads to the idea of space. Space is the ordering of simultaneously existing things: '[T]here can be no space if there are no things to fill it: still, it is distinguished from these things (§17)' (§46). Position and space are external, not internal, characteristics of things because for Wolff it was an evident fact that things could occupy any position whatsoever in space without any alteration of their internal composition (see §§49, 50). Since all external objects are complex and made up of many parts, they must necessarily occupy space. 'When we imagine a manifold of separate things in one [thing], then we have a conception of extension in length, breadth and depth' (§53). Figure is thus understood as the boundary of extension (§54).

The concept or idea of time is arrived at when we recognise that some thing or other gradually is formed just as our thoughts are observed to follow upon one another (*Vernünfftige Gedanken von Gott,* §94). Without awareness of change, we could not imagine time, which is to be understood as an ordering of 'what follows one after another, so that if one takes something as the first, then something else is second and yet something else is third, and so on' (§94). But things do not change because they are in time (§98). While composite things gradually arise through time (see §100), a simple substance (such as the human intelligence) cannot arise over time (see §101).

Wolff's theory, which was later taken up by Alexander Gottlieb Baumgarten in his *Metaphysica* (1739),[16] was challenged as tautologous by Kant:

This definition . . . is tautologous. . . . If we imagine time and space we do not imagine a thing; rather, things can be imagined in time and space. Thought is thus important: that is why Wolff, too, thought that space and time do not exist, because they are not things, and so far he was right. But he takes them for objective conditions of things in themselves, which we dispute, regarding them rather as subjective conditions of sensible objects.[17]

Wolff's definition must not least be seen as tautologous since the definition of space refers to a time predicate ('simultaneous') and the definition of time refers to the separate existence of objects in space.

Whereas it is a conceptual truth that simple things exist because simple things are imperishable (see *Vernünfftige Gedanken von Gott*, §§76, 102, 106), composite things, according to Wolff, are composed of simple things and can therefore perish (§110). Human and animal souls are indeed similar to simple substances (and therefore imperishable); since, however, only the human soul has personality, it alone is immortal.[18] Simple things or substances have no shape, size, or internal movement and therefore fill no space. Bodies, on the other hand, do have these properties because they are composed of parts. 'That which gives a body extension and thus power of resistance is called matter' (§607; see also §§81–2).

Probably the most significant opponent of the Leibniz-Wolff school of philosophy in the pre-Kantian era was Christian August Crusius. Besides his criticism of the concept of sufficient reason, his attack on the doctrine of simple and composite substances is remarkable, though the latter contrasts with the former by being purely theoretical or speculative.[19]

In Chapter 7 of his *Entwurf der nothwendigen Vernunft-Wahrheiten* (1745),[20] 'Of the simple and the compound' (ch. 7, §§103–19), Crusius makes use of the distinction between 'ground of knowledge' (*Erkenntnisgrund*) and 'ground of being' (*Seinsgrund*). On this basis, he criticises the Leibniz-Wolff definition of the simple, which is said to consist in the 'absence of parts' (§105, p. 174). For him the decisive error is that the reality of a compound of parts is proven directly from the distinction between different parts of an idea or thought (see §105, p. 175). Crusius maintains that the essence of an object consists of various characteristics. The essence is simple 'when it is not possible to take away a part of it' (§107, p. 179). And a substance is simple 'when it is not composed of separable substances. Thus a simple substance is only a single metaphysical subject, which stands complete in itself' (§107, pp. 177–8). The point of this definition is that something which is single and complete need not necessarily exist without parts.

Related to this definition is the conception, also directed against Wolff, that simple substances exist 'in a specific *somewhere* or space' (§46, p. 74). If simple substances exist in space and thus have the quality of extension, a central distinction between thinking and bodily substance is removed. That does not, however, mean that all simple substances are material in nature. Ultimately, the division of simple substances is conceptually impossible since this would destroy their completeness and thus their existence. These reflections have the theologically objectionable result that the simple and unique substance, God, might consist of parts.

In this connection, Crusius's distinction between the mathematical and the philosophical points of view is of importance. In mathematics, one views 'the simple abstractum as magnitude' (*Entwurf*, §114, p. 183) along with its variations, modifications, and relations but disregards the things that have the magnitude. This leaves 'the concept of *space* and of being *external to other things*' (§114, p. 184). Space can be divided in thought, so that one eventually arrives at a mathematical point that no longer consists of parts. Mathematical extension is a 'mere concept' and not a 'real object' (§440, p. 855). However, what is possible in mental (that is, analytical) reflection cannot be translated into metaphysics because it would lead to the untenable conclusion that simple, indivisible substances exist. Considered in philosophical terms, 'simple' signifies a substance that can no longer be broken down into actual parts. In mathematical terms, this substance is extended and composite. 'Simple' can thus be understood in two different senses, which represent the difference between the merely conceivable and the actual.

According to Crusius, simple substances have force. A subject is inconceivable without a space which it occupies. From this Crusius concludes that the mathematically simple has no force. One of Crusius's three ontological arguments for the thesis that simple parts constituting a body are not simple in the mathematical sense states that if they were simple the phenomenon of motion could not be explained. In order to explain the movement of a composite, even the smallest parts must be capable of movement (see *Entwurf*, §119, p. 197). The simple substances constituting the body are therefore extended.

In his inaugural dissertation, *De mundi sensibilis atque intelligibilis forma et principiis* (1770), Kant challenges Crusius's thesis that '*to be nowhere* and *not to be*' mean the same thing. Based on his own theory of space and time, Kant charges Crusius with speaking nonsense.[21] Kant gets the basic idea of this critique and of his own theory of the virtual or 'derived' locality of simple mental substances from the German translation of Leonhard Euler's *Lettres à une princesse d'Allemagne* (1768–72).[22] Euler states that it is just as foolish to ask where the spirit or soul is located as to ask 'where an hour is located, although an hour is undoubtedly a something: it can also be something without being tied to a specific place' (Letter 92, 2: 4). The soul is not in any place because it is not extended; nevertheless, it exists. Certainly, in this world it can only operate in a place. According to Kant, the virtual place of a simple soul substance is given by the fact that it is attached to a body through which the soul actually receives sensory impressions. This point is central to the further development of Kantian philosophy for the human soul belongs to the *mundus sensibilis* by virtue of its perceptual forms of intuition – that is, space and time. As a free and spontaneous substance, however, it can determine itself as a member of the *mundus intelligibilis* in accordance with the moral law.[23] In the latter perspective, the soul disregards the restrictions to which its spontaneity is necessarily subjected in cognitive propositions.

When we trace the theory of substance in the authors who more or less directly adopted the Lockean 'way of ideas', the Irish philosopher George Berkeley's main work, *A Treatise concerning the Principles of Human Knowledge* (1710),[24] is the first to be considered. In his view, all our ideas originate in immaterial substances which he calls 'mind', 'spirit', 'soul', or 'my self'.[25] To be able to speak of a substance at all, we must, as Malebranche had already stressed, be able to perceive an activity. Since, however, ideas are completely passive, they cannot be substances. We have immediate awareness only of our own activity, and the immaterial spirit is the only cause of ideas and therefore a substance, while God as highest substance is the cause of all finite substances and ideas.

Berkeley defines the human soul as an 'incorporeal active substance or spirit', a 'simple, undivided, active being' (§§26–7). This being has an understanding which perceives the ideas called forth in us, ultimately by God, and it has a will capable of producing and connecting ideas. The fact that a created substance does not have the power to alter at will the empirically known laws of nature is clear proof that God is the cause of all (real) ideas of our senses (§§33, 90). All ideas deriving from the operation of the human will, on the other hand, are readily changeable (§30). The human soul itself is, however, 'absolutely incapable of annihilation' (§141).

If, as Berkeley maintains, the concept of matter is meaningless and self-contradictory (see §22), what about the reality of the physical world and our ordinary conviction that extended bodies exist in space? In his view, ideas are constituted and connected as if there were a material world. Berkeley does not question our ordinary convictions but only seeks to demonstrate that a material world independent of a thinking substance is impossible (see §90). Since it is epistemologically out of the question for something to exist without being perceived (*esse est percipi*) and material substances do have a form of existence, we must conclude that they exist in the mind of God (§3). However, that also means that the difference between substances and accidents in the physical world – between perception and the object of perception – is abolished since the idea no longer represents the physical world but coincides with it (in God's mind, of course).

This is a fundamental point in Berkeley's philosophy. In his view, nothing has done more to encourage scepticism, atheism, and fatalism than the distinction between things that exist independently of a mind that perceives them on the one hand, and ideas on the other (see §§87, 94). 'From what has been said, it follows, there is not any other substance than *spirit*, or that which perceives' (§7). Moreover, physical objects exist even when no human beings perceive them. The continuity of human experience is thus made totally dependent on a divine substance.

Berkeley mounts a similar critique of the theory of abstraction, which is also central to his theory of space and time. Of space he writes:

[W]hen we attempt to abstract extension and motion from all other qualities, and consider them by themselves, we presently lose sight of them, and run into great extravagancies. All which depend on a two-fold abstraction: first, it is supposed that extension may be abstracted from all other sensible qualities; and secondly, that the entity of extension may be abstracted from it being perceived. (§99)

Against this view, Berkeley maintains that all sensible qualities are equally real and that extended objects therefore always also have colour. No quality, however, can exist unperceived. Ultimately, however, we can know neither how colour and sound, nor figure, motion, or magnitude, arise (§102). This is connected with Berkeley's critique of the conception of a (Newtonian) absolute space: no space can exist independently of what we perceive through our senses. Moreover, we cannot even form an abstract idea of pure space (§116). Without the presence of a body or a movement, an experience of space is impossible. Moreover, we acquire our ideas of space and distance through touch, not vision.[26]

The basic theological motives in Berkeley's philosophy are evident in his critique of Newton's theory of absolute and pure space. If space, like time, could not be understood relatively, we would be faced with a dangerous dilemma: 'of thinking either that real space is God, or else that there is something beside God which is eternal, uncreated, infinite, indivisible, immutable' (*Principles*, §117).

With his concept of substance, Berkeley avoids Cartesian ontological dualism, and his direct realism of ideas gets around the problems connected with the Lockean distinction between primary and secondary qualities. But his own monistic conception of substance rests on theological assumptions which made his whole epistemology unconvincing. Probably no other eighteenth-century epistemology aroused such a flood of polemics and personal attacks. His contemporaries saw him as at once an eminently modern and an objectionable philosopher because he developed the sceptical implications of Locke's 'way of ideas' and presented, as a necessary alternative, a metaphysical theory whose basic premises, in spite of protestations to the contrary, had nothing to do with common sense. David Hume and Immanuel Kant were among the authors who in their fashion took the immaterialism of the Irish philosopher seriously. For Hume, this theory led directly to scepticism, but it was no danger to religion or morals since Berkeley's arguments '*admit of no answer and produce no conviction*'.[27] Kant devoted a section in the second edition of *Kritik der reinen Vernunft* (1787) to Berkeley and Descartes, in which 'material idealism' was to be refuted. While Descartes's idealism was 'problematic', Berkeley represented a 'dogmatic idealism' according to which the existence of objects other than ourselves in space must be considered 'false and impossible'. This position, Kant held, necessitates the unjustifiable assumption that space itself is a property of things (see B 274).

If Berkeley attempts a partial rehabilitation and remodelling of metaphysical theories in connection with Locke's idea-based empiricism, Hume's *Treatise of Human Nature* (1739–40)[28] is decidedly critical of every sort of metaphysics. He opens Book 1 ('Of the Understanding') with the assertion that all our perceptions are simple impressions or ideas, originating either in sensation or in reflection (1.1.1.1). Following Locke, he sets simple ideas in opposition to complex ones (relations, modes, and substance), which are based on an association of simple ideas through the imagination (1.1.4). Whereas ideas of relation, such as resemblance, identity, space and time, and cause and effect are interpreted in partly novel ways, both as to content and function, there is no place for the concept of substance in Hume's epistemology since it starts from impressions considered as independent entities. Substances and modes are nothing 'but a collection of simple ideas, that are united by the imagination, and have a particular name assign'd them, by which we are able to recal, either to ourselves or others, that collection' (1.1.6.2, SBN 16).

The Lockean distinction between sensation and reflection as the sources of all our perceptions did, however, exact a tribute to Cartesian dualism, namely that the untenability of its substance theory be displayed in two separate lines of thought, concerning body and concerning mind. The substance theory of body is critically examined in Book 1, Part 1, Sections 3 ('Of the Antient Philosophy') and 4 ('Of the Modern Philosophy'), and the substance theory of soul or human spirit in Section 5 ('Of the Immateriality of the Soul'). The preeminence that Descartes assigns to the *res cogitans* over the *res extensa* is echoed when Hume declares the mere question of what constitutes a substance to be totally incomprehensible. On the other hand, there is a perceptible antithesis between sensation and reason in connection with the *res extensa* and this issues in an extravagant scepticism. As for the substantial soul, Hume seeks to undermine it by reverting somewhat ironically to Spinoza and the practically relevant argument that the speculative doctrine of the soul as a simple substance must be erroneous since it leads directly to atheism (as Berkeley had already stressed).

The immateriality of the allegedly substantial character of the soul is of central importance since this quality is essential for proving the immortality of the soul. In this connection, Section 6, 'Of Personal Identity', is directly connected with the preceding discussion. Because of Locke's denial of the connection between substance metaphysics and personal identity, the question of personal identity becomes more significant since it can no longer be answered by reference to the simplicity of a soul substance. Since Hume is unwilling to accept Locke's theory of personal identity and unable to formulate a satisfactory one of his own, these considerations, too, end with a sceptical conclusion. The *theoretical* problem of personal identity could be solved only by means of an (untenable) metaphysics of substance: 'Did our perceptions either inhere in something simple and individual, or did the mind perceive some real connexion among them, there wou'd be no difficulty in the case' (*Treatise*, App. 21, SBN 636).

In his discussion of mistaken theories of substance and accident, Hume attempts to establish the basic principles of human nature (see 1.4.3.1, SBN 219). Even the greatest errors in man's theories can be explained naturally but only by those who, like Hume himself, develop the science of man on the basis of observation and experience. Basically, Hume traces such errors back to a misguided imagination, whose constitutive significance for knowledge he nevertheless repeatedly affirms.

Hume approaches the idea of material substance in two different ways and relates them historically to ancient and modern philosophy. The fictions of '*substances*, and *substantial forms*, and *accidents*, and *occult qualities*' are ascribed to the Peripatetics in particular (1.4.3.1, SBN 219). Bodies, in Hume's view, represent nothing but collections of 'several distinct sensible qualities'; and yet from the earliest times it had been maintained that they remain one and the same even as their qualities or accidents change. This is due to an error of the imagination that believes it can connect the succession of interconnected qualities to one and the same object. In order to remove the contradiction of the simultaneous identity of the object and its changing qualities, the imagination 'feign[s] something unknown and invisible, which it supposes to continue the same under all these variations; and this unintelligible something it calls a *substance*, or *original and first matter*' (1.4.3.4, SBN 220). The same process can be discerned with reference to the simplicity and indivisibility of substances (see 1.4.3.5, SBN 221). The Peripatetics assumed that one and the same substance underlies all objects. On the basis of the various substantial forms which are the reason for the diverse qualities of objects, the latter can be divided into various types. The concept of accidents is therefore a natural and necessary consequence of this view. In his critique, Hume has recourse to one of his epistemological principles, according to which every quality is distinct from every other and 'may be conceiv'd to exist apart, and may exist apart' (1.4.3.7, SBN 222).

Hume pours scorn on the theory of occult qualities and of sympathy and antipathy between objects. He thought the ancient philosophers were childish in their thinking; just as children in a rage throw away a stone on which they have hurt themselves, so the Peripatetics ascribed to objects qualities which, properly understood, are nothing but characteristics of human nature. 'There is a very remarkable inclination in human nature, to bestow on external objects the same emotions, which it observes in itself; and to find every where those ideas, which are most present to it' (1.4.3.11, SBN 224).

The basic principle of *modern* philosophy, for Hume, was the theory that colours and noises, for example, are mere impressions in the human mind, derived indeed from external objects but in no way resembling the qualities of those objects (1.4.4.3, SBN 226). At the same time, Hume acknowledges that there are many impressions for which we have 'no external model or archetype' (1.4.4.4, SBN 227). However, modern philosophers draw a false conclusion from this. From the fact that these qualities are not independently existing entities, it is falsely deduced that only primary qualities such as extension and solidity exist in the objects themselves. This theory, which had already been criticised by Berkeley, leads to 'the most extravagant scepticism' (1.4.4.6, SBN 228) because when colours, for instance, are viewed as secondary, dependent qualities, extension and solidity cannot exist independently either. The so-called primary qualities can only be conceived when we also invoke the so-called secondary qualities (see 1.4.4.9, SBN 228–9). But if, for example, we derive the idea of solidity from a sensation, this leads to the contradiction already mentioned between reason and our sensible nature. Bodies are felt by virtue of their solidity. But the solidity is not the same thing as the sensation. From these reflections, Hume concludes that

there is a direct and total opposition betwixt our reason and our senses; or more properly speaking, betwixt those conclusions we form from cause and effect, and those that perswade us of the continu'd and independent existence of body. When we reason from cause and effect, we conclude, that neither colour, sound, taste, nor smell have a continu'd and independent existence. When we exclude these sensible qualities there remains nothing in the universe, which has such an existence. (1.4.4.15, SBN 231)

This proves that the theory of primary and secondary qualities is untenable.

Whereas in the case of external objects we are confronted with contradictions that are peculiar to the object as such, similar contradictions respecting the substance of the soul can only be inferred from the *theories* of 'certain philosophers' concerning its materiality or immateriality (*Treatise*, 1.4.5.1–2, SBN 232). It is characteristic of a typical style of Humean argument that he concludes this debate by declaring it impossible to solve. As in the case of matter and body, we cannot find an idea of our own mind in our stream of consciousness. But discussion of the substance theory of the mind leads to special difficulties.

All ideas are copies of previous impressions. Were we to have an idea of substance, a corresponding impression would have to be shown, and supporters of the substance theory have failed in that regard. And if the definition of substance as '*something which may exist by itself*' is considered adequate, the desired result does not follow (1.4.5.5, SBN 233) for, according to Hume, impressions must be understood as independently existing entities. Consequently, each impression would have to be viewed as a substance, but then all distinction between substance and accident would be empty, and such distinction is the object of every substance theory. Even the question of '*[w]hether perceptions inhere in a material or immaterial substance*' becomes incomprehensible on close investigation. Expounding on his argument, Hume gives positive proof of the impossibility of an idea of substance: 'We have no perfect idea of any thing but of a perception. A substance is entirely different from a perception. We have, therefore, no idea of a substance' (1.4.5.6, SBN 234). Clearly, the question of whether perceptions inhere in material or immaterial substances is unanswerable if we cannot even make sense of it.

Hume does, however, critically examine the best proof available for the immateriality of the soul. Extended objects consist of parts and are therefore divisible; it is impossible for anything divisible to produce a thought or a perception; and the unity of a thought can be guaranteed only if the thinking subject constitutes a simple, indivisible, and therefore immaterial substance.[29] 'Thought, therefore, and extension are qualities wholly incompatible, and never can incorporate together into one subject' (*Treatise*, 1.4.5.7, SBN 234–5). Against this claim, Hume argues that 'an object may exist, and yet be no where', that in fact 'the greatest part of beings' exist without occupying any space.[30] That applies to 'all our perceptions and objects, except those of sight and feeling' (1.4.5.10, SBN 235–6). Materialism therefore seems to be false: 'We cannot refuse to condemn the materialists, who conjoin all thought with extension' (1.4.5.15, SBN 239). But the falsehood of materialism does not entail the immateriality of the soul. In the end, Hume opts for the impossibility of deciding the matter. In accordance with his principle that 'any thing may produce any thing' (1.4.5.30, SBN 247), it is possible to imagine, with Locke, that matter causes thought in us. The 'final decision' is that 'the question concerning the substance of the soul is absolutely unintelligible' (1.4.5.33, SBN 250).

Locke narrowed the concept of substance through the distinction between real and nominal essences; Hume demonstrated its internal discrepancies and contradictions by means of a consistent empiricism; and Étienne Bonnot de Condillac likewise could not find any fundamental use for it. In his sensualistic theory, which first of all was directed against the Leibnizian doctrine of monads, there are no beings which do not exist as predicates of another or which must be seen as their own causes. In his *Traité des sensations*,[31] Condillac starts with the fiction of a marble statue which he gradually endows with the five senses, so bringing it to life in stages. This method is designed to show the contribution of each sense in the acquisition of knowledge. Unlike Locke, Condillac brings out the significance of the genesis of individual cognitive capacities but gives up the Lockean dualism of sensation and reflexion by eliminating the latter. He wants to refute Diderot's accusation that his sensualism leads to a Berkeleyan idealism. All knowledge derives from sensations, and in the second part of his work Condillac singles out the sense of touch as the only sense capable of judging external objects by itself.

The sensations created by the sense of touch are of two kinds. The first are extension, form, space, solidity, fluidity, hardness, softness, movement, rest; the second kind are heat and cold and various sensations of pleasure or pain. The relations of the latter are naturally indefinite. They exist in the memory only because the organs have repeatedly transmitted them. The first, however, have more exactly recognisable relations. Our statue measures the circumference of bodies with her hands, measures space in moving from place to place, determines forms by counting their surfaces and tracing their contours, judges of solidity and fluidity, hardness and softness by testing resistance . . . (*Traité*, II.xi.1)

All our external sensations, therefore, are directly related to extension (§2). Without the sense of touch, the statue could not know anything at all about external objects.

Condillac himself emphasises that such a theory of knowledge, which actually is in danger of confusing the validity of our epistemic judgements with their origins, has no place for the concept of substance. 'But however great the number of objects she [that is, the statue] discovers, no matter how she combines them, she will never attain to the abstract concepts of being, substance, essence, nature etc.; such fantasies are only palpable to philosophers' (II.vii.21). Philosophers falsely assume that by the term 'body' we understand the sum of several qualities without asking themselves what connects them. This something, which Locke still thought of as an unknowable but necessary bearer of these qualities, is mocked by Condillac:

Assuming the statue to be curious to discover how these qualities exist in each combination, she would, like ourselves, be inclined to imagine a something as the subject thereof and if she could give this something a name she would have an answer ready for the philosophers. She would then know as much about it as they did, that is, they know no more than she does. (§22)

But of course Condillac does not deny that the statue develops successive abstract concepts, and he points out the particular importance of duration and space.

Just like Locke before him,[32] Condillac draws attention to the fact that the statue only knows duration because of the succession of her ideas (§23) but conceives time as a line along which she moves from the past into the future with the help of her memory. Whereas she learns duration through the succession of ideas, she learns space through their coexistence. Condillac here starts from the definition of touch as the sense which transmits, distinguishes, and unites several sensations at one point in time; touch is what constitutes bodies (see §24). Gradually the statue thus recognises that space extends beyond her direct experience of it (§25). Just as duration leads her to the idea of eternity, so she is led to the infinity of space (§§25, 26). However, in the end, eternity and infinity are based, as Condillac emphasises, on a deception of our imagination (§27).

In the introduction to *An Inquiry into the Human Mind on the Principles of Common Sense* (1764),[33] Thomas Reid inaugurates an understanding of the 'way of ideas' which has remained influential until the present day. According to this, the importance of the human mind, its abilities, and their use, as demonstrated since the time of Descartes, remains beyond question for all spheres of theoretical and practical philosophy. But Reid saw it as an impossible ambition on the part of modern philosophers to establish a few fundamental principles or laws for the human mind which were as certain as any in the fields of mechanics, astronomy, or optics (Introd., §3, p. 16). The 'ideal system' of Descartes, followed by Malebranche and Locke, necessarily led to scepticism (Introd., §7, p. 23). Berkeley's aim of defeating scepticism had actually prepared the way for it, as Hume had argued (*Inquiry*, Introd., §5, pp. 19–20). And Hume for his part then turned nature into an Epicurean dance of atoms, and the *Treatise* was itself a 'monster' of modern scepticism (*Inquiry*, Introd., §6, p. 22, and ch. 7, Conclusion, §3, p. 210).

Reid organises the chapters of his book according to the five senses of smell, taste, hearing, touch, and sight. This methodology already plainly shows the distance separating him from his English-speaking predecessors; the senses become the measure of investigation, yet there can be no contradictions between them and reason, as in Hume's *Treatise*. Reid's theory of knowledge essentially seeks to prove the unity and harmony of reason with the basic principles of human nature, 'the original constitution of our minds' (*Inquiry*, V.3, p. 59), which also distinguishes it markedly from Condillac's sensualism. The senses can fulfill the functions ascribed to them by Reid exactly because the central points of Locke's 'way of ideas' have been abandoned. According to Reid, we do not perceive merely the idea of a smell but the smell itself, which is a quality of a body (II.8, pp. 38–9), just as colour is not a mere mental perception but a permanent quality of the body itself (see VI.4). Our external perceptions are thus not to be understood as reproductions or copies of bodies but as identical with them (see VI.6).

Central to Reid's epistemology is his theory of natural signs comprehending three classes. The first are those signs whose connection with the specific object is established in nature itself and which we know by experience. They include the laws of mechanics, astronomy, and optics, as well as those of agriculture, chemistry, and medicine (see *Inquiry*, V.3). The second class includes those natural signs whose connection with specific objects is also established in nature but which we discover not by experience or by reason but rather through 'natural principles'. 'Of this kind are the natural signs of human thoughts, purposes, and desires, which have been already mentioned as the natural language of mankind'. Lastly, the third class includes those natural signs 'which, though we never before had any notion or conception of the thing signified, do suggest it, or conjure it up, as it were, by a natural kind of magic, and at once give us a conception, and create a belief of it' (V.3, p. 60). Among other things, Reid is here thinking of the existence of other minds and of the external objects of our experience. These three classes of natural signs are assigned to natural philosophy, to fine arts, and to common sense. In Reid's opinion, philosophy hitherto had failed to explain the last group of signs sufficiently clearly.[34] Since these basic principles of human nature derive neither from reason nor from experience, they must be regarded as 'original' principles.

A new understanding of primary and secondary qualities is also basic to Reid's philosophy. The reason for the distinction between primary and secondary qualities must be sought in the constitution of human nature. All primary qualities, 'by means of certain corresponding sensations of touch, are presented to the mind as real external qualities, the conception and the belief of them are invariably connected with the corresponding sensations, by an original principle of human nature' (*Inquiry*, V.4, pp. 61–2). The primary qualities, according to Reid, represent neither ideas of sensation nor ideas of reflexion and also do not derive from mental acts. The only remaining alternative is to assume that they are original principles of human nature:

[O]ur notions of external existences, of space, motion, and extension, and all the primary qualities of body, that is, the qualities of which we have the most clear and distinct conception . . . have no resemblance to any sensation, or to any operation of our minds; and therefore, they cannot be ideas either of sensation or of reflection. The very conception of them is irreconcilable to the principles of all our philosophic systems of the understanding. (V.6, p. 67)

Just as nature has generally linked signs to specific objects, so too has it provided human nature with specific concepts by which humankind is first enabled to know. 'The conception of extension, motion, and the other attributes of matter, cannot be the effect of error or prejudice; it must be the work of nature' (V.7, p. 70). Nature relieves human beings epistemically to a certain extent, by supplying them with principles that cannot err. This fundamental epistemic devaluation of reason stands in opposition to the metaphysical tradition and at the same time banishes the specter of scepticism. 'All reasoning must be from first principles; and for first principles no other reason can be given but this, that, by the constitution of our nature, we are under a necessity of assenting to them. Such principles are parts of our constitution, no less than the power of think-ing' (V.7, p. 71). The circumstance that our sense of touch acquaints us with 'something external, extended, figured, hard or soft' rests on no 'deduction of reason' but on a 'natural principle'. 'The belief of it, and the very conception of it, are equally parts of our constitution. If we are deceived in it, we are deceived by Him that made us, and there is no remedy' (p. 72). The primary qualities are perceived 'by means of sensation of touch', but these sensations, again, are not images of primary qualities of bodies (such as shape and extension: see V.8, p. 73). Whereas our original perceptions are not acquired but given with our constitution, others, the secondary qualities, are the result of experience. And belief in the existence of external objects is not the result of sensation alone but the effect of instinct (VI.20, pp. 171–2).

Reid is principally concerned with the knowledge of human abilities and their powers, in which original principles play a pivotal role. Consequently, the question of the substantiality of the human soul is not central to his philosophy. This is not contradicted by Reid's idea that the individual mind 'upon the testimony of common sense . . . is a substance, that is, a permanent subject of thought' (VII, p. 217), of which my reason tells me that it is unextended and indivisible.

For Reid the unity and reliability of experience are due to original principles of human nature, with which God has provided us. Reid's theory of knowledge can thus properly be described as a 'Providential Naturalism', which embraces the study of both external and internal nature and – in contrast with Descartes's dictum that nothing is easier to know than one's own self – is attended with considerable difficulties.

It is justly reckoned a valuable branch of human knowledge to know the Structure of the human Body, the Uses of its various parts external & internal, the disorders and diseases to which they are liable & the Proper Remedies. There is a Structure of the Mind as well as of the Body, which is not less worthy to be known. Its various Powers & Faculties are the Workmanship of God no less than the various Parts of the body and no less wisely adapted to their several ends. . . . The knowledge of it is indeed attended with many and great difficulties as I shall afterwards shew. And there is no part of Philosophy in which Speculative Men have run into so many and so great Errors and even absurdities.[35]

Against the background of our survey thus far of the concept of substance in the eighteenth century, Kant's *Kritik der reinen Vernunft* represents an attempt at a new founding of metaphysics, which received decisive impetus from rational-ism, empiricism, and scepticism. While Locke and Hume made it impossible uncritically to accept the traditional substance metaphysics from Descartes to

Wolff, neither the former's empiricism nor the latter's scepticism made empirical laws of nature intelligible. Kant, of course, subjected the traditional substance metaphysics to a fundamental critique insofar as he asked how experience is at all possible for us. But against the background of the transcendental aesthetics, in which space and time are regarded as the pure forms of the sensible manifold of our experience, the distinction between the thing in itself and appearance is used to formulate a doctrine which combines critique of knowledge with metaphysics in such a way that the metaphysics of substance is partially rehabilitated. Without assuming a world of noumenal objects unknowable to us theoretically, the project of a new critical justification of metaphysics loses its – ultimately dogmatic – foundation.[36] Kant's extremely difficult and complex statements about the concept of substance in his main work can only be given in rough outline.

In the *Kritik* Kant tries to relate the understanding, conceived as spontaneous, and our sensibility, conceived as receptive, by means of the triad of understanding, judgement, and reason, in a way that will explain how knowledge of phenomenal objects of experience is possible. The basic problem is how pure concepts of understanding functioning as categories can be applied to the manifold of our sensibility in such a way that, on the one hand, the unity of experience of nature is possible, and, on the other, the need of our reason to understand the unconditioned of all knowledge is accounted for.

In the 'Transcendental Aesthetic' which opens the *Kritik*, Kant argues that we are given all the manifold of our sensibility in the subjective intuitive forms of space and time.[37] Time is the pure intuitive form of internal sense, space of external sense. We can never know those objects which affect our sensibility as they are in their true constitution, as things in themselves, but only as appearances. Matter is the object of outer sense, but it is no *res extensa* in the Cartesian sense because we know it only as appearance. Kant's transcendental aesthetic, in contrast to Wolff's theory of space and time, allows a strict separation between sensible appearances on the one hand and purely intellectual concepts on the other.

This theory, however, raises an issue that parallels the distinction between noumena and phenomena[38] in the 'Transcendental Analytic' of the *Kritik*, and is linked to what Kant calls the transcendental object of our knowledge. He denies the possibility of knowing the essence of things as they exist in themselves, but he cannot avoid speaking of things in themselves which (causally) call forth a manifold in our sensibility (A 494/B 522–3, A 538–9/B 566–7). Objects are given to us in our sensibility, but what is given must be called forth by something other than ourselves. Kant's distinction between the thing in itself and appearance and his transcendental idealism are to this day the subject of extensive exegetic and systematic discussions. In these discussions, it is of special importance whether the thing in itself and the object of experience belong to two different realms of objects or merely represent two different ways of considering the same thing. The former is a metaphysical interpretation, the second a phenomenological or methodological perspectivism designed to overcome the metaphysical implications of Kant's transcendental idealism.[39] It seems doubtful, however, whether the latter reading can be carried through because Kant's two-world theory plays a crucially important role in his practical philosophy.[40]

In the so-called table of judgements in 'Kant's Transcendental Analytic', all epistemic judgements are distinguished according to quantity, quality, relation, and modality. In the 'Table of Categories' (A 80/B 1206), these forms of judgement are then conceived as objects of experience in the framework of transcendental logic and derived from the supposedly complete table of judgements. Here we find the distinction between substance and accident as the relation between 'inherence and subsistence' (A 80/B 106). However, in this context, substance as a pure concept of understanding is not meant metaphysically but represents a category by means of which the objects of experience (and only these) are determined.

After the objective validity of these categories for the manifold of our sensibility has been demonstrated in the chapter 'On the Deduction of the Pure Concepts of the Understanding' (A 84–130/B 116–69), Kant argues in the chapter on 'The System of All Principles of Pure Understanding' for four different synthetic principles a priori that are constitutive for our experience of the world. Like the 'Principle of Temporal Sequence according to the Law of Causality' (A 189/B 232ff.), the 'Principle of the Persistence of Substance' (A 182/B 224) belongs to the analogies of experience.[41] These set out to prove that 'Experience is possible only through the representation of a necessary connection of perceptions' (B 218). Kant goes a good deal further with this than did Hume. Whereas the latter maintained that everything that can be thought of without contradiction can exist, Kant sees the principle of contradiction as merely a negative criterion of truth (see *Kritik* A 154/B 193–4). The highest principles of all judgements of experience are rather synthetic principles a priori.

The central importance of the principle of the persistence of substance is apparent from the fact that it is understood as the first analogy of experience in accordance with the table of categories. This states that 'In all change of appearances substance persists; and its quantum is neither increased nor diminished in nature' (B 224). The proof of this principle starts from the doctrine that all appearances exist in time, which itself does not change since it is the only condition under which a change of appearances by way of succession or identity can be imagined. Since time as such cannot be perceived, Kant concludes that 'it is in the objects of perception, i.e., the appearances, that the substratum must be encountered that represents time in general and in which all change or simultaneity can be perceived in apprehension through the relation of the appearances to it' (B 225). Kant calls this the 'substratum of everything real . . . [the] *substance*, of which everything that belongs to existence can be thought only as a determination'. He concludes that

that which persists, in relation to which alone all temporal relations of appearances can be determined, is substance in the appearance, i.e., the real in the appearance, which as the substratum of all change always remains the same. Since this, therefore, cannot change in existence, its quantum in nature can also be neither increased nor diminished. (B 225)

In other words, determinations of time are possible only when they are based upon a substratum that remains constant through all changes of appearance and all our temporal determinations – that is, one that is not subject to change.

In this way, Kant gave a new significance to the distinction between substance and accident. All change and all simultaneity in the substance are understood as '*modi* of time' (A 182/B 226). Time itself does not change 'but only the appearances in time. . . . Only through that which persists does *existence* in different parts of the temporal series acquire a *magnitude* which one calls *duration*. . . . Without that which persists there is therefore no temporal relation' (A 183/B 226).

In this connection, Kant complained that philosophy up until then had given no satisfactory proof for the fact that substance remains the same through all changes in the world and only accidents change (see A 184/B 227). This is understandable, given the viewpoint of the *Kritik*, that such proof must be given in the form of a synthetic a priori proposition. The possibility of such propositions or judgements can be demonstrated only on the basis of critical philosophy. That metaphysics, correctly understood, concerned the foundation and justification of such judgements was something that, in Kant's view, had remained hidden from all previous writers.[42]

With the reference to something that persists in all appearances, Kant singles out an element in our sensibility that is the actual possibility of using the category for substance. The use of this category for noumenal objects is, however, ruled out (see A 186/B 229). Where the substance is empirically determined, Kant speaks of accidents:

The determinations of a substance, that are nothing other than particular ways for it to exist are called *accidents*. They are always real, because they concern the existence of substance. . . . If we ascribe a special [kind of] existence to this real in substance, (for instance, to motion, as an accident of matter), this existence is entitled inherence, in distinction from the existence of substance which is entitled subsistence. (A 186/B 229–30)

Without the concept of substance, we could never form the concept of change. The second analogy then demonstrates that all changes happen in accordance with the synthetic principle of causality.[43] The third and last analogy shows that 'all substances insofar as they can be perceived in space as simultaneous, are in thoroughgoing interaction' (see B 256).

In the 'Transcendental Dialectic,' which, like the 'Transcendental Analytic', belongs to the transcendental logic (a logic of transcendental illusion, not one of truth), Kant discusses the central topics of traditional metaphysics: soul (rational psychology), world (cosmology), and God (theology). In this, Kant followed the systematics of Wolff, except that, like Crusius, he started with the soul rather than the mind. Critically dissociating himself from the metaphysical tradition, however, Kant is keen to prove that a theoretical knowledge of these three objects is not humanly possible. For example, rational psychology saw the human soul as a simple and numerically identical substance, whose existence, unlike that of external objects, is beyond doubt; this leads Kant to the diagnosis that this discipline actually entangles itself in paralogisms which can be disclosed only by means of his transcendental logic. It had escaped the school of rational psychology that the epistemological use of categories, in the interest of extending our knowledge, is possible only if the categories are applied to the manifold of our sensibility. But this is just what must be denied if this school is not to find itself back in the realm of empirical psychology or anthropology and thus fail at what it set out to show. For Kant, rational psychology is a discipline that seeks to increase our self-knowledge by a syllogistic conclusion from the empirically indeterminate 'I think'. In effect, it tries to make synthetic a priori judgements about the essence and nature of the human soul. However, in contrast to the empiricist and sceptical tradition, Kant does not totally reject the concept of the soul as substance as unfounded or inconsistent but assigns it an indispensable function as a regulative idea for the sciences concerned – in this case psychology (see *Kritik* A 642/B 670ff.).

Cosmology is addressed in the chapter on the antinomies, where the assertions of traditional cosmology are formulated as four theses and antitheses. The thesis of the second antinomy states that 'every composite substance in the world consists of simple parts'. The antithesis to this Leibnizian thesis is that 'no composite thing in the world consists of simple parts' (A 434/B 462, A 435/B 463). Kant dissolves the transcendental illusion of this antinomy by means of his transcendental idealism. That is, the antinomy arises only when it is overlooked that we are not concerned with things in themselves but merely with objects of experience.

To sum up our discussion of the eighteenth-century concept of substance, we must maintain that Locke's theory of knowledge undoubtedly was a significant impulse for the disintegration of the traditional metaphysics of substance. Locke directed the attention of philosophers to man's cognitive abilities, their epistemic results, their number, and their formation. In English-language philosophy, authors as different as Berkeley, Hume, and Reid take up the thread of Locke's 'way of ideas'. From the substance-critical implications of Locke's philosophy, however, they reach various conclusions, ranging from idealism through scepticism to naturalism. On the European continent, Lockean faculty psychology was taken up by writers such as Condillac and Charles Bonnet in France and by Johann Nicolas Tetens, Johann Georg Heinrich Feder, and Christian Garve in Germany, to name but a few, just as Hume and Scottish Common Sense philosophy had a considerable impact on the Continent.[44] Nevertheless, Leibniz and Wolff made sure that the questions of traditional metaphysics of substance were much more intensely discussed and developed in Germany than elsewhere. This still remained the case after Kant's *Kritik* reshaped German philosophy in the 1780s, and various forms of empiricism and Leibnizian rationalism were pushed into the background. Kant could still recognise Moses Mendelssohn's *Morgenstunden*[45] as the 'final legacy of a dogmatizing metaphysics' and as, at the same time, 'its most perfect accomplishment, both in view of its chain-like coherence and in the exceptional clarity of its presentation'.[46] But already in his essay 'Was heisst: Sich im Denken orientiren?' (1786), and in his paper 'Einige Bemerkungen zu Ludwig Heinrich Jakobs Prüfung der Mendelssohn'schen *Morgenstunden*',[47] Kant struck a decidedly polemical note. If Mendelssohn extends the speculative use of reason

> beyond the boundaries of sense through insights . . . then it is no longer possible to restrict it to this object; and as if it is not enough that it then finds a wide field open to all kinds of enthusiasm, it even dares to decide by sophistries on the possibility of a supreme being (according to the concept swelled by religion) . . .[48]

Mendelssohn is thus among the authors who postulate the possibility of a transcendental use of categories to formulate synthetic a priori propositions concerning the noumenal world, and this was directly contrary to the teaching of the *Kritik*.

A central criticism of Kant, in the tradition of German neo-scholastic metaphysics, was mounted by Johann August Eberhard, a follower of Leibniz, who held that Kant owed much more to the latter than he cared to acknowledge. In denying the originality of Kantian philosophy, Eberhard of course also rejected its claim that a transcendental use of the pure concepts of understanding without reference to our sensibility cannot enlarge our knowledge.[49]

The further course of German philosophy increasingly isolated Kant's critical philosophy, arguing that he had neither refuted Hume[50] nor succeeded in providing the premises of his own philosophy. Going back to Spinoza and Leibniz, the early idealist philosophers took up the idea of the re-ontologisation of the Kantian categories, including the category of substance. This process is as characteristic of authors such as the early Fichte and Schelling as of the later Hegel.[51]

NOTES

1 See Roger S. Woolhouse, *Descartes, Spinoza, Leibniz: The Concept of Substance in Seventeenth-Century Metaphysics* (London, 1993).

2 See Aristotle, *Metaphysica*, 1017b14, and *Categories*, 2a11, in *The Complete Works*, ed. J. Barnes, 2 vols. (Princeton, NJ, 1984), 2: 1606 and 1: 4, respectively; René Descartes, *Meditationes de prima philosophia* (1641), translated as *Meditations on First Philosophy*, in *The Philosophical Writings of Descartes*, trans. J. Cottingham, R. Stoothoff, and D. Murdoch, 3 vols. (Cambridge, 1984–91), 2: 1–62, here at *Meditations* III ('quae per se apta est existere'), 30.

3 See Descartes, *Principia philosophiæ* (1644), translated as *Principles of Philosophy*, in *Philosophical Writings*, 1: 177–291 at 210.

4 Thomas Hobbes, *Leviathan, or The Matter, Forme and Power of a Commonwealth Ecclesiasticall and Civill* (1651), in *The Collected Works*, ed. W. Molesworth, 12 vols. (London, 1839–45), 3: Pt. III, §34, p. 393.

5 Baruch de Spinoza, *Ethica ordine geometrico demonstrata* (1677), translated as *Ethics* by S. Stirling, ed. S. Feldman (Indianapolis, IN, 1992), Pt. I, Prop. 11, p. 37; Prop. 14, Cor. 2, p. 40; Pt. II, Props. 1, 2, p. 64.

6 *Ethics*, Pt. I, Def. 1, p. 31; see also Prop. 7, p. 34, Proof; and Pt. I, Prop. 16, Cor. 3, p. 44. See Aristotle, *Metaphysica*, 983a25–32, p. 1555.

7 Nicolas Malebranche, *De la recherche de la vérité* (1674–5), ed. G. Rodis-Lewis, in *Oeuvres complètes*, ed. A. Robinet, 22 vols. (Paris, 1958–84), vols. 1–2 (1962), translated as *The Search after Truth* by T. M. Lennon and P. J. Olscamp (Columbus, OH, 1980), VI.ii.3, pp. 449–51.

8 John Locke, *An Essay Concerning Human Understanding*, ed. P. H. Nidditch, in *The Clarendon Edition* (1975), I.i.2; see also Immanuel Kant, *Kritik der reinen Vernunft*, translated as *Critique of Pure Reason*, trans. and eds. P. Guyer and A. W. Wood, in *Works* (1998), A xii.

9 See Locke, *Essay*, II.xii.6, II.xiii.18–19, II.xxiii, and III.vi. See Michael Ayers, *Locke*, 2 vols. (London, 1991), 2: 15–128. For parallels between Locke and Pierre Gassendi, see Rolf W. Puster, *Britische Gassendi-Rezeption am Beispiel John Lockes* (Stuttgart-Bad Cannstatt, 1991).

10 See Locke, *Essay*, IV.iii.6. See also John W. Yolton, *Thinking Matter: Materialism in Eighteenth-Century Britain* (Oxford, 1984), and Mario Casula, 'Die historische Entwicklung der Frage: Ob die Materie denken kann? Von F. Suarez bis P. J. G. Cabanis. Ein Beitrag zur Einführung in die philosophische Problematik der künstlichen Intelligenz', *Filosofia oggi*, 12 (1989): 407–62.

11 See Gottfried Wilhelm Leibniz, *Monadologie*, (1714), §§1, 3, translated as *Monadology*, in *Philosophical Papers and Letters*, trans. and ed. L. E. Loemker (Dordrecht, 1969), 643–52 at 643.

12 See Locke, *Essay*, II.xxvii.9 and II.xxiii.12; Leibniz, *Monadologie*, §§14, 23. See also K. J. Grau, *Die Entwicklung des Bewusstseinsbegriffs im XVII. und XVIII. Jahrhundert* (Halle, 1916), and Max Dessoir, *Geschichte der neueren deutschen Psychologie* (Berlin, 1902).

13 The triad can be traced back to Leibniz; see Eileen O'Neill, 'Influxus Physicus', in *Causation in Early Modern Philosophy: Cartesianism, Occasionalism and Preestablished Harmony*, ed. S. Nadler (University Park, PA, 1993), 27–55 at 27–8. See also Locke, *Essay*, II.xxvii. See Gerd Fabian,

Beitrag zur Geschichte des Leib-Seele-Problems (Lehre von der prästabilierten Harmonie und vom psychophysischen Parallelismus in der Leibniz-Wolffschen Schule) (Langensalza, 1926).

14 See Christian Wolff, *Vernünfftige Gedancken von Gott, der Welt und der Seele des Menschen, auch allen Dingen überhaupt* (Deutsche Metaphysik) (1719–20), in *Werke*, I.2, ed. C. A. Corr (1983), §753, p. 468, and his *Anmerckungen über die vernünfftigen Gedancken von Gott, der Welt und der Seele des Menschen* (1724), in *Werke*, I.3, ed. C. A. Corr (1983), §269, pp. 439 ff. See also Fabian, *Beitrag*, 41, 224–7.

15 Wolff, *Philosophia prima, sive Ontologia, methodo scientifica pertractata* (1730), in *Werke*, II.3, ed. J. École (1962).

16 Alexander Gottlieb Baumgarten, *Metaphysica* (Halle, 1739), in German as *Metaphysik*, trans. G. F. Meier (Halle, 1766).

17 Immanuel Kant, *Vorlesungen über Metaphysik*, Ak 28: 177–8, translated as *Lectures on Metaphysics*, trans. and eds. K. Ameriks and S. Naragon, in *Works* (1997). However, the quoted passage is not included in this translation.

18 Animal souls are indestructible but – in contrast with the souls of human beings, which have a personal identity – they are not immortal; see Leibniz, *Essais de théodicée Sur la bonté de Dieu, la liberté de l'homme et l'origine du mal* (1710), in *Philosophischen Schriften*, 6: §89, translated as *Theodicy: Essays on the Goodness of God, the Freedom of Man and the Origin of Evil*, trans. E. M. Huggard, ed. A. Farrer (London, 1951), 171; Kant, *Die Religion innerhalb der Grenzen der bloßen Vernunft*, Ak 6: 151, translated as *Religion within the Boundaries of Mere Reason*, trans. G. di Giovanni, in *Works/Religion and Rational Theology*, eds. A. W. Wood and G. di Giovanni; and Wolff, *Vernünfftige Gedancken von Gott*, §573, pp. 350–1.

19 See Reinhardt Finster, 'Zur Kritik von Christian August Crusius an der Theorie der einfachen Substanzen bei Leibniz und Wolff', *Studia Leibnitiana*, 18 (1986): 72–82 at 75. On sufficient reason, see Chapter 13, this volume.

20 Christian August Crusius, *Entwurf der nothwendigen Vernunft-Wahrheiten* (Leipzig, 1745). See also Martin Krieger, *Geist, Welt und Gott bei Christian August Crusius. Erkenntnistheorisch-psychologische, kosmologische und religionsphilosophische Perspektiven im Kontrast zum Wolffschen System* (Würzburg, 1993).

21 Immanuel Kant, *De mundi sensibilis atque intelligibilis forma et principiis* (1770), Ak 2: 385–419, translated as *On the Form and Principles of the Sensible and the Intelligible World*, in *Works/Theoretical Philosophy 1755–1770*, trans. and eds. D. Walford and R. Meerbote (1992). See Heiner F. Klemme, *Kants Philosophie des Subjekts: Systematische und entwicklungsgeschichtliche Untersuchungen zum Verhältnis von Selbstbewusstsein und Selbsterkenntnis* (Hamburg, 1996), 50–5.

22 See Leonhard Euler, *Letters . . . to a German Princess on Different Subjects in Physics and Philosophy*, trans. H. Hunter, 2 vols. (London, 1795). Kant used the German translation, *Briefe an eine deutsche Prinzessinn über verschiedene Gegenstände aus der Physik und Philosophie*, 2 vols. (Leipzig, 1769).

23 Kant, *Kritik der praktischen Vernunft* (1788), Ak 5: 87, translated as *Critique of Practical Reason*, trans. and ed. M. J. Gregor, in *Works/Practical Philosophy* (1996).

24 George Berkeley, *A Treatise concerning the Principles of Human Knowledge* (1710) in *Works*, 2: 19–113.

25 See Pt. 1, sect. 2. Descartes used no fewer than twelve different terms for the *res cogitans*; see also Hartmut Brands, *'Cogito ergo sum': Interpretationen von Kant bis Nietzsche* (Freiburg, 1982), 77.

26 See Berkeley, *An Essay Towards a New Theory of Vision* (1709), in *Works*, 1: 159–276.

27 David Hume, *An Enquiry concerning Human Understanding* (1748), ed. T. L. Beauchamp, in the *Clarendon Edition* (2000), 12.2 fn, SBN 155 fn.

28 Hume, *A Treatise of Human Nature*, eds. D. F. Norton and M. J. Norton in the *Clarendon Edition* (2006).

29 See Ben Lazare Mijuskovic, *The Achilles of Rationalist Arguments: The Simplicity, Unity and Identity of Thought and Soul from the Cambridge Platonists to Kant. A Study in the History of an Argument* (The Hague, 1974).

30 Hume takes up the theme of space and time in the *Treatise*, 1.2, where he rejects the concept of an infinite divisibility of our ideas of space and time. In his concise expositions of the topic in the *Enquiry* (see 12.2, SBN 155–60), geometric proportions are understood as analytic relations.

31 Étienne Bonnot de Condillac, *Traité des sensations*, 2 vols. (London, 1754), I.xi.1, 1: 320–1.

32 See Locke, *Essay*, II.xiv.2–4.

33 Thomas Reid, *An Inquiry into the Human Mind on the Principles of Common Sense*, ed. D. R. Brookes (Edinburgh, 1997), 11–24.

34 For a similar interpretation of Claude Buffier, see Louise Marcil-Lacoste, *Claude Buffier and Thomas Reid: Two Common-Sense Philosophers* (Kingston and Montreal, 1982).

35 Reid, *Practical Ethics, Being Lectures and Papers on Natural Religion, Self-Government, Natural Jurisprudence, and the Law of Nations*, ed. K. Haakonssen (Princeton, NJ, 1990), 105–6. See Descartes, *Meditations*, II, 16–23 at 22–3. Reid took over providential naturalism from his teacher, George Turnbull. See David Fate Norton, *David Hume: Common-Sense Moralist, Sceptical Metaphysician* (Princeton, NJ, 1982), 171.

36 This was immediately stressed by Kant's first critics. See 'Beylage: Ueber den transzendentalen Idealismus', in Friedrich Heinrich Jacobi, *David Hume über den Glauben oder Idealismus und Realismus: Ein Gespräch* (1787), in *Werke*, eds. F. von Roth and F. Köppen, 6 vols. (Leipzig, 1812–25), 2: 304.

37 See Hans Vaihinger, *Kommentar zu Kants Kritik der reinen Vernunft*, 2nd edn., 2 vols. (Stuttgart, 1922), and Reinhard Brandt, 'Raum und Zeit in der "Transzendentalen Ästhetik" der Kritik der reinen Vernunft', in *Rehabilitierung des Subjektiven: Festschrift für Hermann Schmitz*, eds. M. Großheim and H.-J. Waschkies (Bonn, 1993), 441–58.

38 Kant, *Kritik der reinen Vernunft*, A 235/B 294 ff.

39 A systematic defence of Kant's transcendental idealism against Peter F. Strawson's criticisms in *The Bounds of Sense: An Essay on Kant's Critique of Pure Reason* (London, 1966) has been attempted by Henry E. Allison in *Kant's Transcendental Idealism: An Interpretation and Defense* (New Haven, CT, 1983), drawing on Gerold Prauss, *Kant und das Problem der Dinge an sich* (Bonn, 1974).

40 See Klemme, *Kants Philosophie des Subjekts*, 245–70.

41 In what follows, I refer to the revised second edition of the *Kritik* (1787), Ak 3, referred to as 'B'.

42 See the introduction to Kant's *Prolegomena zu einer jeden künftigen Metaphysik, die als Wissenschaft wird auftreten können* (1783), Ak 4: 255–64, translated as *Prolegomena to Any Future Metaphysics that Will Be Able to Come Forward as a Science*, trans. G. Hatfield, in *Works/Theoretical Philosophy after 1781* (2002). See also the 'Vorrede zur zweiten Auflage' of the *Kritik*, B vii–xliv.

43 See Chapter 13 on Causality, this volume.

44 See Günther Gawlick and Lothar Kreimendahl, *Hume in der deutschen Aufklärung: Umrisse einer Rezeptionsgeschichte* (Stuttgart-Bad Cannstatt, 1987), and Manfred Kuehn, *Scottish Common Sense in Germany, 1768–1800: A Contribution to the History of Critical Philosophy* (Kingston and Montreal, 1987).

45 Moses Mendelssohn, *Morgenstunden*, in *Gesammelte Schriften: Jubiläumsausgabe*, eds. F. Bamberger and A. Altmann (Stuttgart-Bad Cannstatt, 1971–), vol. 3.2, ed. L. Strauss (1974), 1–175.

46 Kant, Letter to Christian Gottfried Schütz, November 1785, Ak 10: 428–9, translated in *Works/Correspondence*, trans and ed. A. Zweig (1999).

47 Kant, 'Einige Bemerkungen zu Ludwig Heinrich Jakobs Prüfung der Mendelssohn'schen *Morgenstunden*', Ak 8: 149–55; 'Was heisst: Sich im Denken orientiren?', Ak 8: 131–47. The latter is translated as 'What Does It Mean to Orient Oneself in Thinking?', in *Works/Religion and Rational Theology*, trans. and eds. A. Wood and G. di Giovanni (1996).

48 Kant, Ak 8: 151; see also 143n.

49 See Johann August Eberhard, 'Vorbericht' to the revised edition (Halle, 1783) of the German translation of Baumgarten's *Metaphysica*.

50 This hypothesis is suggested by Gottlob Ernst Schulze in his anonymously published *Aenesidemus, oder Über die Fundamente der Elementarphilosophie* (1792); see the edition by A. Liebert (Berlin, 1911).

51 See Rolf-Peter Horstmann, 'What Is Wrong with Kant's Categories, Professor Hegel?' in *Proceedings of the 8th International Kant Congress, Memphis, 1995*, ed. H. Robinson (Milwaukee, WI, 1995), 3.3: 1005–15.

13

CAUSALITY

HEINER F. KLEMME

The question of the nature and status of causality is basic both for ontology and epistemology. Thus Aristotle emphasised that it is only possible to know (in the full sense of the word) an object if its first cause is known.[1] For Hume, causality is an essential ingredient of 'the cement of the universe'.[2] Obviously, the meaning of causality depends on a series of ontological, metaphysical, and epistemological presuppositions. Insofar as seventeenth- and early eighteenth-century metaphysics is decisively oriented towards the concept of substance, the assessment of the causal power of substances and their interaction will depend on how these substances are determined. Instead, if the ontological concept of a substance is given up, then the problem of understanding ideas and objects as causes or effects arises in quite another way. Not until Locke's critical turn in epistemology was the question of the scope and limits of human knowledge insisted upon, which naturally involved a new understanding of causality. The new theoretical physics and the emerging experimental sciences made it necessary to test causality by empirical standards. Interactions between objects and between intentions and aims of persons were now less frequently demonstrated by rational definitions and more often formulated and confirmed or denied by observation and experience.

It is one of the achievements of eighteenth-century philosophy to have distinguished between general and special laws of causality. Whereas the general law of causality says that without any exception all objects or events are causally connected, the special law of causality states that specific objects of the same class are connected causally with one another. Retrospectively, we can identify three basic and distinct conceptions of causal judgement by which a cause-and-effect relationship between objects is asserted. First, following the Cartesian rationalist tradition, analytical-deductive models were developed, in which cause and effect stand in the same relationship as a premise stands with the conclusion of an argument. The effect was understood as the analytical implication of the cause, exemplifying a necessary connection between them. Since time was generally not understood as a constitutive element of the causal relation, mathematical and geometric relationships were also interpreted as causal relations. The innate knowledge that the degree of reality of the effect can never be greater than that of the cause led Descartes to the idea of God as a *causa sui* from which the existence of the world can be derived.[3] Secondly, for empiricist philosophy, John Locke's *An Essay Concerning Human Understanding* (1690)[4] pointed the way. Locke started from a concept of power, according to which even the ideas of cause and effect can be deduced from observation and experience, so that causal judgements are, to put it in Kant's terminology,[5] synthetic judgements a posteriori. According to Locke, we perceive, in the constant change of things, that qualities and substances begin to exist by reason of the activity of other things. 'From this Observation, we get our *Ideas* of *Cause* and *Effect*. That which produces any simple complex *Idea* we denote by the general Name *Cause*; and that which is produced, *Effect*' (*Essay*, II.xxvi.1). While Locke devotes only two short paragraphs to the ideas of cause and effect, the concept of power, essential for causal judgements, is discussed in detail in a chapter of its own (II.xxi). Power as *active* is the ground of all change in our perceptual ideas; power as *passive* is the object of such change (see II.xxi.2). Since power itself is merely a simple idea, causality can be understood only as a cognitive principle, no longer as a principle of existence. From experience, we know that our understanding and our will are active powers and that humankind is therefore free to think and to act. As corporeal beings, on the other hand, we are not free. Bodies are fundamentally subject to physical necessity, just as a billiard ball, hit by another, cannot choose whether or not to move in a particular direction.

With Lockean empiricism, the problem arises of how the necessity of causal judgements can be accounted for. In the tradition of such seventeenth-century sceptics as Blaise Pascal and Pierre Bayle, who denied the possibility of mathematical evidence in our knowledge of objects, David Hume, in *A Treatise of Human Nature* (1739–40),[6] not only criticises the rationalist concept of causality but also proposes an innovative basis for causal judgements that is entirely dependent on empirical presuppositions.

Thirdly, Immanuel Kant supported the empiricist notion that all empirical judgements are synthetic in nature. But the necessity and unity of experience is ensured, in his view, only when we succeed in the proof of synthetic principles a priori, among which is the 'Principle of Temporal Sequence according to the Law of Causality' (*Kritik*, B 232). With his attempt to develop a complete system of synthetic principles a priori, Kant enters new territory in the history of philosophy.

In addition to the question of the logical status of causal judgements, the eighteenth-century philosophers also debated the question of which object or objects could be causally effective. According to a system developed by Christian

Wolff in the early eighteenth century, it is necessary to distinguish between *metaphysica generalis* (ontology) and *metaphysica specialis* (cosmology, psychology, and theology). According to *metaphysica specialis*, the world (and the things in it), the soul, or God may be causally effective. Wolff also distinguishes three different theories of causal interaction between substances, namely occasionalism (Malebranche), the theory of pre-established harmony (Leibniz), and the theory of *influxus physicus*, which Locke, among others, supported.[7] Wolff believed that these exhausted all possible explanations of causal interactions between substances.

In his *De la recherche de la vérité* (1674–5),[8] Nicolas Malebranche, the most important representative of occasionalism, denied causal relations between substances. Between cause and effect there is a necessary connection (*liaison necessaire*[9]) based on an effective power but one that experience encounters in neither the spiritual nor the physical sphere. Something of which we have no clear and distinct consciousness cannot be caused by us. When we raise an arm, we are conscious of our will to do so but not of how this works on our body. My will is thus merely a *causa occasionalis*[10] for God to make me raise my arm. In experience, we are supplied only with a regular succession, as when we observe that a ball will move when it is hit by another. Although regular succession must never be understood as a causal relation, Malebranche here addresses a point that was of great significance for Hume's causal analysis, and George Berkeley took up Malebranche's idea that external things are not causally effective.[11]

Whereas Malebranche and his followers deny the causality maintained by Descartes between *res cogitans* and *res extensa* for occasionalist reasons, Baruch de Spinoza, in his *Ethica ordine geometrico demonstrata* (1677),[12] believed that only the one absolute free and powerful substance, God, is causally effective. God is seen as the cause of all modes (Pt. I, Prop. 32, pp. 48–9). Causal connections are analytical relations, so that cognition of causes combines cognition of effects (see Pt. I, Axiom 4, p. 32). Cause is transformed from a transient to an immanent principle because there is nothing that is not present in God (see Pt. I, Prop. 18, p. 46).

Leibniz, in his *Monadologie* (written in 1714 but published in 1720), maintains that all rational knowledge rests on two principles. According to the principle of non-contradiction, everything containing a contradiction must be adjudged false. Anything set against or contradicting what is false, on the other hand, is true. According to the second principle, that of sufficient reason (*raison suffisante*, §32, p. 1049), no fact and no statement can be true if there is not sufficient reason why it should be so and not otherwise.[13] These two principles apply in different ways to the two sorts of truth recognised by Leibniz. Whereas truths of reason (*vérités de raisonnement*) are necessarily and analytically true and their opposites therefore impossible, truths of fact (*vérités de fait*) are contingent. The sufficient reason of truths of reason lies in original principles (axioms, postulates), which 'cannot be proved and need no proof' (§35, p. 1049). By contrast, the sufficient reason of truths of fact lies in the order and coherence of all created things. Leibniz is thinking here of both efficient and final causes.[14] The sufficient and ultimate ground in this chain of causality must, however, be outside the contingent sequence of events. God is a necessary and simple substance, and the simple and active substances or monads are also complete (§47, p. 1052). With his theory of pre-established harmony, Leibniz suggested that monads do not affect each other directly or physically but only through the intervention of God (*par l'intervention de Dieu*, §51, p. 1052). Monads, according to a well-known metaphor of Leibniz, have 'no windows' (§7, p. 1044); each monad reflects in itself the whole universe. The correspondence of body and soul can only be explained through pre-established harmony since they follow different laws. Souls follow the laws of final causes, bodies those of efficient causes (see §79, p. 1058), but they always act as if influenced by one another (§81, p. 1058). Since every body belongs to a monad, which constitutes its soul or entelechy (see §19, p. 1047), the efficient causes ultimately coincide with the final causes and thus with God. He alone is pure disembodied spirit (§72, pp. 1056–7) and the efficient cause of our being (see §90, p. 1060). With these reflections, Leibniz turned against Descartes's mechanistic explanation of the body, which Thomas Hobbes had also transferred to the soul.

Christian Wolff, in the ontology of his German[15] and Latin[16] works on metaphysics, attempts to derive the principle of sufficient reason (*principium rationis sufficientis*), which Leibniz did not prove, from the principle of contradiction (*principium contradictionis*).[17] According to Wolff, Leibniz had not considered that it would be a contradiction if a change of objects or a difference between them were not based upon a sufficient reason. An exception to the universal validity of the principle of sufficient reason is impossible.[18] Even contingent truths, which may be recognised in advance by an infinite intelligence, do not exist without sufficient reason (*Ontologia*, §70, p. 47).

Unlike Leibniz, Wolff's cosmology sees the world as a 'series of changeable things' (*Vernünfftige Gedancken von Gott*, §544, p. 332), which are interconnected in time and space and whose changes derive from powers of the independent things (substances: see §§115–19, pp. 60–2). With this goes the distinction between reason and cause: 'Reason is that whereby one may understand why something is and cause is that which contains in itself the reason for another'.[19] The power of a thing constitutes the sufficient reason for a change in condition (see *Ontologia*, §722, p. 542), and the efficient cause is the action that turns possibility into reality.[20] The sufficient reason for changes in things, and therefore for truth, lies in the 'rules of order which one encounters in those things and their changes' (*Vernünfftige Gedancken von Gott*, §145, p. 76; see also §142, p. 74). This order is accepted as a property of the things themselves and represents a *veritas transcendentalis* (see *Anmerckungen*, §43, pp. 90–1), which cannot be understood through experience (*Vernünfftige Gedancken von Gott*, §722, p. 451). The principle of sufficient reason thus serves Wolff to distinguish between truth and falsehood, between reality and dream: in the land of Cockaigne everything happens without sufficient reason and so is not imaginable without contradiction.[21] To God alone the principle of sufficient reason does not apply since he alone is unchanging (see *Anmerckungen*, §43, pp. 90–1).

Christian August Crusius first presented a penetrating critique of Wolff's principle of sufficient reason in his *Dissertatio philosophica de usu et limitibus principii rationis determinantis, vulgo sufficientis.*[22] He argued that all attempts to derive this principle from the principle of contradiction represented either a *petitio principii* or were based on false reasoning (§§11–14). Since the principle of sufficient reason maintains the absolute necessity of things (§5), the abolition of human free will also abolishes morality (§8, p. 30). Crusius modified the principle of sufficient reason, claiming that all things, except actions that are freely performed, have a determining cause and citing as examples physics and mathematics.[23]

According to Crusius, Wolff also failed to distinguish between *causa*, the real cause (*Realgrund*), and *ratio*, the cognitive cause (*Erkenntnisgrund*).[24] The effective cause of each thing goes back to its power to achieve an effect, a power that Crusius termed 'sufficient power' or 'sufficient cause' (*Entwurf*, §31). The principle of sufficient reason cannot derive from the principle of contradiction since cause and effect do not take place at the same time. The concept of causality is formed instead on the basis of the perception of separate events, such as the observation that fire produces warmth (§32). 'Causality therefore is the relation between A and B that the reality of B depends on the reality of A without B being contemporaneous with A or consequent upon it and without B being a part, determinant or inherent quality of A' (§32).

In the most general sense, the concept of reason in Crusius coincides with that of cause. The real cause is to be understood here as a *principium essendi vel fiendi*, in other words as that which 'produces or makes possible, wholly or in part, the thing itself, outside thoughts' (*Entwurf*, §34). The real cause, by virtue of an effective power, produces the thing itself and thus may be termed the effective cause. This must be distinguished from the 'non-effective real cause' (§36), whose mere existence, according to the laws of truth, makes something else possible or necessary. Crusius is here thinking of geometric and mathematical relations, in which the concept of time plays no part. The cognitive or ideal reason, on the other hand, as *principium cognoscendi*, 'convincingly generates cognition of an object and is recognised as such' (§34). This may be a priori or a posteriori.

Regarding the validity of the universal law of causality, Crusius observes that the necessity of assigning to every existing object an effective cause cannot be inferred from the principle of contradiction[25] but rests on a subjective need: 'Imagine some positive object whose non-existence or existence in different form is conceivable: one will then feel compelled to suggest some other object as the origin' (of this different state) (*Entwurf*, §63, p. 113). The same is true of the formation of particular causal judgements, although Crusius, within his empirical causal analysis, also sticks to rational criteria (see §72, p. 124). Many causal connections can be proved by means of demonstrative or probable inferences. But the transition from effect to cause is explained as a matter of internal feeling (§72, p. 125). Necessary causes such as acts of God, in contrast, rest upon substances that are themselves necessary and cannot be derived from any other causes (see §139).

While Crusius's principle of determinant reason applies to real causes, he believes that the principle of sufficient reason applies to ideal causes (see *Entwurf*, §85). Cause and effect are thus strictly separated. Crusius rejects pre-established harmony in favour of the *influxus physicus*.[26] In causes of existence (*Existentialgründe*), the cause and that which is caused coincide. 'In the case of effective causes, the effect must come after its cause, even if the latter's relation to the effect, according to which the production of the effect can be assigned to it as an effective cause, will not follow until the effect is present' (§131).[27] In this way, Crusius is able to distinguish sharply between ontology (*principium essendi*) and logic, or the psychology of knowledge (*principium cognoscendi*), and, in contrast with Wolff, ontology and physics are equally concerned with the real reasons for things. The principle of sufficient reason thus loses its special status in metaphysics. Truth is no longer defined, as by Wolff, as agreement with order, in the widest sense, but is derived from perception. Crusius dissolves the analytical connection between cause (reason) and effect (result). By acknowledging the temporal relation of cause and effect, he invests causal judgements with a dynamic which had no place in Wolff's principle of sufficient reason. With Crusius, a new chapter in the discussion of causality opened in German school metaphysics, which on several issues recalls ideas that occur in Hume's *Treatise*.

While the analysis of causality in continental Europe in the first half of the eighteenth century generally remained within the seventeenth-century metaphysical tradition, English-language philosophy took a different departure with Locke's 'way of ideas'. This applies also to George Berkeley, whose *Principles of*

Human Knowledge[28] sought to combine the analysis of ideas with a new theory of substance. His understanding of causality presupposes the view that the only true cause of ideas is mind (spirit, soul, self), of whose activity we are immediately aware.[29] Ideas themselves cannot be the cause of other ideas because, as we know from experience, they are purely passive. Since the ideas we perceive in 'continual succession' must have a cause, Berkeley introduces the concept of an 'incorporeal active substance or spirit' (§26, p. 52) as a 'simple undivided active being' (§27, p. 52). Such a being has an understanding capable of perceiving linked ideas and a will that produces and connects ideas. Since it is not in human power to alter the 'laws of nature', known to us by experience, this is clear evidence that God is to be viewed as the origin of all (genuine) ideas that are familiar to us through our senses (see §§33 and 90, pp. 54 and 80). In contrast, the ideas that are effects of human will are changeable (§30, p. 53).

All our causal judgements rest on experience; it is impossible to infer an effect from an experiential idea by mere analysis (*Principles*, §31, p. 54). At the same time, the constancy of natural laws is for Berkeley proof of the goodness and wisdom of God. Alluding to the problem of miracles, he nevertheless expresses the view that God may consider 'exceptions from the general rules of Nature' (§63, p. 68) to be necessary in order that humankind will recognise him as God. On the other hand, we are misled by the constancy of natural events to ascribe a power to ideas themselves that enables them to operate causally on each other (see §32, p. 54). Like Malebranche, Berkeley is convinced that there can be no causal relation between ideas. Our supposed causal conclusion that the sun is the source of heat is revealed as an illusion. As opposed to Malebranche, however, Berkeley emphasises that while it is right that God is the only effective cause, the assumption of a passive *res extensa* as '*unknown occasion*' (§68, p. 70) amounts to an assertion that God has created something without a purpose (see §53, p. 63). This makes it clear that Berkeley's expositions of causality are based on a teleological concept of the created world.

The connection of ideas does not imply the causal relation of cause and effect but rather that of sign and thing signified: 'The fire which I see is not the cause of the pain I suffer upon my approaching it, but the mark that forewarns me of it' (*Principles*, §65, p. 69). With his theory of signs, Berkeley develops Locke's theory of language and enters new territory in the history of modern philosophy. The task of the natural philosopher can only be to understand these signs (§66, pp. 69–70), and narrow boundaries to his knowledge are set. The natural philosopher can have no knowledge of effective causes beyond ordinary experience since these exist only in the will of a spirit. He can achieve only a more extensive comprehension of analogies, harmonies, and agreements in nature on the basis of which he may draw probable conclusions (see §105,

p. 87). The validity of general and special laws of causality cannot be derived from experience. In the end, everything, even the uniformity of nature, depends on a '*governing spirit*', God, and his goodness (§§106–7, pp. 87–8).

First, it is plain philosophers amuse themselves in vain, when they inquire for any natural efficient cause, distinct from a *mind* or *spirit*. Secondly, considering the whole creation is the workmanship of a *wise and good agent*, it should seem to become philosophers, to employ their thoughts (contrary to what some hold) about the final causes of things. (*Principles*, §107, p. 88)

The laws of mechanics and the assumption of an a priori necessity in natural events are reduced to observable regularities, but at the same time teleological explanations are introduced (see §§101–17, pp. 85–94). In the knowledge of final causes, Berkeley saw greater dignity than in the attempt to derive particular phenomena from general rules of nature (see §109, p. 89). The existence of God is made plain in the beauty and perfection of his creation (§§146–7, pp. 107–8); he alone 'maintains that intercourse between spirits, whereby they are able to perceive the existence of each other' (§147, p. 108).

Berkeley accepts two central occasionalist theses: first, we can only posit causal connections where we can consciously complete the causal sequence; and second, no causal influence exists at the level of phenomena or experiential ideas. Unlike Malebranche, however, Berkeley assumes that the human will can itself be causally active. It is human beings who walk, not God. All regularities in nature originate with God, and he maintains the intercourse between finite minds. Natural causality is only one form of derived causality resulting from the will of God. Viewed in this light, the knowledge of natural causes coincides with the knowledge of God.

Such an assessment of causality is alien to David Hume. He is the first modern philosopher whose analyses of causality are totally without theological motives. In terms of method, his discussions are based exclusively on observation and experience and operate in the tension between scepticism and naturalism. Since cause and effect is a matter of judgement of objects, Hume first discusses causality in Bk. 1, Pt. 3 ('Of knowledge and probability') of the *Treatise of Human Nature* (1739–40).[30] All reasoning consists in a comparison of objects and discovery of the relations that exist between them. If both objects of comparison are known through the senses, we speak of 'perception rather than reasoning' (1.3.2.2, SBN 73). Not until Bk. 1, Pt. 4 ('Of the sceptical and other systems of philosophy'), which corresponds to a traditional methodological scheme (in the Port-Royal *Logic* of Arnauld and Nicole and elsewhere), is Hume's scepticism fully revealed. The certainty originally attached to impressions and ideas as such is completely lost when we turn to merely probable judgements, thus demonstrating the fallibility of our cognitive capacity (see 1.4.2.47, SBN 212). The resulting scepticism can be controlled only by falling back on nature, which compels us to suspend our scepticism in daily life. Nature, not reason, directs life.

The relation of cause and effect belongs, with those of resemblance and contiguity in time and place, to the principles of association by means of which Hume explains all connections of ideas (*Treatise*, 1.1.4.1, SBN 11). For us, these three principles are 'the cement of the universe'.[31] At the same time, the special significance of causality is made clear in that it is the only relation which can take us beyond the immediate evidence of our senses and our memory.[32] Through observation and experience, according to Hume, we establish that all our causal judgements are characterised by three elements: objects or events, which we call cause and effect, appear contiguously in space and time; the effect succeeds the cause in time; and the connection of cause and effect, in contrast to chance, is considered necessary (1.3.2.5–11, SBN 75–7). Hume's analysis of causality culminates in the question of the necessary connection between objects: Why is it necessary for everything that exists to have a cause (general causal law)? Why do particular causes necessarily have particular effects? (see 1.3.2.14–15, SBN 78).

Since all ideas can be consistently separated in imagination, it cannot be proved, either intuitively or demonstratively, 'that *whatever begins to exist, must have a cause of existence*' (1.3.3.1, SBN 78). To conclude the necessity of the cause from the concept of effect constitutes a *petitio principii*. What was traditionally implied by the concept of *causa sui* Hume here ironically applies to the objects of experience. What is wrong with assuming that all objects of our experience exist without cause (or are their own cause)? The answer is indirectly given in the *Treatise*:[33] it will turn out that the same elements that explained the status of particular causal judgements also explain the universal law of causality (see 1.3.3.9, SBN 82).

Before we turn to the particular law of causality, it should be noted that the problem of causality already exists at two more fundamental levels. In the first place, according to Hume, the constant connection of similar perceptions is a convincing proof (1.1.1.8, SBN 5) that impressions are the cause of our ideas and not vice versa. It is impossible to have an idea that does not originate in an impression.[34] In the *Enquiry*, however, Hume avoids speaking of impressions as the causes of ideas. But he does speak there of custom as the 'cause of this cause' (*Enquiry*, 5.1.5, SBN 43).

Secondly, Hume asserts that impressions (of sensation, not reflexion) themselves have a cause (the 'real cause of any event', *Enquiry*, 6.1, SBN 56) which we, however, cannot know (see *Treatise*, 1.1.1.12, SBN 7). Therefore it cannot be determined whether God, external things or bodies (unknown to us), or our own minds are the cause of our impressions. Hume here deliberately takes up the God-world-mind triad of traditional metaphysics;[35] a fourth object is not possible. However, for real causal analysis, the cause of impressions is irrelevant. Put another way, Hume's causal analysis is compatible with the thesis that all our causal judgements are concerned with mere appearances.[36] Since Hume generally argues with reference to observation and experience, which yet can never deal with the causes of our impressions, the question arises whether he does not go beyond the limits of his empiricism, for he does not dispute that impressions do have a cause.

According to Hume, neither rationalism nor traditional empiricism was in a position to explain the nature of causal judgements. The falsity of the analytical ontological conception is already manifest in the definition of impressions as independently existing entities. Cause and effect are not qualities or relations of our perceptions and therefore cannot be known by reason. Causal judgements are not based upon a comparison of ideas (as is the case with demonstrative judgements) and so cannot achieve any 'knowledge and certainty' (*Treatise*, 1.3.1.2, SBN 70) in the strict sense of the term. The *empirical* conception of causality, according to which causes possess an active power that produces the effect, is untenable because we cannot foresee the effect B from the existence of event A (see *Enquiry*, 7.1.10, SBN 64–5). If we attend to objects as such, each can equally well function as cause and effect. Furthermore, there is as little distinction between effective, formal, material, and final causes as between cause and occasion (see *Treatise*, 1.3.14.33–6, SBN 171–2). Not only do we have no knowledge of the real causes of our impressions, but we are also denied knowledge of the 'secret operation' (1.3.8.13, SBN 104) by which we reach our causal conclusions (see *Enquiry*, 11.30, SBN 148).

If causality can neither be put down to an observable characteristic of things nor be apprehended by reason, the philosopher of human nature is forced to fall back on imagination as the effective power of the perceiving subject. On this interpretation, all our causal judgements are based on impressions of the memory or the senses as well as on the idea of that existence which summons up the impressions in us. They are distinguished from the ideas of the imagination by their great vivacity alone. It is here that Hume introduces the concept of belief.

To believe is in this case to feel an immediate impression of the senses, or a repetition of that impression in the memory. 'Tis merely the force and liveliness of the perception, which constitutes the first act of the judgement and lays the foundation of that reasoning, which we build upon it, when we trace the relation of cause and effect. (*Treatise*, 1.3.5.7, SBN 86)

Only by experience can we deduce the existence of one object from the existence of another. We observe and recall that an object of class A always appears in contiguity with and in temporal sequence with an object of class B. 'Thus in advancing we have insensibly discover'd a new relation betwixt cause and effect, when we least expected it, and were entirely employ'd upon another subject. This relation is their CONSTANT CONJUNCTION' (1.3.6.3, SBN 87). With this relation, Hume has found the sought-after factor in our causal judgements: similar objects always appear in the same relations of contiguity and succession (see 1.3.6.3, SBN 88). But how are we entitled to conclude that one instance of B will follow after one instance of A, when we have previously always observed B to follow A? It could only be a rational inference if future objects were to resemble those of which we have experience, that is, if the future resembled the past. However, first, since we can imagine that the course of nature undergoes change, it can be no demonstrative argument and thus no knowledge in the strict sense of the word. If, secondly, we stick to experience, it can only be a probable judgement; but in this the unity of experience is already presupposed (see 1.3.6.7 and 12, SBN 90, 92). Accordingly, Hume argues, the constant conjunction depends not on reason but on imagination.

In order to prove this positively, Hume refers to the concept of belief. Belief is 'an idea related to or associated with a present impression' (1.3.6.15, SBN 93). The difference between an object in whose existence we believe and one in which we do not believe does not depend on the fact that a new idea has been joined to the object (existence is not a predicate) but only on the way in which we conceive of the object. 'An opinion, therefore, or belief may be most accurately defin'd, A LIVELY IDEA RELATED TO OR ASSOCIATED WITH A PRESENT IMPRESSION' (1.3.7.2 and 5, SBN 94, 95, 96). A present impression is the 'true and real cause' (1.3.8.8, SBN 102) of the idea, which is accompanied by belief. Belief causes 'an idea to imitate the effects of the impressions' (1.3.10.3, SBN 119).

Not reason but custom and habit are thus the guidelines of our causal judgements. They are the only warrant for our belief that the future will resemble the past (see 1.3.12.8, SBN 133–4). They produce in us a felt compulsion to conclude an instance of B from the existence of an instance of A. We owe our causal judgements to a mechanism which operates even in irrational beasts and ensures that only such ideas as are commonly connected in previous experience will achieve the vividness of impressions (see 1.3.14.20, SBN 164–5). The second of the two definitions of cause which Hume gives in the *Treatise* runs: 'A CAUSE is an object precedent and contiguous to another, and so united with it, that the idea of the one determines the mind to form the idea of the other, and the impression of the one to form a more lively idea of the other' (1.3.14.31, SBN 170). Thus the validity of the special causal judgement is proved: '*that instances of which we have no experience, must necessarily resemble those, of which we have*' (1.3.8.13, SBN 104).

Humean causal analysis has disastrous consequences for the *causa sui* theory and hence for rational theology. It excludes that a cause can be known only through its effect (God-creature) and that a cause can be singular, or particular, and have no parallels or similarity with any others (see *Enquiry*, 11.30, SBN 148). Hume's conception of belief rules out acceptance of the existence of a cause that in principle cannot be observed. This is also central to Hume's critique of miracles: we do not believe the evidence of a person who tells of a miracle because such an event by definition contradicts the previously observed course of nature. It is more probable that the witness is not telling the truth than that the course of nature has actually altered (see 10.2, SBN 116–31).

Within his 'science of MAN' (*Treatise*, Intro., SBN xv), Hume not only denies that there are different kinds of causes but also maintains that there is no distinction between *moral* and *physical* necessity (1.3.14.33, SBN 171). By deriving causality from the regularity of observable events, he indicates that even the concept of the efficient cause no longer has any function in philosophy. This also answers the question of the validity of the general law of causality: There is no 'absolute or metaphysical necessity' (1.3.14.35, SBN 172) that every object that comes into existence must have a cause.

Probably the most significant contemporary criticism of Hume's 'doctrine of ideas', his scepticism, and analysis of causality in English-speaking philosophy is that of Thomas Reid, who develops a striking alternative theory, also concerning causation.[37] The structure of Reid's argument is two-tiered. First, he suggests that Hume's criticism of empirical physical causation is mistaken; secondly, he argues that although 'physical causation' is a legitimate concept, Hume is right that it is not real 'efficient causation' but that the latter, pace Hume, is an entirely warranted concept.

The rejection of Hume's criticism of causation is threefold. First, Reid applies his basic epistemological principle, that it is wrong to think of sensation as some sort of image of its object. It makes no sense to seek similarity between a sensation of sweetness and a piece of candy, yet the thoughts that derive from the sensations are meaningfully *about* the sweetness. In the same way, although Hume is right that we cannot locate a sensation ('impression') that pictures the causal link between two perceived events, the thought suggested by the perception can be about the two events as cause and effect.

In addition, there are two arguments directly against the Humean notion of constant conjunction. On the one hand, says Reid, we clearly give causal accounts of events that have not occurred with any constancy, such as unique or first-time occurrences. On the other hand, we are not led by all constant conjunctions to think of their constituents as cause and effect, Reid's example being that of night and day. It is not regularity that identifies causes but rather our judgement regulated by basic principles of common sense and corrected by experience, and systematic correction is what we know as science. In this way, we find the laws of nature that state the 'physical causes' of things.

However, although the scientific laws of nature state which things and events in nature cause which other things and events, they do not tell us the underlying or real cause, what Reid calls the 'efficient cause'. When the motion of one billiard ball is explained by the physical impact of another ball, through reference to the relevant laws of physics, we still do not have an explanation of *why* these relations should hold in the world. In contrast to Hume, Reid thinks that this question of the necessity of the laws of nature can be answered coherently. His solution is in terms of the idea of power. Power belongs only to agents, that is, to beings with minds and will who can judge whether or not to exercise their power. So, while one billiard ball moves 'because' of the impact of the other, there is only such movement at all because some agent exerted power and could have done otherwise. Human agents exert limited powers, but behind the physical causes of nature at large is the efficient cause of God. The laws of nature thus detail the physical causes whose necessity derives from the efficient causation of the divinity.

The second innovation in the theory of causation, whose importance extends far beyond the eighteenth century, is Immanuel Kant's attempt to understand causal judgements as synthetic judgements a priori. According to a famous remark of Kant's in the preface to the *Prolegomena zu einer jeden künftigen Metaphysik* (1783)[38] about the beginnings of his critical philosophy, it was Hume's causal analysis that roused Kant from his 'dogmatic slumber'. On the basis of the Humean exposition in the *Enquiry*, Kant tells us, he had seen the need for a complete assessment of human reason, leading to categories as pure intellectual concepts. Their application to the manifold of our sensibility makes the necessary unity of our experience understandable since man becomes a legislator for nature.

Whether Kant's account of the development of his thought is true or simply a stylisation to invoke the triad of dogmatism, scepticism, and criticism is a continuing source of controversy. If one takes it literally, then Hume's impact on Kant must postdate 1770, the year of Kant's inaugural dissertation, *De mundi sensibilis atque intelligibilis forma et principiis*.[39] In his letter of 21 February 1772 to his former student Marcus Herz,[40] Kant raises for the first time the question of the bearing of pure intellectual concepts and hence the category of causality on the manifold of our sensibility.

For the reception of Hume's philosophy after 1755 in Germany and in particular for the development of Kant's thought after 1770, the critique of Hume's causal analysis by two adherents of Wolff is very instructive. This strikingly highlights the systematic differences between Hume's empiricism and the rationalism of Wolff's followers.[41] Moses Mendelssohn and Johann Georg Sulzer point out that empirical judgements can only be necessary if, contrary to Hume's view, we allow reason or understanding a decisive share in them. Herz also raises this point in his *Betrachtungen aus der spekulativen Weltweisheit*,[42] published in 1771 on the occasion of Kant's inaugural dissertation. In it he reviews Hume's thoughts on the validity of causal law and induction as developed in Section IV ('Sceptical doubts concerning the operations of the understanding') of the *Enquiry*. Herz here refers to Mendelssohn's essay 'Ueber die Wahrscheinlichkeit',[43] which appeared in the second part of his *Philosophische Schriften* (1761), the second corrected edition (1771) of which was known to Kant. Mendelssohn points out in his essay.

All our judgements based upon experience, analogy or induction, have been attacked by the learned sceptic David Hume in his *Philosophical Essays*. The German translation[44] of this work is in everyone's hand and we shall quote the chief objections from the fourth section which he calls *Sceptical Doubts concerning the Understanding*, which generally appear to suspend physical certainty.[45]

Mendelssohn then cites a longer passage from Part II of this section, in which Hume considers why frequent experience tends to make us expect similar effects from apparently similar causes. However, in his exposition and critique of the Humean position, Mendelssohn appears to suffer from a significant misapprehension.[46] Already in the preface to the first edition, he alerts the reader to his purpose of 'defending the correctness of all our experimental reasoning against the attacks of the English philosopher *David Hume*'.[47] The reader of the preface is left with the impression that Hume was determined to leave the validity of particular causal judgements in this disastrous situation. But it is not because he has not understood Hume that Mendelssohn ignores Hume's own justification for particular causal judgements as developed in later sections of the *Philosophical Essays*; it is because they *must* be factually inadequate. This is proved for Mendelssohn when Hume in the fourth Essay (section) unequivocally doubts a causal analysis in which reason plays an essential part. For Mendelssohn it is indubitable that, for instance, 'all voluntary decisions have predetermined certainty; for whatever objectively has no predetermined certainty cannot be known'.[48] No grounds of truth can remain hidden from an 'infinite intelligence' (512, see also 162).

Sulzer pleads a similar rationalist case when he points out, in his 'Anmerkungen über den fünften Versuch', that 'custom, approbation and belief are mere words which do not and can not explain anything, unless one may understand a series of concepts by them'.[49] In the same essay, he writes:

I cannot conceal that this present essay has caused me some bewilderment. I had not supposed that so acute and judicious a man as Mr. Hume could lapse into such a strange kind of philosophising as to give explanations and solutions that scarcely differ by a hair's breadth from the long since rejected introduction of hidden attributes (*qualitates occultae*). (131)

A similar characterisation occurs in Kant's *Kritik der reinen Vernunft*, where Hume's justification of the necessity of causal connections by means of custom is called 'a disturbing proposition' (A 765/B 793), and 'sceptical aberrations' are spoken of which have arisen because Hume – like other dogmatists – 'did not systematically survey all the kinds of *a priori* synthesis of the understanding' (A 767/B 795).

If we follow Mendelssohn's and Sulzer's arguments, then Hume's causal analysis necessarily breaks down because our 'experimental reasoning' cannot be established without a rational element. This, however, is basically the problem that Kant was examining in the early 1770s: in what way are pure intellectual concepts to be applied to the manifold of our sensibility in order to make possible the unity and necessity of experience?

In the *Kritik*, Kant counts 'causality and dependence (cause and effect)' (A 80/B 106) among the categories of relation. The categories in this 'Table of Categories' are exhaustively derived from the so-called table of judgment; they represent pure concepts of the understanding whose objective validity for the manifold of our sensibility is given in the section on their deduction. Since it is impossible to use categories pure and in abstraction from the conditions of our sensibility, the analytical-ontological concept of causation is doomed from the start.[50] The synthetic a priori principle of causality must always relate to an actual manifold given in the pure intuitive forms of space and time (see A 246–7/B 303). The objects we experience are not things in themselves but appearances. However, causality cannot be perceived through the senses either and is not a property given in appearances (A 137–8/B 176–7).

Along with Hume and Locke, Kant thus raises the question of how '*subjective conditions of thinking* should have *objective validity*' (*Kritik*, A 89/B 122). According to Kant, the unity of experience presupposes the a priori necessity of the formal conditions of our knowledge, so the objective validity of the categories as purely synthetic a priori concepts cannot be proved in an empirical deduction, but require a transcendental deduction. Such a necessity cannot be established by laws of association (B 127–8; A 765–6/B 793–4). Nature is thus conceived as a system of experience constituted on a priori synthetic principles. In some places in the second edition of the *Kritik*, Kant holds up for Hume that pure mathematics and the general natural sciences with their a priori knowledge are facts (see B 128), but this seems to be a circular argument that does not take Humean scepticism seriously.

The so-called principles chapter in the *Kritik*, in which the synthetic a priori principles of the understanding are exhaustively developed in accordance with the table of categories, is not an attempt to prove empirical laws of nature in Newton's sense. Nor does the second analogy, on the 'Principle of temporal sequence according to the law of causality',[51] deal with the problem of induction. Induction comes into the work only insofar as it, in Kant's eyes, is an entirely unsuitable method of proving the necessary validity of the general law of causality.[52] But Kant has a more fundamental concern. He wants to justify the a priori legitimacy of comprehending all changes in the world under the 'law of the connection of cause and effect' (B 232). The general law of causality would therefore be valid for all objects of experience, but questions about which objects should be understood as causes and which as effects according to particular causal judgements are no part of the *Kritik*'s transcendental philosophy (see A 135/B 174).

How can the validity of the general law of causality be proved? Presupposing the first analogy of experience about the persistence of substances, Kant understands the change (succession) of appearances as an alteration of the persisting substances. The second analogy states, 'All alterations occur in accordance with the law of the connection of cause and effect' (B 232).

All connections of perceptions go back to the synthetic power of the imagination, which determines the inner sense whose form is time. Through the subjective apprehension of the manifold of sensibility, however, the order of events will remain uncertain. An objective relationship between perceptions is only present when it is determined to be a necessary one. Whereas Hume falls back upon a merely subjectively felt necessity (B 127, B 168) to make the experience of causal relationships understandable, Kant focuses on causality as a pure concept of the understanding that expresses the necessity for a synthetic unity in its application to perceptions.

It is only because we subject the sequence of the appearances and thus all alteration to the law of causality that experience itself, i.e., empirical cognition of them, is possible; consequently they themselves, as objects of experience, are possible only in accordance with this law. (B 234)

In other words, as categories are applied to the succession of representations in the inner sense, this merely subjective sequence becomes an objectively necessary one. This defines an experiential object: 'That in the appearance which contains the condition of this necessary rule of apprehension is the object' (A 191/B 236). The principle of the causal relation is valid for all objects of experience because without it no experience is possible (A 202/B 247).

For Kant, just as for Crusius and Hume, time plays an important role in causal analysis, but whereas for Hume the succession of cause and effect is fundamental, Kant also recognises a simultaneity of cause and effect that is relevant for most efficient causes in nature (A 202–3/B 248).

Having proved the a priori validity of the general law of causality, Kant directs his attention, in the *Metaphysische Anfangsgründe der Naturwissenschaft*,[53] to specific principles of Newtonian physics, applying the synthetic principles a priori to the empirical concept of matter. In the third chapter of this work ('Metaphysical Foundations of Mechanics'), the law of inertia is linked to the category of causality. According to Proposition 3, the second law of mechanics states that 'every change in matter has an external cause' (Ak 4: 543). Thus we are familiar with synthetic a priori laws of nature since without them empirical knowledge would be impossible. In addition, however, there are also particular laws of nature which can only be found out by concrete experience.[54] Particular laws of nature presuppose causality as an a priori synthetic law of nature; only *after* causality has been proved as an a priori synthetic principle can we fall back on induction to discover particular laws of nature.[55]

In a century shaped above all by Hume's and Kant's innovative theories of causality, we may distinguish the following general lines. In continental Europe, following the tradition of the Leibniz-Wolff school, causality continued to be understood as an ontological principle, whereas British empiricism, with Locke and Hume, took an epistemological turn that Kant continued on different premises. While Aristotelianism, with its four different causes, continued to operate in some places well into the eighteenth century, the new scientific advances focused attention exclusively on the efficient cause. Nevertheless, it should not be overlooked that with Kant the concept of *causa finalis* deriving from the reflective power of judgement underwent a significant revival, particularly in his *Kritik der Urtheilskraft*.[56] It was Kant, too, who sought to establish how the causality of a free-acting person can be combined with natural causality.[57]

As in other areas of philosophy, with causality too the limits and capacity of reason are put to the test. Whereas Hume generally uses reason and understanding interchangeably and transforms the theory of judgement in the strictly logical sense into a theory of association of ideas and impressions, Kant differentiates sharply between the scope of reason in the narrower sense and that of the understanding, both of them objects of a critique of reason in the wider sense. And, whereas Hume with his critique of rationalism bases causal judgements on our affective powers, Kant seeks to achieve the necessary validity for the law of causality by probing the extent and limits of human understanding as an a priori faculty.

Despite all their differences, Hume and Kant share a problem in their explanations of causality, which they are not able to solve and which may have contributed to the fact that towards the end of the eighteenth century, influential authors were again looking at causality – and at substance – as a matter of ontology. Both Hume and Kant understand causality as a relation which can only be established between the objects of our experience. But at the same time they asserted that impressions or appearances are caused in us by objects we cannot know. Kant's distinction between thing in itself and phenomenon and the quasi-causal function of the thing in itself gave rise to a lively debate which led to the philosophy of German idealism by way of Friedrich Heinrich Jacobi, Gottlob Ernst Schulze, and others.

Kant's claim to have demonstrated the validity of the general law of causality against Hume was among the controversial topics in the philosophy of the time. In his anonymous work *Aenesidemus*,[58] Schulze offers a detailed critique of Karl Leonhard Reinhold's 'fundamental philosophy' (*Elementarphilosophie*), which was intended to set Kantian criticism on a secure foundation. At the same time, he casts doubt on whether Kant really did refute Hume. According to Schulze, Hume would point to the transcendental dialectic of the *Kritik der reinen Vernunft* and argue that Kant's own attempt to justify objective regularity on subjective grounds itself rests on a transcendental illusion.[59] If cause and effect constitute a category by means of which alone we can determine the manifold of our sensibility, how can we talk of the necessity of causal connections? In contrast with Kant, Schulze demands proof of causality as an objective principle of the things themselves. Just as Kant supplied the results but not the correct premises of critical philosophy, so too with Reinhold: Hume has not been refuted (*Aenesidemus*, 135). With his demand for a justification of the principle of causality as a principle of objects themselves, Schulze reverts to a problem from the beginning of the century, yet he also opens up a new chapter in the history of causality.

NOTES

1 See Aristotle, *Metaphysica*, 983a, in *The Complete Works*, ed. J. Barnes, 2 vols. (Princeton, NJ, 1984), 2: 1555.

2 See note 31.

3 René Descartes, *Meditationes de prima philosophia* (Paris, 1641), as translated in *The Philosophical Writings*, trans. J. Cottingham, R. Stotthoff, and D. Murdoch, 3 vols. (Cambridge, 1984–91).

4 John Locke, *An Essay Concerning Human Understanding*, ed. P. H. Nidditch, in *The Clarendon Edition* (Oxford, 1975).

5 See Immanuel Kant, *Kritik der reinen Vernunft* (1781) in Ak, vol. 4, referred to as A, (1787), 2nd edn., in Ak 3, referred to as B, translated as *Critique of Pure Reason*, trans. and eds. P. Guyer and A. W. Wood, in *Works* (1998): A6/B10 ff.

6 David Hume, *A Treatise of Human Nature* (1739–40), eds. D. F. Norton and M. J. Norton, in the *Clarendon Edition* (2006).

7 See my Chapter 12 'Substances and Modes, Space and Time', this volume.

8 Nicolas Malebranche, *De la recherche de la vérité* (1674–5), ed. G. Rodis-Lewis, in *Oeuvres complètes*, ed. A. Robinet, 22 vols. (Paris, 1958–84), vol. 1, translated as *The Search after Truth*, trans. T. M. Lennon and P. J. Olscamp (Columbus, OH, 1980).

9 Malebranche, *Recherche*, VI.ii.3, trans., 448.

10 'A natural cause is therefore not a real and true but only an occasional cause, which determines the Author of nature to act in such and such a manner in such and such a situation' (*Recherche*, VI.ii.3, trans., 448).

11 For Malebranche's influence on Berkeley, see Charles J. McCracken, *Malebranche and British Philosophy* (Oxford, 1983), ch. 6.

12 Baruch de Spinoza, *Ethica ordine geometrico demonstrata* (1677), translated as *Ethics* by S. Stirling, ed. S. Feldman (Indianapolis, IN, 1992).

13 Gottfried Wilhelm Leibniz, *Monadologie* [1714, first published in a German translation: *Lehr-Sätze über die Monadologie*, trans. H. Köhler, Frankfurt an der Oder, Leipzig, Jena, 1720; first publication of the French original in 1840], ed. É. Boutroux (Paris, 1970), translated as *Monadology*, in *Philosophical Papers and Letters*, trans. and ed. L. E. Loemker, 2 vols. (Chicago, IL, 1956); the volumes are consecutively paginated. In this connection, Leibniz cites §§44 and 106 of his *Essais de théodicée sur la bonté de Dieu, la liberté de l'homme et l'origine du mal* (1710), in *Philosophischen Schriften*, 6: 21–462; see *Theodicy: Essays on the Goodness of God, the Freedom of Man and the Origin of Evil*, trans. E. M. Huggard, ed. A. Farrer (London, 1951), 147, 249.

14 See Leibniz, *Monadology*, §36, 2: 1050, and the references given there to *Theodicy*, §§37, 44, 45, and 49; trans., 94–5, 98–9, 101.

15 Christian Wolff, *Vernünfftige Gedancken von Gott, der Welt und der Seele des Menschen, auch allen Dingen überhaupt*, ed. C. A. Corr, in *Werke*, I.2 (1983).

16 Wolff, *Philosophia prima, sive Ontologia, methodo scientifica pertractata* (1730), in *Werke*, II.3 (1962).

17 Carl Günther Ludovici, 'Satz des zureichenden Grundes', his *Dissertatione de ratione philoso-phandi in genere* (Leipzig, 1730), in Johann Heinrich Zedler, *Grosses vollständiges Universal-Lexikon aller Wissenschaften und Künsten*, 64 vols. (Halle and Leipzig, 1732–50), 64: cols. 395–430; see also John Edwin Gurr, *The Principle of Sufficient Reason in some Scholastic Systems, 1750–1900* (Milwaukee, WI, 1959), 35–49.

18 See Wolff, *Anmerckungen über die vernünfftigen Gedancken von Gott, der Welt und der Seele* (1740), in *Werke*, I.3 (1983), §§14–15, pp. 8–9.

19 Wolff, *Vernünfftige Gedancken von Gott*, §29, p. 15; see also *Ontologia*, §56, p. 39 and §881, p. 652.

20 Wolff, *Vernünfftige Gedancken von Gott*, §120, pp. 62–3; and *Ontologia*, §886, p. 652.

21 See Wolff, *Anmerckungen* §15, p. 32; *Vernünfftige Gedancken von Gott*, §142, p. 75; *Ontologia*, §493, pp. 379 ff. On the subject of dreams and the land of Cockaigne in Wolff, see Sonia Carboncini, *Transzendentale Wahrheit und Traum: Christian Wolffs Antwort auf die Herausforderung durch den Cartesianischen Zweifel* (Stuttgart-Bad Cannstatt, 1991).

22 Christian August Crusius, *Dissertatio philosophica de usu et limitibus principii rationis determi-nantis, vulgo sufficientis* (Leipzig, 1743). In what follows I refer to the German translation,

Ausführliche Abhandlung von dem rechten Gebrauche und der Einschränkung des sogenannten Satzes vom zureichenden oder besser determinierenden Grunde, 2nd edn. (Leipzig, 1766).

23 See Crusius, *Entwurf der nothwendigen Vernunft-Wahrheiten, wiefern sie den zufälligen entgegen gesetzet werden* (Leipzig, 1745), §84.

24 See, in what follows, Carboncini, *Transzendentale Wahrheit*, 204–5.

25 Crusius, *Weg zur Gewissheit und Zuverlässigkeit der menschlichen Erkenntnis* (Leipzig, 1747), §260, p. 471.

26 Crusius, *Entwurf*, §§363–4, p. 485.

27 Crusius, *Weg zur Gewissheit*, §141, p. 258.

28 George Berkeley, *A Treatise concerning the Principles of Human Knowledge* (1710), in *Works*, 2: 19–113.

29 See my Chapter 12, this volume.

30 Hume, *Treatise*; see note 6.

31 Hume, *An Abstract of a Book lately Published: Entituled, A Treatise of Human Nature* (London, 1740); see *Treatise*, Abstr. 35, SBN 662.

32 See Hume, *Treatise*, 1.3.2.3, SBN 74, and his *An Enquiry Concerning Human Understanding* (1748), ed. T. L. Beauchamp, in *The Clarendon Edition* (2000), 4.1.4, SBN 26.

33 Hume does not discuss the general law of causality in his *Enquiry*.

34 The only exception to this is the so-called missing shade of blue; see Hume, *Treatise*, 1.1.1.10, SBN 6.

35 See Locke, *Essay*, IV.xi.1; Hume, *Treatise*, 1.3.5.1, SBN 84, and *Enquiry*, 12.1.13, SBN 153.

36 See Étienne Bonnot de Condillac, *Traité des sensations*, 2 vols. (London, 1754), Pt. 4, ch. 4, in 2:196–200.

37 Thomas Reid, *Essays on the Intellectual Powers of Man* (1785), eds. D. R. Brookes and K. Haakonssen (Edinburgh, 2002), VI. 6; Reid, *Essays on the Active Powers of Man* (1788), in *Philosophical Works*, 511–679, Essays I and IV. See also the extensive discussions in Reid's correspondence with Lord Kames and James Gregory, *The Correspondence of Thomas Reid*, ed. P. B. Wood (Edinburgh, 2002).

38 Immanuel Kant, *Prolegomena zu einer jeden künftigen Metaphysik die als Wissenschaft wird auftreten können* (1783), Ak 4: 253–383, translated as *Prolegomena to Any Future Metaphysics that Will Be Able to Come Forward as a Science*, trans. G. Hatfield, in *Theoretical Philosophy after 1781*, trans. G. Hatfield et al., eds. H. Allison and P. Heath, in *Works* (2002).

39 Kant, *De mundi sensibilis atque intelligibilis forma et principiis* (1770), Ak 2: 385–419; translated as *On the Form and Principles of the Sensible and the Intelligible World*, in *Theoretical Philosophy 1755–1770*, trans. and eds. D. Walford and R. Meerbote, in *Works* (1992).

40 Kant, Ak 10: 123–30; translated in *Correspondence*, trans. and ed. A. Zweig, in *Works* (1999).

41 See Heiner F. Klemme, *Kants Philosophie des Subjekts: Systematische und entwicklungsgeschichtliche Untersuchungen zum Verhältnis von Selbstbewusstsein und Selbsterkenntnis* (Hamburg, 1996), 55–75.

42 See Marcus Herz, *Betrachtungen aus der spekulativen Weltweisheit* (1771), eds. E. Conrad et al. (Hamburg, 1990), 71–3.

43 Moses Mendelssohn's essay was first published in 1756 as 'Gedanken von der Wahrscheinlichkeit' in *Vermischte Abhandlungen und Urtheile über das Neueste aus Gelehrsamkeit* (Berlin, 1756): 3–26, then as 'Ueber die Wahrscheinlichkeit' in Mendelssohn, *Philosophische Schriften* (Berlin, 1761); re-published in *Gesammelte Schriften*, ed. F. Bamberger, vol. 1 (1971); translated as 'On Probability', in Mendelssohn, *Philosophical Writings*, trans. and ed. D. Dahlstrom (Cambridge, 1997), pp. 233–50. See also Manfred Kuehn, 'David Hume and Moses Mendelssohn', *Hume Studies*, 21 (1995): 197–220.

44 Hume's *Philosophical Essays Concerning Human Understanding* (Edinburgh, 1748; later known as the first *Enquiry*) was translated, edited, and published by Johann Georg Sulzer as *Philosophische Versuche über die menschliche Erkenntniss, von David Hume, Ritter. Als dessen vermischter Schriften Zweyter Theil. Nach der zweyten vermehrten Ausgabe aus dem Englischen übersetzt und mit Anmerkungen des Herausgebers begleitet* (Hamburg and Leipzig, 1755).

45 Mendelssohn, 'Ueber die Wahrscheinlichkeit', *Gesammelte Schriften* vol. 1, 505–15. See also his 'Gedanken von der Wahrscheinlichkeit' in the same vol. 156–7.

46 See G. Zart, *Einfluss der englischen Philosophen seit Bacon auf die deutsche Philosophie des 18. Jahrhunderts* (Berlin, 1881), 114.

47 Mendelssohn, *Philosophische Schriften* (1771), 'Vorrede zur ersten Auflage 1761', in *Gesammelte Schriften zur Philosophie und Ästhetik*, 230.

48 Mendelssohn, 'Ueber die Wahrscheinlichkeit', 515.

49 Sulzer, *Philosophische Versuche*, 132.

50 See Kant, *Kritik*, B 289–91; Kant, *Prolegomena*, Ak 4: 313.

51 Kant, *Kritik*, B232; in what follows I refer to the 2nd (B) edition of the *Kritik*.

52 See Kant, *Kritik*, A 24/B 3–5, A 91/B 124, A 196/B 241.

53 Kant, 'Vorrede', in *Metaphysische Anfangsgründe der Naturwissenschaft* (1786), Ak 4: 467–79, translated as *Metaphysical Foundations of Natural Science* by M. Friedman in *Works/Theoretical Philosophy after 1781*.

54 See Kant, *Kritik*, A 216/B 263.

55 See Michael Friedman, *Kant and the Exact Sciences* (Cambridge, MA, 1992), ch. 3.

56 Kant, *Kritik der Urtheilskraft* (1790), Ak 5: 165–485, translated as *Critique of the Power of Judgment*, trans. P. Guyer and E. Matthews, ed. P. Guyer, in *Works* (2000).

57 See also the Third Antinomy in the *Kritik der reinen Vernunft*, A 445/B 473.

58 Gottlob Ernst Schulze, *Aenesidemus, oder Über die Fundamente der Elementarphilosophie* (1792), ed. A. Liebert (Berlin, 1911).

59 Schulze, *Aenesidemus*, 130–3.

14

KNOWLEDGE AND BELIEF

MANFRED KUEHN

I. INTRODUCTION

We are, without doubt, credulous animals. We must believe something. And, as Bertrand Russell once pointed out, in the absence of good grounds for belief, we will be satisfied with bad ones. Philosophers like to think of themselves as more discriminating than others, claiming not only that they are better at distinguishing good grounds of belief from bad ones but also that they are better at resisting badly grounded beliefs. Certain cynics have tried to undermine this belief in philosophy as itself badly grounded, pointing out that there is no position, however implausible and absurd, that has not been held by some philosopher at some time, or arguing that philosophy can provide us only with bad reasons for what we already believe anyway. Still others went so far as to argue that no ground of belief is intrinsically better than any other ground of belief. But most philosophers in the Western tradition, including those called skeptics, have insisted that their enterprise had to do with exposing bad grounds of belief and replacing them with good ones. The philosophers of the eighteenth century were deeply concerned with accomplishing this feat. Indeed, they were trying to expose all kinds of prejudices for what they were and to replace them with justified and true claims.

Belief that is based on good grounds is usually called knowledge. Therefore, we may also say that these philosophers were fundamentally interested in replacing mere belief with knowledge. Yet there was – and is – no agreement on what constitutes 'good grounds'. Philosophical views on the nature of knowledge differ widely and radically. Knowledge and its relation to belief has remained a problem for philosophers. In fact, the problem of knowledge belongs to that relatively small group of problems that gives Western philosophy its characteristic outlook. Knowledge and belief have remained central topics of discussion from the very beginnings of philosophy in Greece until today. Whatever else we may or may not say of the theories of Heraclitus and Parmenides, Plato and Aristotle, the Stoics and the Epicureans, the Skeptics and most of the other philosophical

389

sects or schools of antiquity, it is true that they were fundamentally concerned with the definition of genuine knowledge and the establishment of its relation to mere beliefs. This was not just a theoretical problem but had for them profound implications for the way they lived, for they found that the 'unexamined life is not worth living'.

However, not everyone would agree that knowledge consists of beliefs that are true and in some sense justified. There are some who believe that knowledge and belief have little to do with each other. Thus, Sir Karl Popper, in his paper on 'Epistemology without a Knowing Subject', contrasts 'belief philosophers' with those who are concerned with 'objective contents of thought'. Following Frege, he argues that these objective contents of thought are entirely independent of our subjective psychological states or beliefs. They belong to a world entirely different and distinct from that of subjective mental states.[1] Belief philosophers are most interested in our subjective beliefs and their basis or origin; those who believe in a 'third world' of objective contents of thought are not very interested in such psychological matters. Popper mentions Plato, Hegel, Bolzano, and Frege as prime examples for the objective view and Descartes, Locke, Berkeley, Hume, Kant, and Russell as representatives of belief philosophers. By Popper's definition, the majority of the eighteenth-century philosophers we will discuss – and indeed most of the philosophers we will not discuss – were belief philosophers. Most of them felt that our subjective beliefs, their basis and origins are most important to understanding objective knowledge. Indeed, their philosophical program was to a large extent defined by the problem of how subjective beliefs can give rise to objective knowledge. The fundamental exception was Christian Wolff. And Kant's position, which arose as a response to both Wolff and Hume, is perhaps a hybrid in this regard as well.

Eighteenth-century philosophers, in various ways, were trying to revive ancient approaches to philosophizing and living. Most of them also had some knowledge of the views that had been formulated during the period that is today commonly referred to as the Middle Ages, their view of this period was in general rather negative. During the Middle Ages, the problem of knowledge and belief had been assimilated into the problem of knowledge versus (religious) faith. The thinkers of the eighteenth century tried to escape the problems connected with this religious dimension. In doing so, they were deeply influenced by developments of the preceding century (the beginning of the 'modern' period). It has been argued that all of their problems had their roots in the seventeenth century. This is an exaggeration, but it is true that for understanding the framework in which the problem of knowledge and belief arose for the eighteenth century, it is necessary to know the broad outlines of the discussion of knowledge in the seventeenth century and especially the theories of René

Descartes (1596–1650) and John Locke (1632–1704). Indeed, it would be difficult to overestimate the historical importance of Locke's theory of belief for the eighteenth century. While it might go too far to say that Locke was 'the intellectual ruler of the eighteenth century,' his influence was to a large extent an eighteenth-century phenomenon.[2]

Descartes's conception of knowledge was defined by the problems of the emerging natural sciences in the sixteenth and seventeenth centuries. He wanted to provide the foundation for scientific knowledge. All knowledge was for him 'certain and evident cognition'.[3] He believed that to obtain such cognitions, we must follow a definite method. This method is usually called Descartes's method of doubt. He argued that it was necessary for once to doubt everything, since, he claimed, 'there is not one of my former beliefs about which a doubt may not properly be raised.... So in future I must withhold my assent from these former beliefs just as carefully as I would from obvious falsehoods, if I want to discover any certainty' (*Philosophical Writings*, 2: 14–15). Yet his ultimate goal was clearly not this doubt but rather certain knowledge. Another way of putting this is to say that although Descartes emphasized that we must reject everything that is merely probable and believe only what can be perfectly known and is incapable of being doubted, he thought that what was left over after this exercise was indeed certain knowledge. The only two sources of knowledge Descartes recognized were intuition and deduction (1: 15). Only beliefs that could be shown to be derived from these two sources of knowledge were acceptable to him. Only these beliefs ultimately could be said to possess certainty and evidence. Accordingly, Descartes insisted that knowledge was not just true belief but true belief that was either itself a 'clear and distinct' intuitive cognition or based upon such cognitions by a complete deduction. We must start from subjective beliefs which may or may not be true, and it was only the method that guaranteed objective knowledge. For Descartes, this method was based on mathematics, and it most decidedly did not consist of an empirical inquiry into the physical constitution of the world or ourselves. Our constitution, although not irrelevant, had to be understood from primary truths that themselves were not based on this constitution. This meant that knowledge was essentially independent of sense perception. Yet the criterion of 'clear and distinct ideas' remained one of the most fundamental problems of Cartesianism during the seventeenth century. Arnauld, Spinoza, Malebranche, Pascal, Leibniz, and Bayle had difficulties with this criterion of knowledge, and some of the most fundamental issues in the discussion that took place among the Cartesians can be traced back to confusions having to do with it.[4] The question of whether we have knowledge of things, formulated as a question about whether we have clear and distinct ideas, led to a number of deep epistemological problems that were often considered to be irresolvable in accordance with Cartesian principles.[5] The Cartesians aimed at indubitable knowledge, but they were more successful at raising doubt than at removing it. If Bayle represented the end of Cartesian philosophizing, and many have argued he does, its legacy is a form of fideism in which the difference between knowledge and belief becomes illusory.

John Locke, who in many other ways remained closer to Descartes than is commonly realized, was more skeptical about knowledge independent from sense perception.[6] Indeed, his philosophy represented a decisive shift in the problem of knowledge.[7] Whereas the Cartesians were largely concerned with establishing and applying the proper method in obtaining absolute certainty about all of reality, worrying relatively little about whether this was possible, Locke asked a question that put into doubt large parts of the Cartesian enterprise. He asked a question about the *extent* of knowledge. Thus, Chapter 3 of Book IV is entitled 'Of the Extent of Humane Knowledge'. Locke wanted to investigate how and how much we can know. As he put it:

> This, therefore, being my *Purpose* to enquire into the Original, Certainty, and Extent of humane Knowledge; together, with the Grounds and Degrees of Belief, Opinion, and Assent; . . . It shall suffice to my present Purpose, to consider the discerning Faculties of a Man, as they are employ'd about the Objects, which they have to do with: and I shall imagine I have not wholly misimploy'd my self in the Thoughts I shall have on this Occasion, if, in this Historical, plain Method, I can give any Account of the Ways, whereby our Understandings come to attain those Notions of Things we have, and can set down any Measures of the Certainty of our Knowledge, or the Grounds of those Perswasions which are to be found amongst Men . . . that he that shall take a view of the Opinions of Mankind, observe their Opposition, and at the same time consider the Fondness, and Devotion wherewith they are embrac'd; the Resolution and Eagerness wherewith they are maintain'd, may perhaps have Reason to suspect, That either there is no such thing as Truth at all; or that Mankind hath no sufficient Means to attain a certain Knowledge of it.[8]

Locke's questions were clearly motivated to a significant extent by his rejection of the Cartesian criterion of knowledge. Whether our ideas are clear and distinct is for him a very different concern from the question of whether we have clear and distinct knowledge. To be sure, for Locke, knowledge also has to do with ideas. And ideas are for him 'whatsoever is the Object of the Understanding when a Man thinks' (I.i.8). However, knowledge is for him '*the perception of the connexion and agreement, or disagreement and repugnancy of any of our Ideas*' (IV.i.2). Simply to have a clear and distinct idea is not yet knowledge. Since I may have a rather obscure perception of the relation of two ideas that are by themselves both clear and distinct, clear and distinct ideas do not guarantee certain knowledge (IV.ii.15). Knowledge is characterized by perceptions of the agreement and disagreement of ideas. Locke believed that there were basically three kinds of such perceptions, namely intuition, demonstration, and sensation. Intuitive knowledge is based on immediate perceptions of agreements and disagreements between ideas. In demonstrative knowledge, we must rely on intermediate ideas when we compare two ideas. It needs arguments and proofs, or demonstrations. Sensitive knowledge reaches 'no farther than the Existence of Things actually present to our Senses' (IV.iii.5). Locke argued therefore that the '*extent of our Knowledge* comes not only short of the reality of Things, but even of the extent of our own *Ideas*' (IV.iii.6). Indeed, Locke drew from this far-reaching conclusions about our ignorance of many things that the Cartesians had believed to be both certain and important. Thus, he claims that, strictly speaking, we do not know anything about substance, be it material or immaterial. Nevertheless, we do know many things, and we can be sure about much. Locke is committed to the view that we know things external to us only indirectly – that is, by means of ideas. But this knowledge is nevertheless real as long as there is 'a conformity between our *Ideas* and the reality of Things' (IV.iv.3). And there are two kinds of ideas that we may be sure agree with things, namely, the simple ideas, which enter the mind naturally, and all our complex ideas (except those of substances). The first agree with the things because they are caused by the things external to us and because we are completely passive with regard to them. The second must agree with the things they refer to because they represent no thing in itself apart from the idea; they are archetypes that do not represent copies of other things (IV.iv.3–5). Both mathematics and moral knowledge provide us with examples of such ideas. We can also be sure of the existence of ourselves (by intuition), of God (by demonstration), and of other things (by sensation). On the other hand, there are many things of which we cannot be so sure. We must believe them, or have faith in them. Locke defines belief as 'the admitting or receiving any Proposition for true, upon Arguments or Proofs that are found to perswade us to receive it as true, without certain Knowledge that it is so' (IV.xv.3). It is interesting that belief, for Locke, has always to do with probability, and probability has always to do with demonstration. In fact, he defines probability as nothing

but the appearance of . . . an Agreement, or Disagreement, by the intervention of Proofs, whose connexion is not constant and immutable, or at least is not perceived to be so, but is, or appears for the most part to be so, and is enough to induce the Mind to *judge* the Proposition to be true, or false, rather than the contrary. (IV.xv.1)

Locke believed that, as a matter of fact, most of the assertions we make and act upon are merely probable. They do not amount to knowledge, and whereas some of them have a very high degree of probability, many are rather questionable.

It is therefore an important part of Locke's enterprise to differentiate between knowledge and belief. Yet, the ultimate goal of this inquiry is not so much to transform beliefs into knowledge as simply to identify those beliefs that often pass for knowledge. For it is those that may lead us astray, and when they do so, it may have serious consequences. There are essentially two kinds of 'Inducements of Probability'. The first one concerns a particular matter of fact or particular existence, and the second concerns such things as are 'beyond the discovery of our Senses' (IV.xvi.5). It is especially the latter kind of probability that is important to Locke because it is important in determining the proper boundaries of faith and reason, or between what we can be certain or reasonably convinced of by our own ideas and faculties and what we receive directly by revelation from God. Locke tries to show that there can never be a real conflict between faith and reason if the realms of faith and reason are properly understood. So, for Locke, religion is for the most part a matter of belief or faith, and not knowledge. Although we can know that God exists, most substantive religious claims are matters of faith and thus probabilities. As such, religious claims may outweigh other probabilities, but they can never outweigh '*clear and self-evident Dictates of Reason*' (IV.xviii.10).

The religious implications of Locke's views on knowledge and belief of course received the greatest attention almost immediately. Locke was seen as restricting theology too much and to give too great a power to our natural faculties and knowledge. Yet, there were also other objections. Although the problems posed by skepticism may appear not to be as central to Locke as they were to Descartes, they are far from being absent. Locke's goal was clearly one of disarming skepticism by showing how far our knowledge can reach. His opinion was that 'Men, extending their Enquiries beyond their Capacities . . . 'tis no Wonder that they raise Questions . . . which never coming to any clear Resolution . . . confirm them at last in perfect Scepticism' (I.i.7). He meant to show what can be known and what cannot be known. Yet, he had to admit that many of the things he claimed could be known by ideas might be disputed.

If it be true, that all Knowledge lies only in the perception of the agreement or disagreement of our own *Ideas*, the Visions of an Enthusiast, and the Reasonings of a sober Man, will be equally certain. . . . Castles in the Air, will be as strong Holds of Truth, as the Demonstrations of *Euclid*. That an Harpy is not a Centaur, is by this way as certain knowledge, and as much a Truth, as that a Square is not a Circle. (IV.iv.1)

Locke did not succeed in drawing a distinction between knowledge and belief, and his account of knowledge and belief was therefore ultimately fraught with the same difficulties as that of the Cartesians. These were the problems that the eighteenth century had to face.

II. WOLFF

Christian Wolff (1679–1754) was not only the most influential philosopher in eighteenth-century Germany before Kant, but he was also philosophically the most important. He had many followers. Their names are too numerous to mention all of them. Some of the most important are Ludwig Wilhelm Thümmig (1697–1728), Bernhard Bilfinger (1693–1750), Friedrich Christian Baumeister (1709–85), Johann Christoph Gottsched (1700–66), Georg Friedrich Meier (1718–77), and especially Alexander Gottlieb Baumgarten (1714–62). However, the Wolffians are also very much misunderstood. Traditionally, it has been held that their philosophical project was essentially defined by their concern with working out in a clearer and more systematic fashion the ideas of Leibniz and that they had little use for such philosophical theories as were put forward by Hobbes and Locke, for instance. But this is false. Although they accepted the Leibnizian principles of contradiction, of sufficient reason, of the identity of indiscernibles, and of pre-established harmony as essentially correct, and although they also thought that philosophy was well on its way to becoming an exact science by following the 'mathematical model', they were not always hostile to the British approach, which emphasized experience and the role of sensation in all of knowledge. Wolff was clearly not a 'rationalist' in the sense of discounting empirical observation altogether. In fact, empirical observation formed for him the very starting point, even 'foundation', for philosophy because he thought that by 'means of the senses we know things which are and occur in the material world'.[9] Just like Locke, and very much unlike Descartes, Leibniz, and Hume, Wolff thinks that the senses provide us with real knowledge. Furthermore, he argues that this 'knowledge acquired by the senses and by attention to ourselves cannot be called in doubt' (*Preliminary Discourse*, 3). Wolff calls this knowledge based on the senses 'historical knowledge' and argues that it forms 'the foundation of philosophy'.[10] Indeed, it provides for him 'exact descriptions and firm and immutable principles' (19). In characterizing his approach, Wolff pointed out that he was 'most careful' not to 'surreptitiously introduce [*erschleiche*] anything' and to make 'inferences from reality to possibility', for he thought only 'in this way I keep my concepts pure so that nothing can sneak in whose possibility has not been cognised . . . and in this way I provide the foundation of absolutely reliable inferences in the sciences'.[11] His philosophy was meant to be a marriage of reason and experience (*connubium rationis et experientiae*), and even if this was not meant to be a marriage of equal partners, reason and experience were still partners for Wolff.[12] Thus, although Wolff is usually regarded as a follower of Leibniz, and although the phrase 'Leibnizo Wolffian philosophy' was used even in the eighteenth century to refer to what was understood as a more or less

unified movement, this is fair to neither. Wolff himself insisted rather strenu-
ously that his position was very different from that of Leibniz, and I believe he
was right. He was much more of an empiricist than Leibniz ever wished to be.
When he thus defines philosophy as a 'science of all possible objects, how and
why they are possible', or as 'the science of the possibles insofar as they can
be', and when he thus claims that existence is nothing but the 'complement of
possibility', he does not mean that we can dispense with experience.[13] Experience, or historical knowledge, remains the foundation. 'Experience establishes
those things from which the reason can be given for other things that are and
occur, or can occur'.[14] Although Wolff defines a thing as anything that exists
or might exist and identifies 'reality', 'possibility', and 'what does not involve
contradiction,' he does not believe that we can start our inquiry from just anything that does not involve contradiction. His 'ontology . . . is an analysis of the
logical possibilities for the existence of real entities'. It may well be true that
his philosophy is not about 'existing reality, as it had been before him', but it is
nevertheless about possibles insofar as they can be or actually are.[15]

Yet, Wolff does not give a special place to 'belief' in any sense in his system.
Although Wolff's *Logik* is organized in accordance with the 'three operations of
the mind' (*tres operationes mentis*) – namely, concept, judgment, and inference –
it is less mentalistic than the logic textbooks of many of his predecessors. Indeed,
the words 'mind', 'subject', 'self', and 'belief' do not play a large role in it. His
logic is not so much a logic of the workings of the mind as it is a logic of the
preconditions of knowledge and truth. As such a logic, it cannot do without
referring to mental operations and the faculties, but it is not primarily about
them. Philosophy is not so much concerned with establishing and describing
things as they exist, or as we may be acquainted with them by the senses. Indeed, Wolff's philosophy has been called a philosophy without a subject, and its
strenuous insistence on being per se and 'objectivity' separates it as much from
Leibniz as anything else. In placing so much emphasis on objective contents of
thought, Wolff distinguishes himself from almost all other philosophers of the
seventeenth and eighteenth centuries. For Wolff, things 'which are or occur
possess a reason from which it is understood why they are or occur', and philosophy is the enterprise of finding these reasons and putting them into systematic
order by demonstrating how they are connected. Put differently, whatever exists
or occurs is by that very fact possible. Philosophy's task is to show how they are
possible. Accordingly, 'philosophy is the science of the possibles insofar as they
are possible'. It must demonstrate from 'certain and immutable principles' and
with 'complete certainty' why 'those things which can occur actually do occur'.
Once this has been done, we have also demonstrated the 'reality' of the concepts
of these objects, and we have gone from mere sensible and 'historical' knowledge

to true philosophical understanding. In demonstrating why the things that can occur do occur, Wolff follows essentially Leibnizian lines, appealing to the principles of contradiction and sufficient reason.

Given this program, there remains not much room for *Glaube*, 'belief', or even 'faith'. Indeed, Wolff tells us in his *Logik* that 'Belief concerns... only things that have happened or will happen. For all other things allow of being proved, and they can thus be known. And therefore [it is only] when we must trust the testimony of others that we believe'.[16] Belief for Wolff is nothing but assent to a proposition that is accepted on testimony (*Logik*, 200). Though one might argue that testimony is important, and that we believe many things on the basis of testimony, it is clearly not of primary importance. Belief, for Wolff, cannot be a fundamental epistemic category. It is important for a very narrow spectrum of our knowledge. Indeed, it is something to be minimized. It not only can but should be minimized. Wolff is more of a Cartesian in this respect. Yet, he is different from the Cartesians in that he unquestioningly accepts immediate experience as a reliable source of truth. The Wolffian program is not to eliminate experience but to eliminate belief. Belief means to rely on others, not on oneself. If we did not have to rely on others at all, we would not have to believe either. Therefore, beliefs play no significant role in the Wolffian philosopher's thinking about the world and our knowledge of it. The Wolffian is only incidentally interested in the psychological mechanisms that allow us to know. He is more interested in what might be called the objective contents of thought or in the logical possibility or reality of what we think, and this can ultimately be shown in a completely objective fashion. We neither need nor should we utilize merely psychological or subjective factors in explaining why and how a concept or thought is possible. Yet, this does not mean that Wolff had to disagree with everyone else on substantive matters. In fact, especially the later Wolffians thought that they could incorporate most of what was valuable in other theories. How this was supposed to work can be seen perhaps most clearly from Moses Mendelssohn (1729–86), who is sometimes considered to be 'the last great representative of the Leibniz-Wolffian school'.[17]

III. THOMASIUS AND HIS FOLLOWERS

The views of the Wolffians were not uncontested. Indeed, German philosophy during most of the first half of the eighteenth century was characterized by the conflict between Wolff and the followers of Christian Thomasius (1655–1728). This dispute began at the newly founded University of Halle. The pietistically influenced Thomasians strongly opposed Wolff's rationalism on religious grounds. Some of the Thomasians advocated an almost mystical view of nature, and all exhibited strong fideistic tendencies.[18] 'On the Practical Philosophy of the Chinese', Wolff's formal address to the University of Halle in 1721, was one of the most dramatic public occasions in this dispute. It has also been taken as the starting point of the enlightenment in Germany.[19] Wolff argued in this address that ethics was not dependent on revelation, that Chinese ethics and Christian ethics were not fundamentally different, that happiness need not have a religious basis, and that reason was sufficient in moral matters as in all other matters. The followers of Thomasius were successful in having Wolff expelled not only from the University but even from Prussia (in 1723). The king found persuasive their argument that the principle of sufficient reason and the theory of pre-established harmony could be used to justify desertion from the Prussian army.

In their epistemology as well as in the metaphysical theory of physical influx, the adherents of Thomasius were following a more or less Lockean approach. Yet, they were more interested in the practical consequences of philosophy than in philosophy itself. The most important members of the Thomasian school were Johann Franciscus Budde (1667–1729), Joachim Lange (1670–1744), Andreas Rüdiger (1673–1731), and, very remotely, A. F. Hoffmann (1703–41) and Christian August Crusius (1715–75).[20] Thomasius himself was one of the first professors who taught in German, and his lectures covered very practical matters. Thus he lectured on Baltasar Gracian's *Oráculo manual y arte de prudencia* (1647), which insists on the goodness of man and his perfectibility. This, as well as his defense of Epicureanism and some of his free views on legal matters, not only brought him into conflict with orthodox Lutheran teaching but also close to the Pietists, who were just as opposed to Lutheran orthodoxy but for different reasons. The Pietists emphasized the importance of independent Bible study, personal devotion, the priesthood of the laity, and a practical faith issuing in acts of charity. They formed a highly evangelical movement, insisting on a *personal* experience of radical conversion and an abrogation of worldly success.[21] Thomasius became a Pietist himself for a time, but under the influence of Locke he returned in 1707 to a more rational view of the world – much to the chagrin of his friends and followers in Halle. His most important books in philosophy were his *Einleitung zur Vernunftlehre* (Introduction to Logic) and *Aussübung der Vernunftlehre* (Practical Logic), both of which appeared in 1691, and his *Einleitung zur Sittenlehre* (Introduction to Ethics) and *Ausübung der Sittenlehre* (Practical Ethics) of 1692 and 1696, respectively.[22] Although only the last of these works shows a marked influence of Pietistic teaching, none of them are philosophically rewarding. They are more concerned with making logic and ethics relevant for daily life than in advancing the philosophical discussion. Thomasius seems confident that common sense and good will or 'reasonable love' is all that is needed to make this world a better place. One of the most important functions of logic consists in removing prejudices, or bad beliefs, which for Thomasius result from the influence of our corrupted will. Accordingly, the problem of knowledge and belief is mainly the practical problem of how we can avoid false beliefs and not a deep problem connected with the essential nature of knowledge.

Just like Thomasius, his Pietistic followers regarded most of the classical problems of perception and knowledge as skeptical quibbles of no consequence, believing that ultimately these problems could all be explained as the effect of the Fall on man's faculty of knowledge. For this reason, they were convinced that if the influence of the evil will were to be eliminated, everything would find its proper place and perspective. The Thomasian epistemology was therefore rather meager. Its most distinctive characteristics are (1) an extreme sensationalism, (2) a correspondence theory of truth, (3) rejection of pre-established harmony and acceptance of a theory of physical influx, and (4) the subordination of the faculty of knowledge to that of the will and thus (5) the subordination of philosophy to theology. Although many of their psychological views exhibit a great resemblance to Locke's theories, Thomasians often lacked everything that made Locke philosophically interesting and important, namely, his detailed investigations of particular epistemological problems and their consequences for metaphysics.[23] Crusius, the most important philosopher of the movement, was important for his criticism of the Leibnizian principle of sufficient reason and his own metaphysical and ethical theory but contributed little to the problem of knowledge and belief.

IV. CONDILLAC

Locke was very influential in France.[24] Indeed, many of the most important French thinkers took themselves to be followers of Locke or, perhaps better, continuing the work started by Locke. This is true of Voltaire (1694–1778), who not only appreciated Locke's attempt at drawing the limits of knowledge and belief but also accepted the view that the sphere of true knowledge was rather narrow. Diderot (1713–84), who wrote the entry on Locke in the *Encyclopédie*, just like most other French *philosophes*, liked Locke's epistemology for very much the same reason, and Jean le Rond d'Alembert (1717–83) praised his approach to epistemology in his *Discours préliminaire* of 1751.[25] While it is not always clear whether the French thinkers understood Locke correctly, they were enthusiastic in their acceptance of his empiricism or sensationalism. The most important Lockean among the French was, however, Étienne Bonnot de Condillac (1715–80). His *Essai sur l'origine des connaissances humaines* (1746), which became one of the most influential books of the eighteenth century, builds on

Locke's sensationalism but develops it in a rather different direction.[26] Whereas Locke concentrated on ideas and the mind and had little interest in the signs by means of which we might communicate, Condillac believed the 'use of signs is the principle which unfolds all our ideas as they lye in the bud'. All of this is very interesting in its own right, and it may indeed have been an improvement on Locke's 'impossible term-by-term empiricism.'[27] It may even be a step on the way to the views of Herder and Hamann, which will be discussed later, but it is rather doubtful whether it presented a new theory of knowledge and belief or whether it remained essentially the Lockean account (with a new recognition of the importance of language for knowledge).

V. HUME

The concept of belief is so central in Hume's thought that his philosophy has, not without justification, been called a 'philosophy of belief'.[28] Yet, what precisely Hume's theory of belief was remains hotly contested. Knowledge, by contrast, seems much less prevalent in Hume's philosophical works. Although Part 3 in Book 1 of *A Treatise of Human Nature* is entitled 'Of Knowledge and Probability', and although its first section is called 'Of Knowledge', it seems clear that knowledge is not as important to Hume as is belief.[29] This is an illusion. Knowledge is most important to Hume. It is just that he believes we have very little of it, and much of his philosophical work is concerned with showing this as a fact. For Hume, as for Descartes and Locke, knowledge is characterized by certainty.[30] Knowledge is also essentially tied to reason. Indeed, it forms for Hume one of the three basic kinds of reason. The other two forms are proof and probability. In other words, when Hume calls something 'rational' he means that it is based on knowledge, proof, or probability. Thus he says, 'by knowledge, I mean the assurance arising from the comparison of ideas. By proofs, those arguments which are deriv'd from the relation of cause and effect, and which are entirely free from doubt and uncertainty. By probability, that evidence which is still attended with uncertainty' (1.3.11.2, SBN 124). This might appear to be a rather odd division because it restricts knowledge to a rather narrow sphere, namely, to just one side of what has been called 'Hume's Fork'. According to this doctrine, all 'objects of human reason or enquiry' naturally fall into either of two classes. They are either *Relations of Ideas* or *Matters of Fact*. Relations of ideas are 'either intuitively or demonstratively certain', and their truth does not depend upon the way the world is actually constituted.[31] They are 'discoverable by the mere operation of thought' or they can be known a priori, and they form the subject matter of geometry, algebra, and arithmetic. Matters of fact are radically different. In order to determine whether something is, as a matter of fact, true, I must take a look at the world, and depending on how the world is, a claim about a matter of fact may be true or false. Indeed, it is one of the most important characteristics of a matter of fact that its opposite is always possible.[32] According to Hume's definition of knowledge, we cannot have knowledge of the world.[33] Knowledge is restricted to geometry, algebra, and arithmetic.[34] Yet, we can have proofs and probabilities about the world. These essentially have to do with belief, and since Hume's philosophical analyses are mainly concerned with them, his theory of belief is of central concern.

Hume defines 'belief' as 'A LIVELY IDEA RELATED TO OR ASSOCIATED WITH A PRESENT IMPRESSION'. This is not to be construed as a perfect definition but as a working definition, the best he could offer at the time, given the difficulties of defining such a basic term (*Treatise*, 1.3.7.5, SBN 96). In the Appendix to the *Treatise*, he still attempts to clarify the notion of 'belief', saying it is '*a peculiar feeling, different from the simple conception*' and is 'the manner' in which we conceive an idea. 'An idea assented to *feels* different from a fictitious idea.' The difference is one of force, vivacity, solidity, or firmness. Belief gives ideas 'more force and influence; makes them appear of greater importance, infixes them in the mind, and renders them the governing principles of all our actions' (App. 3; 1.3.7.7, SBN 624, 628–9). Hume's theory of belief is embedded in his theory of ideas. More specifically, it depends on his distinction between impressions and ideas, a distinction which is 'as evident as that betwixt feeling and thinking' (Abstr. 5, SBN 647). Impressions are more lively than ideas. They comprehend all our sensations, passions, and emotions. Ideas are mere copies of these impressions, and they constitute our thinking (1.1.1, SBN 1 ff.). Belief makes our ideas more similar to impressions. It transforms a mere thought into something that could almost pass for an impression, and as impressions seem more real than ideas, so ideas that are believed also seem more real (1.3.10.3, SBN 119). Hume claimed that belief 'seems hitherto to have been one of the greatest mysteries of philosophy; tho' no one has so much as suspected, that there was any difficulty in explaining it'(1.3.7.7, SBN 628).

What are the causes of belief, or how does an idea become vivacious? Hume's answer, in one word, was 'custom'. When we sense something, or have an impression of something, we are naturally reminded of things that are similar to it, or are close, or are causally related to it. Impressions are invariably connected with other impressions or ideas, and if a certain impression is often conjoined with another impression or idea, then whenever I have an impression of it, I will also tend to have an idea of the other. Accordingly, belief arises from a customary conjunction of two impressions or of an impression and an idea. But a 'present impression . . . is absolutely requisite to this whole operation'; and a belief is thus 'a more vivid and intense conception of an idea, proceeding from its relation to a present impression'.[35] Just as beliefs are based on custom and repetition, so is causation based on constant conjunction. And we 'have no other notion of cause and effect, but that of certain objects, which have been *always conjoin'd* together, and which in all past instances have been found inseparable' (1.3.6.15, SBN 93). Hume's analysis of causality and belief are just different aspects of the same project. He wanted to show that as far as our knowledge of the world is concerned, everything depends on habit or custom and thus on belief. Insofar as all reasoning concerning matters of fact is based on the relation of cause and effect, it is all merely probable and all a species of belief rather than knowledge or proof. Locke, who had believed that we could be sure of the existence of ourselves (by intuition), of God (by demonstration), and of other things (by sensation), is clearly wrong if we are to believe Hume. None of these claims amounts to knowledge. Every one of them could be wrong, and this amounts only to belief. This belief is for Hume quite sufficient for leading our ordinary lives as well as for engaging in science. However, it is clearly insufficient for doing the kind of philosophy that Descartes, Locke, and most other philosophers wanted to do. Hume is a skeptic about philosophical justification. Indeed, if we apply strict philosophical standards to our reasoning, we inevitably encounter contradictions. Hume notes a blatant contradiction between beliefs based on the senses and beliefs based on reason. Hume thinks that when we believe in our senses, which we are forced to do by a 'blind and powerful instinct of nature', we take the ideas, presented by the senses, to be the external objects. But, he also thinks that 'no man, who reflects, ever doubted, that the existences, which we consider, when we say *this house* and *that tree*, are nothing but perceptions in the mind, and fleeting copies or representations of other existences, which remain uniform and independent' (*Enquiry*, 12.1.9, SBN 152). So reason leads to a new belief, or a 'new system' that is incompatible with our common-sense view. Yet, this does not mean that the rational view is better. Hume goes on to show that we cannot really trust reason and its 'new system' either. If we accept the view that we can only consider copies of things, we can never be sure whether what we consider as copies actually are copies. In order to be able to determine this, we would have to be able to take an independent point of view and compare the real things with their copies. Since we cannot do this, we cannot prove that the perceptions of the mind must be caused by external objects entirely different from them (12.1.10–11, SBN 152–3). They may just as well have been created by the mind. Thus, in order to get into the 'new system' we need external objects, independent existences, or things in themselves, but we cannot stay within this new system and still hold on to these things. It appears that we have to abandon the point of view prescribed by our senses without getting anything in return since we cannot consistently hold on to the rational point of view (and rationality presupposes consistency). As Hume put it, our belief in the existence of material objects, 'if rested on natural instinct, is contrary to reason, and if referred to reason, is contrary to natural instinct, and at the same time carries no rational evidence with it, to convince an impartial enquirer' (12.1.16, SBN 155). The propositions 'We see external objects' and 'We cannot see external objects' cannot be true together. Either we accept one or the other. Yet each finds, to use the words of Kant, 'conditions of its necessity in the very nature of' the mind. One is based upon the senses and its beliefs, the other on reason and its beliefs. But they not only contradict each other; neither of them is sufficient to allow us to decide for or against either. We cannot decide which proposition is correct. Accordingly, it may not be surprising that Hume makes no attempt to resolve the conflict and simply allows 'the profounder and more philosophical sceptics', who seem to be his mouthpiece, to ask:

Do you follow the instincts and propensities of nature, . . . in assenting to the veracity of sense? But these lead you to believe, that the very perception or sensible image is the external object. Do you disclaim this principle, in order to embrace a more rational opinion, that the perceptions are only representations of something external? You here depart from your natural propensities and more obvious sentiments; and yet are not able to satisfy your reason. (*Enquiry*, 12.1.14, SBN 153–4)

It is our imagination which is at fault. We must follow it because it is the most basic principle of the human mind. Yet, it leads us to contradictions by means of operations that are equally natural and necessary. Hume noted:

No wonder a principle so inconstant and fallacious shou'd lead us into errors, when implicitly follow'd (as it must be) in all its variations. 'Tis this principle, which makes us reason from causes and effects; and 'tis the same principle, which convinces us of the continu'd existence of external objects. . . . But tho' these two operations be equally natural and necessary in the human mind . . . they are directly contrary, nor is it possible for us to reason justly and regularly from causes and effects, and at the same time believe the continu'd existence of matter. (*Treatise*, 1.4.7.4, SBN 265–6)

Moreover, these contradictions are not based upon principles that are changeable, weak, and irregular (such as faculty, occult quality, sympathies, antipathies, or the horror of a vacuum [1.4.3.10–11, SBN 224]). They are based upon those principles in the imagination that are 'permanent, irresistible, and universal . . . [and] are the foundation of all our thoughts and actions, so that upon their removal human nature must immediately perish and go to ruin' (1.4.4.1,

SBN 225). Hume made not the slightest attempt to explain away the contradictions but simply asks:

> How then shall we adjust those principles together? Which of them shall we prefer? Or in case we prefer neither of them, but successively assent to both, as is usual among philosophers, with what confidence can we afterwards usurp that glorious title, when we thus knowingly embrace a manifest contradiction? (1.4.7.4, SBN 266)

Neither reason nor the senses can be trusted because they are both founded on the imagination, and it is not to be trusted either. 'We have, therefore, no choice left but betwixt a false reason and none at all. For my part, I know not what ought to be done in the present case. I can only observe what is commonly done' (1.4.7.7, SBN 268). What is commonly done, of course, is not what philosophers do. In any case, Hume believed he had proved at least indirectly that the philosophical approach was wrong. The philosopher's

> principles, when carry'd farther, and apply'd to every new reflex judgment, must, by continually diminishing the original evidence, at last reduce it to nothing, and utterly subvert all belief and opinion. If belief, therefore, were a simple act of the thought, without any peculiar manner of conception, or the addition of a force and vivacity, it must infallibly destroy itself, and in every case terminate in a total suspense of judgment. But as experience will sufficiently convince any one, who thinks it worth while to try, that though he can find no error in the foregoing arguments, yet he still continues to believe, and think, and reason, as usual, he may safely conclude that his reasoning and belief is some sensation or peculiar manner of conception, which 'tis impossible for mere ideas and reflections to destroy. (1.4.1.8, SBN 184)

So, Hume believed that by reducing our knowledge of the world to belief in his sense, he had actually made it more secure. This does not mean that Hume's theory of belief is irrational, as so many commentators have thought. Though belief itself is more an act of our sensitive than our rational nature, reason nevertheless has a part to play. Probability is, after all, part of reason, and beliefs are always part of a reflexive context.

But this is not the entire story. By reducing most of our knowledge to belief, Hume assimilated knowledge to Locke's faith. Locke's maxim that religious claims may outweigh other probabilities but can never outweigh 'clear and self-evident dictates of Reason' could no longer be applied. The validity of religious claims needed to be questioned in a different, and more radical, way. Hume's theory of belief as being based on regular conjunction does precisely that by pointing out that religious beliefs are founded on particularly singular evidence, namely, on miracles, or exceptions to natural regularities. Therefore, he could argue that

> upon the whole, we may conclude, that the CHRISTIAN Religion not only was at first attended with miracles, but even at this day cannot be believed by any reasonable person

without one. Mere reason is insufficient to convince us of its veracity: And whoever is moved by *Faith* to assent to it, is conscious of a continued miracle in his own person, which subverts all the principles of his understanding, and gives him a determination to believe what is most contrary to custom and experience. (*Enquiry*, 10.2.41, SBN 131)

Hume's theory of belief in this way goes to prove not only that any philosophical justification of religious belief is impossible but also that religious faith, in principle, is incompatible with a rational outlook. Anyone willing to accept as decisive the kind of 'evidence' available for the religious believer will necessarily incline towards irrationalism. Faith has a tendency to undermine a reasonable outlook.

VI. REID

Thomas Reid was Hume's most significant critic and opposed him on many counts. But most significantly Reid saw him as the most dangerous representative of the theory of ideas, or the theory that we perceive by means of ideas. Reid held that we perceive the objects 'immediately', that is, without a third kind of object 'mediating' between ourselves and the world of objects.[36] Rejecting talk of 'ideas', he speaks of 'sensations' and 'perceptions'. Neither sensations nor perceptions are a 'mediating entity'. 'Sensation' was meant to be entirely different from 'idea'. It has three essential characteristics. First, 'sensation' does not have any sort of permanence for Reid. The term refers to an action or operation of the mind that has a definite beginning and a definite end in time. Thus, smelling, for instance, 'is an act of the mind, but is never imagined to be a quality of the mind'. In short, 'its *esse* is *sentire* and nothing can be in it that is not felt'.[37] We sense – that is, feel pain, smell, or hear – at one moment or another. This is a mental act or action. When this action has run its course, nothing remains of it. Secondly, a sensation 'can have no existence but when it is perceived'. In fact, 'this is common to all sensations, that as they cannot exist but in being perceived, so they cannot be perceived but they must exist'. 'It is essential to a sensation to be felt and it can be nothing more than we feel it to be'.[38] To speak of an 'unperceived sensation' makes absolutely no sense for Reid. It is through perception that we can make sense of sensation and not the other way around. Furthermore, though sensation is 'a simple act of the mind', it is given only as part of the complex act of perception. Although it is in the order of nature 'simple', we arrive at it only by abstraction, 'by art and chemical analysis' (*Inquiry*, II.4–5; 30). Thirdly, as simple acts of the mind, 'considered abstractly', sensations do not have reference to objects. Sensations 'hath no object distinct from the act itself' and can thus be differentiated from all other acts of the mind.[39] They get referred to objects in perception.

Our actual sensations – sensations as experienced, that is – are quite different from these simple acts, for they are 'necessarily accompanied' by certain beliefs (*Inquiry*, II.3; 27). Sensations, compel us to believe in certain things. When we have sensations, we must not only believe in 'the present existence of the thing' sensed by us but also believe in 'a mind, or something that has the power of smelling, of which it is called a sensation, an operation or feeling', as well as in a certain 'faculty' that allows us to sense. Finally, there are certain other notions such as cause, extension, solidity, and motion that we must believe in. All these things 'are nowise like to sensations, although they have been hitherto confounded with them' (II.7; 38). Sensations, when considered together with the beliefs that 'necessarily accompany' them, are perceptions. Thus, while sensations in themselves do not have any object and are nothing distinct from what they are felt to be, perception 'hath always an object distinct from the act by which it is perceived'.[40] But this object is not our sensation, it is 'an object which may exist whether it be perceived or not'.[41] The beliefs, which necessarily accompany them, are also simple. For this reason, belief cannot be defined logically.[42] It is 'like seeing and hearing which can never be so defined as to be understood by those who have not these faculties; and to such as have them, no definition can make these operations more clear than they are already' (II.5; 31). Yet, this impossibility of logical definition does not stop Reid from saying interesting and new things about belief. In particular, he tries to elucidate the relation of belief to sensation by means of the 'language analogy'. His main reason for this seems to be his belief that there is a close natural analogy between language and perception anyway:

[T]he objects of human knowledge are innumerable, but the channels by which it is conveyed to the mind are few. Among these, the perception of the external things by our senses, and the informations which we receive upon human testimony, are not the least considerable: and so remarkable is the analogy between these two, and the analogy between the principles of the mind which are subservient to the one and those which are subservient to the other, that, without further apology we shall consider them together.

Spelling out this analogy, he finds, in 'the testimony . . . given by the senses, as well as in human testimony given in language, things are signified to us by signs: and in one, as well as the other, the mind, either by original principles or by custom, passes from the sign to the conception and belief of the thing signified' (*Inquiry*, VI.24; 190). Reid thus differentiates two kinds of relationships between a sign and the thing signified by it. The relation can either be based upon experience or upon principles of the mind. When a certain kind of sound suggests immediately to the mind a coach passing by we are clearly concerned with a belief based upon experience or custom. But, as we have seen already, there were for Reid also many beliefs that 'necessarily accompany' certain sensations. These are original beliefs. 'We cannot get rid of the vulgar notion and belief of an external world', for instance, and even 'if Reason should stomach and fret ever so much at this yoke, she cannot throw it off' (V.7; 68–9, see also VI.20; 169–70).

On the other hand, Reid emphasized repeatedly that he does not believe that it is in our power to give an account of why and how these beliefs follow upon or, better, accompany our sensations. These necessary beliefs are 'instinctual'. 'We are inspired with the sensation, and we are inspired with the corresponding perception, by means unknown.' All Reid will say is that the language analogy is of help here as well. Just as there is a sort of natural language – that is, the one consisting of 'features of the face, gestures of the body, and modulations of the voice', which conveys to us what the other person thinks or feels – so there are certain sensations that conjure up these original principles.[43] He calls the perceptions in which such sensations occur 'original perceptions', and he differentiates them from 'acquired perceptions' in which the relation between the sign and the thing signified depends upon experience or custom. Since Reid cannot explain or define the way in which this happens, he 'beg[s] leave to make use of the word *suggestion*, because [he] know[s] not one more proper, to express a power of the mind, which seems entirely to have escaped the notice of philosophers, and to which we owe many of our simple notions which are neither impressions nor ideas, as well as many original principles of belief' (*Inquiry*, II.7; 38). The sensations suggest to us basic principles and notions not to be found in sensation itself. Just as there is in artificial signs usually no similarity between the sign and the thing signified, so there is none between the sensation and the things suggested by it. We cannot speak of a necessary relation between the sensation and those things suggested by it either. Reid distinguishes three classes of natural signs. The first class consists of those natural signs 'whose connection with the thing signified is established by nature but is discovered only by experience'. All natural sciences are based upon such signs. The second class is constituted by signs 'wherein the connection between the sign and the thing signified is not only established by nature, but discovered to us by a natural principle without reasoning or experience'. These are the natural signs of our thought, purpose, and desire, or what Reid calls 'the natural language of mankind'. The 'third class of natural signs comprehends those which, though we never before had any notion or conception of the things signified, do suggest it or conjure it up, by a natural kind of magic, as it were, and at once give us a conception, and create a belief in it'. Sensations belong to this class.

They suggest to us a mind or an identical self to which they belong, as well as such notions as those of hardness and extension, or our belief in the existence of objects:

It may be observed, that as the first class of natural signs . . . is the foundation of true philosophy, and the second, the foundation of the fine arts, or of taste; so the last is the foundation of common sense; a part of human nature which hath never been explained. (V.3; 61)

Reid never makes clear how many basic principles there are and how precisely they do their work.[44] The only thing he seems to have been certain of is that

there are certain principles . . . which the constitution of our nature leads us to believe, and which we are under a necessity to take for granted in the common concerns of life – these are what we call the principles of common sense; and what is manifestly contrary to them, is what we call absurd. (II.6; 32)

He claimed further that

all reasoning must be from first principles; and for first principles no other reason can be given but this, that, by the constitution of our nature, we are under a necessity of assenting to them. Such principles are parts of our constitution, no less than the power of thinking; reason can neither make nor destroy them; nor can it do any thing without them. (V.7; 71)

In doing so, Reid may be seen to have argued for the necessity of an a priori component in all knowledge. Though this a priori component may appear to be not a necessary logical presupposition but as merely founded in human nature, it would be a mistake to view Reid as a naturalist. The principles he identified were valid not just for us but for any intelligent being.

One of the consequences of this view is that Reid differentiates sharply between a sensation, and the things that are suggested by this sensation but which themselves are not of sensation in the sense that they can be reduced to it. Sensation and thought are different, yet they are united in the act of perception. For Reid, sensation is neither a sort of confused thinking, as it was for most of the rationalists, nor are our abstract notions of space, and so on, rarefied sensations, as they were to most of the empiricists. The principles of common sense are radically different from particular sensations, yet they are known to us only through perceptions. They also provide Reid with a radically different account of knowledge. Whereas for Hume knowledge is essentially restricted to mathematics, Reid clearly believes that we can have knowledge of the world. We can have knowledge of the world because of the principles of common sense, which are not just principles of human nature but principles for any kind of knowledge. They hold absolutely. Reid makes this clearest in his account of moral principles. He argues that Hume's moral sense fails to do justice to moral principles.

If God has given to man a power which we call *conscience*, the *moral faculty*, the *sense of duty*, by which . . . he perceives certain things that depend on his will to be his duty . . . if the notion of duty be a simple conception, of its own kind, and of a different nature from the conceptions of utility and agreeableness, of interest or reputation; if this moral faculty be the prerogative of man, and no vestige of it be found in brute animals; if it be given us by God to regulate all our animal affections and passions; if to be governed by it be the glory of man and the image of God in his soul . . . [then] to seek the foundation of morality in the affections which we have in common with the brutes, is to seek the living among the dead, and to change the glory of man, and the image of God in his soul, into the similitude of an ox that eateth grass.[45]

If Hume were right about ethics, then there would be nothing special about human nature. It would be just more nature. Furthermore, as Reid explicitly points out on the last pages of his *Essays on the Active Powers of Man*,

If what we call *moral judgment* be no real judgment, but merely a feeling, it follows, that the principles of morals, which we have been taught to consider as an immutable law to all intelligent beings, have no other foundation but an arbitrary structure and fabric in the constitution of the human mind . . . [then] beings of a different structure . . . may have different, nay opposite measures of moral good and evil. (V.7; 678–9)

If we were to undergo a change in 'our structure', our moral responses might change in such a way that what is moral now would become immoral, and what is immoral now might become moral. Hume's naturalism leads to relativism. What holds of moral principles holds even more of Hume's principles of belief. Reid holds that moral claims, just like knowledge claims, must admit of being true or false. 'A true judgment will be true, whatever be the fabric of the mind. . . . Nothing like this can be said of mere feelings, because the attributes of true or false do not belong to them'.[46] Reid was led to this view ultimately by such moral and theological considerations. Although these may be themselves ultimately unsatisfactory, his clear formulation of the view that we need a priori principles to account for knowledge and his closely related analysis of the act of perception as a complex phenomenon, involving certain judgment-like operations of the mind, represent important contributions to the philosophical discussion. Although Reid was ultimately a 'belief philosopher', he may also be viewed as someone who aimed at the kind of theory that Wolff was also trying to develop. And it was for this reason that his theory appealed to some of the Germans.

VII. MENDELSSOHN

Mendelssohn was important not just because he upheld the basic tenets of Leibniz and Wolff but also because he advanced them in light of developments that took place in Germany after 1750. As he noted on the occasion of a review of Edmund Burke's *A Philosophical Enquiry Into the Origin of Our Ideas of the Sublime and Beautiful*:

The theory of human sensations and passions has in more recent times made the greatest progress, since the other parts of philosophy no longer seem to advance very much. Our neighbors, and especially the English, precede us with philosophical observations of nature, and we follow them with our rational inferences; and if it were to go on like this, namely that our neighbors observe and we explain, we may hope that we will achieve in time a complete theory of sensation.[47]

What was needed, Mendelssohn thought, was a universal theory of thinking and sensation, and such a theory would cover sensation and thinking in theoretical, moral, and aesthetic contexts.[48] It would be comprised of British observations and German (read Wolffian) explanations. Mendelssohn had definite ideas about the general approach that had to be followed. It had to be shown that the phenomena observed by British philosophers, and traced by them to a special sense were really rational. It is precisely this task that defines one of the central concerns of German philosophers during the final third of the eighteenth century. For moral philosophers, this implied the necessity of showing how moral sense was really practical reason. In a theoretical context, it had to be shown how Hume's 'beliefs' could be reduced to rational principles. As far as the problem of belief and knowledge is concerned, Mendelssohn is accordingly entirely within the Wolffian tradition. He does not consider belief very important in epistemic contexts, and he is convinced that in the end even sensible knowledge can be explained by means of rational principles. In his paper 'Über die Wahrscheinlichkeit' (On Probability) he faces Hume on this fundamental level. In particular, he attacks Hume's claim that he had shown causality to be based on belief and not on reason or rational principles.

Hume had claimed that if causality was based on reason, then whether we observe a certain connection of two events once or many times should not make any difference as to whether we consider it a causal relation. Mendelssohn tries to show that this is false and that probability theory shows why the causal principle is ultimately rational and why particular causal relations can only be established after repeated observations. Furthermore, he draws from these observations a conclusion that must have been rather startling to most members of the Berlin Academy, namely that Hume's analysis is irrelevant to the deeper metaphysical issues with which they themselves were concerned and that all the important problems remained just as they had been before Hume entered the scene. So, as far as experience is concerned, it makes no difference whether the theory of universal physical influx is true, whether occasionalism is true, or whether the system of pre-established harmony is true.[49] Hume's analysis of induction and causality cannot make a difference to these issues. His explanations make a great deal of sense at the phenomenological level, but nobody who really understands what is at issue between Leibniz, Malebranche, and Spinoza would be perturbed in the slightest by Hume's analysis. Indeed, Hume's problem is not only compatible with Leibniz's view but follows directly from the Leibnizian position.[50] Leibniz also argued that efficient causality did not obtain at the level of substances. Monads cannot be causally related in the way phenomena are. Only phenomena are related by efficient causality, which is strictly an experiential concept based on constant conjunction. Thus, Leibniz's metaphysical position requires a Humean analysis at the phenomenal level. Hume's view is already contained in that of Leibniz and Wolff, and Hume's beliefs can be justified by objective contents of thought that do not require appeals to our subjective nature.

VIII. TETENS

Johann Nicolaus Tetens (1736–1807), another important thinker in the period between Wolff and Kant, found Hume's analysis of belief and causation more important than did Mendelssohn. Indeed, the topic of 'subjective necessity of thinking', which is of central importance in Tetens's work, presents in many ways a further development of what Hume and Reid discussed as belief.[51] Yet, the notion of a subjective necessity of thinking is not only a broader notion than the notion of belief, but also represents a significant shift in the problem. What could appear to be merely affective and noncognitive in the work of the British thinkers is for Tetens already at the outset characterized as something cognitive; and one might argue that Reid and Locke, at least, had something similar in mind and that it is not clear that Tetens is contradicting even Hume because the latter calls also reason an 'instinct'. The Wolffian background seems to be responsible to a large extent for this shift. However that may be, the problem of the relation of belief and knowledge becomes for Tetens the problem of how a merely subjective necessity of thinking becomes an objective necessity of thinking, or, more briefly, becomes objective. Tetens discusses this problem with explicit references to Locke, Hume, Reid, and a host of other thinkers. In his two main works, *Über die allgemeine speculativische Philosophie* (On General Speculative Philosophy) of 1775 and *Philosophische Versuche über die menschliche Natur und ihre Entwicklung*

(Philosophical Essays on Human Nature and its Development) of 1777, he not only argues against these thinkers but also tries to push their approach further. It is interesting to note that he sees Hume and Reid as working on a common project and that at times he seems to be annoyed by unnecessary squabbles.

In general, Tetens believes that subjective necessity comes first and that objective necessity comes later. There are three different kinds of subjective necessity, namely, (1) one that is based on the nature of the faculty of thinking, (2) one that is based on the nature of the ideas that are being considered, and (3) one that is based on habit or custom. The last one is the least interesting, and the first one perhaps the most. Tetens argues that Hume and others have misconstrued the problem of knowledge by often mistaking the first kind for the third. It is really the first kind of necessity that is at work in the creation of objective knowledge. Thus Tetens argues that we

know from observation the subjective necessity to think in accordance with general laws of the understanding. We feel that it is impossible for us to think square circles, and that we cannot think an object as different from itself. Upon this subjective necessity we found an objective one. We transfer the impossibility of thinking things differently to things external to the understanding. Our ideas are now no longer ideas within us, but things external to us. The qualities and relations we perceive in the ideas are represented to us as qualities and relations of the objects themselves. They belong to the objects even apart from our thought, and they would have to be recognized by any other thinking being. This is a consequence of instinct. It is an effect of common sense. The old metaphysics has noted something correct in this approach and has accepted as its axiom that truth is something objective.[52]

We cannot help but view things that we encounter in sensation as objectively real and as being objectively connected with one another. This does not mean that we could somehow compare what is given to us in sensation with the objects themselves. It only means that some things given in sensation are necessary in a different way than others. What Tetens really suggests is that we should replace the words objective and subjective with the terms 'subjectively unchanging' and 'subjectively changing'. Objective things are those that never change; subjective things are those that do change. Thus, Tetens's objectivity is not the result of the external characteristics of objects existing apart from us but is rather due to the nature of our understanding. Our laws of thought are not just the laws of thought of human intelligence but the laws of any faculty of thought that is possible. This means knowledge is ultimately dependent on objective laws of thought. Though the details of Tetens's account differ considerably from that of Kant, in broad outline they correspond to what the latter argues in the 'Transcendental Analytic'.

IX. KANT

Kant clearly continues Tetens's approach, although in a different way. Objective knowledge is for Kant based on the structures of the human mind, particularly on the categories and principles of the human understanding that make knowledge possible. There is at least one important difference between Tetens and Kant. Whereas Tetens starts from 'subjectively necessary thinking' and tries to reach objective necessity by extrapolating from what is merely subjective, Kant takes the opposite route, arguing that what is subjectively necessary presupposes or implies objectively necessary structures of the human mind. If we did not have the categories and the principles, we also would not have the three kinds of subjectively necessary claims. This means that even Hume's subjective necessity based upon repeated experience, custom, or habit is possible only given the kind of absolutely necessary structure of the human mind that Kant thinks he has accounted for in his *Kritik der reinen Vernunft*. Belief is subject to the same laws as knowledge. If we did not have the categories and principles, we could not even believe anything about the world. This might be taken to mean that knowledge is in a certain sense prior to belief. And this sense seems to be ultimately not all that different from that of Wolff. However, there is one sense in which Kant has radically departed from Wolff, namely, in his argument of what kind of metaphysics and (in particular) ontology can be justified by this knowledge. For Kant, metaphysics is possible only concerning the conditions that make knowledge possible, and knowledge remains for him much more closely tied to what it is actually possible for us to experience. Accordingly, large parts of Wolff's system that were described as knowledge are either eliminated altogether (such as rational psychology) and other parts are radically changed (such as rational theology), and still other parts gain an entirely new and urgent meaning for Kant (such as moral theology). Belief becomes much more important for Kant than it could ever have been for Wolff. Indeed, it seems to be the ultimate outcome of his entire system.

In an important, but much too little discussed section of his *Kritik der reinen Vernunft*, Kant differentiates between opinion, knowledge, and belief.[53] To explain the distinctions between these three different ways of 'taking something to be true', he further distinguishes between conviction and persuasion as subjective states that are connected with our taking something to be true. And Kant claims that we are convinced of the truth of a certain claim only if we can declare it to be necessarily valid for everyone. Conviction gives rise to assertion. In asserting a certain claim to be true, I expect that everyone who understands what I am saying will have to agree with me. As Kant puts it, 'its ground is objectively sufficient'. Persuasion, on the other hand, has only private validity. If I am merely persuaded that something is true, I cannot, or rather should not, assert it. Persuasion has its ground 'only in the particular constitution of the subject' (A 820/ B 848). Thus, I may be persuaded that the moon is made out of green cheese, but if I were to assert it, I would soon find out that most people would not agree with me.

This shows, according to Kant, that we can know the difference between persuasion and conviction only by communicating with others. 'Persuasion cannot be distinguished from conviction subjectively, when the subject has taken something to be true merely as an appearance of his own mind' (A 821/B 849). In communicating with others, I find out whether a judgment I want to make merely appears true to me or whether it is true. If everyone agrees with me, then, Kant claims, there is 'at least a presumption that the ground of the agreement . . . rests . . . on the object' (A 820/B 848). So when we differentiate between persuasion and conviction, we must take into account both subjective and objective grounds, and the objective grounds are what ultimately count. I can distinguish between the two only insofar as I am a member of a society or a communicative praxis. If I were completely isolated from all other human beings (that is, if I had never been able to communicate in any way with anyone), I could not make a distinction between conviction and persuasion. This is, of course, not to say that whatever I can successfully communicate to someone or other is therefore also objectively valid. If this were true, certain 'postmodern' noises that are clearly no more than persuasion would also become conviction. Rather, communication is a means of identifying what is merely private: that is, persuasion. To determine whether something is indeed objectively valid, or whether I should consider a claim as conviction, requires more.

Kant's distinction between opinion, belief, and knowledge goes as follows: opinion is the conscious acceptance of a claim without either objectively or subjectively sufficient grounds; belief is the conscious acceptance of a claim on the basis of subjective grounds but without any objective grounds; and knowledge is the conscious judgment on the basis of both subjective and objective grounds. As should be clear from this discussion, Kant calls the subjective grounds of knowledge conviction. Its objective ground he calls certainty (A 822/B 850). According to Kant, we should allow ourselves opinions only in matters where we have at least some knowledge. To have an opinion about things of which we have no knowledge at all is wrong. Furthermore, Kant thinks it wrong to have opinions in a subject matter that deals with pure reason alone. Where a priori knowledge is concerned, only certainty will do. To have an opinion in mathematics 'is absurd' (A 823/B 851). Nor is opinion sufficient in moral questions. We should not act simply because we are of the opinion that an action is allowed but should act only if we know that it is allowed. In any of those cases, opinion is, at least according to Kant, clearly inappropriate because they require knowledge. However, when we are concerned with what he calls the 'transcendental use of reason' – that is, when we worry about such questions as whether there is a God, whether we are free, or whether we are immortal – opinion may seem appropriate because here we are not dealing with questions of knowledge. But again Kant thinks it is not appropriate because 'to have an opinion is of course too little' (A823/B851). What we need here is belief. Since belief is the conscious acceptance of a claim on the basis of subjective grounds in the absence of any objective grounds, Kant must show what the subjective grounds are for holding beliefs about God, freedom, and immortality.

One might be tempted to think that this is all there is to the story. Subjective reasons are easy to find. Anything will do as long as we are only concerned with subjectivity, and there are many existential, psychological, or sociological factors influencing a subject to hold certain beliefs about any of these matters. Nor does it seem to matter what we actually believe about these matters since if belief is based on merely subjective reasons then anything goes. However, this would be a mistake. For Kant, 'subjective' does not imply 'arbitrary'. He identifies many structures of the human mind that, although subjective, are still far from arbitrary. We only have to think of space and time as subjective forms of intuition.

Accordingly, Kant need not accept every subjective ground of belief as equally valid or good, and he does not. He holds that even in religion there are good reasons for believing and bad reasons for believing. A bad reason for Kant would be if we believed because it makes us feel better or makes us feel more secure. Such an ultimately hedonistic motivation is not compatible with our dignity. Indeed, the only grounds that are sufficient are rational reasons. Religious beliefs must be understood as fully rational. Although Kant argued that it is impossible for us to know genuinely religious truths, and thus claimed in the *Kritik der reinen Vernunft* that he 'found it necessary to deny knowledge, in order to make room for faith' (B xxx), he also believed that religious belief is essentially rational. Indeed, he argued that

> every belief, even the historical, must of course be *rational* (for the final touchstone of truth is always reason); only a rational belief or faith is one grounded on no data other than those contained in *pure* reason. . . . The *concept* of God and even the conviction of his *existence* can be met with only in reason, and it cannot first come to us either through inspiration or through tidings communicated to us, however great the authority behind them.[54]

Kant's task therefore is to show how a belief can be rational.

Kant believes that he can show that many beliefs are rational from a practical point of view. Thus, if I wish to achieve a certain goal, I may be justified in assuming something, even though I have no objective grounds for believing it. A physician, for example, often needs to go by mere beliefs when she needs to treat a patient but does not know the nature of his illness. However, these pragmatic beliefs are not what interests Kant the most. He finds more interesting certain doctrinal beliefs, beliefs held for theoretical reasons. Kant himself puts forward an argument for such a belief. He claims that if we wish to understand the world as an ordered whole that can be rationally explained in its entirety, we must think of it as having boundaries. We must, Kant argues, at least assume things external to reason. One of these is the existence of God as a designer, for

without assuming an intelligent author we cannot give any *intelligible ground* of it [purposiveness] without falling into plain absurdities; and although we cannot *prove* the impossibility of such purposiveness apart from an *intelligent cause* . . . there yet remains a sufficient ground for *assuming* such a cause. (Was heisst: 'Sich im Denken orientiren?', Ak 8: 138–9)[55]

Kant calls this 'ground' also a '*need* of reason'. We must presuppose something rationally comprehensible in order to approach a full explanation of what is given to us in experience. We must assume God in order to assert the universal applicability of rational explanation. However, this need of reason is not very strong. It does not make a belief in God very urgent. It may be beneficial for making sense of the world, but that may not be a strong enough justification.

Kant, of course, has a stronger justification, and it is found in our morality. There is a moral interest of reason that gives rise to moral belief. Kant most fully develops this argument in his Dialectic of Pure Practical Reason of the *Kritik der praktischen Vernunft*, where he argues that we must postulate or assume as necessary the existence of God because of a practical need of reason. The argument goes roughly as follows: The moral law commands that we should work towards the highest good, so what is commanded as a duty must be possible. Now, the highest good is possible only if happiness and moral worth are proportional to each other. But there is not the slightest connection between our rational will and nature. (Bad things happen frequently to good people, and there is no guarantee that good acts make any difference to the world.) Therefore, in order for morality to make a difference for the good, we must assume 'a cause of all nature, distinct from nature, which contains the ground of this connection, namely of the exact correspondence of happiness with morality'.[56] And this is God.

This argument has puzzled many readers of the *Kritik der praktischen Vernunft*. Many have viewed it as an 'objective' proof of the existence of God, or as a demonstrative argument that is intended to prove the truth of the conclusion 'There is a God', and have rejected it for this reason. Today it is more likely to be viewed as a piece of practical thinking, or something that expresses the existential predicament of somebody who finds himself in a particular situation. Kant was not trying to prove anything but was only concerned with rationalizing something that is essentially non-rational.

Both of these approaches are wrong. What Kant does here is best seen as his attempt to defend a rational faith, or as trying to show again that because of definite and necessary needs of practical reason, we may believe and have a right to believe. The argument has to do with what we can reasonably or responsibly believe, not with what can be asserted as true. It is also meant to establish that we are not necessarily talking irresponsible nonsense when we engage in religious discourse and that it is rational to believe in God. Theism is far from requiring a miracle, and it does not necessarily involve us in contradictions that subvert the principles of our understanding (Ak 5: 132).

If Kant's argument is successful, then morality not only allows us to believe but actually leads us to such beliefs. 'Therefore, we have a warrant of pure reason in its practical use to an extension which is not possible to it in its speculative use' (Ak 5: 50). Although this right does not afford us knowledge about these objects, it does allow us to believe in God and maintain a rational outlook. In fact, belief in God is necessary for such a rational outlook. 'Morality...leads inevitably to religion.'[57] Those who, like Hume, reject religion as irrational and opposed to true morality are wrong. Reason and faith not only do not contradict but actually require each other. Reason has '*a need from an absolutely necessary point of view* and justifies its presupposition' of the existence of God

not merely as a permitted hypothesis but as a postulate from a practical point of view; and, granted that the pure moral law inflexibly binds everyone as a command (not as a rule of prudence), the upright man may well say: I *will* that there be a God.... I stand by this, without paying attention to rationalizations, however little I may be able to answer or oppose them with others more plausible, and will not let this belief be taken from me; for this is the only case in which my interest, because I *may* not give up anything of it, unavoidably determines my judgment. (*Kritik der praktischen Vernunft*, Ak 5: 143)

So Kant's philosophy may be said to end with two articles of belief, or faith: we may believe that God exists and that morality is its own reward (*Kritik der reinen Vernunft*, A 30/B 858). No more no less.

X. THE POST-KANTIANS

Johann Georg Hamann (1730–88), who was one of Kant's closest acquaintances in Königsberg, published in 1759 an essay entitled *Sokratische Denkwürdigkeiten* (Socratic Memorabilia).[58] In it, he tried to show, among other things, that his contemporaries were wrong in trying to supply a rational justification and explication of experience. At its most fundamental level, experience involves beliefs. 'Our own existence and the existence of all things outside us must be believed, and cannot be determined in any other way', he claimed, and he argued that '[t]here are proofs of truth which are of as little value as the application which can be made of the truths themselves, indeed, one can believe the proof of a proposition without giving approval to the proposition itself' (167). Hume, of whom he was 'full' when he wrote this, had shown, he thought, that reason is not given to us to make us 'wise' but to make us aware of our 'folly and ignorance'. We cannot 'eat an egg and drink a glass of water' without believing. And the question that Hamann was raising was that if Hume needs such beliefs 'for food and drink, why does he deny belief when he judges of matters that are higher than sensuous eating and drinking?'[59] Playing on the ambiguity in the German word *Glaube*, which can mean both belief and faith, he accuses Hume of being inconsistent in relying on *Glaube* in epistemic contexts while denying its legitimacy in religious contexts. Hamann believed that any consistent reading of Hume would lead to the view that his argument served as a defense of a fideism, and, indeed, the concluding paragraph of Section X of Hume's *Enquiry concerning Human Understanding* might suggest such a reading. At the same time, Hamann thought that it undermined the very foundations of all intellectual pursuits and enlightenment philosophy.

This view, although first formulated in 1759, received a great deal of attention only after 1785. And the attention it received was not due to Hamann himself but the use to which Friedrich Heinrich Jacobi (1743–1819) put it in the so-called Pantheismusstreit. Jacobi had published in 1785 a book, *Über die Lehre des Spinoza* (On the Doctrine of Spinoza), in which he related that Gotthold Ephraim Lessing (1729–81), a famous and highly respected German playwright, theologian, critic, and good friend of Mendelssohn, had confessed to him that he was a Spinozist and thus also an atheist.[60] The book created a great controversy that overshadowed the reception of Kant's *Kritik der reinen Vernunft* and gave the philosophical discussion a rather peculiar twist. Mendelssohn rose to the defense of Lessing, accusing Jacobi of irrationalism and enthusiasm because he ultimately appealed to faith. Jacobi's defense was to use the ambiguity of *Glaube* in order to argue that if he was an irrationalist, then so was Hume. Quoting long passages from Hume's *Enquiry* in his *David Hume über den Glauben* (1787), Jacobi had no trouble showing that Hume, who could not be suspected of enthusiasm, had used belief (*Glaube*) even more often than he had, and that when he made faith fundamental to all human activities he was in relatively good company.[61] Whatever one may think of the tactic employed by Jacobi, he greatly influenced the younger generation of philosophers, whose Kantianism became strongly colored by Jacobi's, or perhaps more so Hamann's, theory of faith. He attacked especially Kant's view that our knowledge, even though only a knowledge of appearances, presupposed 'things in themselves'. For Jacobi, any acceptance of things in themselves was inconsistent with Kantian idealism and indeed any kind of rationalism. We must believe in the reality of external objects, and this belief is essentially a sensible belief. Once knowledge gets separated from the senses, the belief in external objects cannot be recovered. Using Thomas Reid's theory of belief, Jacobi attempted to develop a realism as an alternative to Kant's idealism. Although this theory was itself rather inconsistent and eclectic, it played a large role in the development of absolute idealism. Indeed, it would be impossible to understand the thought of the post-Kantian generation without it.

Karl Leonhard Reinhold, whose *Briefe über die kantische Philosophie* (Letters on Kantian Philosophy) of 1787 had done a great deal to popularize Kant's philosophy, took a different route. He also found it necessary to criticize Kant (for reasons similar to those of Jacobi). However, he wished to develop his own theory along more or less Kantian lines. Yet his approach was much more ambitious than Kant's. In fact, his stated goal was to expose the foundation of Kant's system and thus for any possible kind of philosophy. He argued that until Hume there had been only two basic systems of philosophy possible, namely, that of empiricism (*Empirismus*) and that of rationalism. The two most important thinkers in those traditions (that is, the ones who developed each of these systems to the greatest perfection they were capable of) were for him Leibniz and Locke. Hume destroyed both empiricism and skepticism by 'refuting the presuppositions of Locke and Leibniz';[62] and Kant discovered a new foundation of philosophical knowledge. It contains 'all that is true and that is contained in the isolated and one-sided systems maintained before him,' and it 'excludes what is not true'. Yet, Kant did not give an adequate foundation for this system. In particular, he did not refute Hume's 'dogmatic skepticism'. Reinhold himself tried to supply the true foundation of Kant's system in what he called the 'fact of consciousness'. Formulated as a principle, this fact amounts to the claim that 'the representation is differentiated by the subject in consciousness from the object and the subject and referred to both'(*Briefe*, 78). Discussions of belief, as found in Hume's and Kant's works, do not have any significant place in this project. In fact, in some ways it constituted a return to a Cartesian approach. Philosophy must be derived from one highest principle. This highest principle is the fact of consciousness, not anything merely factual or historical.

Reinhold's hubris did not remain unchallenged for long, however. In 1792, Gottlob Ernst Schulze published anonymously a book entitled *Aenesidemus oder Über die Fundamente der von dem Herrn Professor Reinhold in Jena gelieferten*

Elementarphilosophie. Nebst einer Vertheidigung des Skepticismus gegen die Anmas-sungen der Vernunftkritik (Aenesidemus, or Concerning the Foundations of the Philosophy of the Elements Issued by Prof. Reinhold in Jena, together with a Defense against the Pretensions of the Critique of Reason).[63] Ernst Cassirer seems to sum up the received view on the importance of the *Aenesidemus* for our understanding of Kant when he claims that in

the *Aenesidemus* the problem of Hume is newly posed. But it now appears in a more significant and more dangerous form, as it speaks the language of critical philosophy itself. The final result of critical philosophy is now being contested on the basis of the concepts and presuppositions of the *Critique of Pure Reason* itself.[64]

One may doubt that this is true. Schulze seems to rely more on Reinhold than on Kant, and his target is clearly not so much the *Kritik der reinen Vernunft* as it is what Reinhold made of it. But however this may be, Schulze's book was seen as undermining Kant's enterprise and as showing that Kant had not succeeded in answering Hume's skepticism about knowledge of the external world. Schulze himself was rather more sophisticated than Jacobi, Reinhold, and almost anyone else in the host of Kantians and anti-Kantians who wrote during this *aetas Kantiana*. He appreciated Reid's subtle analysis of sensation and belief and tried to develop it further in his *Kritik der theoretischen Philosophie*.[65]

However, Schulze was the exception rather than the rule. The mainstream of German philosophy went a rather different route, characterized by such names as Johann Gottlieb Fichte, Friedrich Wilhelm Joseph Schelling, and Georg Wilhelm Friedrich Hegel. The starting point of their philosophizing is to a large extent defined by the works of Jacobi, Reinhold, and Schulze. By the time they begin to publish, Kant has already become part of the historical background. The problems that occupied Locke, Hume, and Reid are still further removed from the problems they find important. Hegel's work *Glauben und Wissen* (1802) bears the subtitle *Die Reflexionsphilosophie der Sub-jektivität in der Vollständigkeit ihrer Formen als Kantische, Jacobische und Fichtesche Philosophie.*[66] What is important to Hegel is not the analysis or discussion of the interplay of knowledge and belief, nor the question of what and how much we can know, but rather such broad questions as the nature and rela-tion of such concepts (or rather the concerns expressed by such concepts) as finitude, subjectivity, objectivity, eternity, God, Being, totality, and others. The last paragraph of this book is characteristic not only of the work as a whole but also of the cultural background against which Hegel's idealism arose. Hegel starts from the claim that the 'pure concept . . . or its infinity, as the abyss of nothingness into which all being sinks, must characterize that eternal suffering which forms the foundation of the religion of the modern period . . . namely, the feeling: "God himself is dead" . . . purely as an aspect of . . . the highest idea'. He then goes on to argue that in this way the pure concept 'must restore the idea of absolute freedom and therewith the absolute suffering or the philosophical Good Friday . . . and thus restore itself and the entire truth and harshness of its Godlessness'. And he ends up claiming that the pure concept can and must find resurrection in this way and in 'the most cheerful freedom'. Jacobi called this kind of philosophy 'nihilism'. I believe most other thinkers of the eighteenth century would have agreed. Hegel clearly transcended the more or less ordinary discussion of knowledge and belief that characterized the eighteenth century. Whether in doing so he succeeded in achieving anything worth our while I do not know (and I am glad that I do not have to decide).

XI. CONCLUSION

Insofar as many of the most important developments in the second half of the eighteenth century are concerned with an attempt to combine the objective Wolffian approach, which is concerned with the possibility of objects or thought contents, with an approach that is more indebted to British sources and emphasizes subjective belief, we can also characterize these developments as the conflict between belief philosophers and philosophers who believe that there can be knowledge without a knowing subject. In the eighteenth century, the latter party lost. With Hegel, the third world seems to have reappeared with a vengeance. It would be difficult, if not impossible, to identify the precise historical causes of these developments, but perhaps this is not necessary for we can still learn some philosophical lessons from the eighteenth-century discussion. The questions, in any case, are still with us.

NOTES

1 Karl R. Popper, *Objective Knowledge: An Evolutionary Approach* (Oxford, 1972), 106f.
2 Leslie Stephen, *The History of English Thought in the Eighteenth Century*, 2 vols. (London, 1876), 1: 86.
3 René Descartes, *The Philosophical Writings of Descartes*, trans. J. Cottingham, R. Stroothoff, and D. Murdoch (Cambridge, 1984–91), 1: 10.
4 See Ernst Cassirer, *Das Erkenntnisproblem in der Philosophie und Wissenschaft der neueren Zeit*, 3 vols. (Darmstadt, 1974), 1: 506.
5 See Steven M. Nadler, *Arnauld and the Cartesian Philosophy of Ideas* (Manchester and Princeton, NJ, 1989), 105f.
6 See Peter A. Schouls, 'The Cartesian Methods of Locke's *Essay Concerning Human Understanding*', *Canadian Journal of Philosophy*, 4 (1974–5): 579–601, and his *In The Imposition of Method: A Study of Descartes and Locke* (Oxford, 1980). See also Roger Woolhouse, 'Locke's Theory of Knowledge,' in *The Cambridge Companion to Locke*, ed. V. Chappell (Cambridge, 1994), 146–171.

7 There were precedents to the Lockean view in the seventeenth century. See, for instance, Rainer Specht, 'Gassendi Analogien in Lockes Theorie des sinnlichen Wissens', *Philosophisches Jahrbuch*, 100 (1993): 267–81.

8 John Locke, *An Essay Concerning Human Understanding*, ed. P. H. Nidditch, in *The Clarendon Edition* (1975), 1.i.2.

9 Christian Wolff, *Discursus praeliminaris de philosophia in genere/Einleitende Abhandlung über Philosophie im allgemeinen*, trans. and eds. G. Gawlick and L. Kreimendahl (Stuttgart-Bad Cannstatt, 1996). All citations refer to the translation *Preliminary Discourse on Philosophy in General*, trans. R. J. Blackwell (Indianapolis, IN, 1963), 3.

10 Wolff, *Preliminary Discourse*, 6. Besides historical and philosophical knowledge, there is also mathematical knowledge, or 'knowledge of the quantity of things' (8). Mathematical knowledge is based on both historical and philosophical knowledge (10).

11 Wolff, *Ausführliche Nachricht von seinen eigenen Schriften, die er in deutscher Sprache von den verschiedenen Theilen der Welt-Weisheit ans Licht gestellet* (Frankfurt, 1726), §28, translated in Hans Lüthje, 'Christian Wolff's Philosophiebegriff', *Kant-Studien*, 30 (1926): 39–66 at 55.

12 See also Cornelis Anthonie van Peursen, 'Christian Wolff's Philosophy of Contingent Reality,' *Journal of the History of Philosophy*, 25 (1987): 69–82; and Charles A. Corr, 'Christian Wolff and Leibniz', *Journal of the History of Ideas*, 36 (1975): 241–62.

13 See Wolff, *Vernünfftige Gedancken von den Kräfften des menschlichen Verstandes und ihrem richtigen Gebrauche in Erkänntnis der Wahrheit* (*Deutsche Logik*), ed. H. W. Arndt, in *Werke*, I.1: 115; *Preliminary Discourse*, 3; and *Philosophia prima, sive Ontologia* (1730), §§134, 174, 574 (115, 143, 574).

14 Wolff, *Preliminary Discourse*, 6. Anything that excludes logical contradiction is not just possible, but it is a possible thing.

15 Van Peursen, 'Wolff's Philosophy', 73.

16 Wolff, *Deutsche Logik*, 201.

17 See, for instance, Allan Arkush, *Moses Mendelssohn and the Enlightenment* (Albany, NY, 1994), 37.

18 George Becker, 'Pietism's Confrontation with Enlightenment Rationalism: An Examination of Ascetic Protestantism and Science', *Journal for the Scientific Study of Religion*, 30 (1991): 139–58.

19 Wolff, *Oratio de Sinarum philosophia practica* (delivered 1721), in *Fasces Prorectorales Successori Traderet* (Frankfurt am Main, 1726); trans. and ed. M. Albrecht, *Oratio de Sinarum philosophia practica/Rede über die praktische Philosophie der Chinesen* (Hamburg, 1985); English translation in Julia Ching and Willard G. Oxtoby, *Moral Enlightenment: Leibniz and Wolff on China* (Nettetal, 1992). See Lewis White Beck, *Early German Philosophy: Kant and His Predecessors* (Cambridge, MA, 1969), 243ff.

20 Johann Jakob Brucker (1696–1770) also deserves to be mentioned. His influential *Historia critica philosophiae*, 4 vols. in 5 (Leipzig, 1742–4), is said to have been the source of Diderot's articles on the history of philosophy in the *Encyclopédie*. See Peter Gay, *The Enlightenment: An Interpretation*, 2 vols. (New York, NY, 1977), vol. 1: *The Rise of Modern Paganism*, 364–8. Christian August Crusius (1715–75) also has close connections to them.

21 Its most important source of inspiration was Philipp Jakob Spener's *Pia desideria* of 1675, but August Hermann Francke (1663–1727) soon made Halle the center of this movement. Pietism remains influential in Germany today. It also had significant effects outside of Germany. See F. E. Stoeffler, *The Rise of Evangelical Pietism*, 2nd edn. (Leiden, 1971).

22 Christian Thomasius, *Einleitung zur Vernunftlehre* (Halle, 1691); *Ausübung der Vernunftlehre, oder: Kurze, deutliche und wohlgegründete Handgriffe, wie man in seinem Kopffe aufräumen . . . solle* (Halle, 1691); *Einleitung zur Sittenlehre* (Halle, 1692); and *Ausübung der Sittenlehre* (Halle, 1696).

23 For details (and a more positive account), see G. Zart, *Einfluss der englischen Philosophen seit Bacon auf die deutsche Philosophie des 18. Jahrhunderts* (Berlin, 1881), 33–72.

24 For a discussion, see Hans Aarsleff, 'Locke's Influence', in *The Cambridge Companion to Locke*, ed. V. Chappell (Cambridge, 1994), 252–89. See also John W. Yolton, *Locke and French Materialism* (Oxford, 1991).

25 Jean le Rond d'Alembert, *Discours préliminaire de l'Encyclopédie*, in *Oeuvres*, 5 vols. (Paris, 1821–2), vol. 1, translated as *Preliminary Discourse to the Encyclopedia of Diderot*, trans. R. N. Schwab and W. E. Rex (Indianapolis, IN, 1963).

26 Étienne Bonnot de Condillac, *Essai sur l'origine des connaissances humaines*, in *Oeuvres philosophiques*, ed. G. Le Roy, 3 vols. (Paris, 1947–51), vol. 1, translated as *An Essay on the Origin of Human Knowledge*, trans. and ed. H. Aarsleff (Cambridge, 2001).

27 See Aarsleff, 'Locke's Influence', 277. See also his *From Locke to Saussure: Essays on the Study of Language and Intellectual History* (Minneapolis, MN, 1982), especially 120–45 and 146–207.

28 See Antony Flew, *Hume's Philosophy of Belief* (New York, NY, 1961); see also Michael Hodges and John Lachs, 'Hume on Belief', *The Review of Metaphysics*, 30 (1976): 3–18 at 5.

29 This seems already clear from merely statistical considerations. The term 'knowledge' appears 27 times in Book I of the *Treatise*, whereas 'belief' appears 80 times. In many books on Hume, the word 'knowledge' does not even make it into the index.

30 David Hume, *A Treatise of Human Nature*, eds. D. F. Norton and M. J. Norton (Oxford 2006), 1.3.1.2, SBN 70.

31 This seems to represent Locke's intuition and demonstration. Locke's sensation becomes matter of fact in Hume.

32 Hume, *An Enquiry concerning Human Understanding*, ed. T. L. Beauchamp, in the *Clarendon Edition* (2000), 4.1.1–2, SBN 24f.

33 See Robert J. Fogelin, *Hume's Skepticism in the Treatise of Human Nature* (London, 1985), 13f.

34 When Hume says 'wherever ideas are adequate representations of objects, the relations, contradictions, and agreements of the ideas are all applicable to the objects; and this we may in general observe to be the foundation of all human knowledge' (*Treatise*, 1.2.2.1, SBN 29), he restricts this to the mathematical disciplines.

35 *Treatise*, 1.3.8.11, SBN 103. This is parallel to his explanation of causality. He explicitly draws that parallel at 1.3.9.19, SBN 117.

36 This does not mean, of course, that we can know objects without any form of mediation whatsoever or that objects somehow enter 'directly' into our mind. Perception is in some sense always dependent upon mediation, and Reid is very much aware of this. See Thomas Reid, *An Inquiry into the Human Mind on the Principles of Common Sense*, ed. D. R. Brookes (Edinburgh, 1997), VI.21, 174.

37 David Fate Norton, 'Reid's Abstract of the Inquiry into the Human Mind', in *Thomas Reid: Critical Interpretations*, eds. S. F. Barker and T. L. Beauchamp (Philadelphia, PA, 1976), 125–32 at 128.

38 Reid, *Inquiry*, II.9, II.3, VI.21 at 43, 27, 175–6, respectively.

39 Reid, *Essays on the Intellectual Powers of Man*, eds. D. R. Brookes and K. Haakonssen (Edinburgh, 2002).

40 See, for instance, the chapter 'Of Extension' in the *Inquiry*.

41 Reid, *Inquiry*, VI.20, 168; see also the discussion on extension in ch. VI.

42 Reid states: 'Every man knows what it is, but no man can define it', *Inquiry*, II.5, 30.

43 Reid, *Inquiry*, II.3, p. 28; II.5, p. 31; VI.20, pp. 170, 172; VI.21, p. 177; VI.24, p. 190.

44 He is much more definite on the number of basic principles in the *Essays on the Intellectual Powers*, VI.5.

45 Reid, *Essays on the Active Powers of Man*, in *Philosophical Works*, ed. W. Hamilton, 2 vols. in 1 (Edinburgh, 1895), 2: V.5, p. 652.

46 Reid, *Active Powers*, V.7, p. 676. Hume, of course, was aware of the possibility of this objection. One may also wonder about one rather curious aspect of Reid's critique of moral sense in *Active Powers*, namely, its lack of references to Hutcheson and Smith. See J. C. Stewart-Robinson and David F. Norton, 'Thomas Reid on Adam Smith's Theory of Morals', *Journal of the History of Ideas*, 45 (1984): 309–21. The same criticisms that apply to Hume also apply to Hutcheson and Smith. Yet, Reid chose not to publish any of them or even to draw explicit attention to these similarities in his published works.

47 Moses Mendelssohn, review of Edmund Burke's *A Philosophical Enquiry into the Origin of our Ideas of the Sublime and Beautiful*, in *Bibliothek der schönen Wissenschaften und der freyen Künste* II (1759; 2nd edn., 1762), 290–1.

48 This is the title of a book by Johann August Eberhard: *Allgemeine Theorie des Denkens und Empfindens* (Berlin, 1776).

49 These seem to be the only relevant theories Mendelssohn recognizes. See Moses Mendelssohn, *Gesammelte Schriften: Jubiläumsausgabe*, eds. F. Bamberger and A. Altmann (Stuttgart-Bad Cannstatt, 1971–) 1: 160. Physical influx, occasionalism, and pre-established harmony exhaust for him the possible metaphysical positions.

50 It also follows from the occasionalist position. See John P. Wright, 'Hume's Criticism of Malebranche's Theory of Causation: A Lesson in the Historiography of Philosophy', in *Nicolas Malebranche: His Philosophical Critics and Successors*, ed. S. Brown (Assen and Maastricht, 1991), 116–30.

51 See Beck, *Early German Philosophy*, 412–25; Giorgio Tonelli, 'Tetens, Johann Nicolaus', in *The Encyclopedia of Philosophy*, ed. P. Edwards, 8 vols. (New York, NY, 1972); and Jeffrey Barnouw, 'The Philosophical Achievement and Historical Significance of Johann Nicolaus Tetens', *Studies in Eighteenth-Century Culture*, 9 (1979): 301–35.

52 Johann Nicolaus Tetens, *Philosophische Versuche über die menschliche Natur und ihre Entwicklung* [facsim. of Leipzig 1777], in *Die philosophischen Werke*, 2 vols. (Hildesheim, 1979), 2: 531f.

53 Immanuel Kant, *Kritik der reinen Vernunft*, Ak vols. 3 (A) and 4 (B), translated as *Critique of Pure Reason*, trans. and eds. P. Guyer and A. W. Wood, in *Works* (1998), A 820/B 848-A 831/B 859.

54 Kant, 'Was heisst: Sich im Denken orientiren?, translated as 'What Does It Mean to Orient Oneself in Thinking,' in *Works/Religion and Rational Theology*, trans. and eds. A. Wood and G. di Giovanni (1996), Ak 8: 131–47 at 140–2.

55 See also *Prolegomena zu einer jeden künftigen Metaphysik, die als Wissenschaft wird auftreten können*, in Ak 4: 253–383, translated as *Prolegomena to Any Future Metaphysics that Will Be Able to Come Forward as a Science*, trans. G. Hatfield, in *Works/Theoretical Philosophy after 1781* (2002).

56 Kant, *Kritik der praktischen Vernunft*, Ak 5: 125, translated as *Critique of Practical Reason*, trans. and ed. M. J. Gregor, in *Works/Practical Philosophy* (1996).

57 Kant, *Die Religion innerhalb der Grenzen der bloßen Vernunft*, Ak 6: 6n, translated as *Religion within the Boundaries of mere Reason*, trans. and eds. A. Wood and G. di Giovanni, in *Works/Religion and Rational Theology*.

58 Johann Georg Hamann, *Sokratische Denkwürdigkeiten für die lange Weile des Publicums zusammengetragen von einem Liebhaber der langen Weile Mit einer doppelten Zuschrift an Niemand und an Zween* (Königsberg, 1759), translated as *Socratic Memorabilia, Compiled for the Boredom of the Public by a lover of Boredom. With a Double Dedication to Nobody and to Two* (1759), trans. J. O. Flaherty (Baltimore, MD, 1967). I shall quote in accordance with this translation.

59 He argued this in a letter to Kant in 1759. See Immanuel Kant, *Works/Correspondence*, trans. and ed. A. Zweig (1999), 52–3. (I have substituted 'belief' for 'faith'.)

60 Friedrich Heinrich Jacobi, *Über die Lehre des Spinoza in Briefen an den Herrn Moses Mendelssohn*, ed. M. Lauschke (Hamburg, 2000).

61 Jacobi, *David Hume über den Glauben oder Idealismus und Realismus: Ein Gespräch*, in *Werke*, eds. F. von Roth and F. Köppen, 6 vols. (Leipzig, 1812–25), vol. 2.

62 Karl Leonhard Reinhold, *Über das Fundament des philosophischen Wissens/Über die Möglichkeit der Philosophie als strenge Wissenschaft* (1791) (Hamburg, 1978), 45; see 48. I quote in accordance with *Between Kant and Hegel: Texts in the Development of Post-Kantian Idealism*, trans. and eds. G. di Giovanni and H. S. Harris (Albany, NY, 1985), 56, 59.

63 Gottlob Ernst Schulze, *Aenesidemus oder Über die Fundamente der von dem Herrn Professor Reinhold in Jena gelieferten Elementarphilosophie. Nebst einer Vertheidigung des Skepticismus gegen die Anmassungen der Vernunftkritik*, ed. A. Liebert (Berlin, 1911).

64 Ernst Cassirer, *Das Erkenntnisproblem*, 1: 57. Translated in *Between Kant and Hegel*, 104 and 135.

65 Gottlob Ernst Schulze, *Kritik der theoretischen Philosophie*, 2 vols. (Hamburg, 1801). Reinhold also learned to appreciate Reid in one of his later phases.

66 Georg Wilhelm Friedrich Hegel, *Glauben und Wissen oder Die Reflexionsphilosophie der Subjektivität in der Vollständigkeit ihrer Formen als Kantische, Jacobische und Fichtesche Philosophie*, in *Werke in zwanzig Bänden*, eds. E. Moldenhauer and K. M. Michel, 20 vols. (Frankfurt am Main, 1971), 2: 287–433, translated as *Faith and Knowledge or the Reflective Philosophy of Subjectivity in the Complete Range of Its Forms as Kantian, Jacobian, and Fichtean Philosophy*, trans. W. Cerf and H. S. Harris (Albany, NY, 1977).

15

SCEPTICISM

RICHARD H. POPKIN

Scepticism was a most important philosophical view at the beginning of the eighteenth century, continuing the development that had started in the Renaissance with the ideas of Montaigne and was then presented by Charron, La Mothe Le Vayer, Gassendi, and Foucher, among others, during the seventeenth century.[1] The major philosophers from Descartes to Locke and Leibniz had struggled to provide answers to the sceptical challenges.

Three major philosophical sceptical works appeared in the first decades of the eighteenth century. There was a new and very erudite Latin and Greek edition of the writings of Sextus Empiricus done by the learned J. A. Fabricius,[2] as well as the first published French translation of Sextus's *Outlines of Pyrrhonism*.[3] Second, the revised and much enlarged second edition of Pierre Bayle's *Dictionnaire historique et critique* appeared in 1702,[4] including the author's defence of what he had said about Pyrrhonism and atheism in the first edition. Third was the posthumous publication of Bishop Huet's very sceptical *Traité philosophique de la foiblesse de l'esprit humaine* (1723), which was quickly put out in Latin, English, German, and later Italian.[5] These provided important bases for discussions of scepticism throughout the eighteenth century.

At the same time, quite a few important attempts to refute scepticism appeared. Learned discussions by Dutch and German professors were published dealing with the origins, causes, and ways of refuting scepticism. Some debated whether Solomon and Job were actually sceptics and whether one or the other should be considered the founder of the sceptical movement. A German dissertation from Kiel in 1706 declared that the Devil was the actual author of scepticism since he made Adam and Eve doubt the word of God.[6] George Berkeley, in his *Principles of Human Knowledge* and *Three Dialogues between Hylas and Philonous (1713)*, sought to rescue philosophy from the scepticism he saw following from the views of Descartes and Locke.[7] Jean Le Clerc, a friend of John Locke, wrote answers to Bayle and, in a review of the 1718 edition of Sextus's *Opera*, set out an almost book-length attempt to refute scepticism.[8]

In 1733, the Swiss philosopher-theologian, Jean Pierre de Crousaz, offered an immense folio volume, *Examen du pyrrhonisme ancien et moderne*, in which he tried to save the intellectual and cultural world from the corrosive influences of Sextus, Bayle, and Huet, which he saw as having disastrous social, moral, and religious effects.[9] Crousaz pictured the Pyrrhonism of Sextus, Bayle, and Huet as a complete menace, which was undermining everything and leading people even to such disasters as the South Sea Bubble and the Mississippi Company financial collapses, as well as weakening religious and moral beliefs. His enormous volume decried the sad fact that the sceptical bacillus was infecting the entire European intellectual world. (Berkeley's philosophy was offered as a case in point.) Though Crousaz went through the arguments in Sextus, Bayle, and Huet, his critique is mainly a lot of invective and argument from catastrophe – if one accepts the sceptics' point, then all sorts of terrible things will follow. Reviewers were not impressed, so two leading figures in the Berlin Academy, its perpetual secretary, Jean Henri Samuel Formey, and Baron Haller, put out abridged versions in French and German.[10]

Crousaz's great crusade against scepticism was ridiculed and answered in an anonymous 'Apologie de monsieur Bayle, ou Lettre d'un Sceptique sur l'Examen du Pyrrhonisme pour servir de réponse au livre de M. de Crousaz sur le Pyrrhonisme', which was included in the 1739 edition of the *Nouvelles lettres de Mr. P. Bayle*.[11] This author suggested that perhaps Crousaz himself was a disguised Pyrrhonist who was actually aiding the sceptics while pretending to attack them. After all, he asked, why are his arguments so bad?

Further, the author contended that, as Bayle and Huet had said, Pyrrhonism leads to the true faith and not to irreligion. A sceptic, the author said, is really in the state that the Gospel prescribes for the faithful. Crousaz's confused and insulting attack convinces sceptical readers that in fact Bayle cannot be answered. So, instead of saving the world from the sceptical menace, Crousaz, in his misguided way, has actually made scepticism stronger!

The new editions of Sextus, plus the full English translation of the *Outlines of Pyrrhonism*, which appeared in the third volume of Thomas Stanley's *History of Philosophy*, first published in 1655 and reprinted into the eighteenth century,[12] made this treasury of classical Greek arguments available to the general intellectual public throughout Europe. Copies of one or another of the editions appear in the libraries of a great many figures all through the century,[13] and Sextus is cited in the writings of most of the well-known and lesser figures of the time.[14]

Bayle's *Dictionnaire* was one of the widely read books of the time, reaching a fifth edition in 1740. Two English translations appeared, and in the latter part of the century a German translation was issued. Bayle provided, in a racy and a scholarly fashion, a huge battery of sceptical arguments against all kinds of current theories in philosophy, theology and science. He attacked the theories of leading thinkers of his time – Malebranche, Locke, Leibniz, and Newton, among others – and showed that their views were 'big with contradiction and absurdity'. He revised the ancient sceptical arguments so that they applied directly to the 'new philosophy' and all sorts of competing theories. He examined the argument of his sceptical contemporary Simon Foucher – that sceptical doubts about the reality of secondary qualities, sounds, tastes, smells, colors, and tactile feelings applied just as well to primary qualities – and showed that it thereby undermined the Cartesian way of knowing reality. Bayle scandalised his contemporaries by arguing that a society of atheists can be more moral than a society of Christians, that Manicheanism is more plausible according to reason and evidence than Christianity, that Pyrrhonism can be of great service to Christianity, and that it is more powerful against the new philosophy than against classical theories. Bayle's arguments plus his scholarly revelation of the foibles of ancient and modern heroes of Judaism, Christianity, kings and queens, political leaders, and theologians provided what Voltaire claimed was 'the Arsenal of the Enlightenment'.

Huet's *Traité*, the third major presentation of sceptical views in the early eighteenth century, was one of the shockers of the time. Huet, who had been tutor to the Dauphin and then bishop of Avranches, was well known for his classical erudition, his scholarship, his attacks on Cartesianism, and his apologetic works about Christianity. He was a well-liked and well-regarded member of the republic of letters who was in touch with scholars all over Europe. (He and Leibniz had much contact.) After he died in 1721, many were startled to find that he had written such a strong presentation of Pyrrhonian scepticism, claiming that it was the proper preparation for accepting the Christian faith. The Jesuits, who had trained him and among whom he lived after his retirement, at first claimed the book was a forgery released to embarrass the Catholic Church and to destroy Huet's reputation.[15] Soon manuscripts in Huet's hand were produced, as well as correspondence indicating that the bishop had sent a copy to Jean Le Clerc in Amsterdam[16] and had shown the work to others in the 1690s.

Huet in the *Traité* sought to picture Pyrrhonian scepticism as the *prisca theologia*, the ancient wisdom that went back to the Bible and had been passed on ever since. He gave a history and outline of ancient scepticism, claimed that both Maimonides and St. Thomas Aquinas were part of the sceptical tradition, and then made sceptics the only present-day thinkers who could deal constructively with the new scientific ideas of the time. He ended by urging his readers to accept a kind of scientific scepticism like that of the leaders of the Royal Society of England and to accept Christianity on faith alone. Bayle, whom Huet did not particularly like, had made the same fideistic proposal throughout his writings. However, in Huet's case, people assumed he was sincere since no one had ever questioned his religious commitment or his piety. In Bayle's case, there was much doubt of his sincerity among his Huguenot brethren, and his Catholic opponents. Interpreters then and now have been fighting over the soul of Bayle, seeing him as anything from a most fervent fideist or a deist to a secret atheist undermining the very foundations of traditional religious belief.[17]

Several bright young men early in the century pored over Bayle's tomes (his four folio volume *Dictionnaire*, plus his four folio volume *Oeuvres diverses*). Young George Berkeley in Dublin, young David Hume in Scotland, and young Voltaire and Denis Diderot in France all immersed themselves in Bayle's arguments.[18] Berkeley thought that he could resolve all sceptical problems by his new principle, *esse est percipere sive percipi*, which dissolved the ontological difference between appearance and reality and with it the force of scepticism. As Berkeley ended the *Dialogues*, he declared that starting from scepticism one ends up avowing the principles of common sense, that what we perceive is what is really there in the world. Berkeley, as we shall see, was seen both as a *sceptique malgré lui* and as one who opened the way for a new, more moderate scepticism that was developed during the French Enlightenment.[19]

In the 1730s, Hume apparently had his own personal sceptical crisis. In his early notebooks, at least half the entries are from Bayle, together with Hume's thoughts on them. When Hume went to France in 1734 to write his *Treatise of Human Nature*, he took with him eight folio volumes of Bayle's writings. He stayed first in Paris with the Chevalier Andrew Michael Ramsay, a Catholic mystic, the teacher of Bonnie Prince Charlie and the leader of the Free Masons. Ramsay had been a Pyrrhonist in his youth and was developing his own theosophical way of dealing with scepticism.[20] Hume read Huet's *Traité* and Sextus at some point in his career. In his *Treatise*, his *Enquiry Concerning Human Understanding*, and his *Dialogues Concerning Natural Religion*, he advanced the most complete presentation of scepticism in modern philosophy.

The *Treatise* begins most optimistically, its author promising to introduce the Newtonian method of reasoning into moral subjects. In the first part of Book I, Hume sought to develop an associationist science of the mind. He argued that all that we are aware of is our impressions, our ideas (which are copies and compounds of our impressions), and our feelings. In the second part of Book I, Hume tried to deal with the sceptical paradoxes that had appeared in Bayle's article 'Zeno of Elea' by his own empirical theory of space and time as modes of perceiving. Then, in the third part of Book I, entitled 'Of Knowledge and Probability', Hume carefully analysed what can be known from our ideas, contending that we can only know what ideas resemble each other, or are contrary to each other, and degrees of quantity or number. All other knowledge claims depend upon something more than the immediate inspection of our ideas.

The most important relation upon which our purported knowledge of anything beyond our immediate ideas and impressions depends is that of causation. Hume then proceeded to show that we know about causes and their effects neither from the inspection of our ideas nor from any reasoning process. How then do we acquire causal information, which 'peoples our world'? Following Malebranche and Bayle, Hume insisted that we do not see events as causing one another, we do not see the power in one object producing effects in another. We only perceive a sequence of impressions and ideas. We cannot infer causal connections because we do not know whether what we have experienced in the past will be like our future experience. Any proof of causality is based upon the assumption that nature will always be uniform, but we have no way of telling whether this principle is true. In fact, we cannot even prove that events must have causes.

Having said all this, Hume then examined the process by which people in fact make causal inferences, a process which, he argued, is not rational or evidential but only psychological, founded upon basic features of human nature. After experiencing one event after another several times, the mind moves immediately, on perceiving one of these events, to a lively idea of the other. There is no justification of this process, only a description of how it operates, based on original principles of human nature, and how in operating it produces strong psychological beliefs about what is beyond our immediate experience. This at best produces probable views rather than knowledge.

Following on this analysis, which would result in a scepticism about knowledge claims concerning matters of fact, Hume then went on in the fourth part of Book I, called 'The Sceptical and other systems of philosophy', to show that the very principles of human nature by which we live as 'rational beings' should actually lead us to complete doubt about our reasoning and our sense experience. He developed a 'scepticism with regard to reason'. Though the rules in demonstrative subjects may be certain and infallible, there is always the problem of whether each of us, as a fallible human being, has applied them correctly. When we check our reasoning, we make a judgement, which is also subject to correction and inspection. This checking of our checking can go on indefinitely, each check yielding only a probable result, so that 'when I proceed still farther, to turn the scrutiny against every successive estimation I make of my faculties, all the rules of logic require a continual diminution, and at last a total extinction of belief and evidence'.[21]

In this discussion, Hume offered a striking development in sceptical argumentation about the reliability of reasoning. Sextus is at his least convincing in offering ways of doubting logic and mathematics. Gassendi had held that the rules of logic were true but that their application posed a problem. Descartes and Pascal had presented ways in which it might be false or dubious if there were a demon influencing our thinking. Hume showed that a judgement of the reliability of any reasoning is questionable. In any reasoning process, there is an empirical element, the reasoner thinks that he or she has reasoned correctly and thinks that he or she can tell that this is the case, and so on. Each of these checks is an empirical claim open to inspection, and each inspection results in a probable view open to further empirical inspection. Hence the purported independent knowledge claims of mathematics and logic turn out to involve human psychological claims that are less than certain.[22]

However, Hume immediately went on from this to insist that although sceptics hold that all is uncertain and that we have no measures of truth and falsehood, nobody was ever sincerely and constantly of this opinion. 'Nature, by an absolute and uncontroulable necessity has determin'd us to judge as well as to breathe and feel' (*Treatise,* 1.4.1.7, SBN 183). This natural determination may account for why we believe what our senses tell us about an independent and continuous world outside ourselves. Each attempt to explain why we believe this ends up in contradictions and absurdities. 'Philosophy wou'd render us entirely *Pyrrhonian* were not nature too strong for it',[23] so we can be grateful that 'nature breaks the force of all sceptical arguments in time'. If it did not, sceptical arguments would not be destroyed or destroy themselves until 'they have first subverted all conviction, and have totally destroy'd human reason' (*Treatise,* 1.4.1.12, SBN 187). But, thanks to nature, the sceptic continues to reason and believe, though he cannot justify doing so. He or she also assents to the belief in the real existence of bodies, although he or she has no way of defending this. 'Nature has not left this to his choice, and has doubtless esteem'd it an affair of too great importance to be trusted to our uncertain reasonings and speculations' (1.4.2.1, SBN 187).

According to Hume, the more we examine and philosophise about what we believe in any area whatsoever, the more we expose the insoluble sceptical difficulties that undermine the bases for any conclusions and convictions whatsoever. We are saved by the benevolent protection of nature whenever scepticism is about to undermine us and lead us into abysses of doubt. Nature distracts us for a while, or keeps us from caring about the status of our beliefs.

In the conclusion to Book I of the *Treatise*, Hume found even this natural consolation inadequate for peace of mind or tranquillity, the original goal of the ancient sceptics.

The *intense* view of these manifold contradictions and imperfections in human reason has so wrought upon me, and heated my brain, that I am ready to reject all belief and reasoning, and can look upon no opinion even as more probable or likely than another. Where am I, or what? From what causes do I derive my existence, and to what condition shall I return? Whose favour shall I court, and whose anger must I dread? What beings surround me? and on whom have I any influence, or who have any influence on me? I am confounded with all these questions, and begin to fancy myself in the most deplorable condition imaginable, inviron'd with the deepest darkness, and utterly depriv'd of the use of every member and faculty. (1.4.7.8, SBN 268–9)

As Hume was sinking into philosophical melancholia and delirium, 'the disease of the learned', which cannot be cured by any scientific or rational remedies, it is nature, and nature alone, that saves him. This happens not by nature providing any answers but by nature diverting him to other interests.

Sceptics from Montaigne to Bayle and Huet had seen the ultimate solution to the sceptical crisis in religious terms, and each had claimed, whether sincere or not, that faith and the grace of God alone could provide the certainty mistakenly sought by human means. Hume seems to have dropped out of the religious world and religious framework and so saw that the answer could come from nature, not supernature. Nature allows us to alternate between pressing sceptical inquiries and accepting unjustified beliefs that lead us to investigations about man and nature, the results of which, of course, are still open to sceptical doubts. Nonetheless, in his last work, the *Dialogues Concerning Natural Religion*, Hume ended with the same refrain found in his sceptical predecessors: '[T]o be a philosophical sceptic is, in a man of letters, the first and most essential step towards being a sound, believing Christian'.[24] However, there is no evidence that Hume himself could make this first step. He was then left with the terrifying realisation of the uncertainty of all of our beliefs and the meaninglessness and emptiness of life. When he became terrified about this, nature kindly took him out of his philosophical closet and allowed him cheerfully to divert himself in the ordinary world.

In sum, Hume had carried the sceptical attack further than Bayle or Huet, raising problems that have been central to philosophical studies for the last two centuries. He offered psychological and biological explanations of how we in fact acquire beliefs and actually believe anything in spite of the sceptical challenge. But our scientific understanding of human nature, to which Hume himself contributed greatly, did not provide any way of answering our quest for certainty or of dispelling the terrors of men without faith.

Hume's picture of the sceptical crisis of natural man, what Pascal had called the misery of man without God, which was to have such an impact later on, was generally ignored by thinkers of his time in both Great Britain and France. As he later said, his *Treatise* fell stillborn from the presses. The few reviewers could not recognise his great contribution and wondered why he was sceptical and why he was so upset by his own sceptical conclusions.[25] As time went on, most who noted Hume's views misunderstood and misrepresented them. In France, where Hume became the intellectual darling and hero of the young *philosophes*, his radical scepticism was practically ignored in favour of a more limited but more influential scepticism. The French Enlightenment figures have usually been seen as too positive in their scientific outlook and their belief in the power of reason to take scepticism seriously.[26] However, as Giorgio Tonelli, and later Ezequiel Olaso, have shown, the *philosophes* presented their own form of scepticism.

This was developed both from their reaction to Berkeley's philosophy, rather than Hume's, and from their own understanding of the messages of Bayle, Locke, and Malebranche. Hume had said that Berkeley's arguments

form the best lessons of scepticism, which are to be found either among the ancient or modern philosophers, Bayle not excepted . . . *that they admit of no answer and produce no conviction.* Their only effect is to cause that momentary amazement and irresolution and confusion, which is the result of scepticism.[27]

French thinkers from Voltaire (who had actually met him) onward saw Berkeley in terms of the radical sceptical possibilities that had been raised after Malebranche and Bayle and of the pure empiricism they drew from the French version of Locke's *Essay*. In assessing Berkeley's contribution, they advanced their own 'reasonable' scepticism as a great improvement over the extreme variety of either Bayle or Berkeley.

The great thought projects, such as those proposed by Condillac and Diderot in the 1740s and 1750s to explain the origins, the acquisition, and the limits of human knowledge in purely empirical terms, building up all knowledge from the sense of touch or from the experiences of a blind person, also involved spelling out what human beings cannot know. Berkeley had set forth a complete empiricism or phenomenalism, but he was either a *sceptique outré* or had a crazy metaphysics-like egoism. To avoid such pitfalls, it was necessary to spell out not only the power of reason but also its weakness.[28]

Rather than continuing in what they saw as the destructive line of Bayle (who gradually disappeared as their hero),[29] the French thinkers offered their own version of constructive scepticism. This involved combining the sceptical side of Locke's views with Gassendi's *via media* between scepticism and dogmatism. French thinkers such as Voltaire, Condillac, Diderot, Maupertuis, Changeux, Turgot, and Condorcet all in one way or another accepted the conclusion of Gassendi, Locke, Fontenelle, and Pascal that all knowledge is subjective. They also agreed that Locke had shown that we cannot possess scientific knowledge that cannot possibly be false. They interpreted Locke as teaching them that all we can know is about our experiences and not about some independent real objects.

Tonelli, who explored this side of Enlightenment thinking more than anyone else, summarised eighteenth-century French scepticism as holding that (1) we cannot know how things are in themselves – all we can know are our own ideas, which do not represent the real essence of their objects; (2) we do not know what matter and spirit are in themselves; and (3) there is no proof for the real existence of bodies or (4) of other finite spirits. This scepticism also cast doubt on any conclusive proof of the existence of God and, in some cases, on the certainty of mathematics.[30]

Along with this kind of scepticism, most of the *philosophes* were developing positive views about knowing enough scientifically to understand the physical world and to improve the human world. As the reform projects became more and more important, it also became clear that the limited scepticism of the *philosophes* was not compatible with the complete scepticism of their good friend, David Hume, 'le bon David'. Turgot, who had perhaps been closest to Hume, finally realised that Hume in his thoroughgoing scepticism completely opposed the *philosophes'* programme for the reform of human understanding and society and that Hume actually was an enemy of what they considered 'enlightenment'. Hume in 1768 wrote to Turgot criticising the view

that human Society is capable of perpetual Progress towards Perfection, that the En-crease of Knowledge will still prove favourable to good Government, and that since the Discovery of Printing we need no longer Dread the usual returns of Barbarism and Ignorance.

To make his point, Hume mentioned bad things that were happening in England. Turgot answered that Hume should not be blinded by small local events but should look at the big picture and realise that human beings and their knowledge are perfectible and that progress is inevitable.[31] Turgot then bade farewell to Hume, now his ex-friend, saying 'Adieu, monsieur – car le tems presse [for time is short]'.

In 1777, the young Jean-Pierre Brissot de Warville, one of the very last of the *philosophes*, suggested to d'Alembert that they join forces to put together an encyclopedia of Pyrrhonism. The aged organiser of the *Encyclopédie* was not interested, but young Brissot, then in his early twenties, worked away at the project. An unpublished 90-page manuscript on Pyrrhonism called *Pyrrhon* exists.[32] In 1782, Brissot published *De la vérité, ou Méditations sur les moyens de parvenir à la vérité dans toutes les connaissances humaines*,[33] exploring whether we can know anything with certainty in any of the sciences. Brissot's work (which has not been studied at all by historians of philosophy) is, perhaps, the most extended presentation of French Enlightenment scepticism. Brissot concluded that the sciences can never reach the final degree of perfection and that it is necessary to doubt continuously. This does not mean we have to reach a universal doubt. Because of sceptical difficulties and human fallibility, there is very little that we can know with any degree of certainty (*Vérité*, 341–58). Brissot wanted to avoid the positive metaphysical views of people such as Malebranche or Berkeley. Sceptics should neither affirm nor deny the existence of bodies. We do not know enough to decide one way or the other. Instead we should just consider the probabilities (*Pyrrhon*, fol. 19v). At the very end of *Vérité*, Brissot said that he hoped to discover in each science the very few truths that there are. He thought it would take him several years to do so. Then, in a footnote at the end, he said that, if his work on legislation and politics permitted, in two or three years he could present a 'tableau' of these truths along with a universal scepticism applied to all of the sciences, and this would constitute a reasonable scepticism (*Vérité*, 361n). Unfortunately, Brissot was guillotined before he could complete his work because he was the leader of the Girondists.

Turgot's leading intellectual disciple, the Marquis de Condorcet (who was an ally of Brissot in trying to end slavery and in advocating liberal reforms during the Revolution), pushed both the sceptical and the optimistic sides of French Enlightenment thought to their highest levels. Condorcet was one of the best mathematicians of the age, and he developed Turgot's proposal to apply mathematics to human problems. Condorcet was also one of the very few persons in France, maybe the only one, who had read Hume's *Treatise of Human Nature*. In fact, he got his clue for applying mathematics to the social sciences from a most confusing section of Hume's text on the probability of chances.[34]

Condorcet developed the most advanced sceptical epistemology of any of the *philosophes* and used his scepticism as support for his positive views and his belief in the unending progress of human knowledge. He had said in the notes to his edition of Pascal's *Pensées* that

all those who have attacked the certainty of human knowledge have committed the same mistake. They have established (nor was it difficult to establish) that neither in the physical sciences nor in the moral sciences can we obtain the rigorous certainty of mathematical propositions. But in wishing to conclude from this that man has no sure rule upon which to found his opinions in these matters, they have been mistaken. For there are sure means of arriving at a very great probability in some cases and of evaluating the degree of this probability in a great number. (quoted in Keith Michael Baker, *Condorcet*, 129)

Condorcet developed his sceptical views from Locke's contention that we cannot arrive at a necessary science of nature due to human limitations. Empirically, we are able to observe what happens but not why it happens. Newton's laws yielded no guarantee that nature will always behave in certain ways and cannot act otherwise. We cannot attain logical demonstrative certainty in the study of nature as we do in mathematics. However, our uncertainty does not lead us into complete scepticism. Although the world may be totally determined, we can only start with what we know about it, namely empirical observations and intuitively recognised relations of ideas. We can induce laws from the empirical facts. However, these laws are only probable because we do not know whether nature will be uniform, and therefore we do not know whether the future will resemble the past. This shows the limits of our empirical knowledge (*Condorcet*, ch. 3).

But, Condorcet pointed out, the development of the mathematics of probability allowed people to formulate a mathematics of reasonable expectation, provided one presumed that nature would remain uniform. This mathematics does not tell us what will happen but rather tells us what human beings can reasonably expect to happen.[35]

In his notes for his inaugural address to the French Academy, Condorcet indicated that scepticism applied even to mathematics. A proposition such as $2 + 2 = 4$ is intuited by us to be certain. The sceptical problem arises when we ask whether we can be sure that our minds will continue to function in the same manner so that the same proposition will seem certain in the future. The kind of doubt that Condorcet was raising has some resemblance to Hume's scepticism with regard to reason in the *Treatise*.[36] But it introduced a new basis for doubt. Mathematics itself became slightly open to question and was empirical inasmuch as it depended on the human psyche operating continuously in the same manner. Mathematics, like physics and the moral sciences, is only probable.

This sceptical conclusion is then turned positive by pointing out that at least the moral sciences can have the same sort of precision and exactitude as the natural sciences and *the same kind of certainty*. Hence, notwithstanding all the sceptical questions, we can know with certainty about the empirical study of nature and about man and society, provided we accept that nature and man will act uniformly. The physical and human sciences can then be developed in terms of probabilities. Our knowledge in these areas can grow endlessly and can be used to improve the human scene, so we have every reason to expect the indefinite progress of human knowledge and the perfectibility of mankind.[37]

On the other hand, Hume, with his basic doubts about man's ability to improve his world, could in his essay on 'The Idea of a Perfect Commonwealth' dismiss the progress-people as political projectors who could do much more harm than good.[38] Nonetheless, Condorcet (who never mentioned Hume in his published works)[39] spent the years before the Revolution offering solutions to problems such as eliminating slavery in the colonies.[40] During the Revolutionary period, he was one of the most active persons in government, writing up proposals for reforming education, law, hospitals, and prisons, writing a liberal democratic constitution, and so on, politically projecting until the end of his career and his life in 1793.

Although Condorcet is mainly remembered for his positive, upbeat optimism, maintained even in the face of the Reign of Terror, he did offer a powerful point for a scepticism with regard to reason. Even if we could resolve Hume's point by some techniques applicable to the present state of our consciousness, how do we know if this will be relevant in the future? Our mental apparatus may change and hence what seems true today may not be in tomorrow's mental world.

Another, and perhaps more forceful, version of the French sceptical view was presented by Jean-Jacques Rousseau, who reacted negatively to Berkeley's ideas. Although he knew Hume personally, lived with him, and had a tremendous personal quarrel with him, he never discussed Hume's philosophy. Rousseau's own version of scepticism appeared most prominently in the confession by the Savoyard vicar in *Émile* and later in *Les Rêveries du promeneur solitaire*.[41] He presented a picture of how one became immersed in and engulfed by a personal *crise pyrrhonienne*, as all one's beliefs were cast in doubt.[42] Perhaps more strongly than his enemy Hume, Rousseau portrayed the frightening inner life of the doubter, which was only overcome by accepting those opinions which seemed the best founded, the most believable, and the most probable, but which could still be questioned. The tranquillity so gained did not eliminate sceptical problems or sceptical moments, but the doubting episodes were short and could be accepted as just unimportant vibrations in an ongoing life. In this, Rousseau's solution resembles that of the *philosophes*. He accepted a basic sceptical attitude that could not be overcome but did not prevent belief and action on some kind of probabilistic basis.

Olaso, in his 'The Two Scepticisms of the Savoyard Vicar', argues that Rousseau went beyond the usual Pyrrhonism of the time, such as that of Hume, in relying on nature as the solution or the way of overcoming doubts. His 'originality consists in having discovered that Nature is not merely a residual and passive state unaffected by the anguish nourished by opinion. Rousseau's great discovery consists in listening to the Voice of Nature in the most hidden part (hidden by civilization) of one's intimacy'.[43] This hidden part, our interior feeling and sentiments, is not necessarily benign or 'rational' or 'commonsensical'. It is just our nature and it is what saves us from accepting views such as Berkeley's. In 1769, Rousseau wrote, 'While all of modern philosophy rejects spirits, suddenly Bishop Berkeley appears and asserts that there are no bodies.' How can we answer '*ce terrible logicien*'. If we withdraw the interior feeling, our sentiments, then 'I defy all the modern philosophers together to prove to Berkeley that there are any bodies'.[44] The same could be said of other beliefs.

In the discussions of scepticism by various French thinkers, Hume's presentation of Pyrrhonism is never discussed. Condorcet was apparently the only one to have read the *Treatise*. They all took the *Enquiries* as basic texts in social and moral thought and ignored the sceptical discussions that were included. In two other quite different intellectual worlds, that of the Prussian Academy in Berlin and that of the Scottish Enlightenment, Hume began to appear as the major figure to be dealt with.

Two Swiss members of the Berlin Academy, Johann Georg Sulzer and Jean Henri Samuel Formey, translated Hume's *Enquiry Concerning Human Understanding* into German (1755) and French (1758) in the 1750s, accompanied by lengthy critical comments. Formey, the indefatigable perpetual secretary, wrote a lengthy critical review. Johann Bernhard Merian translated Hume's *Natural History of Religion* in 1759 at the request of Maupertuis, who could not read English.[45] Formey, in his *Histoire abregée de la philosophie*,[46] devoted a chapter to the modern sceptics up to the time of Huet and Bayle.[47] Formey, Merian, and Frédéric Ancillon wrote many attacks on Hume and on scepticism in general in the proceedings of the Prussian Academy from 1749 to the end of the century. Basically, their approach was to bemoan the unfortunate consequences of scepticism on the contemporary intellectual world and to present the argument from catastrophe. They saw scepticism as *the* major threat of the time to intellectual stability and saw Bayle, Huet, and Hume as having spread the Pyrrhonian poison throughout the republic of letters.[48] Merian in 1793 and Ancillon in 1796 sought to show that it was Berkeley and Hume who had brought about this state of affairs.[49]

One of their associates in the Berlin Academy, Louis de Beausobre, was moved to write a defence of scepticism in his *Le Pyrrhonisme raisonnable*,[50] in which he tried to show that contrary to some other forms of scepticism, Pyrrhonism could do no harm and might even be of help in view of the arrogance and ignorance of the age. Sulzer shared this attitude in part when he said that every dogmatist should have a Pyrrhonist at his side to keep questioning him. Further, he declared, Germany had a greater need of this kind of sceptical prodding than any other country since it had fewer doubters. Moreover, German professors should model their style and exposition on Hume if they want to be understood.[51]

The discussions and denunciations of scepticism by members of the Prussian Academy do not seem to have had much influence in Germany or elsewhere.[52] They were written in French for a Francophone audience but aroused little interest in France itself. In Germany, the members of the Academy had almost no contact with the German university world. Moses Mendelssohn seems to have been the main German intellectual of the time who interacted with them.

A more forceful and most influential form of anti-scepticism developed in Scotland. The philosopher Thomas Reid spent twenty-five years studying Hume's *Treatise* and diagnosing what had led to such scepticism and how to avoid it. He was genuinely affected by Hume's argument and saw that the simple answers offered by theologians were inadequate. What was needed was a fundamental reexamination and reconsideration of the very foundations of modern philosophy since it was by a systematic tracing of basic principles that Berkeley and, after him, Hume, had come to such disastrous sceptical conclusions. Descartes had begun the kind of inquiry that was bound to lead to scepticism but did what he could to stop it. Malebranche and Locke, 'who dug deeper', found it still more difficult to keep this enemy at bay. Berkeley, no friend to scepticism, despaired of rescuing all knowledge and hoped by jettisoning the material world to save the world of spirits. 'But, alas! the Treatise of Human Nature wantonly sapped the foundation of this partition, and drowned all in one universal deluge.' Descartes's system, even with improvements by later writers, 'hath some original defect; that this skepticism is inlaid in it, and reared along with it'.[53] So, as Reid said in his conclusion, 'I observe, That the modern scepticism is the natural issue of the new system [of Descartes]; and that, although it did not bring forth this monster until the year 1739, it may be said to have carried it in its womb from the beginning', as Hume's *Treatise* made clear.[54]

Reid did not discuss the actual modern sceptical tradition from Montaigne to Bayle and Huet but instead made scepticism the internal issue of Cartesianism and Lockean philosophy. In so doing, he detached Hume from his sceptical roots and created an historical mythology that has lasted to the present – that there was an old philosophy, Aristotelianism, and a new philosophy, Cartesianism. The latter spawned scepticism because of its methodological assumptions. Reid did not seem to be aware that Cartesianism had developed as a reaction to a pervasive sceptical movement in France and that this movement continued, battling each new version of the new philosophy, up to Hume.[55] Reid's construction, an inversion of what actually happened in the course of the seventeenth and eighteenth centuries, together with what Kant's world made of it, accounts, I think, for the neglect of the ongoing sceptical movement all through the eighteenth century and for the distortion of the usual historical account of how philosophy developed from Descartes to Kant.

In Reid's analysis, scepticism is the logical outcome of the principles laid down by Descartes. It is incredible – that is, it cannot be believed by rational people – and it contradicts the principles of common sense. Therefore, the examination of what sane, reasonable, commonsensical people do in fact believe and cannot be led to disbelieve by any amount of argument or evidence constitutes the answer to scepticism and provides principles that men can live by and whose truths depend on a conviction of God's veracity.

Reid proudly sent the results of his years of examination, the *Inquiry into the Human Mind on the Principles of Common Sense*, to Hume in 1763 before publication. Hume was not impressed. After studying the manuscript, he told Reid that he had recognised the basic problem but had found no other solution than the one that he had already set forth, namely that nature prevents us from being actual living sceptics, even though we cannot overcome the sceptical difficulties.[56] Reid in reply assured Hume that he believed that Hume's system was solid and that it had destroyed modern philosophy. In fact, Reid had questioned the very assumptions of modern philosophy and then offered his own answer to the sceptical debacle.[57] From Hume's perspective, Reid's work did not seem to be an answer but just another way of saying the same thing, only with a different emphasis. As the early nineteenth-century thinker Thomas Brown is reported to have said, 'Reid bawled out, "We must believe an outward world; but added in a whisper, we can give no reason for our belief". Hume cries out, "We can give no reason for such a notion; and whispers, I own we cannot get rid of it".'[58]

Reid's answer to Hume soon blossomed into a school of philosophy that was important in the British Isles and the United States for more than a century. After the posthumous publication in 1779 of Hume's *Dialogues Concerning Natural Religion*, Reid's disciples became quite abusive of him, stressing the irreligious implications of his scepticism. The best known and most notorious of them, James Beattie, attacked many aspects of Hume's scepticism in his lengthy *An Essay on the Nature and Immutability of Truth, in Opposition to Sophistry and Scepticism*.[59] Beattie scoffed at Hume's views and ridiculed what would happen if people psychologically adopted his scepticism – namely, that their beliefs in science, religion, virtue, and society would be overturned. He pointed out what good commonsensical people believe but never came to grips with Hume's epistemological arguments. However, the last book of Beattie's *Essay* presented a sharp answer to Hume's racist utterances against blacks.[60]

Joseph Priestley, who rejected Hume's views, contended that Reid and Beattie were complete sceptics themselves, worse than the ancient ones: '[T]he ancients professed neither to *understand* nor *believe* anything, whereas these moderns believe every thing, though they profess to understand nothing. And the former, I think, are the more consistent of the two.'[61] A year later, Hume dismissed 'Dr. Reid and . . . that bigotted silly Fellow, Beattie', disowning his *Treatise* as a juvenile work and urging his opponents to criticise his later writings.[62]

In spite of what Priestley and Hume may have thought of the merit or lack of it in the writings of the Scottish Common Sense realists, these works were translated and became popular in Germany. Reid and his disciples were the first to portray the mainstream of English thought as that of the trinity of Locke-Berkeley-Hume, advancing from empiricism to consistent empiricism to total scepticism. Reid and Beattie provided many German thinkers with their information about Berkeley and Hume.[63]

Although most German interest in and knowledge of scepticism during the period seems to have come either through Rousseau's discussion of it or from the Scottish critics of Hume, there was some indigenous interest as well. Ernst Platner published many sceptical aphorisms in the period before Kant.[64] Some, like Immanuel Kant, had examined ancient sources of scepticism and were aware of Bayle's views and others independently.[65] Carl Friedrich Stäudlin, a professor at Göttingen, published the first full-length history of scepticism from Pyrrho to Kant, covering all sorts of major and minor sceptics through the ages.[66] (It is interesting that this history precedes any history of British empiricism or Continental rationalism as significant intellectual movements.)

Kant, in the preface to the *Kritik der reinen Vernunft*, pointed out that the dogmatic builders of metaphysical edifices had been attacked sporadically by the sceptics, who were like nomadic tribes, never settling anywhere. 'But since there were fortunately only a few of them, they could not prevent the dogmatists from continually attempting to rebuild'.[67] Kant said that it was Hume who had awakened him from his 'dogmatic slumbers' in this matter and had made him realise the importance of scepticism and the need to overcome it. Hume had destroyed the hope of establishing universal and necessary knowledge by means of experimental philosophy, the study of the physiology of the understanding advanced by Locke, Newton, and their eighteenth-century disciples. Kant's Copernican revolution in philosophy purported to reveal a compromise between an unconquerable scepticism concerning the possibility of any metaphysical knowledge about the nature of reality and a universal and necessary certainty about the conditions of all possible experiences, constituting genuine knowledge. The central question was not whether knowledge is possible but rather how knowledge is possible. The Kantian answer offered a new resolution to the challenge of scepticism.

Kant said that future philosophers would either have to accept or try to refute his system. It was offered as the final act in the long dramatic struggle between scepticism and dogmatism. But, almost as soon as his answer appeared, a new period in the history of scepticism commenced, initiated by Kant. New forms of scepticism were offered and new, more radical means were offered to escape from these new scepticisms.

Stäudlin, in his *Geschichte und Geist des Skepticismus*, presented the sceptical background which, he claimed, permeated the German intellectual world at the time Kant's philosophy appeared and in terms of which Kant was soon seen as *sceptique malgré lui*. Stäudlin was not an isolated provincial preacher or an idiosyncratic observer. He came from Swabia, studied at Tübingen, where Schelling and Hegel studied a little later, from 1779 to 1784, then became a pastor, travelled extensively in Germany, France, and Switzerland, and spent a year in England. He was appointed professor at Göttingen in 1790.[68] He and Kant corresponded from 1791 to 1798, and Kant dedicated his *Der Streit der Fakultäten* of 1798 to him.[69] Both men were very active in the 1790s in opposing popular disruptive kinds of scepticism. Stäudlin, however, not only favoured what he called 'philosophical scepticism' but saw it emerging at the end of the century from Kant's critical philosophy.[70]

Stäudlin's picture is of a generation whose beliefs were being eroded by a century of sceptical attacks, especially by the dramatic scepticism of Rousseau, and who were undergoing personal traumas as scepticism undermined their religious faith, their family, and their social values. Stäudlin claimed that some of his classmates had committed suicide in their personal *crises pyrrhoniennes*. On a broader scale, revolutions were occurring as a result of the inroads of scepticism. Stäudlin saw both the detrimental effects of and the positive constructive results from what he called 'philosophical scepticism'.

Kant's work appeared in this disintegrating world. Its author thought he had found a basis for a limited certainty about the conditions of all possible experience. Stäudlin and others recognised immediately that this transcendental way of overcoming scepticism actually involved a complete scepticism about whether we could know anything about the nature of the *real* world. Kant was attacked both from the right and from the left. From the right he was challenged by his friend Johann Georg Hamann, a most ardent religious believer.[71] Hamann, who had spent years in England, had studied Hume's writings in the original. He translated part of the *Dialogues* into German, and announced that he found Hume 'the greatest voice of orthodoxy'.[72] Hume and Hamann saw that belief or faith was at the basis of any human understanding of the world. For Hume it was animal or natural faith, whereas for Hamann it was religious faith. Hamann tried to get Kant to see the importance of faith and in fact Kant, in the second preface to his *Kritik der reinen Vernunft*, claimed, possibly to placate Hamann, to have eliminated knowledge in order to make room for faith in the practical realm.[73]

Hamann saw Kant's response to Hume as too weak. He himself rejected the Enlightenment entirely and opted for faith, pure biblical faith. He prepared a translation of the first and last of Hume's *Dialogues Concerning Natural Religion* for Kant to try to make him realise the need for religious faith.[74]

In contrast with this kind of sceptical religious response to Kant was the attack of Gottlob Ernst Schulze, who sought to show that Kantian philosophy, no matter what its author said, led to complete scepticism. Schulze identified himself with the ancient Pyrrhonist Aenesidemus in insisting that no knowledge claims could be justified within Kant's outlook and that Kant's introduction of the 'thing-in-itself' was illegitimate since his whole elegant system dealt only with the realm of appearance, not with what may or may not lie beyond or behind it. Schulze-Aenesidemus contended that, if Kant were consistent, he would end up with just the ancient sceptical view.[75]

Salomon Maimon, a strange Jewish thinker from Lithuania, severely criticised Kant and tried to stake out a sceptical position between Hume and Kant. Maimon, a member of Moses Mendelssohn's circle, attacked Kant's

Kritik der reinen Vernunft as soon as it appeared. On seeing this, Kant wrote that

but a glance at the manuscript soon enabled me to recognise its merits and to see not only that none of my opponents had understood me and the main problem so well, but that very few could claim so much penetration and subtlety of mind in profound inquiries of this sort as Herr Maimon.[76]

Maimon argued that Kant could only establish the categories that applied to experience *post facto*. No guarantee could be found that the categories applicable today will also be applicable in the future, and hence no necessary and universal knowledge about experience is possible. Maimon argued against Hume and Schulze that mathematics and logic had to be a priori, otherwise nothing would make any sense at all. In this he seems to have anticipated basic aspects of logical positivism.

Maimon opened another door when he indicated that the creative powers of the mind, intuition and feeling, a reflection of the power of the infinite mind, could be a way of reaching an understanding of experience. This turn to non-rational (but not necessarily irrational) factors as those that could be constitutive of our knowledge became the opening to Romanticism, or to metaphysical idealism, as developed by Fichte and the young Hegel.[77]

Stäudlin saw the history of scepticism from ancient Greece through to its modern revival culminating in the work of Hume and Kant, with the French Enlightenment figures and Rousseau as important contributors as well, and by 1794 he had joined others in seeing Kant as a *sceptique malgré lui*.[78] Stäudlin reported that he and his fellow students in the 1780s became increasingly sceptical in the period *after* the appearance of Kant's *Kritik der reinen Vernunft*. They doubted their religious views and doubted everything they had been taught.[79] The march from doubts about one's original religious beliefs, to learning to think for oneself, to questioning everything as one searches for reasons for all human knowledge and for objective truth, Stäudlin said, can lead to genuine philosophical scepticism, in which one ceases to look for absolute truth and accepts that all is uncertain and that one can have only personal opinions (*Skepticismus*, 89–93). This kind of scepticism and the sceptic who adheres to it he saw as no enemy of mankind. But another more frivolous type of scepticism is used as an excuse for immorality and debauchery. Scepticism, if adopted as a way of freeing one from all constraints, can lead to something like de Sade's behaviour or to Nietzsche's rejection of accepted morality (96–7).

Stäudlin then went on to portray the social and political consequences of scepticism at the time. 'Our century is the century of revolution in the moral and political world and of the secret political orders.' Confidence in accepted political views and institutions is questioned and undermined, leading to new orders that are also open to question (100). Stäudlin and Kant used scepticism in this way to criticise censorship and undesirable government authority.[80]

If there are many factors leading people into scepticism, what is its effect on them and on society? Ancient scepticism claimed that it brought its adherents peace of mind and that such people would be conformists who would not cause any trouble to society since they would accept its rules and laws undogmatically. Stäudlin refused to believe that this would work in the modern world, pointing out that Bayle, Huet, La Mothe Le Vayer, Montaigne, and Hume accepted, in the moral realm, matters that they doubted in theory (117). He refused to make scepticism the road to faith. Perfect scepticism would destroy *both* reason and faith. So Stäudlin advocated a modest scepticism, regarding metaphysics as open to endless doubt but accepting a kind of subjective certainty. This allows acceptance of the moral teachings of the Gospel without requiring theological justification. It is sufficient to challenge dogmatic science and to seek new outlooks on nature; it becomes a constant urge to advance knowledge and to deflate dogmatism. This modest scepticism Stäudlin saw as the effect of Hume's views, leading in turn to Kant's moderate dogmatism, which again leads to scepticism with its critique of all previous dogmatisms (135–6).

In sum, the eighteenth century began with scepticism in full flower in the form of the texts of Sextus and the presentations of Huet and Bayle. Hume advanced what was to be the most drastic and lasting version. French Enlightenment figures espoused a more mitigated version coupled with their advocacy of the new science and its application to human problems. Rousseau cast some doubts on this. The Scottish Common Sense critics of Hume thought they could base a total rejection of scepticism on its conflict with common sense and ordinary beliefs. Kant, influenced by these many currents, thought he had found a new way of dealing with the sceptical menace. His new way was immediately challenged as either too sceptical or too dogmatic.

So, contrary to my previous view,[81] scepticism was not petering out in the latter half of the eighteenth century. It was taking on different forms and reacting to different ways in which dogmatic philosophers tried to answer the sceptical challenge. Some of its more popular effects involved undermining confidence in the old orders of church and state in Western Europe, breeding a sceptical 'basis' for democratic and tolerant worlds if no traditional system of ideas or institutions could be rationally defended.

Hume was the major presenter of sceptical arguments for the middle and end of the eighteenth century. Others tried to mitigate the force of his complete Pyrrhonism and to show how one could live with it while still promoting the advancement of human knowledge. The closing moments of the century saw what was later to be taken as a new stage of philosophy, Kant's Copernican revolution, almost immediately enmeshed in sceptical attacks and interpreted as another form of scepticism or as leading to new forms of scepticism. The challenges of various post-Kantians sought to show that, on Kant's terms, one really could not *know* anything about the conditions of experience of the world. But none, perhaps with the exception of Hamann, saw the deep scepticism to which this could lead.

I should certainly no longer say, as I did in 1963, 'that the Enlightenment was pretty much a hiatus in the continuous development of scepticism'. Scepticism was an active force throughout the period. Hume may have been its last original presenter, but the tradition of Sextus, Bayle, Huet, and Hume lived on and had to be addressed in one way or another. Scepticism may not have been as deeply and fundamentally troubling as it was for Hume, but in modified form it was part of the basic philosophical discussion of the period. As Stäudlin contended, both popular and elite intellectual movements were affected positively or negatively by the sceptical legacy. At the very end of the eighteenth century, a whole new era of scepticism versus dogmatism was about to be launched in the wake of Kant's supposed resolution of the *crise pyrrhonienne* induced by Hume's arguments. When the nineteenth century began, scepticism was still the spectre haunting European philosophy.

It was only when they thought one had found better answers, and maybe better questions, that historians of philosophy from the mid-nineteenth century could package their past so that the seventeenth century comprised the philosophies of Bacon, Descartes, Spinoza, Locke, and Leibniz and the eighteenth century the philosophies of Berkeley, Hume, and Kant. Hume was no longer a sceptic but the end man of the British empirical trinity – Locke, Berkeley, and Hume.

This might have been comforting had the intellectual world been seen as the triumph of either British empiricism or Continental rationalism. But each of these movements was soon to be confronted with sceptical problems, and so the dialectic of scepticism versus anti-scepticism goes on. As one of Hume's friends wrote:

> The wise in every age conclude,
> What Pyrrho taught and Hume renewed,
> That dogmatists are fools.[82]

NOTES

1 On this, see Richard H. Popkin, *The History of Scepticism from Erasmus to Spinoza* (Berkeley and Los Angeles, CA, 1979), and *The High Road to Pyrrhonism*, eds. R. A. Watson and J. E. Force (San Diego, CA, 1980).

2 Sextus Empiricus, *Opera graece et latine*, ed. J. A. Fabricius (Leipzig, 1718). In the introduction, in the list of promised editions of Sextus, Fabricius mentions that Leibniz was working on a commentary and refutation. Ezequiel de Olaso found some manuscript pages of this in the Leibniz archives at Hanover.

3 Sextus Empiricus, *Les Hipotiposes ou institutions Pirroniennes . . . en trois livres*, trans. C. Huart (Amsterdam, 1725). Huart is the Swiss mathematician Claude Huart. Crousaz claimed that on his deathbed, Huart begged forgiveness for his translation and the effects it had on the intellectual world.

4 Pierre Bayle, *Dictionnaire historique et critique*, 2 vols. (Rotterdam, 1697); 2nd edn., 3 vols. (Rotterdam, 1702). The first edition appeared in 1697. This included four 'Clarifications' answering charges made against the content by the French Reformed Church of Rotterdam.

5 Pierre-Daniel Huet, bishop of Avranches, *Traité philosophique de la foiblesse de l'esprit humaine* (Amsterdam, 1723). A list of editions appears in Lodovico Antonio Muratori, *Delle forze dell'intendimento umano, o sia il Pirronismo confutato, trattato . . . opposto al libro del preteso Monsignore Huet* (Venice, 1745). Two different English translations appeared in London in 1725, both going into a second edition. The German translation of 1724 was reprinted at the end of the century.

6 See the anonymously authored *Q. D. B. V. de Scepticorum praecipuis hypothesibus, secundum constitutionem Fridericianum, praeside Georgio Paschio* (Cologne, 1704), 4.

7 See Popkin, 'Berkeley and Pyrrhonism', in *The Skeptical Tradition*, ed. M. Burnyeat (Berkeley and Los Angeles, CA, 1983), 377–96.

8 Jean Le Clerc's lengthy review of Sextus appeared in the widely read journal, published in Amsterdam, *Bibliothèque ancienne et moderne* 14 (1720): 1–113.

9 Jean-Pierre de Crousaz, *Examen du pyrrhonisme ancien et moderne* (The Hague, 1733). Crousaz wrote an important logic text that appeared in French and English.

10 Jean Henri Samuel Formey, *Le triomphe de l'évidence* (Berlin, 1740); Albrecht von Haller, *Prüfung der Sekte die an allem zweifeln* (Göttingen, 1751).

11 *Nouvelles lettres de Mr. P. Bayle,* 2 vols. (The Hague, 1739). The 'Apologie de Monsieur Bayle' is in vol. 1. Barbier's index of authors of anonymous French texts attributes the work to a M. de Monier, former financial official in Provence.

12 Thomas Stanley, *History of Philosophy*, 4 vols. (London, 1655–62; 2nd edn., 1687). Jean Le Clerc translated it into Latin.

13 A major London book dealer's sale catalogue of 1745 lists both the Latin 1718 edition and the French 1725 edition. See Paul Vaillant, *Catalogue of Books in Most Languages and Faculties* (London, 1745).

14 See Popkin, 'Sources of Knowledge of Sextus Empiricus in Hume's Time', *Journal of the History of Ideas*, 53 (1993): 137–41.

15 See *Mémoires pour l'histoire des sciences et des beaux-arts (Mémoires de Trévoux)* (Trévoux, 1701–67), Juin 1725, 989.

16 See Le Clerc, review of Huet's *Traité, Bibliothèque ancienne et moderne*, 18 (1722): 455–65, in which he said that one cannot doubt the authenticity of the work. In fact, Le Clerc declared that he himself had seen the holograph manuscript, in Huet's hand. Such a manuscript is in the collection of the Remonstrants Biblioteek of Rotterdam.

17 For a discussion of the different interpretations of Bayle's religious intent, see the introduction in Bayle, *Historical and Critical Dictionary: Selections*, trans. R. H. Popkin (Indianapolis, IN, 1965), xi–xliv; and Elisabeth Labrousse, *Bayle*, trans. D. Potts (Oxford, 1983).

18 Diderot's article 'Pyrrhonienne ou sceptique philosophique', vol. 13 of the *Encyclopédie*, contains his tribute to Bayle.

19 See Popkin, 'Berkeley in the History of Scepticism', in *Scepticism in the Enlightenment*, eds. R. H. Popkin, E. de Olaso, and G. Tonelli (Dordrecht, 1997), 173–86.

20 On Ramsay, see G. D. Henderson, *Chevalier Ramsay* (London, 1952). Ramsay's analysis of scepticism, showing its force and offering an intriguing answer, deserves serious consideration. Unfortunately, it seems to have had little influence except upon Hume. Some of Ramsay's

formulations appear in David Hume's *Treatise of Human Nature*, eds. D. F. Norton and M. J. Norton, in *The Clarendon Edition* (2006), 1.1.2 and 1.4.5.

21 Hume, *A Treatise of Human Nature*, 1.4.1.6, SBN 183.

22 On Hume's contribution to the history of scepticism with regard to reason, see Popkin, 'Scepticism with Regard to Reason in the 17th and 18th Centuries', in *The Philosophical Canon in the 17th and 18th Centuries*, eds. G. A. J. Rogers and S. Tomaselli (Rochester, NY, 1996), 33–48.

23 Hume, *An Abstract of a Treatise of Human Nature, 1740*, eds. J. M. Keynes and P. Sraffa (Cambridge, 1938), 24.

24 Hume, *Dialogues Concerning Natural Religion*, ed. N. Kemp Smith (2nd edn., London, 1947), 228.

25 See, for instance, the anonymous reviews in the *Bibliothèque raisonnée des ouvrages des savans de l'Europe*, 14 (1740): 328, and in the *Nouvelle Bibliothèque*, 6 (July 1740): 291–316 and 7 (September 1740): 44–63.

26 This is the reading I offered in my article 'Scepticism in the Enlightenment', *Studies on Voltaire and the Eighteenth Century*, 24–7 (1963): 1321–45. See also *The Skeptical Tradition around 1800: Skepticism in Philosophy, Science, and Society*, eds. J. van der Zande and R. H. Popkin (Dordrecht, 1998).

27 Hume, *An Enquiry Concerning Human Understanding*, ed. T. L. Beauchamp, in *The Clarendon Edition* (2000), 12.1.15n, SBN 155n.

28 See Giorgio Tonelli, 'The "Weakness" of Reason in the Age of Enlightenment', *Diderot Studies*, 14 (1971): 217–44; 'Pierre-Jacques Changeux and Scepticism in the French Enlightenment', *Studia Leibnitiana*, 6 (1974): 106–26; and 'The Philosophy of D'Alembert: A Sceptic beyond Scepticism', *Kant-Studien*, 67 (1976): 353–71.

29 See Pierre Rétat, *Le Dictionnaire de Bayle et la lutte philosophique au XVIIIe siècle* (Paris, 1971). The same thing happened to Hume a little later. See Lawrence L. Bongie, *David Hume, Prophet of the Counter-Revolution* (Oxford, 1965).

30 Tonelli, 'Pierre-Jacques Changeux', 112.

31 See Popkin, 'Hume and Turgot and Condorcet', in *Condorcet Studies II*, ed. D. Williams (New York, NY, 1987), 47–62. The citation from Hume is from *The Letters of David Hume*, ed. J. Y. T. Greig, 2 vols. (Oxford, 1932), 2: 180.

32 Jean-Pierre Brissot de Warville, *Pyrrhon*, Paris: Archives nationales, 446/AP/21.

33 Brissot, *De la vérité, ou Méditations sur les moyens de parvenir à la vérité dans toutes les connaissances humaines* (Neufchâtel, 1782; 2nd edn., 1792). The second edition, which claims on the title page to conform exactly to the original edition, was published just a year before Brissot was guillotined during the Reign of Terror.

34 Keith Michael Baker, *Condorcet: From Natural Philosophy to Social Mathematics* (Chicago, IL, 1975), 135–55.

35 Baker, *Condorcet*, ch. 3; and R. H. Popkin, 'Condorcet's Epistemology and His Politics', in *Knowledge and Politics: Case Studies in the Relationship between Epistemology and Political Philosophy*, eds. M. Dascal and O. Gruengard (Boulder, CO, 1989), 111–24 at 113–15.

36 On Condorcet's knowledge of Hume's *Treatise*, see Baker, *Condorcet*, 139–55 and 181ff.; and Popkin, 'Condorcet and Hume and Turgot', 47–8. Condorcet seems to have been the only *philosophe* who knew of Hume's scepticism with regard to mathematics.

37 Baker, *Condorcet*, 44, 74, and 181–2; and Popkin, 'Condorcet's Epistemology', 114. One always has to remember that Condorcet's most powerful statement of the progress theory and of the perfectibility of mankind was written while the agents of the Reign of Terror were looking for him and that he died, either by his own hand or by execution, just after finishing the *Equisse*.

38 'Of all mankind there are none so pernicious as political projectors, if they have power; nor so ridiculous, if they want it', 'Idea of a Perfect Commonwealth', Essay XVI, in Hume, *Works*, 3: 480 n.1.

39 See Popkin, 'Condorcet and Hume and Turgot'. I could not find any evidence that they ever met when Hume was in Paris. Condorcet wrote an important life of Turgot and had access to Turgot's papers. Somehow Hume is not mentioned in the biography, although he and Turgot were very close at one point.

40 See Popkin, 'Condorcet, Abolitionist', in *Condorcet Studies I*, ed. L. C. Rosenfield (Atlantic Heights, NJ, 1984), and 'Condorcet's Epistemology'. Condorcet was the head of the *Société des amis des noirs*, founded by Brissot.

41 Jean-Jacques Rousseau, *Émile, ou De l'éducation*, Bk. 4, in *Oeuvres*, 4: 489–691, and *Les rêveries du promeneur solitaire*, Deuxième promenade, in *Oeuvres*, 1: 1002–10.

42 The best study of Rousseau in this connection is Ezequiel de Olaso's *Escepticismo e ilustracion: La crisis pirronica de Hume y Rousseau* (Valencia, Venezuela, 1981).

43 Olaso, 'The Two Scepticisms of the Savoyard Vicar', in *The Sceptical Mode in Modern Philosophy: Essays in Honor of Richard H. Popkin*, eds. R. A. Watson and J. E. Force (Dordrecht, 1988), 43–59 at 56. For Hume, the voice of nature has been covered up by barbarism but is becoming evident in more civilized times. Rousseau's more anarchistic view of civilisation leads him to rely on a primitive voice of nature untainted by the arts and sciences or by the so-called civilised world.

44 Rousseau, 'Lettre à M. de Franquières', in *Oeuvres*, 4: 1133–47 at 1139.

45 Hume, *Histoire naturelle de la religion*, trans. J. B. Merian (Amsterdam, 1759).

46 Jean Henri Samuel Formey, 'De la Secte des Sceptiques modernes', *Histoire abregée de la philosophie* (Amsterdam, 1760), 243–8.

47 A much more detailed and less judgemental account of modern scepticism appeared in Johann Jacob Brucker, *Historia critica philosophiae*, 2nd edn., 6 vols. (Leipzig, 1762), 4: Bk. 3, 536–609. Brucker's classification of the schools of modern philosophy provided the framework for the 'canonical' picture that now appears in all textbooks.

48 See Formey's review of Sulzer's translation of Hume, *Philosophische Versuche über die menschliche Erkenntnis*, in *Nouvelle Bibliothèque germanique*, 19 (1756): 78–109 and 311–32; 20 (1756): 57–86 and 268–96; and 21 (1757): 65–81.

49 Johann Bernhard Merian, 'Sur le Phénoménisme de David Hume', presented on 10 October, 1793, in *Mémoires de l'Académie royale des sciences et belles-lettres depuis l'avénement de Fréderic Guillaume II au trône* (Berlin, 1793), 417–37; and Johann Peter Friedrich Ancillon, 'Dialogue entre Berkeley et Hume', presented on 14 April 1796, *Mémoires de l'Académie royale*, proceedings for 1796 (Berlin, 1799), 86–127.

50 Louis de Beausobre, *Le Pyrrhonisme raisonnable* (Berlin, 1755).

51 Sulzer's comments appear in the introduction to his translation of Hume's *Philosophische versuche* (1756).

52 Their overall position is delineated in Ancillon's long 'Essai sur le scepticisme', in his *Mélanges de litterature et de philosophie*, 2 vols. (Paris, 1809), 2: 3–70, which deals mainly with Sextus and Hume.

53 Thomas Reid, *An Inquiry into the Human Mind on the Principles of Common Sense*, ed. D. R. Brookes (Edinburgh, 1997), 1.7, 23.

54 Reid, *Inquiry*, 7, Conclusion, 210.

55 See Popkin, *History of Scepticism*, and *High Road to Pyrrhonism*, eds. R. A. Watson and J. E. Force.

56 Hume to Reid, 25 February 1763, in *Letters*, 1: 375–6.

57 Reid's letter to Hume, 18 March 1763, cited in Hume, *Letters*, 1: 376–7.

58 Thomas Brown, in a conversation reported by James Mackintosh in his *Dissertation on the Progress of Ethical Philosophy, chiefly during the Seventeenth and Eighteenth Centuries*, 2nd edn. (Edinburgh, 1837), 346 fn.

59 James Beattie, *An Essay on the Nature and Immutability of Truth, in Opposition to Sophistry and Scepticism* (Edinburgh, 1770).

60 On this, see Popkin, 'Hume's Racism', in *High Road to Pyrrhonism*, 251–66; and 'Hume's Racism Reconsidered', in Popkin, *The Third Force in Seventeenth-Century Thought* (Leiden, 1992), 64–75.

61 Joseph Priestley, *An Examination of Dr. Reid's Inquiry into the Human Mind on the Principles of Common Sense, Dr. Beattie's Essay on the Nature and Immutability of Truth and Dr. Oswald's Appeal to Common Sense in Behalf of Religion* (London, 1774), xxi.

62 Hume, letter to William Strahan, 26 October 1775, in *Letters*, 2: 301 and fn. 2.

63 Manfred Kuehn, *Scottish Common Sense in Germany, 1768–1800: A Contribution to the History of Critical Philosophy* (Kingston and Montreal, 1987).

64 Ernst Platner, *Philosophische Aphorismen nebst einer Anleitung zur philosophischen Geschichte*, 2 vols. (Leipzig, 1776–82). Platner also published a translation of some of Hume's writings.

65 Giorgio Tonelli, 'Kant und die antiken Skeptiker', in *Studien zu Kants philosophischer Entwicklung*, ed. H. Heimsoeth (Hildesheim, 1967), 93–123; John C. Laursen, 'Kant in the History of Scepticism', in *John Locke und Immanuel Kant: Historische Rezeption und gegenwärtige Relevanz*, ed. M. P. Thompson (Berlin, 1991), 254–68; *The Politics of Skepticism in the Ancients, Montaigne, Hume and Kant* (Leiden, 1992), 195–7.

66 Carl Friedrich Stäudlin, *Der Geschichte und Geist des Skepticismus, vorzüglich in Rücksicht auf Moral und Religion*, 2 vols. (Leipzig, 1794). Stäudlin and Kant became friends, and Kant dedicated a work to him. On their relations, see Laursen, 'Kant in the History of Scepticism', 255–6.

67 Immanuel Kant, *Kritik der reinen Vernunft*, 1st (A) edn. (1781), in Ak 4 (Berlin, 1903), 'Vorrede', A vii–xiv at ix, translated as *Critique of Pure Reason*, trans. and eds. P. Guyer and A. W. Wood, in *Works* (1998).

68 On his life and career, see P. Tschackert, 'Stäudlin', in *Allgemeine Deutsche Biographie*, 56 vols. (Leipzig, 1875–1912), 35: 516–20.

69 Kant, *Der Streit der Fakultäten*, in Ak 7.

70 On Stäudlin, see Laursen, 'Kant in the History of Scepticism', and Popkin, 'New Views on the Role of Skepticism in the Enlightenment', *Modern Language Quarterly*, 53 (1992): 279–97 at 291–5.

71 On Hamann, see Isaiah Berlin, 'The Magus of the North', *New York Review of Books*, 40: 17 (21 October 1993): 64–71.

72 Of the conclusion to Hume's essay 'Of Miracles', Hamann remarked that 'this is indeed orthodoxy and testimony of truth in the mouth of an enemy and persecutor thereof'. See Johann Georg Hamann, *Hamann's Schriften*, ed. F. Roth, 8 vols. in 9 (Berlin, 1821–43), 1: 406.

73 Kant, *Kritik der reinen Vernunft*, 2nd (B) edn. (1787), Ak 3 (Berlin, 1904–11), 'Vorrede zur zweiten Auflage', B vii–xliv at xxx: 'Thus I had to deny *knowledge* in order to make room for *faith*'.

74 Philip Merlan, 'Hamann et les dialogues de Hume', *Revue de métaphysique et de morale*, 59 (1954): 285–9; and 'Hume and Hamann', *Personalist*, 32 (1951): 111–18. Hamann's sceptical fideism led to the position later offered by Kierkegaard. See also Richard H. Popkin, 'Kierkegaard and Scepticism', in *Kierkegaard. A Collection of Critical Essays*, ed. J. Thompson (Garden City, NY, 1972), 361–72, and Walter Lowrie, *Kierkegaard* (London, 1938), 165–7.

75 Gottlob Ernst Schulze, *Aenesidemus oder Über die Fundamente der von dem Herrn Prof. Reinhold in Jena gelieferten Elementarphilosophie. Nebst einen Vertheidigung des Skepticismus gegen die Anmassungen der Vernunftkritik* ([Helmstädt], 1792).

76 Cited in Samuel Atlas, *From Critical to Speculative Idealism: The Philosophy of Solomon Maimon* (The Hague, 1964), 5. Maimon's scepticism is set forth in Chapter 13 of this work. On his career, see his amazing autobiography, *Lebensgeschichte*, ed. J. Fromer (Munich, 1911).

77 See Daniel Breazeale, 'Fichte on Skepticism', *Journal of the History of Philosophy*, 29 (1991): 427–53.

78 On Kant as a sceptic, see also Manfred Kuehn, 'Kant's Transcendental Deduction: A Limited Defense of Hume', in *New Essays on Kant*, ed. B. den Ouden (New York, NY, 1987), 47–82.

79 Stäudlin, *Geschichte und Geist des Skepticismus*, 1: 74–81.

80 See Laursen, *Politics of Skepticism*, 193–212, and 'Kant in the History of Scepticism'.

81 In Popkin, 'Scepticism in the Enlightenment'.

82 This is the original version of a poem by Thomas Blacklock as it appears in Hume's letter of 20 April 1756 to John Clephane, *Letters*, 1: 231.

16

PHILOSOPHY OF LANGUAGE

HANS AARSLEFF

I. INTRODUCTION

The tenor of eighteenth-century philosophy was anti-Cartesian, and the primary vehicle of this reaction was the philosophy of language. In the rationalist view of the seventeenth century, speech served only as the inert outward means for the communication of the prefabricated mental discourse of ideas. In theory as well as in practice, language constituted an epistemological obstacle because it was an easy victim of the seductive inducements of eloquence and persuasion – hence the denunciations of rhetoric that are common in the writings of Galileo, Descartes, and Locke. There were no disputes in geometry because the visual figure delivered its truth without the intervention of communication. But since communication could not be avoided, the new science and philosophy undertook a cognitive appropriation of language, based on the claim that only an emotion-free information language exhibited the true nature of language. Thus language was split in two. One form was considered natural by virtue of being obediently cognitive and descriptive, the other unnatural and in the strict sense allied with the passion and transgression that had caused the Fall. Descartes believed there had been a long-past Golden Age of perfect communication and harmony, a belief that matched the more familiar notion that the origin and nature of language were revealed in Adam's prelapsarian naming of the animals, an act that characteristically transformed silent epistemic vision into postlapsarian sound.[1]

By contrast, the eighteenth century believed in small beginnings and progress toward greater amplitude of communication and knowledge. The pivotal work in these events was Condillac's *Essai sur l'origines des connaissances humaines*, first published in 1746.[2] The *Essai sur l'origines* presented two interlaced arguments. First, the discursivity that is the condition of knowledge is a function of public speech. Secondly, language owes its origin to a combination of instinctually affective communication and reflectively conceived artificial signs. Instinct, sympathy, and reflection are facts of human nature, and they cannot be explained, except insofar as they may be considered divine gifts toward the self-education of humanity. Condillac's *Essai* is the source of the notion that language is the best means for gaining insight into mind and thought, a principle especially stressed by Adam Smith:

The best method of explaining and illustrating the various powers of the human mind, the most useful parts of metaphysics, arises from an examination of the several ways of communicating our thoughts by speech, and from attention to those literary principles which contribute to persuasion and entertainment.[3]

The cognitive appropriation of language that perfectly served the epistemological and descriptive priorities of the seventeenth century made no sense once it had become accepted that communication is creative. Though the seventeenth century was the great age of French eloquence,[4] only the next century could claim to have a doctrine about the source and nature of language, based on the principles of what I shall call rhetorical expressivism.

This development may usefully be seen in two wider perspectives. First, the eighteenth century differed from the seventeenth about the role of social life in human affairs. In the Cartesian view, innateness is compromised by social intercourse. Right reason and knowledge are private achievements, for in this Augustinian view we do not truly learn anything from anybody. God alone is the teacher, and communication is risky. Seen in this light, it took a contract to secure social bonding.

In the eighteenth century, a different view emerged, as shown in David Hume's and Adam Smith's rejection of contract theory because they had other means of accounting for social cohesion, namely, sympathy. This radical cultural shift toward emphasis on natural sociability is illustrated in the frequency with which certain French words occur, based on a survey of 334 texts by 93 authors for the seventeenth century and 488 texts by 156 authors for the eighteenth century. The figures are not directly comparable but still give a striking lesson:[5]

Word	1600–1700	1701–1800
société	620	7168
social	8	838
sociabilité	0	66
sociable	16	222

With such a dramatic shift toward social awareness, all means of communication became of theoretical interest – including music, pantomime, dance, acting, poetry, ballet, and opera – as did the deprivation of communication, such as the conditions of being deaf or blind.

Another perspective is that speech and knowledge come to be seen as aspects of our natural history. In Condillac's conception of the possibility and growth of knowledge, the development of language is a long-term process of repetition, formation of habits, and social interaction. No one before Condillac had so fully and cogently argued that a fundamental human institution is the product of evolving adaptation and functional success over time. It calls to mind Adam Smith's idea of the invisible hand that stirs individuals to action without any forethought or intention about the ultimate effects of their behavior. Speech is not the lone creation of private Cartesian minds. It owes nothing to plotted invention but comes about, as Hume suggests, 'gradually . . . by human conventions without any promise', just like 'two men, who pull the oars of a boat, do it by an agreement and convention, though they have never given promises to each other'.[6] Adam Smith had read Hume, but Condillac had not; however, he still pulled oars with them 'without any promise'. He did so at a time when thinking about language for decades had been dominated by Locke's *Essay Concerning Human Understanding* and by the rising prominence of rhetorical expressivism.

II. LOCKE'S ESSAY

The *Essay* stood at the threshold of the eighteenth century like a Janus figure, and it was chiefly its Book III on 'words and language in general' that made it two-faced. Both Berkeley and Condillac found that Locke's argument went awry because he treated language only after ideas (Book II). It is obvious that Locke was at his most Cartesian on the matter of discourse, taking the position that only the word-free discourse of the mind guarantees true knowledge, just as he also held the rationalist view that syllogistic is trivial, for 'A Man knows first, and then he is able to prove syllogistically. So that *Syllogism* comes after Knowledge, and then a Man has little or no need of it' (*Essay*, IV.xvii.6). This is 'the impossible term-by-term empiricism of Locke and Hume', that was taken over from rationalism.[7]

Condillac found that if Locke had treated language before ideas, he would have realized that his faith in word-free mental discourse clashed with his admission that words often take an active role in thought, as when he observed that like children, we learn most words before having the experience to provide the requisite ideas (*Essay*, III.v.15; III.ix.9); that the complex ideas of mixed modes would either not exist or lose stability without the words that name them because 'it is the Name that seems to preserve those *Essences*, and give them their lasting duration' (III.v.10; see also I.iv.27); and that we hardly ever engage in pure mental discourse, but use words instead, 'even when Men think and reason within their own Breasts' (IV.vi.1; see also I.iv.27). But Condillac's critique was simultaneously a tribute to the forward-looking views by which the *Essay* facilitated the looming intellectual revolution.

Among these views were Locke's insistence that there is no natural connection between the sounds of words and what they signify. The dismissal of this notion released words from any imputation of a nonarbitrary connection grounded in divine origin by virtue of Adam's name-giving, thus clearing the way for the only alternative, human origin. Another important idea was Locke's notion that language is public owing to its social use and its continued modification in speaking. Languages are 'suited only to the convenience of Communication . . . , not to the reality and extent of Things' (*Essay*, II.xxviii.2), and they were 'established long before Sciences', their 'more or less comprehensive terms' having received 'their Birth and Signification, from ignorant and illiterate People who sorted and denominated Things, by those sensible Qualities they found in them' (III.vi.25). Though Locke never treated the origin of language, he made suggestive remarks about the beginners, the beginning, and growth of languages.[8] A third important view was Locke's belief that this process of usage will cause change over time, thus giving each language a particular quality and historical dimension. He noted that even with our great volume of classical scholarship, we still often cannot with certainty get the right sense of classical texts, and he found that the same was true of the reading and interpretation of Scriptures (III.ix.10 and 23). Locke's *Essay* had the effect of expanding our thinking about language into the larger issue of communication in general.

Though the *Essay* ranged so widely over the nature and workings of language beyond the strict needs of epistemology, Locke still found no place for the uses of language on the stage, at the bar, in the pulpit, or in poetry. He remained confident that if we wish to 'speak of Things as they are, we must allow, that all the Art of Rhetorick . . . , all the artificial and figurative application of Words Eloquence hath invented, are for nothing else but to insinuate wrong *Ideas*, move the Passions, and thereby mislead the Judgment' (*Essay*, III.x.34). This reassurance was whistling in the dark, for if words pushed their way into mental discourse, then emotion would enter with them and spoil the cognitive appropriation. For Berkeley, one problem with that appropriation was that the language of the Bible and religion is not cognitive. This led to rhetorical expressivism, an altogether new conception of language that took the place of the rationalist appropriation.

III. RHETORICAL EXPRESSIVISM: THE READMISSION OF EMOTION

In a chapter on the progress of gesture in antiquity, Condillac writes that, at the time of Augustus, mimes had brought their art to such perfection that they could perform entire plays by gestures alone, thus creating unawares 'a language which had been the first that mankind spoke' (*Oeuvres*, II.1.34). This was the ultimate progress of expressivism; it was a form of what Condillac called the language of action, the proto-language of speech that sets humans apart from other animals. But the reaction against the mere information language of the cognitive appropriation had claimed much earlier that emotion and gesture cannot be kept apart from communication.

Best known is Berkeley's identification of the so-called emotive theory of meaning in the 'Introduction' to *A Treatise Concerning the Principles of Human Knowledge* (1710). The 'communicating of ideas marked by words is not the chief and only end of language'. Words also raise passions, induce actions, create beliefs, and may even by their mere sounds, without intervention of ideas, cause such emotions as 'fear, love, hatred, admiration, disdain, and the like'. These effects have no bearing on cognition. 'May we not', Berkeley asked, 'be affected with the promise of a *good thing*, though we have not an idea of what it is?' This is a veiled reference to the apostle Paul, who did not mean to raise 'abstract ideas of the good things nor yet particular ideas of the joys of the blessed', but to make men 'more cheerfull and fervent in their duty'. On this page we also read Berkeley's fullest statement about the 'good things': 'We are told that the good things which God hath prepared for them that love him are such as eye hath not seen nor ear heard nor hath it enter'd into the heart of man.' These words are a conflation of two passages, one from the Collect for the Sixth Sunday after Trinity in *The Book of Common Prayer*, 'O, God who has prepared for them that love thee such good things as pass man's understanding', and the other from I Corinthians 2:9 (which in turn echoes Isaiah 64:4), 'Eye hath not seen, nor ear heard, neither have entered into the heart of man, the things which God hath prepared for them that love him'. In the 'Seventh Dialogue' of *Alciphron*, Berkeley reiterated these principles, again quoting Paul and arguing vigorously that we must accept ordinary usage in all its fullness of expression and communication. Though they do not refer to determinate ideas, such words as 'grace', 'person', 'force', and 'number' are understood perfectly well in common speech.[9]

Berkeley's rejection of the cognitive appropriation in favor of the emotive theory is often said to have been altogether new, but that is not correct. It had already been proclaimed in two popular works. In a chapter on 'what words mean in usage', Arnauld and Nicole in the *Port-Royal Logic* (1662)[10] argued that in addition to the 'principal idea', which is its proper signification, a word often 'raises several other ideas that we can call accessory [*accessoires*] of which we do not take notice though the mind receives the impression of them'. Thus, if someone is told 'you have lied about it', the sense is not merely 'you have said what you know is not true', which pertains to the 'truth of things', but also the accompanying thoughts of contempt and outrage that pertain to the 'truth of usage'. The concept of accessory ideas in usage clearly belongs with emotive meaning in Berkeley's sense.

The same chapter stated that philosophers had not paid sufficient attention to accessory ideas and went beyond Berkeley by emphasizing that these ideas need not all have their source in custom and usage but may also be created by the speaker's tone of voice, facial expression, gestures (often called 'movements' both in French and English), and 'by other natural signs that attach a multitude of ideas to our words', including the affective deviation from standard syntax as in the inversion of normal word order. This stylistic device was often called 'hyperbaton' after a much-quoted section on it in Longinus's *On the Sublime*, recently made widely known in Boileau's French translation (1674).

The chapter in the *Port-Royal Logic* also argued that departure from the 'simple style', which states bare truths, is especially suitable for 'divine truths', which are not merely to be known but chiefly 'to be loved, venerated, and adored by the people'. Here again there is a striking closeness to Berkeley, who used the example of the liar in the draft version of the 'Introduction' to *Principles*.[11] The rhetorical nature of these observations is noteworthy in a work entitled *Logic, or The Art of Thinking*.

The second work to anticipate Berkeley was Bernard Lamy's *La rhétorique, ou l'art de parler* (Rhetoric, or the Art of Speaking) (1675), which until Lamy's death in 1715 went through fifteen steadily expanded and revised French printings, expounding with increasing force and detail the emotive and expressive dimensions of speech.[12] Lamy followed the *Port-Royal Logic* on the primacy of usage (66–72), on accessory ideas exemplified by the liar (39), and on the use of vocal gestures for which he cited interjections (or particles, as he called them) that express 'admiration, joy, disdain, anger, pain' (38–9). Lamy boldly claimed that the passions are good in themselves (343), that people hardly ever act on reason but on imagination and sense (367), and that his book did something unusual in aiming to uncover the foundations of rhetoric (153). Lamy's *Rhétorique* remained a respected authority for much of the eighteenth century.

At this point, oratory begins to blend with sympathy, gestures, and sociability. In its classical formulation, the art of oratory had five parts: invention, disposition, expression, memory, and delivery. Traditionally these parts were given roughly equal importance, but toward the end of the seventeenth century, delivery began to get the most attention as the chief agent of persuasion. This change is evident in Fénelon's *Dialogues sur l'éloquence en général et sur celle de la chaire en particulier* (Dialogues on eloquence in general and on that of the pulpit in particular), published in 1718 but written some forty years earlier.[13] His thesis is that truth will not prevail without eloquence and persuasion and that sermons tend to present ineffectual philosophical argument. In our present fallen state, with man being 'wholly enmeshed in things of sense . . . it is necessary to give physical body to all the instructions one wishes to inject into his soul, and to find images that beguile him', that is by poetry, which, being 'the lively portrayal of things, is as it were the soul of eloquence' (94).

Fénelon found the greatest eloquence in the Old and New Testaments, especially in the prophets and the psalms, which for him surpassed Homer and Plato in grandeur, naiveté, liveliness, and sublimity (131). The example of David showed that 'the oriental nations regarded the dance as a serious art, similar to music and poetry', just as the fact that the ancient Greeks went to war to the sounds of 'trumpets and drums that threw them into a state of enthusiasm and a sort of furor they called divine' showed that even in pagan Greece, 'music, dance, eloquence, poetry had no other purpose but to give expression to the passions and to inspire them in the very act of expressing them' (68). Fénelon paid much attention to the use of gestures in delivery. Citing Cicero, he wrote that the 'action of the body' expresses 'the sentiments and passions of the soul' (99). The Latin word *actio* was Cicero's and Quintilian's term for delivery, and both cited Demosthenes in support of their belief that delivery is the heart of oratory.[14] 'Action', said Cicero, 'influences everybody, for the same emotions are felt by all people and they both recognize them in others and manifest them in themselves by the same marks' (*De oratore*, III.223). The gestures of action, both with voice and body, constitute a universal language that promotes communication and social cohesion.

Classical rhetoric did not have a term for the mysterious something that provides humanity with the means of universal communication, but Lamy suddenly supplied one in the fourth edition of his *Rhétorique*. 'Human beings are bound to one another by a wonderful sympathy [*sympathie*] which naturally makes them communicate their passions'. Thus, a 'person with an expression of sadness on his face causes sadness, just as a sign of joy makes those who notice it share in the joy', and all this, Lamy declared, 'is an effect of the wonderful wisdom of God' (*Rhétorique*, 111–12). In support, Lamy cited some lines from a passage in Horace that Hume also cited to make the same point.[15] The term is Greek, and its philosophical home was in Stoic philosophy, where 'sympathy' is the name for the cosmic harmony that binds all things together in an organized whole of both the physical and the moral worlds. A loan translation appears in ecclesiastical Latin as *compassio*, which in turn produced other loan translations such as the German *Mitleid*. Among the most efficient disseminators of this concept of sympathy and its significance for the growth of sociability was Jean-Baptiste Du Bos, whose *Réflexions critiques sur la poésie et sur la peinture* (1719) was well known to David Hume and Adam Smith.[16]

The rise of rhetorical expressivism met the need to understand language within the entire spectrum of human communication. The seventeenth century believed that speech had its origin in better times before the Fall; with that faith gone, what would take its place? How could we become self-starters? We could not have begun by inventing language by discursive plotting for, in the aporia made popular by Rousseau, this would require that we already had a discourse to work with. However, spontaneous emotive expression, natural sociability, and sympathy provided a proto-language, a background language ensured by action and response without forethought. Rhetorical expressivism became the source of the proto-language that Condillac called the language of action.

IV. CONDILLAC

Condillac admired Locke as the best of philosophers because he had studied how the mind works without reliance on postulates about its essential nature. The rejection of innate ideas was one aspect of this which, with other debts to Locke, is too obvious to need explication. On this basis, however, it is still often believed that Condillac was a close disciple of Locke, even that his *Essai sur l'origines* is merely a short version of Locke's *Essay*. This is doubly wrong. First, whereas Locke sought to protect his mental discourse from the cheat of words, Condillac did the very opposite by making language the generator of discursivity and knowledge. The second reason can be read right off the table of contents to Part Two of *Essai* in such chapter titles as 'The prosody of the first languages', 'The progress of the art of gestures among the ancients', 'Music', 'The origin of poetry', 'The origin of the fable, the parable, and the enigma', and 'The genius of languages'. These chapters concern artistic expression, a subject irrelevant to the foundations of Locke's epistemology.

The argument of *Essai* is based on two principles: that nature begins everything, and that we owe so much to the passions that without them 'the understanding is virtually at a standstill' (I.2.106). There is nothing at all passive or mechanical in this philosophy.[17] With other animals, we share consciousness, attentiveness, reminiscence, and a limited form of the livelier human imagination. But unlike them we are capable of becoming speaking and discoursing creatures. What accounts for this difference we do not know, though with many of his contemporaries Condillac located it in 'our organization' – that is, our organic makeup. Discursivity cannot occur without recall, recall not without memory, and neither without signs. These signs cannot be private but must be public. Since we are born with neither innate ideas nor signs (I.2.35), how do we get the signs?

The brief Introduction to *Essai* presents two concepts that underlie the argument. The aim of *Essai* is 'to reduce everything that pertains to the human mind to a single principle', namely 'the connection of ideas'. This connection has two sources, the first existing among the objects and phenomena we experience, the second among the signs we make for the experiences that matter to us. As we attend to these aspects, they enter the network of connections that expresses our relation to our natural and social environments. We create our own internal version of the external world. The objects of attention come in contextual bunches, forming chains and subchains that the mind can survey and control once it has the requisite signs. This control over attention is called reflection.

The second basic concept is the language of action, which 'has produced all the arts that pertain to the expression of our thoughts: the art of gesture, dance, speech, declamation, the art of recording it, the art of pantomime, of music, of poetry, eloquence, writing, and the different characters of languages.' (Introduction, p. 5 of transl.). The treatment of this proto-language in Part Two will 'show the circumstances in which signs are imagined'. Part One examines the operations of the mind and argues why signs are necessary for thinking.

Condillac distinguishes two kinds of remembering, memory and imagination. Memory evokes only details of an original perception and is often limited to the mere sign for a thing, its name (I.2.18). This second possibility invests memory with the power of recalling what is stored in the mind. Memory enables reflection. For us the important distinction between recall and storage is generally lost because we use the word memory chiefly in the sense of storage. Imagination does not present mere details; unlike memory, it raises entire perceptions with all the circumstances of the original experience; not just a flower, but the flower brought to life with color shadings, scent, leaves, surroundings, and so forth. Such imagination can be evoked only indirectly as, for instance, by first recalling the requisite name. Thus memory enables imagination, leading to a second expanded meaning that takes 'the imagination to be an operation that, in the act of reviving ideas, constantly makes new combinations subject to our will' (I.2.75). This free-ranging imagination is the quality that preeminently belongs to genius (I.2.104). In a later work, Condillac wrote that a person of imagination is a 'creative mind' (*un esprit créateur*) by virtue of joining diverse parts into a single whole that exists only in his own mind (*Oeuvres*, 1: 413a; see also 385a). Since imagination creates synthesis, it is not compatible with analysis; poetry and philosophy are different modes of thought. The great lesson of *Essai* is that speech is the primal act of human creation and that speaking and communicating remain inherently creative acts at all times.

Condillac distinguishes three kinds of signs (I.2.35). First, 'accidental signs' occur when the chance repetition of some perception acts as a sign that triggers an unexpected recall (I.2.15). Condillac calls it reminiscence, and it shows that something stored in memory can suddenly flash vividly to mind with conviction both that it genuinely belongs to memory and that it is not intentionally evoked. Such renewed awareness urges the possibility that with signs we could recall at will, command our attention, and thus become free, creative agents.[18]

Secondly, there are 'natural signs or the cries that nature has established for the sentiments of joy, fear, pain, etc.' (I.2.35). These sounds express affective states of mind but when first produced spontaneously do not differ from accidental signs; we could not repeat them unless the appropriate situation recurred. They cannot therefore be signs for the utterer, but they become so if a hearer, who by sympathy has recognized a natural cry as the expression of a familiar state of mind, in turn deliberately reproduces the sound of the cry with the intent of communication – that is, as a sign carrying an intended meaning.

With that move, the hearer creates an instance of the third category of signs, 'instituted signs, or those that we have ourselves chosen and that have only an arbitrary relation to our ideas'. Here Condillac's language is careless, as he later realized. There are natural cries, but no natural signs, for it takes a mind to know a sign. In the statement on instituted signs, he got ahead of himself, for the very first instituted signs are, though chosen, not arbitrary in relation to our ideas; these signs repeat the sounds of natural cries, which of course are not arbitrary in that sense. However, the very core of his argument was suggested: the first conception of language occurs when the hearer turns the utterer's natural cries into signs. This suggests that the stock of signs may be enlarged by arbitrary signs that will enter usage in the continuing language game that has now begun within a form of life on the analogy of Hume's two rowers. Meaning and language arise only in dialogue.

Without natural cries and gestures we could not become self-starting communicators, and Condillac stresses again and again that nascent speech for a long time needs the support of action. All the modes of expression initially coexisted until, ages later, they emerged as the separate arts that Condillac named in his first statement on the language of action. Thus prose eventually evolves from poetry, ready to serve analysis and cognition. Yet language continues to have many uses; Condillac dismissed the rationalist claim that only the fixed subject-predicate order exhibits the true nature of language.

Condillac was well aware of the problem of getting from action to speech and thought, admitting a seeming impasse for if 'the exercise of reflection can only be acquired by the use of signs', how do we acquire the instituted signs unless some degree of reflection was already possible at an earlier stage? (I.2.49). The answer is that for the hearer the inherent sign function of the natural cries suffices to awaken reflection. 'It is reflection', Condillac wrote, 'that makes us discern the capability of the mind' (I.2.51).[19] From then on, signs and reflection engage in a process of reciprocal improvement. In the chapter on language of action (II.1.3), Condillac refers back to his seeming impasse, remarking that he now gives the solution. By repeatedly hearing spontaneous avowals and engaging in communication within their form of life, speakers came to do by reflection what they had earlier done by instinct. Nature begins everything. The proto-language is part of our natural history.

After eight chapters focusing on the forms of action, Condillac explains that he could not interrupt what he 'wished to say about the art of gesture, dance, declamation, music, and poetry' because they are all so 'closely interrelated as a whole and to the language of action which is their principle'. These eight chapters are the heart of *Essai* (II.1.1–79).

To stress the necessity of signs, Condillac devoted a chapter to the cases of two boys, one of whom grew up as if deaf-mute, the other apart from human society (I.4.13–27). Both were reported around 1700 and had already entered the literature on the subject, as we shall see. The first boy lived in Chartres in the midst of social life, he went to church and outwardly participated in worship by crossing himself, kneeling in prayer, and the like. Then suddenly in his early twenties he began to hear; for some months he listened quietly to what he heard spoken and then began to speak, though haltingly. When theologians asked him what thoughts he had had about God, the soul, and moral good and evil in his past state, it became evident that he had no notion of such matters and even lacked any sense that acts of worship were intentional. Condillac concluded that in his deaf-mute state this young man 'hardly had any idea of what life is' (I.4.18), and he agreed with the source he was quoting that the young man had 'led a mere animal life, wholly occupied with [the] sensible and present objects' that determined his attention. Without hearing and speaking, his social life was so severely limited that he could develop neither memory nor the use of signs, for as the source also said, 'the principal fund of the ideas of mankind is their mutual converse'. In spite of having had the benefit of living in society, he was barely human.

The condition of the other boy was worse, for he was found at the age of about ten living among bears in the forests of Lithuania, making bearlike sounds and crawling on all fours. Like animals he had the use only of accidental signs. He would of course make the natural cries of the passions, but without the opportunity to hear others make similar cries, he could not have suspected that they were 'suited to become signs' by being connected 'with the sentiments they are intended to express' (I.4.25). He could not learn that lesson from the roar of the animals for the important reason that 'their roar does not have sufficient analogy with the human voice'. Each species conforms to an analogy, which in human beings is grounded in the sympathy that is the condition for the proto-language. For Condillac, this is all part of our natural history.

Analogy plays a crucial role. It is a product of comparison and resemblance, and it shows up in all aspects of language – in grammar, phonology, word formation, and style – thus interacting with and mirroring the mind's corresponding effort to create order and coherence in the connection of ideas. It follows that 'the poorer a language is in analogous expressions, the less assistance it gives to memory and imagination' (II.1.147). Since any particular language embodies a ruling analogy, a language that is a mixture of idioms gives less assistance to the mind (II.1.146, see also 151–2). It is this role of analogy that lies behind the notion of language being an organism. Since there is always a variety of possible relations of resemblance, analogy does not act like a deterministic vise on the mind; quite the contrary, it opens scope for creativity.[20]

Condillac's account of signs raised problems both among his contemporaries and also later, often leading to the charge that his account is incoherent. Condillac occasionally exchanged ideas about language with Maupertuis, a distinguished French scientist who was then president of the Prussian Academy in Berlin. In response to an essay on language by Maupertuis, he wrote (25 June 1752) that he wished Maupertuis had shown how the progress of the mind depends on language, continuing that 'I tried to do that in my *Origin*, but I was mistaken and gave too much to signs' (*Oeuvres*, 2: 536a). This has been read as an admission that Condillac was wrong about signs and thus, astonishingly, about the entire argument of his *Essai*. The evidence shows otherwise. Condillac wrote much on language during the rest of his life, in the *Cours d'étude pour l'instruction du prince de Parme* (Course of study for the Prince of Parma) (1775), in his *La logique* (Logic) (1780), and in *La langue des calculs* (Language of the calculus) (1798), without retreating from the argument of *Essai*. By his own admission, *L'art de penser* (Art of thinking; part of the *Cours d'étude*) repeated, usually verbatim, the text of *Essai*. He changed the title of the chapter on how we give signs to ideas (*Essai*, I.4. 1–12) to 'The necessity of signs', adding a note saying that since *Essai*, 'I have completed the task of showing the necessity of signs in my *Grammar* [also in *Cours d'étude*] and in my *Logic*', both with searching chapters on the language of action. Condillac's remark about having given too much to signs cannot be read as an admission of fatal error on a matter at the center of his philosophy.

He meant that he had given insufficient emphasis to social intercourse, as he implied in criticizing Maupertuis for assuming that a single isolated person would ever hit upon the notion of giving signs to ideas. A few years earlier, in letters to the Swiss mathematician Gabriel Cramer,[21] Condillac insisted on the need for social life, with frequent references to his chapter on the two boys, though he admitted that his exposition had not been clear enough. Asked whether natural signs count for nothing, Condillac answered:

[B]efore social life, natural signs are properly speaking not signs, but only cries that accompany sentiments of pain, joy, etc., which people utter by instinct and by the mere form of their organs. They must live together to have occasion to attach ideas to these cries and to employ them as signs. Then these cries blend with the arbitrary signs. That is what I am supposing in several places [he refers to I.4.23–4, II.1.2–3]. But I appeared to suppose the contrary, and thus to make too great a difference between natural and arbitrary signs; and in that I was wrong. (*Lettres inédites à Gabriel Cramer*, 85–6)

This might give the impression that natural cries could be signs before or without social intercourse, but the need for social life is spelled out by what comes next:

That is what my entire system comes down to in this matter. Social intercourse gives occasion 1. to change the natural cries into signs; 2. to invent other signs that we call arbitrary; and these signs (the natural as well as the arbitrary) are the first principles of the development and progress of the operations of the mind. I admit that on all this my work is not clear enough. I hope I'll do better another time (*Lettres*, 86).

The position is thoroughly anti-Cartesian, against solipsism and against the notion that any acceptable explanation of mental life must begin with claims about the mind of the silent, isolated individual. On that view, determinate meaning must precede use; for Condillac, meaning arises only in use and dialogue.

How is it possible to reconcile this argument about communication and knowledge with the widely credited dogma that Condillac's philosophy is most fully represented by the famous statue in his *Traité des sensations* (1754)?[22] The claim is that the statue, if endowed with each of the five senses, becomes a full-fledged human being, ready to acquire and command the entire range of our intellectual abilities. Seen in this perspective, Condillac is said to wish 'to eliminate all autonomous activity from the mind' by making reflection 'depend upon the mechanical association of ideas'. This is the familiar misconception that 'the informal metaphysics of the Enlightenment tended toward a mechanical philosophy which saw nothing artificial in likening man to an animated statue, even as the universe is likened to a watch'. However, such a reading grasps neither the pivotal role of signs and communication nor Condillac's persistent affirmation of the creativity and action of the mind. Like the two deprived boys, the statue is radically speechless because its existence is wholly private and unsocial; its mental life is that of an animal.[23] For Condillac, the essence of humanity is the activity of the mind that is generated when thinking is cycled into action by signs and their use in dialogue. Without language, there is no humanity.

V. INVERSIONS OR THE PROBLEM OF WORD ORDER

Condillac's discussion of inversion brings out the deep implications of his argument that all languages ultimately stem from and still bear some marks of the expressive language of action. In a chapter on 'Music', he observed that compared with Frenchmen, the Greeks had a much livelier imagination because their language was closer to the language of action, which itself is a product of the imagination, while French is so prose-like and analytical that 'it hardly requires more than the exercise of memory' (*Traité*, II.1.51). In a chapter on 'Inversions' (II.1.117–26), he challenged the rationalist term-by-term doctrine, declaring that no one could tell what the natural order was. French must use the order 'Alexander overcame Darius', whereas in Latin '*Alexander vicit Darium*' and '*Darium vicit Alexander*' are equally good. The doctrine that the subject-predicate order was natural might really be a French prejudice since its grammar left no choice in the matter. Latin grammar put little constraint on word order because it left the expression free to create the order that best suited the emotions and the intended emphasis.

In support, Condillac analyzed a passage from Horace and one from Virgil. In plain English, the latter said, 'the nymphs wept for Daphne who lost her life in a cruel death', or, in similar order in Latin, '*Nymphae flebant Daphnim extinctum funere crudeli*'. But Virgil's poetry is '*Extinctum Nymphae crudeli funere Daphnim flebant*'. Here the first four words keep us in suspense until '*Daphnim*' comes like 'the first stroke of the painter's brush', which then quickly completes the picture with '*flebant*'. Thus 'the attributes of a doleful death strike me all of a sudden. Such is the power of inversions over the imagination.' (II.1.120–2). Virgil's poetry emulates the early language of action, which is truer and more spontaneous than the analytical prose that later developed. Much like a painting, Virgil's Latin expression captures the instancy of thought, while the time-bound and linear French can produce only 'a plain narrative'. This implies that the sentence is the unit of meaning; people who are familiar with the language of action know that 'a single gesture is often equivalent to a long sentence' (II.1.51). This is now called semantic holism and contrasts with rationalism, for which individual words are the prime carriers of meaning.

Condillac was pointedly criticized in two long entries in the *Encyclopédie*, on 'Inversions' (8 (1765), 852a–62a), and on language ('Langue', 9 (1765), 249a–66a), by the great universal grammarian Nicolas Beauzée. For him, the original language, being divine and Adamic, exhibited an immutable analytical order reflecting the mind as 'an emanation of the unchanging and sovereign reason of the true light that enlightens everyone who comes into this world'. Citing the Bible and Descartes, Beauzée concluded that a language of inversions was artificial and thus secondary. Condillac's position was as much against nature as a painting of a tree with its roots in the air and its leaves buried in the ground.[24]

For Condillac, the poetic quality of the language of action recaptured by inversion gave vivacity and force, or 'energy' as his contemporaries, especially Diderot, called it. The concept of expressive energy became so well known that by 1782 it gained an entry in the *Encyclopédie méthodique: Grammaire et littérature*:

Energy is the quality that in a single word or in a small number of words causes us to perceive or feel a large number of ideas; or which by means of a small number of ideas expressed by words excites in the mind sentiments of admiration, respect, horror, love, hate, etc., which words alone do not signify.[25]

This is illustrated by a passage from Horace that Condillac used to the same purpose (*Traité*, II.1.121). Written by the splendid Beauzée, the entry began: 'Energy is a Greek word *energeia*, *actio*, *efficacia*; in this sense its roots are in *en* (*in*, dans, en) and *ergon* (*opus*, ouvrage, oeuvre).' Beauzée is saying that the true nature of language is action, not ready to hand in finished work, and that this creativity can best be attained in languages that, like Latin, have a grammar that puts few constraints on word order.

In words widely taken to state the heart of his linguistic thought, Wilhelm von Humboldt declared that language 'in itself is no product (*Ergon*) but an activity (*Energeia*). . . . It is the ever-repeated mental labor of making the articulated sound capable of expressing thought.' Humboldt's distinction between what he in German called *Werk* (work) and *Thätigkeit* (activity) corresponds wholly to the one Beauzée made between the two Greek words and their Latin and French equivalents. Humboldt found the true nature of language in Sanskrit and Greek, which by means of their rich use of inflection could create what he called the 'true inner fixity' of expression. Humboldt hardly arrived at his distinction and its formulation without knowing what had been written about inversion and energy.[26]

Some twenty years after Beauzée's claims for its exclusive legitimacy, the analytical order was celebrated in Antoine Rivarol's less important but better-known *Discours sur l'universalité de la langue française* (1784). In 1783, it won the prize of the Berlin Academy for the famous argument that 'what is not clear is not French', whereas French has remained 'faithful to the direct order as if it was reason itself'. French 'first names the *subject* of the discourse, then the *verb* that is the action, and last the *object* of this action; there you have the logic that is natural to all humanity'. By contrast, Rivarol wrote, languages with inversions are muddled and hard to learn, though they are very favorable to music, which thrives on 'disorder and abandon'.[27]

Condillac had already undermined Rivarol's extravagant opinions in his *Grammaire* (1775):

> The truth is that in the mind there is neither direct order nor inverted order because the mind perceives all its ideas at the same time; it would speak them at the same time if it could speak them as it perceives them. That is what would be natural to it; and that is how it speaks them when it knows only the language of action. It is therefore only in discourse that ideas have a direct or inverted order, for their succession occurs only in discourse. These two orders are equally natural. (*Oeuvres*, 1: 503a)[28]

There cannot be discrete prevenient ideas or mental discourse without the public signs that enable thinking, and we cannot claim to know what a thought was before its expression.

VI. CONDILLAC'S EIGHTEENTH-CENTURY SOURCES

For a work of its kind, *Essai sur l'origines* cites at unusual length from other texts, chiefly from three near-contemporaries of Condillac: the English bishop and man of letters William Warburton, the German philosopher Christian Wolff, and the French critic and historian Jean-Baptiste Du Bos.

Warburton is cited at length in a chapter on 'Writing' (*Essai*, II.1.127–37) and in the crucial chapter on the language of action (II.1.1–12), which draws on a brief section on language in *The Divine Legation of Moses* (1741). Condillac had no English but saw a French translation of Book IV, Section Four of *Divine Legation*, in which he found the term 'language of action' (*langage d'action*) both in the text and in the prominent marginal summaries. Warburton himself never used that phrase nor did he even consistently use the same phrase for that notion. Warburton also argued that in the time of early religion, speech was so rude that the Old Testament prophets often instructed the people by 'actions . . . and conversed with them in signs', to which Warburton added that such 'speaking by action' was also common in pagan antiquity, for instance, by the Delphic oracle.[29] Warburton also said that 'the mutual converse [that] was upheld by a mixed discourse of words and actions' might in time be improved by 'use and custom . . . especially amongst the *Eastern* people [as in the Old Testament], whose natural temperature inclined them to a mode of conversation which so well exercised their vivacity by *motion*' (*Divine Legation*, 83; in French, 120). In other words, development might occur even in this sacred territory. Warburton went further, citing ancient accounts of the origin of language, with people at first living in caves like beasts before gradually gaining speech by mutual assistance – an origin so natural, he said, that it had been credited by several church fathers (81–2; in French 119), although the Bible said that God had instructed Adam in religion and language. Still Warburton thought that this language must 'needs have been very poor and narrow', though it did put man in the position of 'being now of himself able to improve and enlarge it, as his future necessities should require'. Having quoted Warburton's sanction of development, Condillac commented that this observation 'seems very judicious to me', and that when he would now begin his argument with the schematic account of two children alone in the desert after the Fall, it was because he did not think a philosopher could appeal to special dispensation but must limit himself to explaining how things could have come about by natural means (*Essai*, 113–14, note). However, since Warburton's speaking by actions was divine and deliberate, in fact it had little in common with Condillac's involuntary expression of sentiments that formed the basis for his language of action. Probably Condillac chose to cite the English divine in order to bolster the legitimacy of an enterprise that might have easily run afoul of doctrine and church authority.[30]

For his account of the two deprived boys, Condillac referred to Wolff's *Psychologia rationalis* (1736, 1740), where the relevant passage begins: 'The use of speech promotes and enlarges the use of reason; without the use of speech the use of reason is quickly lost.'[31] Like Condillac, Wolff argues that pain and pleasure are grounds of action; that reflection does not occur without words; that reason becomes manifest only by virtue of speech; and that signs and words are necessary for thinking and recall. Wolff is also strong on the enchainment of all things and on the connection of ideas, and he presents the entire architecture of the mind and the process of knowing in terms similar to those of Part One of *Essai*. But there are salient differences. Unlike Condillac, Wolff referred to God as a ground of explanation, and he often likened nature to a clockwork, in contrast with Condillac's preference for organic terms and metaphors. Wolff has no trace of the evolutionary conception of language or the related conception of the language of action. This may explain why Condillac found that Wolff 'did not know the absolute necessity of signs, any more than the manner in which they contribute to the operations of the mind' (I.4.27).[32]

In *Essai*, Condillac cites Du Bos's *Réflexions critiques sur la poésie et sur la peinture* more than any other text. The seven long citations are in chapters on prosody and declamation in Greek and Latin and on the use of pantomime in the ancient theater, and they are all drawn from Du Bos's third volume, 'A dissertation on the theatrical performances of the ancients'. This is a veritable handbook on rhetorical expressivism, and its copious references to Cicero and Quintilian constitute an anthology of passages on expression, gesture, and 'action' in the works of those authors. It is true, therefore, that Condillac 'undoubtedly owes the theory of the language of action and of the language of music to Du Bos',[33] but his debt goes far beyond the actual citations. *Réflexions* has chapters on music (1.360–75; 3.4–60) and on the advantages of poets composing in Latin over those in French (1.246–77). This chapter is about inversion and draws the same conclusions as Condillac did in regard to the poetic benefits of the free word order made possible by the inflections of Latin grammar.

In art, Du Bos gave primacy to emotion, with concomitant celebration of genius and activity. We rate a poem or a painting as we do a ragout, not by analysis of the recipe but by a 'sixth sense' that is 'commonly called sentiment', which is the way the heart works 'by a movement that precedes all deliberation' (*Réflexions*, 2.238–9). The tenor of *Réflexions* is that discursivity lacks the energy and immediacy of wordless communication. Du Bos expounded this subject chiefly in four chapters on dance and pantomime in the ancient theater (3.160–225). 'The gestures of ancient dance must speak, they must signify something, they must, as it were, be a continued discourse' (3.164), a subject he treated most fully in a chapter 'on pantomimes or actors who perform without speaking' (3.202–25). Du Bos relied heavily on Lucian's dialogue on expression and action in the ancient theater, 'The dance'.[34] This spirited work argued that dance brings both pleasure and harmony in the combined uses of music, song, rhythm, ballet, pantomime, declamation, and other forms of expression. In this sense, dance keeps company with eloquence, for dance 'is given to depicting character and emotion, of which the orators are also fond' ('The dance', 247). Thus, for Lucian, dance corresponds to what Condillac in the opening pages of *Essai* called the language of action, which 'has produced all the arts that pertain to the expression of thoughts'.[35]

The similarity of conceptions and arguments in the works of Condillac and the works of the late Wittgenstein may already have crossed the reader's mind. This similarity is not surprising. Both take aim at the Cartesian dualism of body and mind, and their arguments follow analogous paths from a non-Cartesian proto-language to the conclusion that language cannot have emerged from the privacy of the individual mind but is a function of social life and communication. For both, the proto-language provides a firm, doubt-free beginning, and for both that beginning was action. The language of action initiates a game that occurs within a form of life, and, like a game, the language of action carries no implication that it is guided by reason. It is unlikely that Wittgenstein had read Condillac (or Du Bos, Fénelon, and Adam Smith) or had come upon the rhetorical expressivism that prevailed over Cartesian dualism. But attention to Wittgenstein evokes a good sense of Condillac's achievement.[36]

In his own time and for a good while after, his influence was wide and deep. One aspect appealed particularly to the temper of the times. Condillac argued at length that modern arts have developed from seeds sown in the distant past, that the style of the earliest poetry was a function of the particular quality of the language in which it was composed, and that owing to this interdependence good poetry and language tend to flourish together. Languages differ, and each language forms a quality or genius very early by the ruling analogy that is, as it were, its soul. Just as each individual, according to his or her passions, has a particular language, so the genius or 'character of nations shows still more openly than the character of individuals', for a 'multitude cannot act in concert to conceal their passions'. As compatriots, we are proud of our shared preferences and 'happy that they point to our native country in favor of which we are always prejudiced. Thus everything confirms that the language of each nation expresses the character of the people who speak it' (*Essai*, II.1.143). Poets shape the quality of a language, and it becomes a 'painting of the character of each nation's genius' (II.1.161–2).

This mix of language, poetry, history, and nation is totally at odds with the universalism and contempt for individuality that lie at the core of the so-called Enlightenment project. It is true that Condillac did have a concept of 'a well-made language' that might go beyond prose and approach the quality of algebra without ever achieving its perfection. This may sound as if Condillac had in mind a universal or philosophical language, but in the posthumous *La langue des calculs* (Language of the Calculus) (1798) he expressly rejected the possibility of making a transnational, universal language since it would impair or lack the analogy necessary for the proper understanding and use of any language.[37] Condillac did contribute to the universal 'language' of Guyton de Morveau's and Antoine Lavoisier's chemical nomenclature, but the well-made language remained a national language.[38] This was the dominant position in the eighteenth century, foreshadowed by Locke's suggestion that no one 'can pretend to attempt the perfect *Reforming* the *Languages* of the world . . . without rendring himself ridiculous' (*Essay*, III.xi.2).

However, Condillac's influence was more powerful at the poetic end of the linguistic spectrum. One of the truly important cultural events of the latter half of the eighteenth century was the sudden rise of interest in the poetry of the unlettered folk, first in Scotland, where Hugh Blair published his *Critical Dissertation on the Poems of Ossian Son of Fingal* (1763), and then on the shores of the Baltic, where Herder, after reading Blair, became excited by the singing and poetry of the folk he met in the fields and villages outside Riga. This was not a sudden whim but a wish to learn from the nameless art upon which Condillac had conferred dignity and philosophical importance. The aesthetics of Romanticism has its roots in Condillac's philosophy of speech, art, and culture.

VII. DIDEROT

It cannot be doubted that it is to Diderot that we owe the *Encyclopédie*'s copious attention to topics relating to rhetoric, dance, music, pantomime, the stage, poetry, declamation, and other forms of expression – the language of action.

Taken together, these entries constitute the single most notable and innovative feature of that work, and they have shared the usual fate of such reference work entries of flowing anonymously into the minds and discourse of authors who left no evidence of their source. The *Encyclopédie méthodique* was probably an even more important uncredited source. It contained articles that had appeared in the *Encyclopédie* and its Supplement, as well as new entries on topics that had gained prominence in more recent years such as Beauzée's on 'Energie'.[39]

In the 1740s, Condillac occasionally shared meals with Rousseau and Diderot, who, with his good contacts in the book trade, helped the reclusive author find a publisher. As Condillac's first and most influential spokesman, Diderot, in his *Lettre sur les sourds et muets* (Letter on deaf-mutes) (1751), widened the scope of inversion and the language of poetry. Diderot recognized that the problem of inversion raised important issues about the nature of language. How did the unitary gestures of the language of action develop into the analytic order of modern French prose? Could it be known what the basic natural word order had been? And, if so, what was it? How did language solve the problem of converting the simultaneity of a thought into the sequentiality of a sentence? What were the relative merits of poetry and prose? What was the relation between visual and verbal expression? What, if any, was the interdependence of thought and language? How well do speakers and hearers understand one another? And especially, what can we do to improve communication and understanding?

A good rationalist had ready answers to these questions; Condillac's were quite different. About effective communication he would have said that if the aim was affective communication, then the energetic and poetic concentration made possible by Greek and Latin grammar was best, but if the aim was expository clarity suitable for philosophy, then French prose was best. Diderot agreed, and like Condillac he admitted with regret that the perspicuity of French prose had been gained at the cost of 'enthusiasm (*chaleur*), eloquence, and energy'.[40] This loss became the fulcrum of Diderot's lifelong fascination with forms of art and expression. People of genius were rare, and genius could put an entire nation into a temper of fermentation, perfecting knowledge in a marvellously short time. Genius was marked chiefly by its impact on language because creative minds had 'the passion of imagination and thoughtfulness to enrich language with new expressions'.[41] Diderot disagreed sharply with Helvétius's deterministic beliefs that genius is a matter of luck and that people, being shaped by their environment and education, are mostly alike rather than individually different. The individuality of each person was the heart of Diderot's conception of human nature, genius being a unique and wholly unpredictable manifestation of individuality. But there is a problem: what happens to individuality in the process of communication?

If we imagined, Diderot boldly declared, that 'God suddenly gave each individual a language which at every point was analogous to his or her feelings, there would be no understanding at all'. We have been spared that possibility by the very poverty and insufficiency of language, for 'though we all feel differently, we speak alike'. 'Such is the diversity [of feeling] that if each individual could create for himself a language that was analogous to what he is, there would be as many languages as there are individuals'.[42] In successful communication, we surrender part of our individuality, with the consequence that 'we never precisely understand, we are never precisely understood'.[43] Naturally, Diderot wished to recover as much as possible for individuality, and this meant paying attention to the spoken dimension of communication. In an early work, Diderot compared creativity in communication to the efforts of strangers to be understood among speakers whose native language they barely know.[44]

It is an accepted axiom, argues Diderot, that different causes do not produce the same effects. Still, says his interlocutor, two people may have the same thought and express it identically; two poets may write the same lines on the same subject. Since two individuals are different causes, does not the sameness of expression show that the axiom does not hold? Not at all, answers Diderot; the sameness is only a superficial result of the poverty of language. If it were rich enough, the two persons and the two poets would not have a word in common, and the public dimension of sense that ensures understanding would be lost. Now Diderot's friend gets the point, even adding that not having a word in common would be much like the individual differences of what he calls accents in pronunciation. 'That's it', says Diderot,

it is the very variety of accent . . . that makes up for the paucity of words by doing away with the frequent identities of effects that are produced by the same causes. The number of words is limited, while that of accents is infinite. That explains how everyone has his own individual language and speaks as he feels, is cold or warm, vivacious or placid, is himself and only himself, while in regard to idea and expression he seems to be like another person.[45]

Accent belongs to 'the language of nature' that is understood by all; it is what ancient authority called 'the seed-plot of music' – that is, of vocal music. Accent is a sort of singing added to speech. As noted earlier, the term is a translation of the Greek word behind our word prosody. One authority often cited is Cicero's statement that 'there is even in speech a sort of musical play of voice'.[46] Accent is an aspect of rhetorical expressivism. As a vocal gesture within the repertoire of the language of action, it keeps our information prose alive with the poetic qualities of early speech. Diderot's chief aim was to show that language has more uses and forms than appear in the silent, visual, ordered display on the written page. We are wrong to think that our prosy information language exhausts the dimensions of communication.[47] Diderot's celebration of hearing contrasts with the seventeenth century's fixation on seeing. This opposition of ear and eye, orality and vision defines two radically different conceptions of the nature of language.

In the dialogue cited, while taking a walk in the country, Diderot holds forth about painting, art, life, imitation, and expression, but then suddenly interrupts himself to ask his friend,

'We have been conversing for a long time. I suppose you have heard me and under-stood me'. – 'Very well'. – 'Do you think you have heard anything besides words?' – 'Certainly' – 'Well, you are mistaken. You have heard only words and nothing but words. . . . Really, while I was talking you were busy enumerating the ideas subsumed under abstract words; your imagination was hard at work depicting the sequence of inter-linked images in my discourse. You aren't thinking of that. I would have finished talking when you would still be at the first word, at the end of my description before you would have sketched the first outline of my presentation.' 'Yes indeed, you may well be right'.

To drive home his point, Diderot cites some soul-stirring lines of poetry about Neptune, Pluto, the gods, hell, death, and Styx, and then begins to ask his friend a question about the recitation – but is interrupted by his friend: '[T]hat is an astonishing mystery; for without recalling the ideas, without depicting the images, I have all the same felt the impression of that terrifying and sublime passage.' To this Diderot quickly answers: '[T]hat is the mystery of everyday conversation.' Playing on the double meaning of the French word *entendre*, which means both 'to hear' and 'to understand', Diderot has disabused his friend of the myth that understanding does not occur until the exterior language in a process of introspection has been translated into an interior language of ideas.[48]

VIII. THE DEBATE ABOUT LANGUAGE IN THE BERLIN ACADEMY: MICHAËLIS AND SÜSSMILCH

Twelve years after the publication of Condillac's *Essai sur l'origines*, the Prussian Academy in Berlin set this prize-essay topic: 'What is the reciprocal influence of the opinions of the people on the language and of their language on the opinions?' The prize went to a famous professor at Göttingen, the Semitic and Arabic scholar Johann David Michaëlis, for a refreshingly unacademic, readable essay called *A Dissertation on the Influence of Opinions on Language and of Language on Opinions*, full of telling examples. It argued that language is the product of usage by generations of speakers, especially 'the fair sex' and children, who, he said, with no preconceived ideas are full of bold associations of ideas. The learned by contrast play a small role because they tend to have narrow minds and to be 'blinded by prejudices'. Echoing Locke's remarks about the 'ignorant and illiterate people' who shape language, Michaëlis declared that it is 'from the opinions of the people and the point of view in which objects appear to them that language has received its form', which make language 'a democracy in which use or custom is decided by the majority'.[49] In the course of time, 'thousands of people become contributors to that immense heap of truths and errors, of which the languages of nations are the repository' (*Dissertation*, 3). Michaëlis's essay is one of the first statements (one could even say manifestos) of the powerful folk doctrine that was emerging from Condillac's *Essai*.

The papers delivered in the Academy, and usually published in its proceedings, did not favor the divine origin of language, but that doctrine found a strong defender in Johann Peter Süssmilch with two papers in 1756. When these were not published by the Academy, he brought them out in expanded form in 1766 as *Versuch eines Beweises, dass die erste Sprache ihren Ursprung nicht vom Menschen, sondern allein vom Schoepfer erhalten habe.*[50]

Süssmilch's argument deserves attention both in its own right and as an illuminating contrast to Condillac's *Essai*: It takes the form that language is either divine or human. If human, it must be either natural or artificial. Since the sounds made by animals are natural and, for each kind, the same all over the world, human language cannot be natural in this sense. Language must be artificial and must have come about either by chance or by design. Chance can be ruled out since it would entail irregularity and lack of order, and, apart from the uselessness of such a language, all languages, even primitive ones, have rules of perfection and order – that is, design. Human language must be the work of reason and wise choice, which means that 'the first inventors of language' must already have had the use of reason in order to be able to reflect, abstract, and ratiocinate. These operations, however, cannot be performed without the use of signs, which would presuppose the prior possession of reason. Thus human beings cannot have invented language instantly or even gradually, for the latter would entail that mankind for hundreds of years lived as animals or children, incapable of conceiving the intent, let alone the goal, of any improvement. The origin must lie outside mankind in a higher, more intelligent being. It follows that 'our Creator was the first teacher of language', which by a miracle was communicated in the beginning. How this may have happened the essay naturally does not propose to examine; miracles defy explanation and understanding (*Versuch*, 13–17). Although entirely philosophical and without a single biblical citation, Süssmilch's argument confirms Scripture.

He allows that the arts have undergone gradual growth from simple beginnings toward greater perfection but does not admit anything of the sort for language (*Versuch*, 54), thus implying agreement with Condillac's belief in the radical priority of language over other human institutions. The very uniformity of grammar among languages and the free choice of signs display a formal agreement that 'forces us to go back to the one and only teacher and originator of language. . . . The form of language is not like the form of a bird's nest or beehive, which owing to innate instincts must always be formed in the same fashion' (83). Süssmilch's argument comes down to this: no reason without language, no language without reason. This is Rousseau's familiar aporia, which Süssmilch in a late addition to his essay cited in support of his position. The contrast between that position and Condillac's is shown in their conceptions of a human origin for language. Süssmilch saw it as 'invention', the term he consistently used, and Condillac as art and creation. It was a contrast between timeless wisdom beyond human reach and the gradual improvement of expression, communication, discursivity, and reason. Süssmilch made it clear that he had not read Condillac. His essay is one of the first extended treatments of the conflict between faith and natural history, anticipating the thicker debate in the nineteenth century, not least in regard to language.

IX. HERDER

Johann Gottfried Herder in 1770, wrote his prize essay on the origin of language for the Berlin Academy, *Abhandlung über den Ursprung der Sprache*, which was due for submission by the end of the year. It gained the prize and was published by the Academy in 1772. He had by then already published a good deal on familiar themes in language and literature, especially in the first of three anonymous collections of essays on modern German literature, *Über die neuere deutsche Literatur* (1766–7).[51] Herder's debt to his extensive reading of French is obvious. In a fragment called 'On the life stages of a language', Herder repeated Condillac's and Diderot's observations on the birth, formation, and maturity of a language. In the early stage, language was full of gestures, song, accents, music, and pantomime, all of which assisted the sense of speech that was coming into being. Marked by energy, poetry, and inversions, this stage developed through a middle period into the maturity of prose and well-ordered ideas that is the proper discourse of philosophy while also constituting decline and even decadence owing to loss of immediacy of emotive expression.[52]

Another fragment is devoted to inversions, again with emphasis on their prominence in the early affective language before those features gave way to prose, which has no inversions because it follows the order of ideas in the mind. In this context, Herder repeats, with similar analysis, a Latin phrase, *serpentem fuge* ('flee the serpent'), which Diderot in *Lettre sur les sourds et muets* (155–6) had used to argue that the speaker's and hearer's principal concern determines whether inversion occurs in that phrase. If the first concern is fright at the sign of the serpent, there is no inversion, but if escape is the first concern, then inversion occurs because the imperative 'flee' stands at the end.[53]

The fragment on 'Life stages' and the two other early short pieces show knowledge of Condillac's *Essai* and have dates not later than early 1765, possibly even earlier. But in an addendum to *Fragmente* III (1767), Herder wrote that he had recently, through a review published in 1766, come upon a book that cast much light on his 'Life stages'. The book was Condillac's *Essai* which he was now leafing through with delight. The implication is that 'Life stages' was written without knowledge of *Essai*. Unfortunately, Herder was fiddling with the dates, which suggests that his statements cannot always be taken at face value.[54]

In sum, (1) in the 1760s, before *Ursprung*, Herder was familiar with the conception of the language of action and its consequences; (2) he accepted this conception and made it his own to the point of largely repeating Condillac and Diderot; (3) like them he thought of language as speech and communication, not as the prior silent, mental discourse of rationalism; (4) he was committed to expressivism; (5) inversion, poetry, and creativity belonged together; and (6) for these reasons Herder's early principles are not clearly distinguishable from those of Condillac and Diderot. In *Ursprung*, Herder's conception of the nature of language is sharply at odds with his earlier beliefs.

Michaëlis had suggested in his essay that the Prussian Academy in Berlin set a topic on the origin of language, and ten years later it did so: 'Supposing that human beings were left to their own natural faculties, are they in a position to invent language [*d'inventer le langage*]? And by what means will they achieve this invention [*cette invention*]?' The answer was clearly expected to counter arguments, such as Süssmilch's, for divine origin. With no less than thirty-one submissions, this proved vastly more popular than any of the earlier topics.[55]

Ursprung is divided into two parts. In the first, we find Herder's account of the nature and origin of language. It opens with the arresting statement that 'already as an animal does man have language' (Gaier 697, Pross 253). All animals, including humans, naturally express their passions and may thereby elicit sympathetic responses in others, but since the potential for voluntary communication goes unnoticed, human language cannot have its origin here. These merely natural sounds remain 'brutish, the natural law of a sensitive machine' (Gaier 708, Pross 263). The vocal sounds Herder calls 'interjections', which shows that he is committed to Beauzée's rationalist doctrine that interjections are foreign to the true nature of language.[56] But Herder is astonished that anyone has thought it possible to explain the origin of human language from the cry of passion alone,

unless 'the intellect supervenes to use the sound with intent' in the making of a
'human, arbitrary language'. He declares that Condillac's is among such empty
accounts, giving in support an outrageously false report on the case of the two
children in the desert at the beginning of Part Two of *Essai sur l'origines*. This
is a rejection of the language of action, and from *Ursprung* one would never
appreciate that conception nor its crucial role in Condillac.[57]

Herder could hardly have failed to realize that his version of Condillac was
false, for his early writings do not show any such failure. Furthermore, *Essai*
argues that animals and humans share the capacity for reminiscence, whereas
humans alone command the memory that makes recall possible (I.2.39–40).
Though not Cartesian automatons, animals cannot cross the threshold into discursivity. Herder made this point through the familiar organismic principle that
there is 'a unique quality of thinking which, by virtue of its linkage to a certain
organization of the body, is called reason in humans but instinct in animals'
(Gaier 717, Pross 272). This nearly repeats Condillac's statement in the *Traité des
animaux* (1755) that it is no wonder that 'man, who is as superior [to animals] in
regard to organic nature [*l'organisation*] as by the nature of the mind that animates
him, alone has the gift of speech' (*Oeuvres*, 1: 361b). Herder obviously followed
Condillac in connecting the issue of animal language with that of instinct and
reason, for he cited *Traité des animaux* in support of his statement that Condillac
had made animals into human beings, a claim that is manifestly false but often
quoted with approval.

Having closed off one avenue to language, Herder seeks another in what he
sometimes calls *Besonnenheit*, a noun formed from the past participle of a verb
commonly used reflexively (*sich besinnen*), meaning to consider, reflect, discriminate, or show circumspection. Many efforts have been made to distinguish
between Herder's term and Condillac's 'reflection', but Herder in fact uses both
terms interchangeably. It has, for instance, been suggested that *Besonnenheit* is
the ability to direct attention at will, but this is precisely Condillac's explanation
of reflection. For Herder, the crucial event takes this form:

> Man being placed in the state of reflection [*Besonnenheit*] that is peculiar to him, when this
> reflection works freely for the first time [*diese Besonnenheit (Reflexion) zum erstenmal frei
> würkend*], has invented language [*hat Sprache erfunden*]. For what is reflection [*Reflexion*]?
> What is language? This reflection [*Besonnenheit*] is uniquely human and essential to the
> species, as are also language and his own invention of language. (Gaier 722, Pross 276)

Reflection makes it possible to fix attention on some particular 'among the
ocean of perceptions that rush on us through the senses'. For each object singled
out for attention, man will seek a tag (*sich Merkmale absondern*) by which the
object can be marked and recalled. This process begins with onomatopoeic tags.

For our man seeing and hearing a sheep, its bleat becomes the internal tag word (*innerliches Merkwort*) for sheep, and at that moment 'language is invented! Thus the invention of language is as natural and necessary to him as he is a human being' (Gaier 724, Pross 278). This onomatopoeic record of tags derived from the sounds of nature becomes the first human dictionary (Gaier 737, Pross 290). Tags for objects that do not resound are gained by what is known as synaesthesia, which works most powerfully in the early stages of language (Gaier 743–4, Pross 296–9). The second and shorter part of *Ursprung* shows how language subsequently becomes exteriorized as speech.

This account has a baffling feature: subjectively, the invention of language is wholly interior, private, and silent. Herder insists that this reveals the true nature of language.

> The savage, the man alone in the forest, would have invented language for himself, even if he had never spoken it. It was the soul's understanding of itself, and an understanding as inescapable as man was man. . . . [I]t is incomprehensible to me how a human soul could be what it is except by being bound to invent language also without mouth and society. (Gaier 725, Pross 279)[58]

Already in this isolated human being the mental tags were linked to what Herder, with a familiar Cartesian term, calls 'a discourse of the mind (*eine Diskurs der Seele*)'. He could not imagine that while having such strings of thought – now shifting into the first person – 'I would not carry on or strive to perform a dialogue in my mind, with the effect that this internal dialogue will prepare for external dialogue and conversation with others' (Gaier 732–3, Pross 285–7).

There is no explanation why anyone would fix attention on a sheep or on anything else among the ocean of perceptions washed onto the mind by the senses, for emotion, passion, and satisfaction of needs play no role whatever. It is as if the name-giver is moved by an intellectual urge to designate and classify in an epistemological act of cognition. Furthermore, *Ursprung* rules out the possibility of understanding the nature of language in terms of its communicative function.[59] In *Ursprung*, sociability has no place in Herder's conception of the origin and nature of language. It has the unmistakable rationalist cast that rules out expressivism.

Why should Herder so quickly have reversed his position? Bearing in mind that the name-giving in Genesis 'is for Herder, as it were, the schema for his basic philosophy of language',[60] we find a suggestion in *Ursprung* itself when Herder invokes Genesis 2:19–20 about God bringing the beasts of the field and the birds before Adam to see what he would call them. Here, spoken in 'the Oriental style', Herder finds a beautiful way of saying 'just what I am trying to prove', that 'man invented language for himself from the sounds of living nature as signs for his commanding intellect' (Gaier 736, Pross 289). In the final pages of *Ursprung*, Herder returns to the name-giving, reiterating that 'the divine origin has nothing in its favor, not even the testimony of Oriental Scriptures [the Old Testament] on which it relies, for these clearly indicate the human origin of language in the naming of the animals' (Gaier 809, Pross 356). This reading is unorthodox for two reasons: Genesis says that naming occurred before the Fall when Adam still commanded semidivine wisdom, and, secondly, the traditional reading held that Adam knew the natures he named by seeing the creatures, not by hearing them. Thus Herder presents a hybrid Adam who straddles the two realms of lapsarian division, a conception he said more about in writings on Genesis that are contemporary with *Ursprung*.

In the period immediately before *Ursprung*, Herder worked on a manuscript entitled 'About the first documents of the human species. Some observations', which is an early version of a much larger work on Genesis published a few years after *Ursprung*.[61] The latter sections of the early version show 'many analogies' with *Ursprung* – for example, that 'physical nature gave the first dictionary of names'.[62] Furthermore, *Ursprung* proclaims that human language is utterly incommensurable with animal language (Gaier 732, Pross 286); the early work on Genesis complements that it is childish to think that the Bible is God's language, for whatever that language is, it cannot have anything that is 'commensurable' with human understanding. God speaks to humanity in early forms of language, in dialects and national languages, in myth, folksong, and early poetry, all of which are commensurable among themselves by virtue of being human. Obviously, Herder would not have allowed the conceptual absurdity that God might have created several sorts of incommensurable human languages, cultures, and civilizations. In *Ursprung*, animal language stands 'total und inkommensurabel' apart from human language. This was of course also the view of Condillac, as shown by his statement that the Lithuanian boy was cut off from any possible communication with the bears among which he lived owing to lack of mutual 'analogy' between their expressive sounds and sympathetic responses. The early version argues that it is anthropocentric to believe that human language and God's language bear any relation to each other. 'God thinks without words, without symbols, without sentences, without images'.[63]

In the early version, the designative naming is a matter of Adamic hearing, which thus has the same role as in *Ursprung*, whose silent listener to the sounds of nature is a repetition of the openly theological conception of Adam in the early version. The latter also provides a motive for the naming, namely, that Herder did not wish to exalt Adam's naming as a eulogy of his philosophy, science, and theological wisdom but took it instead as an intimation of Adam's first employment in the formation of his mind and of his title to lordship over the earth and the creatures as granted in Genesis. In the naming, he was taking stock of his kingdom.

Since the theology of the early version ruled out appeal to a state of nature, it is not surprising that the first language is silent, private, designative, and formed 'without mouth and society' by the emotion-free intellect alone. Herder had no use for the language of action because its passionate expressivism was foreign to the accepted understanding of Adam's nature.

Ursprung is generally taken to be the definitive statement of Herder's philosophy of language. Yet within a dozen years he not once but twice disowned its argument. In what is generally considered Herder's greatest and also most widely read work, *Ideen zur Philosophie der Geschichte der Menschheit* (1784–91) he proclaimed that language was a divine gift.[64] Also in 1784, in his preface to the German translation of the early volumes of Lord Monboddo's *Of the Origin and Progress of Language*, Herder crowned that work as the best treatment of its subject, though it was incompatible with that of *Ursprung*. For Herder himself, *Ursprung* occupied an anomalous position in his *oeuvre*; this, along with the extreme rarity of its publication until after 1870, casts doubt on the confident claims that are being made for its vast influence. What is more, behind these claims lies a perverse but widely trusted tradition that in defiance of the evidence has made Herder into the expressivist who triumphed over the rationalism now attributed to Condillac. Herder is said to exemplify the purported 'German revolt against the soulless mechanical rationalists of the French Enlightenment'.[65]

X. SCOTLAND

In no country was language written about more widely and diversely than in Scotland, by philosophers, lawyers, clergymen, and literary figures. One reason may be that the union with England in 1707 suddenly set a high premium on a good command of correct English. A philosophical reason, often remarked on by Dugald Stewart, was the warm reception Locke had always enjoyed in the Scottish universities, with chief attention to the *Essay*'s Book Three on words and language. Still more important was probably the attitude reflected in the famous letter to the early *Edinburgh Review* (1756) in which Adam Smith urged the editor to pay as much attention to Continental as to English contributions to the learned world. He especially praised the *Encyclopédie* and its editors, describing its wide coverage: 'Theology, morals, metaphysics, the art of criticism, the history of *belles lettres*, philosophy, the literary history of sects, opinions and systems of all kinds, the chief doctrines of ancient and modern jurisprudence, nay all the nicest subtleties of grammar, are explained in a detail that is altogether surprising'.[66] Not least there was the presence of the Gaelic language, with its rich store of folklore and song, soon to become celebrated in Scottish and pan-European excitement about the poems of *Ossian*, poetry which, as Condillac had suggested, came closer to original truth and imaginative expression than the colorless speech of urban life.

Eager to advance good English and literary taste among his countrymen, Henry Home, Lord Kames, encouraged the young Adam Smith to deliver a series of public lectures on rhetoric and *belles lettres* at Edinburgh in 1748–9. They were subsequently repeated annually at Glasgow University but were never published and are only known from student notes published as *Lectures on Rhetoric and Belles Lettres*.[67] The *Lectures* presented a new and modern form of rhetoric emphasizing communication in general within the tradition from Locke. Instead of the traditional concentration on the principles of oratory in the manner of Aristotle, Cicero, and Quintilian, Smith treated rhetoric as 'the general theory of all branches of literature'. This was a rhetoric that 'must define its function as broadly communicative rather than narrowly persuasive and hence must assert jurisdiction over the forms of historical, poetical, and didactic composition no less than over the traditional forms of oratory'.[68] Smith's entirely new genre of writing about language and literature became vastly influential when American college education made 'rhetoric and belles lettres' the foundation of instruction in the liberal arts. This success had begun immediately with Hugh Blair's popular lectures at Edinburgh from 1759 onward, later published on his retirement in 1783.[69]

Smith did publish an essay entitled 'Considerations concerning the first formation of languages, and the different genius of original and compounded languages' that was a greatly expanded version of his third lecture, 'Of the origin and progress of language'.[70] Smith started from Rousseau's argument that it was virtually incomprehensible how primitive people, as the early language makers must have been, could have 'invented' – the consistent usage of both Rousseau and Smith – words for concepts and relations that imply the possession of great 'metaphysical' sophistication. Smith's first principle is that 'in the beginnings of language . . . every particularly event' was represented 'by a particular word, which expressed at once the whole of that event' (*LRBL*, 218). But given the infinite variety of events, mankind would soon begin 'to split and divide almost every event into a great number of metaphysical parts, expressed by the different parts of speech, variously combined in the different members of every phrase and sentence' (217).

Smith uses Latin illustrations of what he often, without any apparent distinction, calls 'the progress of language' or 'the progress of society'. For example, the two Latin names *Julius* and *Julia* express their distinction of gender without the need of an adjective. Or, in *fructus arboris*, 'the fruit of the tree', the genitive relation in *arboris* is expressed 'as it appears in nature, not as something separated and detached, but as thoroughly mixed and blended with the correlative object', thus surprisingly requiring, in Smith's words, no 'effort of abstraction', no 'effort of generalization', and no 'effort of comparison' (*LRBL*, 211). All those complications come into play the moment the Latin case marker is replaced by the preposition 'of'. Indeed, the prepositions that 'in modern languages hold the place of the ancient cases are, of all others, the most general, and abstract, and metaphysical; and of consequence, would probably be among the last invented' (212). Verbs were at first impersonal, merely expressing an event as in *pluit* (it rains) and *tonat* (it thunders), 'each of them expressing a complete affirmation, the whole of an event, with that perfect simplicity and unity with which the mind conceives it in nature' (216). But 'in the progress of language', those verbs would become personal. 'For the first savage inventors of language', *venit* would mean 'the lion comes', thus in one word expressing 'a complete event, without the assistance of any other' word. But with knowledge of other feared animals, *venit* would become a personal verb that could be used about the coming of any terrible object, such as a bear or a wolf.

If early language was a mass of event words that required little or no metaphysical skill, why did it not last? An answer to this question might, as Smith surely intended, answer Rousseau's puzzle. One reason is that there is a limit to the qualities and relations that can be piled into declensions and conjugations that are added to nouns and verbs, and another is, as mentioned, that the infinity of events would soon demand economy of expression. But, toward the end of 'Formation' Smith suddenly adds a third factor, the mixture of nations that has occurred in history. Children gain perfect command of their native language, but adults learning a new language 'by rote, or by what they commonly heard in conversation, would be extremely perplexed by the intricacy of its declensions and conjugations' (*LRBL*, 220). Instead of the proper case endings, they would use prepositions such as 'ad' and 'de' before nouns. A Lombard who wished to say 'I am loved' but had forgotten the word *amor* would instead say *ego sum amatus* (221). All this creates obvious problems. Why, for instance, were prepositions after all available to serve as an easy fix for a learning problem? It all sounds very much like a version of the difficulty boys have always had learning Latin in school.

The result of 'progress' is clear. Some languages, such as Greek and to a lesser degree Latin, are 'original'; they are largely unmixed and have rich inflectionality, as it were, and consequently few constraints on word order. In contrast, modern languages attained low inflectionality both by mixture and by the resolution of event words into their metaphysical elements; consequently the typical modern language became 'more intricate and complex' in structure while at the same time 'the whole system of the language became more coherent, more connected, more easily retained and comprehended' (*LRBL*, 218). The form of modern languages is prose, which with Smith's constant evocation of progress would seem a desirable result. His entire stance appears rationalistic, almost as confidently as that of Rivarol some twenty years later.

However, in the final pages, Smith, quite surprisingly, leaves no doubt that the original, uncompounded languages are much to be preferred to the modern languages, which (1) are more prolix, requiring, for instance, the expression 'I should have loved' instead of *amavissem*; (2) are less agreeable to the ear, while Greek and Latin have a 'sweetness . . . and variety unknown to any other modern language'; and (3) '[restrain] us from disposing such sounds as we have, in the manner that might be the most agreeable' (*LRBL*, 224). This last point Smith illustrates by comparing some lines translated by Milton with their original in Horace, seeking to show that Milton's English lacked the poetic and creative resources of the Latin. This is the familiar principle powerfully explicated in Condillac's chapter on inversion. It is no surprise, therefore, that Smith, in the final lines of 'Formation', exclaims: 'How much this power of transposing the order of their words must have facilitated the composition of the ancients, both in verse and prose, can hardly be imagined.' By contrast, in modern languages, the 'expression is constantly confined by [their] prolixness, constraint, and monotony'.

'Formation' is a curious performance that seems incoherent in several ways, most obviously in its concluding commitment to the perfection of the classical languages that earlier had supplied examples of the forms whose resolution into their elements illustrated Smith's idea of the progress of language. As he no doubt knew, the distinction between original and compounded languages was already current, though known by other terms. But in the well-known treatments Smith could have known, such as the chapter on inversion in Condillac's *Essai* and Beauzée's entry on that subject in the *Encyclopédie*, the discussion always centered on determining the natural order. In 'Formation', however, this issue is not even raised. 'Formation' has no place for passion or the need for social intercourse because its orientation is entirely 'metaphysical', seeking to account for the 'invention' of the parts of speech on the assumption that such invention would occur all at once in an intentional act.

This rationalist cast is paradoxical. Apart from the sudden reversal at the end, there is the more urgent question of what relation 'Formation' bears to *The Theory of Moral Sentiments*.[71] Since Smith eventually published them in the same volume, he must have had some quite close relation in mind that would become apparent to the reader, but I confess that I see only conflict or at best irrelevance. In 'Formation' there is no trace of the notions of sympathy and the impartial spectator. In contrast, *The Wealth of Nations* (Book I, ch. 2) is evidently linked to *The Theory of Moral Sentiments*. Thus the division of labor 'is not originally the effect of any human wisdom' but 'the necessary, though very slow and gradual consequence of a certain propensity in human nature', namely, 'the propensity to truck, barter, and exchange one thing for another'. This propensity is likely to be 'the necessary consequence of the faculties of reason and speech'.[72] These lines contain in brief Smith's pivotal principle of communication and exchange in the formation of social harmony and individual welfare. But in 'Formation' calculating wisdom is very much at work, and things are not 'invented' in a slow and gradual process. Oddly, 'Formation', except possibly the final pages, shows no conceptual similarity to Condillac's *Essai*, which Smith owned in an early anonymous printing.[73] Smith considered 'Formation' one of his 'favorite performances', and late in life he regretted that he 'had not written more on *language*', a subject, he said, 'of the richest kind, which had not been at all exhausted'. He even said he thought himself 'better qualified for writing such a work than any man in Britain' because he 'had thought often and long upon the subject', as shown in the specimen he had given in 'Formation'.[74]

Dugald Stewart shared Adam Smith's belief that 'the human faculties are competent to the formation of language' (*Works*, 4: 23). He was probably at least as well read in the literature on the subject as Smith and found little to admire in 'Formation', finding 'obvious and formidable' objections against it, such as Smith's belief that great philosophical effort must have gone into the invention of the prepositions that took the place of Latin noun cases. To this Stewart answered 'that the difficulty of explaining the theory of any of our intellectual operations, affords no proof of any difficulty in applying that operation to its proper practical purpose; nor is the difficulty of tracing the metaphysical history of any of our notions, a proof that in its first origin it implied any extraordinary intellectual capacity' (4: 26). It may be difficult to account for the import of 'of' and 'by', but that does not entail that the 'invention of them implied any metaphysical knowledge' in those who first used them. Even young children know the import of such words and use them correctly. This objection Stewart had brought (1: 360–5) nearly verbatim against the same 'metaphysical' difficulties raised by Rousseau and cited in the opening pages of 'Formation'. In Stewart's view, Smith and Rousseau held the same erroneous opinions.

Stewart also argued against Smith's belief that the invention of new parts of speech would occur instantaneously: '[T]he transition from substantives to adjectives, was probably not (as Mr. Smith supposes) a step taken all at once. It is by a process much more gradual and imperceptible, that all improvements in language are made' (*Works*, 4: 28–9). In support, Stewart cited Adam Ferguson's fine statement that

without the intervention of uncommon genius, [we must suppose] mankind in a succession of ages, qualified to accomplish in detail this amazing fabric of language, which, when raised to its height, appears so much above what could be ascribed to any simultaneous effort of the most sublime and comprehensive abilities. (*Works*, 4: 27; 1: 365)

Ferguson and Stewart understood very well that the origin of language could not be imagined without allowing nearly endless ages of imperceptible development. As we have seen, such understanding was rare indeed, and its acceptance in Scotland was one of the notable features of the Scottish Enlightenment. Stewart was not uncritical of Condillac, but he was certain that 'concerning the origin and theoretical history of language, Condillac was one of the first who made any considerable advances' (*Works*, 1: 361). In this regard, Stewart may be indebted to his teacher Thomas Reid.

XI. THOMAS REID

It is difficult to form a coherent picture of Adam Smith's view of language, but Thomas Reid's is perfectly clear; language mattered to him as the vessel of the shared common sense of all people:

[T]he first principles of all sciences are the dictates of common sense, and lie open to all men; and every man who has considered the structure of language in a philosophical light, will find infallible proofs that those who have framed it, and those who use it with understanding, have the power of making accurate distinctions, and of forming general conceptions, as well as Philosophers.[75]

Reid took a very wide view of language as being 'all those signs mankind uses to communicate to others their thoughts and intentions, their purposes and desires'.[76] Signs are natural or artificial. Natural signs formed an initial means of communication because there is 'in the human mind an early anticipation, neither derived from experience, nor from reason, nor from any compact or promise, that our fellow-creatures will use the same signs in language when they have the same sentiments'.[77] We are reminded of Hume's two oarsmen. Without this 'natural language', mankind 'could never have invented an artificial one by their reason and ingenuity', precisely because the natural proto-language must provide the 'compacts and agreements' in communication that must precede the 'invention' of an artificial language. The natural signs are modulations of voice, gestures, and facial expression. All the fine arts are founded on this natural language, which in all respects corresponds to Condillac's language of action. As a warrant for natural language, in his *Essays on the Intellectual Powers of Man*, Reid cites Cicero on the natural expression of emotions and Du Bos on pantomime and other details (486–7). Like Condillac, Reid thought that the virtual displacement of artificial signs for natural ones that is one of the 'refinements of civilized life' has amounted to a 'corruption' of natural language, which has lost the signs that give 'force and energy' to language by making it 'expressive and persuasive'. 'Artificial signs signify, but they do not express' (*Inquiry into the Human Mind on the Principles of Common Sense*, 53).

Reid believed it was important to study the origin of language because 'it tends to lay open some of the first principles of human nature' (*Inquiry*, 51). One of these principles, shared by Condillac and Turgot, is that the primary purpose of language is social, for a 'man, who had no intercourse with any other intelligent being, would never think of language', though once we have language it may be used for 'solitary meditations. . . . But this was not its first intention' (*Intellectual Powers*, 69). In contrast with all the efforts to analyse propositions, none have been made to analyse the 'expression of a question, of a command, or of a promise'. 'Why have speculative men laboured so anxiously to analyse our solitary operations, and given so little attention to the social? I know no other reason but this, that, in the divisions that have been made of the mind's operations, the social have been omitted, and thereby thrown behind the curtain' (*Intellectual Powers*, 70). Reid had the Cartesian tradition in mind, including the theory of ideas that he made it his chief aim to reject.

XII. HORNE TOOKE

The end of the century saw the remarkable publication of two large volumes with the curious title, *The Diversions of Purley*.[78] The work carries a head title in Greek, *Epea pteroenta*, or 'winged words', which refer to 'the artificial wings of Mercury by means of which the Argus eyes of philosophy have been cheated' (1: 27), namely by abbreviations of words that have obscured what the author considers the philosophical perfection of language. The author was John Horne Tooke, who proclaimed that 'the imperfections of philosophy' were chiefly caused by our failure properly to understand 'the perfections of language' (1: 37). He also proclaimed that 'etymology will give us in all languages what philosophy has attempted in vain' (1: 318). Thus etymology becomes the method of the entire work. When we add a third proclamation, we have the foundation of Tooke's system. 'The business of the mind, as far as it concerns language, appears to me to be very simple. It extends no farther than to receive impressions, that is to have sensations and feelings. What are called its operations, are merely the operations of language' (1: 51). This last statement sounds both materialist and somewhat mysterious, aspects well illustrated by one of his typical etymologies. The Latin word *res* for 'thing' is the source of the verb '*reor, that is, I am thing-ed*'. The English verb 'to think' is no different, 'for remember', says Tooke, 'where we now say, *I think*, the ancient expression was – *me thinketh*, that is, *me thingeth, it thingeth me*' (2: 402–6).

The first aim of language is to communicate, and the second is to do so 'with dispatch' in order to make the speed of discourse more nearly approach the speed of thought. Dispatch is created by abbreviation, which is the chief reason that language is not properly understood. Tooke recognized only two kinds of signs or words. Verbs and nouns formed one category. The verb 'must be accounted for from the necessary use of it in communication' (*Diversions*, 1: 27), but Tooke never figures out what to do with it. It is the nouns that matter, for they are the names of the impressions received by the mind. The other category contains all other words, whose nature it is to be 'merely abbreviations employed for dispatch and are the signs of other words' – that is, chiefly of nouns. Abbreviation is Tooke's great discovery, as he often proudly proclaimed. It is especially productive in the explanation of prepositions and conjunctions, as a typical example will show. The preposition 'from' has 'as clear, as precise, and at all times as uniform and unequivocal a meaning, as any word in the language'. Here, as throughout, the proof is etymological. Citing an Old English and Gothic noun 'frum', which, he says, means 'beginning, origin, source, fountain, author', he boldly asserts that '*from* merely means beginning and nothing else'. Thus the phrases 'figs come from Turkey' and 'lamp falls from ceiling' can be converted into 'figs come beginning Turkey' and 'lamp falls beginning ceiling' (1: 341–7). This shows what Tooke means when he says that 'wherever the evident meaning and origin of the particles of any language can be found, there is the certain source of the whole' (1: 147).

Tooke had a method in this seeming madness. He was attacking the philosophy of language that began with Locke. Locke's great mistake was that he judged particles to be 'not truly by themselves the names of any ideas' (Tooke, *Diversions*, 1: 225; Locke, *Essay*, III.vii.2). In fact, Locke's chapter on particles 'should have contained an account of everything but nouns' (1: 41) – that is, of Tooke's category of words that are abbreviations of other words. Tooke's bizarre etymologies provided the basis for his claim that all words, including Locke's particles, are names of impressions of the mind, and furthermore for the astonishing claim that the single true meaning of any word is at all times equivalent to the postulated etymology, as shown in the case of 'from'. These claims have three crucial consequences: (1) that the contexts in which words are used count for nothing in regard to their meaning; (2) that attending to the actual use of words is a confused and even harmful way of seeking their meaning; (3) and that the etymologized word, not the sentence, is the unit of meaning. How speakers in projecting their meanings could be sure to know or at least respect Tooke's etymological determinism is never discussed. Looking back over the eighteenth century, it is obvious that Tooke's doctrines were retrograde, for they reestablished the term-by-term conception of the nature of discourse that had been respected in the seventeenth century. The tenor of the *Diversions* reveals Tooke's mystical notion that language performs the operations normally assigned to the mind, except for the mind's passive reception of impressions.

Our sense of deep confusion and incoherence was not at all shared by Tooke's contemporaries. They were impressed by the aura of great learning created by his profuse citations in many languages, and especially by the apparently boundless knowledge of forms he cited in his etymological arguments, drawn from scores of languages, including Old English and other early Germanic languages. The work was reviewed in more than a dozen journals, in all but one of them favorably. It was considered superior to Plato's *Cratylus* and called 'the most valuable contribution to the philosophy of language, which our literature has produced'.[79] Tooke became the celebrated 'philologer', who, in the words of Erasmus Darwin, had 'unfolded in a single flash of light the whole theory of language, which has so long lain buried beneath the learned lumber of the schools'.[80] Bentham was convinced that Tooke's discovery had laid firm foundations for universal grammar and expected great things from its application to the learning of foreign languages, especially to the benefit of missionaries.[81] Hazlitt thought that Tooke had proceeded 'upon the true principles of science' by treating words 'as the chemists do substances; he separated those which are compounded from those which are not decompoundable. He did not explain the obscure by the more obscure, but the difficult by the plain, the complex by the simple'.[82]

The most important admiring convert was James Mill, who found the *Diversions* 'a profound and satisfactory' investigation, worthy 'to be ranked with the very highest discoveries which illustrate the names of speculative men'.[83] In Mill's *Analysis of the Phenomena of the Human Mind*, a title designed to evoke the chemical analogy, Tooke's philosophy played a critical role by virtue of its demonstration that the complexities of the mind are an illusion that stems from a misunderstanding of the true nature of language.[84] By tracing all words via etymology to the names of impressions, Tooke gave Mill the tools to explain the phenomena of the mind by exclusive reference to sensation and the association of ideas. The doctrine of abbreviation made it possible for Mill to make 'the human mind as plain as the road from Charing Cross to St. Paul's'.[85] It is Tooke's secure place in utilitarian philosophy that makes it impossible to ignore his strange work.

There was one dissenter, Dugald Stewart, in his essay 'On the tendency of some late philological speculations'.[86] Stewart had respect for Tooke's learning but was severely critical of his arguments and conclusions. Language is 'much more imperfect... than is commonly supposed, when considered as an organ of mental discourse'. Even in ordinary daily discourse, our words merely 'suggest *hints* to our hearers, leaving by far the principal part of the process of interpretation to be performed by the mind itself'. This implies, as had been argued in the eighteenth century, that speaking and hearing are reciprocally creative acts. Stewart compared this process to what a sketch of a profile does to the eye. It is not the minute copying 'after nature' that produces the best portrait, but the artist's skill 'in a happy selection of particulars, which are *expressive* and *significant*' (*Essays*, 153–4).

Meaning is contextual. The notion that every word in a proposition presents an idea to the understanding and that the mental act called judgment results from 'the combination and comparison' of these ideas is falsified by 'the fact, that our words, when examined separately, are often as completely insignificant as the letters of which they are composed, deriving their meaning solely from the connection, or relation, in which they stand to others' (*Essays*, 154–5). A 'problematical term' is understood 'by the general import of the sentence' in which it occurs. Naturally, Stewart also rejected the appeal to etymology in philosophical argument, a procedure he found 'altogether nugatory' and serving at best 'to throw an amusing light on the laws which regulate the operations of human fancy' (5: 161).

Stewart's critique of Tooke was cogent, but it did little to stem the reputation Tooke continued to enjoy in England for another two generations. Thanks to James Mill, the philosophy of the *Diversions* was largely taken to be sound, even though it was admitted that the etymologies were hopeless. When comparative historical philology became an academic discipline, Tooke's work was seen as a pitiful and even laughable example of 'pre-scientific' etymology, as if his aim had been to do what the new philologists now flattered themselves to be doing correctly. It was not understood that Tooke's aim was philosophical – that etymology was his method but not his aim.

This failure of understanding holds true in general for the way in which nineteenth-century language study judged the philosophy of language that flourished during the eighteenth century. Rhetorical expressivism, the aesthetics of language, the language of action, communication, sympathy, sociability, Condillac's analysis of inversion, and Diderot's notion of the poverty of language and of the individuality of expression – all these things were disdained or ignored as speculations that need not engage the attention of properly trained academics. This indifference and even hostility created a sort of intellectual void in the nineteenth century, a void that is still being papered over by a goodly amount of bad history.

NOTES

1 See Hans Aarsleff, 'The Rise and Decline of Adam and His *Ursprache* in Seventeenth-Century Thought', in *The Language of Adam/Die Sprache Adams*, ed. A. P. Coudert (Wolfenbüttel, 1999), 277–95.

2 See Étienne Bonnot de Condillac, *Oeuvres philosophiques*, ed. G. Le Roy, 3 vols. (Paris, 1947–51), 1: 3–118. References are to part, section, and paragraph. See also Condillac, *Essai sur l'origines des connaissances humaines*, ed. C. Porset (Paris, 1973), with an introduction by Jacques Derrida, translated as *The Archeology of the Frivolous: Reading Condillac*, by J. P. Leavey, Jr. (Lincoln, NB, 1987). The translation of *Essai* used here is *An Essay on the Origin of Human Knowledge*, trans. and ed. H. Aarsleff (Cambridge, 2001). *Encyclopédie* refers to *Encyclopédie, ou dictionnaire raisonné des sciences, des arts et des métiers*, eds. D. Diderot and J. d'Alembert, 28 vols. (Paris, 1751–72).

3 This is from John Millar's description of Smith's lectures on logic as reported in Dugald Stewart, 'Account of the Life and Writings of Adam Smith LL.D.', in Adam Smith, *Essays on Philosophical Subjects*, eds. W. P. D. Wightman and J. C. Bryce, in *Works* (1980), 269–351 at 274.

4 Marc Fumaroli, *L'age d'éloquence; Rhétorique et 'res literaria' de la Renaissance au seuil de l'epoque classique* (Geneva, 1980: Paris, 1994).

5 Daniel Gordon, *Citizens without Sovereignty: Equality and Sociability in French Thought (1670–1789)* (Princeton, NJ, 1994), 53.

6 David Hume, *A Treatise of Human Nature* [1739–40], eds. D. F. Norton and M. J. Norton, in *The Clarendon Edition* (2006), 3.2.2.10 , SBN 490.

7 John Locke, *An Essay Concerning Human Understanding*, ed. P. H. Nidditch, in *The Clarendon Edition* (1975); Willard Van Orman Quine, 'Two Dogmas of Empiricism', in his *From a Logical Point of View*, 2nd edn. (Cambridge, MA, 1980), 20–46.

8 *Essay*, II.xxii.2, II.xxviii.2, III.i.5, III.vi.46, III.vi.51. On the social and public nature of language in Locke, see James Tully, *A Discourse on Property: John Locke and His Adversaries* (Cambridge, 1980), 12–16; E. J. Ashworth, 'Locke on Language', *Canadian Journal of Philosophy* 14 (1984): 45–73 at 49–51, 72; Lia Formigari, *Language and Experience in Seventeenth-Century British Philosophy* (Amsterdam and Philadelphia, PA, 1988), 135–6.

9 George Berkeley, 'Seventh Dialogue' of *Alciphron, or the Minute Philosopher*, in *Works*, 3: 286–329 at 286, 298, 294–95, 293. The passage on Paul is in 'The First Draft of the 'Introduction' to *Principles*', in *Works*, 2: 137. See also David Berman, *George Berkeley: Idealism and the Man* (Oxford, 1994); Geneviève Brykman, *Berkeley: Philosophie et apologétique*, 2 vols. (Paris, 1984), 1: 462–516, and Brykman, *Berkeley et le voile des mots* (Paris, 1993), 349–401.

10 Antoine Arnauld and Pierre Nicole, *La logique ou L'art de penser*, eds. P. Clair and F. Girbal (Paris, 1965), 93–9. This is Chapter 14 in the 5th edition (1683); it was Chapter 12 in the 1st edition (1662). The fifth edition added Chapter 15, 'About Ideas that the Mind Adds to Those that Are Precisely Signified by Words'. This chapter is also about religious language.

11 Berkeley, *Works*, 2: 139.

12 Bernard Lamy, *La rhétorique, ou L'art de parler*, 4th edn. (Amsterdam, 1699). The first seven issues bore the title *L'art de parler*, but in 1688 the title was changed to *La rhétorique, ou L'art de parler* to take account of the work's new orientation and signalling a movement away from the strict Cartesianism that Lamy professed earlier in his career. Lamy's constant and radical changes constitute an archeological site for the quickly shifting views of language from rational to emotive foundations. See Ulrich Ricken, *Grammaire et philosophie au siècle des lumières* (Lille, 1978), 53–66, and Ricken, *Linguistics, Anthropology and Philosophy in the French Enlightenment: Language Theory and Ideology*, trans. R. E. Norton (London, 1994).

13 François de Salignac de la Mothe-Fénelon, *Dialogues on Eloquence*, trans. W. S. Howell (Princeton, 1951). This edition identifies Fénelon's many references to Cicero, Quintilian, and Longinus. As Howell says (46), the *Dialogues* are 'the earliest statement . . . of what may be said to have become the dominant modern attitude toward rhetoric'. See also Howell, *Eighteenth-Century British Logic and Rhetoric* (Princeton, NJ, 1971), 504–19.

14 See Cicero, *De oratore*, trans. E. W. Sutton and H. Rackham, 2 vols. (Cambridge, MA, 1942), Bk. III, 213, and *Orator*, trans. H. M. Hubbell (Cambridge, MA, 1939), 56; Quintilian, *The Orator's Education*, trans. H. E. Butler, 4 vols. (Cambridge, MA, 1969–79), III.iii.1 and XI.iii.6. In both places, Quintilian says that *actio* and *pronuntiatio* are synonyms for delivery.

15 David Hume, *An Enquiry concerning Human Understanding*, ed. T. L. Beauchamp, in *The Clarendon Edition* (2000), 5.2.18, SBN 220.

16 Jean-Baptiste Du Bos, *Réflexions critiques sur la poésie et sur la peinture* (Paris, 1719), translated as *Critical Reflections on Poetry, Painting, and Music*, trans. T. Nugent, 3 vols. (London, 1748), for example, at 1: 32. The term *sympathie* was rarely used in French at the time, but *sensibilité* either alone or suitably qualified as in 'the natural sensibility of the heart' serves just as well. The *Encyclopédie* has an entry 'Sympathie (*Physiolog.*)' (15 (1765), 736a), which opens with a glowing statement that could have come from Hume or Adam Smith.

17 Nicolas Rousseau, *Connaissance et langage chez Condillac* (Geneva, 1986), 194 (with full bibliography). See *Condillac et les problèmes du langage*, ed. J. Sgard (Geneva, 1982). For a general introduction to Condillac in English, see Catherine Hobbs Peaden, 'Condillac and the History of Rhetoric', in *Rhetorica*, 11 (1993): 136–56. See also François Dagognet, 'L'animal selon Condillac', in Condillac, *Traité des animaux* (Paris, 1987), 9–131. Dagognet dismisses the notion that Condillac was a materialist. See G. A. Wells, 'Condillac, Rousseau and Herder on the Origin of Language', *Studies on Voltaire and the Eighteenth Century*, 230 (1985): 235–46. On Condillac's aesthetics, see Annie Becq, *Genèse de l'esthétique française 1680–1814* (Paris, 1994), 444–64.

18 The entries 'Mémoire (*Metaphysiq.*)' (10 (1765), 326a–28b) and 'Réflexion (*Logique*)' (13 (1765), 885a–86a) in the *Encyclopédie* quote extensively from Condillac's *Essai*. The entry 'Signe (*Metaphysiq.*)' (15 (1765), 188a) quotes, without acknowledgement, *Essai*, I.2.35, which is cast in the first person. Presumably Condillac supplied this entry.

19 See Condillac, *Oeuvres*, 1: 733a, in his *Logique*, I.6: 'It is the use of signs that advances reflection, which in turn contributes to the multiplication of signs'.

20 See Quintilian's remark (*Orator's Education*, IV.vi.1–27) that analogy is a Greek word that was translated as 'proportion' in Latin.

21 *Condillac, lettres inédites à Gabriel Cramer*, ed. G. Le Roy (Paris, 1953), with an illuminating 'Mémoire', 89–109. Le Roy's datings have been revised by Piero Peccato in 'Note sul carteggio Condillac–Cramer', *Belfagor*, 26 (1971): 83–95. Following the Peccato datings, the letter cited is from early 1747. Maupertuis' essay was entitled 'Réflexions critiques sur l'origine des langues et la signification des mots'. In 1750, Anne-Robert-Jacques Turgot remarked on the same passage as Condillac: '[A] single person . . . would never be tempted to find marks to designate his perceptions; it is only in company [*vis-à-vis des autres*] that we seek to do that'. See *Oeuvres de Turgot*, ed. G. Schelle, 5 vols. (Paris, 1913–23), 1: 162.

22 Condillac, *Traité des sensations* (Treatise on the Sensations), in *Oeuvres*, vol. 1.

23 The quoted passages are from Isabel F. Knight, *The Geometric Spirit: The Abbé de Condillac and the French Enlightenment* (New Haven, CT, 1968), 29, 37, 85. It is telling that 'reason' has a long entry in this book's index, but 'imagination' does not occur in it. See also Hans Aarsleff, 'Condillac's Speechless Statue', in *From Locke to Saussure: Essays on the Study of Language and Intellectual History* (Minneapolis MN, 1982), 210–24.

24 Large parts of Beauzée's entries are repeated in his *Grammaire générale*, 2 vols. (Paris, 1767). For word order in Lamy, Condillac, Beauzée, and others, see Ricken, *Grammaire et philosophie*; see also Irene Monréal-Wickert, *Die Sprachforschung der Aufklärung im Spiegel der grossen französischen Enzyklopädie* (Tübingen, 1977), listing 333 linguistic entries in the *Encyclopédie*.

25 *Encyclopédie méthodique. Grammaire et littérature*, eds. N. Beauzée and J.-F. Marmontel, 3 vols. (Paris, 1782–6), I: 713a.

26 Wilhelm von Humboldt, *On Language. The Diversity of Human Language Structure and Its Influence on the Mental Development of Mankind*, trans. P. Heath, introduction by H. Aarsleff (Cambridge, 1988), 49 and liv–lvii. In the *Lettre sur les sourds et muets* (Letter on Deaf-Mutes), ed. J. Chouillet, in *Oeuvres complètes*, eds. H. Dieckmann et al. (Paris, 1975–), vol. 4 (1978), Diderot used *énergie* for a concept central also in his aesthetics. See Jacques Chouillet, *La formation des idées esthétiques de Diderot* (Paris, 1973), 151–257, and his *Diderot poète de l'énergie* (Paris, 1984), especially 27–43.

27 Antoine Rivarol, *Discours sur l'universalité de la langue française* (Paris, 1936), 49–50.

28 See Ludwig Wittgenstein's anecdote in *Philosophical Grammar*, ed. R. Rhees, trans. A. Kenny (Berkeley, CA, 1978), 107, and see his *Philosophical Investigations*, trans. G. E. M. Anscombe (Cambridge, MA, 1997), §336.

29 In William Warburton, *The Divine Legation of Moses*, 3 vols. (London, 1738–41), the section (1741) translated into French is 2: 66–205, the section on language 2: 81–87. See Warburton, *Essai sur les hiéroglyphes des egyptiens, ou l'on voit l'origine et les progrès du langage et de l'écriture, l'antiquité des sciences en Egypte, et l'origine du culte des animaux*, trans. M.-A. L. des Malpeines (Paris, 1744, 1977), where the section on language is at 118–27.

30 It has been argued that Condillac is much indebted to Bernard Mandeville's *Fable of the Bees: or, Private Vices, Publick Benefits* (1729), ed. F. B. Kaye, 2 vols. (Oxford, 1924), and that this debt rests chiefly on the language of action. See Rüdiger Schreyer, 'Condillac, Mandeville, and the origin of language', *Historiographia linguistica*, 5 (1978): 15–43. This is untenable; see Aarsleff, Introduction to *Origin*, xxxiii, note.

31 Christian Wolff, *Psychologia rationalis methodo scientifica pertractata* (Frankfurt, 1740 edn.), in *Werke*, II.6: §461.

32 For Wolff, see Ulrich Ricken in Ricken et al., *Sprachtheorie und Weltanschauung in der europäischen Aufklärung* (Berlin, 1990), 212–36; Aldo Scaglione, 'Direct vs. Inverted Order: Wolff and Condillac on the Necessity of the Signs and the Interrelationship of Language and Thinking', *Romance Philology*, 33 (1980): 496–501; Gianni Paganini, 'Signes, imagination et mémoire. De la psychologie de Wolff à l'*Essai* de Condillac', *Revue des sciences philosophiques et théologiques*, 72 (1988): 287–300.

33 Chouillet, *Formation*, 239.

34 See *Lucian*, 8 vols. (Cambridge, MA, 1913–67), vol. 5, trans. A. M. Harmon (1936), 209–89. The original Greek title is *Peri Orcheseos*, in Latin *De Saltatione*.

35 See Basil Munteano, *Constantes dialectiques en littérature et en histoire* (Paris, 1967), 139–71, 219–34, and 297–374.

36 For a fuller discussion of Wittgenstein and Condillac, see Aarsleff, Introduction, in *Origin*, pp. xxxiv–xxxviii.

37 Condillac, *Oeuvres*, 2: 463a–b, 471a; Hans Aarsleff, 'Origin of Universal Languages', *Language and Society*, 6 (1977): 281–8 at 286; N. Rousseau *Connaissance*, 281; Ricken et al., *Sprachtheorie*, 247; Umberto Eco, *The Search for the Perfect Language*, trans. J. Fentress (Oxford, 1995), 289–90. On analogy, see also note 20.

38 Antoine Lavoisier, *Méthode de nomenclature chimique* (Paris, 1787). Lavoisier relied chiefly on Condillac's *Logique*. See Marco Beretta, *The Enlightenment of Matter: The Definition of Chemistry from Agricola to Lavoisier* (Canton, MA, 1993).

39 See note 24 above.

40 Diderot, *Lettre sur les sourds et muets*, 164–5. On Diderot's *Lettre*, see Chouillet, *Formation*, 151–257; Franco Venturi, *Jeunesse de Diderot (1713–53)*, trans. J. Bertrand (Paris, 1939), 237–82. On Diderot's poetics, see Marie-Louise Roy, *Die Poetik Denis Diderots* (Munich, 1966).

41 Diderot, *Oeuvres complètes*, 7: 196, in Diderot's long entry 'Encyclopédie' in the *Encyclopédie*.

42 *Réfutation suivie de l'ouvrage d'Helvétius intitulé l'Homme*, in *Oeuvres*, ed. Laurent Versini, 5 vols. (Paris: Robert Laffont, 1994–7), vol. 1, *Philosophie*, pp. 777–923, at pp. 816 and 780. Passages on the themes of individuality, genius, and speaking occur throughout Diderot's writings; see, for example, the 'First satire', *Oeuvres complètes*, 12: 3–30.

43 Diderot, *Oeuvres complètes*, 17: 193, toward the end of *Le rêve d'Alembert*.

44 Diderot, *Lettre sur les aveugles* (Letter on the Blind) (1749), in *Oeuvres complètes*, 4: 41.

45 Diderot, *Oeuvres complètes*, 16: 219–20; that is, the *Salon de 1767* in the section (174–237) devoted to seven paintings by Joseph Vernet. For the first six paintings, Diderot creates the fiction that he and his friend are observing landscapes during a walk in the country.

46 Cicero, *Orator*, 57: '*Est autem etiam in dicendo quidam cantus obscurior.*'

47 See Wittgenstein's oft-repeated arguments to the same effect; for example, his *Zettel*, trans. G. E. M. Anscombe, eds. G. E. M. Anscombe and G. H. von Wright (Oxford, 1967), §§150, 151, 160, 161, and his *Philosophical Investigations*, I §304.

48 Diderot, *Oeuvres complètes*, 16: 217. See Wittgenstein, *Zettel*, §163: '[I]t is wrong to call understanding a process that accompanies hearing'. See also Wittgenstein, *Philosophical Investigations*, §329.

49 Johann David Michaëlis, *A Dissertation on the Influence of Opinions on Language and of Language on Opinions* (London, 1769), 12–13, 2–3. In the section on ancient history in his course of study for the Prince of Parma, Condillac included a chapter under the same title (*Oeuvres*, 2: 90–4); here he said that the essay topic was proposed by Maupertuis. 'Opinion' means 'thinking' or 'manner of thinking'. 'Ideas' would have given the question an unwanted intellectual and rationalist bias. Michaëlis's essay was published in German in 1760 and in French in 1762, with a supplement that presented one of the best available arguments against the possibility and desirability of a universal or philosophical language. The English version was translated from the French and reissued in 1771, simultaneously with a Dutch translation. Maupertuis initiated the debate on language in the Academy with two papers that are printed in *Varia linguistica*, ed. C. Porset (Bordeaux, 1970), 22–118. On the debate and its participants, see Aarsleff, *From Locke to Saussure*, 146–209.

50 Johann Peter Süssmilch, *Versuch eines Beweises, dass die erste Sprache ihren Ursprung nicht vom Menschen, sondern allein vom Schoepfer erhalten habe* (Berlin, 1766). See Bruce Kieffer, 'Herder's Treatment of Süssmilch's Theory of the Origin of Language in the *Abhandlung über den Ursprung der Sprache*: A Re-Evaluation', *The Germanic Review*, 53 (1978): 96–105.

51 Johann Gottfried Herder, *Über die neuere deutsche Literatur. Fragmente*, commonly known as *Fragmente* I, II, and III, in *Werke*, ed. W. Pross (Munich, 1984–), vol. 1, *Herder und der Sturm und Drang 1764–1774* (1984). Vol. 2, *Herder und die Anthropologie der Aufklärung* (1987) contains *Abhandlung über den Ursprung der Sprache* at 251–357. Johann Gottfried Herder, *Frühe Schriften 1764–1772*, ed. U. Gaier, in *Werke*, ed. M. Bollacher, 10 vols. (Frankfurt am Main, 1985–2000), vol. 1 (1985), where *Ursprung* is at 695–810. Both editions are richly annotated. For the dating of the *Fragmente*, see Gaier, 1007. Subsequent references are, wherever possible, to both 'Pross' and 'Gaier'.

52 'Von den Lebensaltern einer Sprache', in Gaier, 181–6. Gaier's notes refer to relevant passages in *Essai*: Gaier, p. 1035 to *Essai* II.1.§§158–63; p. 1036 to II.1.§§14–15; p. 1037 to II.1.§§66–79 (the chapter 'On the Origin of Poetry'); p. 1039 to II.1.§76 and II.1.§§155–6. See also Gaier, 947, 960. Diderot on the life stages of language is in *Lettre sur les sourds et muets*, 166–7.

53 Gaier, 216–22, referring to *Essai*, II.1.§§80–126, II.1.§94, II.1.§84, and II.1.§§1–12. Herder's remark on no inversions in the mind (219) echoes Diderot in *Lettres sur les sourds et muets* (163–4). See Eric A. Blackall, *The Emergence of German as a Literary Language 1770–1775* (Cambridge, 1959), 451–6. Herder's enthusiasm for inversion was so great that he considered it a form of 'the German freedom' that German poets enjoyed, with the implication that French poets did not have that freedom (221).

54 Gaier, 537. On the fiddling with the dates, see Aarsleff, *From Locke to Saussure*, 152; Gaier, 871–2, 944; and especially Jörn Stückrath, 'Der junge Herder als Sprach- und Literatur-theoretiker – ein Erbe des französischen Aufklärers Condillac?', in *Sturm und Drang: Ein literaturwissenschaftliches Studienbuch*, ed. W. Hinck (Frankfurt am Main, 1978), 81–96.

55 For the Academy's official French wording of the topic, see Gaier, 909–10.

56 On Herder's reading of Beauzée's entries in the *Encyclopédie*, including the great entry on 'Langue', see Pross, 907, 934, 949.

57 For Herder's misrepresentation of Condillac, see Rudolf Schottlaender, 'Die verkannte Lehre Condillacs vom Sprachursprung', *Beiträge zu romanischen Philologie*, 8 (1969): 158–65.

58 The phrase 'without mouth' may be an echo of a passage in Du Marsais's famous entry on 'Construction' in *Encyclopédie*, 4 (1754), 73b: 'Thought in so far as it is only in the mind without regard to speaking, needs neither mouth, nor tongue, nor the sound of syllables'. This in turn is, as Du Marsais points out, taken from the *Confessions*, XI.iii, in which Augustine explains that 'in that inward house of my thoughts', truth comes without language, which is always fallible and open to doubt. Augustine and Du Marsais offer impeccable rationalist credentials. For Herder's reading of 'Construction', see Pross, 906.

59 See Hans Dietrich Irmscher, 'Nachwort', in Johann Gottfried Herder, *Abhandlung über den Ursprung der Sprache*, ed. H. D. Irmscher (Stuttgart, 1966), 162.

60 Irmscher, 'Nachwart', 162.

61 The early version was first published as, 'Ueber die ersten Urkunden des menschlichen Geschlechts: Einige Anmerkungen', in Herder, *Werke*, vol. 5, *Schriften zum Alten Testament*, ed. R. Smend (1993), 11–178. The large work is *Älteste Urkunde des Menschengeschlechts*, 2 vols. (Riga, 1774–6).

62 See Günter Arnold, 'Das schaffhauser Urmanuskript der 'Ältesten Urkunde des Menschengeschlechts' und sein Verhältnis zur Druckfassung', in *Bückeburger Gespräche über Johann Gottfried Herder 1988*, ed. B. Poschman (Rinteln, 1989), here 56 and 60.

63 Herder, *Werke*, 5: 28–9.

64 See Herder, *Ideen zur Philosophie der Geschichte der Menschheit*, in *Werke*, vol. 6, ed. M. Bollacher (1989), 138 (IV.iii).

65 Noel Annan, *Our Age, Portrait of a Generation* (London, 1990), 274. Behind this fundamental misconception lies the work of Isaiah Berlin. See, for example, *Mind and Language*, ed. Samuel Guttenplan (Oxford, 1975), and, following Berlin's lead, Charles Taylor, 'The Importance of Herder', in *Isaiah Berlin, a Celebration*, eds. E. Margalit and A. Margalit (London, 1991), 40–63. Compare Stephen K. Land, *From Signs to Propositions: The Concept of Form in Eighteenth-Century Semantic Theory* (London, 1974), 71, and Hans Aarsleff, 'Herder's Cartesian *Ursprung* vs. Condillac's Expressivist *Essai*', in *Language Philosophies and the Language Sciences: A Historical Perspective in Honour of Lia Formigari* (Münster, 1996), 165–79.

66 Adam Smith, 'Letter to the *Edinburgh Review*,' in *Essays on Philosophical Subjects* (see note 3), 242–54, 247.

67 Smith, *Lectures on Rhetoric and Belles Lettres*, ed. J. C. Bryce, in *Works* (1983) (LRBL).

68 Wilbur Samuel Howell, 'The New Rhetoric Comes of Age: Adam Smith's Lectures at Edinburgh and Glasgow', in Howell, *Eighteenth-Century British Logic and Rhetoric* (see note 12),

536–76; here 547 and 575, also in *Essays on Adam Smith*, eds. A. S. Skinner and T. Wilson (Oxford, 1975), 11–43.

69 Hugh Blair, *Lectures on Rhetoric and Belles Lettres* (Edinburgh, 1783), ed. H. F. Harding, 2 vols. (Carbondale IL, 1965). By 1861, there had been at least one hundred separate issues plus translations into French, German, Spanish, and Italian. Blair says 'several ideas have been taken from a manuscript treatise on rhetoric, part of which was shown to me, many years ago, by the learned and ingenious author, Dr. Adam Smith'. (1: 381, note).

70 'Formation' is in LRBL, 201–26, first published in 1761 (Introd., 27). For the Rousseau passage, see *Discourse on the Origin and Foundation of Inequality among Men* in Rousseau, *The Discourses and Other Early Political Writings*, trans. and ed. V. Gourevitch (Cambridge, 1997), 145–9, with the two famous aporias about no society without language and vice versa and about the need of language for thinking about having language. Its arguments were criticized by Condillac in *Oeuvres*, 1: 433, and by Dugald Stewart in *Dissertation Exhibiting the Progress of Metaphysical, Ethical and Political Philosophy since the Revival of Letters in Europe*, in *Works*, ed. W. Hamilton, 11 vols. (Edinburgh and London, 1854–60), 1: 361–5.

71 Smith, *The Theory of Moral Sentiments*, eds. D. D. Raphael and A. L. Macfie, in *Works* (1976).

72 Smith, *An Inquiry into the Nature and Causes of the Wealth of Nations*, eds. R. H. Campbell, A. S. Skinner, and W. B. Todd, 2 vols., in *Works* (1976), I.ii.1–2.

73 See Land, *From Signs to Propositions*, 80–7 and 154–81; Hiroshi Mizuta, *Adam Smith's Library: A Supplement to Bonar's Catalogue with a Checklist of the Whole Library* (Cambridge, 1967). Adam Smith owned all of Condillac's works published during the latter's lifetime, except the *Logique*. See also Gabriel Girard, *Vrais principes de la langue françoise*, to which Smith referred as inspiration for 'Formation' (*Essays*, 338). He owned several editions of Lucian, of whom he says that 'in a word there is no author from whom more real instruction can be found' (*LRBL*, 51). Part II of Smith's essay 'Of the imitative arts', especially *Essays*, 187–90, and the fragment 'Of the affinity between music, dancing, and poetry' (210–13), show indebtedness to Lucian's dialogue 'The dance', which, as we have seen, became influential through Du Bos's *Réflexions*. Smith also owned other French works that are closely relevant to his professed interest in language.

74 Henry Mackenzie, *Literature and Literati: The Literary Correspondence and Notebooks of Henry Mackenzie*, ed. H. W. Drescher, 2 vols. (Frankfurt am Main, 1989 and 1999), vol. 2: *Notebooks 1763–1827*, 213.

75 Thomas Reid, *Essays on the Intellectual Powers of Man*, eds. D. R. Brookes and K. Haakonssen (Edinburgh, 2002), 466–7.

76 Reid, *An Inquiry into the Human Mind on the Principles of Common Sense*, ed. D. R. Brookes (Edinburgh, 1997), 51.

77 Reid, *Inquiry*, 193. In a note to Reid's chapter 'Of Natural Signs', William Hamilton wrote that 'this whole doctrine of *natural signs*, on which his philosophy is in great measure established, was borrowed by Reid, in principle and even in expression' from certain passages in Berkeley, including the fourth dialogue, Sections 7–12, of *Alciphron*. A comparison of the relevant passages does not support that claim. See Reid, *Philosophical Works*, ed. W. Hamilton, 2 vols. in 1 (Edinburgh, 1895), 122b. In a note on p. 146a, Hamilton said, on the authority of Dugald Stewart, that 'there is no ground for thinking that Reid was at all acquainted with the writings' of Condillac. Reid's closeness to Condillac's conceptions and the overlap of citations make that claim implausible, as does a remarkable letter in which Reid gives a striking overview of his theory of language; see Letter 102, to James Gregory, 26 August 1787, in *The Correspondence of Thomas Reid*, ed. P. B. Wood (Edinburgh, 2002).

78 John Horne Tooke, *Epea ptepoenta, or, The Diversions of Purley*, vol. 1 (London, 1786, 2nd edn. 1798), vol. 2 (London, 1805), both 'printed for the author'. There were four English reissues

during the nineteenth century. See Hans Aarsleff, *The Study of Language in England 1780–1860* (London, 1983), 44–114.

79 *Annual Review*, 4 (1805): 675–9.

80 Erasmus Darwin, *Zoonomia; or, the Laws of Organic Life*, 2 vols. (Dublin, 1800), 1: 601 (§xxxix.8.3; in 3rd edn., §xxxix.12.3).

81 Jeremy Bentham, *Works*, ed. J. Bowring, 11 vols. (Edinburgh, 1843), 8: 185 and 188 (Appendix to *Chrestomathia*, 1816).

82 William Hazlitt, *Complete Works*, ed. P. P. Howe et al., 21 vols. (London, 1930–4), 11: 55–6 ('The Late Mr. Horne Tooke', in *The Spirit of the Age*, 1825).

83 *Literary Journal*, (1806), 15.

84 James Mill, *Analysis of the Phenomena of the Human Mind*, 2 vols. (London, 1878).

85 British Museum MSS. 33, 155, Mill to Place, 8 October 1816, as quoted in Elie Halevy, *The Growth of Philosophic Radicalism*, trans. M. Morris (London, 1928), 451.

86 Dugald Stewart, *Philosophical Essays* (1810), in *Collected Works*, ed. W. Hamilton, vol. 5; here pp. 149–88.

17

RHETORIC

PETER FRANCE

Socrates . . . in his discussions separated the science of wise thinking from that of elegant speaking, though in reality they are closely linked. . . . This is the source from which has sprung the undoubtedly absurd and unprofitable and reprehensible severance between the tongue and the brain.

Cicero, *De oratore*, III.xvi

I. THE RHETORICAL TRADITION AND THE PHILOSOPHICAL CRITIQUE

It may seem strange – it would certainly have seemed strange twenty years ago – to include a chapter on rhetoric in a history of philosophy. Is not rhetoric, the art of fine speaking and unscrupulous persuasion, essentially at odds with philosophy, the pursuit of truth and wisdom? This opinion is as old as Plato's attacks on the Sophists; it attained new prominence in seventeenth- and eighteenth-century Europe and has dominated thinking about the subject ever since. I shall argue here, in the light of the recent revival of rhetorical studies[1] (including the rehabilitation of the Sophists), that relations between the two disciplines in the eighteenth century were less antagonistic and more complementary than has often been asserted.

Rhetoric and philosophy were 'disciplines' in the literal sense of the word: subjects taught in schools and colleges. As a rule, philosophy – which included science – was studied after the supposedly more elementary classes in rhetoric; in the *collèges* of eighteenth-century France, it was normal for pupils to leave school once their rhetoric was completed, leaving philosophy to specialists. On the other hand, the Renaissance, with its Ciceronian ideal of the orator as universal man, had encouraged a reversal of this order in some establishments, and certain educationalists continued to argue for this on the grounds that good communication presupposes knowledge of the matter to be communicated.

Rhetoric still held a central position in education and culture over much of eighteenth-century Europe. What then did it teach? Given the time span and the number of countries involved, any generalisations are bound to be fragile.[2] Rhetoric as a discipline had been fully established in classical Greece and Rome; the Renaissance had seen a return to the complete body of theory enshrined in the texts of Aristotle, Cicero, and Quintilian. In the eighteenth century, this full-scale, traditional rhetoric (sometimes called Ciceronian) remained strong, particularly in Catholic Europe, and found its classic form in the Jesuit colleges until they were shut down in the 1760s. It was partly the active study of a dying language, Latin, though this was being displaced by the vernacular in rhetoric classes all over Europe. It was also, increasingly, an apprenticeship in literary appreciation, the formation of polite taste. But, above all, it was an art of oral and written communication; as such, it was traditionally divided into five parts: *inventio*, the finding of material; *dispositio*, the ordering of material; *elocutio*, the verbal form; memory; and *pronuntiatio*, divided into gesture and delivery.

In many places, a much reduced form of the subject was preferred. Ramus, in the sixteenth century, had allocated *inventio* and *dispositio* to dialectic, leaving rhetoric (notably in seventeenth-century England) as essentially a stylistic doctrine whose minute description of figures of speech helped give the subject a bad name. Elsewhere, particularly in eighteenth-century Scotland, rhetoric was reformulated to suit modern demands. In some places, rhetoric was banished entirely from the curriculum as undesirable or ineffectual; such was the case in the *Realschulen* (secondary schools) of the German Pietists or, at the very end of the century, prefiguring more modern developments, in the *Écoles Centrales* of the French Revolution. If we consider Europe as a whole, however, the outright refusal of rhetoric was unusual. Most of the educated male population had some formal training in the subject, and for many it was at the centre of their schooling. The philosophers of the Enlightenment lived in a culture profoundly shaped by an art of communication and argumentation which had its roots in classical antiquity.

A well-established but oversimplified view would have it that rhetoric succumbed in the seventeenth and eighteenth centuries to the assaults of the new philosophy – to which were added, in the early nineteenth century, the effects of romantic aesthetics. The authors of a recent essay on the 'rhetoric of inquiry' affirm that 'under the onslaught of a Method claiming neutrality and universality, rhetoric fell precipitously from favour in the seventeenth century'.[3] This is misleading insofar as rhetoric continued to thrive as a practical discipline. Rumours of its death were much exaggerated; as Brian Vickers writes in his *In Defence of Rhetoric*, 'the danger is that historians take such calls for the banishment of rhetoric as proof that this duly took place',[4] whereas in reality logical or scientific language remained, to quote a recent historian of rhetoric, 'the marginal discourse of an avant-garde elite'.[5] Nonetheless, it is true that the criticism of Descartes, Hobbes, Locke, and their many followers undermined rhetoric in the long term and in the short term robbed it of a degree of prestige and even respectability, so that philosophers such as Condillac, who continued to be concerned with the thing itself, tended to fight shy of the word.

There are a number of *loci classici* for the denunciation of the art of eloquence. Descartes provides perhaps the best known of these in his *Discours de la méthode*, where rhetoric is caught up in the wholesale rejection of humanist Jesuit schooling and dismissed as useless:

Those who have the strongest reasoning powers, and who digest their thoughts best in order to render them clear and intelligible, are always the best at persuading, even if they speak Breton and have never learnt rhetoric.[6]

A rhetorician would of course object that the programme outlined here (clarity, well-digested thought) is visibly indebted to the discipline under attack, and Descartes himself, like many opponents of rhetoric, was a practised communicator. A constant feature of this debate is that critics of rhetoric are skilled rhetoricians.

Following Descartes, the influential *Port-Royal Logic* of Arnauld and Nicole denounced in particular the doctrine of topics; these were the 'places' or general heads (similarity, difference, definition, and so forth) under which a speaker could search for all the material relevant to a given case. According to the Port-Royalists, they produced obfuscating verbiage at the expense of clear reasoning on the facts of a case.[7] Even worse, from a Cartesian point of view, was the rhetorician's reliance on probability (in other words, what corresponds to the general opinion) rather than the clear and distinct 'evidence' that can emerge intact from the test of methodical doubt. In other words, rhetoric seemed incompatible with the emerging scientific method – although it should be noted that Arnauld was fully alive to its value in such fields as preaching; he defended the appeal to the passions and imagination in a famous polemic against the puritanical François Lamy in the final years of the seventeenth century.[8]

England as well as France contributed to the attack on rhetoric. Again this applied largely to scientific communication; the Royal Society, recommending plain speaking ('the language of artisans, countrymen and merchants before that of wits or scholars'), deplored the irrational effect of figures of rhetoric: 'They are in open defiance against reason, professing not to hold much correspondence with that, but with its slaves, the passions. Who can behold, without indignation, how many mists and uncertainties these specious tropes and figures have brought on our knowledge?'[9]

The influential voice of John Locke was added to the anti-rhetorical chorus. In *Some Thoughts Concerning Education*, speaking from his experience as an

Oxford tutor, he condemned rhetoric (especially Latin rhetoric) as ineffectual and time-wasting, though he does suggest his own simplified English-language rhetoric involving exercise, application, good rules, and good examples (for example, Cicero) and focussing on the type of communication most important for gentlemen, the letter. It is in *An Essay Concerning Human Understanding*, however, that Locke launches his most damaging attack:

All the art of rhetoric, besides order and clearness, all the artificial and figurative application of words eloquence hath invented, are for nothing else but to insinuate wrong ideas, move the passions and thereby mislead the judgement; and so indeed are a perfect cheat.[10]

As with Descartes, the art of communication is reduced to 'order and clearness'. As against an art of persuasion, Locke and his school aim for a form of language adequate to facts, words being made to reflect the clear ideas of things.

Such is the tradition of argumentation, already established by 1700, on which philosophical opponents of rhetoric will continue to draw throughout the eighteenth century – a new line is opened up by Kant in his *Kritik der Urtheilskraft*,[11] where the deceits of rhetoric are opposed to the higher truth of poetry. The main heads of accusation are that rhetoric is (1) deceptive and unscrupulous; (2) concerned with probability rather than truth; (3) time-wasting in its concentration on Latin and outmoded exercises; and (4) ineffective and perhaps entirely superfluous since true eloquence comes from nature and cannot be taught. It is principally the third and fourth of these, implying that rhetoric is foolish rather than dangerous, which find expression in what are probably the best-known eighteenth-century broadsides against the traditional discipline, those contained in d'Alembert's *Discours préliminaire* to the French *Encyclopédie* and in the article 'Collège' which he contributed to that compendium of Enlightenment thinking. These mock the 'pedantic puerility' of 'amplifications' and similar college exercises and dismiss the figures of rhetoric ('so dear to certain modern pedants') as beneath contempt.[12]

The actual practise of the colleges was in 1750 by no means as grotesque as d'Alembert claims and was already evolving in the direction he would have preferred. Nor did this partisan attack by an enemy of the Jesuits prevent the *Encyclopédie* from including many quite traditional articles on various aspects of rhetoric. One should note, moreover, that d'Alembert was fully aware of the need for eloquence in civil life. Indeed, part of the point of his attack was not so much to dismiss rhetoric as to suggest that Jesuit rhetoric was to the art of oratory what Scholasticism was to true philosophy. Since persuasive speech was as needed in the modern world as it ever had been, this left it open for the new age (the age of philosophy) to imagine a new rhetoric. D'Alembert did not think that eloquence depended on teaching and wrote in his *Encyclopédie* article 'Elocution' that 'elocution is no more than the husk of eloquence'; in this article he nevertheless outlined the principal rules of the art, basing himself on the 'masters' (Cicero, Quintilian, and others) but offering his own independent-minded reflections. Not being a teacher, he never tried to produce anything like a full-scale philosophical rhetoric. Across Europe, however, we can trace the attempts of many eighteenth-century philosophers to adapt traditional rhetoric to modern needs, in some cases going so far as to offer a radically new theory of communication.

II. PHILOSOPHICAL RHETORIC

In the schools and universities, the same teachers often taught rhetoric and philosophy. In the Jesuit and Oratorian colleges, it was common for the teachers to move up from class to class with their pupils; in Scottish universities (at Edinburgh, for instance, before the founding in 1762 of a new chair of rhetoric and belles lettres), rhetoric classes were among the duties of the professors of logic, moral philosophy, or metaphysics. Professionally, therefore, many philosophers – using the term in its broad eighteenth-century sense – found themselves obliged to teach rhetoric or its equivalent; the list includes Vico in Naples, Lomonosov in St. Petersburg, Adam Smith in Glasgow, Condillac as tutor to the Prince of Parma, and Priestley at the dissenting academy of Warrington. Rather than simply going through the usual motions, these writers, and many others, attempted to rethink the discipline, whether to reject traditional approaches or to marry them with the demands of the modern world and the new philosophy.

Wilbur Samuel Howell, in his important studies of logic and rhetoric in seventeenth- and eighteenth-century Britain,[13] has used the term 'new rhetoric' to designate a non-traditional approach to communication – particularly to learned communication – which was developed primarily in England and Scotland. Inspired by Locke – but also by French precursors, including Arnauld, Bernard Lamy, and Fénelon – teachers such as Adam Smith, Hugh Blair, George Campbell, Joseph Priestley, and the American John Witherspoon elaborated a communicative strategy which was different from logic but avoided the pitfalls of Ciceronian rhetoric.

According to Howell, the 'new rhetoric' had six distinguishing features:

1. the extension of the field of rhetoric to include both learned communication and belles lettres as well as oratory;
2. the use of 'non-artistic' proofs, that is, those furnished by the subject itself rather than the use of *topoi*;

3. the priority given to inductive proof as opposed to the syllogism or its rhetorical counterpart, the enthymeme;
4. the refusal of mere probability as opposed to scientific certainty;
5. the preference of a simpler form of speech than that associated with Ciceronian oratory;
6. hostility to tropes and figures of speech. (Howell, 441–7)

In part, this is advice on how to write philosophical or scientific papers for a nonspecialist audience. Insofar as the 'new rhetoric' goes beyond this – and Smith, Priestley, and other teachers were certainly aiming at a more general theory taking in all kinds of speech and writing – the most important recommendations are probably those calling for a straightforward, natural style. This is what lies behind Smith's condemnation of Shaftesbury's *Characteristicks*[14] (one of the bugbears of the Scottish rhetoricians, and not only on stylistic grounds):

[I]t is plain this author had it greatly in view to go out of the common road in his writings and to dignify his style by never using common phrases or even names for things, and we see hardly any expression in his works but what would appear absurd in common conversation.[15]

Whether in philosophical writing or ordinary life, Smith's guidance warns against the 'excesses' of a rhetoric in which exuberance and amplification are highly valued. At times, particularly when talking of the theory of the tropes ('a very silly set of books'), he seems impatient with the whole rhetorical enterprise as it is enshrined in the work of a Quintilian (an author much admired by his compatriot Blair). However, it is not difficult to find parallels in previous centuries for his praise of naturalness, and Vickers is probably right to see Howell's new rhetoric as one more episode in a long-standing battle between functional and decorative conceptions of the art. He is right, too, to take issue with Howell's teleological view of the subject, his prejudice in favour of plainness.[16] Even so, one can hardly deny that the new (Lockean, Cartesian) philosophy left its mark on some of the more remarkable rhetorical writings of the eighteenth century. Since Howell has dealt at length with the British, it may be useful here to illustrate this point in more detail from one of the most original philosophical rhetorics of the age, *L'art d'écrire*[17] of Condillac, a treatise that exercised considerable influence on the French *Idéologues* at the end of the century.

The work is never described by its author as a rhetoric. Within the *Cours d'étude*, which he composed from 1758 to 1767 for his young pupil, the Prince of Parma, it is one of four treatises – a grammar, an art of writing, an art of reasoning, and an art of thinking – all of which, says the author, can be subsumed under a single heading, the art of speaking (*l'art de parler*).[18] However, *L'art de parler* was the subtitle of *La rhétorique*, the famous rhetoric book by Bernard

Lamy, first published in 1675, and Condillac's use of the term is a clear reference to rhetoric, even though he tends to avoid the word and sometimes speaks with disdain of rhetoricians.

Throughout *L'art d'écrire*, rhetoric and philosophy are indissolubly linked. Speaking well, Condillac tells his pupil, depends on thinking well, which in turn depends on *analysis*. The ideal is to reflect in speech or writing the proper association of ideas (*liaison des idées*), each idea being represented by the appropriate expression. If our thinking and speaking are faulty, this stems largely from the bad habits picked up in childhood, as Condillac explains in his *Essai sur l'origine des connaissances humaines*: '[I]f, reflecting on the children we see, we remember the state we have passed through, we will recognize that there is nothing less exact than the use we ordinarily make of words'. We can, however, observe that whenever we express ourselves effectively, we conform to 'the principle of the closest possible association [*la plus grande liaison*]'.[19] This is demonstrated at the beginning of *L'art d'écrire* by a detailed analysis of an Academy speech given by Racine; Condillac shows how Racine's text corresponds, both in its overall structure (paragraphs, order of sentences) and in its detailed form (punctuation, sentence construction), to a well-ordered thought process.

Some of Condillac's remarks are quite elementary (his pupil was still very young), but they correspond to an important philosophical position – that language is the instrument that allows us to analyse our ideas. But if speaking well depends on thinking well, it does not follow that, as Boileau put it in a famous line, 'what is properly conceived, is clearly expressed'. It is possible to think clearly but write obscurely, since it 'is also necessary to learn the successive order in which you must communicate the ideas which you perceive simultaneously' (*Cours d'étude*, I: 539). Writing is an art that can be taught, and success in this art can be decisively judged by recourse to the criterion of *liaison des idées*. Although many of Condillac's stylistic preferences (such as for Racine and Bossuet) are quite familiar from French classical criticism, his specific criterion does allow him to be quite independent at times. Thus he defends ellipsis, often condemned by grammarians as incorrect, on the grounds that when well used it has the effect of bringing the ideas expressed into closer connection with one another.

In addition to the *liaison des idées*, Condillac distinguished two other qualities essential to good writing: *netteté* and *caractère*. The former is unproblematic; it involves ordering one's ideas in such a way as to avoid anything that might interfere with correct comprehension of the thought expressed. Positive and negative examples from French classical literature are used to hammer home a lesson that does not differ from the precepts of Descartes and Locke.

All I have said so far might suggest that Condillac is a strict devotee of a distinctly puritanical 'new rhetoric'. His second essential quality, *le caractère*, takes him into more interesting, and more traditionally rhetorical, areas. It designates the specific coloration of any particular thought, deriving from the nature and situation of the writer or speaker – and indeed of the reader and listener. If *netteté* means ordering the basic ideas correctly, *caractère* depends on the 'turns of phrase' (*tours*) that allow one to express a thought 'with all its modifications' (*Cours d'étude*, 1: 547). Every thought is seen in a particular light by a particular individual, and it is this personal, emotional element that the *caractère* of good writing will communicate. In practice, many of the turns of phrase turn out to be the familiar tropes and figures so often scorned by philosophical enemies of rhetoric; Condillac, while dogmatically critical of certain stylistic affectations, turns out to be surprisingly tolerant of certain liberties. Metaphors, for instance, as long as they correspond to a correct view of things, 'are never so beautiful as when they are remote [*tirées de loin*]' (1: 565).

What we see here is one of the constants of philosophical rhetoric in the second half of the century, the interest in the psychology of figurative expression. This is most impressively put by John Millar, recalling in 1793 the distinctive quality of Adam Smith's lectures:

The best method of explaining and illustrating the various powers of the human mind, the most useful part of metaphysics, arises from an examination of the several ways of communicating our thoughts through speech, and from an attention to the principles of those literary compositions which contribute to persuasion and entertainment.[20]

What is proposed here is more than training in good composition and good taste. Rhetoric, approached in this way, is less an art than an essential constituent of the 'science of man' which dominates so much eighteenth-century philosophy. In theory, moreover, there was no reason for the philosophical rhetorician to privilege one style over another since all were equally revealing of the workings of the mind and could be studied with scientific detachment.

In practice, the rhetorical teaching of writers of this 'psychological' school, such as *The Philosophy of Rhetoric* of George Campbell (who exploits a vein opened up by Lord Kames's *Elements of Criticism*) or Joseph Priestley's *A Course of Lectures on Oratory and Criticism*, is fairly prescriptive.[21] They offer guidance on effective writing based on a psychology of literary reception rather than what we would now call an expressive stylistics. Priestley, for instance, publishes his *Lectures* as an 'illustration of the [Hartleyan] doctrine of the association of ideas'.[22] It is the association of ideas that underpins his defence of the despised topics, which are seen as corresponding to the normal working of the mind. The same doctrine governs his treatment of rhetorical *dispositio*, an independent-minded discussion of the various ways of ordering material and their effect on the reader's or listener's thought processes, and his advice on the most effective use of metaphor and simile.

In analysing the effect of figures of speech, Priestley stresses the pleasure produced in the reader by the mental activity that is needed to move between figurative and literal uses of a word. The same approach is perhaps most fully developed in a rather forbidding work by the Italian philosopher Cesare Beccaria, better known for his work on crime and punishment. His unfinished *Richerche intorno alla natura dello stile* (ca. 1770)[23] starts from the observation that existing works on poetics and rhetoric, although they give excellent advice, fail to trace back to their psychological sources the pleasure or displeasure given by works of literature. Beccaria was not a teacher; his discussion of these matters is offered in a spirit of disinterested curiosity, although it does lead to practical advice on effective writing. In his view, the choice of expressions can be understood quantitatively; the reader must be assailed by the greatest possible number of strong ideas, and this is done by means of the accessory ideas and sensations aroused by the words chosen. On the other hand, the mind cannot cope with more than four or five ideas at once without feeling confused or bored; this fact of human nature offers a basis for preferring a style that is both concise and sufficiently complex to provide the pleasure of mental activity.

The art of writing and speaking outlined by Condillac or the Scottish rhetoricians may be seen as an Enlightenment rhetoric, deriving from Descartes, Locke, and others an insistence on clear and properly connected ideas. At the beginning of the eighteenth century, however, there was one important philosopher whose rhetorical theories were directed *against* the new philosophy. Giambattista Vico, little attended to in his day, although later hailed as a 'universal precursor', was for several decades professor of rhetoric at Naples. One of his duties was to give inaugural addresses at the beginning of the academic year, and in some of these, notably that of 1708 entitled *De nostri temporis studiorum ratione*,[24] he compared traditional and modern study methods in such a way as to show the limitations of the all-conquering geometrical method of Descartes. Vico was a post-Baconian modern in his ambitions but was unwilling to forgo the advantages of Renaissance humanism, where rhetoric had a central role. Nor was this view confined to the inaugural discourses; it is implicit in his *Princípi di una scienza nuova* (Principles of a new science), with its rehabilitation of imagination and poetry as fundamentally creative rather than ornamental,[25] it is explicitly repeated in letters written after the publication of his masterpiece, notably that of 12 January 1729 to Francesco Solla, and it is put into practice in his textbook, the *Institutiones oratoriae*.

Against the new mathematical, critical method, which is good only for scientific specialists (if that), Vico promotes a public philosophy concerned with the life of human beings in civil society. Here the Cartesian search for absolute certainty is out of place. To refuse the probabilities of rhetorical persuasion is to refuse the reality of life, 'for nature is uncertain, and the chief, indeed the sole, end of the arts is to assure us that we have acted correctly' (*Scienza nuova*, 39). What is needed is the practical wisdom that rhetoric promotes.

Where the Port-Royalists had attacked the topics, Vico, in his address *De antiquissima italorum sapientia*, stresses their indispensable role in philosophical inquiry.[26] Like Priestley many years later, he argues that they lead us to see all sides of a question. To be confident, like the Cartesians, in the certainty of what appear to be clear and distinct ideas is to be easily deceived; what one needs is to 'range through all the general heads of the topics with a critical torch'. In Vico's words, 'the critical method may be the art of true oratory, but topics is the art of eloquent oratory' (73); the two are equally important and need to be combined in educational practice. Since, however, young people are best placed to cultivate invention and imagination, the teaching of topics should precede that of critical method. Whereas Descartes deplores the lasting effect of childhood errors – and by extension of the childhood of humanity – Vico sees the creative value of the youthful and primitive imagination and seeks to incorporate it into his philosophy. Without this element, philosophy is for him an arid discipline; he remarks that in Cicero's time philosophy was eloquent, but now 'it is taught in such a way as to dry up all of the springs which make oratory convincing, eloquent, pointed, ornate, well-ordered, full, expressive and impassioned' (42).

Vico's ideal philosopher is thus not so much the isolated scientist, logician, or metaphysician but the citizen concerned for the life of the *polis* (even if, as he admits, the rise of monarchy has reduced the scope for political oratory). In saying this, he is not refusing the claims of truth but calling for philosophers 'who are also courtiers, who care for truth, but of the kind that is seen' (hence his admiration for Bacon). The rhetorically aware and ethically concerned philosopher, with his knowledge of 'the nature of the human mind, its passions, and how they are related to civil life and eloquence', will know the importance of 'common sense' – not Descartes's radical 'good sense' but the consensus of citizens about the probable truth.

It follows from this that passionate persuasion is not alien to philosophy but a necessary adjunct to it (as for many preachers it was to the pure word of God). Vico opposes his own rhetoric to that of the Cartesians in this eloquent passage:

As for eloquence, the same men [Cartesians] declare that their own method of study, far from causing inconvenience, provides the greatest of benefits. 'How much better it is', they claim, 'for true arguments to make that impression on the mind that unites with reason and can never be separated from it, than to sway the passions by those charms of oratory and fires of eloquence which, when they are extinguished, allow the mind to return to its natural inclinations.' But what is one to do if eloquence is concerned not with the mind, but with the passions? . . . Eloquence is the power of persuading people to duty, and the persuasive orator is he who produces in the listener the degree of passion that he desires. (*De antiquissima italorum sapientio*, 44)

It is of course a professor of rhetoric who is speaking, but one for whom, as for Cicero, the divorce of rhetoric and philosophy is a development greatly to be deplored. In this, Vico appears as the most important precursor of the twentieth-century so-called *nouvelle rhétorique*, the return to an Aristotelian art of argumentation championed by Chaïm Perelman.[27]

III. RHETORICAL PHILOSOPHY

Vico's defence of rhetoric against the new philosophy seems to have been little read at the time. His call for philosophers who are also 'courtiers' does, however, correspond to a characteristically eighteenth-century view of philosophy. The philosopher lives in the world; he (the philosopher being a male in this discourse) owes it to his fellows to communicate his ideas, to persuade people, to persuade society. The model of communication is as much the crusade as the seminar – and this of course implies a rhetoric.

It may be objected that we are talking here of two different things: the philosopher as searcher for truth and the philosopher as ideologue. But one feature of this period is precisely the convergence of the two – a neat example being the statement in the *Encyclopédie* article entitled 'Philosophe' that 'reason demands that he study and work to acquire sociable qualities'. The justification of philosophy and science is their ability to serve the needs of society, and this implies addressing a broader public than fellow philosophers – who are themselves not simply disembodied intellects. To use an old emblem, the open hand of rhetoric is needed as well as the closed fist of logic. Writers must adapt themselves to an audience, using the skills of the orator to win a hearing for their ideas. This involves, among other things, the choice of the appropriate genre (treatise, essay, dialogue, letter, and so on), the attempt to convey the desired image of the writer (what the rhetoricians knew as *ethos*), and the adoption of the right kind of style to fit the subject and the audience.

This stress on the public role of the philosopher is particularly evident in the *philosophes* of the French Enlightenment – who were certainly philosophers in their own time, even if they do not bulk large in many histories of philosophy. Fontenelle, who lived from 1657 to 1757, provides an emblematic case. He was a cautious man, and a famous anecdote recounts him saying: 'If I had my hand full of truths, I would take care not to open it.' Even so, as perpetual secretary of the French Academy of Sciences, he was one of the *philosophes* who did most, in his accounts of the proceedings of the Academy, his obituaries (*éloges*) of deceased Academicians, and his many other writings, to bring the new philosophy to the attention of the public. As such, he was given an honourable place in the roll call of the fathers of enlightenment in d'Alembert's *Discours préliminaire d'Encyclopédie*. Praising his clarity, precision and method, d'Alembert adds:

> He even dared to lend Philosophy the ornaments which seemed most foreign to her, and which she seemed obliged to deny herself the most severely, and this daring was justified by the most general and the most gratifying success. (*Encyclopédie*, I: xxx–xxxi)

The reference here is above all to a work published in 1686 but belonging in spirit to the eighteenth century, Fontenelle's *Entretiens sur la pluralité des mondes*.[28] This consists of dialogues between a philosopher and a lady about the new Cartesian cosmology; the inclusion of the female speaker implies communication with the nonspecialist world of polite society. The choice of the sociable dialogue form is essential. In the case of the *Entretiens*, it is a popularising genre, as it had been in Descartes's *Recherche de la vérité* (The Search for Truth); elsewhere, notably in Diderot's writings, it is rather the necessary road to knowledge, understanding, and belief and less a device for making ideas more attractive than a part of the very process of philosophising.

In Fontenelle's popularising, the 'flowers' of eloquence are hung on the 'thorns' of reason. One of these flowers is comparison. In order to open his interlocutor's mind to the possibility of imperceptible yet substantial change in the order of things, the philosopher imagines the short-lived roses in a garden, reasoning thus: 'We have always seen the same gardener, in roses's memory no other has been seen. He has always been as he is, certainly he does not die like us, he does not even change', and asks: 'Would the roses' reasoning be correct?'[29] Interestingly, this passage is referred to by Diderot in his own dialogue between a scientist and a woman about science and cosmology, *Le rêve de d'Alembert*. The woman, Mademoiselle de Lespinasse, remarks how charming it is and wishes that philosophers would talk or write that way more often. The scientist, Bordeu, replies that such frivolity is hardly suitable to the discussion of serious questions.[30]

Despite Bordeu's objection, such ornaments are not untypical of the way French Enlightenment philosophy adapts itself to the elite world of the salons. In such a situation, the philosopher is an amphibian. As the anonymous Jesuit who authored *Mémoires de Trévoux* put it in 1751, 'when one is making observations in a physics laboratory, . . . everything is done with the simplicity of nature and reason, . . . but when one comes to communicate the new discoveries to the public, then is the time to speak a little to the imagination, to borrow colours'.[31] Such a demand might be irksome to the philosopher; in his *Essai sur la société des gens de lettres avec les grands*, d'Alembert remarks wryly: 'In England they were content with Newton being the greatest mathematician of his time; in France they would have wanted him to be agreeable into the bargain.'[32]

When d'Alembert makes this contrast, he is of course using an idealised England, as Voltaire had before him, to point up the shortcomings of France. In fact, in England as across the Channel, philosophy often felt the need to appear in an 'agreeable' guise. This was true also in Scotland, as it developed its enlightened culture. Hume, a Scottish partisan of French politeness, provides good examples, in theory and practice, of the rhetoric of philosophy.

In his day, Hume was better known to the general public as a historian and essayist than as a philosopher of the mind. In an early essay, 'On Essay Writing' (included in the 1742 editions of the *Essays Moral and Political* but thereafter omitted), Hume notes that 'the separation of the learned from the conversible world seems to have been the great defect of the last age' and is glad to observe that 'in this age' the gap is being narrowed by such persons as the essay writer, 'an ambassador from the domains of learning to those of conversation'.[33] The politeness to which the essays contribute is an essential component of the Enlightenment programme; it means polishing and softening the manners of society, preferring civilised debate to rancorous disputation. Of course, the philosopher, like the good rhetorician, must avoid frivolity, flattery, and the unscrupulous use of art to beguile the reason. Eloquence is not without its problems, but it is essential.

As an 'ambassador', then, Hume wrote essays; he also, like Shaftesbury, Berkeley, and Diderot, wrote dialogues. The *Dialogues concerning Natural Religion* are not pedagogical, like Fontenelle's *Entretiens*, but embody what reads almost like genuine debate, with the powerful use of persuasive eloquence by all three speakers. Hume's preface, moreover, offers a fascinating discussion of the dialogue form. He is obviously uneasy at the familiar rhetorical dressing up of philosophical ideas, regarding it as unnatural and time-wasting, but claims that in the case of religious inquiry, the form is justified both by the familiarity of the subject and by the undecidability of the issues raised. So, he writes, 'the book carries us, in a manner, into company, and unites the two greatest and purest pleasures of human life, study and society'.[34]

Of particular interest are the opening pages of Hume's *Enquiry concerning Human Understanding*, a deliberately more accessible reworking of material from the *Treatise of Human Nature*.[35] Here he contrasts the 'easy' and 'accurate' modes of philosophising. The first is rhetorical in nature; its aim is to encourage its readers to live well rather than to think properly; it does so by 'represent[ing] the common sense of mankind in more beautiful and more engaging colours' (*Enquiry*, 1.4, SBN 7). 'Common sense' is the general opinion, the verisimilitude that seemed so important to Vico; 'colours', a word associated with cosmetic falsehood by Descartes, evokes the riches of rhetorical *elocutio*. Hume is full of apparently genuine praise for this easy method (which we today should hardly call philosophy at all) as being the more useful and bringing the more durable fame. Addison, for instance, 'perhaps will be read with pleasure, when Locke shall be entirely forgotten' (1.4, SBN 7).

Hume himself, however, is committed in the *Enquiry* to the 'accurate' method, which he describes as a rebarbative enterprise. It will appeal to few readers, but it is essential for it means examining what would otherwise go unexamined; only in this way can the new science of human nature be advanced. Hume uses some 'colours' of rhetoric, notably metaphor, to present this second way. Where the 'easy' philosopher is a painter, enchanting the senses with his pictures, the 'accurate' writer is seen as weighing, scrutinising, and examining minutely.

What then is the relation between these two pursuits? The same person can no doubt engage in both, as Hume himself does. He tends, however, to present them as opposites: on the one hand, what we would now call philosophy or science, on the other, literature and eloquence. This gives such pairs as Aristotle versus Cicero, Malebranche versus La Bruyère, or Locke versus Addison. And for all the prestige attached to the 'easy', it does in fact depend on the 'accurate'. Hume talks of the 'subserviency' of the latter to the former but in such a way as to make it clear that the accurate philosopher is the pioneer. Indeed this whole introductory section may be seen as a skilful argument in favour of the less eloquent form of philosophy.

Hume seems then to be establishing a dichotomy between a fundamental philosophy of inquiry, relatively untouched by rhetorical concerns, and a popularising rhetoric of communication with the general public. This distinction would seem highly dubious to much modern theory, which stresses the rhetoricity of all forms of discourse. In fact, the separation proposed by Hume is by no means an absolute one. The end of the chapter suggests the possibility of 'reconciling profound enquiry with clearness, and truth with novelty', of gaining the critical purchase on error offered by the accurate method while still 'reasoning in this easy manner' (*Enquiry*, 1.17, SBN 16). The body of the *Enquiry* bears witness to Hume's success in this undertaking.

Although at the end of Section VII of the *Enquiry* Hume again distances himself from the 'flowers of rhetoric', his whole approach is persuasively rhetorical. This is inevitable not only because he is wooing a broader public than in the *Treatise* but because, as he himself declares, he is concerned with questions that admit no certainty and where proof is dependent on producing arguments of greater effectiveness. Again and again he appeals to what Vico would have called the 'common sense' of humanity with phrases such as the one that opens

Section II: '[e]veryone will readily allow'. If one thinks of the mocking echo of such common-sense axioms at the beginning of Jane Austen's *Pride and Prejudice* ('It is a truth universally acknowledged, that a young man in possession of a good fortune must be in want of a wife'), one realises that this universality is often quite local.[36] So when Hume, discussing 'secret powers', writes: 'Our senses inform us of the colour, weight and consistence of bread; but neither sense nor reason can ever inform us of those qualities, which fit it for the nourishment and support of a human body' (4.2.16, SBN 33), his appeal to the 'common sense' of his day seems less convincing two and a half centuries later.

It would be tedious to enumerate the many elements that make up Hume's philosophical eloquence. One notices such features as the symmetrical short sentence to clinch a line of argument ('The most lively thought is still inferior to the dullest sensation' (2.1, SBN 17)), the unavoidable and eloquent recourse to metaphor ('while we march through such difficult paths, without any guide or direction' (4.1.3, SBN 26)), and more broadly the appeal to what Hume calls the affections. This is particularly evident in such passages as the defence of scepticism, where he defends his position with Ciceronian verve:

Nothing, therefore, can be more contrary than such a philosophy to the supine indolence of the mind, its rash arrogance, its lofty pretensions, and its superstitious credulity. Every passion is mortified by it, except the love of truth; and that passion never is, nor can be carried to too high a degree. (5.1.1, SBN 41)

The appeal to the emotions is a part of what from a rhetorical point of view is most striking in this work: the establishment of a relationship between author and reader – a relationship which often resembles that of speaker and interlocutor. This also involves what the rhetoricians called *ethos*, the creation, mainly by indirect means, of an image of the speaker that predisposes the audience in his favour. In the opening section, we have seen the real or apparent modesty with which Hume allows greater value to the 'easy' philosophy; this is coupled, however, with the acceptance of a heroic and necessary task, that of 'carrying the war into the most secret recesses of the enemy' (superstition). But lest this should seem bombastic, the man of good humour adds: 'We must submit to this fatigue, in order to live at ease ever after' (1.12, SBN 12). And throughout the work, although a vehement and aggressive tone surfaces from time to time, the dominant impression given by the writing is that of the modest, reasonable, good-humoured, and witty person of good company, a practitioner of the politeness he so much favoured.

As well as creating an image of himself, Hume seeks to involve the reader in his inquiry, to accompany him on his search for truth. It is our, the readers', experience that is being appealed to in such formulas as 'it will be readily allowed', and Hume makes a constant use of the pedagogical 'we' to bind his readers to himself (for example, 'If we consider the matter more narrowly, we shall be apt to draw a quite opposite conclusion' (8.1.1, SBN 80)). He also seeks to anticipate their reactions, noting for instance, on the problem of liberty and necessity, that 'it is no wonder, if a sensible reader indulge his ease so far as to turn a deaf ear to the proposal of such a question' (8.1.2, SBN 81). This is part of a more broadly dialogic approach in which the argument proceeds to a large extent by opposition to commonly held views or probable objections.

In Section XI of the *Enquiry*, indeed, echoing the *Dialogues concerning Natural Religion*, Hume abandons his direct conversation with the reader in order to record what purports to be a dialogue between himself and 'a friend who loves sceptical paradoxes' (11.1, SBN 132). What is more, the bulk of this section is made up of a *prosopopeia*, a speech invented by the paradoxical friend for Epicurus addressing the 'more philosophical part' of an Athenian audience. The rhetorical nature of this operation is underlined by Hume, who notes that his opponent has had recourse to the 'artifice of the demagogues of old' (11.24, SBN 142), insinuating himself into his hearer's favour by appealing to principles that he is known to profess. If Hume chooses this elaborately rhetorical mise-en-scène for his quite strenuous argument at this point, it is clearly because here more than elsewhere the philosopher is engaging with public, political concerns.

There is of course nothing surprising in all this. A rhetorical element is an inescapable part of any philosophy – as indeed of any linguistic communication. Nor is this a matter for concern; to point to the argumentative, probabilistic, affective, literary side of philosophical discourse is by no means to endorse Paul de Man's melodramatic affirmation that 'rhetoric radically suspends logic and opens up vertiginous possibilities of referential aberration'.[37] Indeed one of the virtues of much eighteenth-century philosophical writing – in spite of the attacks on rhetoric outlined at the beginning of this chapter – is precisely the easy acceptance of this unavoidable interpersonal and indeed literary dimension of philosophising. It may nevertheless be interesting to conclude by considering one important philosopher of the period who was far from comfortable with his own outstanding communicative skills: Jean-Jacques Rousseau.[38]

For different reasons, Rousseau was unhappy with both labels: philosopher and orator. To many of his contemporaries, however, he was an exemplary figure of the type of eloquent public philosopher praised by Vico. From the work that first brought him to the attention of the European public, the *Discours sur les sciences et les arts*, he displayed unrivalled mastery of the art of presenting radical and searching arguments on political, moral, and cultural issues to a wide educated audience.[39] What is more, he varied his approach according to circumstances. His first two discourses, entries for public competitions of the Academy of Dijon, show some of the traditional eloquence of the public speaker – it is interesting to note that the first discourse, like Hume's *Enquiry*, incorporates a classicising *prosopopeia*, although Rousseau's Fabricius is more of a declaimer and less of a reasoner than Hume's Epicurus. In reply to critiques of the discourses, Rousseau had recourse to the epistolary form, which he was to use to great effect in his public letters to Voltaire (on providence) and to d'Alembert (on the theatre) and in his great works of self-defence, the *Lettre à Christophe de Beaumont* and the *Lettres écrits de la montagne*.[40] His most influential works, however, were cast in fictional or semi-fictional form, the novel *La nouvelle Héloïse* (*Julia*) and the treatise on education, *Émile*, which he saw as the summation of his philosophical work.[41] By contrast, in his more abstract and forbidding treatise on political right, *Du contrat social*, he tried to avoid passionate persuasion and rely entirely on 'the force of reasoning'.[42] And finally, towards the end of his life, he too attempted the dialogue mode (in *Rousseau juge de Jean-Jacques*), though in a far less 'easy' manner than Hume.[43]

While adapting the form to the occasion, Rousseau was constantly concerned with creating the right impression of himself (or as he would have said, to allow his true self to be seen) and with maintaining contact with the reader. This is particularly visible in the introductory pages of his works, but on every page we hear the voice of the writer, who reasons or jokes with his reader, apologises, expostulates, throws down challenges, or seeks to make us share his emotions. Rousseau's highly wrought prose, by turns vehement, simple, brutal, or sentimental, created a sensation in its day. His eloquence is visible equally in the abrupt challenge of such openings as 'All things are good as they come from the hands of the creator; all things degenerate in the hands of man' (*Émile*) or in poetic developments worthy of Pascal, which can only really be appreciated in the original:

De ces contradictions naît celle que nous éprouvons sans cesse en nous-mêmes. Entraînés par la nature et par les hommes dans des routes contraires, forcés de nous partager entre ces diverses impulsions, nous en suivons une composée qui ne nous mène ni à l'un ni à l'autre but. Ainsi combattus et flottants durant tout le cours de notre vie, nous la terminons sans avoir pu nous accorder avec nous, et sans avoir été bons ni pour nous ni pour les autres. (*Émile*, 4: 251)

(From these contradictions springs that which we constantly feel in ourselves. Carried by nature and by men along opposite roads, forced to divide ourselves between these different impulses, we follow an intermediate route which leads neither to one destination nor to the other. Divided and drifting in this way as long as we live, we finish our lives without having found inner harmony, and without being of any good to ourselves or to others.)

It may seem like the language of a preacher, but it is situated in a radical philosophical discussion of nature and culture. Rousseau himself saw no reason why he should divorce himself, his emotions, and what he called his 'warmth' (*chaleur*) from his reasoning. Contemporaries, however, if they were hostile to his positions, often used his eloquence as a stick to beat him with, treating him as a 'sophist' – in other words, someone who did not believe what he was saying and was arguing only for effect and victory. (Such was the view of Dr. Johnson, himself described by Boswell as 'when he chose it...the greatest sophist that ever wielded a weapon in the schools of declamation'.) Such attacks were deeply wounding to Rousseau, for whom insincerity was one of the worst of crimes. He was forced to take them into account, nevertheless; it was because of them that he wrote *Du contrat social* in a relatively dry manner, and later, in the *Lettres écrits de la montagne*, we find him protesting: 'I beg my readers to be so kind as to leave my fine style on one side, and concentrate on whether my reasoning is good or bad' (3: 686).

The example of Rousseau suggests the dangers lying in wait for Vico's oratorical philosopher; eloquence can be a two-edged weapon. Even so, in the eighteenth century philosophy and rhetoric were allies of a kind. Philosophers might condemn traditional rhetoric or aspire to make it more philosophical; in their writing practice, as they addressed the reading public, they still had to overcome what Cicero called the 'severance between the tongue and the brain'.

NOTES

1 See, for instance, Marc Fumaroli, *L'age de l'éloquence; Rhétorique et 'res literaria' de la Renaissance au seuil de l'époque classique* (Geneva, 1980); *Rhetoric Revalued*, ed. B. Vickers (Binghamton, NY, 1982); *The Recovery of Rhetoric: Persuasive Discourse and Disciplinarity in the Social Sciences*, eds. R. H. Roberts and J. M. M. Good (Bristol, 1993); *Histoire de la rhétorique dans l'Europe moderne*, ed. M. Fumaroli (Paris, 1999).

2 See Françoise Douay-Soublin, 'La Rhétorique en Europe à travers son enseignement', in *Histoire des idées linguistiques*, ed. S. Auroux, 2 vols. (Liège, 1992), 2: 467–507.

3 *The Rhetoric of the Human Sciences: Language and Argument in Scholarship and Public Affairs*, eds. J. S. Nelson, A. Megill, and D. N. McCloskey (Madison, WI, 1987), 6.

4 Brian Vickers, *In Defence of Rhetoric* (Oxford, 1988), 201.

5 M. Sides, 'Rhetoric on the Brink of Banishment: d'Alembert on Rhetoric in the *Encyclopédie*', *Rhetorik*, 3 (1982): 111–24 at 112.

6 René Descartes, *Oeuvres philosophiques*, ed. F. Alquié, 3 vols. (Paris, 1963–73), 1: 574. The quotation comes from Part I of the *Discours de la méthode* (Discourse on Method). Translations into English are my own unless otherwise indicated.

7 Antoine Arnauld and Pierre Nicole, *La logique ou l'art de penser*, eds. P. Clair and F. Girbal (Paris, 1965), 232–4.

8 See Basil Munteano, *Constantes dialectiques en littérature et en histoire* (Paris, 1967), 354–60.

9 Thomas Sprat, *History of the Royal Society* (London, 1667), 113.

10 John Locke, *An Essay concerning Human Understanding*, ed. P. H. Nidditch, in *The Clarendon Edition* (1975), 508.

11 Immanuel Kant, *Kritik der Urtheilskraft*, in Ak 5, translated as *Critique of the Power of Judgment*, trans. P. Guyer and E. Matthews, ed. P. Guyer, in *Works* (2000).

12 Jean le Rond d'Alembert, *Discours préliminaire de l'Encyclopédie* (Paris, 1894), 44–5, as well as the article 'Collège' in the *Encyclopédie*; see also d'Alembert's entry 'Elocution'.

13 See in particular Wilbur Samuel Howell, *Eighteenth-Century British Logic and Rhetoric* (Princeton, NJ, 1971).

14 Anthony Ashley Cooper, Earl of Shaftesbury, *Characteristicks of Men, Manners, Opinions, Times*, 3 vols. (London, 1711).

15 Adam Smith, *Lectures on Rhetoric and Belles Lettres*, ed. J. C. Bryce, in *Works* (1983), 8.

16 Brian Vickers, 'Rhetorical and Anti-Rhetorical Tropes: On Writing the History of *Elocutio*', *Comparative Criticism*, 3 (1981): 105–32.

17 Étienne Bonnot de Condillac, *L'art d'écrire* (Art of Writing), in *Oeuvres philosophiques*, ed. G. Le Roy, 3 vols. (Paris, 1947–51), vol. 1. Page references are to this edition.

18 Condillac, *Cours d'étude pour l'instruction du prince de Parme* (Course of Studies for the Instruction of the Prince of Parme), in *Oeuvres philosophiques*, 1: 403.

19 Condillac, *Essai sur l'origine des connaissances humaines*, in *Oeuvres philosophiques*, 1: 105, translated as *An Essay on the Origin of Human Knowledge*, trans. and ed. H. Aarsleff (Cambridge, 2001).

20 Quoted in Smith, *Lectures*, 11.

21 George Campbell, *The Philosophy of Rhetoric*, 2 vols. (London, 1776); Henry Home, Lord Kames, *Elements of Criticism*, 2 vols. (Edinburgh, 1774); Joseph Priestley, *A Course of Lectures on Oratory and Criticism* (London, 1777).

22 Priestley, *Lectures*, i.

23 Cesare Beccaria, *Richerche intorno alla natura dello stile* (Researches Concerning the Nature of Style), in *Edizione Nazionale delle opere di Cesare Beccarias*, vol. 2: *Scritti filosofici e letterari*, eds. L. Firpo, G. Francioni, and G. Gaspari (Milan, 1984).

24 Giambattista Vico, *De nostri temporis studiorum ratione* (On the Study Methods of Our Time). This and Vico's other inaugural discourses are in Volume 1 of his *Opere*, eds. G. Gentile and F. Nicolini, 8 vols. in 9 (Bari, 1914–41). Volume 5 contains correspondence, including the letter to Solla, and Volume 8 gives lengthy extracts from the *Institutiones oratoriae*, a work based on his lectures, 1711–41, but not published until recently, edited by G. Crifò (Naples, 1989). The translations given here are taken from Vico, *Selected Writings*, trans. and ed. L. Pompa (Cambridge, 1982), to which page numbers refer.

25 Vico, *Princípi di una scienza nuova d'intorno alla comune natura delle nazioni* (Naples, 1725).

26 Vico, *De antiquissima italorum sapientia ex linguae latinae originibus eruenda*, 3 vols. (Naples, 1710), translated as *On the Ancient Wisdom of the Italians*, in *Selected Writings*.

27 See Chaïm Perelman and Lucie Olbrechts-Tyteca, *La nouvelle rhétorique: Traité de l'argumentation*, 2 vols. (Paris, 1958), translated as *The New Rhetoric: A Treatise on Argumentation*, trans. J. Wilkinson and P. Weaver (Notre Dame, IN, 1969). On Vico and Perelman, see Alessandro Giuliani, 'Vico's Rhetorical Philosophy and the New Rhetoric', in *Giambattista Vico's Science of Humanity*, eds. G. Tagliacozzo and D. P. Verene (Baltimore, MD, 1976), 31–46.

28 Bernard le Bovier de Fontenelle, *Entretiens sur la pluralité des mondes* (Conversations on the Plurality of Worlds), ed. R. Shackleton (Oxford, 1955).

29 Fontenelle, *Entretiens*, 141.

30 Denis Diderot, *Le rêve de d'Alembert*, in *Oeuvres complètes*, eds. H. Dieckmann et al. (Paris, 1975–), 17: 132.

31 Anonymous, *Mémoires de Trévoux* (April 1751), 797–9.

32 Jean le Rond d'Alembert, *Essai sur la société des gens de lettres avec les grands* (*Essay on the Association of Men of Letters with the Great*), in *Oeuvres*, 5 vols. (Paris, 1821–2), 4: 349.

33 David Hume, *Essays: Moral, Political, and Literary*, ed. E. F. Miller (Indianapolis, IN, 1987), 533–7.

34 Hume, *Dialogues concerning Natural Religion*, ed. N. Kemp Smith (Oxford, 1935), 158.

35 Hume, *An Enquiry concerning Human Understanding*, ed. T. L. Beauchamp, in *The Clarendon Edition* (2000), 1.1–17, SBN 5–16.

36 Jane Austen, *Pride and Prejudice*, ed. R. W. Chapman (Oxford, 1988), 3.

37 Paul de Man, *Allegories of Reading: Figural Language in Rousseau, Nietzsche, Rilke and Proust* (New Haven, CT, 1979), 10.

38 Page references for Rousseau's works are to his *Oeuvres*. On Rousseau's rhetoric, see Peter France, *Rhetoric and Truth in France: Descartes to Diderot* (Oxford, 1972), 235–64.

39 Rousseau, *Discours sur les sciences et les arts* (Discourse on the Sciences and the Arts), in *Oeuvres*, vol. 3.

40 Rousseau, *Lettre à Christophe de Beaumont* (vol. 4); Lettres écrits de la montagne (Letters from the Mountain) (vol. 3), in *Oeuvres*.

41 Rousseau, *Julie, ou La nouvelle Héloïse* (vol. 2); *Émile, ou De l'éducation* (vol. 4), in *Oeuvres*.

42 Rousseau, *Du contrat social ou Principes du droit politique* (On the Social Contract or Principles of Political Right), vol. 3.

43 Rousseau, *Rousseau juge de Jean-Jacques* (Rousseau the Judge of Jean-Jacques), in *Oeuvres*, vol. 1.

18

AESTHETICS

RUDOLF A. MAKKREEL

Aesthetics in the broad sense goes back at least as far as Plato's speculations about different types of beauty and the value of the arts. It is not until the eighteenth century, however, that aesthetics as distinct from traditional philosophical reflection on art comes into its own. This new discipline of aesthetics is more inclusive than a philosophy of the arts per se because it is concerned primarily with the appreciation of the sensory aspects of experience, whether derived from nature or the arts. Nature is also considered in terms of its ability to arouse aesthetic pleasure. In fact, some eighteenth-century thinkers found the purest instances of beauty and sublimity in the contemplation of nature. The variety of aesthetic responses that humans exhibit in relation to both nature and art required a philosophical and psychological reexamination of the human cognitive and critical faculties – one that would give feeling and imagination a larger role than before. Moreover, insofar as aesthetics raises the question of taste, it addresses social conventions concerning fashion, human manners, and other cultural practices that are contiguous with the arts.

The new discipline of aesthetics also introduces a more systematic consideration of the arts themselves. Whereas traditional reflections on art by Plato, Aristotle, Augustine, and others tended to deal with only some of the arts and mainly in terms of their import for philosophy and theology, we now see an increased consideration of the inherent character and unity of the fine arts. As noted by Paul Kristeller in his essay on 'The Modern System of the Arts', the modern notion of the arts as the fine arts – the arts of poetry, painting, sculpture, architecture, music, and dance – only came into being at the beginning of the eighteenth century. The traditional notion of art (*techne*) was applicable to many kinds of skill. The arts were not sharply distinguished from the crafts and included what we would call scientific and philosophical disciplines. The scheme

I wish to acknowledge the helpful comments I received on an earlier draft from Dennis Dugan, Knud Haakonssen, Donald Rutherford, Frances Tanikawa, Stefano Velotti, and Erdmann Waniek, and the bibliographical work of Daniel Richardson.

of the seven liberal arts of late antiquity – grammar, rhetoric, dialectic, arithmetic, geometry, astronomy, and music – makes specific reference to only one of the fine arts. Poetry, to be sure, can be linked to grammar and rhetoric, but the three visual arts were excluded and relegated to the level of the manual crafts.[1]

In the late seventeenth century, the Quarrel of the Ancients and the Moderns provided the occasion to more clearly distinguish between the arts and the sciences. The success of the natural sciences induced reflection on the reasons why there is such clear progress in certain disciplines and not in others. Charles Perrault claimed that 'in all sciences and in those arts whose secrets can be measured and calculated, we clearly prevail over the ancients'.[2] But in arts such as poetry and rhetoric, where taste and imagination are requisite, no such superiority can be proved. These arts aim to produce a beautiful effect. Elsewhere, Perrault approaches the modern conception when he speaks more generally of the *beaux arts* (beautiful or fine arts) and adds music, architecture, painting, sculpture, optics, and mechanics to the list. His account is still slightly too broad due to its inclusion of optics and mechanics, which do not meet the subsequent specification that the fine arts produce aesthetic pleasure.

The most explicit eighteenth-century aesthetic formulation of the system of the fine arts is to be found in Charles Batteux's influential work *Les beaux-arts réduits à un même principe*. Batteux distinguishes three kinds of art: mechanical arts 'that have as their object the needs of man',[3] the beautiful or fine arts which aim to produce pleasure, and a mixed kind of art which is both useful and pleasurable. Music, poetry, painting, sculpture, and dance or the art of gesture are the fine arts par excellence. Rhetoric and architecture are mixed arts. In his concluding chapter on the union of the fine arts, Batteux argues that the theatre can integrate not only poetry, music, and dance, as they represent human actions and passions, but also architecture, painting, and sculpture, as they provide the place and scenery for a dramatic spectacle.

Just as important as this process of the thematisation of the fine arts is the lively discussion of a whole range of aesthetic categories beyond the traditional philosophical concept of beauty. In his translation of *On the Sublime* (traditionally attributed to Longinus), Boileau had already transformed the sublime from a mere rhetorical concept – the so-called grand style – to an attribute that characterises a special type of experience. With the new interest in the nature and meaning of aesthetic experience as such, a variety of qualities and emotions came to be examined: grandeur, wonder, novelty, grace, and dignity. Moreover, in its reflections on imagination and taste, the new discipline dealt with the moral and epistemological import of aesthetic impressions and judgements.

The diverse literary, critical, and philosophical ideas involved in the rise of modern aesthetics resist interpretation according to a single overarching theme or dominant movement. We can see in the aesthetic reflections of the eighteenth century varied, often unexpected, mixtures of the different approaches discriminated by Wilhelm Dilthey in his 'Three Epochs of Modern Aesthetics':[4] the rationalist, normative approach rooted in seventeenth-century Cartesian France and Leibnizian Germany; the empirical, psychological analysis of sense impressions initiated in the eighteenth century; and the historical-cultural approach, which would become prominent in the nineteenth century. Kant's transcendental aesthetics can be regarded as the most ambitious effort to combine these three approaches, mediating rationalist and empirical aesthetics while setting the stage for the historical understanding of art.[5]

In what follows, we will concentrate on five main developments generated more on the basis of specific aesthetic problems than on the basis of general approaches. In the first section, we will see the increasing incorporation of aesthetic content within the forms and principles derived from a rational framework: the efforts, especially in the Cartesian tradition, to relate rational critical standards to the more natural aspects of aesthetic experience; and the attempts, following Leibniz and Shaftesbury, to find aesthetic counterparts to logical rationality. Section II will examine the developing interest in aesthetic sensibility. It will deal not only with the analysis of sense impressions and their specific aesthetic effects but also the mediating functions of feeling and imagination. In Section III, some of the questions raised by the Quarrel of the Ancients and Moderns are related to the problem of the historical and cultural conditions of genius in the arts. The fourth section will deal with the problem of expression and meaning in the arts, ranging from early debates about the role of allegory to Kant's account of beauty as the symbol of morality. The final section, on aesthetic and moral values, begins with Hume's essay on the standard of taste and moves from empirical attempts to arrive at rules of criticism to Kant's transcendental critique of taste. It concludes with a discussion of the broad humanising role of aesthetics as articulated by Schiller.

I. THE RATIONALIST BACKGROUND OF AESTHETICS

In examining how the French rationalist tradition gradually incorporates more natural aspects of aesthetic experience, it will be useful to take Nicholas Boileau as a starting point. His *L'art poétique* of 1674 embodies both the critical norms of classical poetics and a rational method for applying them. Boileau affirms the three dramatic unities of action, time, and place by declaring:

> we, that are by Reason's Rules confin'd
> will, that with Art the Poem be design'd
> ... [to] leave a strong Impression in the mind (Canto III).[6]

Although Boileau's concern for distinctness in art has been regarded as Cartesian in spirit,[7] he does not seem to fully share Descartes's distrust of the senses and passions. His art appeals mainly to the intellect, to be sure, but there is a kind of optimism that emotions 'if decently exprest, will raise no vitious motions in our breast' (Canto III).

1. Rational form versus natural content

When we turn to the *Traité du beau* (1715) of the French-speaking Swiss thinker Jean-Pierre de Crousaz, we find a sharper Cartesian opposition between sense and reason. Whereas the ideas we have on the level of the intellect are within our control, the feelings that fill our heart control us.[8] Accordingly, Crousaz distinguishes two kinds of beauty, an intellectual beauty which can be judged calmly by principles of good taste, and a more arbitrary, felt beauty which confounds taste with fancy. Artists must satisfy not only the rational demands of taste but also the emotional demands of their audiences. From the standpoint of feeling, boredom is the most unbearable state, from which the public seeks relief by means of lively sensations. Accordingly, it can be entertained by things that are great, novel, or diverse (74). The pleasures that these qualities produce can add to the beauty of art but do not constitute it, according to Crousaz. In the final analysis, the artist must subordinate our natural interest in diversity to the rational demand for uniformity, thereby giving rise to regularity, order, and proportion (14).

In his *Essai sur le beau* of 1731, the Cartesian Yves-Marie André introduces a *tertium quid* between the two kinds of beauty distinguished by Crousaz.[9] There is, according to André, a God-created natural beauty that mediates between essential or rational beauty on the one hand and artificial or imaginary beauty on the other. Essential beauty manifests an uncreated geometrical order of things. Natural beauty is volitional, like artificial beauty. However, it is not the product of a potentially capricious human choice but of God's sublime edict 'Let there be light' (18). Because natural beauty relates to the way that colour and light are pleasing to the eye, we can appeal to Newtonian optics in order to mediate between reason and imagination and thus restrict the caprice of the latter (20–1). There are in turn three kinds of artistic beauty according to André: a beauty of genius based on a knowledge of essential beauty, a beauty of taste based on an enlightened opinion about natural beauty, and a purely capricious beauty, where any opinion counts as much as any other and which is at best appropriate for the comic theatre. Whereas in Crousaz the natural was considered fanciful and irrational, in André the natural is neither rational nor irrational but legitimated as having been created by God.

In Charles Batteux's *Les beaux-arts réduits à un même principe* (1746), we find an even stronger emphasis on the natural. Although all the arts are conceived rationally by means of a formal principle of imitation, their content is far from rational. While appealing to the traditional principle of imitation, Batteux transforms it from a cognitive principle of truth (*le vrai*) to one of artifice or pleasing verisimilitude (*le vraisemblable*) (86). Truth in art is shown to derive from an emotional demand for natural content. Instead of disparaging feelings and the human heart, in the manner of Crousaz, for being the source of a capricious desire to be entertained by exotic diversity and novelty, Batteux claims that people are interested in what is familiar or close to them. Since self-love is seen as the 'spring of all the pleasures of the human heart', it follows that 'the closer something is to me the more it will touch me' (129, 128). The arts can thus only arouse an interest in their subject matter if the latter remains close to our own nature and the nature around us. This subject matter need not always be pleasurable; indeed, we are often fascinated by suffering, as in tragedy. It is the imitation principle in the service of taste which nevertheless insists on deriving pleasure from art. Our heart seeks the truth about the things around us – even if what is disclosed is sorrow and upheaval – while imitation engenders pleasure by fashioning order out of disorder.

In a reversal of traditional rationalism, it is now the heart which seeks natural truthfulness, whereas the principle of imitation produces artifice. By itself, imitation can only create artificially perfected objects, from which we derive a disinterested intellectual pleasure. But when related to our emotional demand for psychological veracity, imitation serves to 'temper emotion when its excess becomes disagreeable. It makes amends to the heart when it suffers excessively'(*Les beaux-arts*, 135). For Batteux, as subsequently for Rousseau, emotional plausibility must always prevail over the beautifying demands of imitation – that is, nature over taste.

Whether grudgingly or not, the rationalist tradition by Batteux's time had increasingly acknowledged the role of the natural and sensory aspects of aesthetic experience. Accordingly, contrasts between Continental rationalism and British empiricism have to be drawn with care. One difference which does become discernable, however, is that even for a limited rationalist like Batteux, reason continues to be the primary determinant of what constitutes good taste, whereas for the empiricists there are many equiprimordial factors which properly influence good taste.

2. Aesthetic counterparts to rationality

In contrast with the dualistic rationalism of Descartes, Leibniz proposes that the relation of sense and reason be conceived as a continuum. This allows him to link the aesthetic features of experience to a larger rational universe. Instead of dismissing the confusions of sense and sentiment as irrational, Leibniz finds there a harmonious, if unconscious, reflection of the cosmos. As he writes in 1714, 'Each soul knows the infinite, knows all, but confusedly. . . . Our confused perceptions are the result of the impressions which the whole universe makes upon us'.[10] It is this approach, which delights in finding unity in multiplicity on all levels of experience, that inspired the development of German aesthetics and created a more fruitful relation between rationalism and aesthetics.

In British aesthetics, Shaftesbury had set forth a comparable view in holding that the greatest beauty lies in the interconnectedness of things. In 'The Moralists', Shaftesbury lays out a sequence of three orders of beauty, proceeding from (1) mere inert or surface forms to (2) 'forms which form, that is, which have intelligence, action, and operation',[11] to (3) the creative principle of a forming capacity. This ever-deepening search for the formative power which engenders order moves from the external forms of the particular things which please the senses to the more pervasive inner forms which inform the world as a whole and satisfy the intellect. As in the works of Leibniz, there is a teleological sense that local beauty is indicative of a larger-scale beauty of a world alive with order. Shaftesbury is perhaps more explicit about the moral implications of this vision. His notion of the 'inward eye' necessary to discern the 'inward form' of human beauty ultimately points back to a moral 'inward character'(*Characteristicks*, 137, 132, 278). This relation between beauty and morality is subsequently articulated by Francis Hutcheson into two complementary special senses: an aesthetic internal sense which discerns 'the beauty of regularity, order and harmony' and a moral sense 'which makes benevolent Actions appear Beautiful'.[12]

Whereas Shaftesbury's influence on aesthetics went more in the direction of value appreciation, Leibniz inspired the more epistemological direction taken by Alexander Baumgarten. In defining the new discipline of aesthetics as the 'science of sensible knowledge',[13] Baumgarten envisioned its scope as not limited to the fine arts. In the Prolegomena of his *Aesthetica* (1750–8), he foresees it as also relevant to all the liberal arts and the practical activities of daily life. Aesthetics has philological, hermeneutical, exegetical, rhetorical, and other applications (§4). Baumgarten did not carry out his full program and concentrated mainly on the cognitive conditions for the appreciation of beauty. Even his applications to the fine arts tend to be limited to literature.

Baumgarten defines beauty as 'the perfection of sensible knowledge' (*Aesthetica*, §14, 6). Christian Wolff had already described beauty as the sensible and pleasurable appearance of perfection. From Wolff's standpoint, the same rational perfection can be appreciated sensibly as well as conceptually. But Baumgarten's point is different, namely, that despite being a lower form of knowledge than conceptual knowledge, sensible knowledge nevertheless has its own perfection. Conceptual knowledge is both clear and distinct; sensible knowledge cannot be distinct, but it can develop clarity in ways not explored by logic. In his *Reflections on Poetry* of 1735, where the term 'aesthetics' was first used, Baumgarten interpreted the difference between the clear and the distinct as a difference in modes of clarity. A clear representation differs from an obscure one by having enough marks or characteristic traits (*notas*) to distinguish it from other representations.[14] For a clear representation to also become distinct, it must be made 'intensively clearer' by having its marks internally articulated (*Reflections*, 43). Distinctness requires the logical explication of marks within marks in order to deepen or purify the clarity of a representation. The perfection of aesthetic knowledge does not lie in this internal logical articulation. Rather, its aim is to make representations 'extensively clearer' by widening their scope to encompass ever more marks (43).

This 'extensive clarity' is later called 'richness' in the *Aesthetica*. Such richness leaves an extensively clear representation confused rather than distinct, but, as Ernst Cassirer has pointed out, aesthetically this confusion should be conceived neutrally as a confluence that is not at all tantamount to disorder.[15] Baumgarten is exploiting Leibniz's insight that the more characteristics are compressed into a single representation, the more it becomes suggestive of order. By gaining extensive clarity, an aesthetic representation may become less distinct within, but it gains a determinacy which allows it to become more clearly distinguishable from without – that is, from other representations. This realisation allows Baumgarten to relate the richness (*ubertas*) of extensive clarity to the specificity that singles out a concrete individual.[16] As Baumgarten had already argued in his *Reflections on Poetry*, the task of the poet is not to describe in terms of abstract universals but to vividly portray individuals 'determined in every respect' (*Reflections on Poetry*, 43).

Baumgarten's student Georg Friedrich Meier had a greater immediate influence with his more popular, and therefore perhaps unfairly dismissed, aesthetics. In his three-volume *Anfangsgründe aller schönen Wissenschaften* (1754), Meier used and applied many of the distinctions first made by Baumgarten in his lectures but never fully worked out in his unfinished *Aesthetica*. Expanding on Baumgarten's suggestion that clarity and richness of aesthetic representations contribute to the 'life of knowledge'(*Aesthetica*, §22), Meier describes the liveliness of aesthetic representations with considerable psychological detail. A lively representation does not merely engage our cognitive faculty; it also engages our desires and thus fills the whole mind. The more lively a representation, the more beautiful it can become.[17] Like Baumgarten, Meier makes use of the concept of imitation, but he diminishes its importance by defining it as 'a striving to make something similar to something else' on the basis of 'wit' (*Anfangsgründe*, 2: 377–8). As a consequence, only children are serious imitators; adults imitate by applying a self-conscious wit or by making playful allusions. Another result of this kind of imitation is parody (2: 382–3).

By making wit such an important aesthetic power, Meier also pays more attention to the imagination and lists as its three main perfections: scope (*extensio*), strength (*intensio*), and lastingness (*protensio*) (*Anfangsgründe*, 2: 277–89). Whereas wit by itself can extend the scope (*extensio*) of the imagination, the cooperation of acumen or discernment (*Scharfsinnigkeit*) is required if the representations being compared are not to lose their individual strength (*intensio*). This appeal to acumen allows the various clear representations that make up a whole work to 'be aesthetically proportional to one another' (2: 496). However, if the parts of a whole are recognised as proportional to each other, they must have been differentiated in some way. This suggests a kind of imaginative differentiation as the aesthetic counterpart to conceptual distinctness. Whereas logical acumen enables us to articulate representations from within, imaginative acumen must be able to differentiate representations from without.

Another of Meier's overlooked contributions is his effort to provide the application of aesthetics to hermeneutics, which Baumgarten had merely anticipated. Meier relates hermeneutics to what he calls the last faculty of sensible knowledge, one which involves using signs as a way to come to know something else. When a represented relation between a sign and what is designated is natural, then we have a natural sign; when the relation is based on a voluntary choice of a thinking being, then we have an arbitrary or artificial sign. Regarding this latter arbitrary relation, we can proceed either from the designated matter to invent a sign for it by means of a heuristic *ars characteristica* or from the sign to the designated matter by means of a *hermeneutica* (*Anfangsgründe*, 2: 615). In his *Versuch einer allgemeinen Auslegungskunst* (1757), Meier defines interpretation as based on a clear rather than distinct knowledge of the meaning of sensible signs. The main principle of Meier's sensible hermeneutics is that of reasonableness (*Billigkeit*),[18] which is the aesthetic counterpart of rationality. According to this principle, one must interpret artificial, humanly created signs as perfectly appropriate to their subject matter until the opposite can be proved. Just as natural signs are known to be perfectly appropriate in a rational Leibnizian world, so must artificial signs be assumed to have been chosen reasonably if we are to draw as much meaning as possible from them. Having shown that the liveliness of many compressed characteristics within an aesthetic representation is sufficient to specify a determinate individual, the aim of the interpretation of linguistic characteristics is similarly to obtain a grasp of individual meaning contexts.

Johann Winckelmann, the historian of ancient art, also studied with Baumgarten. Still upholding the imitation theory of art, he pays his dues to both the rational and sensory aspects of knowledge. Beauty must be recognised by the intellect and felt by the senses. For example, while beauty is constituted primarily by the design of things, colour can also be a contributing factor. Despite his stress on aesthetic form, Winckelmann admits in his *Geschichte der Kunst des Alterthums* (1764) that form cannot be geometrically distinct. In his discussion of the ideal in art, Winckelmann indicates that it is not derived from universal concepts – as are geometrical figures – but is arrived at intuitively from many particulars. 'The formation of beauty is either individualistic, that is, directed at the singular, or it involves a selection of beautiful parts from many individuals and their combination into a unity, which we call *idealistic*.'[19] By choosing the most beautiful parts from different human beings and unifying them into one ideal whole being, the artist still only reaches a particular embodiment of beauty. The artistic ideal is a concrete whole which is not to be confused with an abstract universal.

The perfection of art for Winckelmann lies in the proper balance between beautiful form and emotional expressiveness. Before we can deal adequately with this problem, as well as with Moses Mendelssohn, the other important rationalist aesthetician, we need to examine the nature of aesthetic feeling and emotion. We will see that although Mendelssohn also interprets beauty as the recognition of perfection, he approaches it more in terms of a subjective feeling than in terms of the objective traits of our representations. The next section concerns a shift from a primarily object-oriented aesthetics, based on the rational principle of imitation, to a more subject-oriented aesthetics which deals as much with the felt effects of an aesthetic impression as with its descriptive analysis.

II. AESTHETIC EFFECTS ON THE SUBJECT

The turn to the sensible and emotional effects of art is made evident by l'abbé Jean-Baptiste Du Bos, who asserts that the stimulation of passions is the main task of all the arts. Our greatest need is to overcome boredom and, as a consequence, the more powerfully we are moved, the better the aesthetic effect. Thus Du Bos observes: '[M]en generally find more pleasure in the theatre from weeping than from laughing.'[20] We have seen that Crousaz made a similar point in speaking of the artist's need to satisfy the emotional demands of the public, but with Du Bos the arousal of feeling is no longer considered a subordinate task. He declares in his *Réflexions critiques sur la poésie et sur la peinture* (1719) that a merely beautiful landscape by itself does not interest us unless it also portrays human beings who can move us (I.6, 54).

Du Bos's *Réflexions* was perhaps the first work to effectively counter Horace's *ut pictura poesis* by insisting on a sharp distinction between painting and poetry

(*Réflexions*, I.44, 463). Acknowledging that they are alike in having as their primary aim to touch and move our sentiments, Du Bos locates their difference in the manner and efficacy of their doing so. Initially, Du Bos appears to be giving the overall advantage to poetry because it can tell us more about things than can a painting, which is restricted to one moment. A poet can also express more of our thoughts and our sentiments (I.13, 84–7). However, Du Bos comes to the less common conclusion that painting deserves the higher ranking. Because painting uses natural signs rather than the artificial signs of poetry, it has a more powerful effect in moving us. A whole painting can directly affect the eye, whereas the words of a poem can only affect our imagination by degrees, one after the other (I.40, 415). Of course, tragedy as performed on the stage can 'incorporate an infinite number of visual scenes within itself' and thus can combine the advantages of both poetry and painting (I.40, 423).

The imagination, being less direct than sight, is also less effective in touching the heart. When it comes to genius, the imagination is similarly downplayed against the power of observation. The true enthusiasm of genius derives not from the power to invent allegorical personages but from the capacity to un-cover infinite differences among natural human beings. A fertile and correct imagination remains true to nature without copying it literally. Verisimilitude rather than truth is the aim of imitation. Du Bos preserves the principle of imi-tation but without its traditional cognitive intention. It is not reason or intellect which determines our taste but sentiment or a sixth sense (II.22, 342). The best aesthetic judgement is not a function of having more learning but of having a more delicate sensibility.

1. *Modes of sensibility*

For the fullest recognition of sensibility and its most detailed analysis, we must go to Great Britain, where Shakespeare and Milton had already successfully transgressed the classical rules. Whereas on the Continent it was generally as-sumed that in the Battle of the Ancients and the Moderns, the Ancients had proved their superiority in the arts and the Moderns in science, John Dennis's *The Advancement and Reformation of Modern Poetry*, published in London in 1701, claimed that the 'Ancients are not in themselves so strong [in poetry] as to make the Moderns despair'.[21] Moderns have surpassed the Ancients in comedy, but even in serious literature Milton has transcended them. The proper end of the arts, according to Dennis, is not only to arouse human passions but also to engender enthusiasm. The best way to ensure enthusiasm is to return to the sublime themes of religion. The reformation of modern poetry will come from reconciling passion and reason by means of the exalted vision of Christianity.

The importance of Dennis lies in bringing to the British the interest in the sublime that had been awakened by Boileau's translation of Longinus. For Boileau, the sublime involves the experience of something extraordinary or marvelous as found in a single thought or a striking image. Dennis goes on to characterise the sublime as a kind of enthusiastic terror. According to Samuel Monk, Dennis thought of beauty and sublimity as continuous: 'his sublime is simply the highest beauty. . . . The distinction of first establishing the sublime as a separate category, is due to Addison'.[22]

Actually, Joseph Addison's use of the word 'sublime' is restricted to poetic language. While he writes in *The Spectator*, #285 (1711–12), 'It is requisite that the Language of an heroick Poem should be both perspicuous and sublime',[23] his parallel and more general aesthetic contrast is between beauty and greatness. These together with the uncommon provide the three main sources of pleasure for the imagination (209). Addison was one of the first to reflect aesthetically on the way the English ever since Bacon and Shakespeare have taken delight in imagination and fancy. Addison speaks of the imagination as an expanded mode of sight, which in turn may be regarded as a more delicate kind of touch or feeling (206). As such, the imagination provides pleasures, which are 'not so gross as those of Sense, nor so refined as those of the Understanding' (207). We can see how the imagination operates as an intermediary power by examining how it draws pleasure from greatness, the uncommon, and beauty.

It is in its response to greatness that the imagination seems most like the understanding. The imagination revels in surveying large objects and landscapes because any spacious horizon is to it 'an Image of Liberty' (*The Spectator*, 209). Addison declares that wide and undetermined prospects are as pleasing to the imagination as speculation about the infinite is to the understanding. Nevertheless, the enthusiasm of the imagination for the great, the elevated, or the sublime also points to the limits of this faculty. It enjoys the feeling of unboundedness caused by what is *great*, but it cannot 'take in anything that is *very great*' (emphasis added).[24] Its inability to keep up with the understanding in its pursuit of the infinite may not be a defect of the imagination as such, according to Addison, but only of the way it functions in conjunction with the body. He ends by speculating that in the hereafter, 'the Imagination will be able to keep Pace with the Understanding, and to form in itself distinct Ideas of all the different Modes of Quantities of Space' (219). It is possible then that the imagination is not merely a lower, sensible faculty limited to clear ideas but is potentially a higher faculty capable of distinct ideas, at least concerning space.

When the imagination derives pleasure from what is uncommon or new, it enjoys being surprised. Here again the imagination seems to resemble the understanding by exhibiting an intellectual curiosity. Whereas relative to the great

it enjoyed being expanded, which seems to occur through homogeneous incre-
ments, now it enjoys being offered variety or heterogeneity. But if there is intellectual pleasure to be derived from the variety of the new, it is rather superficial:
'[T]he Mind is every Instant called off to something new, and the Attention
not sufficient to dwell too long, and waste itself on any particular Object' (210).
The pleasure derived from the uncommon consists less in being attentive than
in being diverted.

The final source of pleasure for the imagination is 'Beauty, which immediately
diffuses a secret Satisfaction and Complacency through the Imagination' (211).
Throughout his treatment of beauty in *The Spectator* #412, Addison stresses the
prominent role of colours in delighting the eye. He briefly mentions the beauty
of 'the Symmetry and Proportions of Parts, in the Arrangement and Disposition
of Bodies', for which the intellect might be stimulated to attempt an explanation
(212). But since the satisfaction derived from beauty is called 'secret', it does not
seem to involve any intellectual understanding.

Addison claims that beauty 'gives a Finishing to any thing that is Great or
Uncommon' (211). But if beauty can round off what is great or sublime, then
beauty and sublimity are still far from being contrasted in the manner of Burke
and Kant.

Another discussion that throws light on Addison's plea for the importance of
the imagination is his attempt to relate it to a proper critical account of wit. He
builds on Locke's distinction between wit as finding resemblances among ideas
and judgement as finding differences. Citing Locke to the effect that wit is displayed when the fancy connects ideas that have a 'Resemblance or Congruity',
Addison modifies this account by declaring that not all resemblances exhibit wit
(104-5). For a resemblance of ideas to be witty, it must also give '*Delight* and
Surprize to the Reader. . . . [I]t is necessary that the Ideas should not lie too near
one another in the Nature of things; for where the Likeness is obvious, it gives no
Surprize' (105). Simple associations of ideas can account for many close-range
resemblances, but not until the imagination expands our horizon do resemblances become interesting. Only resemblances among things that are distantly
related or varying in nature can cause the surprise and delight that satisfy the
imagination.

Hutcheson, by contrast, claims that the basic pleasures caused in us by beauty
and virtue are not acquired through the imagination but are sensed directly. His
aesthetic internal sense, to which we alluded earlier, can now be defined as 'a
passive Power of receiving Ideas of Beauty from all Objects in which there is
Uniformity amidst Variety'. Despite the reference to the rational formula of
uniformity amidst variety, the enjoyment felt does not involve the activity of
comprehending order. There is no 'innate idea' that relates aesthetic pleasure and

intelligible order (*Inquiry*, 53). Thus Hutcheson admits that there seems to be no necessary connection between the regularity of objects and our finding pleasure in them (32). The relation has been arbitrarily but wisely established by God to allow us to make disinterested determinations about beauty without activating the interests of the will. Similarly, our moral sense allows us to see benevolent activities as beautiful. We can immediately sense the virtue of intending the good of others, antecedent to any calculation of our own advantage or interest (see 75, 84). Both physical and moral beauty give us disinterested pleasures which may be diminished by custom in the former case or by the calculation of self-interest in the latter. But these pleasures as such cannot be obliterated.

Edmund Burke's *A Philosophical Enquiry into the Origin of our Ideas of the Sublime and Beautiful* (1757) rejects Hutcheson's appeal to a special disinterested internal sense of beauty. Taste does not depend on any 'superior principle'[25] but can be derived from the most basic human passions. The sublime is related to the passions concerning self-preservation. Developing the idea that the sublime is evoked by something terrible, Burke shows it to involve our strongest passions, namely, those associated with danger to our survival. When we confront the terrible directly, it causes terror, but if we confront it indirectly through the imagination or from a distance, this painful terror is transformed not into a positive pleasure but into what Burke calls the relative pleasure of 'delight' (34). The result is a 'delightful horror, a sort of tranquility tinged with terror' (123).

Beauty for Burke is a function of our passions relating to society and the propagation of the sexes. Whereas lust finds indiscriminate sexual pleasure, love is a mixed passion which finds itself drawn to particular beings by their beauty. The pleasure found through the love of beauty is related to sexual desire without being reducible to it. No matter how refined the negative delight of the sublime and the positive pleasure of the beautiful may become, they remain inseparable from the interests of life. The delightful horror of the sublime is seen as an 'exercise necessary for the finer organs', but the usual intelligible features of beauty and sublimity are discounted relative to their practical functions in life (123).

Burke, like many others in the eighteenth century, associated the beautiful with delicacy and femininity and the sublime with greatness and masculinity. I would like to point to two at least partial deviations from this kind of linkage in the works of Thomas Reid and Mary Wollstonecraft. Reid, as a proponent of common sense, is suspicious of general aesthetic formulas. Especially critical of Hutcheson's principle of uniformity and variety, Reid allows each kind of being to have its relative beauty if it is well-fitted for its purpose. This means that females and males will exhibit different kinds of beauty: 'Signs of strength, etc., is [sic] a beauty in the male; that of delicacy is beauty in the female.'[26] Whatever stereotype Reid may have had about the sexes, neither sex is given a monopoly on beauty, nor is the masculine made the source of our ideal of sublimity. 'The proper and true object of grandeur or sublimity is the Supreme Being' (*Lectures on the Fine Arts*, 39). Mary Wollstonecraft resists sexual stereotyping as such by distinguishing between 'a pretty woman, as an object of desire', who displays a kind of natural beauty, and 'a fine woman, who inspires more sublime emotions by displaying intellectual beauty'.[27] Sublimity retains its superiority by being considered a noble form of beauty, but it is no longer reserved for men. However, it has been suggested that sublimity 'remains a masculine attribute' for Wollstonecraft, 'although one which males themselves have lost. Taken up by women it is desexualized.'[28]

Whereas Burke departed quite radically from Hutcheson by replacing a postulated and passive internal sense for beauty with a set of aesthetic passions related directly to the external world, Alexander Gerard attempts to improve Hutcheson's approach by incorporating activity into internal sensibility. Gerard used the concept of taste to expand Hutcheson's internal sense to encompass imagination and custom. In his prize-winning *An Essay on Taste* (1759), Gerard defines taste as an aggregate of several internal senses which allow us to derive pleasure from novelty, grandeur or sublimity, beauty, imitation, harmony, ridicule, and virtue. Far from being original senses implanted in us by a wise Creator, the internal senses are '*derived* and *compounded* faculties, liable to alteration'.[29] Taste is therefore formed only gradually, 'subject to the law of *habit*' (92).[30] An internal sense for Gerard is an imaginary or 'reflex' sense 'supplying us with finer and more delicate perceptions, than any which can be properly referred to external organs' (1–2). The internal sense of novelty is 'reflex' because it involves the accompanying awareness that what I now see I have never seen before. Similarly, to develop an internal sense of the sublime, I must relate the immensity of an object to the simplicity of its composition. The comparison of these two qualities definitive of the sublime requires me to use my imagination, or, in the case of objects signified by language, to rely on the association of ideas. The internal or reflex sense of beauty requires me to relate three qualities in an object: not only uniformity and variety, but also proportion, which 'consists not so much in relations of the parts precisely measurable, as in a general aptitude of the structure to the end proposed' (33). There is no longer anything contingent about the pleasurableness of these qualities, as Hutcheson had claimed, but the continuity between aesthetic pleasure and the ends of cognition means that the disinterestedness of the aesthetic is sacrificed.

The internal sense of ridicule is added by Gerard to bring a diverting moment into taste: 'its object is in general *incongruity*, or a surprising and uncommon mixture of *relation* and *contrariety* in things' (62). Whereas the appreciation of beauty presupposes an awareness of proportion or congruity among the parts of an object, the appreciation of ridicule or humour requires a sensitivity for something misproportioned or incongruous. The internal sense of harmony is included to deal with the beauties of language and music. Most interesting is what Gerard says about the importance of expression in music. By expression, music 'acquires a fitness, becomes adapted to an end, and agitates the soul with whatever passion the artist chuses' (60). Finally, the moral sense is regarded as the paramount internal sense, for by it we are led to give our 'joyful approbation' to virtuous characters as imitated by artists and to feel disapproval for vicious characters.

All these internal senses cooperate to constitute what Gerard calls the 'sensibility of taste' (102). The refinement of taste goes beyond this sensibility to include 'acuteness of judgment' and 'long and intimate acquaintance' with what has so far met the highest expectations of good taste (114). There is a further quality of taste, correctness, which it is the function of criticism to promote. To be a critic or have a correct taste, one 'must not only *feel*, but possess that accuracy of discernment, which enables a person to *reflect* upon his feelings with distinctness, and to explain them to others' (170). Criticism requires a philosophical perspective such as the one applied by Aristotle when he generalised from the productions of Greek tragedians.

An attempt at such a critical approach to taste was made by Lord Kames in his *Elements of Criticism* of 1761. Like Gerard, Kames distinguishes a large range of aesthetic qualities, but he no longer attaches special internal senses to them. Whereas the external senses produce different kinds of perceptions, Kames speaks merely of a generic internal sense which is the source of consciousness.[31] Instead of focusing on what is required to be appropriately appreciative of the aesthetic qualities of objects, Kames, like Burke, considers their psychological effects on us. Yet, he at least partially satisfies Gerard's definition of a critic because he analyses aesthetic qualities into their component parts to explain how the spectator responds.

Kames gives a causal account of our aesthetic experiences. Distinguishing grandeur and sublimity as greatness of magnitude and elevation, respectively, he proceeds to claim that they produce effects in us which resemble their causes: 'A great object makes the spectator endeavour to enlarge his bulk. . . . An elevated object . . . makes the spectator stretch upward' (*Criticism*, 102). Although not fully convincing about these resembling effects produced by great and elevated objects, Kames is quite careful in analysing what qualitative elements these objects must possess. The expansive effect of grandeur is supposed to be pleasing, but more 'serious' than the effect of beauty, which is that of 'sweetness and gaiety'. Kames continues by asserting that 'though regularity, proportion, order, and colour, contribute to grandeur as well as to beauty, yet these qualities are not by far so essential to the former as to the latter' (103). Both grandeur and sublimity involve a much greater scope than beauty, which makes any strict observation in them of regularity and other such qualities inappropriate, if not impossible. By means of grandeur, a continuum is created between beauty and sublimity.

Whereas Addison and Gerard gave great prominence to our sense of novelty, Kames rates it as relatively unimportant. In contrast with Addison, who linked novelty to surprise, he links it to wonder. Even familiar things can surprise us if they are met unexpectedly. Conversely, if I travel to India to see an elephant, I will not be surprised by my novel experience of one, merely full of wonder. Novelty is aesthetically unimportant because it is a subjective attribute which relates differently to different individuals according to their past experience.

2. Aesthetic emotions and feelings

What distinguishes Kames's approach from the earlier analyses of aesthetic sensibility is the care with which he defines our emotional responses to the qualitative aspects of experience. His effort to distinguish aesthetic emotions from passions allows us to relate him to the efforts by the Germans to distinguish the aesthetic response from the volitional response.

Although all the senses can arouse feelings in us, only some move us emotionally. Kames writes: 'Of all the feelings raised in us by external objects, those only of the eye and the ear are honoured with the name of *passion* or *emotion*' (*Criticism*, 24). Since the fine arts aim at affecting us through just these two senses, they can be judged by the emotions they are capable of producing. Kames distinguish an emotion from a passion by proposing that the former is simply 'an internal motion' of the mind which 'passeth away without desire', whereas the latter goes over into the desire to act. Since the pleasurable state produced by a work of art or a beautiful garden 'is seldom accompanied with desire', it is best called an emotion (27).

Kames's claim that aesthetic emotion as such need not produce desire has been assumed to mean that for him aesthetic pleasure is disinterested. But his statement that aesthetic emotion is seldom accompanied with desire is an observation about experience which makes no normative claim. If aesthetic pleasure were essentially disinterested, it could not possess the beneficial social effects which Kames attributes to the arts. Indeed, he is perfectly willing to have tragedies arouse what he calls the 'passion of sympathy', especially if the spectator's desire to actively come to the aid of the protagonist is preempted by the poet expressing the sentiments appropriate to this desire. Sentiments are defined as 'thoughts prompted by passion' (202). Since a sentiment is a kind of mitigated desire, we can see delineated here a kind of quasi-interested, but not disinterested, aesthetic response.[32]

Kames's insistence that art must have an ideal presence for the spectator has also been taken to support the view that aesthetic representations have a kind of imaginary virtual status that removes them from the real world of human interests. But ideal presence for Kames has none of the artifice of imaginary production and all the imposed reality of 'a waking dream' (49). By ideal presence, Kames means that I lose awareness of what is really present in my own situation to become totally absorbed by some other state of affairs. The imagination may be useful in this process, but it is often not as powerful as memory in producing the illusion of ideal presence. In general, Kames gives a rather perfunctory account of the imagination's aesthetic contributions. In this he differs markedly from the German-speaking aestheticians to whom we can now proceed.

The Swiss critics Johann Jacob Bodmer and Johann Jacob Breitinger stress the importance of the imagination much in the manner of Addison. Both came in conflict with the Wolffian rationalist critic Johann Christoph Gottsched. Whereas Gottsched was concerned with limiting the role of metaphorical imagery in tragedy for fear of diminishing its seriousness, Breitinger's *Critische Abhandlung von der Natur, den Absichten und dem Gebrauche der Gleichnisse* (1740) calls for a logic of imagination which would assure such imagery a proper role in all poetry, including tragedy. Just as the logic of reason is structured in terms of concepts and propositions, the logic of imagination functions in terms of images and metaphors (*Gleichnisse*).[33] In his *Kritische Betrachtungen über die poetischen Gemälde der Dichter* of 1741, Bodmer agrees with Addison that the imagination is attracted to what is too great for its capacity.[34] The task of the poet is to produce powerful impressions in the reader's imagination. The three main aesthetic qualities that the material world places at the disposal of the poet are beauty, greatness, and the overpowering (*das Ungestüme*). Beauty is simply pleasing, greatness causes surprise and wonder (they do not seem to be distinguished as they are by Kames), the overpowering can be repulsive and frightening, yet poets can, through their imagination, extract from it a delight (*Ergetzen*). This, as we saw, would also be Burke's term for our response to the terror of the sublime. Indeed, it seems that without using the term 'sublime', Bodmer's distinction between the great and the overpowering is roughly that of Kant's mathematical and dynamical sublime.

In 1758, one year after Burke's *Enquiry*, Mendelssohn published *Ueber das Erhabene und Naive in den schönen Wissenschaften*,[35] where he distinguishes two kinds of immensity that can inspire the imagination. The first is an extended boundlessness which is called greatness and produces a dizzying thrill. The second kind of immensity is an intensive boundlessness that overpowers us. 'Power, genius, and virtue possess an unextended immensity, which also arouses a thrilling sensation or feeling, but which has the advantage of not ending with the satiation and disgust that the tiresome uniformity of extended immensity tends to produce'.[36] This intensive immensity of power is called sublime. Mendelssohn differentiates greatness from sublimity in that our response to the latter alone exhibits an inward and moral dimension. With this, Kant's distinction between the mathematical and dynamical sublime is even more closely approximated. The sublime produces in us an admiration 'which is comparable to a flash which blinds us in an instant and then disappears' (*Ueber das Erhabene*, 177). However fleeting the effect of the sublime, it leaves us with an impression of nobility.

Although a rationalist who expects perfection in the arts, Mendelssohn looks for it not so much in cognitive terms, as did Baumgarten, as in affective terms. Having minimised the importance of the cognitive pleasure involved in imitating reality, Mendelssohn develops a disinterested, non-volitional conception of aesthetic pleasure. In his *Morgenstunden* of 1785, Mendelssohn locates the pleasure found in beauty in a distinct faculty of approval or approbation (*Billigungvermögen*), which mediates between our cognitive faculty and our faculty of desire.[37] The approbation of beauty in nature and art involves a calm, contemplative sensibility (*Empfindung*) which is 'without the least stirring of desire' and 'far removed from the longing to possess it' (*Morgenstunden*, 61). Mendelssohn seems to align himself with those, such as Sulzer and Kant, who espouse the importance of feeling (*Gefühl*); however, he clings mainly to the term *Empfindung*.

In his satirical essay 'Die Bildsäule', Mendelssohn uses the term *Gefühl* exclusively for the feeling of touch as located on the surface of our body. Here feeling involves physical contact or touch and is set beside sight as the other basic sense by which the materialists claim we know the world. For Mendelssohn, *Gefühl* seems to be the outwardly directed sense of touch and *Empfindung* the inwardly directed awareness of whatever is sensed or felt.[38] If each sense has its peculiar *Empfindung* or sensibility, then the question becomes how these sensibilities can be compared. Are some senses reducible to others? Are they translatable?

Insofar as these questions concern aesthetics, we must go back to Denis Diderot, who took up the much-discussed problem of Molyneux of whether a man blind from birth who suddenly begins to see can immediately recognise the shapes he had learned to distinguish by touch. Diderot rejects the problem as artificial for no sense can perform its functions apart from practice. It is true that 'he who uses his eyes for the first time sees only surfaces without knowing anything of projection'.[39] But the previously blind person would already have developed a sense of surface by means of touch even though touch is primarily responsible for the projection of depth. This derivative sense of surface would now be recognised as having its own immediacy. Sight and touch normally support each other, but if one of them is inoperative or deficient, the other can still gradually perfect itself in relation to experience at large. Those who are blind or deaf can compensate for their loss by perfecting their other senses. There is no aesthetic hierarchy of the senses according to Diderot. Touch can be trained to become more delicate and aesthetically sensitive than sight. The tendency to restrict aesthetic sensibility to sight and hearing should thus be questioned. Indeed, the eye can be considered as the most superficial of the senses (*Early Philosophical Works*, 165). Although amused by Castel's colour clavichord for playfully correlating musical notes and coloured fans, Diderot rejects the assumption that each note has a definite meaning which can then be translated into its colour equivalent (172). There is thus no reason to think that there is an internal or common sense that can unify the various senses.

The ideas of taste as inner feeling (*Gefühl*) in the work of Johann Georg Sulzer and of taste as pure feeling based on a *sensus communis* in Kant's work will raise the question of the translatability of the senses to a metaphorical level where harmony rather than synthetic unity is expected. We turn first to the Swiss aesthetician Sulzer, who headed the philosophical section of the Berlin Academy in the last years of his life. His *Allgemeine Theorie der schönen Künste* (1771–4) is an encyclopedia of the fine arts which was reissued and expanded after his death because it embodied much of what was best in German Enlightenment aesthetics. In the entry on taste, Sulzer first defines it as the faculty of sensing beauty. We call beautiful that which pleases without our knowing what it is or what it is useful for. 'Thus beauty pleases not because the intellect finds it perfect or because moral feeling finds it good, but because it flatters the imagination by exhibiting itself in an agreeable shape.'[40] Taste is 'the inner feeling (*Gefühl*) whereby one becomes sensitive to (*empfindet*) the charms of what is true and good' (2: 375).

Sulzer is often seen as having divided the soul into three parts or faculties: intellect, moral feeling, and taste.[41] But it is not clear whether taste as the feeling of beauty is a faculty wholly distinct from moral feeling. Sulzer asserts that the intellect, moral feeling, and taste 'can be regarded as the same faculty applied to different objects'. Moreover, he characterises taste as bringing about a harmony or 'coordination of all the mental faculties', which allows us to feel at once what the intellect can only know piecemeal (*Allgemeine Theorie*, 2: 374). As such, taste is the power of feeling things and their connectedness in a more lively manner than normal. To feel things in a lively (*lebhafte*) manner is to sense them both strongly and quickly – that is, to be stirred. The arts serve this purpose not just to amuse or entertain us but to 'arouse a lively feeling for truth and goodness' (1: 47).

In order to exalt feeling from the level of bodily touch, Sulzer may have allied it too closely with moral feeling. It is Kant who distinguishes aesthetic feeling from our moral ends by carefully defining aesthetic judgements as 'disinterested'.[42] They involve neither the interests aroused by the contents of sense, which reduce pleasure to the level of what is empirically agreeable (*angenehm*) or charming, nor the interests of reason, which demand that we approve (*billigen*) what is good. Pure aesthetic pleasure is a free imaginative enjoyment (*Wohlgefallen*) of the formal aspects of sense – like an unexpected favor.[43] Without mentioning Mendelssohn, Kant nevertheless disputes his claim that aesthetic pleasure can be disinterested by virtue of being a function of a faculty of approval (*Billigungsvermögen*). The incipiently moral notion of approval is replaced in Kant by the notion of assent. The pleasure found in beauty is defined more neutrally by Kant as the 'feeling of the promotion of life' (*Kritik der Urtheilskraft*, Ak 5: 244). Since it has no goal outside itself but merely tends to maintain and reproduce itself, this pleasure exhibits a purposiveness without a definite purpose.[44] To assign beauty a definite purpose would be to link it to a kind of perfection. In order to preserve the disinterestedness of aesthetic pleasure, Kant gave up the rationalist search for perfection in beauty.

In epistemological terms, aesthetic pleasure involves an indeterminate felt harmony of the cognitive powers – imagination and understanding – which is purposive for knowledge in general but not determinate enough to produce new knowledge (see Ak 5: 217–19). Aesthetic judgements are thus not determinant judgements giving us more information than we already have about objects in the world. They are reflective judgements about our response to the qualities of objects already known. Like Baumgarten, Kant claims that aesthetic judgements are about singular objects, but he differs in not attributing to them any special knowledge that allows us to single out these objects as determinate individuals. Our pleasure in the aesthetic form of the object is at the same time a clue for imagining a greater overall order in the world (Ak 5: 301). But this affinity between a judging subject, an aesthetic object, and a systematic world order is indeterminate at best.[45]

The response we feel to beauty in objects of nature and in works of art is subjectively universal in that we expect others to agree with our disinterested assent (Ak 5: 214).[46] Such agreement can also be regarded as necessary 'under the presupposition that there is a common sense' (Ak 5: 238).[47] This common sense is not, however, a sense that unites all the external senses discussed by Mendelssohn and Diderot. Kant had already dealt with the problem of the possible discontinuity of the outer senses by relating them to the a priori form of inner sense in the *Kritik der reinen Vernunft*. There the imagination served as a kind of common sense by extracting from the outer senses and linking what is relevant to a mathematically and conceptually ordered objective world. By contrast, the common sense appealed to in the *Kritik der Urtheilskraft* to account for agreement in taste relates our own subjective faculties by means of a felt or formal harmony that is also communicable to other human subjects (Ak 5: 238–9). Kant calls it a *sensus communis* or 'a communal sense . . . , that in its reflection, takes account (*a priori*) of everyone else's way of representing in thought' (Ak 5: 293). Taste is for Kant a mode of sensibility or feeling about which we can reach a reflective agreement but not a determinate consensus.

To be able to have this felt but reflective enjoyment of beauty, we must abstract from the sensuous content of an object and apprehend its formal features. The sublime is often contrasted with beauty by being thought to be formless, but when Kant says that the sublime can also (*auch*) be found in a formless object, he implies that it is possible to find sublimity in well-formed objects as well (Ak 5: 244). What is more important is that in sublime pleasure we are overwhelmed 'by the feeling of a momentary inhibition of the vital powers and the immediately following and all the more powerful outpouring of them' (Ak 5: 245). The sublime provides a more complex feeling than beauty. To the extent that the imagination is overwhelmed by what is mathematically great and dynamically overpowering, the sublime is actually displeasurable. It is only because we are forced in upon ourselves and discover the superiority of our reason that we can draw pleasure from what is physically overwhelming. The sublime does not give a positive pleasure as does beauty but a negative pleasure that contains a measure of self-abnegating respect for reason. This respect is moral in the case of the dynamical sublime but theoretical in the case of the mathematically sublime (Ak 5: 259–60). We will return to the problem of the relation between aesthetic sensibility and moral reason in the last sections of this chapter.

III. ORIGINALITY, HISTORICAL CONTEXT, AND GENIUS

Eighteenth-century aesthetics also manifests a great interest in the conditions of creativity, and we see an increasing number of works on the nature and role of genius. Much of the discussion of genius was inspired by the Quarrel of the Ancients and the Moderns. If, as most thought, the Ancients possessed a superiority in the arts,[48] this could be explained by the peculiar historical circumstances that allowed original genius to flourish untrammeled by traditional rules. The response to this can be either to accept this explanation but minimise the importance of genius by placing more emphasis on the civilising virtues of good taste or to attempt to restore the possibility of genius by rejecting learning and imitation.

In France, Du Bos stressed the organic and environmental determinants of genius. According to him, each genius traverses a unique path, but one determined by local conditions rather than chosen by an inventive imagination. Du Bos considers genius to be the product of 'a fortunate arrangement of the brain as well as of the quality of the blood' that nourishes it (*Réflexions*, II.ii, 14). The latter is influenced by the quality of the air we breathe, and this in turn by 'emanations from the earth' caused by temperature and climate (II.xiv, 251). Climatic conditions are used to attempt to explain why England produced excellent poets and musicians but no great painters (the most important artists for Du Bos) (see II.xi, 160). Montesquieu adds religious and political constraints as historical factors to be considered in judging the quality of art. The Egyptians had the ability to design well but fell short of the Greeks in their art because their religion did not allow them to experiment freely to give their shapes movement and grace.[49]

Diderot also posits an organic basis for genius but stresses its visceral sources and dependence on humours. There is always something unpredictable about genius because like greatness it 'is usually the result of a natural equilibrium among opposite qualities'.[50] Genius is defined as the capacity to see a situation at a glance and understand it without any studious gaze.[51] Whereas genius is an instantaneous gift of nature, taste is the product of long study. The products of genius thus always have something 'irregular, precipitous, and savage'[52] about them. As distinct from the beautiful and regular products of taste (Virgil, Racine), the products of genius (Homer, Shakespeare, Milton) are sublime. It follows from this that works of taste conform to the conventions of their historical age, whereas the products of genius transcend them: 'Milton is constantly violating the rules of his language' ('Génie', 583a). The excesses of genius make it productive in the case of Rameau but destructive in the case of his nephew. Even the triumphs of genius are a mixed blessing, for they can retard subsequent artistic development by encouraging servile imitations (*Rameau's Nephew*, 298).

Voltaire, the quintessential Enlightenment *philosophe*, is much more troubled by the tension between genius and taste than Diderot. Although Voltaire claims to respect the inventiveness of genius, he thinks that we profit much more from those who go on to refine and perfect the contributions of genius. The price of originality is imperfection. We need to combine the crude originality of a genius, who acknowledges no master, with the talent to imitate and improve on masters. Only by means of the art of imitation can civilisation progress and taste improve. To insist on the constant introduction of genius would be to endanger this progress.

If Voltaire stands at one extreme in urging that genius be made to conform to the societal demands of taste, the English poet Edward Young stands at the other extreme in urging that genius must above all remain true to its own nature. Whereas Voltaire sees in imitation a means for human progress, Young regards imitation as servile and mechanical. In his *Conjectures on Original Composition* (1759), Young writes: '[B]y a Spirit of *Imitation* we counteract nature, and thwart her design. She brings us into the world all *Originals.* . . . [H]ow comes it to pass that we die *Copies*?'[53] Young's simple recipe for poetic genius is to look within and nurture 'the native growth of thy own mind' rather than to look back at the learning that our heritage can give us (24).

In his *Essay on Original Genius* (1767), William Duff regards learning and critical judgement as unfavourable to poetic genius but as necessary for philosophical and scientific genius. All genius is characterised by inventive imagination, but whereas in philosophy this power manifests itself in a greater accuracy, in poetry it does so in a greater compass.[54] To define the inventive imagination, Duff distinguishes it from the kind of imagination involved in wit and humour. The purpose of wit and humour is to entertain us; they exhibit a 'quick and lively Fancy' in assembling images that can excite pleasantry or ridicule (58). There is something superficial about this fancy as it hurries from idea to idea without allowing us 'time to conceive any of them distinctly' (59). Fancy is contrasted with a 'vigorous, extensive, and Plastic Imagination' characteristic of genius (58). There are thus two kinds of imagination, the plastic imagination of genius, which invents 'new associations of ideas', and fancy, which is restricted to already existing associations (7). No matter how 'vivacious' or quick fancy may be, it lacks the vigour of the plastic imagination to create new associations or combinations of ideas (59). Duff's distinction between fancy and plastic imagination seems a striking anticipation of Coleridge's separation of fancy from imagination as esemplastic power. However, Duff's plastic imagination still makes use of the power of association, whereas Coleridge's esemplastic imagination transcends it.[55]

Gerard also relates genius to invention and imaginative association. He writes in *An Essay on Genius* (1774) that genius 'requires a peculiar vigour of association. In order to produce it, the imagination must be comprehensive, regular, and active.'[56] The comprehensiveness necessary for genius involves surveying the ideas of others – that is, the world of learning. The second requisite attribute of imagination – regularity – is the capacity 'of avoiding foreign, useless, and superfluous conceptions, at the same time that none necessary or proper are passed by' (47). Regularity consists in not pursuing those associations that lead away from the subject at hand. Activity, the third attribute of genius, means that it must be self-motivated in associating ideas and not allow external causes to divert it from its own design or project. When ideas are associated with 'vigour', they make up a coherent whole. What is to be avoided is a 'false fertility' that leads to 'such ideas as are connected with the last that was present, yet have no connexion either with the former ones, or with the main design' (49).

Gerard expects genius to abide by principles of association, but not so much in terms of the commonly formulated rules of habitual and external aggregation as in terms of a kind of internal organisation. Indeed, he notes that the great inaugural geniuses never had available to them any explicit rules they could follow. But nevertheless they observed implicit laws. Gerard concludes that 'critics discovered the rules which they prescribe, only by remarking those laws by which true genius, though uninstructed, had actually governed itself' (72–3). Explicit rules of poetry à la Aristotle can only be formulated in retrospect and prescribed for epigones.

When we move to Germany, we find the seeds of an intermediate response to the genius–taste debate in the works of Winckelmann. In his *Geschichte der Kunst des Alterthums*, Winckelmann sketches a theory of the historical development of the arts that prizes neither the originality of genius nor the perfectability of taste. According to Winckelmann, all the visual arts manifest three prominent stages: (1) a stage that involves producing simple shapes from material, (2) a stage that delineates more complex proportional forms, and (3) a final decorative stage marked by superfluity and excess (*Geschichte der Kunst*, 15). The first, necessary stage, in which people delight in giving shape to materials such as clay, can be found in all nations. The second stage aims at representing human beauty. This stage requires the ability to draw a well-proportioned body while allowing its beauty to express human qualities – demands that are only seldom met. Here the Greeks excelled because they lived in a sunny and moderate climate which encouraged the development of both natural beauty and the perfection of the arts. Also, the Athenians were blessed with a government that fostered the free celebration of the arts. As much as artists of later times could learn from the models provided by the Greeks, their attempts to improve on them have led to decorative excess. The balance achieved by the Greeks of a delicate feel for beauty and human expressiveness constituted a rare perfection that subsequent artists could not rival. Thus Michelangelo's statues display an excessively hard beauty, according to Winckelmann, and Bernini's an exaggerated expressiveness. Winckelmann's threefold historical scheme, in which the middle phase is the only perfect one, will find many successors, including Hegel's well-known distinction between the symbolical, classical, and romantic styles of art.

Johann Gottfried Herder, best known for his attempts to define German self-identity at the dawn of the Sturm und Drang period,[57] applied a more radical historical perspective to the arts, or more properly to their poetic or creative source. Whereas art seeks perfection and completion, poetry is the process of beginning anew. Herder was greatly influenced by Johann Georg Hamann, who held that 'poetry is the mother tongue of the human race.'[58] Since poetry is an inceptive force, there are no timeless standards for it, according to Herder. 'Poetry is a Proteus among peoples, which changes its shape with each national language, ethical outlook, custom, temperament, climate, even accent.'[59] It is thus inappropriate to establish Homer's accomplishments in the Greek language as a model for other national literatures as they begin to flower in their own time. Each nation produces its indigenous poetry with its own incommensurable value. In his *Ideen zur Philosophie der Geschichte der Menschheit* (1784–91), Herder acknowledges the role of material conditions in explaining national differences, but he adds a teleological perspective, not in order to posit some external goal but to articulate a variety of self-generating inner perfections. Each national outlook is but one human expression of a multifarious divine perspective on reality. A similar duality has been shown to exist in Herder's approach to genius: especially in his youth he regarded it like a Socratic *daemon* or divine spirit that accompanies and guides poets in their original linguistic productivity; on the other hand, he also treated it as a natural disposition or fortuitous proportion of mental faculties.[60]

Kant rejected the teleological speculations of his former student Herder and developed a more explicit theory of genius that seeks to balance the claims for originality and taste. Genius is defined by Kant as 'the inborn predisposition of the mind (*ingenium*) through which nature gives the rule to art'. Kant explicates this nature as 'nature in the subject', which gives the rule to art 'by means of the disposition of its faculties' (*Kritik der Urtheilskraft*, Ak 5: 307). Thus, for him genius involves a fortuitous relation among the cognitive faculties of understanding and imagination (Ak 5: 317). Kant reduces the claim that genius is a divine guiding spirit to an etymological hypothesis (Ak 5: 308). The rule given to art is not a definite rule that could be learned. Genius is marked by originality, meaning that it follows no prior standards. But its products may not be original nonsense and must be able to make sense to others. For this reason, Kant warns that the wings of genius need to be clipped by the discipline of taste. The second attribute of genius is that its products are exemplary, namely, a standard for the judgement of others. Thirdly, the creative process of genius cannot be scientifically explained or transmitted by rule (Ak 5: 307–8).

Kant departs from the positions of Duff and Gerard[61] in asserting that genius exists only in the arts, not in science. Kant's overall position is that nature, through the medium of genius, prescribes rules to the beautiful arts, but that science prescribes rules to nature. In the case of science, the rules are formal rules of determinant judgement that make possible the experience of the objects of nature conceived as constituting an impersonal external world: nature outside the subject. In the case of art, we saw that genius draws on a more restricted nature: 'nature in the subject', or human nature. The rules of genius establish standards for aesthetic or reflective judgement where we also consider how the subject fits into nature: nature as the human context. Whereas the scientist prescribes laws to nature in general on the model of the understanding, artistic genius prescribes a different kind of contextual order which we can feel ourselves part of.

This aesthetic order is, according to Kant, an analogue of rational order. Thus he claims that genius creates aesthetic ideas, which are the imaginative counterparts to rational ideas. The artist's imagination assumes a role complementary to that of reason in striving to complete our experience. This is most fully displayed in the poetic imagination:

The poet ventures to make sensible rational ideas of invisible beings, the kingdom of the blessed, the kingdom of hell, eternity, creation, etc., as well as to make that of which there are examples in experience . . . sensible beyond the limits of experience, with a completeness that goes beyond anything of which there is an example in nature, by means of . . . imagination. (Ak 5: 314)[62]

Whereas rational ideas are concepts for which we have no adequate intuition, aesthetic ideas are intuitions for which we have no adequate concept. Both ideas transcend experience, but in the one case we exceed it abstractly or austerely and in the other in a more concrete or suggestive way that actually stimulates our thinking. Thus Kant claims that an intuitively charged aesthetic idea 'occasions much thinking (*denken*), without, however, any one definite thought (*Gedanke*), i.e., *concept*, being adequate to it' (Ak 5: 314). Although Kant consistently rules out intellectual intuition (that is, intuitive conceptualisation based on rational ideas), his notion of genius introduces the possibility of intuitive thinking inspired by aesthetic ideas. Such intuitive thinking cannot be adequately expressed in determinate concepts, yet as we will see in the next section, it can be expressed and symbolised by language.

IV. EXPRESSION AND MEANING IN THE ARTS

With the increasing stress on the subjective experiences of the aesthetic spectator and creative genius, the problem of expressing this inner life became more urgent. Most eighteenth-century aestheticians who speak of expression still do so within the framework of an imitation theory of art. Accordingly, expression is often conceived as the process of finding external signs corresponding to discrete mental contents. In the first half of this section, we will see that for a few thinkers signs can also express the life of the human subject in a more sweeping manner, not so much to describe states as to draw a character. The second half will deal with the way signs relate to one another as part of a medium and make certain types of expression more appropriate in one art than in another.

1. Expression as characterisation

We saw Du Bos claim on the basis of his distinction between natural and artificial signs that painting, by its use of natural signs, can have a more direct effect on us than poetry. Burke, by contrast, argues for the greater importance of poetry in arousing emotions. Poetry cannot 'succeed in exact descriptions so well as painting does', but its true task is 'to affect rather by sympathy than imitation' (*Inquiry*, 157). Words do not resemble the things they refer to, but they can, according to Burke, represent the effect things have on our mind more powerfully than even the most exact visual representation. Poetic language has the power to move us, to arouse our sympathy, to infect us, as it were, with the passions of others.

Kames also argues for the greater effectiveness of poetry. Painting can make a 'deeper impression than words', but words can raise our passions to greater heights (*Criticism*, 51). In his analysis of signs as means of expression, Kames distinguishes between voluntary and involuntary signs to argue that poetry too can have a natural effect. Clearly, all involuntary signs, such as the grimace that attends pain and the trembling that accompanies terror, are natural, but not all voluntary signs are artificial or arbitrary. Some voluntary signs of passion, such as the words used to express an agitated state of mind, may be arbitrarily chosen, but the tone in which I utter my particular words will have a shrillness that is quite natural and universal. Kames's main concern is to show that many voluntary signs of passion are natural. Apart from expressing passions in words, we express them in gestures and actions with 'a surprising uniformity. Excessive joy is expressed by leaping, dancing, or some elevation of the body; excessive grief, by sinking or depressing it; and prostration and kneeling have been employed by all nations, and in all ages, to signify profound veneration' (193).

However, Kames also points out that the passions adjust themselves to a person's character. They 'receive a tincture from every peculiarity of character: and for that reason it rarely happens, that a passion, in the different circumstances of feeling, of sentiment, and of expression, is precisely the same in any two persons' (*Criticism*, 203). What mediates between a felt passion and its expression are sentiments or thoughts that must be in tune with characteristic traits of a person. Kames in effect moves from expression as mere externalisation toward expression as characterisation in the sense of bringing out what is distinctive.

To what extent the expression of emotion also reflects a person's overall character is not clear from the writings of Kames. It is, however, explicit in the work of Archibald Alison, who uses expression as a principle of unity and composition. In his *Essays on the Nature and Principles of Taste* (1790), Alison describes how we can understand a landscape painting first from the standpoint of imitation and then from the standpoint of expression. When we judge it for its imitative qualities, we compare the parts of the painting to their originals to evaluate the representational skills of the artist. But when we judge the landscape painting for expression, we look for its overall or unifying character. Alison writes: 'As our knowledge of the expressions of nature increases, our sensibility to the beauty or to the defects of composition becomes more keen.'[63] He indicates that the initial language of imitation speaks only to the eye and the intellect. The language of expression, however, requires 'interpretation' by the imagination and the heart (90).

Strictly speaking, neither the original landscape nor its imitation on the canvas can be classified as beautiful in themselves. They only become beautiful as *'signs or expressions* of such qualities, as, by the constitution of our nature, are fitted to produce pleasing or interesting emotion' (emphasis added) (144). For Alison, association is one of the main ways by which qualities of matter can come to be interpreted as expressing qualities of mind. As employed in the empirical analysis of aesthetic impressions, the principle of association has often been criticised by Dilthey and others for leaving our experience of a work of art a mere aggregate of separate elements. Alison, however, stands as a notable departure from this widespread tendency among British thinkers when he distinguishes between the ordinary association involved in our everyday experiences and a special aesthetic association in response to beauty.[64] Whereas in ordinary association separate ideas are related to each other in temporal succession, aesthetic association produces an overall emotive connectedness in a beautiful object. Whatever may be the character of the first emotion inspired by a beautiful scene, 'the images which succeed seem all to have a relation to this character; and if we trace them back, we shall discover not only a connexion between the individual thoughts of the train, but also a general relation among the whole, and a conformity to that peculiar emotion which first excited them' (61). If the beautiful object is natural, then the emotional unity derives from the character of the spectator; if it is a product of art, it can be interpreted as being expressive of the compositional genius of the artist.

2. The means of expression

On the Continent, much of the debate concerning expression in the arts was instigated by Winckelmann's view of the proper relation between emotional expressiveness and beautiful form. According to Winckelmann, expression is the source of meaning, but beautiful individuating form is necessary for aesthetic pleasure. The artist should only express emotions calm enough to be compatible with pleasurable forms and not allow an exaggerated expressiveness to distort beauty. Thus, Winckelmann claims that in accordance with the ethos of ancient Greece a great man such as Laocoön had to be represented as trying to suppress his suffering (*Geschichte der Kunst*, 176). To portray him as screaming in pain would go against his dignity as well as against our ideals of beauty.

In his *Laocoön* of 1766, Gotthold Lessing criticises Winckelmann for thinking that crying out when in pain is incompatible with the Greek conception of nobility of soul. He turns to the heroes of Homer and Sophocles to show that while being 'above human nature in other respects', they 'remain faithful to it in their sensitiveness to pain . . . and in the expression of this feeling by cries, tears, or invectives'.[65] While disputing Winckelmann's general injunction against the expression of agitated emotions, Lessing does allow that their visual portrayal is limited by considerations of beauty. Laocoön's pain should not be fully expressed in a statue, for to fix his scream in marble would distort his facial features and render them ugly. But Lessing insists that such a restriction of expressiveness does not apply to the literary arts. Lessing explains this in terms of the basic difference in the way in which painting (all the visual arts) and poetry (all the literary arts) imitate reality: the former uses forms and colours in space, and the latter articulates sounds in time. These sensuous media set the conditions for what can be appropriately or best expressed in each kind of art. The figures and colours of painting are best used to represent bodies and their visible properties; the articulated sounds of poetry are best used to represent actions. To be sure, poetry can also depict bodies, 'but only by suggestion through actions', and painting can imitate actions, but only by what can be suggested by bodies at one point in time (*Laocoön*, 78). If visual artists are to suggest the Laocoön story, they should not choose the climactic moment of a scream. 'There is nothing beyond this, and to present the utmost to the eye is to bind the wings of fancy' (19). To depict a scream would fix a natural evanescent phase of an action into a permanent but repugnant state. However, the poet Virgil could legitimately allow Laocoön to shriek in pain because there it is a mere momentary phase in the unfolding of a larger action.

The discussion of appropriate means of expression also comes to life in the controversy over the use of allegorical figures in painting. Du Bos questioned the neoclassical expectation that allegorical figures be included in landscape painting. Such embodiments of traditional ideals can only be understood through learning and therefore tend to work against the more direct expressive effects of natural signs. Winckelmann, however, continues to accept the use of allegory as pointing to the ideal beauty which he sought in the visual arts. Lessing, in turn, attacks the 'mania for allegory' as an attempt to make the painting a 'silent poem, without having considered to what degree it is able to express general ideas . . .' (*Laocoön*, 5).

Mendelssohn's treatment of allegory occurs in his discussion of the appropriate means of expressing sublime states of mind. In his essay *Ueber das Erhabene*, he claims that the sublime in art can most readily exert its overpowering effect through a 'naive or unaffected expression, which allows the reader or spectator to think more than what is said to him' (179).

A naive expression must be more than a simple expression. It should also exhibit nobility if it is to be suggestive of something important. Mendelssohn accepts the use of allegory but warns that one should not have to think, reflect, or strain one's wit to guess the meaning of allegorical signs. Allegories 'must be both natural and intuitive, that is, the nature of the sign must be grounded in the nature of what is designated' (*Ueber das Erhabene*, 159). But this is unfortunately not the case when the soul is represented by the image of a butterfly.

In his reflections on means of expression, Mendelssohn also uses a twofold scheme of the arts, but it is no longer the painting–poetry dichotomy used by Du Bos and Lessing. Instead, he distinguishes between the literary arts (*schöne Wissenschaften*), which use the artificial signs of language, and the fine arts (*schöne Künste*), which use natural signs, either visual or auditory. This means that music is no longer considered an appendage to poetry as in Lessing. Instead, it assumes a central role among the fine arts. Music is not merely a sequential art as is commonly thought. Since music uses both melody and harmony, Mendelssohn considers it successive as well as simultaneous in nature.

Herder goes a step further by introducing a threefold scheme of the arts which he bases on the three fundamental metaphysical concepts of space, time, and force. In his *Kritische Wälder* (1769), he writes: '[T]he arts that deliver *works* produce their effect in space; the arts that work by means of *energy*, in time; the various species of fine letters, or rather the only one, poetry, works by means of *force*.'[66] Concerning the arts of space, Herder rejects the traditional way of making painting or design definitive. Sculpture is more fundamental than painting because it addresses our sense of touch, the tactile source of feeling. The proper generic designation for the spatial arts is 'plastic' according to Herder. The temporal arts, music and dance, should really be called energetic arts. Music, for instance, cannot be defined as just a succession of sounds *in* time because it also creates its effect on us *through* time. What is essential to music and dance is their capacity to express energy through time. Finally, Herder makes the point against Lessing that the action portrayed in epic and tragic poetry is not reducible to a sequence of temporal moments. 'Action arises when *successivity comes from force*' (*Kritische Wälder*, 120). For Herder, poetry constitutes a third genus of art, which is more powerful and encompassing than the plastic and the energetic arts because it expresses force or felt meaning.

Kant also sets forth a threefold division of the fine arts in his theory of expression. Expression involves not only seizing thought in definite concepts or words but also fixing intuition in visual forms and discerning the modulations of sense in tonalities. These three modes of expression are necessary for full communication and can be called verbal articulation, visual gesticulation, and tonal modulation, respectively. They are then used by Kant to distinguish three kinds of fine art: the arts of speech, the formative arts, such as painting, sculpture, and architecture, and the arts of the beautiful play of sensations, whether of sound or colour.

We saw that an aesthetic idea of genius involves intuitive thinking that strives to complete our experiences like a rational idea. However, its intuitive thought content is indeterminate and its relation to rational ideas is merely felt. Expression is necessary to give aesthetic ideas a sensible form. Kant elaborates this only for language as a medium of expression. In §59 of the *Kritik der Urtheilskraft*, he shows that a linguistic expression can be an arbitrary *sign* based on the associations of ordinary experience or it can be a *symbol* that also presents (*darstellt*) some affinity with what is thought. The mere expression of an aesthetic idea provides no more than an external sensible form for its intuitive content. When the aesthetic idea is also presented symbolically, its indeterminate intuitive content is explicated imaginatively into more specific 'aesthetic attributes' which generate analogies with rational ideas (Ak 5: 315). The symbol as an imaginative presentation of an indeterminate idea of reason is the analogue of a schema in Kant's *Kritik der reinen Vernunft*, which is an imaginative presentation of a determinate concept (or rule) of the understanding. When Kant suggests that the aesthetic imagination 'schematizes without a concept' (Ak 5: 287), this can be interpreted to refer to the process of symbolisation.[67] The cooperation of expression and symbolical presentation can be illustrated by two poetic lines cited by Kant:

Die Sonne quoll hervor, wie Ruh aus Tugend quillt. (Ak 5: 316)

The first line gives sensible expression to the ordinary experience of the sun rising; the second line creates a presentational analogy between the rational idea of virtue and an aesthetic state of tranquillity. Once we move beyond the experiential synthesis of the sunrise to aesthetic attributes such as tranquillity and flow, we rise to a level of more suggestive reflective affinities that provide the background for Kant's claim that 'the beautiful is the symbol of the morally good' (Ak 5: 353). This symbolic relation between beauty and goodness is a complex one. At this point, we can say that being based on reflective judgement and analogy, the relation is at best indirect and requires interpretation. Unlike Meier, Kant did not explicitly develop an aesthetically based hermeneutics. Yet he speaks of a 'true interpretation' (*Auslegung*) of beauty in nature as showing aesthetic feeling to be 'akin to the moral feeling'.[68]

The general assumption of all those writers we have studied concerning the role of expression in art is that the meaning of a work of art derives from its relation to something outside it, whether that be the creative subject, the natural world, or something supersensible such as Kant's rational ideas. Karl Philipp Moritz, author of the novel *Anton Rieser* and a friend of Goethe, seems to be an exception to this when he claims that a beautiful figure 'should not mean anything, should not speak of anything outside itself. Instead, it should speak only of itself, of its inner being by means of its outer surfaces. It should become significant through itself.'[69] This is perhaps the strongest formulation of his well-known conviction that beauty is that which is complete or perfect in itself (*das in sich selbst Vollendete*). But this definition does not make the work of art as autonomous as it might appear. It is meant to counter the view of Mendelssohn and Sulzer that the purpose of art lies in its pleasurable output for us. Moritz insists that our input is necessary for the true existence of the work of art. 'We can very well exist without looking at beautiful artworks, but they cannot well exist as such without our gaze.'[70] The perfection of the work consists in presenting us with a self-sufficient whole, but through the input of our gaze it continues to imitate the world. Moritz thus clearly stops short of later theories of art for art's sake.[71]

V. THE STANDARD OF TASTE: AESTHETIC AND MORAL VALUE

The proper relation between beauty and goodness and between taste and morals is one of the most vexing problems in the aesthetics of the eighteenth century. Rousseau is quite equivocal on this question in *Émile* (1762), where taste is dismissed as 'the art of knowing all about petty things' that are at best entertaining and yet acknowledged as presupposing good morals and as worth cultivating.[72] Émile's taste is to be cultivated by spending some time in the society of Paris, but it can remain unspoiled only by soon leaving Paris and returning to nature. 'Émile will get more of a taste for the books of the ancients than for ours, for the sole reason that the ancients . . . are closest to nature and their genius is more their own' (343).

To the extent that the models of taste established by the ancients were no longer so generally accepted in the eighteenth century, the problem of the standard of taste came to be an urgent one. Here Hume's essay 'Of the Standard of Taste' (1757) played a central role. Hume is said to have developed a perceptual model of aesthetic judgement[73] whereby taste is not made subservient to moral and religious standards. But he does not exclude moral judgements from his evaluation of art, for he remarks that the 'want of humanity and of decency, so conspicuous in the characters drawn by several of the ancient poets, even sometimes by Homer . . . , diminishes considerably the merit of their noble performances, and gives modern authors an advantage over them.'[74]

Hume begins by noting that it is relatively easy to agree about general values but difficult to decide what instantiates them. We all applaud beauty and justice but find that our sentiments are quite diverse when it comes to deciding whether a particular object is beautiful or a particular act is just. Given this situation, it is 'natural' for us to seek a 'rule, by which the various sentiments of men may be reconciled' (268).

Hume first considers a position that denies the possibility of any such rule for taste. It holds that taste involves subjective sentiments that refer to nothing beyond themselves. Beauty is not an objective property of things but exists merely in the mind. Because there is no objective standard or rule, it is 'fruitless to dispute' about our varying tastes. Although this position is derived from sceptical philosophising, it has become proverbial and 'seems to have attained the sanction of common sense'. We have here a rare convergence of scepticism and common sense. There is, however, an opposing position, also assumed to be a species of common sense, which holds that not everyone is right in judging the relative worth of artistic products. Accordingly, those who pronounce the 'sentiment' that there is 'an equality of genius between Ogilby and Milton' are dismissed as 'ridiculous' (269). Note that in this view, the meaning of 'sentiment' has shifted from mere subjective feeling to an opinion about something objective.

'All the general rules of art', Hume writes, 'are founded only on experience and on the observation of the common sentiments of human nature', but the feelings of men will not always 'be conformable to these rules' (270). General rules allow us to discern great disparities in artistic quality, such as between Ogilby and Milton, but they are less helpful when the disparities are less great. Moreover, if we are too rigid in applying them, we will be left with merely insipid works.

In matters of taste, the rules of common sense are no substitute for what Hume calls 'good sense'. Taste involves developing the finer emotions, and this requires favourable circumstances that rarely exist. To be 'a true judge' of the fine arts requires 'strong sense, united to delicate sentiment, improved by practice, perfected by comparison, and cleared of all prejudice' (277–8). How will we know whether all these conditions have been met? Hume himself recognises a problem here but indicates that he has at least shifted the debate from the domain of felt sentiments to that of matters of fact. One can now bring arguments to bear on the relative strengths of different people's sensibility and education and begin to form a consensus about the ideal aesthetic judge and his or her taste. Against the objection that a present consensus may be just a fashion, Hume counters that since certain poets, such as Virgil, have endured the scrutiny of critics for more than a thousand years, we can assume that at least their work meets the standard of taste.

In the work of Kames, we see an explicit connection made between aesthetics and moral judgement. In the concluding chapter of his *Elements of Criticism*, he claims that taste concerns propriety in morals as well as in the fine arts. In both cases, we can rely on common sense. The standards of common sense in morals are more definite because here uniformity is more urgent than in the fine arts, which concern our leisure. Were the standard of taste in fine art 'clear and authoritative, it would banish all difference of taste, leaving us no distinction between a refined taste and one that is not so; which would put an end to all improvement' (*Criticism*, 444). Again refinement becomes an issue in taste; many are ineligible to decide what constitutes the common sense of mankind. Kames asserts that coarse bodily labour leaves us aesthetically insensitive and that voluptuousness extinguishes the sympathetic affections central to taste in both the moral and aesthetic senses. Although refined aesthetic taste is more prevalent in the higher classes, the fine arts encourage an inclusive social sympathy available to all. Even people 'addicted to the grosser amusements', often 'approve of those who have a more refined taste'.[75] Even though they themselves do not live up to it, they recognise 'a common standard with respect to the dignity of human nature' (442).

In contrast with Hume, Gerard is willing to allow even felt sentiments a role in the establishment of taste, for he believes that they contain a reference beyond themselves. To be sure, a sentiment 'is not an *image* of a quality inherent in the object; but it is the natural *effect* of it'.[76] As such an effect, it can be measured not as true or false but as more or less appropriate. As we saw before, there is for Gerard a sensible or felt aspect to the sentiment of taste that is rooted in our internal senses. But there is also a judgemental aspect to taste that can be made more discerning by measuring whether our sentiments are appropriate responses to the works of art. This is not a question of finding either an ideal aesthetic observer or pointing to works that have stood Hume's durability test for universality. That Virgil is still approved by Europeans does not mean that he would be appreciated by Asians (see *Essay on Taste*, 233). No work has come close to receiving universal approbation. A more limited, inductive standard of taste becomes available by observing what specific qualities in objects cause pleasing aesthetic sentiments. If in considering these qualities we find certain common ones, then we have the basis for comparing the degree to which they manifest themselves in different objects and deciding which object 'deserves the preference' (260). This kind of analysis of works of art into their common pleasure-producing elements is the task of criticism. Having found such common qualities, criticism can 'furnish principles for deciding between discordant appreciations' and determine what constitutes correct taste (253).

With Kant we move from an inductive approach for finding specific rules of taste to a transcendental approach concerning the possibility of rules of taste in general. Both Hume and Kant begin by taking into account the actual divergences of taste, but whereas the British tend to proceed comparatively to find inductive generalisations, Kant proceeds reflectively to consider their universal conditions. British criticism looks for standards of taste by deriving from actual sentiments whatever necessary rules it can to judge the quality of works of art. Kant's critique of taste moves from actual judgements of taste back to the transcendental conditions that make their universality possible.

Transcendental philosophy is essentially regressive in method. In the *Kritik der reinen Vernunft*, Kant asks what transcendental conditions make objective knowledge of nature possible. They are shown to be the a priori formal conditions that allow us to legislate a general lawful order to natural events. In the *Kritik der praktischen Vernunft*, Kant's transcendental question concerns the possibility of moral action. Here his answer is that we can be moral only if we freely submit to the moral law and legislate it to ourselves and others alike. The transcendental problematic of the *Kritik der Urtheilskraft* does not introduce yet a third sense of law but opens up the possibility that natural and moral laws – the necessity of what is and the necessity of what ought to be – may at some point come to be in harmony. The felt harmony of aesthetic pleasure is a promissory note in that direction.

Kant's transcendental deduction of taste seeks to show 'how it is possible that something could please merely in the judging (without a sensation of the senses or a concept) and that . . . the satisfaction of one can also be announced as a rule for everyone else'.[77] This rule is a priori but only subjective because it is based on neither a sensation nor a concept but on a pure feeling of a formal relation among our faculties. Insofar as the harmony of my cognitive faculties felt in apprehending the form of a beautiful object is also the harmony of these faculties necessary for knowledge in general, Kant claims that we can assume it to be universal in nature. To be sure, there is no concept by which I can prove universal agreement by an objective determinant judgement. I can only impute the agreement of others by means of a transcendental rule of reflective judgement. This transcendental rule is the principle of the *sensus communis*, which allows for the possibility that a singular aesthetic feeling may be communicable and provide the basis for universal reflection. Whenever I pronounce an aesthetic judgement, I expect such agreement because I regard my judgement as more than a pronouncement of a private liking. I cannot be certain in any particular case, however, that I have made a pure aesthetic judgement without any private liking influencing me.

Kant's transcendental critique of taste merely legitimises the possibility of universal agreement in matters of taste and provides no normative criteria for deciding about particulars. Yet in the 'Dialectic of the Aesthetical Judgement', Kant does offer some further orientation for dealing with differences in taste. Like Hume, he starts with two commonplaces about taste: (1) 'everyone has his own taste', and (2) 'there is no disputing about taste'. The first translates into

Hume's 'It is fruitless to dispute.' The second commonplace could be translated into the stronger claim that it is impossible to dispute because there are no definite concepts whereby we can settle differences of taste. Kant introduces a third alternative: there are 'quarrels' about taste that cannot be settled definitively like conceptual disputes but that nevertheless lead us to move beyond our own private tastes and are resolvable in a more general way. It is obvious that quarrels about taste cannot be based on determinate concepts of the understanding, but Kant speculates that they may refer to an indeterminate concept of reason, namely, the idea of 'the supersensible substratum of appearances' (*Kritik der Urtheilskraft*, Ak 5: 341). This suggests that different judgements of taste may in some sense be resolved by being oriented toward the idea of humanity. Such a resolution is confirmed in §60, where Kant concludes that 'the propaedeutic for all beautiful art . . . seems to lie, not in precepts, but in the culture of the mental powers through those prior forms of knowledge that are called *humaniora*, presumably because *humanity* means on the one hand the universal *feeling of participation* and on the other hand the capacity for being able to *communicate* one's inmost self universally' (Ak 5: 355). Kant expects this humanising propaedeutic to produce a 'mean' between the refinement of high culture and the originality of natural simplicity, which when brought together furnish a 'correct standard for taste' (Ak 5: 356). This suggests that beauty as a symbol of morality serves not only to intuitively illustrate our rational ideas about virtue but also to humanise them.

The orientation toward humanity is carried further by Friedrich Schiller in his letters *Über die ästhetische Erziehung des Menschen* (1793–5), where aesthetics is applied beyond merely giving a standard of taste to projecting an ideal of human-ity. Writing while the Reign of Terror in France was shaking the Enlightenment faith in progress and freedom through reason, Schiller argues that a harmonious political state cannot be attained 'as long as the split within man is not healed'.[78] The aim of aesthetic education is to produce well-rounded individuals in whom there is a harmonious balance among all their powers. The one-sided favouring of the senses leads to savagery; reliance on reason alone leads to barbarism. To become truly civilised, we must be able to balance the sense impulse, which desires variety of content, with the form impulse of reason, which desires unity. This balance is attained in the play impulse, which combines both the sense and form impulses. Whereas the sense impulse is governed by natural necessity and the form impulse by rational necessity, play cancels both kinds of necessity, thereby raising us to the level of freedom.[79]

Schiller play impulse develops what Kant had suggested about the play of the imagination. But Schiller is also critical of Kant's moral rigorism when he writes that our education is defective if our 'moral character is able to assert itself only by sacrificing the natural' (*Erziehung*, 19). Instead of Kant's morality of duty, he proposes an ideal of noble conduct where there is an 'aesthetic transcendence' of duty. Noble conduct, according to Schiller, aesthetically exceeds the demands of the moral law because it flows from a generosity of character that not only enjoys its own freedom but wants to 'set free everything around it, even the lifeless' (167n). Nobility involves the creative freedom of the artist to give a living shape to dead matter and the beneficent freedom of the statesman-artist to endow all human beings with the right to develop themselves as citizens.

We have seen the rise of aesthetics as a new discipline internally delineating the fine arts and developing its own concepts for the analysis of sensory experience. But the recognition that aesthetic experience and the systematic study of the arts have their own validity did not lead to the absolutisation of art during the eighteenth century. Although Moritz points in that direction, he is no advocate of art for art's sake. The full spectrum of eighteenth-century aesthetics is well illustrated in the works of William Hogarth, who on the one hand was concerned with isolating the most beautiful type of line and on the other hand produced engravings depicting life with all its everyday problems. When inaugurating the new discipline of aesthetics, Baumgarten expressed the hope that it would have a broader application than to the fine arts alone. We saw indications of its hermeneutic relevance in the works of Meier, Alison, and Kant. Beginning with Shaftesbury, we also found many eighteenth-century thinkers relating their examination of taste and sensibility to moral questions. Even the claim that aesthetic judgements are disinterested is made by Hutcheson, Mendelssohn, and Kant within a moral framework for aesthetics. To be sure, doctrinal ethical concerns, especially as they are related to religion, are often suspended in art, and many aestheticians resist the excessive allegorisation pointing away from this world to another spiritual world. Kant reverses this direction by relating supersensible rational ideas back to the level of feeling and intuition in his theory of symbolisation, but beauty as a symbol remains oriented toward morality and the standard of taste toward the idea of humanity. Finally, with Schiller we have the far-reaching use of aesthetic categories to broaden our understanding of human freedom and of what it means to be truly human. Thus, overall, the multifaceted development of eighteenth-century aesthetics is characterised by a concern for both the distinctive qualities and the general philosophical significance of aesthetic experience and expression.

NOTES

1 See Paul Oskar Kristeller, 'The Modern System of the Arts', reprinted in *Problems in Aesthetics*, ed. M. Weitz (London, 1970), 117.

2 Charles Perrault, *Parallèle des anciens et des modernes en cequi regarde les arts et les sciences* (Paris, 1690), 175.

3 Charles Batteux, *Les beaux-arts réduits à un même principe*, ed. J.-R. Mantion (Paris, 1989), 82.

4 Wilhelm Dilthey, 'Three Epochs in Modern Aesthetics and Its Present Task (1892)', in *Selected Works*, eds. R. A. Makkreel and F. Rodi (Princeton, NJ, 1985–), 5: *Poetry and Experience*, 175–222.

5 Alfred Baeumler, who conceived aesthetics up to Kant in terms of the problem of defining individuality, specifically underscores its relevance for the rise of modern historical consciousness. See Alfred Baeumler, *Das Irrationalitätsproblem in der Ästhetik und Logik des 18. Jahrhunderts bis zur Kritik der Urteilskraft* (Darmstadt, 1974), x.

6 Nicholas Boileau, *L'art poétique*, in *Oeuvre diverses* (Paris, 1674), translated as *The Art of Poetry*, trans. W. Soames (London, 1683), 31–2, 38.

7 K. Heinrich von Stein, *Die Entstehung der neueren Ästhetik* (Stuttgart, 1886), 35, 36, 48.

8 See Jean-Pierre de Crousaz, *Traité du beau* (Amsterdam, 1715), 8.

9 Yves-Marie André, 'Premier discours', in *Essai sur le beau* (Paris, 1770).

10 Gottfried Wilhelm Leibniz, *Principes de la nature et de la grâce, fondés en raison*, in *Die philosophischen Schriften*, ed. C. I. Gerhardt, 7 vols. (Berlin, 1875–90), vol. 6, translated as *The Principles of Nature and of Grace, Based on Reason*, in *Selections*, ed. P. Weiner (New York, NY, 1951), 530.

11 Anthony Ashley Cooper, Third Earl of Shaftesbury, *Characteristicks of Men, Manners, Opinions, Times*, ed. J. M. Robertson, 2 vols. (Indianapolis, IN, 1964), 2: 132.

12 Francis Hutcheson, *An Inquiry into the Original of Our Ideas of Beauty and Virtue; in Two Treatises*, 4th edn. (London, 1738), 75.

13 Alexander Gottlieb Baumgarten, *Aesthetica* 2 vols. (Frankfurt, 1750 and 1758).

14 Baumgarten, *Meditationes philosophicae de nonnullis ad poema pertinentibus: Reflections on Poetry*, trans. K. Aschenbrenner and W. B. Holther (Berkeley, CA, 1954), 41. See also Baeumler, *Das Irrationalitätsproblem*, 200–1.

15 Ernst Cassirer, *Die Philosophie der Aufklärung* (Tübingen, 1932), translated as *The Philosophy of the Enlightenment*, trans. F. C. A. Koelln and J. P. Pettegrove (Princeton, NJ, 1951), 346.

16 Baumgarten, *Aesthetica*, §§22, 561.

17 See Georg Friedrich Meier, *Anfangsgründe aller schönen Wissenschaften*, 3 vols. (Halle, 1754–9), 1: 60.

18 Meier, *Versuch einer allgemeinen Auslegungskunst* (Düsseldorf, 1965), 107. See also Rudolf A. Makkreel, 'The Confluence of Aesthetics and Hermeneutics in Baumgarten, Meier, and Kant', *The Journal of Aesthetics and Art Criticism*, 54 (Winter 1996): 65–75.

19 Johann Joachim Winckelmann, *Geschichte der Kunst des Alterthums*, in *Werke*, 2 vols. (Stuttgart, 1847), 1: 132.

20 Jean Baptiste Du Bos, *Réflexions critiques sur la poésie et sur la peinture*, 3 vols. (Dresden, 1760), Pt. I, §1, p. 1.

21 John Dennis, *The Advancement and Reformation of Modern Poetry* (London, 1701), 5.

22 Samuel Monk, *The Sublime: A Study of Critical Theories in XVIII-Century England* (Ann Arbor, MI, 1960), 54.

23 Joseph Addison and Richard Steele, *Selections from The Tatler and The Spectator*, ed. R. J. Allen (New York, NY, 1966), 182.

24 Addison and Steele, *The Spectator*, 218.

25 Edmund Burke, *A Philosophical Enquiry into the Origin of Our Ideas of the Sublime and Beautiful*, ed. A. Phillips (Oxford, 1990), 19.

26 *Thomas Reid, Lectures on the Fine Arts* (1774), ed. P. Kivy (The Hague, 1973), 45.

27 Mary Wollstonecraft, *Vindication of the Rights of Woman* (1792), ed. M. B. Kramnick (Harmondsworth, 1975), 134.

28 Paul Mattick, Jr., 'Beautiful and the Sublime: Gender Totemism in the Constitution of Art', *The Journal of Aesthetics and Art Criticism*, 48 (1990): 300.

29 Alexander Gerard, *An Essay on Taste*, 3rd edn. (Edinburgh, 1780), 91.

30 This no doubt reflects the influence of Hume, who will be treated in Section V on the standard of taste.

31 Henry Home, Lord Kames, *Elements of Criticism* (London, 1824), 447.

32 Paul Guyer makes a related point when he argues that Kames preserves a sense of aesthetic disinterestedness without insisting on detachment from other sources of value. See *Kant and the Experience of Freedom* (Cambridge, 1993), 78–9.

33 Johann Jacob Breitinger, *Critische Abhandlung von der Natur, den Absichten und dem Gebrauche der Gleichnisse* (Zurich, 1740), 3.

34 Johann Jacob Bodmer, *Kritische Betrachtungen über die poetischen Gemälde der Dichter* (Zurich, 1741), 212.

35 By *schöne Wissenschaften* Mendelssohn means the belles lettres: the literary arts and rhetoric.

36 Moses Mendelssohn, *Schriften zur Philosophie, Aesthetik und Apologetik*, 2 vols. (Leipzig, 1880), 2: 173.

37 Mendelssohn, *Morgenstunden*, in *Gesammelte Schriften* (Stuttgart-Bad Cannstatt, 1971–), vol. 3.2: *Schriften zur Philosophie und Ästhetik*, ed. L. Strauss (1974), 62.

38 Mendelssohn, 'Die Bildsäule', in *Schriften zur Philosophie, Aesthetik und Apologetik*, 2: 239, 241.

39 Denis Diderot, *Early Philosophical Works*, trans. and ed. M. Jourdain (Chicago, IL, 1916), 137.

40 Johann Georg Sulzer, *Allgemeine Theorie der schönen Künste*, 2 vols. (Leipzig, 1771–4), 2: 371.

41 See Armand Nivelle, *Kunst- und Dichtungstheorien zwischen Aufklärung und Klassik* (Berlin, 1971), 55.

42 Disinterestedness characterises the judgement of taste in its first moment of quality.

43 See Immanuel Kant, *Kritik der Urtheilskraft*, Ak 5: 210, translated as *Critique of the Power of Judgement*, trans. P. Guyer and E. Matthews, ed. P. Guyer, in *Works* (2000).

44 Purposiveness without a purpose characterises the judgement of taste in its third moment of relation. See Kant, *Kritik der Urtheilskraft*, Ak 5: 222, 236.

45 See Rudolf A. Makkreel, *Imagination and Interpretation in Kant: The Hermeneutical Import of the 'Critique of Judgment'* (Chicago, IL, 1990), Chapters 3 and 8, where this affinity is interpreted as both a felt and reflective relation through which the subject orients itself.

46 Universality characterises the judgement of taste in its second moment of quantity.

47 Necessity characterises the judgement of taste in its fourth moment of modality.

48 Dennis was an exception to this in that he believed Milton to have transcended the ancient poets.

49 See Charles-Louis de Secondat de Montesquieu, 'De la manière gothique', in *Voyages de Montesquieu*, 2 vols. (Bordeaux, 1896), 2: 367–75.

50 Denis Diderot, *Rameau's Nephew and Other Works*, trans. J. Barzun and R. Bowen (Indianapolis, IN, 1964), 59.

51 See Diderot, 'Sur le génie', in *Oeuvres esthétiques*, ed. P. Vernière (Paris, 1968), 20.

52 Diderot, 'Génie', in *l'Encyclopédie ou Dictionnaire raisonné des sciences, des arts et des métiers*, eds. D. Diderot and J. le Rond d'Alembert, 35 vols. (Paris and Amsterdam, 1751–80), 7: 582b. The authorship of this article is disputed. Jean-François de Saint-Lambert claimed it as his own, but Herbert Dieckmann thinks that great parts of it 'must have been either inspired or revised by Diderot himself'. See Dieckmann, 'Diderot's Conception of Genius', *Journal of the History of Ideas*, 2 (1941): 151–82 at 163, n. 19.

53 Edward Young, *Conjectures on Original Composition*, ed. E. J. Morley (Manchester, 1918), 19, 20.

54 See William Duff, *An Essay on Original Genius; and Its Various Modes of Exertion in Philosophy and the Fine Arts, Particularly in Poetry* (1767) (Gainesville, FL, 1964), 33.

55 Thus John L. Mahoney is incorrect to assert that Duff's 'wit and humour are not to be equated with imagination'. See Mahoney's Introduction to Duff, *Essay*, xii. The fancy exhibited in wit and humour is merely a non-inventive or non-plastic form of imagination.

56 Alexander Gerard, *An Essay on Genius* (1774), ed. B. Fabian (Munich, 1966), 41.

57 Robert E. Norton argues that Herder is much less dismissive of traditional and Enlightenment views than has been thought in his *Herder's Aesthetics and the European Enlightenment* (Ithaca, NY, 1991).

58 Johann Georg Hamann, 'Aesthetica in nuce: A Rhapsody in Cabalistic Prose', in *Eighteenth Century German Criticism*, ed. T. J. Chamberlain (New York, NY, 1992), 81.

59 Johann Gottfried Herder, *Sämmtliche Werke*, ed. B. L. Suphan, 33 vols. (Berlin, 1877–1913), 18: 134.

60 Nivelle, *Kunst und Dichtungstheorien*, 156.

61 Whereas Gerard had contrasted the self-prescribed implicit laws whereby artistic genius functions with the externally prescribed explicit rules of art critics, within Kant's critical philosophy the conditions of genius must be contrasted with the already normative conditions of ordinary and scientific experience. In both cases, there is a self-prescription – in the case of ordinary and scientific experience by means of explicit laws and in the case of genius by implicit rules.

62 See Kant, *Kritik der Urtheilskraft*, §49, Ak 5: 157–8.

63 Archibald Alison, *Essays on the Nature and Principles of Taste* (New York, NY, 1854), 89.

64 Duff distinguished a special mode of association characteristic of genius merely by its being able to create new associations. Gerard does anticipate Alison's unifying type of association, but he limits it to genius. Gerard does not explain how an overall sense of unity is generated.

65 Gotthold Ephraim Lessing, *Laokoön, oder, Über die Grenzen der Mahlerey und Poesie* (Berlin, 1766), translated as *Laocoön: An Essay on the Limits of Painting and Poetry*, trans. E. A. McCormick (Indianapolis, IN, 1962), 9. All page references are to this edition.

66 Johann Gottfried Herder, *Kritische Wälder, oder, Betrachtungen, die Wissenschaft und Kunst des Schönen betreffend, nach Massgabe neuerer Schriften* [1769], in *Sämmtliche Werke*, 3: 137 (1878), translated as *Critical Forests: First Grove*, in *Eighteenth Century German Criticism*, ed. T. J. Chamberlain (New York, NY, 1992), 119 (translation altered). Page references are to the translation.

67 Kant's imaginative symbols as non-rule-bound schemata were already anticipated in Giambattista Vico's account of imaginative universals. See *The New Science*, eds. T. G. Bergin and M. H. Fisch (Ithaca, NY, 1948), §§209, 381, 933, 934; also Donald Verene, *Vico's Science of Imagination* (Ithaca, NY, 1981), ch. 3.

68 *Kritik der Urtheilskraft*, Ak 5: 301. For a discussion of the hermeneutical import of aesthetic ideas and reflective judgement, see Makkreel, *Imagination and Interpretation in Kant*, chs. 6 and 7.

69 Karl Philipp Moritz, *Schriften zur Ästhetik und Poetik*, ed. H. J. Schrimpf (Tübingen, 1962), 112.

70 Moritz, 'On the Concept of That Which Is Perfect in Itself', in *Eighteenth Century German Criticism*, 247.

71 See Erdmann Waniek, 'Karl Philipp Moritz's Concept of the Whole in his "Versuch einer Vereinigung ... " (1785)', *Studies in Eighteenth-Century Culture*, ed. H. C. Payne, 12 (1983): 218.

72 Jean-Jacques Rousseau, *Émile ou De l'éducation*, in *Oeuvres*, vol. 4, translated as *Émile* by A. Bloom (New York, NY, 1979), 344, 341. Page citations refer to this translation.

73 See Peter Kivy, 'Recent Scholarship and the British Tradition: A Logic of Taste – The First Fifty Years', in *Aesthetics: A Critical Anthology*, eds. G. Dickie, R. Sclafani, and R. Roblin (New York, NY, 1989), 626–46.

74 David Hume, 'On the Standard of Taste', in *Works*, vol. 3: *Essays: Moral, Political, and Literary*, 282–3.

75 A similar sympathy among sentiments about taste is attributed to Hume by Theodore Gracyk in his 'Rethinking Hume's Standard of Taste', *The Journal of Aesthetics and Art Criticism*, 52 (1994): 169–82.

76 Gerard, *Essay on Taste*, 214.

77 Kant, *Kritik der Urtheilskraft*, Ak 5: 281. For critical treatments of Kant's deduction of taste, see Donald W. Crawford, *Kant's Aesthetic Theory* (Madison, WI, 1974), and Paul Guyer, *Kant and the Claims of Taste* (Cambridge, MA, 1979). Crawford claims that Kant's own deduction is incomplete and can be completed by means of his later discussion of the relation of beauty to morality. According to Guyer, 'Kant's analysis of the moral significance of taste fails to complete his own deduction of aesthetic judgment' (394).

78 Friedrich Schiller, *Über die ästhetische Erziehung des Menschen in einer Reihe von Briefen*, in *Werke*, ed. A. Kurtscher, 10 vols. (Berlin, 1907), vol. 8, translated as *On the Aesthetic Education of Man*, trans. E. Wilkinson and L. A. Willoughby (Oxford, 1967), 45.

79 Here Schiller is the first to exploit the double meaning of *aufheben* (to cancel and to elevate), which becomes central to the dialectical thought of later idealists.

19

THE ACTIVE POWERS

JEROME B. SCHNEEWIND

In 1751, in the *Discours préliminaire* for the great encyclopedia he and Denis Diderot were editing, Jean d'Alembert proclaimed a simple scheme for organising 'the sciences of man'. The divisions of this science, he said,

are derived from the divisions of his faculties. The principal faculties of man are the *understanding* and the *will*; the *understanding*, which it is necessary to direct toward *truth*; the *will*, which must be made to conform to *virtue*. The one is the object of *logic*, the other is that of *ethics*.[1]

D'Alembert's dichotomy was not one of the novel ideas put forward in the *Encyclopédie*. It had forerunners in antiquity, and Descartes used a revised form of it. Locke seemed to use a similar classification, but he stated it in different terms, and for good reason. If we speak of understanding and will as faculties of mind, he said, we may be tempted to suppose that the words 'stand for some real Beings in the Soul, that performed those Actions of Understanding and Volition'. But the idea that there are 'distinct Agents' in us breeds nothing but confusion.[2] Locke chose to talk of the powers of the mind and, without making a fuss about it, sometimes classified them as active and passive (see, for instance, *Essay Concerning Human Understanding*, II.xxi.72).

Leibniz also objected to the 'personification or mythology' in which the will is imagined as 'alone active and supreme . . . like a queen . . . whose minister of state is the understanding, while the passions are her courtiers'. Taken literally, the view would be incoherent, leading to an endless multiplication of faculties to explain how the will can take account of reasons produced by the understanding. The truth is that it is 'the soul, or the thinking substance' that understands, feels, and decides to modify its active force (*sa force active*) in producing our actions.[3]

For comments on drafts of this essay, I would like to thank Knud Haakonssen, Elijah Millgram, Susan James, and Charles Larmore. I am particularly grateful to Natalie Brender for her comments and for her expert assistance on numerous matters of detail.

Later writers tended to follow Locke and Leibniz in explaining mental life in terms of varied powers of a single mind. They thereby avoided the difficulty of explaining the unity of mind posed by explanations in terms of different parts or faculties.[4] In what follows, I outline the various ways in which philosophers from Locke and Leibniz through Kant understood the mental powers associated with 'the will' or connected with action. I suggest that the opposition between Leibniz and Locke set the terms for eighteenth-century discussion of these issues. Hence, after noting briefly, in Section I, the changing metaphysical background to discussions of human activity, I present (Section II) the view sketched by Leibniz and worked out by Wolff and then (Section III) that given by Locke. The Leibnizians held the basically Stoic view that the activities of the mind, including its desires and decisions, naturally tend toward order because all of them represent some aspect of an objectively good and orderly universe. Locke found no such natural, inherent tendency toward order in our decisions. They can be controlled, he held, only by deliberately imposed sanctions. Most of those who accepted Locke's denial that the desires and the will are naturally ordered were repelled by his thesis that external intervention is essential to bring order into human action. Morality, they held, can come from within. Their efforts to show how this is possible fall roughly into three groups.

Some asserted that natural self-interest is so strong that it enables us to govern the passions. Knowledge of where our true private interest lies is thus what gives us control of ourselves.

Those who rejected egoism held that we possess unselfish as well as selfish desires. We also have a moral faculty or sense capable both of showing us the proper ordering of our desires and of helping us to achieve it.

Proponents of both these lines of thought, such as the Wolffians, accepted determinism. Against them, a third school asserted that we possess a unique kind of agency because we have a free will. We are able to order our decisions in accordance with the eternal moral truths discerned by our intellect, regardless of the strength of our desires.

The actual history was, of course, not as simple as the categories suggest. In Sections IV through VII, I discuss the complex British debates on the issues. German philosophers who opposed Wolffianism took the third line. In Section VIII, I discuss the first major German philosopher to oppose the Wolffians with a strong doctrine of free will, Christian August Crusius. In Section IX, I turn to the views of J. N. Tetens, who used both Lockean and Leibnizian ideas in constructing an empirically based libertarian view. Then, in Section X, I describe Kant's views about freedom and desire, which responded to all these discussions among his predecessors. In Section XI, I conclude with a brief look back and then comment on the turn the post-Kantians gave to Kant's view of the will.

I. ACTIVITY AND PASSIVITY

The concepts of activity and passivity as they were used in classifying human powers during the eighteenth century were themselves the outcome of complex and protracted arguments about science, religion, and metaphysics. Aristotle held that active powers enable whatever has them to transmit new forms to substances possessing the passive power to receive those forms. In *Les passions de l'âme* (*The Passions of the Soul*), Descartes rejected this way of understanding action and passion. Whatever happens or is done, he said, 'is generally called by philosophers a "passion" with regard to the subject to which it happens and an "action" with regard to that which makes it happen'.[5] For instance, matter, on Descartes's view, is caused to move at first by God; thereafter, physical change is no more than the transmission of motion to new configurations of corpuscles, each of which is passive when receiving motion and active when passing it on. In this sense, an active body does not differ in any essential way from a passive body. Another Cartesian distinction between action and passion does involve essentials. God's will is wholly active; so too is the human will, the feature of our constitution making us resemble God. In some circumstances, such wills can determine themselves to act in entire independence of anything external to them. This spontaneous exercise of active power differs in kind from the activity displayed by things without wills, which is simply the passing along of motion originating elsewhere.

Descartes's theory of the will helped provoke a sharp reaction. Nicolas Malebranche, the foremost opponent of the belief that anything in the created world could possess genuinely active power, argued that it would be impious and dangerous to locate real power anywhere except in God. If we believe that created beings – particularly human beings – can cause happiness, we might begin to worship them instead of God. Moreover, only God has such power that what he wills *necessarily* occurs. Any other alleged cause serves only as the occasion on which God exerts his power to bring about what we call the effect. We can see this because we can understand what it would be like for the cause to occur without the effect occurring. If a genuine cause makes its effect come about necessarily, then only God is such a cause. Piety as well as logic thus requires the admission that only God possesses truly active power.[6]

Leibniz argued strongly against Malebranche's occasionalism. Locke simply ignored it. He unhesitatingly ascribed active power to created beings and proceeded without apology to track down the source of our idea of it.[7] Newton likewise attributed active powers to natural objects without any fear of irreverence. Thus the greatest scientist of the period as well as its two most influential philosophers validated the thought that humans may – among other things – be truly active.

In doing so, however, they opened the way to a further problem. Leibniz held that all events in the world are determined by some antecedent cause. Newton's theory was widely taken to give determinism and even mechanism the support of the most successful science ever seen, and Locke avowed himself a supporter of Newton. The question then was whether human beings exert their powers only in accordance with deterministic laws such as Newton's laws of motion. If active powers are always caused to act by something outside themselves, then their possessors are not truly originators of their actions.[8] How then can they be capable of moral responsibility or possess any more dignity than stones or trees or horses? Newtonian science seemed to make a Cartesian will just as unthinkable as Malebranchean metaphysics did. Eighteenth-century inquiry about the domain of the will was framed by the question of whether between God and nature there is any conceptual room for powers in the human mind that make our agency different in kind from that of natural objects.

II. THE LEIBNIZ-WOLFF THEORY

Leibniz was deeply critical of Newton's physics and Locke's philosophy. For our purposes, the disagreements between Leibniz and Locke on action, will, and passion are of central importance. They determined the basic outlines of eighteenth-century thought on these topics. Leibniz's position, expounded unsystematically in scattered writings, was drawn together into a massive system of unsurpassed thoroughness and scope by Christian Wolff. Accepting the main Leibnizian views – about monads, the principle of sufficient reason, and the pre-established harmony – he elaborates their consequences far more fully than Leibniz himself ever did. He analyses the passions, he gives an account of will and its place in action, and he argues for a specific way of understanding the difference between being active and being passive. In doing so, he explains freedom, showing how there can be alternatives for the will to choose between and how the will can be the source of its choice.

In Germany, the Leibniz-Wolff philosophy remained the dominant academic orthodoxy until the middle of the eighteenth century. Locke produced no similar orthodoxy, but his admirers all rejected the major points contained in the Leibniz-Wolff understanding of the metaphysics and psychology of action. If we understand the kind of view they rejected, we shall have a better grasp of the positive points they were making. Wolff's exposition of the Leibnizian theory in his *Vernünfftige Gedancken von Gott, der Welt und der Seele des Menschen* (Reasonable Thoughts on God, the World, and the Soul of Man) is a serviceable guide.[9]

The soul, on this view, is a simple, noncorporeal substance. Like any existing thing, its essence is constituted by its power, and because it is simple, it can have only one power (*Gedancken*, §§742–5). Basically this is the power of representing the world as the world impinges on the soul via the body associated with it. Representations (*Vorstellungen*) can have different degrees of clarity and distinctness, but whether clear or dark, explicit or obscure, they all essentially carry propositions about the world (§§198–9, 206, 209). The senses, imagination, memory, reflection, understanding, desire, and will are all to be understood as different ways in which the soul represents the world (§747).

Wolff's position thus entails that each specific instance of each kind of mental activity, from sensation to conceptual reasoning, from desiring to willing, is constituted by two factors: its definite propositional content and the degree of its clarity and distinctness. Since there is only one power in the soul, and content and degree of clarity and distinctness are the only dimensions of manifestations of that power, there is nothing else from which mental states can get their identity. Sensations, for instance, may be clear representations – I see clearly that green is not red – but they are indistinct (*undeutlich*) since I cannot say exactly what constitutes the difference between red and green (§214). Yet there is some set of truths about that difference, and if I perceived colours distinctly I would know it. Memory and reflection, involving reiterated operations on representations, enable us to have clearer and more distinct concepts, to form judgements, and to make inferences. To see how passions and will arise from representations, we must bring in a new consideration.

Like Leibniz, Wolff sees the world and everything within it in terms of perfection and imperfection. 'The harmony of the manifold' is Wolff's definition of the perfection of things (§152). Complex entities contain a number of parts working harmoniously together to attain an end. The more parts they contain and the simpler the principles of their organisation toward that end, the more perfect they are. This world, Wolff argues, is the most perfect of all possible worlds since all its parts work together as fully and as simply as possible to express God's glory (that is, his infinite perfection) (§§982, 1045, 1049–51). If Voltaire's *Candide* made a laughingstock of Leibniz's view that this is the 'best of all possible worlds', it was for him, as for Wolff, a direct a priori inference from the proposition that God, being infinitely wise, powerful, and good, could not act without a reason and so could not choose to create any world other than the best possible one. I discuss later the problems this thesis raises for freedom of the will. Here we must note the way in which degrees of perfection are involved in the passions.

The tie is quite direct. When we recognise, or think we recognise, perfection, we feel pleasure. Indeed, to feel pleasure is just to have an intuition of perfection (*ein Anschauen der Vollkommenheit*) (*Gedancken*, §404).[10] In speaking of intuition, Wolff refers to an uninferred representation without intending to imply that no error is possible. We can get pleasure from mistaken representations of perfection as well as from accurate ones (§405), and the amount of pleasure we feel must be absolutely proportional to the amount of perfection we intuit.[11] Pleasure and displeasure or pain (compare §§417–18, 421) are tied to good and ill through the central definitional claim that 'what makes us and our condition more perfect is good' (§422). Thus the intuitive awareness of good is what brings, or more accurately constitutes, pleasure. And pleasure and pain, so understood, are the building blocks out of which the passions are constituted.

We can clearly tell pleasure from pain, but both of them remain indistinct representations of perfection, or good and ill (§§432–3). Insofar as they are indistinct, they give rise to sensuous desire. Such desire is 'an inclination of the soul toward something of whose goodness we have an indistinct conception' (§434). Just as we can tell green from red without being able to say what makes each the colour it is, so can we tell that we like the taste of a specific wine without being able to say what it is in the wine that makes it more perfect than a wine we dislike. Our pleasure represents the good confusedly and indistinctly, and the inclination to drink, Wolff says, is thereupon necessary since the soul is necessarily inclined toward whatever pleasure represents to it as good (§878).

The specific passions are essentially characterised by the kind of good or pleasure that constitutes them, taking into account also the relations in which we stand to that good. Desire and aversion arise directly, Wolff maintains, from pleasure and pain (§§434, 436). When we are disposed to take pleasure in the happiness of another person, we are said to love that person, and such love in turn can give rise to notable happiness or unhappiness on our part, according to whether the other fares well or ill (§§449–53). Wolff is careful not to suggest that in loving another we are seeking only our own enjoyment or benefit. (Leibniz thinks that the pleasure we get from acts of love is essential to our being moved to perform them, thus allowing a strain of egoistic thinking to enter his psychology.)

Wolff gives brief and conventional accounts of the other passions. Envy, for instance, is the disposition to see another's misfortune as good – that is, to take pleasure in it. Sympathy, by contrast, is the disposition to be pained by the misfortune of another (§§460–1). Remorse is displeasure at something we have done, shame a displeasure at the thought of the bad opinion others will have of us due to some imperfection of ours (§§464–5). These definitions of desires and feelings, very much in the vein of those offered by Descartes and Spinoza, lay the groundwork for the Leibniz-Wolff theory of the will.

When passions rise to a noticeable degree of strength, Wolff says, they are called affects (§441). Affects pull us this way and that, and we remain their slaves as long as they stay indistinct (§491). But there is a way out of such slavery.

We can think something good through clear and distinct representations as well as through obscure and indistinct ones. The effort to attain more perfection is essential to our being. Hence, insofar as we are moved by indistinct representations, we are doing less of what we essentially will and are therefore passive. As our ideas become more distinct, we are acting more as we essentially will to act. Since distinct ideas give us more power than indistinct ones, they make us more active (§§115, 744, 748, 755–6).

Our essential striving toward perfection or good in general constitutes our will (§492). Will and desire are not different in kind from 'the representative power of the soul' (§879). A representation of something as perfect is simply a representation that inclines us toward it. Will differs from desire only because in willing we compare amounts of perfection presented by different ideas and move toward the greatest. What finally moves our will is our reason for acting, and Wolff follows Leibniz in stressing that the will has no power of choice in the absence of a reason or motive (*Bewegungsgrund*).[12] It may seem that we can make choices where we are wholly indifferent, but this is never the case, although often the cognitions of perfection that move us are below the level of consciousness (§§496–8, 508–9). Moreover, we never choose what seems to us the worse in preference to what seems the better, though, again, we may not be aware of the sensuous desires influencing us (§§503–7).

The mind has no dispositions to act other than its motives. Hence we always necessarily act for what we represent as the greatest good or perfection available to us. Both Leibniz and Wolff, moreover, think that God has created the best possible world. Thus it seems that not only do our representations of good and ill determine our actions but that these representations could not have been other than they are and therefore that we could in no sense act in any way other than we do. How, within this framework, can we be free?

Leibniz's *Theodicy* is an extended answer to this question, and Wolff's views are very similar. Both theorists are concerned with making two points. One is that despite the determinism implicit in the 'best of all possible worlds' thesis, we have alternatives from which to choose and we must make choices. The other point is that the determination of the will by representations of perfection allows conceptual room for action to be fully voluntary. These two points seem to Leibniz and Wolff to add up to a defence of human freedom sufficient to underpin morality, and Wolff adds that any less deterministic conception of freedom would in fact undercut morality.

Admitting that we necessarily choose what seems to us the best alternative, Leibniz says that the necessity involved is not absolute or metaphysical but hypothetical. Absolute necessity is the kind involved in mathematics, where the opposite of what is necessarily true is not even conceivable. Hypothetical necessity does not involve the inconceivability of the opposite. What is chosen is necessary as means to an end. Hence we know what it would be like not to do what we do even if, given our end, we necessarily do it. Even God has this choice when he makes the best possible world real: he must create that world, but not because no other choice is conceivable (*Theodicy*, 61, 334, 387). This world is necessarily chosen only on condition that God wills the best.

How, then, can we be free? Are we free to have or not have the ends we have? Could God have a different end? All one can mean in asking this, Leibniz thinks, is whether we are spontaneous when we act, or 'have within us the source of our actions' (*Theodicy*, 303). We cannot be asking whether we choose to have the will we have. The will is a settled disposition to obtain the greatest good, and we cannot without absurdity ask whether we will to have that will, 'else we could still say that we will to have the will to will, and that would go on to infinity' (151). Insofar as what we pursue is something that we distinctly perceive to be good, we are acting as we most want to act. No more than that could meaningfully be required in order for us to be acting from our own will, or voluntarily.

The will, Wolff says, is like a pair of scales, immovable if both sides are equal and moving only through greater weight on one side. Does this rule out freedom? Only, he replies, on a false conception of freedom as the ability to choose either of two alternatives without any reason for a preference (*Gedancken*, §§510–11). On that view, he asserts, all moral truth is destroyed. Morality requires that representations of good and bad have a reliable effect on human action:

If you throw that out of the window, then all certainty in morality collapses, since one cannot influence the human soul except through representations of the good and the bad. Even in the commonwealth, obligation as based on punishment rests on the fact that man does not want ill and does want good, and avoids what he thinks good in order to escape a greater ill. (*Gedancken*, §512).

What we need for morality is freedom defined as 'the ability of the soul through its own power of choice [*Willkühr*] to choose, between two equally possible things, that which pleases it most' (§§514–19).

III. LOCKE

Locke's theory of the passions and the will offered an empiricist alternative to the Leibniz-Wolff position. It also posed a problem which concerned philosophers throughout the century following its publication. Locke's account comes mainly from two chapters of *An Essay Concerning Human Understanding*, in which he uncovers the origins of our ideas of the desires and the will and discusses the will's freedom.

The passions take their rise, he says, from pleasure and pain. Since these are simple, we can obtain ideas of them only from our own experience of them. We call 'good' whatever is 'apt to cause or increase Pleasure . . . in us', Locke says, but he does not say that the feeling represents its cause (*Essay*, II.xx.1–2). Leibniz says he agrees with Locke's view that the good is 'that which is apt to cause or increase pleasure', but the agreement is less than Leibniz makes it seem. In a later section, Leibniz speaks of 'our inevitably confused ideas of pleasure and pain', discussing the advantage we get from their being confused and indistinct. But Locke does not speak of pleasure and pain as involving confusion and indistinctness. Indeed, because they are simple they cannot do so.[13]

When the thought of something produces pleasure, we feel the passion called love for that thing. Love, however, is not desire. Desire occurs only if we find ourselves uneasy in the absence of things we think of as pleasing. The uneasiness felt is what we call desire, and the strength of the desire is the strength of the uneasiness. We do not desire things in proportion to the amount of good we think them to have. We can even know that something would please us without feeling any uneasiness at our lack of it. In a crucial passage, Locke remarks that 'whatever good is propos'd, if its absence carries no displeasure nor pain with it; if a Man be easie and content without it, there is no desire of it, nor endeavour after it' (*Essay*, II.xx.6).

Locke uses his new account of desire to construct some quite standard illustrative accounts of particular desires and passions. Fear is uneasiness at the thought of a likely evil, anger is uneasiness 'upon the receit of any Injury, with a present purpose of Revenge', envy is uneasiness caused by the thought of someone's having a good we want and think he should not have (II.xx.10–13). Locke notes that passions have variable effects on the body – some people blush from shame and some do not – but excuses himself from giving a full treatment of the passions, thinking that these examples show how we get the ideas of the remainder.

The discussion of power, by contrast, occupies the longest chapter in the book. As Locke himself emphasises, he drastically revised his views after the publication of the first edition. Much of the revision is due to the thesis that we do not necessarily pursue what we think would be our greatest good (II.xxi.35, 71–2). Locke begins with the idea of power. We note changes in things affected by other things and note changes in our ideas when we choose to alter them. From these observations, we come to the idea of a power to make change and a power to receive it – active and passive powers. It is quite possible that matter has only passive power. In any case, the clearest source of the idea of active power is 'reflection on the Operations of our Minds'. We can alter our thoughts and also 'barely by a thought of the Mind' we can make our bodies move. Noticing this experience gives us the simple idea of active power, and with it we can define the idea of will. It is the idea of our power to call up ideas for consideration and to prefer moving, or not moving, parts of our bodies. Voluntary acts thus are those 'consequent to such order or command of the mind' (II.xxi.1–5).

What then is liberty? Locke first gives a quite Hobbesian account. I am free if nothing outside me prevents me from doing what I will or makes me perform that action should I will to refrain. A free act is not the same as a voluntary act. If I prefer to stay in a room with someone whose company I like, I stay voluntarily even if the doors are locked. But I am not freely there because, should I will to leave, I could not (II.xxi.8–11). Leibniz objected that there is a sense of 'freedom to will' that Locke here ignores. It stands for a condition opposed to that of 'imposition or constraint, though an inner one like that which the passions impose. . . . [O]ne's mind is indeed not free when it is possessed by a great passion, for then one cannot will as one should, i.e. with proper deliberation' (*Nouveaux essais*, II.xxi.8). Locke does in fact take up the issue.

The will is a power of the mind, he reminds us, and since freedom is also a power, it makes no sense to ask whether the will is free. A power cannot have a power. The power of choosing or preferring is no more either free or unfree than the power of speaking or dancing (*Essay*, II.xxi.14–19). But, because men wish to avoid all thoughts of guilt, they ask whether we are free to will. This question, arising from fear of damnation, entangles us in endless perplexities (II.xxi.22).

The answer is brisk. Where we are faced with a choice, we are not free not to will. We must choose one way or another. That would end the matter were it not that men persist: are we at liberty to will whichever alternative we please? Here Locke loses patience. The question is absurd; anyone who answers it must fall into an infinite regress since a will to will would itself need to be explained by yet a further willing, and so on (*Essay*, II.xxi.24–5).[14]

There is a further question about willing that Locke thinks is not absurd and which he answers. What determines the will to 'this or that particular Motion or Rest?' What determines us to do this or that specific action? Locke's answer is that it is the strongest uneasiness presently felt. To elaborate on this, he returns to the view of desire outlined in the previous chapter of the *Essay*, chapter 20 (II.xxi.29).

Desire is felt uneasiness. Will is different from desire. Introspection shows it to be a different simple, and we can decide or will to do something we do not want to do. The will is determined by uneasiness at the thought of some absent good, but the uneasiness may not be aroused by 'the greater good in view' (II.xxi.30–1). The drunkard knows sobriety would be better for him, yet he decides to drink; the sinner continues to sin although he knows that God rewards with infinite eternal joys those who reform. If the will were determined by the prospect of the greatest good, behaviour of this kind would be inexplicable (II.xxi.32–8). But if the greatest present uneasiness moves the will independently of the amount of good in view, it is no mystery.

Happiness is always what we desire, and happiness consists of 'the utmost Pleasure we are capable of, and *Misery* the utmost Pain'. But not all people are affected in the same way by the absence of various goods. One person may be indifferent to what another desires. Desire is only contingently aroused by various thoughts of goods, and 'all good, even seen, and confessed to be so, does not necessarily move every particular Man's *desire*; but only that part . . . as is consider'd, and taken to make a necessary part of his happiness'. There is no question of confusion and indistinctness here: 'Men . . . may have a clear view of good, great and confessed good, without being concern'd for it, or moved by it' if they take their happiness to be complete without it (*Essay*, II.xxi.38–43). True enough, we all unfailingly seek to avoid severe bodily pain, and we avoid what other evils we can. But in desire and pursuit, there is no uniformity from person to person. Since 'the same thing is not good to every Man alike', philosophers have wasted their time in debating about the highest good (II.xxi.54–5). In heaven, God will accommodate differences of taste in providing for our happiness. 'For that being intended for a State of Happiness, it must certainly be agreeable to every one's wish and desire: Could we suppose their relishes as different there as they are here, yet the Manna in Heaven will suit every one's Palate' (II.xxi.65).

How does this bear on the issue of liberty? The most pressing removable uneasiness determines the will. But usually many uneasinesses are felt together. We find by experience that we are able to suspend action, and refrain from trying to remove our present uneasinesses, at least while we reflect on what makes us uneasy and consider which of the objects of desire will truly be best for us. This suspension of action, Locke says, is 'the source of all liberty; in this seems to consist that, which is (as I think improperly) call'd *Free will*' (*Essay*, II.xxi.47). When we keep our uneasinesses from moving our will, we are not showing our indifference to good and ill.[15] Far from it: we are trying to assure that our will comes to be moved by the greatest good available to us. The power of suspending action, by increasing our ability to cause our will to be moved by the most durable uneasinesses, increases our freedom by leading us to do what we most want to do, which is to increase our happiness. Locke knew and was quite possibly influenced by Malebranche's view that the only action one can perform is to suspend action and do nothing while the amounts of good available to one pass before the mind and determine one to act.[16]

For both the Leibniz–Wolff view and Locke, then, will is to be explained in terms of reflection about our desires for specific goods. But there is a critical difference, shown in Locke's insistence that will is not itself a desire. On the Leibniz-Wolff view, will itself determines choices between desires because it is itself the standing desire for the greatest good, and all desires are commensurable in terms of the amounts of good they promise. To will is simply to go for the most good, or most perfection. For Locke, the matter is much more problematic. The greatest perceived good does not necessarily determine the will; the strongest removable uneasiness does. Suspension of action enables the uneasinesses to pull and tug until one wins. But beyond saying that some thought of good must be involved, Locke tells us nothing about what determines the strengths of present uneasinesses. Nor indeed could he. There is too much variability among people for any general truths about sources of desire to hold. We necessarily seek our own happiness, and it seems to be up to us to decide what goods to make part of our happiness; but once again Locke has no way of saying how we are to decide or what determines our decision.

The fact that we pursue our happiness does not settle the matter because until we make some pleasure part of our specific happiness its absence will not arouse uneasiness and hence not motivate us. Locke holds, moreover, that we can change our tastes. People can 'correct their palates' or learn to like substances, such as tobacco, which are healthful even if at first distasteful (*Essay*, II.xxi.69). But of course we must first will to do so, and Locke says nothing about how we are to develop enough uneasiness at the absence of improved tastes to determine our will.

Hobbes took our overriding fear of death to impose some order on our passions. In the Leibniz-Wolff view, the objective amounts of perfection provide for inner order. But no positive ordering principle seems available for the Lockean inner world. The Lockean will, although an active power different from motives, has no inner rational ordering principle. The strengths of uneasinesses or desires are not necessarily proportional to the amounts of good in the ideas that cause them; and all the will does is to give the uneasinesses time to fight it out.

In his ethics, Locke invokes God's laws backed by threats of punishment and reward to produce more order in human affairs than civil laws and a concern for public opinion can create. Aside from its unpalatable implications for religion and human relations, it is not clear that this can work for Locke. Distance in time weakens the present uneasiness caused by threats (*Essay*, II.xxi.63); people are not, as we have seen, moved by the promise of heavenly rewards. Locke devotes much space to warning us about the dangers of miscalculation in deliberating about what to do. But he never explains what moves us to suspend action and deliberate, a point criticised by Leibniz and Collins.[17] Nor does he tell us how we can bring ourselves to feel a dominant uneasiness in the absence of our greatest good once we see where that is.

Locke's claim that the will is not determined by beliefs about the good amounts to saying that the springs of action are fundamentally irrational. If he is right, personal order as well as social stability seem to be attainable only through some sort of external pressure – either God's punishments or social sanctions. It is understandable that later thinkers, even while accepting much of Lockeanism, should have sought to explain human action in ways that show how we can control what we do.

At the end of Section I, I outlined the three main ways in which later thinkers who accepted Locke's view of the passions tried to respond to what they took to be his unacceptable theory of the will. In what follows, I discuss first, in Sections IV and V, the determinist alternatives and then the various versions of the third line of response.

IV. MORAL SENSE AND EGOISM

The debates on these issues of passions, will, and self in morality were touched off by the striking work of Anthony Ashley Cooper, third Earl of Shaftesbury, who had been tutored by Locke. Shaftesbury reacted strongly against Locke's motivational theory, which he thought no less egoistic than Hobbes's, and against the Lockean belief that morality must invoke divine sanctions. Locke portrays agents with no way of determining what goods to make part of their own happiness and without any internal source of moral self-control. Shaftesbury ties these issues together.[18] If I have no way of telling which goods are to be included in my happiness, or which desires are to constitute my self, Shaftesbury fears I will be left to the whims of passion and have no stable self. 'The man in anger has a different happiness from the man in love.'[19] If my passions are governed only by fancy, I am no better than a madman. 'If I vote with Fancy, resign my opinion to her command, and judge of happiness and misery as she judges, how am I myself?' (*Characteristicks*, III.ii, 209).

What, then, enables the self to distance itself from its fancies and impose its own idea of happiness? Shaftesbury does not propose reason for the job. ''Tis a due sentiment of morals which alone can make us knowing in order and proportion, and give us a just tone and measure of human passion' (II.iii, 181). Though he sometimes speaks of a moral sense, he gives no elaborate theory about its nature, but its function is clear. It is to tell us when our passions and desires form a harmonious whole. A harmonious self elicits approval, and whatever is approved is virtuous. Inner harmony makes the agent happy as well as virtuous. We understand what goods to make part of our happiness when our moral sentiment tells us the virtuous relations our desires should have to one another.[20]

Self-control for Shaftesbury is therefore not dependent on will, of which indeed he has a low opinion. Even if there is a free will (he does not say there is), 'Humour and Fancy . . . govern it. . . . [I]f there be no certain inspector or auditor established within us to take account of these opinions and fancies . . . we are . . . little like to continue a day in the same will' (*Soliloquy: Or, Advice to an Author*, I.ii, 122). The internal auditor cannot be merely a calculative power or a Leibnizian will as a desire for the greatest good because, for Shaftesbury as for Locke, it is not the amount of good involved that influences action but the particular directions in which one seeks one's happiness. The moral sentiment alone, Shaftesbury thinks, can show us which way to go. But although the moral sentiment alone can give one enough unity so that one can be a single agent, Shaftesbury's psychology seems to be rather simply deterministic: the strength of our feelings is what explains which of them we act upon. What ultimately differentiates this view from Hobbes's is that for Shaftesbury we have genuinely altruistic impulses and an independent moral sentiment which can throw its weight into the balance as well. He does not use the vocabulary of active and passive power, nor does he so much as mention suspension of action by means of will and the inner liberty Locke thinks it gives us.

Numerous critics responded to Shaftesbury's rejection of the selfish theory of motivation. Probably the most famous, and certainly the liveliest, is Bernard Mandeville. In *The Fable of the Bees* (1714), he offered a witty and plausible alternative to Shaftesbury's portrayal of the generous other-directed sentiments.[21] Although he gives no systematic analysis of the passions, Mandeville sees both the principle and the particulars of our behaviour through the eyes of an egoist. '[I]t is impossible', he says, 'that Man, mere fallen Man, should act with any other View but to please himself' (*Fable*, 1: 348). If we rescue a baby about to fall into a fire, 'the Action is neither good nor bad, and what Benefit soever the Infant received, we only obliged our selves; for to have seen it fall, and not strove to hinder it, would have caused a Pain, which Self-preservation compell'd us to prevent' (1: 56). Man loves company, no doubt, but he loves it 'as he does every thing else, for his own sake' (1: 341).

These comments suggest that Mandeville has a theory compelling him to find a way to analyse every action as being done at the agent's own pleasure and consequently directed toward the agent's own good. Yet at the same time he sets as a standard for judgement an austere morality demanding that we be completely self-sacrificing. If we are truly charitable, for instance, we transfer 'part of that sincere Love we have for our selves' to others, with no expectation of benefit, not even gratitude or public recognition (*Fable*, 1: 253 ff.). Such virtue may be rare, but Mandeville seems to think it possible. If he really does, then his egoism is less an attempt at a pure theory than a device allowing him to mock pretensions to virtue while showing – in a fashion everyone took to be Hobbesian – that society could operate quite well if no one were ever benevolent or disinterested.

Although Shaftesbury tended to rely not so much on explicit argument as on the immediate appeal of his portrait of human nature, his position seemed convincing to innumerable readers, including the many who, like Kant, read him in French or German translation. In hard-line egoists such as Mandeville, and later Helvétius, Shaftesbury aroused only scorn. One of his admirers, Francis Hutcheson, set out to provide some argumentative backing for Shaftesburyan views in his *An Inquiry into the Original of Our Ideas of Beauty and Virtue* (1725) and other early works. Taking Mandeville as his open target, and assuming that even he would allow that we at least *seem* to have benevolent and disinterested affections, Hutcheson argues that appearances are not misleading. We respond so differently to benevolence and to pure self-interest – approving the former but not the latter and feeling affection for those who are kind but not for those who are purely selfish – that the unselfish affections must be allowed to have a real part in our lives. We cannot get ourselves to have such affections either by simply deciding to have them or by seeing that it pays to have them. Moreover, we do not appreciate the benevolence of others only for the benefits it brings us. We do not cease to love a generous friend the instant she loses all her wealth. We do not love indiscriminately anyone who could give us equivalent assistance. And it is plainly ludicrous to try to explain parental affection, ties to our neighbours, and love of our country by saying that we all think it benefits us to have them.[22]

A year after Hutcheson confronted psychological egoism with these inconvenient facts, Joseph Butler published some further objections to it. Perhaps the most significant are those that involve his distinction between self-interest and what he calls the particular passions. The former is our long-term concern for the attainment of our own happiness. By itself, it does not determine what will make us happy. It is our specific desires – our wants for some things and not others – that determine what will please or displease us. The particular passion of hunger has food as its object; other passions lead us to desire money or fame or the success of our children or the relief of suffering among the ill. Self-interest would have nothing to do were it not that the passions put us upon a variety of projects, but the passions are not themselves self-interested, nor do they aim always at the agent's own good or benefit. Once we understand the nature of particular passions, we have no difficulty admitting that while some of them may indeed move us to benefit ourselves, some move us directly to help others, and some, such as an obsession with gambling, motivate actions that can harm the agent.[23]

If self-interest is the desire for one's own happiness or one's own pleasure, we must admit that it is the particular passions that allow us to take pleasure in things or be made happy by having them. If I did not desire food, Butler says, I would not enjoy eating; if my only desire were the desire for happiness, nothing would make me happy since nothing could give me pleasure. Butler points out that any particular passion is obviously the agent's own passion. One might be tempted to slide from noticing this to thinking that when one acts from a passion, one is acting to gratify one's own desire, or to do exactly what one wants, from which one might conclude that whenever we act from a particular passion we are acting for our own interest or selfishly. This, however, is a mere verbal confusion: that I act from my own desire is a trivial truth, implying nothing about the object of my desire. But it is the object of desire that determines whether or not someone is acting for his or her own interest, and the facts make it plain that we often act for the good of others.[24] Butler here reveals the confusion that caused many writers – Leibniz included – to suppose that any desire that moves me must be a desire for my own pleasure, and so for my interest, simply because in acting from it I act as I please.

The critics of psychological egoism faced a problem the egoists did not. Among the many available springs of action, which should be followed? Butler claimed that conscience would tell us. He abstained, however, from giving any account of how exactly the directions of conscience might become efficacious. Although he believed in free will, he felt no need to develop a theory of how it is possible or how it works.[25] He thus left a problem for his libertarian followers Price and Reid, whose views I discuss later.

Hutcheson was not quite so reticent about the workings of the moral sense. For present purposes, it must suffice to say that he offers a deterministic account of its force. Whatever else it may be, distinctively moral approval is an enjoyable feeling. We want both the approval of others and our own approval. Since approval is caused only by benevolent desires, our own desire for approval is not selfish. It is rather a mark of our being made for society. Approval and disapproval are thus socially efficacious forces; and as the desire to be approved can motivate us to develop our own benevolence, the moral sense can shape our own character as well as guide us in action.[26]

Neither Hutcheson nor Butler forced the partisans of self-interest, even in Britain, to admit defeat, and one of them, John Gay, in 1731 offered an ingenious theory to show how one could concede Hutcheson's factual claims (he does not notice Butler) while still insisting that there is no need to admit original and irreducible benevolent desires in the human constitution. His theory rests on an appeal to the association of ideas, our tendency, noticed in antiquity and referred to by Descartes and Locke, to think of one thing upon seeing or thinking of something else with which the first has frequently been associated. Gay thinks we all pursue only our own happiness in all our voluntary actions. We take pleasure in the thought of what brings us happiness, and we learn that helping others pays off because those we help give help to us in turn. Hence we come to think with pleasure or approval of those who help us. Eventually we associate our own pleasure so strongly with the thought of benevolent action, both in ourselves and in others, that conscious awareness of our original selfish end is not necessary to awaken it. We are, Gay says, like a miser who initially wants money for its purchasing power and comes to want it for itself. We retain out of habit principles of action and feeling originally acquired for reasons of private interest. Hutcheson's data thus do not force us to postulate original benevolent impulses: association provides a simpler and therefore more satisfactory explanation of the undoubted fact that we act and approve without conscious thought of our own benefit.[27]

Egoism, sometimes bolstered by associationism, became a major eighteenth-century articulation of the Lockean alternative to the Leibniz-Wolff theory of the passions. Gay's kind of associationist theory of the passions was elaborated at length by David Hartley, whose treatise, published in 1749, bears a title – *Observations on Man, his Frame, his Duty and his Expectations* – suggesting his plan to link psychology, morality, and religion. Hartley argued that through association we can move from crass selfishness to unselfish devotion to God and our neighbour.[28] In France, egoistic views were used not to defend religion but to attack it. Helvétius, for instance, acknowledging Hobbes as one of his sources, simply spells out the basic points of an egoistic theory with no sense that it had been criticised. Like Hartley, he thinks that our desires are educable and can be shaped in ways that lead us to help others. True virtue is nothing but a desire for the general happiness; men can be so trained or so situated that they find pleasure in bringing it about. We must not expect to make men virtuous by asking them to sacrifice their pleasure for the public good; one can make them so 'only by uniting personal interest to the general interest'.[29] In present society – and this is Helvétius's real point – almost everyone is corrupt, taking pleasure in purely private goods or in goods limited to some small group, such as the Jesuit order. His egoistic theory turns into a tool for unmasking hypocrisy. Allowing the possibility of genuine virtue – 'probity', as he calls it – he hopefully finds room for the existence of people who might desire to reform the corrupt system in which all now live.[30]

V. HUME: ORDER THROUGH NATURE

The most sophisticated and thoroughgoing of the empiricist replies to Locke's denial of any sufficient inner principle of order came from David Hume. He also gave the fullest determinist account of active powers or human agency. Claiming to apply Newtonian methods to the human realm, he portrays us as being fully part of nature, with all our behaviour just as much caused by antecedent events as the behaviour of stones. Nature, he finds, happens to be orderly without being purposive. We are made with a sympathetic ability to feel as others feel, numerous passions leading us to aid one another, and moral feelings reinforcing these passions. No threats from external powers are needed to make us virtuous. Were it not for misguided opinions, mostly about supernatural matters, our inner constitution would enable us to live happily together.

Hume uses 'laws of association' to give reductionist analyses of central concepts such as cause, continuity of objects over time, and personal identity.[31] But, unlike Gay, he does not give reductionist analyses of the concepts involved in explaining feeling and action. For Hume, the desires and passions are not representational: they are essentially simple. Pride and humility, love and hatred, will, and the moral feeling are all indefinable impressions (*Treatise of Human Nature*, 2.1.2.1, 2.2.1.1, 2.2.12.1, 3.1.2.1–4, SBN 277, 329, 397, 470–2). Moreover, self-love does not serve for Hume, as it does for Gay, as a central explanatory principle. Hume disparages the very concept. The feeling of love, he says, is always directed toward 'some sensible being external to us; and when we talk of *self-love*, 'tis not in a proper sense' (2.2.1.2, SBN 329). He accepts the existence of a Butlerian concern for our own good on the whole and even allows himself to call it self-love (3.2.1.10, SBN 480). For Hume, the desire of our own good is neither our sole nor most important motivation, nor the basic explanation of the passions (3.2.2.5, SBN 487). In these ways, he is not an associationist about the passions.

Hume offers a psychology as complex as Butler's. Some of our central passions have ideas of good and ill among their causes, but others do not. There are desires that 'arise from a natural impulse or instinct, which is perfectly unaccountable'. Desires for revenge or for the happiness of friends, as well as hunger and lust, 'produce good and evil, and proceed not from them' (*Treatise*, 2.3.9.8, SBN 439). Of desires that are directly caused by thoughts of good and ill Hume has little to say, and that little is conventional. The mind instinctively tends to 'unite itself with the good'. Desire of this type arises from thoughts of good considered alone. When we believe the good is certain or probable, we feel joy; the thought of certain or probable evil causes sorrow. Hume gives only hope and fear more than perfunctory attention (2.3.9, SBN 438 ff.). These passions themselves are not complicated by concepts other than those of good and ill, certainty and uncertainty. Hume is more interested in the feelings of pride and love, and their opposites, whose explanation involves many more ideas.

For Hume, pride is an 'agreeable' simple impression that can arise not only from the thought of our own beauty, wealth, or power but also from the thought of our own virtue. It is a special feeling of being pleased with oneself caused by the thought of something especially valuable or admirable as having an especially close connection to oneself; and it causes no specific desire (*Treatise*, 2.1.7.7–8, SBN 297). Love is another agreeable simple impression, a feeling of pleasure in the thought of another person caused by the lover's thought of something especially good possessed by the one loved. Love is in itself not a motive at all. True, Hume thinks it is 'always follow'd by a desire of the happiness of the person belov'd', but this separate benevolent desire requires that we think of the happiness of the object of love, which we do not always do. Love might have been conjoined with malevolence. Its connection with benevolence, Hume says, is just 'an arbitrary and original instinct implanted in our nature' (2.2.6.3–2.2.7.1, SBN 367–8).

Pride as well as love helps to bind people to one another. To feel pride is, roughly, to take pleasure in other people's esteem, and esteem is a form of love (2.2.5.1 and 3.3.4.2n, SBN 357 and 608n). Moral approval is also a form of love – of purely human love (see, for example, 3.3.1.19, 26, 30–1, SBN 584, 589, 591). We are approved, or loved with the distinctive feeling we call moral approval, on account of the aspects of our character that make us agreeable or useful to ourselves or others, not because we comply with divine commands or absolute laws. Our enjoyment of this love and our pride in our virtue as well as in our wealth, status, and outstanding abilities indicate our sociable nature. Morality and the economy of the passions thus function to benefit everyone in this life. The passions are naturally conducive to order.

Hume does not say that the impressions and ideas involved in the passions are indistinct or confused. Passions themselves may mingle, and one passion may be 'mixt and confounded with' another (*Treatise*, 2.3.9.12, SBN 441).[32] But the causes or objects of the passions are not presented through confused ideas in such cases. Hume goes out of his way to explain the agitation involved in some feelings without any appeal to indistinctness of idea. Sometimes the passions are violent, producing great agitation and making us disregard long-term consequences. This is because similar passions when produced by related causes may reinforce one another. Uncertainty about the outcome of action may also produce agitation. But indistinctness in the ideas causing the passions does not figure among the causes of violent feeling (2.3.4.3–10, SBN 420–2).

Thus quite generally for Hume there are only contingent connections be-tween beliefs (lively ideas) and feelings such as pride, or desires for specific objects. Because each passion is 'an original existence . . . and contains not any representative quality' reason has only an indirect role to play in our active life. Reason, Hume is notorious for saying, is the slave of the passions (*Treatise*, 2.3.3.4–5, SBN 415). All it can do is present them with a set of beliefs that will trigger the force that constitutes desire. Reason does not determine the amount of force – the strength of the desire – its representations may cause. If it presents two alternatives, I may happen to prefer a greater to a lesser evil – destroying the world rather than getting my finger scratched, for instance – or I may not. Reason cannot decide me (2.3.3.6, SBN 416). To control a passion, we must bring some other passion to bear on it.

Our sympathetic responses to other people's feelings have just that function. To understand others is not merely to represent a counterpart of what they feel. It is to feel it; and the counterpart feelings affect our behaviour. For instance, we feel with all those who benefit from stable property laws, and these feelings are stronger than those we get from feeling with those who benefit from breaking the laws. Hence we feel disposed to obey the laws, and our moral sentiments reinforce that disposition. Sanctions may be needed, but only at the margin. Sympathy and our own desire to have the approval of others and ourselves make us basically sociable. Order arises from the natural interaction of the feelings.[33]

We mistakenly think that the regularity in our lives is the work of reason, Hume suggests, because some passions are 'calm' and only some are violent. A calm desire for, say, a career that demands long training may be strong enough to motivate someone for years, yet it may not erupt in conscious perturbations; a highly disturbing outburst of desire may not be sufficient to move us to act. It is easy to think of durable calm passions as 'determinations of reason' because they feel more or less the same. No matter how they feel, what moves us is wholly different from the faculty that 'judges of truth and falsehood' (*Treatise*, 2.3.3.8, SBN 417; see also 2.3.8.13, SBN 437–8).

As I have indicated, anti-egoists could be as determinist as associationist egoists or they could believe in free will. Hume, anti-egoist and admirer of Butler though he was, continues the determinist line of thought with no reticence. His treatment of the issue is the classical exposition of the claim that determinism is compatible with the only sort of liberty needed to sustain morality.

Hume agrees with Locke in considering will to be different in kind from desire. Will is a simple impression, Hume says, which '*we feel and are conscious of, when we knowingly give rise to any new motion of our body, or new perception of our mind*' (*Treatise*, 2.3.1.2, SBN 399). Unlike Locke, however, he gives the will no clear role to play, even though he treats it as the immediate cause of action. Hume never mentions suspension of action as something we can do because we have a will. He is interested in whether the will is causally determined, and if so by what; and his theory would proceed in the same way if he dropped the term 'will' and asked only whether we are causally determined to act as we do and, if so, how.

Having argued in the first book of the *Treatise* that causation essentially involves no more than constant conjunction of the objects that are causes and effects and the habit in the observer of inferring from the idea of the cause to the idea of the effect, Hume uses this analysis to answer his question about the will or action. The point he makes seems simple. We find ourselves with desires for various ends and beliefs about how to attain them. When we act, desires, aroused by beliefs, serve as motives. Our actions follow our motives as regularly and predictably as stones fall when dropped. If the latter exemplify causation and necessity, so do the former. Nowhere is there less regularity in the human world than in the natural one. The confidence we all have that other people, and we ourselves, will act in predictable ways is evidence that we form habits of expectation about people no less than about things. If causal necessity governs what happens in the physical world, it therefore also governs what happens in the human world; if freedom is incompatible with necessity, then to assert human freedom requires a belief that a billiard ball freely chooses to move when hit (2.3.1.14, SBN 404).

For Hume, the only important kind of freedom is compatible with the only comprehensible kind of necessity. He has no desire to defend the liberty of indifference, the ability to choose without a reason. He is only concerned with 'the liberty of *spontaneity*', or the liberty that comes from the absence of coercion (*Treatise*, 2.3.2.1, SBN 407–8). When we can do what we desire to do, we are as free as we can be or need to be. To insist on more, Hume says, would be to threaten morality and religion. His argument here is the same as Wolff's: laws, whether human or divine, are usually supposed to be 'founded on rewards and punishments'. If these had no necessary influence on our behaviour, laws would be pointless. Moreover, if we possessed liberty of indifference, there would be only random ties between our character and our behaviour. We could then hardly think of holding one another accountable for what would be chance actions. Determinism is not incompatible with morality; it is presupposed by it (2.3.2.5–7, SBN 410–12).

What, then, are 'the influencing motives of the will' (2.3.3 title, SBN 413)? We have already seen that deliverances of reason are not among them. The 'actions of the will' (2.3.2.8, SBN 412) are caused by particular desires of whatever variety. The love of moral approval plays a role, as does self-interest. Custom, imagination, and distance in time and space from desired ends also affect what we do. Taking all these considerations together, Hume concludes that no specific laws of motivation can be stated. There are too many forces interacting within us, and the play of forces is diversified by too many factors, to be formulated. Philosophy must confess that the principles determining action are for the most part 'too fine and minute for her comprehension' (2.3.8.13, SBN 438). The science of man demonstrates the certainty of determinism without giving us a single determinist law.

VI. AGENCY REVITALISED

In France as in Britain, there were many other writers who worked out determinist views of action and passion along Lockean lines. Adam Smith's views are perhaps the most interesting. His analyses of the passions in *The Theory of Moral Sentiments* (1759) rest on a completely nonrepresentational understanding of their nature. This comes out with great clarity in his account of the way we estimate the appropriateness or inappropriateness of feelings. We do so, Smith says, through our ability to feel sympathetically what another feels and to compare it with what we ourselves would feel in like circumstances. If our feelings would be as strong as the other person's, we approve; if we would feel less strongly, we say her feeling is excessive or exaggerated. There is no suggestion that we estimate the amount of good or evil to which the other is responding and approve or condemn her feelings or desires as they are or are not commensurate with that amount.[34] Subtle as his account of assessment is, Smith, like the far less imaginative French materialists and egoists, makes no effort to move the study of active powers beyond a determinist framework.[35] That effort was made by British and German thinkers motivated by concerns about both religion and morality that they thought their determinist opponents could not accommodate.

Many Christian thinkers held that Locke's system, later aided by associationism, opened the door not only to determinism but to materialist exclusion of all spiritual reality, God's included. Neither Leibnizian nor Lockean accounts of will seemed to them able to explain how we could have the psychological resources to act independently of our desires. But this, they held, is what morality requires. They found it necessary to rethink action and to take Newton into account in doing so.

Hume was aware of the religious opposition to determinism. In presenting his theory, he was trying in part to undermine the views of two of its critics, Samuel Clarke and George Berkeley. These two disagreed deeply about morality, but they were at one concerning active power.

Clarke, a highly placed if unorthodox Christian minister, was also a successful expositor and defender of Newton's physics. His Boyle Lectures of 1704 and 1705 aim at refuting Hobbes and Spinoza, whose materialism and necessitarianism amount, he insists, to atheism. In attacking them, he is also seeking to go beyond Locke and Leibniz.[36]

Clarke begins by arguing that there must of necessity be one eternal, nonmaterial, unchanging, infinite being who is the cause of all other things and who himself is a self-activating agent. This being must be free because '*Intelligence* without *Liberty . . .* is really *. . . no Intelligence* at all. It is indeed a *Consciousness*, but it is merely *a Passive One*; a Consciousness, not of Acting, but purely of being Acted upon'. (Boyle Lectures, I.ix, 548). God's freedom enables him, as Clarke makes clear in his correspondence with Leibniz, to choose between alternatives even when it does not matter which alternative he chooses.[37] Newton had indeed thought that God intervenes in the world, restoring it to order. Hence for him the universe is not a closed clockwork mechanism. It is open to spontaneous action from the deity. And if from the deity, then why not from us? Clarke is drawing on such views in his Boyle Lectures as well as in his later controversy with Leibniz. In general, however, there is a special kind of necessity underlying God's choices. It is a necessity of *fitness*, requiring that things be as they are in order not to diminish 'the Beauty, Order, and Well-being of the Whole' (ix, 550). This is not an 'absolute necessity', entailing that there is a contradiction in supposing the contrary (iii, 528). Alternatives are conceivable even if unfit. To act as one does because the fitness of things makes such action necessary is 'consistent with the greatest Freedom and most perfect Choice. For', Clarke continues, 'the only Foundation of this Necessity, is such an unalterable Rectitude of Will, and Perfection of Wisdom, as makes it impossible for a Wise Being to resolve to Act foolishly; or for a Nature infinitely Good, to choose to do that which is Evil' (ix, 551).

It is thus a mistake to argue that liberty is a conceptual impossibility because every event, including volitions, must have a cause. Those who say this 'ignorantly confound *Moral Motives* with *Physical Efficients*, between which Two things there is no manner of relation'. Avoid this confusion, Clarke is saying, and you can see that choices made from motives are free, while being morally necessary (ix, 553).

So much for God's freedom: now for human freedom. God is proven to be omnipotent, and from this it follows that he can give creatures the power of beginning movement (Boyle Lectures, x, 557). When we act, we experience ourselves as we would if we possessed the power of self-motion (x, 557–8). This no more demonstrates that we have the power than sensory experience proves the existence of an external world. But the bare possibility that we might be without such power, like the bare possibility that the material world does not exist, should worry no one. Against Malebranche, Clarke simply points out – as Reid was to do later – that our possession of self-moving power does not make us independent of God. He freely gives us the power, and he can take it away.[38] Since the power of self-motion coupled with intelligence is liberty, Clarke thinks he has done enough to show that our wills are free. What remains is to dismiss all arguments against it as being due to the 'Fundamental Errour' of failing to distinguish clearly between '*moral Motives*, and *Causes Physically Efficient*' (I.x, 565 ff.).

Clarke's treatment of morality shows that he considers motives to be reasons, different in kind from felt desires and not dependent on them. God is guided by reasons given by his knowledge of certain self-evident axioms about the eternal fitnesses of things; we can and ought to be guided by them as well. Knowledge of the axioms, as such, serves as our motive. We do not need additional considerations of punishment and reward to be moved to do what 'right Reason' moves us to do (II.i.7, 628). Thus the earlier argument to show that intelligence entails agency is transposed to human beings to support the claim that we can act from reasons arising not from desires but solely from knowledge of moral truths.

Clarke's liberty is not a Hobbesian absence of external impediments. It is a liberty we have even in prison (I.x, 566). It is an inner power different in kind from desire. It is not the Cartesian will, which necessarily assents to clear and distinct representations and can choose only where there is confusion and indistinctness.[39] It is neither the Leibnizian tendency to seek the greatest perfection nor the Lockean ability to suspend action. What is liberty, then? Clarke regrettably devotes more effort to refuting his opponents than to developing his own position. He is content to say that liberty consists in a person's 'having a continual Power of choosing, whether he shall Act, or whether he shall forbear Acting'. He does not tell us anything about how we choose whether to act or forbear. Nor does he tell us how the motives constituted by our knowledge of eternal fitnesses relate to the urges and impulses due to our needs and desires. What he does make clear is that morality depends on our ability to be moved by our knowledge of eternal truths. That ability is at the core of what he calls the 'Power of Agency or Free Choice (for these are precisely Identical terms)' (I.x, 566).

In the phrase just quoted, Clarke makes what I believe is the first use of the term agency in its modern philosophical context. The *Oxford English Dictionary* shows only one earlier use, in 1658, which is not clearly a philosophical one. It then gives a citation from Jonathan Edwards dated 1762. As we shall see, Berkeley, Hume, and Price used the term before then, and in 1731 Edmund Law, referring to Clarke, described the word as 'generally including the power of beginning *Thought* as well as *Motion*'.[40] The view that humans are agents is of course not new, and Bishop Bramhall, controverting Hobbes a half century before Clarke, had supported views like his.[41] But Clarke brings a new consideration into his defence of liberty. For Leibniz, desires can be controlled directly by reason because they are themselves implicitly rational. Lockean desires are not, and they cannot be so controlled. Clarke agrees with Locke on this point. Leibniz and Locke think of the will as being determined by the strength of various desires. Clarke does not mention strength when he speaks of moral motives and the kind of necessity they involve. He thinks they are the wrong kind of thing to have that sort of property.[42] Knowledge of moral axioms and the desire for happiness are incommensurable, yet both enter into explanations of our action. Strength of desire is one kind of determinant of action. Knowledge of normative truth must be a different kind, playing a unique role in our decisions because it possesses what Butler later called authority. We experience ourselves as deciding which of these incommensurable kinds of consideration to follow. Clarke's innovation here is to see free agency as providing the only possible explanation of how we can do so.

Berkeley takes up Clarke's new term to raise an important problem. He is notorious for his thesis that the physical world is reducible without remainder to ideas, which exist only in the mind. Ideas are necessarily and by their nature, he thinks, wholly and utterly inactive: 'there is nothing of power or agency included in them'.[43] They cannot even *represent* action. Hence all change in the so-called physical world is due to God's action on ideas. Spirit alone, which is simple and substantial, is active. Only spirits understand and, more importantly, exercise will. We experience this because we know we can call up ideas at our pleasure. 'This making and unmaking of ideas doth very properly denominate the mind active'.[44]

The concept of will or agency poses a problem for Berkeley of which he is well aware. Ideas are passive and can only represent what is passive. If spirit is active, we can therefore have no idea of it or of its components, understanding and will. We have instead what Berkeley calls notions, which, unlike ideas, cannot be perceived.[45] He does not make it clear just how notions are known and what relation the existence of imperceptible understanding and will have to the things whose existence is constituted by their being perceived.

Berkeley's difficulties on these matters point to an apparent problem for philosophers who tried to follow Locke in allowing legitimacy only to ideas that can be derived from sensory and introspective experience of ideas and reflection on it. If Berkeley is right, agency of the kind he and Clarke think necessary for morality is a notion that cannot be explained in those terms.

Hutcheson and Hume, of course, did not wish to make room for any such concept. Hume sees no need for the kind of agency Clarke invokes. He takes note of appeal to '*a false sensation or experience*' of liberty only to dismiss it (*Treatise*, 2.3.2.2, SBN 408). Moreover, in reinforcing his conclusion that reason is only the slave of the passions, he argues explicitly against Clarke's claim that knowledge of truth alone can motivate (3.1.1.18–26, SBN 463–8). Hume's theory of causation is itself directed in part against Clarke. Agency is just another synonym for cause, Hume says (1.3.14.4, SBN 157), and his analysis of causal necessity tells us all there is to know about it. There is, he insists, 'but one kind of *necessity*, as there is but one kind of cause . . . the common distinction betwixt *moral* and *physical* necessity is without any foundation in nature' (1.3.14.33, SBN 171). Henry Home, Lord Kames, attacking Clarke explicitly, relies on Hume's denial that there can be different kinds of necessity, asserts that action is necessarily determined by the strongest desire or aversion, and assumes what Clarke is trying to combat, that '[a]ll our principles of action resolve into *desires* and *aversions*'.[46]

Faced with Hume's systematic determinist account of action and morality, those who wished to defend the Clarke-Berkeley view of agency were forced into major attacks on the empiricist position.

VII. AGENCY DEFENDED

I shall consider here only two of the British philosophers who attempted to defend a Clarkean view of agency and morality, Richard Price and Thomas Reid. Both acknowledge a debt to Bishop Butler. They follow him in distinguishing particular desires, whose objects are specific objects or states of affairs, from more general principles such as self-love and benevolence, in rejecting the thesis that all voluntary action is self-interested, and in refusing to see all of morality as stemming from a single principle, such as that of benevolence. They also accept another of Butler's central claims: that there is a difference between the strength of a desire or principle of action and what he calls its authority. We can see that the two are distinct, Butler says, by considering that even when we do not have any desire to do something for our own long-term good – for instance, visit the dentist – we recognise that we ought to, and that recognition is our awareness of the authority of a principle of prudence. Authority of a higher kind belongs to the dictates of conscience, or our general awareness of moral directives. We can be guided, Butler believes, by the authority of prudence or conscience even when their strength is less than that of the desires they require us to control. He thus claims, with Clarke, that the different kinds of considerations involved in action are incommensurable, but he does not say how 'authority' can move us.[47]

Price and Reid go beyond Butler in elaborating the psychology of moral action. 'The human mind', says Price in his one philosophical work, the exceptionally acute *Review of the Principal Questions in Morals* (1758),

would appear to have little order or consistency in it, were we to consider it as only a system of passions and affections, which are continually drawing us different ways, without any thing at the head of them to govern them, and the strongest of which for the time necessarily determines the conduct. But this is far from being its real state.[48]

The Lockean vision Price calls up of the mind's lack of any internal principle of order is falsified by the 'moral faculty' which appropriately governs 'all our other powers' (215n). To explain the operations of the moral faculty, Price finds that he must reject the Lockean epistemology and assert, with Cudworth, that reason is not, as in the works of Locke and Descartes, a purely passive power; it is an active power and is the source of our agency.

For our purposes, the key part of Price's rejection of Locke's epistemology lies in his claim that reason is itself a source of simple ideas. He is driven to this by what he takes to be the inadequacies of Hutcheson's account of moral approval. If Hutcheson were right, approval would simply be a sensation derived from the way our mind operates, telling us nothing about 'the real characters of *actions*' (15).[49] We need not agree. Reason does what sense cannot. It generalises and compares where sense is confined to particulars. Reason discerns, sense merely suffers (21). Many of our ideas – of solidity, substance, duration, space, infinity, contingency, necessity, causation, or power – cannot be explained as originating from purely sensory information. Hume sees this but draws the wrong conclusion. The correct response is not to deny or redefine the ideas as he does but to admit the creative power of reason and the narrow bounds of sense (22–35). Reason, Price holds, gives us simple ideas by giving us intuitive truths of which the simple ideas are constituents. Thus actions, like other things, have a nature, and being right or being wrong is a necessary part of it. Reason, discerning this, gives us these moral ideas. We cannot coherently imagine a rational being unable to distinguish right from wrong and, if actions had no moral nature, God could have no grounds for performing one act rather than another or preferring one end to another (48–9). He could act only arbitrarily.[50]

Awareness of moral truth, Price allows, is always emotionally coloured. But feelings are not all there is to moral ideas. Feelings are aroused by knowledge of moral truth, not constitutive of it. No new sense is needed to account for feelings of approval and the pleasure we take in contemplating virtue. Our cognitions cause them. These feelings also have a definite moral function. It is not that our moral ideas are confused and indistinct, but reason's deliverances would be too slow and weak in many cases to move us to act properly were they not seconded by feelings or what Price calls instinctive determinations. We need both 'a *perception of the understanding*, and a *feeling of the heart*' to prompt us effectively (61–2).[51]

Moral sentiments are not the only feelings aroused by knowledge. Our passions and desires generally have conceptual origins. We cannot understand the idea of happiness without coming to desire it, regardless of who has it. Similarly, we must admire and desire truth, knowledge, and honour, once we understand what they are (70–3). Price's thought seems to be that when objects are conceived in certain ways, they awaken the appropriate feelings or desires. If such 'affections' are strengthened by instinctive determinations, they are 'passions', but in all cases grasp of a concept is the crucial source (74). Although brief on these matters, Price clearly disagrees not only with the Leibniz-Wolff approach, since he does not construe the passions as involving indistinct ideas, but with the Humean approach as well. The instinctive determinations do no more than add strength to affections which get their energy as well as their direction from rational concepts. Price goes so far as to claim that were we sufficiently rational, we would have no need of the instinctive appetites to move us to action (76-7).

Price brings this apparatus to bear on his central concern when he discusses the virtuous agent's motives. The virtuous agent must first possess liberty, 'the power of *acting* and *determining*'. By this Price means not that an agent's actions must have no cause but that the agent must be the cause of them. There cannot be a '*foreign* cause' for what I think of as my own volition. It is absurd to suppose that 'I determine *voluntarily* and yet *necessarily*'. Price thus thinks the Hobbesian view is obviously false. If we do not allow '*agency*, free choice, and an absolute dominion over our resolutions', there is no room for morality (181-2).

The second requisite for morality is intelligence. Self-motion or activity can exist without intelligence, but intelligence cannot exist without liberty. Since we are plainly intelligent, we must have liberty, or so Price suggests without spelling out his argument at any length (183-4). Liberty and reason together make an agent capable of virtue, and Price argues that only the motivation arising from the belief that a given act is morally right or morally good – only the intention to do the act as one that is called for by morality – constitutes the agent's virtue. He has no doubt that we all 'continually feel, that the perception of right and wrong excites to action'. Excitement to action 'belongs to the very ideas of moral right and wrong', and morally appropriate action will ensue from seeing that the ideas apply to a case 'whenever there is nothing to oppose it'. Price thinks that there is no sensible question to be asked about 'why a *reasonable* being acts *reasonably*' (185-7).

Hume had argued that because moral awareness moves us to action, and reason alone never moves us, it follows that moral awareness does not come from reason. Price, agreeing that moral awareness moves us to action, insists that moral awareness comes from reason and so concludes that reason is an active power. Like Clarke, he distinguishes the motive or reason for action from '*physical efficients*' or causes. The former is the '*occasion*' upon which the agent determines to act, but not an external force moving her (183n, 211). Voluntary action always requires 'the *physical possibility* of forbearing it', but this, he adds, is entirely compatible with its being quite certain that the act will be done (244-5).

Liberty, for Price as for Clarke, is an all-or-nothing attribute, not something we can have in varying degrees (209–10). When Price takes up the relations of moral and non-moral motives (which Clarke does not discuss), he creates a difficulty for himself. The two kinds of motive can cooperate in leading to an action, and they can conflict. The strength of our non-moral motives always threatens to overwhelm or outweigh the moral motive, but we can strengthen the latter indefinitely. Thus Price seems to allow, as Clarke does not, that reasons and desires operate in the same field of force. The 'spring of virtue', he says, which should repel the forces of temptation, may be 'relaxed or broken' (207). He seems to be defending agency in a Newtonian world by adding to physical forces those derived from concepts.

Price agrees with Butler in criticising Shaftesbury for treating motives only in terms of commensurable strengths. The latter failed to see that moral motives claim an *authority* over the others (190n). Yet Price does not show how authority can be factored into the field of forces in which moral motives may lose. He recognises an incommensurability in considerations prompting us to action but does not treat the will as that which explains how we can decide among incommensurable potential motivations. He treats it instead as that through which we are able to respond to reasons of a kind that override considerations coming from desires. Hence he does not explain how we can be acting freely when our moral reasons are not strong enough to win the day against non-moral or immoral reasons.

Thomas Reid published his *Essays on the Active Powers of Man* (1788) toward the end of a long academic career.[52] They were preceded by *An Inquiry into the Human mind on the Principles of Common Sense* (1764) and by the *Essays on the Intellectual Powers of Man* (1785). In all these works, Reid opposes Hume's reductionist version of empiricism and defends what he took to be 'common sense' beliefs, themselves rooted deeply in experience. Common sense about action and morality turns out to be quite definitely Christian. In this respect as in many others, Reid's views are closely allied with those of Clarke and Price. Like them, he aims to defend moral accountability in a divinely ordered universe by showing that we can freely determine ourselves to live by the precepts of a code that requires more than the pursuit of happiness. In *Active Powers*, he fights not only Hume, whose necessitarianism he takes to entail atheism, but also Leibniz, who was not an atheist but as strongly necessitarian as Hume and to be rejected just as emphatically (I.6, 624–5).

For our purposes, Reid's views centre on two points: one concerns active power and causation generally and our status as agents, the other our ability to determine our will freely and the way in which this ability enables us to guide ourselves by considering reasons for action. Before turning to these points, we must note Reid's views on desires and other motivations.

Reid's position is as pluralistic as that of Butler and Price. Desires take all sorts of objects and are not reducible to any single principle. They are impulses toward objects as represented in thought. When they cause agitation and cloud thinking, they are passions, but Reid does not say that the thoughts eliciting them must be indistinct. All of them, even anger and resentment, serve good purposes when not excessive, and they do not exhaust our motivational repertoire. Reid follows Price in arguing that some rational ideas themselves motivate. It takes reason to construct the idea of our own good on the whole and to recognise the basic axioms of morality. These thoughts give us reasons to act which, as we shall see, can be effective in determining what we do. Hume is quite wrong in thinking reason is only the slave of the passions. Without reason we would lack some of our most important motivations.

The belief that some things act and others are acted on is one of the fixed points of common sense belief that Reid refuses to doubt. The distinction is made in all languages. Everyone understands it, and so has the idea of power. It is absurd to speak of passive power: 'passive power is no power at all' (*Active Powers*, I.3, 519a). The proper contrast with 'active power' is 'speculative power', the general ability displayed in seeing, hearing, recalling, judging, reasoning, and so forth (I.1, 515a). The idea of power is simple. It is not acquired through sense or reflection but is known only indirectly, through that which we observe it to bring about (I.1, 514a-b). If Locke was mistaken in many ways about power, he was correct in holding that 'the only clear notion or idea we have of active power, is taken from the power which we find in ourselves to give certain motions to our bodies, or a certain direction to our thoughts' (I.5, 523a). Our power is what accounts for this ability, and when we attribute power to God, we think of him as being like us (IV.2, 604a).

Given that we have wills, how do we fit in with the causally ordered world in which we live? Reid never challenges the common sense belief that every event or change must have a cause (IV.2, 603a). But he does raise questions about the common sense way of speaking of one natural event as causing another. We must not take such language literally any more than we now take it literally when we say that the sun is rising. Because we cannot obtain knowledge of causation or power through our senses (here Reid accepts Hume's view), all that we really know about nature is lawlike sequences of events. That is enough to gratify our curiosity, teach us what to expect, and show us how to make things happen (I.6, 526b; IV.3, 606b–7a). Regularities do not constitute causes, whatever Hume may think, but they give us all we need where nature is concerned. God may move natural things directly, or through intermediaries, or by means of an initial command; it is unimportant as well as impossible to decide. 'It is only in human actions, that may be imputed for praise or blame,' Reid says, 'that it is necessary for us to know who is the agent', and here we can often enough tell (I.6, 527b).

What matters is the act of will, or volition. Desire and appetite can take almost anything imaginable as their objects, but will can take as its object only 'some action of our own', either thinking or bodily movement, which we have a thought of and believe to be in our power (I.7, 531a–3a). To will it is to determine ourselves to do such an act. Only actions coming from the will are voluntary (I.7, 531a; IV.2, 601b). Reid freely allows that neither he nor anyone else knows how determinations of the will control thoughts or make the body move (I.7, 528a). The central question, for him as for Locke, is, what determines the will?

There are two alternatives. Any specific volition is determined either by the person whose will it is or by some other being. Reid thinks that in cases of free volition the person whose will is involved is the cause of the volition. Here he comes to his central claim about human active power. We simply possess the power to determine our wills to do this or that, to act or to refrain. Because causation is the exertion of a basic active power, and not constant conjunction, Reid offers no account of what this kind of determination is and sees no need for further inquiry about causes. To deny that persons can determine their own wills is to deny that persons are efficient causes, and so that they are free and accountable. To admit that they are agents is to admit that agents can cause their wills to opt one way or another. We may ask why they made the choice they made but that, as we shall see, is not necessarily to ask what caused the agent to determine her will as she did. It may be a question of reasons (IV.1, 601a–4a).

A conception of agent causation is thus central to Reid's account of liberty and morality. Agency is not always involved in explaining our actions. Reflex acts, or what very young children do or what we do when seriously ill or corrupted by vicious habits, may not be explicable in terms of agency. But when our agency explains why we determined our will as we did, then, Reid says, we are free, and for the actions that ensue we are fully accountable.

It is no surprise that Reid does not accept the Humean position that motives necessarily determine the will. Like Clarke, he argues that motives are not efficient causes at all. A motive 'is not a thing that exists, but a thing that is conceived', and so it is not the right kind of entity to enter into causal relations (*Active Powers*, IV.4, 608b). The necessitarians suppose the world to be composed of inert matter, never acting and always acted upon. Since they think the behaviour of intelligent beings is part of such a world, they think motives work on will in proportion to their strength and direction. But if we consider rational beings as genuine agents, then we must say that motives *influence* action in the way that advice does, not that they cause it. Some of Reid's most effective arguments are directed against the necessitarian view that motives determine the will in accordance with their strength.

Reid raises, for the first time, the question of how we know the strength of a motive. If we know it only because of its outcome, then the claim that motives are effective in proportion to their strength is empty. If the contrary motives are of the same kind, we can compare strengths: a bigger bribe provides a stronger motive than a smaller bribe. But, Reid asks, '[W]hen the motives are of different kinds, as money and fame, duty and worldly interest, . . . by what rule shall we judge which is the strongest motive?' (IV.4, 608b).

Reid offers two rules. Suppose I am hungry but afraid to eat. These feelings act directly on the will, bypassing my reason. That one is strongest which I find most difficult to resist. It wins the 'animal test' of strength (IV.4, 611b). Now consider rational motives, which spring from our awareness of moral principles, or our thought of our own greatest good. The beliefs involved may not cause feelings in us, but they are motives nonetheless. Should these motives conflict, then that one is strongest which represents what is most our duty, or most for our interest. It passes the 'rational test' of strength (IV.4, 612a).

Does the strongest motive always determine the will? Leaving aside cases where we determine our will with no motive – as when we pick one coin rather than another to pay a debt – the answer is negative. Sometimes the strongest animal motive prevails, sometimes the strongest rational motive (IV.4, 612a). Since we have the power of acting without a motive at all, 'that power, joined to a weaker motive, may counterbalance a stronger' (IV.4, 610a). It is thus within our power to act as the *rationally* strongest motives advise. Good agents are those who habitually do so. Reid does not ask what brings it about that some agents are habitually good and others not.

Having explained the conceptual framework needed to make sense of free agency, Reid goes on to consider whether in fact we are free. Of the three arguments he gives to show that we are, two are familiar. Everyone, he says first, is conscious of deliberation and voluntary exertion, and our moral lives are structured around our experience of ourselves as free agents. Reid here backs the Clarkean argument with his own general epistemological principle that fixed points of common sense must be true (IV.6, 616b ff.).[53]

The second argument rests on the thesis, for which Reid argues in earlier sections of the *Active Powers*, that morality imposes a unique kind of requirement upon us. Its demands are thus incommensurable with those involved in satisfying our desires. This brings out the significance of the fact that we accept accountability for our actions. On the common sense view, accountability requires that we must be able to do what we see we ought to do (IV.7, 621a). Since frequently we ought to act in opposition to the motive that according to the animal strength rule is strongest, we can do so, although not so necessitated. Thus we can determine our own will either way, which means, of course, that we are free. Given accountability in this sense, moral praise and blame mean what common sense has always taken them to mean. In the necessitarian system, they must be given a new and quite unacceptable meaning (622b).

Finally, Reid points to prudence in support of his thesis. He accepts the Lockean assumption that there is among our desires no natural ordering toward the good, not even toward the agent's own greatest good. The fact that we can make and carry out long-range plans is therefore evidence that we are not mere mechanisms moved by the varying strengths of our desires but agents able to determine our own wills (*Active Powers*, IV.8, 623b).

Reid's theory of the active powers provided the version of strong libertarianism most influential in British, French, and American thought in the early decades of the nineteenth century. The other eighteenth-century libertarian view that came to be widely influential developed in Germany, among thinkers aware of Locke, Clarke, Shaftesbury, Hutcheson, and Hume but ignorant of Butler, Price, and Reid's work on active powers.[54] Its central opponent was the Leibniz-Wolff theory.

VIII. THE WILL AND GOD'S LAWS

Aside from Wolff, the most interesting eighteenth-century German philosopher before Kant was Christian August Crusius (1715–75). A Lutheran pastor and the leading critic of Wolffianism, Crusius put his considerable philosophical ingenuity at the service of essentially reactionary Christian apologetics. Although his great treatise on ethics, the *Anweisung vernünftig zu leben* (Guide to Rational Living) was published in 1744, a year prior to his metaphysical treatise, *Entwurf der nothwendigen Vernunft-Wahrheiten* (Sketch of the Necessary Truths of Reason), the positions defended in the later work are obviously drawn on in the earlier one.[55] The philosophy of Crusius is highly systematic, deliberately opposing Leibniz and Wolff on almost every major issue.

Crusius is concerned above all with showing that human beings are accountable for their own acts and that their primary responsibility is to acknowledge their total dependence on God by freely obeying his commands. God created, sustains, and oversees the world, but it is a world containing various kinds of agents with their own powers. Something has a power when it contains the possibility or necessity of another thing. Only substances have powers. One substance has a power when there is something within it on account of which another substance can come or continue to be, or alter its condition (*Entwurf*, 112–13). There are passive as well as active powers, and, more importantly, basic as well as derived powers. Derived powers may be explained in terms of basic powers; basic powers belong to the essence of what has them and can not be explained further (121–3). Some attributes are powers simply by existing. Thus the sides of a triangle make its angles what they are. In contrast with these existential powers, other powers change what exists, and these are active powers (*thätige Kräfte*).

Among active powers, some are self-activated, not set in action by anything external to their substance (*Entwurf*, 135–7). Crusius argues that there must be such powers because otherwise there would have to be an infinite series of activators before anything could change. The acts originating in self-activation are called basic actions (139). God must, of course, have this kind of power, but we have it as well: it is the basis of our freedom and our accountability (140–3).

Crusius offers three arguments to show that we are free. First, we experience ourselves as originators, capable of acting or changing course or not acting at all, and we can choose between indifferents – equally good means to our ends, for instance (*Anweisung*, 51–2). Next, we know that there are divine moral laws and that we are obligated to obey them, but we could not be so obligated were we not free (53–4). Crusius's central argument is much more unusual. It is that unless the world contains agents with free will there would be no reason for God to create it. Without free agents in a world, everything in that world would really be done by God himself. Hence 'created beings would obtain through their reality no other relation to God than what they already had in the mere state of possibility, namely, that their being and essence depended on him'. This would mean that God could have no formal purpose in making a possible world real. But God does nothing in vain, and hence any real world must contain free agents (53). Because of free will, created beings can come into kinds of relations with God – moral relations – that would otherwise be impossible. Free will is the power making these relations possible, and they justify God in making a possible world real. Morality is the point of existence (*Entwurf*, 504–8, 638, 669–70).

What, then, is will? Crusius gives an original answer: will is 'the power of a mind to act according to its representations'. It is the effort to make real something represented (*Anweisung*, 4; *Entwurf*, 866). Will as active power contains various strivings, some constant and some intermittent. These are our desires, which are thus aspects of the will. Desire is not essentially due to need or lack. It is one form of the will's exercise of its activity. The representation that stimulates a desire serves as a potential end for us. To adopt a possible end is to decide to realise what is represented, to make it exist, or come to possess it. Thus, where the understanding moves from one idea to another, the will takes us beyond the realm of thinking and so is neither a part of the understanding nor simply derivable from it (*Anweisung*, 9–11; *Entwurf*, 867–9). The Leibniz-Wolff school is thus mistaken in holding that since all we can do is represent, every mental occurrence must amount to moving from one representation to another. For them, desire is the desire for new representations and will is the movement to new representations. But this change in what we think, as Crusius sees it, is not genuine action at all.

Acts of will, or volitions, for Crusius always bring to the representations that elicit them an otherwise absent thrust toward realisation. Beings who can think must have wills because otherwise their representations of the world would be pointless. 'The understanding', Crusius says, in the first modern proclamation of the primacy of the practical, 'exists for the sake of the will' (*Anweisung*, 4; *Entwurf*, 886).

Pleasure and good as well as desire are explained in terms of will. Pleasure is what we feel when we are in a condition we have willed (*Anweisung*, 24). The good itself is simply what is in conformity with a will or with desire (*Anweisung*, 29; *Entwurf*, 326–7). Good is thus a relative concept, unlike the concept of perfection. Things are more or less perfect as they are more or less able to be causes of other things or as they have more or less power (*Entwurf*, 296–300). Crusius thinks that we, like God, always desire perfection, and hence that the perfect is in fact the good, although the concepts are different. But the desire for perfection explains little because there are many kinds and degrees of perfection, and – contrary to Leibniz – no single 'most perfect' or 'best' state toward which we might aim. For Crusius it is, of course, pointless to say, as Leibniz and Wolff do, that we always will the good. Goodness presupposes but does not explain the activity of will. It is thus no surprise to find Crusius insisting that there are innumerable kinds of objects of desire and refusing to try to explain them in terms of self-interest or any other single factor.

Many of our desires originate from other desires, as the desire for a means does from the desire for an end. Since this cannot go on forever, there must be basic desires, and at least some of these must be essential to the mind. Basic desires, given to us by God, cannot be wicked and must be shared by all. As forms of will, desires require representations. Innate desires must therefore carry innate ideas with them (*Anweisung*, 109–15). But it is important to distinguish derivative desires from basic ones. The desire for happiness, for instance, is not basic. It is only the desire to enjoy the gratification of our specific desires and therefore presupposes their existence (119–28). Crusius holds that no general explanation of particular desires can be given (128–9).

Although the desire for happiness is derivative, there are basic human desires or drives. Crusius identifies three. The first is the desire to increase our own appropriate perfection (*Anweisung*, 133–4). Against the Leibniz-Wolff school's use of this desire, Crusius argues that it is the origin not of all striving but of the desires for truth, clarity, good reasoning, the arts, bodily improvement, freedom, friendship, and honour (135–44). The second basic desire is for community with those in whom we find perfection (145). This leads us, among other things, to feel a general moral love or a desire to help others (148–50). The third desire is 'the natural drive to recognise a divine moral law' (157). This is evident in our drive of conscience (*Gewissenstrieb*), a sense of indebtedness which moves us to do our duty and carry out our obligations.

To act from our awareness of God's laws, Crusius thinks, we must be free, and he makes several points about the freedom that enables us to obey those laws. Freedom is not just the absence of external hindrances to doing as we please. Nor is it acting for what we perceive as the greatest available amount of good or perfection. If there were only Leibnizian freedom, he argues, 'all our virtue would be turned into mere good luck' since it would depend on our having a constitution enabling us to acquire knowledge and on our being so situated as to get it (*Anweisung*, 46). Crusius thinks Leibniz does not avoid fatalism. If his 'hypothetical necessity' is to offer real alternatives of action, then the ends involved must be chosen by genuinely self-determining agents of a kind for which Leibniz leaves no room (*Entwurf*, 203–10).[56] If we are truly free, then, even given constant antecedents and circumstances, we can determine ourselves to act in several ways (*Anweisung*, 44–5; see *Entwurf*, 140–5). 'Whenever we freely will something', Crusius says,

> we are deciding to do something for which one or several desires already exist in us.... Freedom consists in an inner perfect activity of will, which is capable of connecting its efficacy with one of the currently active drives of the will, or of omitting this connection and remaining inactive, or of connecting it with another drive instead of with the first. (*Anweisung*, 54–5)

In one way, the Crusian will is more like the Leibnizian than the Lockean one. It contains within itself its own rules for making choices among the alternatives presented to it by desires and drives. These are all forms of will, but they are not commensurable. The drive of conscience, for instance, is different in kind from desire. Hence the Crusian will is much more complex than the Leibnizian. It does not direct us to maximise perfection. It tells us to follow a moral code as well as rules of prudence, both inherent in the will. When these rules seem to conflict, we are to follow God's laws above all else. What enables us to do so is, first, the fact that conscience provides a permanent basic drive and, second, the fact that our will is free. We feel the charm of the various representations to which the will's strivings respond, but we are not determined by them. We can turn the will away from them and 'connect its efficacy' with our conscientious feeling of obligation.

What allows Crusius to make this claim is his distinction between physical causes and motives or exemplary causes, which are reasons justifying proposed actions. He argues that the Leibnizian principle of sufficient reason systematically and inexcusably overlooks this distinction, collapsing radically different kinds of reason (*Grund*), the physical and the moral, into one (*Anweisung*, 204–6; *Entwurf*, 112–55; see also 865–6). Crusius feels no hesitation in allowing cognitive reasons causal efficacy in moving bodies in a material world. Granting physical determinism a large part in explaining the behaviour of inanimate objects, he thinks that total determinism is unacceptable. It allows neither for morality nor for miracles (*Entwurf*, 723–5). Mind, however, is spiritual substance, and both God and humankind must be able to alter the course of events. Indeed, in the end, only God and ourselves possess truly active powers (776–7). If determinism cannot account for these things, so much the worse for it.

IX. EMPIRICAL EVIDENCE FOR FREE WILL

Crusius's incorporation of moral knowledge into the will implied a rejection of the classical distinction between understanding and will. In 1777, J. N. Tetens rejected it more elaborately in his *Philosophische Versuche über die menschliche Natur und ihre Entwicklung* (Philosophical Essays on Human Nature and its Development).[57] He replaced the classical dichotomy with a threefold division not of faculties but of powers, making sensibility a separate power of receiving sensations from the external world or one's own body and giving it the function of supplying data to the other two powers, the understanding and the will (*Versuche*, 1: 618–26). Tetens also reassigned the attributes of passivity and activity, leaving sensibility alone purely passive and finding as much activity in the understanding as in the will (see 2: 20–1). Since Kant reportedly kept Tetens's work on his desk as he wrote the *Kritik der reinen Vernunft*, historians have understandably investigated this aspect of Tetens's thought, expounded in his first volume.[58] They have generally overlooked his reflections on free will and human perfectibility, the topics of the second volume and, for Tetens, the point and justification of the whole (*Versuche*, Vorrede, 1: xxxv–xxxvi).

Tetens, sometimes described as 'the German Locke', knew the work of the British philosophers thoroughly, as well as the work of French theorists such as Condillac and Bonnet, who were influenced by them. He had, however, no single allegiance. Tetens admires Leibniz and Wolff and remarks at one point that the 'foreigners' have left much obscure (*Versuche*, 1: 427). But he rejects the central Leibniz-Wolff thesis that all mental functioning including pleasure and desire can be explained in terms of representation. He is equally doubtful whether association can explain everything. He allows that knowledge must come from experience but takes experience to teach us far more than Hume admits. It teaches us, for instance, that causation is more than paired events always occurring in the same sequence. Real power is involved. We get the idea of power from our own feelings, but it is justifiable (Tetens never succeeds in explaining exactly how) to take our inner experience of necessary connection as showing that objective powers exist in external objects as well as in ourselves (1: 312–16, 322–7; 2: 564–8).[59]

The concept of the mind's self-activating power is central to all of Tetens's accounts of mental functioning. Self-activity is involved, for example, in transforming sensations into thoughts. Possession of it is also presupposed by the ability to act freely. Water flowing out of a hole in a jug displays a self-activating power, as does a tensed spring when it is released, but neither is free. Freedom is a power over oneself, going beyond the ability of the soul to have effects upon itself (as the Leibnizians think). 'The *positive power* through which we have ourselves in our own control when we are active requires a *simultaneous inner capacity* or readiness to do, under unaltered circumstances, the opposite of what we do. This capacity to be otherwise active . . . persists during the whole action if this is a free action in its entirety to its end' (*Versuche*, 2: 6–7). Free agents thus possess more powers than merely self-activated agents. They possess the ability to initiate action, the ability to apply this ability, and the ability not to act, or to do something else entirely. Because they possess this third power, free beings are more fully the originators of their actions than merely spontaneous agents (2: 125).

Tetens rests all his basic claims on experience. The threefold division of mental powers is intended as an explanation of observable phenomena (*Versuche*, 2: 625). So also is the claim that some self-activating agents are free agents. This raises a difficult question. Since the power to do otherwise is never used, how do we know that anything has it? Tetens adduces several kinds of data, which serve as his arguments to show that we are free.

Most importantly, self-awareness gives us a sensation of being able to do otherwise. That sensation may be erroneous, as are some sensory data about the external world, but occasional error does not – despite Berkeley – show that the sensation is always wrong (*Versuche*, 2: 9–19, 131). Moreover, we experience the power to do otherwise as a series of impulses, interrupting the action, to do otherwise. Consequently, freely chosen actions do not proceed in the uninterrupted and unvarying way that unfree actions do (2: 16). Compare human action with the behaviour of the famous automata that Vaucanson made: there are many more forces at work in the former and many more irregularities in their observable performances. When people are swayed by a single passion, and so not free, they act more nearly like machines (2: 126–7).

Observations such as these, made by the 'experimental physics of the soul', require freedom for their explanation (*Versuche*, 2: 43). We should also like to know how it works. Tetens perhaps goes to unnecessary lengths to differentiate a stimulus that merely sets off an inherent self-activating power from an external power working through the capacities of the soul (2: 50–8). He has more difficulty in accommodating freedom to the fact that the power to act and the power to act otherwise are determined by reasons or motives.

Tetens does not deny that there are sufficient reasons leading these powers to act. The principle of sufficient reason is solidly based on experience, which shows that there is 'a fully determining cause, a sufficient . . . reason' for whatever occurs (*Versuche*, 2: 131–2, 137). Motives provide such reasons for action. The sensation of freedom presents itself to us as the power to resist the temptation offered by motives (2: 32). In having motives, we of course have ideas of the acts they give us reason to perform. To act freely, we need not have distinct ideas. We can freely control ourselves even if we feel strong passions aroused by swarms of confused ideas (2: 37). In being motivated, we are presented with an idea of an act as pleasing or unpleasing to us, and our active power is generally stimulated to efficacy (*Wirksamkeit*) by what seems most pleasing to us. Even in cases where the alternatives are indifferent, something occurs to us as a reason to choose, perhaps only that first is best. Given the reason, we act, and the reason fully explains why we act. Sometimes we are overpowered by desire, but where we are free, this is because we could choose not to do what we do. How can this freedom-giving ability be efficacious while there exists a necessary connection between the reason for acting and the act?

Tetens's answer is not wholly clear. He explains that causal laws hold only if there is no hindrance to their operation. A falling cannonball will break a china jug, but not if someone removes the jug from its path. Similarly, it seems, the most pleasing thought of an action will invariably stimulate the agent's self-activating power to efficacy unless the equally present self-activating power to do otherwise intervenes. Hence even when the agent did the act, he had the full power not to do it and could have used his ability to apply that power – his *Willkühr*, or ability to choose – to activate it. But this is all that is required for the agent to be free. To deny that this is possible is to commit oneself to what Tetens takes to be the absurd view that no one could ever do what he did not do. Experience shows that agents could have done what they did not do.

Morality, like freedom, has its source in the self-activating power of the agent, and morality is not thinkable without freedom (*Versuche*, 2: 124).

A being that does *good* out of inner natural necessity – does it not possess a *splendid* nature? But yet this natural goodness is not *free* goodness, and a *free* being, with an *equal* power for good, will have *more inner goodness* and be a *greater* being, because it works with a greater inner power which also has the power to do evil. (2: 27)

Morality and freedom are also tied to reason, without which no ideas of alternative actions are possible. Virtue requires us to control our passions in the name of ideas of right and duty. 'This inner self-power [*Selbstmacht*] of the soul over its sensations and drives, this ability to rule them according to distinct ideas, is the essence and true spirit of virtue' (2: 656). Goodheartedness without self-activation through these ideas can be wicked. Only insofar as goodness springs from reasoned self-control is it meritorious. A self-controlling fully active being is 'the most sublime and most fully worthy of respect of God's creations' (2: 657–8). Tetens seems, in these remarks, to be preparing for an argument, like Clarke's or Price's, from the fact that we can decide between incommensurable reasons to the need for a special power. But he does not argue this way. His defence of free will rests on the empirical, not the moral, evidence for it.

X. KANT: DESIRE AND TRANSCENDENTAL FREEDOM

Kant held that a truly scientific psychology is impossible, and he wrote no treatise on the passions.[60] Nonetheless, from his early cosmological treatise to his final 'posthumous work', he showed a deep interest in the will and its relation to feeling and desire. In the *Kritik der Urtheilskraft* (1790), he presented a theory about the kind of disinterested pleasure that we take in beautiful and sublime works of art and nature. His other discussions of these subjects show his concern with the practical bearing of affects and passions and with our need to control and guide them. He had definite views on health and the prudent conduct of life, but his overriding practical concern was morality.[61]

Kant arrived at the original central idea of his moral theory by about 1765, well before he had come to the main points of his critical views on knowledge.[62] Morality, as he came to think of it, requires us to act independently of our desires. It may dictate that we do what we have the strongest aversion to doing and what in no way serves even our long-term self-interest. Although we often fail to act as we ought, we must be able to do so. Hence we must have a power to do what we do not do. What is it, and how can we know about it?

We know that Kant found Tetens's views on freedom unhelpful, but he could hardly have been indifferent to the questions asked.[63] Moreover, Tetens's extended contrasts of the Leibniz-Wolff theory of the passions and the will with the more empirical British theories would have kept these positions fresh in Kant's mind while he was working on the *Kritik der reinen Vernunft*. He had defended an essentially Wolffian view of freedom in an important early essay[64] but also admired Crusius, so whether he knew Clarke's work or not, he was familiar with a non-Wolffian view of free will supported by moral and a priori arguments. His own views thus respond to all the kinds of theories we have been considering.

However Wolffian Kant was when young, he began to leave Wolff's views behind him under the influence of Shaftesbury, Hutcheson, and Hume. By 1764, he was using a Lockean view of the passions in analysing mental disturbances.[65] In later writings, he abandoned Wolff's view of the passions no less completely than he rejected his theory of knowledge and his theory of freedom. As opposed to the Leibniz-Wolff thesis that the mind has only one power, Kant holds that there are three quite separate aspects of its functioning: knowing, feeling, and desiring. I begin with a brief look at Kant's mature understanding of the last two.

There are three kinds of feeling that we call pleasure. The kind of pleasure connected with desire, Kant insists, is purely subjective. It carries no information about its causes outside us nor even any about us. We think otherwise only if we overlook the ambiguity of the word 'sensation' (*Empfindung*), which may refer to the cognitive representations we obtain through our various senses or to the feeling (*Gefühl*) with which we respond to them (*Kritik der Urtheilskraft*, 5: 206). No logical inference from a representation or concept to a feeling of pleasure of this kind is possible (5: 170). What one person finds pleasant another may not. There can be no question of error here; tastes simply differ (5: 212). This kind of pleasure differs from both aesthetic pleasure and the pleasure that arises from morally motivated choice.

Because pleasure and pain show only the relation of a representation to the subject with the feelings, they 'cannot be explained more clearly in themselves'. We can make them 'recognizable in practice', however, by specifying their results (*Metaphysik der Sitten*, 6: 212). To do so, we must look at a different aspect of the way the mind works, the *Begehrungsvermögen*, or capacity for desire (*Kritik der Urtheilskraft*, 5: 177–8).[66]

We must begin with Kant's explanation of a goal or end. He distinguishes two kinds of events. Some come about through natural causality. Others come about only because a conscious being first represents them and is then moved to bring them about by this representation of them. If we think that some state of affairs can exist 'only through a concept of [it]', we are thinking of it as an end. The thought of the effect here precedes the cause – someone's action – and determines the agent to cause the state of affairs to exist (5: 219–20). The faculty of desire is defined as 'the faculty to be, by means of one's representations, the cause of the objects of these representations' (*Sitten*, 6: 211). When a representation of something causes in me an incipient effort to make it exist, I think of it as my end; I desire it. Since this is different both from having a non-moving thought of something and from taking pleasure in the thought or reality of something, Kant postulates a separate power in the mind to account for it.

How then is pleasure related to desire? There are various ways. Sometimes a pleasure precedes and causes a desire. Alternatively, I may have a propensity for the object of the desire, even before experiencing it and the pleasure it gives me. If I do, then after experiencing the object I will have a habitual desire for such things or an inclination toward them. I can also have desires for objects I have never experienced or thought of. These urges are instincts; pleasure does not cause them but may come from their gratification (*Sitten*, 6: 212; *Religion innerhalb der Grenzen der bloßen Vernunft*, 6: 28n). In addition to these differing connections, one general link between feeling and desire is observable. When I feel prompted to leave the condition I am in, the state is painful; when I feel prompted to stay in it, it is pleasant. Kant thinks, in an almost Lockean way, that pain must precede enjoyment. I must be prompted to leave one state before I enjoy being in another one (*Anthropologie in pragmatischer Hinsicht*, 7: 230–1; see also 7: 235).

Since the capacity of desire is a capacity for a certain kind of causality, it is not passive receptivity as the capacity for feelings of pleasure and pain is. Even the excessive desires we call passions are not, for Kant, passive. Settled desires or inclinations are passions when they are so deeply rooted that they make it difficult for us to use reason to compare them with one another and with our other desires (*Anthropologie*, 7: 265; *Sitten*, 6: 408). Similarly, we are sometimes agitated by a feeling (*Affekt*) not because of its intensity but because it tends to make us fail to compare it with the rest of our pleasures and pains (*Anthropologie*, 7: 254). When we are unreasonable in having passions and emotions, for Kant it is not because they misrepresent the world, as the Leibnizians think, or are caused by false beliefs, as Hume holds. It is because they cause us to fail to use reason to put them in perspective.

If we were being reasonable, we would consider each of our feelings, desires, inclinations, and passions in the light of the totality of what we want. Since we possess reason as a part of our cognitive capacity, we tend to form idealised notions of totalities in practical as well as in theoretical matters. The idea of the satisfaction of all our desires is the idea of happiness. Kant would thus have agreed with Reid in thinking that the desire for happiness is a rational one. But whereas Butler thought that we all too often fail to desire it, Kant thinks it is naturally an inevitable object of desire.

The desire for happiness does not, however, provide an inner source of order. More strongly than Locke, Kant thinks our desires unstable. Each person's conception of happiness fluctuates so greatly that even if nature were at our command, no natural law could guarantee us satisfaction. Contentment is not possible. Human nature 'is not of the sort to call a halt anywhere in possession and enjoyment and to be satisfied' (*Kritik der Urtheilskraft*, 5: 430; see *Anthropologie*,

7: 234–5). The problem is made worse, in Kant's eyes, because he thinks – here following Jean-Jacques Rousseau – that many of our desires and passions are social. They do not arise simply from bodily or other needs taken by themselves, as do our desires for sex, the well-being of our offspring, and human company. They arise when we begin to compare ourselves with other people. Envy, ingratitude, and spite are social in this way (*Religion*, 6: 27), as are our desires or manias for honour, power, and wealth (*Anthropologie*, 7: 268).

Although in the *Grundlegung zur Metaphysik der Zitten* Kant claims that a reasonable person would wish to be free of all inclinations, in the *Religion* he rejects this view. We cannot get rid of our desires, and they are not to be condemned. Morality requires us only to control them, and insofar as we get better at doing so, they may become more nearly capable of being satisfied. But there is no natural harmony among them, nor would theoretical knowledge of the world introduce it. If anything enables us to harmonise them, it is our rational capacity for prudence (*Religion*, 6: 58).

Moral as well as prudential self-control is possible because reason is as much a part of our nature as are the passions and desires. In its theoretical activity, reason enables us to know the world, while practically it enables us to direct our actions freely in a way that other living things in the world cannot. Kant's views on the nature of practical freedom and how we know of it changed significantly from book to book. They are among the most difficult of his theories, and commentators tend to disagree about them. Some points, however, are reasonably clear.

First, the freedom that Kant defends is not merely the ability to act as we choose but an inner ability to control our choices. Freedom does not require the absence of determining grounds for our choice. An indeterministic, lawless freedom – a power to act randomly – is thinkable, but Kant has no desire to defend it. He rather defends, like Leibniz and Wolff, freedom in the sense of spontaneity. A free act is one whose determining ground lies wholly within the agent. But, along with Crusius, Kant rejects the Leibnizian account of spontaneity. When Leibnizian agents act freely, they act on reasons, which they have because of a long chain of antecedent events, springing ultimately from God's decision to make the best world. Their choices, Kant thinks, are *pre*-determined, not merely determined. The determining grounds of their acts were in earlier times and are no longer in their power. Spontaneity requires that my grounds originate in me now.

Second, our knowledge that we are free cannot rest on any empirical grounds. The weakness of Tetens's empirical arguments may have helped to convince Kant of this. In any case, the systematic results of the *Kritik der reinen Vernunft* make it absolutely impossible to ground belief in freedom on experiences such as our feeling of freedom when we decide or on theoretical arguments concerning the need for an uncaused first cause. We must take our experienced world to be fully determined. Psychological events, like spatial events, necessarily follow from prior causes (*Grundlegung*, 4: 427). But the first *Kritik* argues that it is equally impossible for either experiential or a priori arguments to prove that we cannot have free will.

Third, since theoretical reasoning leaves open the question of freedom, only practical considerations can settle it. Here Kant agrees with the Clarkeans. Moral considerations are different in kind from grounds for action drawn from desires, yet we do make choices between them. We have empirical awareness of desires. Our awareness of moral considerations comes to us in what Kant calls 'a fact of reason' (*ein Factum der Vernunft*) (*Kritik der praktischen Vernunft*, 5: 42). We are each unavoidably aware, he believes, of particular obligations to specific acts, regardless of what we feel or desire. Such obligations are unavoidable or, as Kant says, 'categorical'. They entitle us to complete practical assurance that we *can* do as we ought, and so warrant our belief that we are free in the requisite way. No antecedently determined grounds cause us to act. We can ignore our desires and act as we know we ought.

Fourth, in his *Die Religion innerhalb der Grenzen der bloßen Vernunft* and the *Metaphysik der Sitten*, Kant speaks of two separate powers as being involved in the explanation of freedom. There is first the will (*Wille*), which is our own reason in its practical capacity. It functions to place permanent rational requirements on action, both prudential and moral. With Leibniz, and unlike Locke and Clarke, Kant sees the will as containing its own principles for decision making. But with Crusius, and against the Leibnizians, he does not think the principles direct us to consider only the goods and ills that will result from the alternatives before us. Practical reason essentially requires formal consistency in our choices. We in our rational aspect demand this of ourselves as we consider the projects for action proposed by the desires that arise from ourselves in our empirical aspect.

It follows that whenever a desire prompts us to act for an end, the rational demand for consistency is also evident to us. The power of choice (*Willkür*) is what enables us to decide between them. We might have the power of choice even if we did not have the kind of practical reason we have. It would act where the alternatives are indifferent; otherwise, its choices would be determined by the relative strengths of desires and passions. As morality shows us, however, *Willkür* can be determined by purely rational requirements imposed by the self as rational. The will itself is neither free nor unfree. As pure practical reason, it always gives us the option of acting solely on internal spontaneous grounds. The power of choice, which can opt for morality or against it, is a free power. Because we can choose, we never have to accede to desires that, although certainly part of ourselves, are determined by what is not part of ourselves.

Of the many questions raised by Kant's view, I can consider only three. First, how can desires be tested for consistency? Since Kant thinks, with Hume, that desires are blind causal forces, which in themselves are neither rational nor irrational, he holds that they are not tested directly. Collaborating with reason, desires somehow present us with proposals for action. Kant explicitly declines to give any empirical psychological explanation of how this happens (*Grundlegung*, 4: 427). What results is a rationally testable 'maxim', a proposal to act in a definite way in given circumstances to attain a specific end. Reason can test the maxim for consistency in ways that Kant explains in detail in his ethics. We use our power of choice either to adopt or reject the proposal, and we then act accordingly.

Second, what leads us to make the choices we do? We can choose to ignore the requirements of reason or to comply with them, in prudential or in moral matters. Is the free power of choice undetermined? Kant wrestles with this problem in the *Religion*. He gets as far as saying that we must suppose, given the empirical evidence about human behaviour, that each of us makes a fundamental free choice whether to prefer actions in our own interest or those required by morality when the two conflict. Once this choice is made, the rest are explicable; why it is made as it is – for the worse – is inexplicable (*Religion*, 6: 32–9).

Finally, how is it possible that a demand for rational consistency, even elaborated as Kant thinks it can be into a full system of ethics, can have an empirically observable effect on our behaviour? How can action determined by such a non-temporal reason be fitted into the determinist psychology Kant accepts? He tells us that no answer is possible. The *Kritik der reinen Vernunft* has set strict limits on what we can know. The aspect of the self that produces desires is phenomenal. The aspect that is the rational will is noumenal. Only transcendental argument can warrant it. Morality shows us that we possess the ability to act for reasons independent of desire. But nothing noumenal can enter into causal explanations of anything in the phenomenal realm. We here reach the limits of our ability to understand our active powers.

XI. CONCLUSION

Two issues dominate eighteenth-century debates about the active powers. One is whether our desires are themselves implicitly rational, as representations of good or perfection, or whether they are non-rational forces within the psyche. The other is whether all kinds of considerations that we take into account in making decisions are commensurable or whether morality gives us grounds for action that are incommensurable with grounds arising from desire.

If desires are inherently rational, then knowledge alone can produce moral order in them and in our actions. If, as the Lockeans held, they are not rational, then some other source of order must be found. Those who believed that all reasons for action are commensurable had no need to appeal to a strong separate power of willing to explain the decisions we make. They could argue that choice is determined by the strength of our desires, whether or not it is complicated by a moral sense that reinforces some desires and not others. Those who saw morality as requiring us to act regardless of desire had to postulate a will in order to explain the fact that we sometimes decide to act morally. They also felt forced to claim that such a will, or power of agency, must be independent of the causal laws that Newton had shown to determine the physical world.

Libertarians before Kant argued for an empirically discoverable freedom operating, in ways they never managed to explain, within the physical world. Kant thought their efforts failed. He shared with them, however, the belief in the incommensurability of moral and desire-based reasons and in our ability to act against our desires. To save agency in a determinist world, he exiled the source of our freedom to a realm beyond experience.

Kant's way of preserving agency had fateful consequences in German thought. Kant himself took the idea of a source of agency beyond all merely empirical appearances to be available only for practical purposes – only in connection with morality and never with speculative knowledge. Later thinkers dropped the restriction. In the works of Fichte and even more in those of Schopenhauer, the hidden source of freedom became a metaphysical principle explaining appearances. Active power, which the late seventeenth-century occasionalists chased out of the world, returned at the beginning of the nineteenth century as its inner essence.

NOTES

1 Jean le Rond d'Alembert, *Discours préliminaire de l'Encyclopédie* (Paris, 1894), translated as *Preliminary Discourse to the Encyclopedia of Diderot*, trans. R. N. Schwab and W. E. Rex (Indianapolis, IN, 1963), 149. D'Alembert did not use the label 'psychology' for the systematic study of the understanding and will. In 1732, Christian Wolff published his *Psychologia empirica*, and in 1734 his *Psychologia rationalis*. The books initiated the use of the term as the name for a distinct discipline, but it was slow to catch on.

2 John Locke, *An Essay Concerning Human Understanding*, ed. P. H. Nidditch, in *The Clarendon Edition* (1975), II.xxi.6, 20.

3 Gottfried Wilhelm Leibniz, 'Remarques sur le Livre de l'origine du mal, publié depuis peu en Angleterre', in *Philosophischen Schriften*, 6: 400–36 at 416, translated as 'Observations on the Book concerning "The Origin of Evil"', in *Theodicy: Essays on the Goodness of God, the Freedom of Man and the Origin of Evil*, trans. E. M. Huggard, ed. A. Farrer (London, 1951), 405–32 at 421.

4 See, for example, Law's note in William King, *An Essay on the Origin of Evil* (*De origine mali*, 1702), trans. E. Law (London, 1731), 153n; Abraham Tucker, *The Light of Nature Pursued* (1768), 4 vols. (Cambridge, MA, 1831), 1: ch. 1, §17, p. 46; Johann Nicolas Tetens, *Philosophische Versuche über die menschliche Natur und ihre Entwicklung* (1777), in *Die philosophischen Werke*, 2 vols. (Leipzig, 1777).

5 René Descartes, *Les passions de l'âme*, in *Oeuvres*, 11: Pt. I, §1, translated as *The Passions of the Soul*, in *The Philosophical Writings of Descartes*, trans. J. Cottingham et al., 3 vols. (Cambridge, 1984–91), 1: 328.

6 For Malebranche's views, see *The Search after Truth* (*De la recherche de la vérité*, 1674–5), trans. T. M. Lennon and P. J. Olscamp (Columbus, OH, 1980), VI.ii.3, 446–52; *Discourse on Metaphysics* (*Entretiens sur la métaphysique et sur la religion*, 1688), trans. W. Doney (New York, NY, 1980), Seventh Dialogue, 145 ff.

7 For Leibniz, see *On Nature Itself* (1698), in Gottfried Wilhelm Leibniz, *Philosophical Papers and Letters*, trans. and ed. L. E. Loemker (Dordrecht, 1969), 498 ff. Locke did not discuss the occasionalism when he criticised Malebranche in his posthumous *Examination of P. Malebranche's Opinion of Seeing All Things in God*, in *Posthumous Works of Mr. John Locke* (London, 1706), 141–213.

8 For a clear statement, see Clarke's Fifth Reply in his correspondence with Leibniz: the question of liberty, he says, is 'whether the *immediate physical Cause* or *Principle of Action* be indeed *in* him whom we call the *Agent*; or whether it be some *other Reason sufficient*, which is the *real Cause* of the Action, by operating upon the Agent, and making him to be, not indeed an *Agent*, but a mere *Patient*'. Samuel Clarke, *Works*, ed. B. Hoadly, 4 vols. London, 1738), 4: 674.

9 Christian Wolff, *Vernünfftige Gedancken von Gott, der Welt und der Seele des Menschen, auch allen Dingen überhaupt* (1719–20), ed. C. A. Corr, in *Werke*, I.2 (1983). Hereafter cited as *Gedancken*, followed by the section number. Wolff had a European audience through his own lengthy Latin versions of his works and also through French versions. Jean Deschamps published French summaries of the foundations of the system in 1741 and 1743 and abridgements of the two Latin psychology volumes in 1747. Jean Henri Samuel Formey's six-volume *La belle Wolfienne*, which appeared between 1741 and 1753, covered most of Wolff's teaching. Alexander Gottlieb Baumgarten's *Metaphysica* (1739 and many later editions), a textbook from which Kant regularly taught, contains a comprehensive outline of the Leibniz-Wolff philosophy. It was translated into German by G. F. Meier in 1766 for use in his own classes.

10 '*Voluptas* est intuitus, seu cognitio intuitiva perfectionis cujuscunque, sive verae, sive apparentis', in Christian Wolff, *Psychologia empirica* (Frankfurt, 1738), §511. In *Werke*, II.5, Wolff says we owe the idea to Descartes.

11 As Jean École notes (*La métaphysique de Christian Wolff*, 2 vols., in *Werke*, III.12.1–2: 269), Wolff sometimes speaks of pleasure and pain as consequences of intuitions. If he means to treat pleasure and pain as non-representative states of mind, he is departing from his basic theory rather seriously. In either case, the feeling will be proportional to the perfection perceived.

12 Wolff gives *motiva* as the Latin equivalent for *Bewegungsgrund*.

13 Leibniz, *Nouveaux essais sur l'entendement humain*, eds. A. Robinet and H. Schepers, in *Sämtliche Schriften*, VI.6 (1962). Page citations refer to the translation, *New Essays on Human Understanding*, trans. and eds. P. Remnant and J. Bennett (Cambridge, 1981), II.xx.2, §6.

14 In *The Concept of Mind* (London, 1949), ch. 3, 62–82, Gilbert Ryle criticised the concept of volition or willing by arguing that it generates an infinite regress and is therefore useless in explaining action. Both Leibniz and Locke refuse to take willing as itself an action of the kind that requires a willing in order to be done. See Leibniz, *Nouveaux essais*, II.xxi.23.

15 Locke has some harsh words concerning those who claim that liberty of will essentially involves its 'Indifferency' to good and ill; See *Essay*, II.xxi.48 and especially 71. But he thinks we can be indifferent in matters of no importance; see II.xxi.44.

16 See Jean Michel Vienne, 'Malebranche and Locke: The Theory of Moral Choice, a Neglected Theme', in *Nicolas Malebranche: His Philosophical Critics and Successors*, ed. S. Brown (Assen and Maastricht, 1991), 94–108.

17 Leibniz, *Nouveaux essais*, II.xxi.47; Anthony Collins, in *A Philosophical Inquiry concerning Human Liberty* (London, 1717), 39. The objection still seemed worth making to Priestley in 1777: 'a determination to suspend a volition is, in fact, *another volition*, and therefore, according to Mr. Locke's own rule, must be determined by the most pressing uneasiness' (Joseph Priestley, *The Doctrine of Philosophical Necessity Illustrated* (1777), §I, in *The Theological and Miscellaneous Works*, ed. J. T. Rutt, 25 vols. in 26 (London, 1817–32), 3: 447–540 at 461).

18 References to Shaftesbury are to page numbers in Anthony Ashley Cooper, 3rd Earl of Shaftesbury, *Characteristicks of Men, Manners, Opinions, Times*, ed. J. M. Robertson, 2 vols. (London, 1900).

19 Treatise III, 'Advice to an Author', in *Characteristicks*, vol. 1, Pt. 3, §i, p. 192.

20 Shaftesbury's main account is given in Treatise IV, 'An Inquiry concerning Virtue or Merit', in *Characteristicks*, vol. 1, especially Bk. I, Pt. 2, §iii and Bk. II, Pt. 1, §ii, pp. 251–5 and 282–5.

21 References are to Bernard Mandeville, *The Fable of the Bees: or, Private Vices, Publick Benefits*, ed. F. B. Kaye, 2 vols. (Oxford, 1924).

22 Francis Hutcheson, *An Inquiry into the Original of Our Ideas of Beauty and Virtue; in Two Treatises* (London, 1725). For these arguments, see Treatise II, 'An Inquiry concerning Moral Good and Evil', §2, 125–49.

23 Joseph Butler, *Fifteen Sermons Preached at the Rolls Chapel*, I, §§6, 7, in *Works*, ed. J. H. Bernard, 2 vols. (London, 1900), vol. 1: 27–31.

24 Butler, *Sermons*, XI, §§5–9, vol. 1: 138–42.

25 On conscience, see *Sermons*, Preface, §§25–9, vol. 1: 11–13; also Sermon I, §8, vol. 1: 31–3; Sermon II, §§8–11, vol. 1: 44–7; Sermon III, §4, vol. 1: 63–4. On free will, see Butler, *The Analogy of Religion, Natural and Revealed, to the Constitution and Course of Nature,*, Pt. I, ch. 6, in *Works*, 2: 102–18.

26 Hutcheson's first account of the moral sense is in the first part of *An Inquiry*, the 'Inquiry Concerning Moral Good and Evil', §I, Pts. 1, 2, 4, 5; §II, Pt. 3; §V, Pts. 1, 3, and 7.

27 John Gay, *Preliminary Dissertation concerning the Fundamental Principle of Virtue or Morality*, in King, *Essay on the Origin of Evil*, xi–xxxiii.

28 See also *An Enquiry into the Origin of the Human Appetites and Affections* (1747), in *Four Early Works on Motivation*, ed. P. McReynolds (Gainesville, FL, 1969), published anonymously and attributed to one James Long about whom nothing else is known. McReynolds publishes another development of Gay's kind of associationism which has also been attributed to Long; see McReynolds's introduction, xxvi–xxix.

29 Claude-Adrien Helvétius, *De l'esprit*, (1758), Discours II, ch. 15, p. 119. See also the anonymous English translation, published in London the following year, 81.

30 On probity, see Helvétius, *De l'esprit*, Discours II, chs. 5 and 11. A similar use of psychological egoism is to be found in the work of d'Holbach. See Paul-Henri Thiry d'Holbach *Système de la nature ou Des loix du monde physique et du monde moral*, 2 vols. (London, 1770, but probably printed in the Netherlands).

31 References to Hume are to *A Treatise of Human Nature*, eds. D. F. Norton and M. J. Norton, in *The Clarendon Edition* (2006).

32 It is interesting that the few cases where Hume says that important ideas are confused concern theoretical issues, such as the relation of the taste of a fig to the physical fig (*Treatise*, 1.4.5.13,

SBN 238) or aspects of our idea of liberty (2.3.1.13, SBN 404). In discussing curiosity, Hume likens the association of two ideas to a chemical mixture which produces a compound perceptibly unlike either of its elements (2.3.10.9, SBN 452). The chemical analogy became important to nineteenth-century associationists, but Hume does not use it elsewhere.

33 For Hume's views on justice, see *Treatise*, 3.2.1–2; on sympathy, see 2.1.11 and 2.2.5.

34 Adam Smith, *The Theory of Moral Sentiments*, eds. D. D. Raphael and A. L. Macfie, in *Works* (1976), I.i.3–4.

35 See Long, *An Enquiry* (see note 31); Abraham Tucker (pseudonym Edward Search), *The Light of Nature Pursued* (1768), 4 vols. Cambridge, MA, (1831); Joseph Priestley, *Writings on Philosophy, Science and Politics*, ed. J. A. Passmore (New York, NY, 1965); Jean Offray de La Mettrie, *L'homme machine*, in *Oeuvres philosophiques*, 2 vols. (Berlin, 1774), vol. 1; and d'Holbach, *Système de la nature*.

36 The first set of Clarke's lectures is titled *A Demonstration of the Being and Attributes of God: More Particularly in Answer to Mr. Hobbs, Spinoza, and their Followers*, the second *A Discourse Concerning the Unchangeable Obligations of Natural Religion, and the Truth and Certainty of the Christian Revelation*. I give references to the two sets as Boyle Lectures I and Boyle Lectures II, with proposition number and the page number in his *Works*, 2: 513–77 and 579–733. Other references to Clarke are to other volumes in the *Works*.

37 See the Leibniz-Clarke correspondence in Clarke's *Works*, vol. 4.

38 Clarke, *Remarks upon a Book, entitled, A Philosophical Enquiry concerning Human Liberty* (1717), in *Works*, 4: 734; Thomas Reid, *Essays on the Active Powers of Man*, in *Philosophical Works*, ed. W. Hamilton, 8th edn., 2 vols. in 1 (Edinburgh, 1895), 2: I.ii, 517b: 'All our power is, without doubt, derived from the Author of our being; and as he gave it freely, he may take it away when he will'.

39 Assent to truth is a passive operation of the understanding, Clarke says, and it does not 'determine' the active power. See *Works*, 4: 716–18 and *Remarks Upon a Book*, 722–3.

40 King, *Essay*, 156 note.

41 See John Bramhall, *A Defence of True Liberty from Ante-cedent and Extrinsecall Necessity* (London, 1655).

42 See, for example, Clarke, *Works*, 4: 723, 734.

43 George Berkeley, *A Treatise concerning the Principles of Human Knowledge* (1710), Pt. I [no more publ.], §25, in *Works*, 2: 51; see §32; *Three Dialogues between Hylas and Philonous* (1713), Dialogue III, in *Works*, 2: 231.

44 *Principles*, §§25, 28.

45 On notions, see, for example, *Principles*, §142.

46 Henry Home, Lord Kames, *Essays on the Principles of Morality and Natural Religion* (Edinburgh, 1751), Pt. I, Essay III, 172–3, 174; see also 167, 193.

47 Butler, *Sermons*, II and III, in *Works*, 1: 40–60.

48 Richard Price, *A Review of the Principal Questions in Morals*, ed. D. D. Raphael (Oxford, 1974), 215n.

49 For Hutcheson, to feel approval is one way of taking pleasure in someone's action. He says it resembles liking a piece of music rather than contemplating a truth. See his *Illustrations of the Moral Sense*, ed. B. Peach (Cambridge, MA, 1971), §I, 136. The *Illustrations* were originally published as a supplement to *An Essay on the Nature and Conduct of the Passions and Affections* (1728).

50 Price (*Review*, 20n) refers for support to Ralph Cudworth's *A Treatise concerning Immutable and Eternal Morality* (London, 1731), published posthumously in aid of the Clarkeans. Cudworth died in 1688.

51 Price here tries to correct Butler, who says that moral awareness may be considered as 'a sentiment of the understanding, or as a perception of the heart; or, which seems the

truth, as including both' ('Dissertation II: Of the Nature of Virtue', §1, in Butler, *Works*, 2: 287).

52 Citations of Reid are to page and column of these essays, indicated as *Active Powers*, in his *Philosophical Works*, vol. 2.

53 Kames argued in 1751 that the feeling of having the ability to make a free choice is 'delusive' and attempted to explain why we have been given such a misleading feeling; see Kames, *Essays*, 183–5. Jonathan Edwards replied, forcing Kames to modify his position. See Edwards, 'Remarks on the Essays on the Principles of Morality and Natural Religion, in a letter to a minister of the Church of Scotland'. In *The Works of Jonathan Edwards* (New Haven, CT, 1957–), 1: *Freedom of the Will*, ed. P. Ramsey, 443–65, especially Ramsey's introduction. Reid continues the attack.

54 Only Tetens knew Reid's work, and he knew only the *Inquiry*. His own major work was published prior to Reid's late lectures on theoretical and practical philosophy. See Manfred Kuehn, *Scottish Common Sense in Germany, 1768–1800: A Contribution to the History of Critical Philosophy*, (Kingston and Montreal, 1987), ch. 7.

55 References are to Christian August Crusius, *Die philosophischen Hauptwerke*, eds. G. Tonelli, S. Carboncini, and R. Finster, facsimile of Leipzig, 1744–7 edition (Hildesheim, 1964–). Volume 1 contains *Anweisung, vernünftig zu leben*, in four parts, and vol. 2 contains *Entwurf der nothwendigen Vernunft-Wahrheiten*, in three parts. The main treatment of will is in *Anweisung*, Pt. I, 'Thelamatologie', a term Crusius seems to have invented. Some of the material is reiterated in the *Entwurf*. Numbers refer to pages in the two respective volumes.

56 He also accuses Leibniz of altering the meaning of 'free' to suit his philosophy (*Entwurf*, Pt. III, ch. 1, §388, vol. 2: 752).

57 Tetens, *Versuche* (see note 4).

58 Ernst Cassirer, *Kant's Life and Thought*, trans. J. Haden (New Haven, CT, 1981), 194. For discussion of Tetens, see Lewis White Beck, *Early German Philosophy: Kant and His Predecessors* (Cambridge, MA, 1969); Kuehn, *Scottish Common Sense*; and Günter Gawlick and Lothar Kreimendahl, *Hume in der deutschen Aufklärung: Umrisse einer Rezeptionsgeschichte* (Stuttgart-Bad Cannstadt, 1987).

59 The way Reid parallels these views is remarkable, but there is no reason to suppose that he had even heard of Tetens.

60 *Metaphysische Anfangsgründe der Naturwissenschaft/Metaphysical Foundations of Natural Science* (1786), Vorrede, in Ak 4: 467–79 at 471. See also Kant's *Vorlesungen über Metaphysik*, Ak 28: 2.i, 679, translated as *Lectures on Metaphysics*, trans. and eds. K. Ameriks and S. Naragon, in *Works* (1997). Also cited are *Anthropologie in pragmatischer Hinsicht* (1798), Ak 6: 117–333, translated as *Anthropology from a Pragmatic Point of View*, trans. and ed. M. J. Gregor (The Hague, 1974); *Grundlegung zur Metaphysik der Sitten* (1785), Ak 4: 385–463, translated as *Groundwork of The Metaphysics of Morals*, trans. and ed. M. J. Gregor, in *Works/Practical Philosophy* (1996); *Kritik der praktischen Vernunft* (1788), Ak 5: 1–163, translated as *Critique of Practical Reason*, trans. and ed. M. J. Gregor, in *Works/Practical Philosophy*; *Kritik der reinen Vernunft* (1781), Ak 4; 2. Aufl. (1787), Ak 3, translated as *Critique of Pure Reason*, trans. and eds. P. Guyer and A. W. Wood, in *Works* (1998); *Kritik der Urtheilskraft* (1790), Ak 5: 165–547, translated as *Critique of the Power of Judgement*, trans. P. Guyer and E. Matthews, ed. P. Guyer, in *Works* (2000); *Metaphysik der Sitten* (1797–8), Ak 6: 203–493, translated as *The Metaphysics of Morals*, trans. and ed. M. J. Gregor, in *Works/Practical Philosophy*; *Die Religion innerhalb der Grenzen der bloßen Vernunft* (1793), Ak 6: 1–202, translated as *Religion within the Boundaries of mere Reason*, trans. and eds. A. Wood and G. di Giovanni, in *Works/Religion and Rational Theology* (1996).

61 For Kant's views on health, see 'Versuch über die Krankheiten des Kopfes'/'Essay on Illnesses of the Head' (1764), Ak 2: 257–72. His manuscript notes, 'De Medicina corporis, quae

philosophorum est'/'On Philosophers' Medicine of the Body' (1786 or 1788), Ak 15: 939–53, are translated in *Kant's Latin Writings: Translations, Commentaries and Notes*, trans. L. Beck et al. (New York, NY, 1986), 217–43. See also *Der Streit der Fakultäten* (1798), §3, Ak 7: 97–116, translated as *The Conflict of the Faculties*, trans. M. J. Gregor and R. Anchor, in *Works/Religion and Rational Theology*. Kant's views on the conduct of life are scattered through his lectures on ethics; some are presented more compactly in the *Anthropologie*, for example, Pt. I, Bk. 2, §§60–6, and Bk. 3, §§75–6 and 82–8, in Ak 7.

62 See Josef Schmucker, *Die Ursprünge der Ethik Kants in seinen vorkritischen Schriften und Reflektionen* (Meisenheim am Glan, 1961); Dieter Henrich, 'Hutcheson und Kant', *Kant-Studien*, 49 (1957–8): 49–69, and 'Über Kant's früheste Ethik', *Kant-Studien*, 54 (1963): 404–31.

63 See the letter of Marcus Herz, April 1778, Ak 10: 125.

64 *Principiorum primorum cognitionis metaphysical nova dilucidatio/A New Elucidation of the First Principles of Metaphysical Cognition* (1755), §II, Ak 1: 391–410, translated in Kant, *Works/Theoretical Philosophy 1755–1770*, trans. and eds. D. Walford and R. Meerbote (1992).

65 'Essay on Illnesses of the Head', Ak 2: 261.

66 The German is often translated as 'faculty of desire', but *Vermögen* means 'ability', 'power', or 'capacity' as well as 'faculty'. The latter term should be avoided in view of its misleading connection with a faculty psychology which Kant did not accept.

20

EDUCATION

GERAINT PARRY

Education was a topic that held a central place in the concerns of eighteenth-century philosophy. The connection between philosophy and education goes back, of course, to Plato. However, for the eighteenth century, education had a particularly significant role to play. The term 'Enlightenment' applied to much of the period hints clearly at this – implying a process of 'enlightening', of education or re-education. Kant's celebrated definition of enlightenment as man's exodus from tutelage employs vocabulary that is redolent of that of education. The great *Encyclopédie* of Diderot and d'Alembert was an educational enterprise.

All societies engage in a process of conscious social reproduction, and education is part of that process. This in part explains the frequency with which philosophers, and particularly political thinkers, have written treatises on education. These writings seek to transmit to the new generation, via teachers, what is considered by present and previous generations to be of most value in their political, social, and moral arrangements. In this respect, educational treatises offer an indirect insight into the preoccupations of a particular epoch. In the case of those treatises written by major philosophers, the educational prescriptions contained within curriculum proposals are reinforced by epistemological foundations.

Educational philosophy is not, however, entirely concerned with the transmission of tradition. Educationists can also be innovators as well as assimilators. They may be seeking a reorientation of ideas and behaviour which will be achieved and secured through the mediation of the generations to come. If the existing political and social establishment is incapable of extensive reformation, it may be possible to achieve change by shaping the mentality of its successors. The children will remedy the failings of their parents.

Both features – transmission and innovation – are important in eighteenth-century philosophies of education.[1] To the considerable degree that Enlightenment thought involved a rejection of the past, this implied a form of learning which rejected the idea of imitation that was central to humanist philosophies of education. Appeals to nature and reason should displace appeals to authority

608

in the teaching of children. Yet this anti-authoritarianism was necessarily re-strained by the limits to Enlightenment radicalism. Educational treatises were still not written with the education of the poor primarily in mind, and atti-tudes towards female education remained ambivalent. Moreover, even absolutist regimes came to perceive that in an 'age of reason' new modes of legitimation were required which might be achieved through the supervision of a system of national education.

The most significant figure in eighteenth-century history of the philosophy of education was John Locke. In very many respects, Locke set the terms of debate even for those who were to disagree with many of his educational proposals. Rousseau, who might be regarded as Locke's chief rival for pre-eminence in this sphere, was concerned both to acknowledge his predecessor's contributions and to indicate in which respects he departed from them. Locke's *Some Thoughts Concerning Education* was first published in 1693. It was in its fourth edition by 1699, and the fifth edition (the first English edition of the eighteenth century) came out in 1705. Repeated printings and translations appeared throughout the century.[2]

In certain respects, Locke's influence was remarkable in that it can be difficult to discover one piece of child-rearing advice by Locke which had not appeared in earlier literature. Similarities to some of the educational ideas of Montaigne in particular have often been noted. Nevertheless, Locke's proposals, as well as being written in an accessible style, were underpinned by an approach to human capacities which appealed powerfully to eighteenth-century sensibilities. Moreover, the impact of the thoughts on education cannot be separated from Locke's reputation as the author of *An Essay Concerning Human Understanding*. The educational work draws strength from its consistency with the analysis of the understanding.[3]

Some Thoughts Concerning Education is a work more central to Locke's project than might appear from its provenance as an occasional work arising from let-ters to a friend advising him on the upbringing of his son in the calling of a country gentleman. Whilst Locke denied that the work constituted a complete, systematic treatment of the topic ('Epistle Dedicatory', 80), its subject matter was highly pertinent to his epistemological, political, and theological enter-prises. One of the unifying threads in Locke's work is the concern with the appropriate conditions for assent. The second paragraph of the *Essay* states that the book is concerned with the grounds on which one may properly assent to propositions. Knowing how and when to give assent based on evidence is also the theme in *Of the Conduct of the Understanding*, originally projected as a chap-ter of the *Essay* and closely related in its themes to Locke's educational work.[4] Fundamental to Locke's politics is the question of the conditions under which rational persons would assent, or consent, to place themselves under government. Locke's educational objective is to prepare the minds of children so that they can examine in a rational manner whether they should grant or withhold assent to the propositions about the world, morality, religion, and politics with which they will be faced in adult life.

If the educational writings reflect the concern of Locke's other major works, these in turn frequently raise issues related to child development. In the *Essay*, Locke repeatedly illustrated the genesis of ideas by observation of the ways in which children acquire knowledge.[5] Most significantly for educational philosophy and practice is that the environment of the child is the prime source of its ideas. Whilst Locke also insisted upon the active operation of the mind in producing complex ideas, the inference for education lay in the importance of shaping the environment of the child from its earliest days so as to influence the ideas which it might acquire.

Locke's political thinking was premised on a view of political subjects as adult persons who had been educated to a condition of reason and moral responsibility. A major political object was to oppose the paternalist practices of those absolute rulers who treated subjects as if they were children incapable of self-management. Such procedures, Locke asserted, ran contrary to the true model of paternal or, rather, parental behaviour, which did not consist in repressive absolute rule over children but in educating them to a condition of freedom and reason. Once they had reached this age of discretion, their period of immaturity and supervision (nonage) came to an end, along with parental governance.[6] *Some Thoughts Concerning Education* offers guidance to parents who wish to bring up a child (a son, given political realities) to take his place in a civil society in which he can judge whether to give assent to its constitution and laws.[7]

Locke's education is hence a training for a station of responsibility in civil life. The idea of responsibility is itself intertwined with Locke's conception of the 'person' as 'a Forensick Term appropriating Actions and their Merit' and hence as belonging 'only to intelligent Agents capable of a Law, and Happiness and Misery'.[8] Merit and blame can be attached to persons because they are capable of rational reflection on their actions, which distinguishes humans from other beings in the order of nature. Humans can guide their behaviour by reference to a norm of conduct, whether civil law or, more fundamentally, the law of nature and reason. This implies that, unlike the brute beasts, humans are not straightforwardly driven by their desires. In an important revision to the *Essay*, Locke came to argue that what activates the will is an 'uneasiness' at the absence of something the person recognises to be good and capable of providing pleasure (II.xxi.34–47). However, before the will is activated, human beings are able to exercise a distinctive power of suspending the execution of their desires, enabling them to stop and deliberate before reaching any decision. Such a power of acting or not acting and of delaying decisions is liberty (II.xxi.8). This God-given power is 'the great privilege of finite intellectual Beings' (II.xxi.52). It permits moral agents to 'stand still, open the eyes, look about', to examine the good and evil of an action 'as far forth as the weight of the thing requires' (II.xxi.67, 52). The exercise of this freedom is an obligation as well as a motive since it enables a person to pursue true happiness and real bliss. Failure to employ such liberty results in overly hasty and mistaken conclusions. Deliberation should render a person presently uneasy at the absence of what is necessary to genuine happiness. Neglect or abuse of this liberty is culpable (II.xxi.56).

Agents can guide their behaviour in accordance with the laws which regulate human life. These are the divine law (or law of nature), the civil law, and the law of reputation or opinion (II.xxviii.7). In all cases, individuals must use their reason to judge whether they can assent to the prescriptions which an authority (religious, political, or public opinion) claims to derive from the laws. Blind, unthinking acceptance is morally irresponsible. Education should be designed to produce this habit of deliberation in the child so that as an adult he will use his power of liberty to reflect rationally before giving his assent to propositions. Education is vitally important since, in one of Locke's most celebrated pronouncements, 'of all the Men we meet with, Nine Parts of Ten are what they are, Good or Evil, useful or not, by their Education' (*Thoughts*, §1, 83).

This assertion about the malleability of man is of profound significance for education since it appears to grant it immense influence over the formation of character.[9] The child is considered 'only as white Paper, or Wax, to be moulded and fashioned as one pleases' (*Thoughts*, §217, 265). Locke's view of the child appears to follow from his rejection in the *Essay* of innate ideas and his account of the mind at birth as *tabula rasa*, or white paper (*Essay*, II.i.2). The mind acquires ideas from experience, which begins within the womb. The child is not born with any knowledge of logical or moral truths, nor is it tainted by original sin as that idea is ordinarily understood. Every child is, however, born capable of discovering knowledge. Age, experience, and education bring one to the condition of reason. This initial view of the child at birth has liberating and potentially egalitarian consequences. The differences between people in adult life appear to be the consequence of their upbringing rather than of any natural features. This, however, has to be qualified because of the importance Locke also attaches to the active powers of the mind. Human beings reflect on their experience and construct more complex and abstract ideas; generally, they employ their understandings. Though all have similar capacities, many neglect their understanding even when they have the time and leisure to cultivate their minds. In part, this results from natural differences in their dispositions or 'tempers' which disincline some people from energetic self-development.[10]

An important cause of the neglect of the understanding is, however, the lack of a proper training in its conduct from an early age. This is what Locke's educational writings are designed to provide. The remedy for neglect is to be found in cultivating good mental habits. Locke's emphasis on habit raises tensions often found in education. Habit is designed to make certain behaviour second nature and can appear to involve disciplining the child to conform to certain established practices.[11] Yet Locke is also aiming, in a manner to be important in enlightenment thought, to habituate the future adult to the spirit of criticism and independent thought which involves healthy scepticism towards received opinion.

The appropriate habits should be inculcated from earliest infancy when the mind is most like blank paper. In particular, the child must get into the habit of mastering its immediate inclinations and resisting the pressures to satisfy immediate pleasures (*Thoughts*, §45, 111). Accordingly, the child is not constantly to be indulged. It should also be habituated to a hardy life by exposure to cold weather and by a healthy, spartan diet. The objective is to subject children to discipline and authority early in life, which will enable parents to influence their minds from the outset and then to relax their regime as the children become more amenable to rational argument.[12] Ultimately, they will have completely internalised their conduct so that it will never appear alien. From then onwards, they can be trusted by their elders.

Essential to Locke's educational project, therefore, is a developmental view of the child's mental capacity (*Thoughts*, §81, 142–3). Even when being disciplined, children must be treated as children. The instruction should not go beyond what they can grasp. Like adults, they are prompted by pleasure and pain and, to be effective, learning must be made pleasurable. They should be allowed to play, and learning itself can be 'made a Play and Recreation' so that they will positively desire to be taught (§148, 208). As the child becomes older, more formal lessons become appropriate. Throughout, children should be motivated to learn. Severe discipline, such as beating, should be avoided where possible. It invokes fear and produces a slavish, fearful demeanour quite opposed to Locke's moral and political aims (§§50–2, 113–14). Rewards and punishments should consist in praise and disgrace. The law of reputation operates from early years. Children wish to earn the good opinion of their parents, which should be gained by their consistently conducting themselves rationally and industriously (§§54–8, 115–17).

As important as formal teaching in the process of education is the adult behaviour surrounding the child. The wax-like nature of the mind means that, in a favourite phrase of Locke, we 'take a Tincture from things near us'.[13] It is therefore essential for adults to set good examples for the children and prevent the servants from offering bad models (*Thoughts*, §82, 143). There is a human tendency to prefer the short term over the long term, to be backsliding (*Conduct*, passim). The cure must lie in the pressure of virtuous opinion combined with constant exercise of the rational, critical faculties (*Conduct*, sect. 4, 220). The two elements are combined from childhood when the parent both encourages curiosity – 'the great Instrument Nature has provided, to remove that Ignorance, they were born with' – and responds to it with rational answers to the child's questions (*Thoughts*, §118, 182–3).

Such an education might be considered appropriate for any responsible person, but *Some Thoughts Concerning Education* was also specifically designed for the son of a country gentleman. Locke's pupils are the descendants of those rational and industrious persons described in *Two Treatises of Government* who have wisely used their labour to accumulate wealth and property. As a consequence, their sons 'by the industry and parts of their ancestors, have been set free from a constant drudgery to their backs and bellies' (*Conduct*, sect. 7, 224). Unsurprisingly, Locke is keen that children learn early the clear meaning of property, as 'a peculiar Right exclusive of others', and the principles of justice that derive from this notion (*Thoughts*, §110, 171). Locke does not have in mind that his pupils become scholars, which is a distinct calling and requires leisure and advanced study of a more specific curriculum. Instead the focus is more utilitarian. A knowledge of Latin is useful but not its grammar or the ability to write Latin verse. French should be learned by practice. The command of written and spoken English is paramount. Such a preference for the vernacular in teaching was a theme common to educational reformers throughout Europe. Political geography is to serve as an introduction to mathematics and geometry. Chronology leads to history, 'which is the great Mistress of Prudence and Civil Knowledge' (§182, 237–8). Specifically, an English gentleman, whether a Justice of the Peace or a Minister of State, must know the history and principles of 'our *English* Constitution and Government, in the ancient Books of the *Common Law*' (§187, 239–40). This is to be set in a context of a knowledge of moral philosophy and natural law, as found in Cicero, Grotius, and Pufendorf. As well as study, the pupil should learn how to keep accounts by being permitted practice in the running of his expenses. This will not help him get an estate but will assist in preserving it. The position of gentleman is a calling. It carries civil and legal responsibilities. Failure to exercise the mental faculties that education has trained will have significant consequences. If instead of such exercise the English gentleman reverts to type and lives in his country house, devoting himself to hunting and claret, he will, Locke comments sarcastically, 'give notable decisions upon the bench, at quarter-sessions, and eminent proofs of his skill in politics, when the strength of his purse and party have advanced him to a more conspicuous station' (*Conduct*, sect. 3, 211–13).

The country gentleman is a member of the English ruling class. What differentiates him from the lowest levels of society – the day labourers – is not any natural gifts but the economic opportunities he has to develop these gifts. This, however, raises significant issues concerning the eighteenth-century educational project. If all are equally a blank paper at birth, then the very poorest should be as capable of development through education as the advantaged. This is shown, Locke points out, by the achievements of those children of the poor who have been assisted by private charity (sect. 6, 222). The natural parts are the same (sect. 8, 206 and sect. 4, 195). The lack of understanding of the poor is thus the result of their lack of opportunity for education. By the unalterable state of things, they are condemned to labour to fill their bellies in an unending and unchanging way of life. They cannot be expected to develop their minds, apart from devoting themselves to the understanding of religion as revealed in the gospels, for which they have sufficient time on the sabbath.[14] The poor and the unemployed face institutions of discipline and correction rather than the liberal education open to the gentleman.

Locke opened up to the eighteenth century the radical potential of education in re-shaping and reconstructing all men, even enabling them to develop the critical spirit which was to be the *Leitmotiv* of the Enlightenment. Yet, Locke drew back in the face of what he took to be the 'realities' of an inegalitarian society. He thus left two questions for eighteenth-century followers: whether human beings were almost entirely the products of education and whether society had the will to permit education to initiate a radical reconstruction of the social order. Locke left a further legacy to eighteenth-century educational thought. His emphasis was on the positive effect of education in making nine parts out of ten in human conduct. But his discussion of the importance of pupils finding truth for themselves in step with their mental development and his rejection of much in traditional rote learning also permitted an alternative, more negative view of education as enabling self-discovery – an approach to be elaborated by Rousseau. Both sides in the dialogue between positive and negative education in the eighteenth century owe something to Locke.

Positive education followed along parallel paths in France and Britain.[15] In each instance, there was a line of descent from Locke. It led via Condillac to Helvétius in France and via Hartley to Priestley, Catharine Macaulay, and ultimately Bentham and James Mill in Britain. All based their educational programmes on a sensationalist psychology.

In his *Traité des sensations* (1754), Condillac sought to establish that reflection, which for Locke was the second source of ideas, could be regarded as sensation.

All the faculties are generated by the senses. Sensations leave impressions which can be compared and judged. Each sensation, moreover, produces a feeling of pleasure or pain. These feelings are compared, and the soul desires to bring about the pleasurable sensations. In *De l'esprit* (1758) and the posthumously published *De l'homme, de ses facultés intellectuelles et de son éducation* (1772), Helvétius pursued the implications of this sensationalist position for education.[16] The soul passively receives sensations from its environment. These sensations are pleasurable or painful, and we seek to recall and reproduce those effects that are pleasurable. Self-love leads to a search for happiness and the desire for power, which consists in control over the factors that produce pleasure. All the passions are aspects of self-love.

Ideas and passions are ultimately attributable to sensations derived from the environment. At birth, human beings are equal in that they lack ideas. Differences between them are the result of their environment, which is never precisely the same for any two individuals.[17] In a broad sense, people are educated throughout their lives by the environment in which they live, and it is this conception which led Helvétius to his much quoted pronouncement that 'l'éducation peut tout'(education can do all).[18] In a narrower sense of education, the teacher makes use of the same processes. The great potential of education is that, in principle, it could control the environment of the child in such a way that the child would experience only the set of sensations that would be beneficial to the individual and society. Such total control is, however, impossible, and much of the formation of any individual is due to other factors such as friends, books, and mere chance. Nevertheless, the tutor or school can work on the child by confronting it with appropriate learning experiences. If done in a striking and repeated manner, it will engage the interest of the child, who will pursue knowledge or a certain path of conduct out of pleasure. Self-love is channelled in useful directions using rewards and punishments to reinforce the instruction.

The excitement of education consists in the opportunity to construct useful citizens. Helvétius regards the view that human beings are shaped by their constitutions or dispositions as offering an excuse for lazy teachers who can blame their own failures on the pupil's alleged innate lack of capacity. Genius is also not inborn but is created and can be promoted by positive education. Morality can be taught in the same way as knowledge. The pupil is encouraged to discover that the pursuit of the general interest will be rewarded and respected and will bring personal pleasure. There is no inborn moral sense, nor can moral conduct be promoted by religious principles. Self-love is to be directed towards social benefit, assisted by a moral catechism that will displace the absurdities taught by religious catechisms. Helvétius has less to say about the specifics of the educational curriculum. Social utility is its leading theme. The young child's sensations are relatively similar and controllable. The adolescent is confronted with a greater variety of experiences arising from society in general and the customs promoted by the form of government. Helvétius favours public education over domestic tuition because the love of country should come before family affection, and civic virtue will be promoted more effectively and consistently in schools (*De l'homme*, I.ii.8, 113). The promotion of the modern sciences and of the indigenous over the dead languages is characteristic of eighteenth-century educational reformers' concern for social and economic progress.

A very similar concern for social utility permeates British educational thought. The counterpart to Condillac is David Hartley, whilst Joseph Priestley played much the same role as Helvétius in the application of sensationalist ideas to education as well as being an influential teacher.[19] In his *Observations on Man* (1749), Hartley, like Condillac, sought to modify Locke by establishing that the source of all ideas was sensation.[20] His distinctive contribution was the theory of the 'association of ideas', which he adapted from Locke. Sensations are the result of vibrations in the brain transmitted through the ether. Repeated sensations leave traces in the brain, giving rise to ideas. Some of these sensations are regularly associated together and will trigger off corresponding ideas. Language connects words with certain ideas and, by association, with further ideas and the words that designate them. Sensations can be pleasurable or painful. Human beings rapidly learn this and seek to pursue those sensations that offer pleasure. Since humans are identical at birth, if it were possible to expose them to precisely the same sensations and associations, all differences between them would vanish or be made to do so. Pertinent to education, Hartley suggests that if one could unravel the links between the sensations and associations, one would be able to improve the good associations and root out the immoral ones (Pt. 1, ch. 1, sect. 2, prop. XIV, 52).

Both Joseph Priestley in his *Miscellaneous Observations Relating to Education* (1780) and Catharine Macaulay in her *Letters on Education* (1790) asserted that the advances in the science of the human mind achieved by the new philosophy of associationism provided the grounds for their educational proposals.[21] Both also argued that through repeated associations of ideas in the mind it would be possible to inculcate habits that would conform to the principles of morality.[22] Priestley divides education into 'natural', acquired from ordinary life, and 'artificial', which communicates knowledge more speedily and in a more organised manner than does nature. Artificial education should commence early since it is a struggle for later sensations and associations to displace those that have been already implanted. Contrary to Locke, and also to Rousseau, Priestley argues that it can be important to establish some ideas in the child's mind before it is ready to comprehend them fully. Accustoming the child by repetition to kneel in church impresses on its mind the idea of reverence to divine power, first as a mechanical habit that only later is grasped rationally. Priestley acknowledges that this could be used to inculcate any idea (to indoctrinate, as we might say) but asserts that all education is a process of 'prejudicing' children in favour of our own opinions (*Miscellaneous Observations*, sect. XI, 90). In morality, the education can commence on the basis of authority and then through a system of rewards and punishments bring the pupil to associate the idea of virtue with certain types of conduct. Ultimately the well-raised person will appear to act from disinterested principles.

Priestley's educational programme was designed for those intended for an active life in government, law, the professions, and the sciences. Based on the courses given at the Warrington Academy, one of the 'universities' for those religious dissenters not admitted to Oxford and Cambridge, Priestley advocated courses in history (including commercial history), trade policy, laws, accounting, and applied mathematics. The mode of teaching should incite interest and stimulate questions and debate through involving students in writing theses. The old humanistic learning had ceased to be relevant to modern society. Traditional divisions between the learned and the unlearned needed to give way and be replaced by an education directed towards the common interests of the nation.

That positive education could be a tool in promoting national development was immediately recognised in Britain, France, and elsewhere in Europe. Helvétius pointed out that the science of man might enable the legislator to guide the motions of 'the human puppet'.[23] Catharine Macaulay acknowledged that it was in the power of government to effect an improvement in civilisation through the capacity to direct the course of impressions.[24] Proposals for systems of national education, which would become typical of the nineteenth century, were widely disseminated.[25] Among the best-known were the anonymous *De l'éducation publique* (1762) and the *Essai d'éducation nationale* (1763) by La Chalotais.[26] Among the many French contributions were notable essays by Philipon de la Madelaine, Le Mercier de la Rivière, and Coyer.[27] During the Revolutionary period, the most significant of the many projects was probably Condorcet's *Rapport et projet de décret sur l'organisation générale de l'instruction publique* (1792).[28] In Germany and Austria, the welfarist philosophy of Christian Wolff and the statist theories of the Cameralists, such as Justi and Sonnenfels, combined to subsume education into the general policing function of the absolute state.[29] The happiness of the state required a population trained to contribute to welfare, including specialist advanced training for those involved in the management of the state and its economy.[30] Despite often sharp differences in certain of their philosophical and economic foundations, the national education projects of German and French absolutism had much in common. They sought to harness the potential resources of the state for the promotion of the common good. This was partly an economic task, resulting in schemes for a more practical or vocational curriculum for the lesser bourgeoisie, merchant, and artisan classes. It was also a matter of moral regeneration, directing self-love from childhood onwards to social and patriotic ends. Pupils were seen, in the phrase of La Chalotais, as 'the children of the state'. At the very least, they were not seen as subject to the exclusive domestic instruction of the parents. State paternalism challenged traditional domestic patriarchalism. National education provided a uniform direction. Hence La Chalotais advocated state schools with secular teachers, employing state-authorised textbooks to shape the minds of children who, according to Condillac, are without experience. In these ways, absolutist states in particular were able to inculcate moral discipline in their subjects in place of the employment of coercion.[31] Subjects would become citizens by uniting their own wills and happiness with that of the whole. Hence Le Mercier de la Rivière argues that the enlightened ruler will, through a system of instruction, guide subjects to happiness rather than confront them with violence, torture, and the gallows.[32]

In more liberal regimes as well, education could be seen as a national interest. Thus Adam Smith regarded basic education as a public good to be supported by government on the grounds of its economic benefits and its contribution to ensuring a well-ordered and supportive citizenry.[33] In the United States, educationists recognised that different circumstances required a different form of schooling.[34] Citizens should be furnished with the intellectual capacities to defend their rights in the new nation. Republican civic virtue, encouraged by a study of American history, heroes, and values, would supplement the mechanical protections afforded by the constitution. If the educational projects did not provide for full equality of schooling opportunity, they did not reflect the divisions of class and estate which so apparently conflicted with the logic of Enlightenment ideas in Europe.[35] This very potential for national social transformation afforded by education led some of its advocates, however, to question the desirability of its control by the state. Helvétius, for example, regarded the form of government as one of the major educational forces affecting the young. Despotic and liberal governments promoted and rewarded quite different kinds of manners and virtues. Despotism discouraged citizen activism and rewarded only conduct that advanced the happiness of the despot. Reform of school education would be pointless if not reinforced by corresponding changes in the educative effects of government. Education had to be congruent with the political system. A liberal, progressive education needed an environment in which there was freedom of expression for a range of views. Accordingly, despite the eulogy of Catherine II and Frederick the Great in the Preface of *De l'homme*, Helvétius contended that moral enlightenment through education required a reform in the structure of government. To safeguard such enlightenment from the threat arising from the tendency towards despotic control over the liberty of expression, large states should be subdivided into federated republics, each with guarantees of autonomy.

A similar reluctance to countenance state control over education was shared by the British sensationalist advocates of positive education. Priestley linked the issue to civil liberty and religious toleration. He rejected a suggestion in John Brown's *Thoughts on Civil Liberty, on Licentiousness and Faction* (1765) that, as in Sparta, there should be a prescribed code of education binding on the community.[36] Priestley acknowledges that such a code would prevent faction but at the cost of imposing uniformity of thought. If education 'makes the man', a single method of education would produce only one kind of man and not a variety.[37] In a similar vein, Catharine Macaulay argued that speculations concerning state education such as those advanced by Plato were designed to 'form man for the use of government, and not government for the use of man.[38] She was less concerned with defending the natural right of a father to bring up his child whether as a rogue or an honest man than with protecting the wider liberties of society against governments that cannot be trusted.

Positive educationists had no doubts that government itself had an educative role to play in the sense that it should support and transmit norms of virtuous conduct by its own example and by its system of punishments and, especially, rewards. The performance of duty should come to be so inextricably associated with personal happiness that virtue could become second nature. In this a good government enhanced the effects of a good education in constructing humanity. Whether this should entail governmental control of education, with the risk of thwarting innovation, remained a question that continued to divide those who shared the same conception of education and its methods into the nineteenth century and, to some degree, beyond.

The idea of 'negative' education proceeds from an acknowledgement of the widespread contemporary belief in the power of positive education to reconstruct humanity but condemns this project as an attempt to denature and distort human potential. The prime exposition was to be found in Rousseau's *Émile ou De l'éducation* (1762).[39] This tale of an ideal education of a boy, Émile, by his tutor and of the education of Sophie, the female counterpart, was immensely popular throughout Europe and transformed the educational agenda.[40] Negative education consisted in protecting the child from vice and error.[41] In his *Discours sur les sciences et les arts* and *Discours sur l'origine et les fondements de l'inégalité parmi les hommes*, Rousseau had argued that man had been born good but had been corrupted by an exploitative and divided society. Accordingly, any positive education conducted by tutors representative of such a world and designed to fit the child into so-called civilised society would have the effect of producing a corrupt adult. The alternative was a form of education that conformed to 'nature'. It would allow the child to unfold with the least interference from human artifice. Such education would be no less effective than the positive version, but it would produce a person who was not artificial but who, through a process of self-discovery, was self-made or autonomous. Such a man (female education followed a different course) would be able to withstand the pressures of modern society and would think his own thoughts.

Émile is guided at every step in this discovery by a tutor, and it is often pointed out that this appears to be as artificial an education as any other.[42] However, Rousseau wishes the tutor, who has the entire authority of a father, to be understood as the 'minister of nature' (*Émile*, 639/317). He so arranges the life of the pupil that the child will encounter nature and learn from it. But the child can only learn at the point permitted by nature. Rousseau argues, like Locke, that education must be suited to the child's development but holds that Locke, and still less his successors such as Helvétius, did not pursue this insight correctly. They constantly sought to treat the child as a rational creature before it could acquire such a capacity. Contrary to Helvétius, the young child does not receive ideas but images. The brain is like a mirror which reflects back objects which do not enter. A child may learn words but will not acquire ideas until it develops an active capacity of judgement (344/107). Rather than seek to impress ideas prematurely on the child's mind, the tutor should confront him with sensations from nature that will encourage his interest and desire for discovery. The first natural factor in the child's development should be the mother's breast. Rousseau's call for breastfeeding rather than the employment of wet nurses was possibly his single most widely known pronouncement (255–60/44–7). Like Locke, he also wished the young child to be exposed to the cold and the rain, to run barefoot, and eat a healthy diet in order to develop his hardiness.

The confrontation with nature is intended to make the child dependent on 'things'. Conventional education aims at making men who are dependent on other men and, consequently, who are neither free nor moral. Dependence on nature or the recognition of necessity is not inconsistent with freedom (*Émile*, 311/85, 320/91). Émile will grow up to accept as legitimate only a rule of law that he had discovered to be necessary and right, not one that is the product of transmitted opinion. This process of discovery starts young but in a 'natural' manner in the course of the child's free play. He learns to measure by estimating whether he can jump across a stream. The child acquires knowledge of astronomy as a result of a need to find his way home for lunch by the direction of the sun when he is 'lost' (through the tutor's contrivance) in a wood. Practical interest drives this discovery learning. He does not learn science so much as the methods of science that will equip him for new situations. For similar reasons, as he grows older, Émile learns skills, such as carpentry, requiring manual labour, which is part of nature and will both be useful and make him independent of other men. The art of education often consists in delaying the acquisition of knowledge until the right time. Thus Émile is not encouraged to learn to read early. Books offer the substitute experience of others instead of the experience of reality, representations rather than things themselves. Émile's first book is *Robinson Crusoe*, an account of an isolated man's struggle to cope with nature (455/184–5). When Émile needs to learn about society and other men, his reading starts with the history by Thucydides on the grounds that, more than any other similar work, it confines itself to sheer facts without the interpolation of human judgements. Thus the reader retains his independence.

The need to learn about society occurs with the onset of puberty around the age of fifteen. Gradually the child has been acquiring ideas and the power of judging, which is reason. Morality presupposes such a capacity of judgement and choice. Up to this stage, Émile's morality has been limited to the belief that one should not harm others. The young child should not be taught ideas of duty. It does what it wants to do, but it is made to want only what the tutor, standing for nature, wants. The child does what is necessary, and terms of morality such as 'ought' do not arise. With the capacity for reason comes the advent of morality. Puberty also brings with it the desire for companionship and problems of the relations with others (*Émile*, 490/212). The tutor must now exercise extra care over education. There is more need of positive instruction and reasoned explanations. The relationship of tutor and pupil changes to one of friendship, based on the child's new capacity for affection. More significantly still, the pupil will come to wish for enlightened guidance and will authorise the educator to instruct him. He will declare that he will obey the tutor's laws and, in language reminiscent of the phrase 'forced to be free' in *Du contrat social ou Principes du droit politique*, will ask the tutor to 'force me to be my own master and to obey not my senses but my reason' (651–2/325).

Rousseau here raises one of the central justifications of education and one of its dilemmas. The child is to be constrained for the sake of its ultimate rationality and freedom. In Émile's case, some form of autonomy is supposedly safeguarded since he has now chosen his subordination to the educator. The culmination of his education occurs when, after being guided through the temptations of so-called civilised society and after learning the principles of government, he tells the tutor that he has chosen to 'remain what you have made me' (*Émile*,

855/471). Émile, recognises that he has been taught to be independent of the wills and opinions of others but to be free in recognising his dependence on 'necessity'. For Émile, this consists in living a quiet, withdrawn, and largely self-sufficient rural life. Shorn of its elements of the romantic novel, the message in Émile is that the educated man will be one who thinks and bravely expresses his own thoughts, resists public opinion and fashion, seeks for himself the laws of science and nature, and generally acts out of what he has discovered necessarily to be his duty. Rousseau is aware that this is an impossible dream. It is one that can only be approximated, he believes, through negative education in the child's early years and destroyed by positive education. It is intended as a guide to the teaching of autonomy.

Émile is an account of the education of an autonomous individual, but Rousseau in his role of political philosopher was also a theorist of public education for citizens. In *Émile*, he declared these two forms of education to be incompatible. One was concerned with creating a person independent of the wills of others, the other with a citizen who was dependent on the community for his existence and meaning. For the latter, Rousseau recommended Plato's *Republic* or the practices of Sparta (*Émile*, 249–50/39–40). It was, he declared, pointless to write about citizen education when, in the modern world, there were no citizens but only subjects. Nevertheless, notably in *Considérations sur le gouvernement de Pologne* and in the *Lettre à M. d'Alembert*, Rousseau explored the nature of public education in the manner of Plato.[43]

The citizen is not an individual complete in himself but a fraction of a whole (*Émile*, 249/39–40). In the absence of his fatherland, he is a mere cipher (*Pologne*, 966/19). National education creates the citizen by shaping his soul so that he will be patriotic by 'necessity'. An officially designated national curriculum will be taught entirely by native citizens. It will cover national literature, geography, and history (especially of the country's heroes). Beyond the schoolroom, the child's games should consist of competitions in public ceremonies for which the citizen spectators would award the prizes (*Pologne*, 967–8/21–2). Even here, negative education is important in that avoiding vices is the prelude to creating civic virtue. Adult education is as crucial as childhood formation. In the manner of Sparta, there should be national games and festivals in which citizens participate. Distinctive religious rites and customs should mark and unite a people as they do the Jews. National dress should be encouraged. The effect will be to set countrymen apart from foreigners and encourage a genuine commitment to the laws and customs (*Pologne*, 956–66/4–18). In the *Lettre à M. d'Alembert*, the same theme is explored in opposition to the proposal by d'Alembert that Geneva should rescind its ban on theatres. Rousseau regards this ban as the assertion of the general will of Genevans who have been educated to uphold the distinctive austere culture of their homeland. In contrast to the passive role of spectators at a conventional theatre, Rousseau extols the public festivals and dances of the city in which citizens participate and are themselves the actors (*Lettre*, 114–25/125–37). This is an instance of a participatory and educative democracy in which citizens both learn and teach others about their laws, customs, rights, and responsibilities. There is, as it were, a self-enacting national curriculum. The individual is dependent on the community's general will, which has created him, and he is in no way alienated by this dependence, which has the feeling of necessity.

The relationship between the private education offered to Émile and the public education of the citizen presents a puzzling problem for interpreting Rousseau. One response is to accept Rousseau's own assertion in *Émile* that the two forms of education are irreconcilable. They concern themselves with two distinct ideals of life in Rousseau's work – the isolated, self-sufficient individual and the participating citizen. With scarcely any opportunities for true citizenship in the modern world, the alternative was Émile's education for individual autonomy. Alternatively, it has been argued that Rousseau's participatory popular government, portrayed in *Du contrat social*, presupposes the staunch, virtuous individual resulting from Émile's education who will be free in obeying laws that he has participated in making himself.[44] It is noted, in support, that when Émile learns about political institutions it is by means of a précis of *Du contrat social* (*Émile*, 836/49). Turning the argument around, it could be claimed that the regime of *Du contrat social* is the one least incompatible with Émile's upbringing and represents the only country to whose institutions Émile might be prepared to give his full allegiance whilst retaining his independence.[45]

The distinction drawn between positive and negative education, as represented by Helvétius and Rousseau, respectively, was appreciated by other eighteenth-century writers but was by no means always reflected in their educational advice. Responses were often more eclectic, picking up attractive ideas from both Locke and Rousseau in particular. Johann Bernhard Basedow offers an example of this tendency.[46] He was the founder in 1774 of the Philanthropinum, a progressive school in Dessau admired by Kant. Also associated with the Philanthropinum was Joachim Heinrich Campe, author of highly popular conduct books, propagandist for reformist education, sympathiser with the French Revolution, and tutor to Wilhelm von Humboldt.[47] Although sometimes portrayed as a follower of Rousseau, whom he certainly eulogised, Basedow's writings display the influence also of Locke and, in his national education proposals, of La Chalotais. Basedow produced a vast output of educational works, parts of which amounted to a type of teaching package with textbooks for children, manuals for teachers, and advice books for parents guiding them through the proposed curriculum and materials, as well as a manual on the education of princes. Whilst Basedow draws from Rousseau in advocating education through play and learning by discovery, he adapts these in a pragmatic manner that radically alters Rousseau's intentions. He proposes sample 'scripts' for the children's games through which, in opposition to Rousseau, they will positively learn moral precepts. Supplementing the materials to undertake small scientific experiments are copperplate representations of nature, with the appropriate lessons to be drawn set out. In common with both Locke and Rousseau, Basedow insists on the need to respect the child's developing capacities, but he is closer to Locke in his objective of accustoming the pupil to the use of reason as early as is feasible. Basedow shares with many eighteenth-century educationists the preference for teaching through the native language, rather than Latin, but rejects Rousseau's thoroughgoing view that a young child needs only one language.

A common response to Rousseau, in all his many-sided genius, was that he over-dramatised and exaggerated for effect. Educationists admired Rousseau's sensitivity to childhood and, above all, his call for the freeing of children's physical energies and curiosity. They were sceptical, however, of the success in acquiring a solid knowledge if these principles were pushed too far and the child left uninstructed.[48] The positive theory of Helvétius received a similar form of criticism, especially well-expressed by Diderot. In opposition to Helvétius, Diderot argues that the mind at birth is not entirely blank and that, consequently, human beings are not infinitely malleable.[49] Whilst lacking in ideas, they do possess sensibility and particular dispositions, and they differ to some extent in their capacity for judgement. This is shown by the contrasts between the genius and the ordinary individual which cannot, as Helvétius supposed, be traced back simply to environment and interest. Diderot opposed the view that human nature could be shaped entirely by external forces. Consequently, education was a means of developing what is within the child's nature. The upshot of Diderot's critique of Helvétius was to moderate the extreme consequence of sensationalism. In the course of a point-by-point summary of his differences with Helvétius, he qualified the emphatic egalitarianism and countered the celebrated 'education can do all' with the more modest 'education can do much' (*Refutation*, 356).

Going beyond attempts to moderate the extremes of positive and negative education were those that appear to have sought a form of synthesis. Kant's *Über Pädagogik* may be viewed in this light.[50] It is not an extended treatise but a compilation of lecture notes for a course on pedagogy given over a period of years at Königsberg University, and this origin may explain some of the apparent inconsistencies in its classificatory system of aspects of education.[51] Nevertheless, the issue of education plays a not insignificant role in Kant's moral philosophy. It was, famously, the reading of *Émile* that gave the impetus to Kant's conceptions of autonomy and the moral law, and Kant presented to educational philosophy the recurrent problem of how the discipline of teaching could be rendered compatible with the end of individual autonomy.

Kant opens the lectures with this dilemma. Man is said to be the only being who needs education. Young animals require feeding but otherwise are led by instinct to become all they are capable of being. By contrast, human beings become fully human only through education. Without instinct, they have to work out a rational plan of life which is only possible with the assistance of others by the art of education.[52] Education includes physical 'nurture', 'discipline', 'instruction', and 'moral training'. Kant favours the hardy physical upbringing for children already advocated by both Locke and Rousseau. Physical exercise can include forms of play that train the mind as well as the body. 'Discipline' is the 'negative' aspect of education, but Kant's employment of the term is much more limited than Rousseau's. It consists in restraining natural unruliness, which undermines the development of reason. Thus children are sent to school initially not for substantive knowledge but to accustom them to sitting still and learning obedience to the laws of mankind and, ultimately, the laws of reason (Ak 9: 441–3, 449–50/3–15, 18). Whilst Kant wishes young children to have time for play and to be as free as possible, consistent with the freedom of others, they must also learn to work. He rejects the progressive ideas that all learning can be in the form of play (470–2/64–7).

'Instruction' is 'positive' and consists of the formal school curriculum and of guidance in the conduct of social life. The child acquires from school the ability to pursue a vocation and guidance in the virtues of social conduct and citizenship (455/32). Moral training comes last in the temporal order in the sense that it supposes that persons have developed the capacity to obey principles they have discovered for themselves by the use of reason. On the other hand, all aspects of education should from the outset be informed by this moral purpose by treating the pupil as a potential moral subject. Thus discipline is a prerequisite for learning obedience to any law, including that made by oneself.

Although morality consists in acting according to maxims the reasonableness of which one sees oneself and which in this way come from oneself, this is something that has to be cultivated in the child. This can begin with accustoming the child from early on to following rules of life, even down to regular sleeping patterns, and then to obeying the school rules or maxims. Obedience to necessity, can originate in compulsion and gradually become voluntary. There may be echoes of Rousseau in this subjection to necessity, but Kant is insistent that early in life this is explicitly seen as a matter of duty and not mere inclination, which might have to be resisted, as when a child must be taught to regard promise keeping as fundamental to good character (480–2, 487/77–82, 94). Children need to learn duties by rules and examples that lead them to understand the reasons that underpin them. Only then will they do right on the basis of their own maxims rather than from habit or from rewards and punishments.

Moral teaching can take two forms. For the beginner, instruction could be in the form of a catechism in which by question and answer the pupil comes to appreciate the ideas of duty. As pupils advance, this is displaced by dialogue in which the tutor presents case studies of moral dilemmas which both parties debate in a mutually beneficial learning engagement.[53] This mutuality should ensure that moral education cannot degenerate into mere socialisation. The educator can, by the combination of discipline, instruction, and moral training, provide the most favourable conditions for the development of a moral character. It helps to raise one from animality to the level of humanity. However, there is a fundamental limit to positive education. The tutor cannot make the pupil virtuous. A duty is an object of free choice. It cannot be produced from without. For Kant, the guiding factor in all education and also one of its greatest problems is how to unite submission to restraint with the child's capability of exercising its freedom, for which the restraint is necessary (Ak 9: 453/29). It is a formulation which has set the agenda for much liberal philosophy of education, particularly in the latter half of the twentieth century.

The synthesis of eighteenth-century positive and negative education that has most influenced practical pedagogy is that of Heinrich Pestalozzi. As a theorist, Pestalozzi was inspired by Rousseau, but crucially he was also a teacher whose schools, particularly at Yverdon, became almost places of pilgrimage for progressive educators. Pestalozzi's impact was made not only by his theoretical writings but by his practical pedagogic techniques. Both were disseminated in a large corpus of work but notably in two popular writings – *Lienhard und Gertrud*, published in four parts between 1781 and 1787, and *Wie Gertrud ihre Kinder Lehrt* (1801).[54] The former portrays, in the form of a novel, Gertrude the ideal mother, whose methods of practical teaching in her simple Swiss household serve as the model for educators. The latter outlines the philosophy and methodology which underpin the Pestalozzian approach.

Central is the conception of the natural development of the child's faculties. Pestalozzi is a prime source of the influential, if profoundly ambiguous, image of education as horticulture. The child is like a tree whose latent capacities unfold. The initial task of the teacher is largely negative, consisting of preventing damage to this natural growth.[55] This requires an understanding of the natural laws of human development. Hence education is not merely a matter of letting the child alone but, more positively, the art of guiding it to make sense of its environment.

This presupposes an appreciation of the stages in the evolution of intellectual and moral capacities. Pestalozzi saw the process of intellectual development as leading to the attainment of ideas that could be succinctly defined. At birth, the child is unable to differentiate between the sense impressions it receives. The first stage in education consists in learning to distinguish between the ideas received from different objects (*Bestimmtheit*). Second, the child learns how to provide a clear description of an object in its various aspects (*Klarheit*). Third, it will learn how to define it with precision (*Deutlichkeit*). Corresponding to this process of intellectual development, the teacher should first guide the child to distinguish objects by number, then to appreciate their shape, and then to name them so that it can recall the ideas of the object to mind. Number, form, and language constitute the three basic aspects of the world and the fundamental topics of education. With more detailed and extensive knowledge, the child's ideas gain in clarity until it is able to appreciate the essential qualities of an object and to define it.[56]

Learning should also follow a movement from the concrete to the abstract. Pestalozzi insisted that the child must grasp an idea for itself out of its own experience, a process termed *Anschauung* which, according to context, may imply sense impression, passive receptivity, more active reflection, or intuitive understanding. The teacher's task is to place the child in a situation in which it can experience objects concretely and then, from the vantage point of adult understanding, steer it to acquire clear ideas and ultimately to produce precise definitions. Such teaching requires a sensitivity to the capacity of the individual child to move in a continuous process from one stage to the next. Young children, with whom Pestalozzi was primarily concerned, should gain a concrete grasp of things in lessons based on immediate experience. Thus Gertrude taught her children to distinguish and number the panes of glass in the cottage window. Form was to be taught by physical handling, observation, and drawing of common objects or by excursions into the countryside to examine its contours and textures.

Although Pestalozzi conceived these methods as providing a general educational grounding, he was also concerned with fitting pupils for a working life since, unlike Locke, Rousseau, Basedow, or Kant, his instruction was directed primarily to the children of the less well off. Teaching not only had to be adapted to individual capacities but, in some tension with that objective, should equip children with the skills required in the adult lives they would probably live. The most talented children of the poor should be encouraged to develop. The generality should receive instruction that would allow them to work satisfactorily but would not make them frustrated with their lot. Country children needed skills to make them self-reliant. Urban pupils required flexible skills to allow them to adapt to industry's changing requirements. A radical, emancipatory vision was tempered by a recognition of the pupils' likely stations and duties.[57]

Moral education pursues a developmental path similar to that of intellectual education. The objective, revealing the influence of Rousseau and (directly or indirectly) of Kant, is to produce a person who knowingly wills what is right and pursues it as a law governing conduct. Moral education begins with the senses, not with reason. Its starting point is the direct experience (*Anschauung*) of the love and trust of the mother. The child learns sympathy in the home and gradually extends this feeling under the guidance of the school, which should exemplify such qualities. But feelings are insufficient, and blind nature can lead astray. Children must acquire clearer ideas of moral behaviour and understand its vocabulary. They must learn to discipline themselves, often through work, so that they can appreciate the meaning of rules. Instead of relying on feelings, they must come deliberately and autonomously to choose what is right even in the face of a world which is not loving but corrupt. The process of moral education should be one where sense impressions are subordinated to convictions, desires to benevolence, and benevolence to the righteous will. But although the moral education of the child culminates in the exercise of judgement, for a long period it remains a matter of feeling (the heart) rather than reason or, as he puts it, 'the business of the *woman* before it begins to be the business of the *man*'.[58] Morality is, for Pestalozzi, the most important goal of education and a crucial aspect of the harmonious development of all the human faculties, which was one of his major themes.

Pestalozzi's influence was widespread and diffuse partly, one may suspect, because his ideas are often unclear and inconsistent and because his pedagogic proposals were susceptible to different practical interpretations.[59] His view that life educates has been a watchword of 'progressive education' down to John Dewey. Pestalozzi's associate Joseph Neef opened a school in America and was to join Robert Owen at the New Harmony colony. Friedrich Froebel, founder of the Kindergarten, albeit critical of aspects of Pestalozzi's theory and practices after visits to Yverdon, shared the developmentalist account of nature and of the unfolding and harmony of the child's capacities. Johann Herbart, many of whose influential ideas on education were propounded whilst he was holder of Kant's former Chair at Königsberg, was a sympathetic critic of Pestalozzi, suggesting that his broad pedagogic and moral objectives foundered because of inadequate psychological and ethical underpinnings. In Prussia, Fichte, another of Pestalozzi's visitors, in his *Reden an die deutsche Nation* (1807–8), advocated a system of education, using Pestalozzian methods, as an instrument of national regeneration. Wilhelm von Humboldt, whose own concept of *Bildung* as the harmonious realisation of individual potential has affinities with Pestalozzian ideas, was the official in charge of education in Prussia and sent observers to Yverdon. New elementary schools employing Pestalozzian teaching methods, along with teacher training colleges, were part of the reform. How far such corporatist education was consistent with Pestalozzi's own emphasis on encouraging individual autonomy and with his distaste for collectivism is questionable. His approach was one to be exploited, like those of more conventional educators, in the growing movement to view education as an instrument of national development.

These projects of national regeneration or creation through education supposed notions of citizenship that did not necessarily include all classes. Despite the apparently universalist epistemology underlying eighteenth-century educational philosophy from Locke onwards, pedagogic proposals frequently did not extend to the education of the poorest sectors of society beyond a minimal level. Locke's thoughts concerned the sons of gentry; Rousseau's Émile was the son of a wealthy man; La Chalotais denied the common people any education in reading and writing (on which Voltaire specifically complimented him). Basedow and Priestley devoted their efforts to the instruction of the middle class, and even the Americans were as much concerned with developing a new political elite, albeit in Jefferson's case on the basis of universal elementary schooling.[60] There were nevertheless many practical ventures and theoretical projects for the education of the poor. Some in Germany were inspired by the Pietist pedagogy of August Hermann Francke's schools at Halle, which combined some basic education with vocational training.[61] In Britain, Francke influenced the Charity School Movement, itself satirised for its alleged futility by Bernard Mandeville.[62] Others in Germany and Austria were moved in their concern for the poor by utilitarian conceptions of the interest of the state. For Christian Wolff and for the Cameralists, an appropriate level of education might fit the poor to play their supportive part in the functional state order.[63] In France, there was a major debate, in which both leading and lesser lights amongst the *philosophes* were engaged, over the education of the poor as part of a national system.[64] In each case, however, whether the arguments were couched in terms of a person's religious calling or his or her social role and function, the conclusion generally drawn was that the poor required an education that was limited to religious or moral instruction and basic literacy and numeracy. Often indeed, literacy was deemed superfluous. A more demanding education was perceived as a distraction from the life of socially necessary labour, a stimulus to seek to rise to positions for which there was already an oversupply of candidates, and, broadly, a dangerous source of discontentment. Among those who pursued the educational implications of a potentially egalitarian account of the acquisition of ideas were Helvétius (at least implicitly), Pestalozzi, Condorcet, and (setting aside slaves) Jefferson. For them, universal basic education was a consequence of human equality. For the large part, however, as in other spheres, the theoretical belief in equality and meritocracy did not commit educational philosophers to practical projects that would call the class system fundamentally into question.

Similar considerations affected attitudes towards the education of women. Sensationalist psychology is gender neutral. Some minor writers did claim that the wax of the female mind was softer than that of the male and, hence, more susceptible to immediate impressions and appearances. This rendered them unfit for the sustained thought necessary in public affairs, science, and philosophy.[65] However, even some more significant educational thinkers failed to pursue the full implications of their account of mental processes for the requirements of female education. Even when it was accepted that males and females possessed the same basic mental equipment, it could nevertheless be contended that the distinctive social role of women demanded that they should receive the education appropriate to performing it. Hence it remained an assumption common to educationists with different philosophical positions that women needed at best a training in domestic economy and religion. One of the most widely published works continued to be Fénelon's *De l'éducation des filles* (1687), which asserted the mental incapacity of women for politics, philosophy, and theology, warned against encouraging curiosity lest it make what became known as bluestockings, and confined education largely to household management, which could require basic reading, writing, and handling of accounts.[66]

The most thoroughgoing defence of gender difference was in Book V of *Émile*, where Rousseau recounts the education of Sophie to become Émile's ideal partner. The argument rests on a notion of natural complementarity based on sexual roles. Women exist for the pleasure of men, but both sexes are differently equipped to control the excesses of passion. Men are provided with reason, women with modesty. The education of each sex must correspond with their distinct natures. Female education must cultivate the inclination both to modesty and to the qualities that are attractive to the well-educated male as represented by Émile. These include domestic skills and also simplicity of manner, adornment, and beauty. Female character inclines women to the particular rather than the general and renders them unsuited to philosophical or scientific reasoning and also to public affairs, which for Rousseau is concerned with law and the general will. So although Rousseau recommends an active outdoor upbringing for young girls, this should lead to a preparation for an adulthood, as in the ancient world, in which women remain within the private sphere of the household.[67]

Whilst Rousseau met with approval from some educators such as Basedow, who quotes *Émile* extensively on the role of women,[68] others rejected fundamentally the concept of difference. Priestley argued that women needed the same educational resources as men.[69] Helvétius, in a brief comment, blamed the inadequacies of female education simply on the inconsistency of the instruction to which they were exposed.[70] Condorcet, both in his major political writings and his Report on Education to the National Assembly in 1792, treated women as equally capable of reason and as appropriate recipients of virtually identical education.[71] The most emphatic rejection of Rousseau and insistence on the consequences of post-Lockean epistemology came from the liberal feminists Catharine Macaulay and Mary Wollstonecraft. Macaulay's *Letters on Education*, pouring ridicule on Rousseau, dismissed the notion of sexual difference as irrelevant to education. Claims of male distinctiveness had been employed to the advantage of men and had resulted in the repression of women and their treatment as property. A common education would improve both male and female character.[72] Wollstonecraft's *Vindication of the Rights of Woman* similarly rejects conceptions of either a distinct feminine mentality or virtue.[73] The consequence is that the work becomes largely a vindication of equality of education for males and females. In the face of an England where the vast majority of men lacked political rights, the route to female emancipation lay in the first place through educational reform rather than through the franchise. Some authors indeed justified the education of women less as a right in itself than because of its contribution to male citizenship. Women were, in the home, the mothers and teachers of the republic. Pestalozzi's Gertrude was the model teacher, and maternal domestic teaching was fundamental to the first stages of learning. Hence Pestalozzi's girl's school was a form of teacher training establishment with a curriculum virtually identical to that for boys. The theme was forcefully taken up in America, where writers such as Noah Webster and Benjamin Rush argued that if the republican spirit was to be inculcated in future citizens, their mothers must also be educated in the distinctive history, politics, and culture of the new nation.[74]

Struggles over education invariably involve inclusion and exclusion – the incorporation or exclusion of classes, the canonicity of texts, and the rise and fall of disciplines. Education is never neutral and invariably has a political dimension. At the beginning of the eighteenth century, to the degree that one can speak of an educational system, it was controlled by religious establishments. As the vehicle for transmission of religious values, education was an inevitable target for Enlightenment reform. If the eighteenth century was an age of pedagogy, it is because educational reformers could rest their case on what they could claim was a science of psychology explaining the acquisition of ideas. The potential existed to imprint well-founded principles on the mind of the child. Conversely, the manner in which falsehood had been transmitted was exposed, and the minds of the new generations could be isolated from the sources of prejudice.

Education was therefore a technology for Enlightenment available to society. The potentiality was readily seen by governments, thereby ushering in the modern age of national education. The transmission systems could thus be employed by ruling elites. As well as a liberating force, it could be a means of discipline and control. Hence Michel Foucault included the school in his account of the growth of modern surveillance in the eighteenth century, culminating in Bentham's Panopticon, which was a design for a school as well as a prison.[75] The liberal Enlightenment recognised the danger to liberty and innovation, and the deep connection between political and educational governance was to be debated through the following century and beyond.

Eighteenth-century psychology and education also gave rise to a deepened appreciation of child development. Rousseau's negative education was designed to protect the new generation from the values transmitted by modern society and to release the child's faculties. However paradoxically artificial Rousseau's tutorial arrangements may be, he gave impetus to the 'child-centred' approach to education which, through Pestalozzi, Froebel, and their successors, has constituted a major tendency in subsequent pedagogy. It is a tendency which remains controversial because of its continuing challenge to formal methods of transmitting knowledge and ideas.

It was also during this period, from Locke onwards, that education became more self-consciously concerned with teaching the young to be critical and autonomous rather than with imitation of a set of values on which there could no longer be consensus. Traditionalists readily perceived the potentially revolutionary connection between progressive education and progressive politics – the rejection of authority in school paralleling that in society.[76] This posed new problems of reconciling critique with continuity and, as Kant pointed out, of disciplining whilst respecting autonomy. In this way, too, the eighteenth century helped to set the modern educational agenda.

NOTES

1 Among many general histories of education of the period, see James Bowen, *A History of Western Education*, 3 vols. (London, 1972–81), vol. 3: *The Modern West: Europe and the New World*. Selective but penetrating is G. H. Bantock, *Studies in the History of Educational Theory*, 2 vols. (London, 1980–4), vol. 1: *Artifice and Nature, 1350–1765*, vol. 2: *The Minds and the Masses, 1760–1980*; see also *Thinkers on Education*, ed. Z. Morsy, 4 vols. (Paris, 1995). An influential study of child rearing has been Philippe Ariès, *L'enfant et la vie familiale sous l'ancien régime* (Paris, 1960), translated by R. Baldick as *Centuries of Childhood* (London, 1962); but see also Linda A. Pollock, *Forgotten Children: Parent-Child Relations from 1500 to 1900* (Cambridge, 1983).

2 Accounts of the editions and translations can be found in John Locke, *Some Thoughts Concerning Education*, eds. J. W. Yolton and J. S. Yolton, in *The Clarendon Edition* (1989), 48–67,

and Locke, *The Educational Writings*, ed. J. L. Axtell (Cambridge, 1968), 15–17, 98–104. References to *Some Thoughts Concerning Education* are to the Yolton and Yolton edition but cite paragraph number as well as page.

3 Much of the literature on Locke bears directly or indirectly on education, but in addition to the introductions to *Thoughts* by Yolton and Yolton and by Axtell, see in particular Nathan Tarcov, *Locke's Education for Liberty* (Chicago, IL, 1984); Peter A. Schouls, *Reasoned Freedom: John Locke and Enlightenment* (Ithaca, NY, 1992); Margaret J. M. Ezell, 'John Locke's Images of Childhood: Early Eighteenth Century Responses to *Some Thoughts Concerning Education*', *Eighteenth-Century Studies*, 17 (1983–4): 139–55; Samuel F. Pickering, Jr., *John Locke and Children's Books in Eighteenth-Century England* (Knoxville, TN, 1981); M. G. Mason, 'How John Locke Wrote *Some Thoughts Concerning Education, 1693*', *Paedagogica Historica*, 1 (1961): 244–90; M. G. Mason, 'The Literary Sources of John Locke's Educational Thoughts', *Paedagogica Historica*, 5 (1965): 65–108.

4 *Of the Conduct of the Understanding*, §33, in *Works*, 10 vols. (London, 1801), 3: 185–265.

5 See John W. Yolton, *Locke: An Introduction* (Oxford, 1985), 124–31.

6 Locke, *Two Treatises of Government*, ed. P. Laslett (Cambridge, 1967), *Second Treatise*, ch. 6, §§52–76.

7 See Yolton and Yolton, Introduction to Locke's *Thoughts*, 25–8; Tarcov, *Locke's Education for Liberty*, 79–83.

8 Locke, *An Essay Concerning Human Understanding*, ed. P. H. Nidditch, in *The Clarendon Edition* (1975), II.xxvii.26.

9 See John Passmore, 'The Malleability of Man in Eighteenth-Century Thought', in *Aspects of the Eighteenth Century*, ed. E. R. Wasserman (Baltimore, MD, 1965), 21–46; Passmore, *The Perfectibility of Man* (London, 1970).

10 The extent to which Locke acknowledges differences in natural dispositions is a matter of dispute among interpreters. See Yolton, *Locke: An Introduction*, 19–20, 24–9; James Tully, *An Approach to Political Philosophy: Locke in Contexts* (Cambridge, 1993), 188–241; W. M. Spellman, *John Locke and the Problem of Depravity* (Oxford, 1988).

11 Influenced partly by the work of Foucault, some scholars have stressed the element of disciplining in Locke's educational thought. See Tully, *Approach to Political Philosophy*, 179–241; Uday Singh Mehta, *The Anxiety of Freedom: Imagination and Individuality in Locke's Political Thought* (Ithaca, NY, 1992), 119–67. On education and discipline, see also note 31.

12 *Thoughts*, §§40–1, pp. 109–10; §§95–7, pp. 157–60; *Two Treatises, Second Treatise*, ch. 6, §§58, 67–9.

13 *Thoughts*, §67, 126; also §146, 207; *Conduct*, §27.

14 *Essay*, IV.xx.2–3; *Conduct*, §2, 190; §4, 206–7; §8, 206–7; *The Reasonableness of Christianity*, in *Works*, 7: 1–158 at 157–8.

15 Overviews of French educational thought can be found in Georges Snyders, *La pédagogie en France aux XVIIe et XVIIIe siècles* (Paris, 1965); Roger Chartier, Dominique Julia, and Marie-Madeleine Compère, *L'éducation en France du XVIe au XVIIIe siècle* (Paris, 1976). Still useful is Gabriel Compayré, *Histoire critique des doctrines de l'éducation en France depuis le seizième siècle*, 2 vols. (Paris, 1879), 2: Bks. 5–7. Overviews of British educational thought may be found in the general histories cited in note 1. For the latter half of the century, see Brian Simon, *The Two Nations and the Educational Structure, 1780–1870* (London, 1974).

16 See Mordecai Grossman, *The Philosophy of Helvetius, with Special Emphasis on the Educational Implications of Sensationalism* (New York, NY, 1926); Ian Cumming, *Helvetius, His Life and Place in the History of Educational Thought* (London, 1955).

17 Claude-Adrien Helvétius, *De l'homme, de ses facultés intellectuelles et de son éducation*, 2 vols. (London, 1773), 1: §2, ch. 1, 78.

18 The title of ch. 1 of §10 of *De l'homme*, 2: 332.

19 See Lutz Rössner, *Pädagogen der englischen Aufklärungsphilosophie des 18. Jahrhunderts* (Frankfurt am Main, 1988); Ruth Watts, 'Joseph Priestley and Education', *Enlightenment and Dissent*, 2 (1983): 83–100; Basil Willey, *The Eighteenth-Century Background: Studies on the Idea of Nature in the Thought of the Period* (London, 1940), chs. 8 and 10.

20 David Hartley, *Observations on Man, his Frame, his Duty, and his Expectations*, 6th edn. (London, 1834).

21 Joseph Priestley, *Miscellaneous Observations Relating to Education. More especially, as it respects the Conduct of the Mind. To Which is Added, An Essay on a course of Liberal Education for Civil and Active Life* (Cork, 1780), x; Catharine Macaulay Graham, *Letters on Education with Observations on Religious and Metaphysical Subjects* (London, 1790), Preface, p. v and Pt. 1, Letter 3.

22 Macaulay, *Letters on Education*, Pt. 2, Letter 8; Priestley, *Miscellaneous Observations*, xiii.

23 Helvétius, *De l'homme*, 1: ch. 2, p. 4.

24 Macaulay, *Letters on Education*, Pt. 2, Letter 8, 171–6.

25 Compilations of such national plans include *French Liberalism and Education in the Eighteenth Century: The Writings of La Chalotais, Turgot, Diderot and Condorcet on National Education*, ed. F. de la Fontainerie (New York, NY, 1932); *Une éducation pour la démocratie*, ed. B. Baczko (Paris, 1982); *Schriften zur Nationalerziehung in Deutschland am Ende des 18. Jahrhunderts*, ed. H. König (Berlin, 1954); *Essays on Education in the Early Republic*, ed. F. Rudolph (Cambridge, MA, 1965).

26 [Anonymous] *De l'éducation publique* (Amsterdam, 1762); Louis-René de Caradeuc de la Chalotais, *Essai d'éducation nationale ou Plan d'études pour la jeunesse* (Paris, 1763). A translation of La Chalotais appears in *French Liberalism and Education*, ed. la Fontainerie, 40–169. The authorship of *De l'éducation publique* is discussed in Harvey Chisick, *The Limits of Reform in the Enlightenment: Attitudes toward the Education of the Lower Classes in Eighteenth-Century France* (Princeton, NJ, 1981), 100.

27 [L. Philipon de la Madelaine] *Vues patriotiques sur l'éducation du peuple, Tant des villes que de la campagnes, Avec beaucoup de notes interessantes* (Lyon, 1783); [P. P. F. J. H. Le Mercier de la Rivière] *De l'instruction publique; ou Considérations morales et politiques sur la nécessité, la nature et la source de cette instruction* (Stockholm, 1775); [G. F. Coyer] *Plan d'éducation publique* (Paris, 1770). These and many other works are analysed in Chisick, *Limits of Reform*. See also Roland Mortier, 'The 'Philosophes' and Public Education', *Yale French Studies*, 40 (1968): 62–76; R. R. Palmer, *The Improvement of Humanity: Education and the French Revolution* (Princeton, NJ, 1985).

28 Marie-Jean-Antoine-Nicolas de Caritat, marquis de Condorcet, *Rapport et projet de décret sur l'organisation générale de l'instruction publique* (Paris, 1792), translated as 'Report on the General Organization of Public Instruction', in *French Liberalism and Education*, ed. la Fontainerie, 323–78. See Catherine Kintzler, *Condorcet, l'instruction publique et la naissance du citoyen* (Paris, 1984).

29 Christian Wolff, *Vernünfftige Gedancken von dem gesellschafftlichen Leben der Menschen und insonderheit dem gemeinen Wesen*, in *Werke*, I.5, ed. H. W. Arndt (1975); Johann Heinrich Gottlob von Justi, *Die Natur und das Wesen der Staaten, als die Grundwissenschaft der Staatskunst, der Policey und aller Regierungswissenschaft, desgleichen als die Quelle aller Gesetze* (Berlin, Stettin, and Leipzig, 1760), §§271, 277; Justi, *Gesammelte Politische und Finanzschriften über wichtige Gegenstände der Staatskunst, der Kriegswissenschaften und des Cameral- und Finanzwesens*, 3 vols. (Copenhagen, 1761–4), 1: 59–61 and 3: 219–48; Joseph von Sonnenfels, *Grundsätze der Polizey, Handlung und Finanzwissenschaft*, 2 vols. (Vienna, 1768), 1: 106–17, §§93–102.

30 On Cameralism, absolutism, and education, see, for example, James Van Horn Melton, *Absolutism and the Eighteenth-Century Origins of Compulsory Schooling in Prussia and Austria*

(Cambridge, 1988); Keith Tribe, *Governing Economy: The Reformation of German Economic Discourse 1750–1840* (Cambridge, 1988), 19–118; Gerald Grimm, 'Die Staats- und Bildungskonzeption Joseph von Sonnenfels' und deren Einfluss auf die österreichische Schul- und Bildungspolitik im Zeitalter des aufgeklärten Absolutismus', in *Staat und Erziehung in Aufklärungsphilosophie und Aufklärungszeit*, eds. F.-P. Hager and D. Jedan (Bochum, 1993), 53–66; *'Das pädagogische Jahrhundert': Volksaufklärung und Erziehung zur Armut im 18. Jahrhundert in Deutschland*, ed. U. Herrmann (Basel, 1981); *Aufklärung als Politisierung – Politisierung der Aufklärung*, eds. H. E. Bödeker and U. Herrmann (Hamburg, 1987); Anthony J. La Vopa, *Grace, Talent and Merit: Poor Students, Clerical Careers, and Professional Ideology in Eighteenth-Century Germany* (Cambridge, 1988).

31 On the concept of discipline, see Gerhard Oestreich, *Neostoicism and the Early Modern State*, trans. D. McLintock, eds. B. Oestreich and H. G. Koenigsberger (Cambridge, 1982), ch. 15; Michel Foucault, *Discipline and Punish: The Birth of the Modern Prison*, trans. A. Sheridan (Harmondsworth, 1991), 195–228; Marc Raeff, *The Well-Ordered Police State: Social and Institutional Change through Law in the Germanies and Russia, 1600–1800* (New Haven, CT, 1983); Wolfgang Neugebauer, *Absolutistischer Staat und Schulwirklichkeit in Brandenburg-Preussen* (Berlin, 1985); Frank-Michael Kuhlemann, *Modernisierung und Disziplinierung: Sozialgeschichte des preussischen Volksschulwesens 1794–1872* (Göttingen, 1992).

32 Le Mercier de la Rivière, *De l'instruction publique*, 41–2.

33 Adam Smith, *An Inquiry into the Nature and Causes of the Wealth of Nations*, eds. R. H. Campbell, A. S. Skinner, and W. B. Todd, 2 vols., in *Works* (1976), 2: 758–814.

34 For example, Noah Webster, *On the Education of Youth in America* (Boston, MA, 1790), reprinted in *Essays on Education*, ed. F. Rudolph, 41–78.

35 Amongst the voluminous literature on early American education, see Bernard Bailyn, *Education in the Forming of American Society: Needs and Opportunities for Study* (New York, NY, 1972); Lawrence A. Cremin, *American Education: The Colonial Experience, 1607–1783* (New York, NY, 1970); Cremin, *American Education: The National Experience, 1783–1876* (New York, NY, 1980); Lorraine Smith Pangle and Thomas L. Pangle, *The Learning of Liberty: The Educational Ideas of the American Founders* (Lawrence, KS, 1993).

36 John Brown, *Thoughts on Civil Liberty, on Licentiousness and Faction* (Newcastle upon Tyne, 1765).

37 Joseph Priestley, *An Essay on the First Principles of Government, and on the Nature of Political, Civil, and Religious Liberty*, 2nd edn. (London, 1771), §IV, 76–109.

38 Macaulay, *Letters on Education*, Pt. 1, Letter 2, 10.

39 Jean-Jacques Rousseau, *Émile ou De l'éducation*, in *Oeuvres*, vol. 4. The translation cited is *Émile, or On Education*, trans. A. Bloom (Harmondsworth, 1991).

40 The vast literature on Rousseau's political thought is invariably relevant to his educational theory. More specifically on education, see the Introduction by Pierre Burgelin to the *Oeuvres*, lxxxvii–clii; Introduction by Michel Launay to *Émile* (Paris, 1966); Introduction by Allan Bloom to his translation of *Émile*; Peter Jimack, *Rousseau: Emile* (London, 1983); Jean Chateau, *Jean-Jacques Rousseau: sa philosophie de l'éducation* (Paris, 1962); William Boyd, *The Educational Theory of Jean Jacques Rousseau* (London, 1911); David M. Steiner, *Rethinking Democratic Education: The Politics of Reform* (Baltimore, MD, 1994), chs. 3–4; Pierre Burgelin, *La philosophie de l'existence de J-J Rousseau* (Paris, 1952); Tracy B. Strong, *Jean-Jacques Rousseau: The Politics of the Ordinary* (Thousand Oaks, CA, 1994); Geraint Parry, 'Learning to be Men, Women and Citizens', in *The Cambridge Companion to Rousseau*, ed. P. Riley (Cambridge, 2001), 247–71.

41 *Émile*, 323/93 (The second set of page numbers refers to the translation). Rousseau also referred to 'my inactive method', 359/117.

42 See, for example, Bantock, *Artifice and Nature*, 266–86.

43 *Considérations sur le gouvernement de Pologne et sur sa réformation projettée* (1782), in *Oeuvres*, vol. 3, translated as *The Government of Poland*, trans. and ed. W. Kendall (Indianapolis, IN, 1985); Rousseau, *Lettre à M. d'Alembert sur son article Genève dans le VIIe volume de l'Encyclopédie, et particulièrement sur le projet d'établir un Théatre de Comédie en cette ville*, in *Oeuvres complètes*, eds. B. Gagnebin and M. Raymond, vol. 5 (1995), translated as *Politics and the Arts: Letter to M. d'Alembert on the Theatre*, trans. and ed. A. Bloom (Ithaca, NY, 1968).

44 See, for example, Peter Gay, *The Enlightenment: An Interpretation*, 2 vols. (New York, NY, 1977), vol. 2: *The Science of Freedom*, 548–9; Burgelin, Introduction to *Émile*, in *Oeuvres*, cv–cvi.

45 Jimack, *Rousseau: Emile*, 18–28; Chateau, *Jean-Jacques Rousseau: sa philosophie de l'éducation*, 139–56; Julia Simon, 'Natural Freedom and Moral Autonomy: Émile as Parent, Teacher and Citizen', *History of Political Thought*, 16 (1995): 21–36; Geraint Parry, 'Thinking One's Own Thoughts: Autonomy and the Citizen', in *Rousseau and Liberty*, ed. R. Wokler (Manchester, 1995), 99–120.

46 Major works include Johann Bernhard Basedow, *Das Elementarwerk. Ein Geordneter Vorrath aller nöthigen Erkenntnis. Zum Unterrichte der Jugend* (Dessau, 1774); *Das Methodenbuch für Väter und Mütter der Familien und Völker*, 2nd edn. (Leipzig, 1771); *Agathokrator: oder Von Erziehung Künftiger Regenten* (Leipzig, 1771). On Basedow and philanthropinism, see still A. Pinloche, *La réforme de l'éducation en Allemagne au dix-huitième siècle: Basedow et le philanthropinisme* (Paris, 1889). See also Wiltraut Finzel-Niederstadt, *Lernen und Lehren bei Herder und Basedow* (Frankfurt am Main, 1986); Heikki Lempa, *Bildung der Triebe: Der deutsche Philanthropismus 1768–1788* (Turku, 1993).

47 On Joachim Heinrich Campe, see Ludwig Fertig, *Campes politische Erziehung: eine Einführung in die Pädagogik der Aufklärung* (Darmstadt, 1977); Christa Kersting, *Die Genese der Pädagogik im 18. Jahrhundert: Campes 'Allgemeine Revision' im Kontext der neuzeitlichen Wissenschaft* (Weinheim, 1992). Campe's major contribution lay in editing and organising a collective work of essays on the new education: *Allgemeine Revision des gesammten Schul- und Erziehungswesens von einer Gesellschaft praktischer Erzieher*, 16 vols. (Hamburg, 1785–92).

48 Examples would include Helvétius, *De l'homme*, 2: §5, 1–59; Macaulay, *Letters on Education*, Pt. 1, Letters 3 and 4, 15–32, and Letter 23, 131–5.

49 Denis Diderot, *Réfutation suivie de l'ouvrage d'Helvétius intitulé l'Homme*, in *Oeuvres complètes*, eds. J. Assézat and M. Tourneux, 20 vols. (Paris, 1875–7), 2: 275–456.

50 Immanuel Kant, *Über Pädagogik*, in Ak 9; translated as *Kant on Education*, trans. A. Churton (London, 1899).

51 See Paul Moreau, *L'éducation morale chez Kant* (Paris, 1988); Luc Vincenti, *Éducation et liberté: Kant et Fichte* (Paris, 1992); Barbara Herman, 'Training to Autonomy: Kant and the Question of Moral Education', in *Philosophers on Education: New Historical Perspectives*, ed. A. Oksenberg Rorty (London, 1998), 255–72.

52 *Über Pädagogik*, Ak 9: 441–6/1–11. (The second set of numbers indicates sections of the translation.)

53 Kant, *Metaphysik der Sitten* (1797–8), in Ak 6: 203–493 at 478–84, translated as *The Metaphysics of Morals*, in *Works/Practical Philosophy*, trans. M. J. Gregor (1996).

54 J. H. Pestalozzi, *Lienhard und Gertrud: Ein Buch für das Volk* (1781), in *Sämtliche Werke*, eds. A. Buchenau, E. Spranger, and H. Stettbacher, 29 vols. (Zurich, 1927–96), vols. 2–3; abridged translation, *Leonard and Gertrude*, trans. E. Channing (Boston, MA, 1885); *Wie Gertrud ihre Kinder Lehrt. Ein Versuch den Müttern Anleitung zu geben, ihre Kinder selbst zu unterrichten, in Briefen* (1801), in *Sämtliche Werke*, 13: 181–389 translated as *How Gertrude Teaches Her Children: An Attempt to Help Mothers to Teach their own Children*, trans. L. E. Holland and F. C. Turner (London, 1904).

55 Pestalozzi, *Rede an sein Haus an seinem zwei und siebenzigsten Geburtstage den 12. Jänner 1818* (1818) in *Sämtliche Werke*, 25: 275–9; translation in *Pestalozzi's Educational Writings*, eds. J. A. Green and F. A. Collie (London, 1912), 195–6.

56 *Wie Gertrud Lehrt*, 254–8; trans. 85–9.

57 Pestalozzi, *Mémoire über Armenversorgung mit spezieller Rücksicht auf Neuenburg (Armenerziehungs-Anstalten)* (1807), in *Sämtliche Werke*, 20: 73–192 at 111–13, 167–73.

58 *Wie Gertrud Lehrt*, 341–9; trans.181–90; The quotation occurs on p. 190 of the translation.

59 On the ambiguities in Pestalozzi's thought, see Bantock, *The Minds and the Masses, 1760–1980*, 64–90; Kate Silber, *Pestalozzi*, 4th edn. (London, 1976); Michael Heafford, *Pestalozzi: His Thought and Its Relevance Today* (London, 1967); Michel Soëtard, *Pestalozzi ou La naissance de l'éducateur: Étude sur l'évolution de la pensée et de l'action du pédagogue suisse (1746–1827)* (Bern, 1981).

60 See James B. Conant, *Thomas Jefferson and the Development of American Public Education* (Berkeley and Los Angeles, CA, 1962), 1–19.

61 August Hermann Francke, *Schriften über Erziehung und Unterricht*, ed. K. Richter (Berlin, 1871). See Wolf Oschlies, *Die Arbeits- und Berufspädagogik August Hermann Franckes, 1663–1727: Schule und Leben im Menschenbild des Hauptvertreters des Halleschen Pietismus* (Witten, 1969); Melton, *Absolutism and Compulsory Schooling*, 23–59.

62 See Mary Gwladys Jones, *The Charity School Movement: A Study of Eighteenth Century Puritanism in Action* (Cambridge, 1938); Bernard Mandeville, *The Fable of the Bees; or, Private Vices, Publick Benefits*, ed. F. B. Kaye, 2 vols. (Oxford, 1924). For 'An Essay on Charity and Charity Schools' and 'A Search into the Nature of Society', see 1: 253–369.

63 See Melton, *Absolutism and Compulsory Schooling*, and see also references in note 31.

64 See Chisick, *The Limits of Reform*; Harry C. Payne, *The Philosophes and the People* (New Haven, CT, 1976). See also references in note 27.

65 John Brown (of Newcastle upon Tyne), *On the Female Character and Education: A Sermon Preached . . . at the Anniversary Meeting of . . . the Asylum for Deserted Female Orphans* (London, 1765), 6–9; Thomas Franklin, *A Sermon Preached in . . . the Asylum for Female Orphans* (London, 1768), 9–15. On education and women, see *Woman and Society in Eighteenth-Century France: Essays in Honour of John Stephenson Spink*, eds. E. Jacobs et al. (London, 1979); Jane Martin, *Reclaiming a Conversation: The Ideal of the Educated Woman* (New Haven, CT, 1985); Alice Brown, *The Eighteenth-Century Feminist Mind* (Brighton, 1987); Londa Schiebinger, *The Mind Has no Sex? Women in the Origins of Modern Science* (Cambridge, MA, 1989).

66 François de Salignac de La Mothe-Fénelon, *De l'éducation des filles*, in *Oeuvres*, ed. J. Le Brun, 2 vols. (Paris, 1983–7); English version in *Fénelon on Education*, trans. H. C. Barnard (Cambridge, 1966).

67 *Émile*, 704–5/366. In addition to the works cited in note 40, significant studies of Rousseau on female education include Pierre Burgelin, 'L'éducation de Sophie', *Annales de la société J-J Rousseau*, 35 (1959–62): 113–37; Joel Schwartz, *The Sexual Politics of Jean-Jacques Rousseau* (Chicago, IL, 1984); Margaret Canovan, 'Rousseau's Two Concepts of Citizenship', in *Women in Western Political Philosophy*, eds. E. Kennedy and S. Mendus (Brighton, 1987), 78–105.

68 Basedow, *Das Methodenbuch*, 316–76. Campe's radicalism also reaches its limits at this point; see *Väterlicher Rath für meine Tochter: Ein Gegenstück zum Theophron. Der erwachsenern weiblichen Jugend gewidmet* (Frankfurt, 1790). Conservatives were in agreement; see Ernst Brandes, *Betrachtungen über das weibliche Geschlecht und dessen Ausbildung in dem geselligen Leben*, 3 vols. (Hanover, 1802).

69 Joseph Priestley, *Reflections on Death: A Sermon on Occasion of the Death of the Rev. Robert Robinson*, in *The Theological and Miscellaneous Works*, ed. J. T. Rutt, 25 vols. in 26 (London, 1817–32), 15: 404–19 at 419; see Ruth Watts, 'Joseph Priestley and Education', 88–9.

70 Helvétius, *De l'homme*, 1: §I, ch. 10, 38–9.

71 Condorcet, *Rapport*, 47; trans. 369–70. Particularly robust advocacy of political rights and education for women from a minor writer of the period is found in J. Courdin, *Observations philosophiques sur la réforme de l'éducation publique* (Montpellier, 1792).

72 Macaulay, *Letters on Education*, Pt. 1, Letters 3–4 and 22–4.

73 Mary Wollstonecraft, *Vindication of the Rights of Woman, With Strictures on Political and Moral Subjects* (London, 1792); see also her *Thoughts on The Education of Daughters* (London, 1787).

74 Benjamin Rush, *Thoughts upon Female Education, Accommodated to the Present State of Society, Manners, and Government in the United States of America* (Boston, MA, 1787), in *Essays on Education*, ed. F. Rudolph, 25–40; Webster, *On the Education of Youth in America*, 68–70.

75 Foucault, *Discipline and Punish*, 195–228.

76 In Germany, the Burkean Ernst Brandes saw the 'Rousseauian-Basedowian' project as a significant factor in an egalitarian social and political revolution. See Ernst Brandes, *Ueber das Du und Du zwischen Eltern und Kindern* (Hannover, 1809). For an earlier British defence of experience against speculation and innovation in education, see Vicesimus Knox, *Liberal Education: or, A Practical Treatise on the Methods of Acquiring Useful and Polite Learning*, 3rd edn. (London, 1781). For his almost Burkean defence of experience against speculation and innovation, see in particular Introduction, 2–3, 102–4, 171–2, 385–415.